HUDSON TAYLOR

AND THE

CHINA INLAND MISSION

THE GROWTH OF A WORK OF GOD

JAMES HUDSON TAYLOR

In middle life, about the time when his appeal " To Every Creature " was issued.

HUDSON TAYLOR

AND THE
CHINA INLAND MISSION

THE GROWTH OF A WORK OF GOD

DR. & MRS. HOWARD TAYLOR

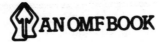

AN OMF BOOK

© OMF INTERNATIONAL
(formerly China Inland Mission)

First printing, 1918
This printing, 1996

ISBN 9971-972-64-6

OMF Books are distributed by
OMF, 10 West Dry Creek Circle, Littleton, CO 80120, U.S.A.
OMF, 5759 Coopers Avenue, Mississauga, ON L4Z 1R9, Canada
OMF, Belmont, The Vine, Sevenoaks, Kent, TN13 3TZ, UK
and other OMF offices.

Library of Congress Cataloging-in-Publication Data

Taylor, Frederick Howard.
   Hudson Taylor and the China Inland Mission: The Growth of a
Work of God / Dr. and Mrs. Howard Taylor; OMF International
[1995].
   xi, 640 p. [4] leaves of plates. Includes index.
   ISBN 9971-972-64-6 (hardcover)
   1. Taylor, James Hudson, 1832-1905. 2. China Inland Mission.
3. Missions—China.
Taylor, Howard, Mrs., joint author.
BV3427.T3 T35-1995

OF HIM

THROUGH HIM AND TO HIM . . .

TO WHOM BE GLORY

FOREWORD

" THE founder of the China Inland Mission was a physician, J. Hudson Taylor, a man full of the Holy Ghost and of faith, of entire surrender to God and His call, of great self-denial, heartfelt compassion, rare power in prayer, marvellous organising faculty, energetic initiative, indefatigable persever-ance, and of astonishing influence with men, and withal of childlike humility."

PROFESSOR WARNECK.

" Surely never was man better fitted for his work than he for the difficult undertaking of founding and conducting a great interdenominational and international mission in million-peopled China. The China Inland Mission was con-ceived in his soul, and every stage of its advance sprung from his personal exertions. In the quiet of his heart, in deep unutterable communings with God, the mission had its origin, and it remains his memorial. On that noble monument, not of perishable marble, and in characters not of man's inditing, his name is written. His dust sleeps now in China. Silence has fallen on the lips which long pleaded China's cause, but the effects of the plea remain in the con-version of thousands called out of heathen darkness into God's marvellous light, and the existence of a mission whose present influence and future growth are beyond our powers to estimate. To God be all the glory.

" The missionary spirit is the spirit of Jesus, the spirit of the Incarnation and the Cross. Not then to the instrument of the Master, however dear, however noble, but to the Master Himself be all the praise, Who lives to carry on by His own unfailing resources and chosen instrumentalities His work of the redemption of a fallen world, to the high and glorious issues of His eternal Kingdom."

H. GRATTAN GUINNESS, D.D.

CONTENTS

ix

PART IV

THE GOD OF THE IMPOSSIBLE

1871–1877. AET. 39-45.

PART V

BURIED LIVES: MUCH FRUIT

1878–1881. AET. 46-49.

PART VI

THE RISING TIDE

1881–1887. AET. 49-55.

PART VII

WIDER MINISTRY

1888–1895. AET. 56–63.

PART VIII

"WORN OUT WITH LOVING"

1895–1905. AET. 63–73.

ILLUSTRATIONS

PART I

THE BACKSIDE OF THE DESERT

1860–1866. AET. 28–34.

Thou on the Lord rely,
So safe shalt thou go on ;
Fix on His work thy steadfast eye.
So shall thy work be done.

.   .   .   .

Far, far above thy thought,
His counsel shall appear,
When fully He the work hath wrought
That caused thy needless fear.

CHAPTER I

IF THOU FORBEAR TO DELIVER

SEPT. 1865. AET. 33.

IT was an anxious moment for the young missionary—
fraught with possibilities of which he was keenly conscious.
From an early hour that morning he had been alone with
God, pleading for abiding results from this meeting. Now
the great hall with its sea of faces lay before him ; but how
weak he felt, how inadequate to the opportunity ! And no
one was expecting his message. A stranger at Perth and
indeed in Scotland, it had only been with difficulty he had
persuaded the leaders of the Conference to give him a few
minutes in which to speak on China—that vast empire with
its four hundred millions, a fourth of the entire human race,
about which his heart was burdened.

"My dear sir," the Convener had exclaimed, scanning
the introductions of this unknown Hudson Taylor, " surely
you mistake the character of the Conference ! These
meetings are for *spiritual edification.*"

But the missionary was not to be denied, nor could he
see that obedience to the last great command of the risen
Saviour was out of keeping with spiritual edification. To
him it seemed rather to lie at the root of all true blessing,
and to be the surest way to a deepened experience of fellowship with God. It was at no little cost, however, that he
ventured to urge this point of view ; for those were not days
when foreign missions occupied a place of much importance,
and his dread of public speaking was only less than his

3

sensitiveness about putting himself forward.[1] But the facts, the great unseen realities, burned as a fire within him. He could not be at Perth in the midst of the Conference and see those multitudes of Christian people, intelligent, influential, and caring deeply about spiritual things, without longing that they should see and feel needs incomparably greater than their own.[2]

And now the moment had come. Trembling from head to foot as he rose, Hudson Taylor could only grasp the rail of the platform and command voice enough to ask his hearers to unite with him in prayer to God. To *Him* it was easy to speak ; and unusual as this beginning was, even for a missionary address, it arrested attention and opened the way to many a heart. For there was about that prayer a peculiar reality and power. More simple it could not have been, and yet it revealed a sacred intimacy that awakened longing for just such confidence in and certainty of God. A strange hush came over the people before the prayer ended, and then all else was forgotten in scenes to which they found themselves transported.

For the missionary came at once to the heart of his message. Back again in thought in the land of his adoption, he was travelling by native junk from Shanghai to Ningpo. Among his fellow-passengers, one Chinese, who had spent

[1] In the train on his way from Aberdeen to Perth, Mr. Taylor had written to his wife in London, his chief helper in prayer :
" Sept. 5, 1865 : Through God's goodness I have got some letters of introduction to Perth. May the Lord help and guide and use me there. My hope is in Him. I do desire not to please myself, but to lay myself open for China's sake. I much need to add to faith courage : may God give it me."

[2] One of the very few gatherings which, at that time, united Christians of all denominations, Perth was taking much the place in Scotland that the Barnet Conference (afterwards moved to Mildmay) occupied in London. The occasion of Mr. Taylor's visit to Perth was the third Conference, presided over in the City Hall by the Revs. J. Milne of Perth and Macdowall Grant of Arndilly, and attended by Messrs. Stevenson A. Blackwood, R. C. Morgan of *The Revival* (afterwards *The Christian*), the Rev. Hay Aitken of Penzance, Brownlow North and other visitors from England, as well as by such well-known Scottish leaders as the Revs. Andrew Bonar, J. Macpherson, Moody Stuart, M'Gregor of Dundee, Yule of Cargill, General Macdowall, George Barbour, Esq., of Bonskeid, Messrs. Colville and Gillett of Glasgow, and Mr. Jenkinson of Edinburgh, who in the Carrubber's Close Mission had for six years been dealing almost nightly with anxious inquirers, seeking and finding salvation, an outcome of the great Revival of 1859. The Conference was attended by about two thousand people.

some years in England and went by the name of Peter, was much upon his heart, for, though not unacquainted with the Gospel, he knew nothing of its saving power. Simply he told the story of this man's friendliness and of his own efforts to win him to Christ. Nearing the city of Sung-kiang, they were preparing to go ashore together to preach and distribute tracts, when Mr. Taylor in his cabin was startled by a sudden splash and cry that told of a man overboard. Springing at once on deck he looked round and missed Peter.

"Yes," exclaimed the boatmen unconcernedly, " it was over there he went down ! "

To drop the sail and jump into the water was the work of a moment ; but the tide was running out, and the low, shrubless shore afforded little landmark. Searching everywhere in an agony of suspense, Mr. Taylor caught sight of some fishermen with a drag-net—just the thing needed.

"Come," he cried as hope revived, " come and drag over this spot. A man is drowning ! "

" *Veh bin*," was the amazing reply : "It is not convenient."

" Don't talk of convenience ! Quickly come, or it will be too late."

" We are busy fishing."

" Never mind your fishing ! Come—only come *at once* ! I will pay you well."

" How much will you give us ? "

" Five dollars ! [1] only don't stand talking. Save life without delay ! "

" Too little ! " they shouted across the water. " We will not come for less than thirty dollars."

" But I have not so much with me ! I will give you all I've got."

" And how much may that be ? "

" Oh, I don't know. About fourteen dollars."

Upon this they came, and the first time they passed the net through the water brought up the missing man. But all Mr. Taylor's efforts to restore respiration were in vain. It was only too plain that life had fled, sacrificed

[1] Worth at the time more than thirty shillings.—J. H. T.

to the callous indifference of those who might easily have saved it.[1]

A burning sense of indignation swept over the great audience. Could it be that anywhere on earth people were to be found so utterly callous and selfish ! But as the earnest voice went on, conviction struck home all the more deeply that it was unexpected :

"Is the body, then, of so much more value than the soul ? We condemn those heathen fishermen. We say they were guilty of the man's death—because they could easily have saved him, and did not do it. But what of the millions whom we leave to perish, and that eternally ? What of the plain command, ' Go ye into all the world and preach the Gospel to every creature,' and the searching question inspired by God Himself, ' If thou forbear to deliver them that are drawn unto death, and those that are ready to be slain ; if thou sayest, Behold, we knew it not ; doth not He that pondereth the heart consider it ? and He that keepeth thy soul doth not He know it ? And shall He not render to every man according to his works ? ' "

China might be far off and little known ; we might silence conscience by saying that its vast population was largely inaccessible ; but every one of those men, women, and children was a soul for whose salvation an infinite price had been paid ; every one of them had a right to know that they had been ransomed by the precious blood of Christ, and to have the offer of eternal life in His Name. While we were busy about other things, quite profitably occupied it may be, they were living, dying without God and without hope—a million every month in that one land passing beyond our reach.

Rapidly, then, Hudson Taylor arrayed before his hearers facts that recent prayer and study had burned afresh upon his soul. Not the coast-board provinces only, to which the little band of Protestant missionaries was confined, but the great unreached interior, every part indeed of the mighty empire passed in review. To most if not all present it was a revelation. Millions upon millions of their fellow-creatures,

---

[1] It was on Friday, October 10, 1856, that this incident took place, when young Hudson Taylor was returning to Ningpo with Mr. J. Jones, whose colleague he became a little later.

unknown, unthought-of, were brought out of the dim mists of forgetfulness, and put before them in such fashion that their claim upon Christian hearts could never again be disregarded. Missionary addresses were not wont to be of that order. It was not speaking, so much, about these startling facts as letting the light of God fall upon them—making those present see as the speaker saw, hear as the speaker heard, GOD's view, GOD's verdict upon the matter.

And what a verdict that was!

In Scotland, with its population of four millions, several thousand ministers were needed to care for the spiritual interests of people already flooded with Gospel light. China, with a hundred times as many precious, immortal souls, had not even one Protestant missionary, on an average, to every *four millions*. Moreover, its ninety-one missionaries of all societies were not by any means evenly distributed. They were gathered in a few, a very few, centres near the coast. Confined to the treaty ports, they were in touch with a mere fringe of the population of the provinces in which they were found; while beyond lay the vast interior, inhabited by two hundred millions of our fellow-creatures, amongst whom no voice was raised to tell of salvation, full and free, through the finished work of Christ. Yet we believe that "the wicked shall be turned into hell, and all the nations that forget God." Amazing inconsistency, appalling indifference to the revealed will of Him Whom we call Master and Lord, and to the deepest needs of the human soul!

It was for these inland provinces and dependencies the speaker pleaded—populous regions as large as all the countries of Europe put together, in which no Protestant missionary was yet to be found.

"Do you believe that each unit of these millions has an immortal soul," he questioned searchingly, "and that there is 'none other name under heaven given among men' save the precious name of Jesus 'whereby we must be saved'? Do you believe that He and He alone is 'the Way, the Truth, and the Life,' and that 'no man cometh unto the Father' but by Him? If so, think of the condition of these unsaved souls, and examine yourself in the sight of God to see whether you are doing your utmost to make Him known to them or not.

" It will not do to say that you have no special call to go to China. With these facts before you, you need rather to ascertain whether you have a special call to stay at home. If in the sight of God you cannot say you are sure that you have a special call to stay at home, why are you disobeying the Saviour's plain command to go ? Why are you refusing to come to the help of the Lord against the mighty ? If, however, it is perfectly clear that duty—not inclination, not pleasure, not business—detains you at home, are you labouring in prayer for these needy ones as you might ? Is your influence used to advance the cause of God among them ? Are your means as largely employed as they should be in helping forward their salvation ? "

Recalling an experience, the pain of which could never be forgotten, Mr. Taylor went on to tell of a Ningpo convert who, full of joy in his new-found faith, had inquired :

" How long have you known this Good News in your country ? "

" We have known it a long time," was the reluctant answer ; " hundreds of years."

" Hundreds of years," exclaimed the ex-Buddhist leader, " and you never came to tell us ! "

" My father sought the Truth," he added sadly, " sought it long, and died without finding it. Oh, why did you not come sooner ? "

" Shall we say that the way was not open ? " continued the speaker. " At any rate it is open now. Before the next Perth Conference twelve millions more, in China, will have passed forever beyond our reach. What are we doing to bring them the tidings of Redeeming Love? It is no use singing as we often do :

'*Waft, waft ye winds the story.*'

The winds will never waft the story ; but they may waft *us*.

" The Lord Jesus commands us, commands us each one individually—' Go,' He says, ' Go into all the world and preach the Gospel to every creature.' Will you say to *Him*, ' It is not convenient ' ? Will you tell Him that you are busy fishing—have bought a piece of land, purchased five yoke of oxen, married a wife, or for other reasons cannot obey ? Will He accept such excuses ? Have we forgotten that ' we must all stand before the judgment seat of Christ,' that every one may receive the things done in the body. Oh, remember, pray for, labour for the unevangelised millions of China, or you will sin against your own soul ! Consider again whose Word it is that says :

"'If thou forbear to deliver them that are drawn unto death, and those that are ready to be slain ; if thou sayest, Behold, we knew it not ; doth not He that pondereth the heart consider it ? and He that keepeth thy soul, doth not He know it ? And shall not He render to every man according to his works ? ' "

So deep was the impression that the meeting broke up almost in silence. Many sought the speaker afterwards, to inquire about the work in which he was engaged and to offer such help as they could give. Far and wide reports were carried, both of the address and that Hudson Taylor was about to return to China. With no denomination at his back, no Committee even or promise of supplies, he was taking with him a party of fellow-workers to attempt nothing less than the evangelisation of the inland provinces of that great empire. And he was so calm about it, so sure that God had called them to this seemingly impossible task and would open the way before them ! Amazed at his faith and vision, men felt almost as if a prophet had risen up among them, and one of the larger churches was filled with an audience eager to hear more of the projected mission.[1]

Further openings resulted, as it was found that Hudson Taylor was no visionary though he had his God-given vision. Quiet, practical, steeped in prayer, his words had weight and influence. Reports of his addresses appeared in not a few religious journals. Friends made at these meetings were among his faithful helpers through all the after-years, and to this day there are those who remember with thankfulness the coming of this servant of God into their lives at the Perth Conference of 1865.

What was it that lay *behind* the faith and vision, making them far other than a Utopian dream ? What had been the life, the character, the heart-experiences that led to the launching in this unexpected way of the China Inland Mission ?

---

[1] " I spoke on China yesterday," Mr. Taylor wrote from the Conference, " and have one or more meetings to-morrow for this purpose exclusively. I am staying with General Sir Alexander Lindsay. . . . I should not wonder if many men are raised up for China."

CHAPTER II

HIDDEN YEARS

1860–1864. Aet. 28–32.

In the heart of the East End of London, among the toilers of Whitechapel, Hudson Taylor had made his home. Invalided from China in 1860, it had been like a death-sentence to be told that he must never think of returning unless he wished to throw his life away. Six and a half years of strenuous work in Shanghai, Ningpo, and elsewhere had taken heavy toll of a constitution none too strong at the outset, and with a delicate wife and child it looked for a time as though he would never see China again.[1]

His one consolation in leaving the converts in Ningpo had been that he could serve them in England. A hymn-book and other simple works in their local dialect were much needed, and above all a more correct translation of the New Testament with marginal references. Immediately on landing, the young missionary had thrown himself into the task of getting the Bible Society and the Religious Tract Society to undertake these publications, and so engrossed was he with meetings, interviews, and correspondence that almost three weeks elapsed before he could visit his beloved parents in Barnsley.

Then came the question as to where to settle. If he should be detained at home but a year or two, Mr. Taylor was anxious to make the most of the time. No thought of

---

[1] The story of Mr. Taylor's first period of work in China will be found in *Hudson Taylor in Early Years : The Growth of a Soul*, published by the China Inland Mission and the Religious Tract Society, to which this volume forms the sequel.

a holiday seems to have entered his mind. Furlough to him simply meant an opportunity for finding fellow-labourers and fitting himself and them for future usefulness. His colleagues in Ningpo, Mr. and Mrs. J. Jones, whose work (unconnected with any society) had been the means of much blessing, were no longer equal to the burdens pressing upon them. Even before Mr. Taylor left, five additional helpers had been appealed for, and much prayer was being made in the faith that they would be given. Meanwhile tidings were none too good from the little mission.

" You know what it is to have a sick child at a distance," Mr. Taylor wrote to his parents, after two months in England, " and we are feeling separation from children in the Lord who are spiritually sick. But what can we do ? We can scarcely go back at once. I know how we are needed, but the object sought in our coming home does not yet seem gained. It is true that our friends (Mr. and Mrs. Jones) are apt to look on the dark side of things ; so we must hope for the best, and join our prayers with yours for God to work in the hearts of the dear but feeble lambs of His flock, redeemed with His own precious blood. Oh, yes ! He will bear the lambs in His bosom. He loves them more than we do."

Curbing his eagerness to be back in China, Mr. Taylor had decided to complete his medical studies and take his diplomas. Facing the broad thoroughfare of Whitechapel stood his old Alma Mater, the London Hospital. Its doors were open to him, and turning resolutely from an easier line of things he brought his wife and children to East London, renting a house on a side street near the hospital, that no time might be lost in going to and fro to attend his lectures, etc.

Here, then, at No. 1 Beaumont Street, began the discipline that was to lengthen out, little as Hudson Taylor expected it, until he was ready for the wider vision that was yet to dawn upon him. Four years were to elapse—quiet, hidden years—in which little apparently was to be accomplished, while God was doing the real, the inner work which was to bear fruit not in Ningpo only but in every part of China.

Well was it that the young missionaries could not foresee all that lay before them. At twenty-nine and twenty-four, long patience is not easy. They were in England truly, but with every thought, every breath, loving China, living for China ! In addition to his medical studies, they had undertaken the important task of revising the Ningpo Testament, the Bible Society having agreed to publish a new edition. They were in correspondence also with candidates for the mission, and as health improved their hope brightened that a couple of years might set them free—medical degrees obtained, Romanised publications in hand, and the fellow-workers given about whom they were waiting upon God. And it was to be *four* years before the Pillar of the Cloud moved for them even a little ; four years that were to bring them but *one* missionary, and in which, though Mr. Taylor's medical studies were completed, the revision was to prove a task that grew upon their hands. Yet it was right, all right, and the one way to answer their deepest prayers.

A glimpse into the daily life of that little home in Beaumont Street, so different from the sordid scenes about it, is afforded by the recollections of the Barnsley candidate who came up during the first year Mr. Taylor was in London. Through his Class Leader, Mr. Henry Bell, he had been interested in China, though without for a moment supposing that he could himself become a missionary.

" James," said Mr. Bell one day, " I have a job for you. Will you undertake it ? "

" What is it, sir ? "

And the unexpected reply had been, " Go to China."

Hudson Taylor's appeal for workers had reached Barnsley before his return to England, and often was the matter remembered in prayer in the old home on the Market Place. Dropping in to tea, the good old-fashioned Yorkshire meal, Mr. Bell had learned that spiritual qualifications were needed rather than high educational attainments. This turned his thoughts to the young mechanic who was his right-hand helper in open-air meetings and wherever a soul was to be won. Telling him all he knew of the opening, Mr. Bell repeated his question :

" Will you go ? "

" I will," replied Meadows, " if God is calling me. But I must have time to pray over it."

The faith principles of the mission caused him no apprehension, nor did the difficulties of the language. He was ready to give up good business prospects, and go out looking to the Lord alone for supplies. But he must know assuredly that he was being led of God.

" So I fasted," he wrote long after, " and going into my workshop one dinner-hour, knelt down and definitely asked the Lord, ' Shall I go ? '

" The answer that came then and there was, ' Go, and the Lord be with thee,' and I have never regretted from that day to this (nearly fifty years later) that I acted upon it."

When the time came for his first visit to London, it was with immense interest he looked forward to being in Mr. Taylor's company. To see something of a missionary's life at close quarters had more attraction for him than all the wonders of the great city. Making his way to the address given, he was scarcely surprised to find himself in a poor neighbourhood. Mr. Taylor, he knew, was studying medicine at the London Hospital, and it was natural he should live near at hand. But the poverty of the little house itself did somewhat take him aback, when he got over the surprise of being welcomed by a Chinese in native gown and *queue*. The cottage he had left in Barnsley possessed more of comfort, as he soon discovered, than the scantily furnished rooms which contented the missionaries. They and their Chinese helper (none other than Wang Lae-djün of Ningpo [1]) seemed to have little time for housekeeping, so keen were they on the chief work in hand, the revision of the New Testament. In a study devoid of all but actual necessaries, he found Mr. Taylor engrossed with Mr. Gough over a knotty point of translation,[2] and it was some time before they could do more than give him a cordial welcome. So interested

[1] For the conversion of this remarkable man and his early labours, see *The Growth of a Soul*, p. 477 *et sqq.*
[2] The Rev. F. F. Gough of the Church Missionary Society, also on furlough from Ningpo, who had joined Mr. Taylor in the revision.

was he, however, in all that was going on that he forgot the bareness of the room, the low fire in the grate, though the day was bitterly cold, and the well-worn dress of the man whose spirit seemed in such contrast with his surroundings !

And at table it was the same. Lae-djün was both cook and laundryman, and the table linen no less than the provisions told of the secondary place given to such details. But the conversation made him oblivious of the cooking, and he was surprised to find himself unruffled by things that would have upset his peace of mind at home. The " gentle, earnest piety " of the missionaries deeply impressed him, as did their absorbing devotion to the work they had left, which was never far from their thoughts. The appalling fact of a million precious souls, month by month, perishing in China for lack of the Gospel was *real* to them, and found some adequate, corresponding reality in their daily life. Poor as they were—and it was not long before he discovered that they had no means in hand, or even in prospect, with which to send him to China—he was glad to accept such leadership, and to go out simply as a " Scripture-reader " when before long funds were provided.[1]

And Hudson Taylor's care of his one missionary was not unworthy of this confidence. He had known what it was to be alone, in need, and apparently forgotten during his first years in China, and nothing that could be done by correspondence and attention to business details should be omitted to further the efficiency and well-being of his fellow-workers. Careful though he was of every penny, he invested in a good account-book and a file for letters, and the clear entries in his own handwriting testify to the faithfulness with which he discharged these responsibilities. Mr. Meadows's only complaint, indeed, in his early correspondence illustrates the regularity with which he was cared for.

" James Meadows speaks of being well and regularly supplied with money," Mr. Taylor wrote to his mother a year after the

---

[1] Mr. Meadows and his bride sailed for China in January 1862, first of the five workers prayed for to reinforce Mr. and Mrs. Jones in the Ningpo Mission.

young couple had gone out. " His only dissatisfaction is that his friends, knowing him to be looking to God only, would be anxious, while he is receiving remittances as regularly as though he had a salary. He seems distressed, in fact, at their being so regular and sufficient, as though such a state of things were incompatible with leaning upon God alone. I have explained in my reply that this is not the case, and that as neither he nor I have any promise of another farthing from any one, we need to look to the Lord constantly to supply us as He sees fit."

By this time Mr. Taylor's medical studies were completed and his diplomas taken. He had worked hard for them, gaining valuable experience in hospital practice ; and now, the strain of examinations over, he was more free to look ahead.

" We have many difficulties before us," he had written home some months earlier.[1] " I do not see my way at all ; but it is enough that He does Who will guide, and supply all our need. . . . I wish Barnsley were not so far away. But when we get *Home* we shall be all together. . . . We must not seek our rest here, must we ? We must press forward, counting everything (and that includes a great many things) but loss, that we may ' win Christ and be found in *Him*.' "

Of these hidden years of work and waiting little would have been known in detail but for the preservation of a number of brief journals whose very existence was unsuspected. Providentially brought to light while these pages were being written, they fill a gap hitherto passed over in silence. Here they lie upon the table, twelve thin paper-covered notebooks, worn with years, but not one of them missing. Beginning soon after Mr. Taylor's medical degrees were taken, they cover a period of three years, up to and a little beyond the Perth Conference.[2] Daily entries in his small clear writing fill the pages, which breathe a spirit words are poor to express.

Scarcely a day is recorded in which he did not have correspondence, visitors, meetings, lessons in Chinese to give to intending missionaries, medical visits to pay to friends or suffering neighbours, attendance at committees,

---

[1] In a letter of July 27, 1862.
[2] *I.e.* December 1862 to the end of 1865.

or other public or private engagements *in addition* to the revision of the Ningpo Testament.   That the latter was his chief occupation, and one to which he devoted himself with characteristic thoroughness, is evident from the journals. Every day he noted the number of hours spent in this work alone, and one frequently comes across such entries as the following :

April 13, 1863 : Commenced with Mr. Gough at 10 A.M. and worked together about eight hours.   Revision, total nine hours.
April 14 : Revision nine hours.
,,   15 :   ,,   ten and a half hours.
,,   16 :   ,,   eight hours.
,,   17 :   ,,   eleven and a half hours.
,,   18 :   ,,   eleven hours.
,,   19, Sunday : Morning, wrote to James Meadows, . . . had service with Lae-djün.[1]   Afternoon, took tea with Mr. John Howard, having walked to Tottenham to inquire after Miss Stacey's health.   Evening, heard Mr. Howard preach.   Proposed to Miss Howard, as subjects for prayer, that we should be helped in revision—to do it well and as quickly as is consistent with so doing.   Walked home.[2]
April 20 : Revision twelve hours.
,,   21 :   ,,   eleven hours.
,,   22 :   ,,   ten hours.
,,   23 :   ,,   twelve hours.
,,   24 :   ,,   nine and a half hours.
,,   25 :   ,,   thirteen and a half hours.
Several answers to prayer to-day. . . . Thanks be to Him.

Thus the record runs on, putting to shame our easy-going service by its intensity and devotion.   And this was a returned missionary, detained at home on account of seriously impaired health through equally strenuous labours in China !

[1] The only Chinese Christian within reach, Lae-djün was not neglected spiritually.   Regularly, as the journals testify, Mr. Taylor spent hours with him on Sunday, tired though they must often have been : hours of prayer and Bible study that had not a little to do with Lae-djün's subsequent usefulness as the first and for thirty years one of the most devoted native Pastors in the China Inland Mission.

[2] The walk to and from Tottenham, twelve miles in all, must have been fatiguing to Mr. Taylor ; but he had strong conscientious objections to Sunday travelling, and felt the effort well repaid by intercourse with the Howards and other friends, and the helpful fellowship of the Brook Street Meeting

April 26, Sunday: Morning, heard Rev. T. Kennedy on
" Do thyself no harm." (Appropriate surely !) Afternoon, lay
down, having headache and neuralgia. Evening, with Lae-djün
on Heb. xi., first part. Mr. Gough promised to begin to-morrow
not later than 10.30. May God prosper us in our work this week,
and in all other matters be our help and guide.

April 27 : Revision seven hours (evening at Exeter Hall).

„ 28 : „ nine and a half hours.

„ 29 : „ eleven hours.

„ 30 : „ five and a half hours (B.M.S. meetings).

May 1 : „ eight and a half hours (visitors till 10 P.M.).

„ 2 : „ thirteen hours.

„ 3, Sunday, at Bayswater : In the morning heard Mr.
Lewis, from John iii. 33 ; took the Communion there in the
afternoon.[1] Evening, stayed at home and engaged in prayer
about our Chinese work.

May 4 : Revision four hours (correspondence and visitors).

„ 5 : „ eleven and a half hours.

„ 6 : „ seven hours (important interviews).

„ 7 : „ nine and a half hours.

„ 8 : „ ten and a half hours.

„ 9 : „ thirteen hours.

„ 10, Sunday : Morning, with Lae-djün on Heb. xi., first
part—a happy season. Wrote to James Meadows. Afternoon,
prayer with Maria about leaving this house, about Meadows,
Truelove, revision, etc. Wrote to Mr. Lord.[2] Evening, heard
Mr. Kennedy on Matt. xxvii. 42 : " He saved others, Himself
He cannot save." Oh! to be more like the meek, forbearing,
loving Jesus. Lord, make me more like Thee.

But it was not work only, it was faith and endurance
under searching trial that made these years so fruitful in
their after-results. The testing permitted was chiefly along
two lines, those of the Ningpo Testament and the supply
of personal needs. Mr. Taylor, it should be recorded, never
at any time received financial help from the funds of the

[1] Bayswater was the home at this time of Mr. and Mrs. B. Broomhall,
the beloved sister Amelia, for many years Mr. Taylor's chief correspondent.
The Rev. W. G. Lewis was the minister of the Baptist Church, of which
Mr. Taylor had become and long remained a member.

[2] The Rev. E. C. Lord of Ningpo, formerly of the American Baptist
Missionary Union, was a highly esteemed friend of Mr. Taylor's. Although
very busy in his own work, he found time to replace Mr. Jones in the
pastoral oversight of the Bridge Street Church, and to give much help to
Mr. Meadows. Mr. Jones had had to leave China in broken health, and
reached the better Home before the journey could be completed.

Mission.   Even in these early days he felt it important to be entirely independent, in this sense, of the work.   He had long been looking to the Lord in temporal matters as in spiritual, proving in many wonderful ways the truth of the promise, " No good thing will He withhold from them that walk uprightly."   These years, however, in East London were marked by very special exercise of mind in this connection, and some periods of extremity never afterwards repeated.   Such, for example, were the autumn days in 1863, of which we read as follows :

October 5, Monday : Our money nearly spent.   Paid in faith, however, what was owing to tradesmen and servants. Found a very sweet promise for us in our revision work, 1 Chron. xxviii. 20.   Revision seven hours.

October 9 : Our money all but gone.   O Lord, our hope is in Thee !   Revision six and a half hours.   Mrs. Jones, Mrs. Lord, May Jones and Baby came from Bristol.   (So they were responsible for quite a party.)

October 10 : Revision nine and a half hours. . . . Went with Mrs. Jones to see Mr. Jonathan Hutchinson, who kindly refused to take any fee.   Only 2s. 5½d. left, with the greatest management.

> I must have all things and abound,
>   While God is God to me.

October 11, Sunday : Morning, with Lae-djün.   Afternoon, engaged in prayer.   Evening, went to hear Mr. Kennedy.   We gave 2s. to-day to the collections, in faith and as due to the Lord.

It is not surprising to find, as the week wore on, special evidences of the Lord's watchful care.   He was permitting their faith to be tested for sufficient reasons, but He was not unmindful of them in the trial.   Early in the week Mrs. Jones' sister came up from the country, bringing " a goose, a duck, and a fowl," with other good things, for the household ; and a day or two later a relative called with more than thirty pounds for Mr. and Mrs. Taylor's personal use.

Once, and once only, was there a liability that could not be met, for they sedulously obeyed the injunction, " Owe no man anything, save to love one another."   It was the summer of 1864, the close sultry season so trying in East

London. Ever since the beginning of August supplies had been running low, and on the 12th a brief entry closed with the words :

The tax-gatherer called, and I was obliged to defer him. Help us, O Lord, for Thy Name's sake.

Next day was Saturday, and there was little or nothing in hand. Seven and a half hours were given to revision just as usual, though the children's nurse had to be told the situation in case she might wish to leave.

Sought to realise that it is in weakness and need the strength of Jesus is perfected

is the entry that shows how deeply their hearts were exercised.

That night, though late, a friend who had left the house returned, and putting seven pounds into Mr. Taylor's hand begged him to accept it. Five pounds reached him by post on Monday, and thirty-five during the course of the week. Thus he was confirmed in the confidence that, for them at any rate, to give all their time and strength to the Lord's work and quietly wait His supplies was the right way.

On yet another occasion that little home in Beaumont Street witnessed some hours of anxious suspense. A quarter's rent was due immediately after a summer holiday in Yorkshire, and the day before the landlord was to call for it Mr. Taylor returned from Barnsley (where he had left his family) and went to the desk in which he had placed the money in readiness. To his surprise, instead of finding the amount expected, it was *a pound short*, and a moment's reflection assured him that the mistake was due to carelessness on his own part, which he had now no means of rectifying. For how to make up that missing pound he knew not, and the landlord—a quick-tempered, hard-spoken man—was to call the following morning.

There was more prayer than sleep that night, but the early post brought no relief. Slowly the minutes wore on, Mr. Taylor listening for the knock that did not come. After an hour or two he began to breathe more freely, though in intervals of work all day the anxiety returned, and when night came he gave himself again to prayer. Next morning, in a more friendly spirit than usual, the landlord appeared. He had been hindered, he explained, in starting for business the day before, and had been too late to call. Such a thing was most unusual, he could not account for it.

"But I can," interposed his tenant thankfully; "for only by this morning's post have I received a sovereign needed to make up the rent !"

Meanwhile, what of the bright hopes with which Mr. Taylor had entered upon the work entrusted to him by the Bible Society ? To obtain a correct version of the New Testament—not in Chinese character but in Roman letters, representing the sounds of the local dialect, and thus comparatively easy both to read and understand—was an object worthy of considerable sacrifice. With the help of Wang Lae-djün and Mrs. Taylor, who was as much at home in the Ningpo dialect as in English, he hoped to accomplish it in reasonable time. After a beginning had been made, he was joined also by the Rev. F. F. Gough of the C.M.S., whose knowledge of Greek as well as Chinese enabled him to translate with confidence from the original. They were thus well qualified for the work, and progress was not hindered by lack of diligence. But the task itself proved far more laborious than they had anticipated, extended as it was to include the preparation of marginal references.

Moreover it met, strange to say, with the strongest opposition. Persons whose position gave them weight criticised the undertaking at the Bible House to such an extent that, once and again, it seemed as if it must be abandoned, and this not at the beginning, but after months and years of toil, during which Mr. Taylor's friends and the Mission circle had become interested in the matter. To fail after having sacrificed so much, delaying even his return to China, was a possibility that cost him keen distress. Yet he had to face it, especially when Mr. Gough seemed on the point of giving way. For two or three months the situation was painful in the extreme. Brief entries in the little journal show how keenly Mr. Taylor felt it, though working on in the faith that all would yet be well.

Sept. 21 (1863) : Spent the morning in fasting and prayer. . . . Mr. Gough went to see Mr. Venn,[1] and I began a letter to the Secretary of the Bible Society.

Sept. 27, Sunday : Morning, with Lae-djün. Afternoon, engaged in prayer with Mr. Gough. Evening, heard Mr. Kennedy on Hos. vi. 1, a very valuable sermon. (" Come, and let us return unto the Lord : for He hath torn, and He will heal us ; He hath smitten, and He will bind us up.") May we turn to Him again, and again find His favour in our revision work.

Forty-three hours were given to revision that week, in spite of much distress.

Oct. 4, Sunday : Morning, with Lae-djün on Romans ii. Afternoon, read Hebrews, in Conybeare and Howson. Evening, took the lead at Mr. Scott's " Twig Folly " Meeting. Determined by God's help to live nearer to Him, and thus ensure His blessing in our work.

But the difficulties only increased, until Mr. Gough could go on no longer.

" Humanly speaking there is little hope of the continued aid of either the C.M.S. or the Bible Society," Mr. Taylor wrote to his mother on Oct. 7. " For *this* I care but little, as the Lord can easily provide the funds we need. But the help of Mr. Gough in the remainder of the work is very desirable, and under these circumstances it is improbable that we should have it. I would ask special prayer then.

" I. That the C.M.S. and the Bible Society may be brought to that conclusion which will be most for the glory of God and the *real* (not apparent) good of the work.

" II. That, if, as is almost certain, they throw up the revision, and if it be most for the good of the dear converts of Ningpo, Mr. Gough may be induced to continue his share in it.

" III. That if he should not do this, we may be guided aright as to our path—whether simply to reprint the Epistles and Revelation, or in some measure to revise them, correcting where we can any glaring errors ; or whether to give up the work altogether.

" My present full conviction, not a little confirmed by the character of the opposition to our work, is that it is of the Lord,

[1] Hon. Secretary of the Church Missionary Society.

and that He is saying to us, ' Be strong and of good courage and do it : fear not, nor be dismayed ; for the LORD GOD will be with thee, until thou hast finished all the work for the service of the house of the Lord.' If this is really His will, by His grace I will go forward. May He teach me if it be not so.

" ' Whatsoever ye shall ask in My Name, that will I do, that the Father may be glorified in the Son.' Plead this promise, dear Mother, in behalf of our work. And may He, whose we are and whom we serve, guide us aright."

Nothing is more striking in the records of the period than Mr. Taylor's dependence upon prayer, real dependence for every detail, every need. He leaned his whole weight on God, pleading the promises. Was it Lae-djün's affairs, the wife and child who needed him, or the difficulties of their long task ; was it a question of health, their own or the children's, of house - moving, money for daily bread, or guidance as to their return to China ?   All, all was brought to their Heavenly Father with the directness of little children, and the conviction that He could and would undertake, direct, and provide.   It was all so real, so practical !

Equally characteristic was the faithfulness with which he followed when the Lord's way was made plain. Barely two weeks after the above letter was written, the Bible Society reached a decision which bound him more than ever to the revision.

" There is no intention of taking it out of your hands," wrote his friend Mr. Pearse, forestalling the letter of the Committee. " They are evidently satisfied with what you are doing, and the way you are doing it."

This meant that the Romanised Testament would be completed, and greatly rejoiced Mr. Taylor as a definite answer to prayer ; but it meant also that he was pledged more than ever to his part of the work—and the years were passing on. With returning strength the longing grew upon him to be back in China, especially when the death of Mr. Jones left the Bridge Street converts almost without pastoral care. Great changes had swept over Ningpo with the devastations of the Tai-ping Rebellion.   After indescribable sufferings the population had largely lost faith in idols which could not protect even themselves, and many were ready as never before for the consolations of the Gospel. Mr. Meadows, bereaved of wife and child, was in sore need of companionship, and the native Christians of spiritual help. Everything pointed, humanly speaking, to Mr. Taylor's return, and increased his longing to be in direct missionary work once more. Important as the revision was, he was young and craved activity and the joy of winning souls to Christ. Yet did not the very answers to prayer that had been so marked bind him to continue the work that was detaining him, and carry it to completion ?

But all the while another longing was taking possession of his soul, looming large and ever larger with strange persistence. Do what he would, he could not escape the call of inland China, the appeal of those Christless millions for whom no man seemed to care. On his study wall hung the map of the whole vast empire ; on the table before him lay the ever-open Bible ; and between the two how close and heart-searching the connection ! Feeding, feasting, upon the Word of God, his eye would fall upon the map—and oh, the thought of those for whom nothing was prepared !

" While on the field," he wrote, " the pressure of claims immediately around me was so great that I could not think much of the still greater need farther inland, and could do nothing to meet it. But detained for some years in England, daily viewing the whole country on the large map in my study, I was as near the vast regions of the interior as the smaller districts in which I had personally laboured—and prayer was the only resource by which the burdened heart could obtain any relief."

Laying aside their work, for Mr. Gough in measure shared this experience, they would call Mrs. Taylor and Lae-djün, and unitedly pour out their hearts in prayer that God would send the Gospel to every part of China. And they did more than pray. Alone, or together, they interviewed the representatives of the larger missionary societies, pleading the cause of those unevangelised millions. Everywhere they were met with sympathy, for the facts were their own argument ; but everywhere also it was evident that nothing could, or rather would be done. The objections raised were

twofold : in the first place, financially, any aggressive effort
was impossible.   Neither the men nor the means were forthcoming.   And were it otherwise, those remote provinces
were practically inaccessible to foreigners.   True the treaty
of 1860 provided for journeys and even residence inland,
but that was merely on paper, and everywhere the conclusion
was the same : " We must wait until God's providence
opens the door ; at present we can do nothing."

These objections, however, did not lessen the need or
bring any lightening of the burden.   Returning to the East
End and his quiet study, Hudson Taylor found himself still
challenged by the open Bible, the ever-accusing map.   The
Master had said nothing about politics or finance in His
great commission.   " Go ye . . . Lo, I am with you."
"All the world . . . all the days "—so read command and
promise.   Was He not worthy of trust and utmost allegiance?

And there were others who thought as he did, friends
and candidates of the Mission who gathered weekly for
prayer at Beaumont Street.   Ever since the outgoing of
Mr. and Mrs. Meadows this meeting had been held on
Saturday afternoons.   Few though they were in number,
the spirit of prayer was so outpoured that for a couple of
hours at a time those fervent hearts went up in continued
supplication.   Thus as the silent years drew to a close, with
their restraining providences and all their deepening and
development, to the man upon his knees came at length
some apprehension of that for which also he was apprehended
of God.

CHAPTER III

THERE WRESTLED A MAN WITH HIM

1865. AET. 33.

AMONG those who attended the prayer meeting at Beaumont Street, none were more interested in the Ningpo Mission than the tall silent merchant and his wife who came up from their beautiful home in Sussex. As the owner of large starch works Mr. Berger was a busy man, but his chief interest lay in the extension of the Kingdom of God. Brought up in the Church of England he had been converted early in life under unusual circumstances. At an evening party he was talking with a girl of his own age when, to his surprise, she introduced the subject of religion. So evident was her sincerity, and the joy she found in Christ as a personal Friend and Saviour, that the young man was deeply moved. In the midst of that gay company he realised the emptiness of all the world can give, apart from the one thing needful. No special sense of sin seems to have come to him till later, but then and there he received the Lord Jesus as his Saviour, " and went behind the drawing-room door to hide his tears of thankfulness."

He was still under forty when he met Hudson Taylor for the first time, then a lad of twenty-one on the eve of sailing for China, and was attracted by his spirit.[1] Correspondence increased the interest, and when the missionary was invalided

[1] As much was to grow out of this association, it is interesting to recall that the introduction was through a mutual friend, Mr. George Pearse of the Stock Exchange, Secretary of the Society that was sending the young missionary to China, who, after the Hackney Meeting one Sunday morning, took Hudson Taylor and his friend (later on his brother-in-law), Mr. B. Broomhall, to dine with the Bergers, then living at Hornsey Rise.

home seven years later, no warmer welcome awaited him, outside his family circle, than the welcome of Mr. and Mrs. Berger to Saint Hill.[1] From that time their house was open to him and his, and the prolonged task that kept him in London served to deepen the friendship.

With more experience of the world as well as in spiritual things, Mr. Berger was fitted to be just the adviser Hudson Taylor needed, and in his gentle wife Mrs. Taylor found almost a mother's sympathy. Saint Hill, indeed, became a real oasis to all the family at Beaumont Street. How good it was to escape at times from the squalid surroundings of Whitechapel to the hills and lanes of Sussex! The fine old house and grounds, sloping down to a little lake with meadows beyond, were a paradise to the children, quite apart from the good cheer Mrs. Berger's hospitality provided. It was a perfect friendship; and with no family of their own, the Bergers had room in their hearts for all the interests of the Mission.

As time went on and Mr. Taylor became increasingly burdened about the need and claims of inland China, Mr. Berger shared with him much of the exercise of heart involved. He knew of Mr. Taylor's efforts to induce various societies to extend their operations to those waiting provinces, and was in sympathy with his thought of utilising a class of labourers hitherto little drawn upon. But it was in the growing sense of personal responsibility that the chief bond of union lay. Accompanying Mr. Taylor to a farewell meeting for a young worker about to join Mr. Meadows, he was surprised to find a small poor church, without a single influential member, undertaking the whole of his support. The joy with which they were making sacrifices brought to Mr. Berger a new sense of the privilege of giving and suffering for Jesus' sake, and the earnestness of Mr. Taylor's address moved him to a definite resolve. Rising at the close of the meeting he said that what he had seen and heard overwhelmed him with shame because he had done so little, comparatively, for the cause of Christ. It filled him with

---

[1] The beautiful mansion near East Grinstead to which they had moved from London.

joy also ; and he had determined that night to do ten times more, yes, by the help of God, a hundred times more than he had hitherto attempted.[1]

Thankful as Mr. Taylor must have been for this step forward, how little either he or Mr. Berger can have anticipated the developments for which provision was thus being made ! Yet they were near at hand. For to himself also matters were assuming a new urgency. Added to the consciousness ever present with him of passing souls in China, had come another thought :

" They perish—a thousand every hour of the day and night—and this while to me, as to every believer, is given power to ask in prayer whatsoever we will ; to ask *without limit* in the name of Jesus."

Little wonder the burden was intolerable !

By this time a change had come in his immediate surroundings. A growing interest in the Ningpo Mission and an increasing number of candidates made it necessary to seek larger quarters. A home had been found in Coborn Street, a couple of miles farther east, where Mile End merges into the more residential neighbourhood of Bow, and side streets aspire to modest gardens shaded by welcome trees. One would hardly have thought that number 30, with its one window beside the hall-door, could have offered any serious difficulty through excess of size ; but the entry in Mr. Taylor's journal was as follows :

Sept. 28 (1864) : Revision five hours. Went with Mr. Gough to seek a house : found the way closed in all but one direction. The house seemed too large for us, but Mr. Gough offered to pay the difference between it and our present rent.

A week later the result was recorded :

Oct. 5 : Revision two and a half hours. . . . We prepare for moving to-morrow. Prayer was answered in our finding a man who would help us to remove reasonably.

---

[1] It is interesting that this experience took place on March 13, 1865, little more than three months before Mr. Taylor himself met the crisis of his life on the sands at Brighton.

Oct. 6 : Came to 30 Coborn Street, Bow. Paid eighteen shillings for removing. Took Truelove to Bryanstone Hall, and lectured on China.

Eighteen shillings for the transport of all their worldly belongings ! And not only so : a day sufficed for packing, it would seem, and even less for settling into the new home. For Mr. Taylor " lectured on China " within a few hours of taking possession, and thereafter, as may be seen from the journal, the revision and other work proceeded just as usual. What a light it casts upon the largeness of his aims and the lowliness of his spirit !

Here, then, a fresh start had been made in October 1864, the sitting-room, extending from front to back on the ground-floor, being much appreciated for the prayer meeting which was increasing in numbers. The revision of the Ningpo Testament was still the main task, though Mr. Gough was expecting to complete it single-handed, as the time seemed near for Mr. and Mrs. Taylor's return to China. Candidates were coming and going, and new cycles of interest were opening up.

" We need your prayers," Mr. Taylor wrote to his mother at the beginning of 1865. " The responsibility resting upon us is increasing very much. I must have more grace and wisdom from above or shall utterly fail. May He Who *giveth* ' more grace ' grant me to live increasingly in His light. We have received a hundred pounds toward the expense of outfit, etc. ; pray for what more may be needed, perhaps nine hundred or a thousand pounds "

—for he was hoping to take with him six or seven new missionaries.

And then, just as all seemed ready for advance, an unexpected happening changed the current of events and closed the way again indefinitely. A fine new steamer was about to sail for China, and the owner, hearing of Mr. Taylor's party, offered free passages to a couple of missionaries. Two of the young men were ready in time and embarked at Glasgow ; but a stormy voyage down the Irish Channel so upset one of them that he turned back from Plymouth, fearing he had mistaken his calling. This was, of course, a keen disappointment to Mr. Taylor, who was concerned also that the passage and outfit should be lost. Right nobly a young farmer from Aberdeenshire stepped into the gap, putting off his marriage, which was about to take place, that he might redeem the situation. He had been long engaged, and it was naturally felt that his fiancée, also an accepted candidate, should follow him as soon as possible. Funds and a suitable escort being provided in answer to prayer, she sailed a fortnight later, and Mr. Taylor was left minus *four* of his prospective party. Of the remainder, strange to say, one wanted more time for preparation, a second was unable to free himself from home claims, and a third had not fully made up his mind about going ; so there was nothing for it but to pray and wait until the way should open.[1]

Meanwhile, moreover, Mr. Taylor had been drawn into a new undertaking, which was absorbing time and thought. Early in the year the pastor of the church to which he belonged (who was editor also of the *Baptist Magazine*) had asked for a series of articles on China with a view to awakening interest in the Ningpo Mission. These Mr. Taylor had begun to prepare, and one had even been published, when Mr. Lewis returned the manuscript of the next. The articles, he felt, were weighty, and should have a wider circulation than his paper could afford.

" Add to them," he said earnestly ; " let them cover the whole field and be published as an appeal for inland China."

This seemed incompatible with Mr. Taylor's many engagements, but when his departure was unexpectedly delayed he saw the opportunity and set himself to take advantage of it. Even before his party had been broken up, the study necessary for these papers was bringing to a crisis the exercise of mind through which Mr. Taylor had been passing. Compiling facts as to the size and population of every province in China, and making diagrams to show their

---

[1] With the sailing of the bride-elect the prayer was fully answered which had been going up since 1860, for five additional workers for the Ningpo Mission. The five thus sent out were: Mr. Meadows (who had already lost his wife in China), Miss Notman, Messrs. Barchet and Crombie, and Miss Skinner (Mrs. Crombie).

neglected condition, stirred him to a desperate sense of the sin and shame of allowing such a state of things to continue. Yet what was to be done ? The number of Protestant missionaries, as he had discovered, was diminishing rather than increasing. Despite the fact that half the heathen population of the world was to be found in China, the missionaries engaged in its evangelisation had actually been reduced, during the previous winter, from a hundred and fifteen to only ninety-one. This had come to light through his study of the latest statistics, and, naturally, added fuel to the fire that was consuming him. But he had done all that was possible. No one would move in the matter   He must leave it now, until the Lord—— But somehow that was not the final word.

Leave it, when he knew that he, small, weak, and nothing as he was, might pray in faith for labourers and *they would be given* ? Leave it, when there stood plainly in his Bible that solemn word, " When I say unto the wicked, Thou shalt surely die ; and thou givest him not warning, nor speakest to warn the wicked from his wicked way, to save his life ; the same wicked man shall die in his iniquity, but *his blood will I require at thy hand* " !

" I knew God was speaking," he said of this critical time. " I knew that in answer to prayer evangelists would be given and their support secured, because the Name of Jesus is worthy. But there unbelief came in.

" Suppose the workers are given and go to China : trials will come ; their faith may fail ; would they not reproach *you* for bringing them into such a plight ?   Have you ability to cope with so painful a situation ?

" And the answer was, of course, a decided negative.

" It was just a bringing in of *self*, through unbelief ; the devil getting one to feel that while prayer and faith would bring one into the fix, one would have to get out of it as best one might. And I did not see that the Power that would give the men and the means would be sufficient to keep them also, even in the far interior of China.

" Meanwhile, *a million a month* were dying in that land, dying without God. This was burned into my very soul. For two or three months the conflict was intense. I scarcely slept night or day more than an hour at a time, and feared I should lose my reason.   Yet I did not give in.   To no one could I speak freely, not even to my dear wife.   She saw, doubtless, that something was going on ;   but I felt I must refrain as long as possible from laying upon her a burden so crushing—these souls, and what eternity must mean for every one of them, and what the Gospel might do, would do, for all who believed, if we would take it to them."

The break in the journal at this point is surely significant. Faithfully the record had gone on for two and a quarter years ;   but now—silence.   For seven weeks from the middle of April, lovely weeks of spring, there was no entry.   First and only blank in those revealing pages, how much the very silence has to tell us !   Yes, he was face to face with the purpose of God at last.   Accept it, he dare not ;   escape it, he could not.   And so, as long ago, " there wrestled a man with him until the breaking of the day."

It was Sunday, June 25, a quiet summer morning by the sea.   Worn out and really ill, Hudson Taylor had gone to friends at Brighton, and, unable to bear the sight of rejoicing multitudes in the house of God, had wandered out alone upon the sands left by the receding tide.   It was a peaceful scene about him, but inwardly he was in agony of spirit. A decision had to be made and he knew it, for the conflict could no longer be endured.

" Well," the thought came at last, " if God gives us a band of men for inland China, and they go, and all die of starvation even, they will only be taken straight to heaven ;   and if one heathen soul is saved, would it not be well worth while ? "

It was a strange way round to faith—that if the worst came to the worst it would still be worth while.   But something in the service of that morning seems to have come to mind.   God-consciousness began to take the place of unbelief, and a new thought possessed him as dawn displaces night :

Why, if we are obeying the Lord, the responsibility rests *with Him,* not with us !

This, brought home to his heart in the power of the Spirit, wrought the change once and for all.

" *Thou*, Lord," he cried with relief that was unutterable, " *Thou* shalt have all the burden ! At Thy bidding, as Thy servant I go forward, leaving results with Thee."

For some time the conviction had been growing that he ought to ask for at any rate two evangelists for each of the eleven unoccupied provinces, and two for Chinese Tartary and Tibet. Pencil in hand he now opened his Bible, and with the boundless ocean breaking at his feet wrote the simple memorable words : " Prayed for twenty-four willing skilful labourers at Brighton, June 25, 1865."

" How restfully I turned away from the sands," he said, recalling the deliverance of that hour. " The conflict ended, all was joy and peace. I felt as if I could fly up the hill to Mr. Pearse's house. And how I did sleep that night ! My dear wife thought Brighton had done wonders for me, and so it had."

CHAPTER IV

THE MISSION THAT HAD TO BE

1865. AET. 33.

NEW life, evidently, had come to Hudson Taylor with the decision taken that June Sunday on the sands at Brighton, for he was up with the lark next morning and off to London at 6.30 A.M. No record remains of that day, save that Mrs. Taylor was cheered to see him better, and that he went to have special prayer with one who was wishing to join the mission, whose way was beset with difficulties. But next day brought just the practical step that might have been expected:

> June 27: Went with Mr. Pearse to the London & County Bank, and opened an account for the *China Inland Mission*. Paid in £10 : 0 : 0.

It is the first appearance of the new name.

Thereafter the little journal scintillates with its repetition, as though writing it in full were in itself a satisfaction. Thus, after the prayer meeting of the following Saturday, July 1:

> Gave Miss Faulding a receipt for a pound for the China Inland Mission.
> July 3: Breakfasted with Lady Radstock. . . . Mr. Berger took tea with us and stayed till 7 P.M. He promised £80 to £100 for printing-press and type, and £150 towards the China Inland Mission.
> July 4: Miss Faulding brought 3/6 from Regent's Park Chapel for the China Inland Mission.

It is all so sweet and natural—the overflowing of a young heart just as full as a mother's with her first-born !

And then came days of activity in striking contrast with the silence of preceding weeks. Complete surrender to the will of God not only set the joy-bells ringing, it gave the clue to much that before had seemed perplexing, and started the suspended energies on a clear course. Delays and difficulties explained themselves, and how thankful Mr. Taylor felt for the restraining Hand that had kept him from leaving England previously, and had returned that unpublished manuscript for a purpose he little anticipated. Now he had something to write about, something definite to lay before the Lord's people, new power in pleading the cause of inland China, and an object worthy of highest endeavour. He had found himself at last, found life's best and deepest, not in the way of his own choosing, but in the " good works which God had before ordained " that he should walk in them.

The change soon made itself felt, and the little house at Coborn Street was more than ever busy. An unexpected introduction to Lady Radstock led to interesting developments, and all through the summer and autumn Mr. Taylor had a succession of engagements that brought him into touch with influential circles. He was preparing also for the outgoing of Mr. J. W. Stevenson, who for some months had been with him in London, and of a newer candidate from Scotland, Mr. George Stott.   In the midst of outfitting and business details it was not easy to run off for luncheon with titled people, and drawing-room meetings at which everybody appeared in evening dress. It rather took away Mr. Taylor's breath at first !   But it had come about entirely apart from his seeking, and in such a way as to leave no doubt that the One Who had led him to settle in East London was opening to him also the drawing-rooms of the West.

A week only after his visit to Brighton he had gone to spend Sunday with his sister at Bayswater, doubtless to seek her prayerful sympathy and that of her husband, Mr. Benjamin Broomhall, in the step just taken. As the hour for public worship drew near, instead of going as usual to

the chapel of which he was a member, Mr. Taylor sought
definite guidance as to where he should worship that morning.   Passing down Welbeck Street, it came to him to join
the little company of " Open Brethren " who had a meeting
there.   This he did, finding much refreshment in fellowship
with them at the Table of the Lord.

It so happened that among the requests for prayer read
out toward the close of the meeting was one that seemed
in danger of being forgotten.   Nobody took it up, and Mr.
Taylor feared the service might close without united remembrance of this special need.   The circumstances were quite
ordinary—a case of illness, involving long-continued suffering
—but, stranger though he was, he could not let the appeal
for spiritual help pass unnoticed.

" Who was that ? " inquired the Dowager Lady Radstock
afterwards, deeply impressed by the simplicity and helpfulness of his prayer.

On learning that the visitor was Hudson Taylor, a
missionary from China, she desired to see more of him.   The
outcome was an invitation to breakfast at Portland Place
the following morning, and the commencement of a friendship with several members of the Waldegrave family that
became fruitful in blessing for China.

Staying with Lady Radstock at the time was a married
daughter, who on returning to her Norfolk home arranged
for a visit from Mr. Taylor.   It was not easy to get away
from all there was to be done, but Lady Beauchamp was
planning a series of meetings to occupy several days, and
Mr. Taylor felt the importance of the opportunity.   It was
only by working all night he finally completed arrangements
for the outgoing party (Mr. Stott and the Stevensons), and
even then he had to write on the train a farewell letter full
of suggestions and messages.   Almost bewildering must it
have been to turn from these preoccupations to the programme before him at Langley Park.   But Sir Thomas and
Lady Beauchamp and their family were thoroughly in
sympathy with the aims and spirit of their guest.   Even
the children were drawn to him, and loved to hear his stories
about China.   One indeed, who as a member of the Mission

was to be Mr. Taylor's chosen companion in China and elsewhere, remembers to this day " the pig-tail and chop-sticks " and much beside that came with that welcome visitor to Langley Park.[1]

So warm was the sympathy of the parents that they desired to help the Mission financially, though no appeal had been made for money and no collections taken. All the more, perhaps, for this reason, Mr. Taylor's host and hostess wished to give as a matter of privilege ; but their generosity in other directions had left them little in hand for the purpose. After praying over it, however, the thought suggested itself :

" Why not trust the Lord about the conservatories, and contribute the amount almost due for insurance ? "

Langley Park possessed extensive greenhouses, and winter storms were apt to be serious near that east coast. But, definitely committing the matter to Him Who controls wind and wave, the cheque was drawn and the premium paid into the Mission treasury. The sequel Mr. Taylor never heard till long after, nor indeed that the gift had been made possible in this way. But the Lord knew ; and when a few months later a storm of exceptional violence broke over the neighbourhood, He did not forget. Much glass was shattered for miles around, but the conservatories at Langley Park entirely escaped.

The little leather-bound account-book that shows the receipt of this gift on the day of Mr. Taylor's return to London shows also many contributions from the Portland Place circle. The late Lord Radstock, Lady Beauchamp's brother, became a warm supporter of the Mission, and was frequently in correspondence with Mr. Taylor at this time. Meetings arranged by him in his town house and elsewhere laid the needs of China on many hearts, and it was a wonderful encouragement in launching the new enterprise to have such an accession of sympathy.

It was not all talk and meetings, however, in those early

[1] The Rev. Sir Montagu Beauchamp, C.F., who after thirty years of devoted service in China has recently succeeded to the title, through the lamented death of his brother, Col. Sir Horace Beauchamp, Bart., at the front.

days. Though the branches were spreading out, the roots were striking deeper in quiet hours of thought and prayer. With Mr. Berger especially, many were the consultations held upon practical questions, and as responsibilities increased it was an untold comfort to have his help in bearing them.

" When I decided to go forward," said Mr. Taylor of this summer, " Mr. Berger undertook to represent us at home. The thing grew up gradually. We were much drawn together. The Mission received its name in his drawing-room. Neither of us asked or appointed the other : it just *was so*."

And what shall be said of the still more intimate help of the life nearest of all to his own—the tender love, the spiritual inspiration and practical wisdom of the one who shared his every experience ? To Mrs. Taylor, necessarily, the new departure meant more than to any other ; for, young as she was, not yet thirty, she had to mother the Mission as well as care for a growing family. To take four little children out to China was no light matter, and when the object in view is remembered—nothing less than to plant messengers of the Gospel in every one of the unopened provinces—a mother's heart alone can realise what hers must often have felt. It was not her husband's faith, however, upon which she leaned, great as were her joy and confidence in him. From girlhood, orphaned of both parents, she had put to the test for herself the Heavenly Father's faithfulness. Family burdens and the pressure of need might come, and this immense responsibility be superadded, but her resources did not fail, for she drew moment by moment upon " all the fulness of God."

The chief work that claimed Mr. and Mrs. Taylor after the decision at Brighton was that of completing the manuscript returned by Mr. Lewis. It may have been easy to say, " Add to it, let it cover the whole field and be published as an appeal for inland China," but to carry out the suggestion was another matter. Little information was to be had about that great closed land, and to make its needs real and appealing needed a touch other than they could give. The writing meant much study, thought, and prayer. Too

busy during the week to obtain quiet, they gave what time
they could on Sunday, without neglecting public worship,
to this important task.   Together in the little sitting-room
at Coborn Street they prayed and wrote, wrote and prayed.
China's Spiritual Need and Claims was the outcome.

" Every sentence was steeped in prayer," Mr. Taylor recalled.
" It grew up while we were writing—I walking up and down
the room and Maria seated at the table."

Turning the pages thoughtfully, one feels again the power
that touched and moved readers of that book for more than
a generation.   There is evidence in every paragraph not
only of painstaking study, but of the spirit of prayer in
which it was written.   It is skilfully adapted to its purpose,
and, what is more, one stands from first to last in the light
of God.   *His* word it is that comes to one, His point of view
from which there is no escaping.   There is no self about it,
no turning of the thought to man.   The writer scarcely
appears in the whole book.   Mr. Berger is referred to by
name, and so are the members of the Mission already in
China or on the way thither, but Hudson Taylor is absent
to a remarkable degree.

First, very briefly, the reader is reminded that every act
in this life and every omission too has a direct and important
bearing on the future—his own and that of others.   It is
pointed out that we are to pray not as the heathen who use
vain repetitions, nor as the worldly-minded who ask principally if not solely for their own benefit.   " After *this* manner
therefore pray ye," putting the kingdom of God first, and
His righteousness.

How this is to be done is set before us in the example of
our Lord Himself : " Let *this mind* be in you which was also
in Christ Jesus."   How did HE act in view of the sin and
suffering of a lost world, in view of His knowledge of the
will of God ?   Was it not these things, the very conditions
we too have to meet, that brought Him out of His Heaven
to limitless depths of self-emptying, even to " the death of
the cross " ?   Grievously have His people failed in following
that example.   With the large majority of our fellow-men

still destitute of the knowledge of salvation, how can we, owing everything to the sacrifice of the Son of God, remain comfortable and unconcerned in a life of self-pleasing ?

Then, turning from other fields, attention is centred upon China—its antiquity, extent, population, early efforts to introduce Christianity among its people, and the history of Roman Catholic propaganda. A survey of Protestant missions is given, showing great progress since the days of Morrison, but bringing out the startling fact that even in the seven provinces in which such work had been begun there were still *a hundred and eighty-five millions* " utterly and hopelessly beyond the reach of the Gospel." What this meant, and further, that beyond these again lay the eleven inland provinces—*two hundred millions more* without a single witness for Christ—is emphasised by comparisons and diagrams prepared with the very heart's blood of the writer. As one reads, the mind almost reels before such a situation. No wonder this man is burdened ! No wonder he cannot get away from the awful sense of responsibility. And he looks upon it all, makes the reader look upon it all, *with God*. That is where the deep solemnity comes in. One is standing in the light of eternity, in the presence of the crucified, risen Lord of Glory. His unconditional command, " Go . . . I am with you alway," is sounding on and on, while with it mingles the low wail of thousands, passing hour by hour into Christless graves. It is profoundly, unutterably real. " A million a month in China are dying without God," and we who have received in trust the Word of Life, we are responsible. It was not China's need alone that called the Inland Mission into being, it was *China's claim.*

The overwhelming greatness of the task before the Mission is felt rather than dwelt upon, for yet another Reality shines out from these pages, preoccupying mind and heart. Than the greatness of the need, one thing only is greater—the fact of God : His resources, purposes, faithfulness, His commands and promises. " All power is given unto Me . . . go ye *therefore*." That is enough ; that alone could be enough. The need is great, immensely great ; but

God is greater, infinitely greater.   And this God the writer knows, has proved, trusts.

Hence it follows that the principles of the new Mission are simply an adjustment of these two considerations—the need to be met and GOD.   HE stands behind the work He has called into being.   The writer has no other resources, absolutely none, and he desires no other.   Every problem resolves itself into a fresh appeal to God, for there can be no need unmet in Him.

We have to do with One Who is Lord of all power and might, Whose arm is not shortened that it cannot save, nor His ear heavy that it cannot hear ; with One Whose unchanging Word directs us to ask and receive that our joy may be full, to open our mouths wide that He may fill them ; and we do well to remember that this gracious God, Who has condescended to place His almighty power at the command of believing prayer, looks not lightly on the blood-guiltiness of those who neglect to avail themselves of it for the benefit of the perishing. . . .

Feeling, on the one hand, the solemn responsibility that rests upon us, and on the other the gracious encouragements that everywhere meet us in the Word of God, we do not hesitate to ask the great Lord of the Harvest to call forth, to *thrust* forth twenty-four European and twenty-four native evangelists, to plant the standard of the Cross in the eleven unevangelised provinces of China proper and in Chinese Tartary.   To those who have never been called to prove the faithfulness of the Covenant-keeping God in supplying, in answer to prayer alone, the every need of His servants, it might seem a hazardous experiment to send twenty-four European evangelists to a distant heathen land, " with *only God to look to* " ; but in one whose privilege it has been through many years to put that God to the test in varied circumstances, at home and abroad, by land and sea, in sickness and health, in dangers, in necessities and at the gates of death, such apprehensions would be wholly inexcusable.[1]

---

[1] " The writer has seen God, in answer to prayer, quell the raging of the storm," Mr. Taylor continued, " alter the direction of the wind and give rain in the midst of prolonged drought.   He has seen Him, in answer to prayer, stay the angry passions and murderous intentions of violent men, and bring the machinations of His people's foes to nought.   He has seen Him, in answer to prayer, raise the dying from the bed of death, when human aid was vain ; has seen Him preserve from the pestilence that walketh in darkness, and from the destruction that wasteth at noonday.   For more than eight years and a half he has proved the faithfulness of God in supplying his own temporal wants and the needs of the work in which he has been engaged."   See *Hudson Taylor in Early Years : The Growth of a Soul*, especially pp. 429-492.

Instance after instance is given from Mr. Taylor's experience of direct, unmistakable answers to prayer, and the deduction drawn is that with such a God it is safe and wise to go forward in the pathway of obedience—is indeed the only safe and wise thing to do.

When he comes to touch upon the practical working of the Mission, the application of Scriptural principles is just as direct. Not much is said, for the organisation is of the simplest, but Bible precedents cast light on every problem. The writer is dealing with an unchanging God, and confidently expects Him to work in the same way still. The very greatness of the need, considered in the light of Divine not human resources, called for methods as new and distinctive as the proposed sphere of the Mission itself.

How could the work be limited, for example, to any *one* section of the Church of Christ ? No denomination, however generous its support, could be equal to it, just as no one class in society could provide the labourers needed. The Mission must be free to accept " willing, skilful workers," no matter what their Church connection or previous training, provided they were wise to win souls, men and women who knew their God and could sink lesser differences in the one great bond of union.

Then as to funds : how could the Mission, possessing nothing, promise stated salaries to its members ? How could Mr. Taylor let them look to *him* for support ? All that was sent in answer to prayer he would gladly use for or distribute among his fellow-workers, but more than that he could not promise, except that under no circumstances would he go into debt for the Mission any more than for himself. Each individual member must know that he or she was sent of God, and must be able to trust Him for supplies—strength, grace, protection, enablement for every emergency, as well as daily bread. No other basis would be possible. If the Mission were to be fruitful, were to continue at all amid the perils that must be faced, it could only be as each one connected with it contributed his quota of faith in the living God.

" We had to consider," Mr. Taylor said of this period,
" whether it would not be possible for members of various
denominations to work together on simple, evangelistic lines,
without friction as to conscientious differences of opinion ?
Prayerfully concluding that it would, we decided to invite the
co-operation of fellow-believers irrespective of denominational
views, who fully held the inspiration of God's Word, and were
willing to prove their faith by going to inland China with only
the guarantee they carried within the covers of their pocket
Bibles.

" That Word had said, ' Seek first the Kingdom of God and
His righteousness, and all these things (food and raiment) shall
be added unto you.' If any one did not believe that God spoke
the truth, it would be better for him not to go to China to propagate the faith. If he did believe it, surely the promise sufficed.
Again, ' No good thing will He withhold from them that walk
uprightly.' If any one did not mean to walk uprightly, he had
better stay at home ; if he did mean to walk uprightly, he had
all he needed in the shape of a guarantee fund. God owns all
the gold and silver in the world, and the cattle on a thousand
hills. We need not be vegetarians.

" We might indeed have had a guarantee fund if we had
wished it ; but we felt it was unneeded and would do harm.
Money wrongly placed and money given from wrong motives are
both to be greatly dreaded. We can afford to have as little as
the LORD chooses to give, but we cannot afford to have unconsecrated money, or to have money placed in the wrong
position. Far better have no money at all, even to buy food
with ; for there are plenty of ravens in China, and the Lord
could send them again with bread and flesh. . . .

" Our Father is a very experienced One. He knows very
well that His children wake up with a good appetite every
morning, and He always provides breakfast for them, and does
not send them supperless to bed at night. ' Thy bread shall
be given thee, and thy water shall be sure.' He sustained three
million Israelites in the wilderness for forty years. We do not
expect He will send three million missionaries to China ; but if
He did, He would have ample means to sustain them all. Let
us see that we keep God before our eyes ; that we walk in His
ways and seek to please and glorify Him in everything, great
and small. Depend upon it, GOD's work done in GOD's way
will never lack GOD's supplies."

It was men and women of faith, therefore, who were
needed for the Inland Mission, prepared to depend on God

alone, satisfied with poverty should He deem it best, and confident that His Word cannot be broken.

Much else comes out in these earnest pages, and much that is *not* said is significant by its absence.   There is no mention even of a Committee, no reliance upon organisation or great names.   The entire direction of the Mission was to be in the hands of its founder, himself the most experienced of its members, who like a General on active service would be with his forces in the field.   So natural does this arrangement seem that one hardly recognises the greatness of the innovation, or that in this as in other new departures Hudson Taylor was making a contribution of exceeding value to the high politics of missions.   He had simply learned from painful experience how much a missionary may have to suffer, and the work be hampered, if not imperilled, by being under the control of those who, however well-intentioned, have no first-hand knowledge of its conditions, and are, moreover, at the other side of the world.

Another striking absence is that of any pleading for financial help.   It is mentioned that an annual expenditure of five thousand pounds might be anticipated when the outgoing party of ten or twelve should be added to those already on the field.   Mr. Berger's address is given as Mr. Taylor's representative in England, to whom gifts might be sent by any desiring to have fellowship with the work.   And for the rest, the quiet words express a sense of *wealth* rather than need, " although the wants are large, they will not exhaust the resources of Our Father."

Finally, there is not a word about Government protection or dependence upon treaty rights.   Many instances are given of *Divine* protection in the dangers inseparable from pioneering work such as the Mission looked forward to. Unarmed, in native dress, and claiming no aid from Consular authorities, the writer had found times of peril to be always times of proving the watchful care of One Who is a refuge better than foreign flag or gunboat.   It is God who looms large, not man.

" He can raise up, He will raise up ' willing, skilful men ' for every department of our service," was the quiet conclusion.

" All we are now proposing to do is to lay hold on His faithfulness Who has called us into this service, and in obedience to *His*
call and reliance on *His* power to enlarge the sphere of our
operations, for the glory of His name Who alone doeth wondrous
things.

" The question, however, might be raised as to whether the
interior of China, though evidently needing the Gospel and
nominally open to us by treaty-right, will in point of fact prove
accessible ?   We would answer this question by another : When
the Lord Jesus gives a definite command, is it our place to ask
whether it can be obeyed or not ?   The terms of His command
are explicit . . . and He answers every objection, meets every
difficulty at the very outset by assuring us that *all power* is
given unto Him in heaven and on earth ; that He Who is true,
and therefore can neither fail nor forget, Who hath the key of
David to open or to shut as pleaseth Him, is with us *always*,
even unto the end of the world.

" The dangers and difficulties will be neither few nor small,
but with Jesus for our Leader we may safely follow on.   These
dangers, difficulties and trials, while leading to a deeper realisation of our own weakness, poverty and need, will constrain us
also to lean more constantly, to draw more largely, to rest more
implicitly on the strength, the riches, the fulness of Jesus. ' In
the world ye shall have tribulation,' but ' in Me . . . peace,'
will be the experience of those engaged in the work.   If it be
for God's glory, for the benefit of His cause and the true interest
of those concerned, the times of greatest trial and danger will be
the times when His delivering power will shine forth most conspicuously ;   and if otherwise, His sustaining grace will prove
sufficient for the weakest servant in the conflict. . . .

" Let but devoted labourers be found, who will prove faithful
to God, and there is no reason to fear that God will not prove
faithful to them.   He will set before them an open door, and
will esteem them of more value than the sparrows and the lilies
that He clothes and feeds.   He will be with them in danger,
in difficulty, in perplexity ;   and while *they* may be utter weakness, *He* will work through them in power.   They may cast
their bread upon the waters, but His Word shall not return unto
Him void :   it shall accomplish that which He pleases, and prosper
in the thing whereto He sends it. . . . It is upon past Ebenezers
we build our Jehovah-Jireh.   ' They that know Thy Name will
put their trust in Thee.' "

Little wonder that faith of this sort, so uncalculating
and withal so practical, made a strong appeal to Christian

hearts ! Finished by the middle of October, the manuscript was first of all submitted to Mr. and Mrs. Berger at Saint Hill.

" The Lord caused them to be interested," we read in Mr. Taylor's journal.

Interested they certainly were ! for Mr. Berger forthwith undertook to meet the expense of publication, and urged that the pamphlet should be ready for the Mildmay Conference, to be held ten days later. The earlier sheets were already in the press, and the goodwill of the printer was not lacking. By sitting up all night to correct proofs, Mr. Taylor managed to return the last batch in time, and had the satisfaction of receiving a consignment for distribution on the opening day of the meetings.

Only six weeks previously he had been in Scotland and had found himself at Perth, as we have seen, during a similar Convention. The deep impression made by his address on that occasion had affected Mildmay circles, for the latter was the mother-conference with which Perth was in close connection. Convened by the Rev. W. Pennefather, Vicar of St. Jude's, it had a definite Church of England element, but its platform included ministers and laymen of other connections, and from the Continent as well as Great Britain and America. Deeply spiritual in tone, it attracted the leaders of the young evangelistic movements that had sprung out of the Great Revival, to whom Mr. Taylor's line of things made naturally a strong appeal. With Mr. Pennefather's cordial approval, the pamphlet was distributed among the many hundreds who attended the Conference, and few went away from those days of waiting upon God without a quickened sense of responsibility in view of China's need.

Many were the letters that reached Mr. Taylor during the weeks that followed, showing that the book was doing its quiet work, and that in widely differing circles the C.I.M. was hailed with thankfulness as a Mission that had to be. Offers of service came from the students' hall, the business counter, and the mechanic's shop. Invitations for meetings were numerous, and so great was the demand for literature that *China's Spiritual Need and Claims* had to be reprinted within three weeks.

" I have read your pamphlet on my way down here," wrote Lord Radstock from the Isle of Wight, " and have been greatly stirred by it. . . . I trust you may be enabled by the Holy Ghost to speak words which shall thrust forth many labourers into the vineyard. Dear Brother, enlarge your desires ! Ask for a hundred labourers, and the Lord will give them to you."

Reinforced by a cheque for a hundred pounds, this characteristic letter was doubly welcome, though its "*ask for a hundred labourers*" must have been rather startling in that day of small things !

Meanwhile preparations for a party of ten or twelve were going forward, and in the midst of other engagements proved almost more than Mr. Taylor could manage. The Coborn Street house, far from being too large, was now wholly inadequate, and the next-door premises falling vacant, they were glad to rent them also, thus doubling their accommodation.

" The revision is now going on," he wrote to his mother in November. " We have reprinted the pamphlet, and have missionary boxes on the way. I am preparing a magazine for the Mission, furnishing a house completely, setting up two fonts of type for China, teaching four pupils Chinese, receiving applications from candidates and lecturing or attending meetings continually—one night only excepted for the last month. I am also preparing a New Year's address on China, for use in Sunday Schools, and a missionary map of the whole country. . . . Join us in praying for funds and for the right kind of labourers, also that others may be kept back or not accepted, for many are offering."

Was there a need just then for a reminder that work cannot take the place of prayer ? Overwhelmingly busy, it certainly would not have been surprising if that little circle had been tempted to curtail quiet times of waiting upon God. It was in love, in any case, that the closing year was shadowed by an anxiety so distressing as to bring them to their knees as never before. In one of the houses, strangely quiet now, Mrs. Taylor lay in a critical condition. Serious illness had so reduced her strength that when an operation became necessary there was little hope that she could live through it.

"It is very solemn to feel that all our married happiness may be so near its close," Mr. Taylor wrote to his parents in Barnsley. "She is resting happily in Jesus. . . . Ask grace for me to mean and say, 'Thy will be done.'"

Three weeks later, his loved one spared to him, Mr. Taylor was reviewing the progress made since that memorable Sunday at Brighton with all that it had brought. Besides the eight fellow-workers already in China, twenty or thirty others were desiring to join the Mission.

"How much we need guidance both for them and for ourselves," he wrote to the wider circle of his prayer-helpers. "We have undertaken to work in the interior of China, looking to the Lord for help of all kinds. This we can only do in His strength. And if we are to be much used of Him, we must live very near to Him."

The last day of December was set apart, therefore, as a day of fasting and prayer at Coborn Street, fitly closing the year that had witnessed the inauguration of a Mission so completely dependent upon God.

CHAPTER V

ACCORDING TO HIS WORKING

1866. AET. 34.

To understand aright the fruitfulness of this period it should be borne in mind that Mr. Taylor, among others, was reaping the aftermath of the great Revival of 1859. That wonderful spiritual awakening had not only swept thousands into the Church of Christ ; it had prepared the way for a new order of things, an up-springing of individual faith and effort, characterised by love for souls and new resourcefulness in seeking their salvation. It was a day of new departures in the development of lay agency, and a striking fulfilment might be seen in many directions of the prophecy of Joel : " Also upon the servants and the handmaids in those days will I pour out my Spirit."

To mention a few only of the evangelical movements that had their beginnings in that formative time : Mrs. Ranyard was pioneering a way for the work of Biblewomen, and Mrs. Bayley for that of Mothers' Meetings ; Miss Macpherson had just commenced Gospel services in Bird Fair, and the rescue of little waifs from the lowest slums of London ; Miss Robarts, Mr. (afterwards Sir George) Williams, and others, were laying the foundations of the Young Men's and Young Women's Christian Associations ; Mrs. Daniels and her helpers were developing work for soldiers, with their special needs ; and Mr. and Mrs. Pennefather, at Mildmay, were launching out in the training of Deaconesses for all manner of home missions. All these were making use of the consecrated energies of young

converts in their first love, many of them comparatively
" unlearned and ignorant men," but no opening had as yet
been found for a similar employment of lay agency on the
foreign field.

"When travelling in England, Scotland, and the north of
Ireland in 1859 and '60," wrote a Christian leader from the
Continent, " I repeatedly asked myself, ' Where is the channel
through which simple-hearted labourers brought to Christ through
these remarkable Revivals, wishing to devote themselves to
missionary work in foreign lands may reach their object ? ' But
I found no such channel.   All the colleges for missionary training
require a preliminary education which one would seek in vain in
youths of this sort.   To raise a missionary agency of a humbler
kind seems to me to be a special design of our Lord at this juncture,
for the carrying out of which He has prepared His instruments
in different countries, independently of each other." [1]

Into this prepared soil the seed-thought of the China
Inland Mission was providentially cast.   It could not have
come at a better time.   Christian hearts were kindled to
fresh devotion, drawn together in a new sense of oneness,
and awakened to the fact that God by His Holy Spirit was
using a class of workers hitherto largely excluded from the
spiritual ministries of the Church.   Manifestly the Mission
was suited to meet an urgent need.   New fields must be
entered, new gifts called forth, and here came an organisation
embodying these very ideas with a quiet faith and simplicity
that commended itself to the spiritually minded.

" The very thing, come let us help it ! " was the response
awakened in many a heart.

Young people in workshop and office heard of it and were
encouraged.   Perhaps in such a mission, place might be
found for faith and love even without much learning of the
schools ?   So thought Rudland, for example, at his forge
in a Cambridgeshire village, when a printed report of Mr.
Taylor's address at Perth came to him as a call from God,
In a neighbouring farmhouse lived Mr. Merry, his Sunday
School teacher, who with Mrs. Merry and her sister, Miss
Annie Macpherson, had been the means of blessing to many

---

[1] Herr Spittler, connected with " The Pilgrim Mission " of St. Chris-
chona, near Basel, Switzerland.

in the neighbourhood. They had visited London to see something of the Revival movement, and through them its quickening influences had reached Eversden and the surrounding villages. Meetings had been held in the farmhouse kitchen at which Rudland and several of his companions were converted, and great was the joy with which they gathered round the open Bible with Mr. Merry as their teacher, beside the big log-fire. When the young man wanted to know more about China and the Inland Mission it was to these friends he turned. But the Merrys could tell him nothing, Miss Macpherson could tell him nothing, and even a minister in Cambridge whom he walked miles to consult was unable to supply information. Still, Rudland could not forget the appeal of those Christless millions ; and when Miss Macpherson, on her return to London, sent him a ticket for the Mildmay Conference (1865) it immediately came to him that there he might meet Mr. Taylor.

But his employer had also a great desire to go to the Conference. He and Rudland could not both be spared from the forge. It cost a struggle—but the younger man, feeling it was what the Lord would have done in his place, gave up his cherished hope and offered his master the ticket. Before leaving, the latter promised to write about the meetings and bring back a full report, but for reasons best known to himself he said nothing about China or the Inland Mission. Unable to learn even whether Mr. Taylor had been at the Conference, and not knowing where or how to reach him, Rudland was much perplexed. He could not get away from the burden of souls in China—a thousand every hour of the day and night perishing " without God." On the wall of the forge two passages of Scripture daily confronted him, " Quench not the Spirit " and " To him that knoweth to do good and doeth it not, to him it is sin." Yet what could he do but pray ?

Meanwhile his master, loath perhaps to lose so good an assistant, sought to discourage the ambition Rudland had at heart.

" See," he said one day with a Chinese book in his hand,

" this is the language they talk over there ! Do you think you could ever learn it ? "

" Has anybody else learned it ? " was the quiet reply.

" A few."

" Then why not I ? "

And the yellow pages with their strange hieroglyphics only made him pray the more that the Lord would open his way to China.

After that it was not long before another book reached him with a letter from Miss Macpherson. Settled now in East London she had found the answer to Rudland's question. The pamphlet was *China's Spiritual Need and Claims*, and the letter asked him to join her the following Saturday in going to the prayer meeting at Coborn Street. Too thankful for words, the young man put the letter before his master.

" Yes, you must take a day or two," said the blacksmith. " But as sure as you cross this threshold you are on your way to China ! "

With what interest the pamphlet was studied as Rudland travelled up to London, and how eagerly he drank in every impression of the missionary circle at Coborn Street ! That prayer meeting—could he ever forget it ? The crowded room, the map on the wall, the freedom of spirit, the unceasing flow of prayer and praise all deeply impressed him. But it was the manifest presence of God and earnestness of all concerned that drew to the Mission that day one of its most successful labourers.[1] In Mr. Taylor he found a man of absorbing purpose, to whom perishing souls in China were *real*, and who lived for one thing only, to fulfil the purpose of God in their salvation. Reality, simplicity, intensity— it was the same impression everywhere, the very essence of the new Mission.

But how easy with such a spirit to overlook the con-

[1] From Mr. Rudland's centre at Tai-chow-fu three other cities were opened during his lifetime and thirty-seven out-stations. In connection with these, over 3000 persons have been baptized ; and at the time of Mr. Rudland's death, in 1912, there were more than 1500 communicants. He had translated into the local dialect the whole New Testament and a large part of the Old, printing himself edition after edition on the Mission press, for which he was responsible.

sideration due to the work of others ! Mr. Taylor had now many openings. He was a man with a message, and a message Christian people wanted to hear irrespective of the denomination he or they might represent. The Mission drew its friends and workers from church and chapel alike, and the proposed sphere of its operations was so vast as to call forth unusual interest.

It might have been, as Mr. Taylor felt from the first, quite possible to rob Peter to pay Paul, or in other words to deflect interest and gifts from previously existing channels. Every effort on behalf of China and other heathen lands was more than needed, and he longed that the new work should, by the blessing of God, be helpful to all and a hindrance to none. But how to avoid trespassing, in this sense, on the preserves of others was a problem not easy of solution.

To cut at the root of the difficulty, he and Mr. Berger, his chief adviser, saw that the faith-principles of the Mission must be carried to the point of making no appeals for money nor even taking a collection. If the Mission could be sustained by the faithful care of God in answer to prayer and prayer alone, without subscription lists or solicitation of any kind for funds, then it might grow up among the older societies without the danger of diverting gifts from their accustomed channels. It might even be helpful to other agencies by directing attention to the Great Worker, and affording a practical illustration of its underlying principle that " God Himself, God *alone*, is sufficient for God's own work."

Was money after all the chief thing, or was it really true that a walk that pleases God and ensures spiritual blessing is of more importance in His service ? But for the quiet years in Beaumont Street in which, like Paul in Arabia or Moses at the backside of the desert, Hudson Taylor had been shut in with God, he might have given a different answer to this and many other questions.

" In my shortsightedness," he wrote of that period largely occupied with work on the Ningpo Testament, " I had seen nothing beyond the use that the book with its marginal references would be to the native Christians. But I have often realised since that without those months of feeding and feasting on the Word of God I should have been quite unprepared to form, on its present basis, a mission like the China Inland Mission. In the study of that Divine Word I learned that to obtain successful labourers, not elaborate appeals for help, but first, earnest prayer to God ' to thrust forth labourers,' and second, the deepening of the spiritual life of the Church, so that men should be unable to stay at home, were what was needed. I saw that the Apostolic plan was not to raise ways and means, but to go and do the work, trusting in His sure promise Who has said, ' Seek ye first the Kingdom of God and His righteousness, and all these things shall be added unto you.' "

The chief need, as he saw it, was faith in God for such an increase of spiritual life among His people as to *produce the missionary spirit*. Not money, not the collection was to him the object of a meeting, but to get people under the power of the Word and into fellowship with God.

" If our hearts are right," he often said, " we may count upon the Holy Spirit's working through us to bring others into deeper fellowship with God—the way the work began at Pentecost. We do not need to say much about the C.I.M. Let people see God working, let God be glorified, let believers be made holier, happier, brought nearer to Him, and they will not need to be asked to help."

And the satisfaction of that way of working was that people would be sure to help their own missions first, the Church work for which they were responsible. They would probably increase their gifts, indeed, to those objects, for there is no heart as generous as one that is " satisfied with favour and full with the blessing of the Lord." And if they wanted, over and above, to help the China Inland Mission, such gifts would be given with prayer and followed by prayer that would immeasurably increase their value. It was no figure of speech with Mr. Taylor when he said, as he often did, that he would rather have a consecrated shilling, representing real spiritual fellowship, than an unconsecrated pound ; and gifts given spontaneously, apart from solicitation or the pressure even of a collection, were more likely to have that quality. It was a strange sort of deputation work, perhaps, but it left the speaker free in spirit, occupied with God rather than man, and more eager to *give* than to get.

Then there were other problems, many of them—such as how to test and train candidates, how to organise the Mission in China and carry on the work at home.   But though these were duly considered among the friends who met at Saint Hill, Mr. Berger's illustration of the tree was manifestly in point.

" You must wait for it to grow," he said, " before there can be much in the way of branches.   First you have only a slender stem with a few leaves or shoots.   Then little twigs appear. Ultimately these may become great limbs, all but separate trees : but it takes time and patience.   If there is life, it will develop after its own order."

Thus they were content with little to begin with in the way of organisation.   Essential, spiritual principles were talked over with the candidates, and clearly understood as the basis of the Mission.   A few simple arrangements were agreed to in Mr. Berger's presence, that was all.

" We came out as God's children at God's command," was Mr. Taylor's summing up of the matter, " to do God's work, depending on Him for supplies ; to wear native dress and go inland.   I was to be the leader in China, and my direction implicitly followed.   There was no question as to who was to determine points at issue."

In the same way Mr. Berger was responsible at home. He would correspond with candidates, receive and forward contributions, publish an *Occasional Paper* with audited accounts, send out suitable workers as funds permitted, and keep clear of debt.   This last was a cardinal principle with all concerned.

" It is really just as easy," Mr. Taylor pointed out, " for God to give *beforehand* ; and He much prefers to do so.   He is too wise to allow His purposes to be frustrated for lack of a little money ; but money wrongly placed or obtained in unspiritual ways is sure to hinder blessing.

" And what does going into debt really mean ?   It means that God has not supplied your need.   You trusted Him, but He has not given you the money ; so you supply yourself, and borrow. If we can only wait *right up to the time,* God cannot lie, God cannot forget : He is *pledged* to supply all our need."

But upon the many conferences on these and kindred subjects at Saint Hill we must not linger. Time was getting short. It was hoped that Mr. Taylor and his party would sail in May, and much had to be got through in the way of preparation. In answer to all inquiries as to how many would be going with him, the leader of the Mission could only reply :

If the Lord sends money for three or four, three or four will go ; but if He provides for sixteen, we shall take it as His indication that sixteen are to sail at this time.

Not that this meant uncertainty in his own mind. He had little doubt that the larger number would be provided for, and though no solicitation was made for money, the matter was not left to drift. He believed that to deal with God is at least as real as to deal with man ; that when we get to prayer we get to work, and work of the most practical kind. Two thousand pounds, as nearly as he could tell, would be needed if the whole party were to be sent out ; and in preparing the first *Occasional Paper* of the Mission, early in the new year (1866), Mr. Taylor mentioned this sum. The MS. went to press on the 6th of February, and that very day a noon prayer meeting was begun at Coborn Street for funds. Faith did not mean inaction. From twelve to one the households gathered for daily united waiting upon God, the would-be missionaries realising that their first work was to obtain—from Him Who was so ready to give—whatever would be necessary for as many of their number as He was sending forth.

Mr. Taylor was not able to be present, himself, on many of these occasions. Invitations for meetings were so pressing that, the Bible Society having released him from his long task,[1] he was giving as much time as possible to deputation

[1] In January 1866 Mr. Taylor relinquished into the hands of his colleague, the Rev. F. F. Gough, the work that had occupied so large a part of his time for four and a half years. Finally completed by the Rev. George Moule (afterwards Bishop in mid-China), the book became, as a C.M.S. authority stated, " of the greatest value to Christians throughout the province " (Che-kiang).

work. Day by day he was with the little group at Coborn Street, however, in spirit, and they rejoiced to hear how their prayers for him were being answered.

For in the midst of many responsibilities he was kept wonderfully free from anxiety, and ready to take advantage of every opportunity for deepening interest in China. With little experience in such matters, he was scarcely conscious, perhaps, of the way in which he was gaining the confidence of spiritually minded people wherever he went. He only knew that in answer to prayer many were moved to help ; that one opening led to another, and that the Lord seemed to have prepared hearts in all the Churches, upon which He was laying the burden of China's perishing millions.

Meeting in Liverpool, for example, the young evangelist H. Grattan Guinness, Mr. Taylor accepted his invitation to Dublin to address the members of a theological class Mr. Guinness was teaching in his own house. Going ahead to make preparations, the latter had much to tell about the new Mission, and especially its leader, who, in faith, was attempting no less a task than the evangelisation of inland China. Needless to say, the young men assembled at the hour of Mr. Taylor's arrival were on the tip-toe of expectation. John McCarthy was there, and Charles Fishe and his brother, little thinking they were that night to hear the call of God to their life-work. Tom Barnardo was there also, a bright lad of twenty whose interest in China, dating from that evening, was to bring him to his own among the waifs and strays of East London.[1] Mr. and Mrs. Guinness, too, were unconsciously waiting the touch that was to lead first themselves, then all their children, into the work of foreign missions and thus to result in the training of more than a thousand evangelists for the dark places of the earth.[2]   It

---

[1] T. J. Barnardo, coming to Coborn Street as a candidate for the China Inland Mission, was advised by Mr. Taylor to study medicine, and introduced accordingly to the London Hospital. His sayings and doings were a source of constant amusement to the missionary household. In his Bible he had written " Tom Barnardo, China " ; and long after the work for waifs and strays began which has attained such wonderful proportions, he fully intended leaving it to others and going out himself to the land of his prayers and longings.

[2] Mr. and Mrs. Grattan Guinness were also attracted to East London by their interest in the new Mission. " Strangely enough," as he wrote of

was a company worth coming over to meet, hidden though these developments were in the unknown future.

But what a shock of surprise, not to say disappointment, the members of the class experienced when the door opened and their visitor appeared! Or, had he not come after all? What—that young, slender, fair-haired man, so small in contrast with their teacher's familiar figure! Surely there must be some mistake? But no, Mr. Guinness was undoubtedly introducing Hudson Taylor: and taking it all in in a flash, Barnardo—who was less in stature, even, than the stranger—whispered to McCarthy, " Good, there's a chance for me! " and was all attention.

Oh, the riveted interest, the burning hearts of that hour, as the young men listened to all Mr. Taylor had to tell!

" I think I see him now," wrote John McCarthy after nearly forty years in China, " so quiet, so unassuming in manner and address, but so full of the power of God! I found that night not only the answer to many prayers as to my sphere of service, but the God-given leader in the work to which the Lord had called me. The little talk in his room after the meeting, and the simple prayer to God for guidance, are among the most treasured memories of my life. The bond then formed between us has only grown and strengthened: it has never known a strain. And the blessing his love and prayers have been to me, eternity alone can reveal."

Ten or more promising candidates for the Mission resulted from that Irish visit, and permanent friendships

---

this experience, " Harley House—for more than thirty years our Missionary Training Institute—is but a few steps from Coborn Street, where Mr. Taylor received his first volunteers for the China Inland Mission. How little, when I visited the small, crowded home of the out-going ' *Lammermuir* party,' did I imagine that close to that spot we were to build a college which should train more than a thousand evangelists for the foreign field. . . . About a hundred of our students have become missionaries in China, some of them being numbered among the martyrs of the Boxer Outbreak. The acquaintance between Dr. Howard Taylor and our beloved daughter Geraldine, which subsequently led to their marriage, arose from Dr. Taylor's residence in East London while studying for several years at the London Hospital. All these things were linked together and connected with Hudson Taylor's choice of that humble home in Coborn Street, amid the poverty and obscurity of East London, for the reception of the ' *Lammermuir* party.' It would be impossible to estimate the results for good in East London and throughout the world which have followed the selection of that lowly dwelling in the mighty city."

were made with Henry Bewley, William Fry, and other leaders in Christian work. In Belfast Mr. Taylor had remarkable openings among the Presbyterians. He had recently given several days in Liverpool and Manchester to meetings of the English Presbyterian Synod, speaking by request on his association in China with their beloved missionary, the Rev. William Burns. To stimulate ministers and people to more generous support of their own Swatow mission was his object, and he rejoiced in the successful issue no less than when gifts and prayers were called forth for the Inland Mission.

" I feel little doubt," he wrote to Mrs. Taylor from Belfast, " that this effort to stir up the Presbyterians here will result in their sending several additional missionaries to China. If the English Presbyterian Mission will only follow up the interest awakened in Liverpool, etc., they will easily obtain funds for the support of three or four men."

Long long after, impressions made by this work were still fresh in the minds of many with whom Mr. Taylor then came in contact. A man burdened, deeply burdened, a man God-conscious had moved from place to place, everywhere awakening longing for the same God-consciousness. It made no difference whether meetings were large or small, influential or apparently otherwise ; he gave the best he had to give, and so earnestly that other hearts could not but come to share the burden. At Birmingham, for example, the night was so stormy that it seemed as if there could be no meeting at all. Mr. Taylor was tired, and the fireside at Spark Hill looked specially attractive as the rain poured in torrents. No one could get to the Severn Street Schoolroom, his kind hostess assured him, and it would be taken for granted that the meeting would not be held.

" But was it not announced for to-night ? " asked Mr. Taylor quietly. " Then I must go, even if there is no one but the doorkeeper."

And there, in that almost empty schoolroom, the presence of the Lord was so real that both speaker and hearers felt it to be one of the best meetings they ever attended. Half the little audience of eight or ten, as Mr. Taylor often mentioned, either became missionaries themselves or gave one or more of their children to the foreign field, while the remaining half were from that day earnest and prayerful supporters of the C.I.M.

On his return to London, Mr. Taylor took the opportunity of going over the Mission cash-book to see how far the daily prayer for funds had been answered. In the first five weeks of the year, up to the 6th of February, when the noon meeting was begun, a hundred and seventy pounds had been received. Another five weeks had now elapsed, and eagerly he made the reckoning necessary to compare the periods. Only the day before he had received from Liverpool, as a result of his recent visit, a gift of no less than six hundred and fifty pounds, from a gentleman who upon reading Mr. Taylor's pamphlet was impressed with the importance of making sacrifices that the Gospel might be preached to the Christless millions of inland China. Deeply interested, Mr. Taylor was anxious to see how far other hearts had been moved in the same direction, and what was the surprise and thankfulness with which he discovered that all they were praying for—not the smaller but the larger sum—was actually in hand! Mr. Richard Houghton's generous gift had made up the contributions of that second period of five weeks to almost two thousand pounds ; so that not only was prayer answered, it was manifest also that all the praying band were to go forward without delay to China.

The question then was what to do with the *Occasional Paper*, which had not yet been sent out. Delayed by a fire at the printing office, it had only been received that very day (March 12), and already the need of fifteen hundred to two thousand pounds of which it made mention had been supplied. Some explanation must be made to this effect ; and so it came about that the first issue of the magazine which was to represent the Mission had to have an inset slipped into each number saying that the whole sum needed for passages and outfits was already in hand—" the response of a prayer-hearing God through His believing people."

" We were reminded of the difficulty of Moses," wrote Mr. Taylor some years later, " and of the proclamation he had to send throughout the Camp to prepare no more for the building of the Tabernacle, as the gifts in hand were more than sufficient. We are convinced that if there were *less* solicitation for money and *more* dependence upon the power of the Holy Ghost and the deepening of spiritual life, the experience would be a common one in every branch of Christian work."

One more campaign of meetings was fitted in after this, in response to urgent invitations from the western counties. Mr. Taylor was specially glad to be going in that direction, as it gave the opportunity of paying a farewell visit to Bristol. In spite of many responsible and pressing occupations in caring for a family of over eleven hundred orphans,[1] Mr. Müller followed with keen interest the development of the China Inland Mission. He gave time whenever Mr. Taylor visited him to careful consideration of matters connected with the work, his judgement being no less valued than his helpful spirit. Only a few months previously Mr. Taylor had taken an outgoing party to Ashley Down, that they might have the privilege of meeting this man of God.

" Had an hour with Mr. Müller," he wrote on August 22. " He spoke most preciously on the call and spirit of the missionary ; on the consecutive reading of the Scriptures ; on prayer and faith in God ; on obstacles and thorn hedges."

And again next day :

Mr. Müller spoke on communion with God being before work for God ; on the need of not acting uncertainly ; on mixing freely with the people, and restraining the speaking of English among ourselves (in the presence of Chinese who could not understand) ; and finally promised to pray for the party.

How much his prayers meant the outgoing missionaries could not but realise when they went over the Orphan Houses and saw those hundreds of children, sheltered and provided for without a penny of endowment, without an appeal of any kind for help, or even making their wants known. From the very commencement of his Christian life Mr. Taylor had been profoundly influenced by this quiet

[1] Shortly thereafter increased to two thousand, and later on to double that number.

consistent testimony to the faithfulness of God ; and now that he was himself being led out along similar lines, he valued more than ever Mr. Müller's prayerful sympathy.

In Malvern, Bath, and other places no little interest was aroused by the story Mr. Taylor had to tell and the spirit in which he came. Rising early to travel, and speaking once, twice, and three times a day, he found his strength taxed to the utmost ; but in spite of a large correspondence which kept him busy even in the train, he managed to write a pencilled line to his mother as he was nearing Exeter (April 18, 1866) :

It is joy to work for such a Master ! My soul is often filled to overflowing, and it is an honour to be spent in such a cause. If the labour is great, and the difficulties numerous and formidable, the strength—" all might, according to His glorious power " —is greater, and the reward will be so too. No service can be happier even now, but the reward is not yet, and it is eternal.

To the young people with whom he came in contact this joy in the Lord was no less attractive than to their elders. The missionary was young himself, and his burning words had the more power.

" They gave several of us a sleepless night," recalled Miss H. E. Soltau, whom Mr. Taylor met on this visit for the first time, " and linked myself and dear Agnes (then about to be married to Mr. Richard Hill) with the Mission from that hour." [1]

When one remembers how much that one life has meant to China, and the love and veneration with which the writer

[1] No fewer than six members of this family (of which the father, Mr. Henry W. Soltau, was then at the height of his great usefulness by voice and pen as a Bible teacher) have for longer or shorter periods been connected with the C.I.M.—as well as the son-in-law mentioned above and a grand-daughter, Miss Mabel Soltau, now in China. Messrs. George and Henry Soltau were members of the first Council, formed in 1872, and the latter went with Mr. J. W. Stevenson to Burma to attempt the opening up of Western China. Mr. William Soltau, prior to his devoted work in France, gave much assistance in the home department. Mr. Richard Hill, who had been largely instrumental in forming the Council, became its Hon. Secretary, and rendered valued service in this and other capacities for nearly forty years. Mrs. William Warren (Miss Charlotte Soltau), in her Training Home for missionaries in Melbourne, prepared not a few of its first Australian workers ; and Miss H. E. Soltau (assisted latterly by Miss Elsie Soltau and Miss Edith Smith) was for many years entirely responsible for the Women's Department in London, sending out hundreds of workers and following them with helpful ministrations.

of those lines is regarded by the women of the Inland Mission, one cannot but realise that Mr. Taylor's brief visit to Exeter, difficult though it had been to fit in, resulted in one of the best gifts God ever gave to the work of foreign missions.

Back again in London, for we must not dwell upon his intercourse with the saintly Robert Chapman and others,[1] Mr. Taylor found himself plunged in a very vortex of business and farewell meetings. It was the end of April, and in May the party was to sail for China. Apart from Mrs. Taylor, who was slowly convalescing from her recent illness, there was no one who had any experience of the conditions to which they were going. Everything had to pass through Mr. Taylor's hands ; yet, as the candidates from Dublin noticed, he was ready with helpful sympathy to meet the endless requests with which he was greeted and followed.

" Whatever needed doing, he seemed to know just how to do it," wrote Mr. McCarthy. " Questions as to printing (lithographic or common), engraving, purchase of materials for outfits or supplies, and the thousand-and-one things that come up in connection with a large party setting out for a foreign land, all were found to have light thrown upon them by a reference to the leader who was supposed to know everything, and who really did seem to have learned something about any and every matter however remotely connected with the work."

But all this time, strange to say, they had no ship in view to take them to China. Avoiding the expensive " overland " route, via Suez, Mr. Taylor wished to travel round the Cape, and was seeking a sailing-vessel of which

---

[1] Saturday was the day Mr. Robert Chapman set apart for special waiting upon God, though it was his habit to rise always at or before daylight and give hours to fervent intercession—and this until he was well over ninety years of age. His " workshop " claimed him, however, in a special way at the close of every week. It was his sanctum, containing little but his turning-lathe and a shelf on which he could lay his open Bible. Here he spent hours at a time, denying himself on Saturdays to any and every visitor, and going without his midday meal that he might be the more free in spirit. The mechanical occupation of the lathe he found helpful to a connected line of thought ; so looking at the Bible from time to time, or dropping on his knees in prayer, he would turn out plates and trenchers, his mind occupied the while with the eternal interests of the Kingdom of God. " Dear Brother," he exclaimed on meeting Mr. Taylor again six or seven years later, " *I have visited you every day since you went to China.*" Who can tell how much the Inland Mission owes to the prayers that went up from that hidden corner in Barnstaple ?

they might engage the entire accommodation. As the party was to consist of eighteen adults and four children, the cabin space of an ordinary three-master would be none too much, and there were decided advantages for so long a voyage in being the only passengers. But here was already the beginning of May and a suitable ship had not been found. Daily the matter was remembered in the noon prayer meeting at Coborn Street, the out-going missionaries not only asking for a Christian captain, but for a crew every one of whom might find blessing through the voyage. Mr. Taylor was not anxious ; he was sure the Lord would meet the need in good time, though he would have been glad to have it settled.

Just then, on the 2nd of May, he was due in Hertfordshire for an important meeting, Colonel Puget, brother of the Dowager Lady Radstock, being his host and Chairman. To this new friend it seemed a peculiar arrangement to have a missionary meeting without a collection, but understanding it to be Mr. Taylor's wish the announcement had been made accordingly. When the time came, however, and the speaker proved unusually interesting, Colonel Puget realised that people would give generously if only they had the opportunity.

Rising therefore at the close of the address, he said that interpreting the feelings of the audience by his own, he took it upon himself to alter the decision about the collection. Many present were moved by the condition of things Mr. Taylor had represented, and would go away burdened unless they could express practical sympathy. Contrary therefore to previous announcements, an opportunity would now be given—— But at that point Mr. Taylor interposed, asking to be allowed to add a few words.

It was his earnest desire, he said, that his hearers *should* go away burdened. Money was not the chief thing in the Lord's work, especially money easily given, under the influence of emotion. Much as he appreciated their kind intention, he would far rather have each one go home to ask the Lord very definitely what He would have them do. If it were to give of their substance, they could send a contribution to their own or any other society. But in view of the

appalling facts of heathenism, it might be much more costly
gifts the Lord was seeking ; perhaps a son or daughter or
one's own life-service. No amount of *money* could save a
single soul. What was wanted was that men and women
filled with the Holy Spirit should give *themselves* to the work
in China and to the work of prayer at home. For the
support of God-sent missionaries funds would never be
lacking.

"You made a great mistake, if I may say so," remarked
his host at supper. "The people were really interested.
We might have had a good collection."

In vain Mr. Taylor explained the financial basis of the
Mission and his desire to avoid even the appearance of
conflicting with other societies. Colonel Puget, though
sympathetic, was unconvinced.

Next morning, however, he appeared somewhat late at
breakfast, explaining that he had not had a good night. In
the study, after handing Mr. Taylor several contributions
given for the Mission, he went on to say :

"I felt last evening that you were wrong about the
collection, but now I see things differently. Lying awake
in the night, as I thought of that stream of souls in China,
a thousand every hour going out into the dark, I could only
cry, 'LORD, what wilt Thou have *me* to do ? ' I think I
have His answer."

And he handed Mr. Taylor a cheque for five hundred
pounds.

"If there had been a collection I should have given a
five-pound note," he added. "This cheque is the result
of no small part of the night spent in prayer."

It was Thursday morning the 3rd of May, and at the
breakfast-table, a letter had reached Mr. Taylor from his
shipping agents offering the entire accommodation of the
Lammermuir, about to sail for China. Bidding farewell to
his now deeply interested host, he returned to London, went
straight to the docks, and finding the ship in every way
suitable, paid over the cheque just received on account.
This done, with what joy he hastened to Coborn Street with
the tidings !

So the time came at length for the quiet, unostentatious start.   To see God working—to look up to Him moment by moment, conscious of " His arm " to enfold, " His right hand " to protect and guide, and " the light of His countenance "—was more to that little band than thousands of gold and silver.

" Utter weakness in ourselves," Mr. Taylor wrote before setting out, " we should be overwhelmed at the immensity of the work before us, were it not that our very insufficiency gives us a special claim to the fulfilment of His promise, ' My grace is sufficient for thee ; My strength is made perfect in weakness ' "

PART II

LAUNCHING OUT INTO THE DEEP

1866–1868. AET. 34–36.

Nothing before, nothing behind:
 The steps of faith
Fall on the seeming void, and find
 The rock beneath.

WHITTIER.

CHAPTER VI

MY PRESENCE SHALL GO WITH THEE

1866. AET. 34.

HUMAN nothingness, divine sufficiency—the one just as real as the other—was the atmosphere of those last days at Coborn Street. None could come and go without feeling it. Among packing-cases and bundles the Saturday prayer-meetings were held, friends from far and near crowding the room, sitting up the staircase and on anything that came to hand. Upon the wall still hung the great map ; on the table lay the open Bible ; and all else was lost sight of.

"Our great desire and aim," Mr. Taylor had written in his pamphlet, "are to plant the standard of the Cross in the eleven provinces of China hitherto unoccupied, and in Chinese Tartary." [1]

"A foolhardy business !" said those who saw only the difficulties.

"A superhuman task !" sighed others who wished them well. And many even of their friends could not but be anxious.

"You will be forgotten," was the chief concern of some. "With no Committee to represent you at home you will be lost sight of in that distant land. Claims are many nowadays. Before long you may find yourselves without even the necessaries of life !"

[1] "Your plan of seeking to plant two missionaries in each of the unoccupied provinces is a noble one," wrote the Rev. William Burns from Peking in January of this year (1866), " and if, by the help of God, it is but half accomplished, a great step will have been taken in advance, and the necessities of China will become more visible and clamant in the view of all the Protestant Churches."

69

" I am taking my children with me," was Mr. Taylor's reply, " and I notice that it is not difficult for me to remember that the little ones need breakfast in the morning, dinner at mid-day, and something before they go to bed at night. Indeed, I could not forget it. And I find it impossible to suppose that our Heavenly Father is less tender or mindful than I."

Little wonder that the quietness and simplicity of it all, combined with such aims, such faith, drew out the sympathy of many hearts ! [1]

Over the dark blue sea, over the trackless flood,
  A little band is gone in the service of their God :
The lonely waste of waters they traverse to proclaim,
  In the distant land of Sinim, Immanuel's Saving Name.
They have heard from the far-off East the voice of their brother's
    blood :
  A million a month in China are dying without God. . . .

No help have they but God : alone to their Father's hand
  They look for the supply of their wants in a distant land.
The fulness of the world is His—' All power ' in earth and heaven ;
  They are strong tho' weak, and rich tho' poor, in the promise He
    has given.
'Tis enough ! they hear the cry, the voice of their brother's blood :
  A million a month in China are dying without God. [2]

Never surely were travellers more prayed for, as the long months of the voyage wore on, and none could have more needed such aid. Sailing from London on the 26th of May, it was the end of September before they reached Shanghai ; and very determined were the onslaughts of the enemy, first to wreck the unity and spiritual power of the missionary party, and then to wreck the ship on which they travelled, sending

[1] The Rev. Alexander M'Aulay, then a minister in East London, saw a good deal of Mr. Taylor and his fellow-workers at this time. " I watched very closely the manner and spirit of those about to proceed to China," he said as President of the Wesleyan Conference ten years later. " I was delighted to find the spirit of self-sacrifice very deep in every one of them, so far as I could discern. They were given to prayer, and had all the elements about them that were likely to make them successful missionaries in any field to which God might call them."

[2] From *The Voice of thy Brother's Blood*, by H. Grattan Guinness.

them all to the bottom.   But from the hour of parting, when they were commended to God in the stern-cabin of the *Lammermuir* by Mr. Berger and a company of those nearest to them, they were daily sustained in this most important way.[1]

And prayer was wonderfully answered on board that little sailing-ship tossed on the mighty deep.   Most of Trinity Sunday, their first whole day at sea, they were anchored awaiting a favourable breeze.   Freedom from much motion gave opportunity for morning and evening services and for rest which was greatly needed.   Next day was occupied with putting things in order and steadying the heavy baggage, piled up in the corners of the saloon upon which the cabins opened.[2]   On Tuesday regular studies were begun, Mr. Taylor taking a class in Chinese every morning and Mrs. Taylor another in the afternoon.

" I should like you to have a peep at us when we are gathered together," she wrote to Mrs. Berger, " just to see how happy we all are !   God ever keeps us so. . . . The Captain and crew number thirty-four, which with our own party makes fifty-six souls on board."

After that came rougher weather, when many were down with sea-sickness and Mr. and Mrs. Taylor, in the absence of of a stewardess, had their hands full.   By the time Madeira was reached almost all " had their sea-legs," and great advance had been made in getting into touch with the crew. From that time on, all across the Atlantic (for their course took them westward almost to Brazil) round the Cape of Good Hope and up to the East Indian Islands, the weather was wonderfully fine—few gales and no distressing heat.

[1] The Saturday prayer-meeting was continued by Mr. and Mrs. Gough (the widow of Mr. J. Jones of Ningpo) in their home on Bow Road, near Coborn Street.   Another weekly prayer-meeting was held by Mr. and Mrs. Berger at Saint Hill, who also kept up the noon half-hour daily, no matter what guests or occupations they might have.   There were praying circles also in Scotland, Ireland, and the provinces, in which the needs of the mission found constant remembrance.

[2] This they had all to themselves, with its three port-holes at the stern, and sky-light over the table from the poop deck.   Immediately outside this saloon (or " stern-cabin ") was the main-mast, forward of which lay the well-deck with officers' quarters, and the forecastle.   The *Lammermuir* was a three-masted iron sailing-ship of 760 tons burden.

Eleven and a half weeks were occupied in this part of the voyage, weeks chiefly memorable for the change they brought to many a life on board.

For the sailors had been watching these unusual passengers, whose company they had looked forward to with anything but satisfaction. One missionary would have been bad enough, but a whole ship's load of them ! It was " a pretty go," as the first mate told his wife before leaving, and more than he " wished they were out of it." For the *Lammermuir* carried a godless crew, though the Captain was a Christian. This was a great help, as he gave permission for Sunday services and put no hindrance in the way of intercourse with the men. But the latter held aloof for some time, and the missionaries were wise enough to give them plenty of line.

There are some things, however, that cannot be hid, chiefest of which is the fragrance of Christ in a spirit made loving and helpful by His presence. This was not lacking on board the *Lammermuir*, and before long it began to be strangely attractive. Hardly knowing what it was that drew them, the men found their hearts open to spiritual influences as never before. The missionaries, after all, were not such a bad lot ! When a difficult piece of forging had to be done, Nicol, the Scotch blacksmith, was better at it than any of themselves. Jackson and Williamson, the carpenters, were always ready to lend a hand ; and in the absence of a ship's doctor Mr. Taylor's surgical skill, gladly placed at their disposal, was invaluable. Then he gave capital lectures—talks on the eye, the circulation of the blood, first aid to the injured, etc., which helped to pass the time. And there was more than that. Seen at close quarters, these people were downright happy—always busy, always kindly, and given to singing.

It was queer, that part of it ! for what could there be in the life they had chosen to make them want to sing ? Yet morning, noon, and night, in the stern-cabin with their harmonium or out on deck, whether two or three alone or the whole company together, they seemed never to tire. True it was only hymns they sang, but what could touch

deeper chords ? " Yes, we part, but not for ever," " Jesu,
Lover of my soul," " Rock of Ages, cleft for me "—to them
it all seemed so real !

> Thou, O Christ, art all I want,
> More than all in Thee I find. . . .

Yes, it was plain enough : religion *meant* something to these
people. And little by little not a few on board, instead of
wishing themselves out of it, began to wish they were in it
in any real sense.

" The Captain, officers, and crew are most kind to us," Mr.
Taylor wrote at the beginning of the voyage. " The cabin
steward is a Christian. May God give us to see many conversions
ere we leave the vessel."
" The friendly feeling only increases," he added a week later.
" Continue to pray for us: God is answering. . . . What we need
is more of His grace, more faith, more devotion to Him, more love
for souls. May these be given us for Jesus' sake."

Before ever they had seen the *Lammermuir*, or the crew
had been engaged for the voyage, much prayer had been
made for those with whom they were to travel all the way
to China. Very definitely they had asked for a ship's-
company to whom the Lord would bless His Word. That
prayer was still going up, both on board and at home, and
they were eagerly looking for the answer. " A voyage
across the ocean will not make any one a soul-winner," as
Mr. Taylor often said ; but these fellow-workers, whatever
they may have lacked in some directions, possessed that
personal knowledge of God which makes men keen about
bringing others to know Him too.

And Mr. Taylor's example helped them not a little.
Soul-winning was to him as it had always been, the very
object of his existence as a Christian. For this he lived,
prayed, laboured ; and amid the many responsibilities that
had come upon him he was still, in this sense, the true
missionary. He encouraged his fellow-workers also in
putting prayer, definite, believing prayer, before any other
means to bring about conversion, and in seeking to live the
life that makes such prayer possible. Well he knew how

easy it is on board ship to drift into an unhelpful spirit, and lose all influence for good over others.   Novel-reading, waste of time, and self-indulgence at table were carefully watched against, and the daily prayer-meeting kept up which registered unerringly the spiritual temperature of the little company.   Chinese study and useful reading occupied a good part of the day ; Mr. Taylor himself having a Greek Grammar on hand, and Wordsworth's Commentary on Leviticus.   But the eternal welfare of those with whom they travelled was sought directly, as well as in these indirect but potent ways.

The conversion of the second officer, twenty-five days out from Plymouth, was a welcome answer to prayer, and was quickly followed by that of two of the midshipmen. This was the beginning of an awakening among the crew which continued for some time.   Concern about spiritual things began to lay hold of them, and there was great joy among the missionaries as one after another came out into the light.

" I can give you but little idea," Mr. Taylor wrote to Mr. Berger, " of the precious answers to prayer we have received, and of the blessed change wrought in some of these men.   Four of them were Romanists ; now they are resting on the finished work of Christ and prizing His words. . . . We hope to see others brought in before long . . . for did we not ask God to gather a crew to whom He would bless His Word, and will He not continue to answer ?   Dear Mr. Berger, I do wish you could have been with us some times when we have received special answers to prayer. Our joy has literally overflowed, and we have longed that our friends at home could know of the blessing poured out upon us.

" As is often the case, God has singled out some who seemed most unlikely, and who at first manifested the greatest opposition to the Gospel. . . . Others again being foreigners with little knowledge of English seemed difficult to reach, but the Lord has opened their hearts. . . .

" We commenced by having service on Sunday morning in the saloon, with Captain Bell's permission.   A few of the sailors came. Then the young men started an afternoon meeting in the forecastle, held thrice weekly.   Nor were our sisters less active. Mary Bell began a Bible Class, which soon grew into a meeting for reading the Scriptures and for prayer every night, Mrs. Nicol and others joining her. Some were converted, and these meetings became general. . . . Miss Desgraz undertook reading with the four Swedes, Miss Faulding with a German, Miss Bausum with the cook and a South Sea Islander. Miss Barnes holds a reading-class for all who wish to improve themselves in English, and has been blessed to the conversion of several ; while the other brethren and sisters have taken part in personal conversations and public meetings."

High-water mark was reached early in August, when the first mate, who had been a savage bully among the men, experienced a real change of heart. For a month or more his wretchedness had been pitiable ; but though under deep conviction of sin, it was not without a desperate struggle he was able to break with the old life and enter into peace in believing.

" Had a special prayer-meeting for the conversion of Mr. Brunton," is the entry in Mr. Taylor's journal for August 3.

And the following morning :

" Could not retire without seeing Mr. Brunton. Read to him at 12.30, when he came from his midnight watch, part of Mackintosh on Exodus xii. (the Passover). After much conversation and prayer, the Lord brought him into liberty. First, told my dear wife and Miss Blatchley (their friend and secretary), then Mr. Williamson, who rose and joined me in praise and thanksgiving to God. Then I went to awake Mr. Sell, though it was 2.30 A.M. Oh, how glad our hearts were ! " [1]

---

[1] " Mr. Brunton's conversion was very interesting," wrote Miss Rose, who was going out to be married to Mr. Meadows. " For several weeks he was miserable. He had been brought up a Roman Catholic, and there were many prejudices to overcome. Every means was used to help him, and again and again requests came from those who were going to converse with him, that they might be prayed for. One night Mr. Sell came running down from the deck at twelve o'clock saying that Mr. Brunton had just asked him to go to his cabin and pray with him. Two of us were up and we united in prayer : but he did not find peace that night, nor for many weeks following.

" By the first week in August, matters came to a climax, and it was felt that if he were to be saved it must be at once. He was wretched . . . it seemed a life and death question. The enemy was determined not to let him go, and the struggle was fearful. On the night of the 3rd his watch ended at twelve o'clock, Mr. Taylor went just after and had a long conversation with him, those who were up retiring to the stern-cabin for prayer. When Mr. Taylor came down and the answer had not yet been given, he and another continued in prayer till three o'clock. The Bible Class next day was turned into a prayer-meeting, another special meeting

The news was quickly known all over the ship, and deep was the impression next day when this officer called out his watch and told them personally what God had done for his soul.   One young midshipman to whom he spoke gave his heart to the Lord, and several of the crew who had been halting between two opinions were brought to decision.

August 4: A day of great things: Carter, Dixon, and the steward (Russell) professed to find peace through believing. Had a protracted meeting, till midnight, to praise the Lord and seek the conversion of all hands.   At midnight, Mr. Brunton, Carter, and Dixon joined us, and we gave thanks together.

At the request of the crew, the daily meetings were now moved from the steward's cabin to their own quarters, where a larger number could be accommodated.

" Our first meeting in the forecastle was held the night before last," Mr. Taylor wrote on August 22.   " Many of our own number and most of the sailors were present.   It was truly a pleasant sight !   Card-playing had for some time given place to Bible reading, and foolish songs to hymns.   But now they and we were met as believers—brothers and sisters from various parts of the new and old world and from the islands of the sea—all journeying toward the same blessed home.   Some were seated on sea-chests, some on planks, some on chairs that we had brought, some on various parts of the ship's fittings, while a few—half-ashamed to be seen, yet drawn by something they themselves, perhaps, did not understand—were hiding behind the capstan or hanging about the doors.   The meeting commenced with the hymn :

> Come let us join our cheerful songs
> With angels round the throne.

Mr. Sell then engaged in prayer, and was followed by a converted

---

was called in the forenoon ; and a third would have been held later, but bad weather prevented it.   God, however, knew the longing of our hearts, and took the work into His own hands.   Mr. Taylor again met Mr. Brunton at midnight, in his cabin ; and while he was explaining to him the passage, ' When I see the blood, I will pass over you,' light broke !   He saw the plan of salvation ; peace and joy took possession of his heart ; and he at once poured out his soul to God in praise and prayer—remembering us each one by name, all who were unsaved on board, and his own wife and children.   Mr. Taylor was so overjoyed that he went and awoke Mr. Sell, to tell him the good news.   The latter got up and woke me, and at three in the morning we gave thanks together.   It is impossible to describe the rejoicing of that day !   You know what it is to have the burden of souls upon your hearts, and the joy that follows their conversion."

West Indian, who in broken English poured out his heart to God.
A passage in John was read and conversed about. Another hymn
was sung ; prayer followed ; and Miss Barnes, who had just come
in, gave thanks for the conversion of one of the men who had been
in the deepest distress for some time, and with whom she had
been speaking on deck where his duty detained him.   Then one
of the sailors asked for, ' O happy day, that fixed my choice.'
Prayer was again offered and the meeting closed with

> Come, ye that love the Lord,
> And let your joys be known. . . .

Then followed such a shaking of hands, such mutual exhortations
and expressions of Christian love as did one good to see and hear.
Truly, the Lord is wonderfully answering the prayers of His dear
people who are bearing us up at the throne of grace."

"August 23 : Such a happy meeting again last night ! The
second of the four Swedes has found peace, and three others
present were seeking Jesus. The first mate (Mr. Brunton) led
us in prayer, as did also three of the sailors ; and the joy was so
great that it was with difficulty I could get the meeting concluded
half an hour after the time had come for doing so."

Among themselves, also, the missionaries had helpful
meetings, and several days were given entirely to waiting
upon God, in view of all that lay before them.

" On Saturday afternoons we join in Spirit with friends in
China and at home," Mr. Taylor continued to Mr. Berger, " praying for the good of the mighty empire toward which we are
journeying. Our minds are kept in peace as to the future.
Were we never to reach China, we should all rejoice in the work
God has done on the *Lammermuir* ; and if permitted to reach our
destination, He Who has led hitherto will be with us and will
guide us by a plain path."

Gladly would one leave the record of the voyage at this
point, telling only of the wonderful deliverance from shipwreck in the China Sea with which it ended. But to do so
would be untrue to facts, and untrue moreover to universal
experience. Who does not know, with any spiritual life
at all, that where God is working the devil is sure to be
busy ; and that the nearer one seeks to live to the Lord
Himself, the more painful are the consequences of grieving
Him ? They were only little things that had come in

between one and another of the party. Big temptations
would have defeated their own end ; but little criticisms,
little coldnesses, little jealousies had brought in disunion
that led to serious results. Prayer was hindered ; and
to the grief of all concerned, the work of the Holy Spirit
was so checked, that *for one whole month* no souls were
saved, and some who had been anxious remained sin-
burdened and undecided. It was a startling experience,
and deeply searching : a whole month without conversions,
at a time when already many of the men had come over the
line and others seemed ready to do so ! And in their
troubled hearts the missionaries themselves knew what was
hindering.

Yet it was so hard to get right, to get right and to keep
right with one another ! It was painful light on the inspired words, " Behold, how good and how pleasant it is for
brethren to dwell together in unity . . . for *there* the Lord
commanded the blessing, even life for evermore." The fact
that they were living, most of them, in true fellowship with
God made the grief of failure the more distressing. It made
it also the more needful for the Lord to let that grief be felt.
Evidences of the self-life in those who had not come so near
to Him might be less disastrous in their results ; but " whom
the Lord *loveth* He chasteneth." It is the fruitful branch
He purges, that it may bring forth " more fruit."

To Mr. Taylor, needless to say, these developments
caused deep concern. Could he by more watchfulness have
safeguarded his fellow-workers and prevented misunderstandings ? Could he now, prevailing first with God, bring
them to a better mind, and restore " the unity of the Spirit
in the bond of peace " ?

" This morning," runs a note in his journal early in July,
" had some conversation with Mr. Nicol about the present state
of matters. Sell joined us and afterwards Williamson, and we
decided on holding a special meeting for confession and prayer
for the increase of love and unity. Spoke to most of them
privately, and affectionately urged the need of a better spirit.
We met in the evening, and the Lord was with us indeed. I
trust He gave to all present a real desire to be united in love."

But the danger was a recurring one, and a couple of months later a spirit of discord again crept in. It was on different grounds this time and with other members of the party, but the outcome was the same—criticism, discontent, loss of power and blessing.

" Almost all the party deploring the want of more unity and love," is the record for September 8. " The Lord make bare His arm on our behalf."

The notable thing is that they *did* deplore it; that they saw and felt the danger; could not go on in such a condition, even on ship-board, and gave themselves to heart-searching before the Lord. Prayer and fasting again turned the tide : for to those who humble themselves before Him it is still true, " When the enemy shall come in like a flood, the Spirit of the Lord shall lift up a standard against him."

Then the adversary changed his tactics. Unsuccessful in wrecking the spiritual usefulness of the party, it seemed as though " the Prince of the Power of the Air " let loose his fiercest legions, determined on the destruction in one way or another of the infant mission. For fifteen days and nights the stress of storm and tempest lay upon them. Caught in one typhoon after another they beat up the China Sea all but a wreck—sails gone, masts gone, everything gone but their steadfast hope in God. Of the beginning of this terrible experience Miss Blatchley wrote :

On Monday morning (September 10) the sun rose as usual and the wind was fair, but in the afternoon the weather became squally. The wind increased, the glass was steadily falling, and before night it was but too clear that we were on the edge of a typhoon. The night was fearfully rough, with a wild sea. The rain descended as if the clouds were coming down bodily, while the raging of the wind made it exceedingly difficult to pass orders. More than once all the men on duty were nearly swept overboard by heavy seas. In the darkness little could be done. We could only watch, and commend ourselves and more especially the crew to God's keeping. . . .

All Tuesday the glass continued to fall, and the wind and sea were unabated. But we were beginning to hope from the direction of the wind that we were on the outer edge of the typhoon.

On Wednesday the sun was visible, the rain ceased and the glass was no longer falling. We were safe ; we had a fair wind, and toward noon sighted Formosa. . . . So we renewed hope of reaching Shanghai on the Saturday following. But on Thursday, a strong gale blew right ahead, with a tremendous sea on, so that we were driven out of our course. . . . This gale continued all Friday. Moreover, we were now among shoals and breakers. Heavy seas were sweeping the decks, loosening things from their lashings. Many of the sailors were ill, and the storm we had already passed had weakened the ship, rendering her very unfit to meet another gale. We were all feeling worn out with want of rest, with the perpetual tossing, our wet clothes, etc., and were longing to reach our desired haven. We were, indeed, within a couple of days' good run of it : but the wind continued adverse, and we had constantly to tack, with the prospect of having to beat all up the China Sea in the teeth of a N.E. simoon.

At last with longing eyes we sighted Fu-kien on Tuesday the 18th of September. The waters were becoming pale, earnest of our approach to the Yangtze. But we were still beating to windward, and continued to do so all Wednesday, not only making nothing, but not even holding our own, for we lost some twenty knots or more. It was tedious work, but we kept up courage and cheered our weariness by constant communion with Him Who is our hope and our salvation. The old, familiar hymns had now new meaning. While the winds raged, we sang " Jesu, Lover of my soul," " Rock of Ages," " O God, our help in ages past," and others. We could not always raise our voices above the storm, but at least they mingled with it, they and it praising God.

In the night especially we had prayer, because the darkness prevented much from being done or attempted about the ship. Of course *rest* was out of the question. When the tempests were upon us we were tossed up and down as if our iron ship were nothing—now on the crest of a wave, now in a deep valley, now thrown on her port, now on her starboard side, almost dipping her yard-ends into the sea, and again plunging forward, her fore-castle right under water. In this condition we were wearying for land . . . and it would have been with despairing feelings we watched the wind increase . . . but for the assurance that God's arm was closely round us, and at the same time ruling all powers.

Twelve days the storm had been upon them, but the worst was yet to come.

" It is useless to attempt to describe," wrote Miss Faulding,

" what passed on Saturday, Sunday and Monday " (Sept. 22–24). " The sea washed our lea bulwarks away, and seemed as if it would carry everything before it. Our mainsail was torn to ribbons ; the jib-boom and fore, main and mizen masts were carried away, and it seemed impossible we should weather it. I am glad to say we were all kept calm, ready for life or death. We were making water fast. The broken masts were hanging over our heads as if by a thread, swinging about fearfully and threatening every moment to fall—which if they had done, the deck or side of the vessel must have been staved in, and we should have gone down in a few minutes. I did feel so thankful that you could not know ; for I had the strongest conviction that our lives would not be lost."

But for the courageous example of Mr. Taylor,[1] and indeed all the missionary party, things would have gone very differently however. In outward prosperity, during the earlier part of the voyage, they had been learning something of their spiritual foes and " the need," as Mr. Taylor wrote, "of having our souls stayed upon God, and of clinging to Him in ceaseless prayer " ; now it was His purpose to teach them in a different way, " the blessedness of trusting Him in the hour of human helplessness and danger." Of those last, worst days he wrote :

Friday, Sept. 21 : The gale increasing and having all the appearance of another typhoon, we had prayer together from time to time during the afternoon and night. The decks were swept by the sea in a manner I have never before witnessed.

Saturday, Sept. 22 : The jibs and stay-sails gave way early this morning. So fearful was the sea that the men refused to go out and secure them. The Captain and first Mate went on

---

[1] " All through the storm," said Mr. Rudland, " Mr. Taylor was perfectly calm. When almost at its height the men refused to work any longer. The Captain had advised all to put on life-belts. ' She can scarcely hold together two hours,' was his verdict. At this juncture he was going to the forecastle, where the men were taking refuge, revolver in hand. Mr. Taylor went up to him. ' Don't use force,' he said, ' till everything else has been tried.' He then went in quietly and talked to the men, telling them he believed God would bring us through, but that everything depended upon the greatest care in navigating the ship, in other words, upon the men themselves. ' We will all help,' he added; ' our lives are in jeopardy as much as yours.' The men were completely reassured by his quiet demeanour and friendly reasoning, and with officers, midshipmen, and the rest of us went to work in earnest at the wreckage, and before long got in the great iron spars that were ramming the side of the ship."

the forecastle . . . the men followed, but soon all had to be recalled as the vessel was driving into the sea. Soon after this the lea, upper bulwarks, began to give way, and before long all this side was overboard. Next, the jib-boom and flying jib-boom gave way, followed immediately by the foretop and top-gallant masts and the maintop-gallant mast. They hung by the wire shrouds, swinging about most fearfully, owing to the heavy rolling of the ship.

The appearance of things was now truly terrific. The decks full of water, which poured over both sides as she rolled, were encumbered with floating spars, tubs, buckets, casks, etc. Besides the danger of being washed overboard, there was no small risk of having one's limbs broken by moving timbers, torn from their moorings. Prayer to God was our only resource. The sailors, paralysed, gave up work. The probability seemed that our hours, if not minutes, were numbered. I kissed the dear children, and with the young men of our party went out and set to work, hoping to encourage others. Commending ourselves to God, we began to secure the floating things and cut away the wreckage. This stimulated some of the crew to help us. Many of the smaller things washed overboard, and the larger we secured from time to time, for the fury of the waves was such that no lashings would stand long. The water-casks having been swept away no fresh water was procurable, for we dared not open the tanks in the gale. Cooking was out of the question, and we had to eat a little biscuit and cheese or butter from time to time. Through God's blessing the wreck of the fore masts and jib-booms was safely got over the side. The main mast was swinging fearfully, and water was going down into the hold in large quantities by the foot of the mast and by the anchor pipes, the covers of which had been washed away. These places were now secured, and as the afternoon was far advanced no more could be attempted.

We were still in very bad shape. Rolling fearfully, the masts and yards hanging down were tearing our only sail (the main lower top-sail) and were battering like a ram against the main yard. The deck from forecastle to poop was one scarcely-broken sea. The roar of the water, the clanging of chains, the beating of the dangling masts and yards, the sharp smack of the torn sails made it almost impossible to hear any orders that might be given. Providentially the moon was bright and the night light. Though all were tired out, there was little sleeping. About 10 P.M. the mizen top-gallant royal mast gave way, and with the royal yard hung swinging about. The rain and spray beat desperately, and the force of the wind was such that it was impossible to stand on the poop without holding

on. Captain Bell kept moving about, though so unwell—half
his face paralysed.

Sunday, Sept. 23 : Very weary in body we recommenced
at 6 A.M. . . . The pumps were got to work, and ropes being
carried into the saloon the ladies helped in pumping. . . . The
rolling continued to be very heavy, and at times the decks were
one sheet of water, rushing and roaring in a way to appal the
stoutest heart. The ship began to labour very heavily, leading
us to think that she was taking water, but of this we could get
no certainty. Worn out after a hard day's work, we did not
attempt a service, but lay down for a little rest. This was often
disturbed by unusually heavy seas and rolls, when it seemed as
though we must be going down at once. But after a while she
would get more quiet, and moonlight and lessening wind gave
rise to hope.

Although the storm was blowing over, this second
Monday was the most anxious day of all. Every one on
board was worn out ; the pumps would not work, and they
were shipping water fast. What it must have been to Mrs.
Taylor with the little ones about her may be better imagined
than described.

" But it was sweet to rejoice in God through all," she wrote ;
" to rest in past proofs of His love, independently of present
circumstances ; and I entered into Habakkuk's song as never
before, ' *Yet* will I rejoice in the Lord ; I will glory in the God of
my salvation.' "

CHAPTER VII

TO SEARCH OUT A RESTING-PLACE

1866.   ÆT. 34.

IT was a bright September Sunday, five days after the storm passed away, when the *Lammermuir* at length came to anchor off the foreign settlement of Shanghai. Her broken, dismantled condition made her an object of general curiosity among the gaily-painted junks and foreign shipping; but when it became known that she only carried missionaries, albeit the largest party that had yet come to China, interest soon subsided, and beyond a few facetious remarks in the papers little notice was taken of the new arrivals.

To themselves that quiet Sunday was specially grateful. They did not go ashore, and out on the river were protected from many visitors. Their hearts were full of thankfulness for recent deliverances—more wonderful, even, than they realised at the time. A vessel coming in soon after their own proved to have lost sixteen out of a ship's company of twenty-two, while on the *Lammermuir* none were missing or seriously injured; and no sooner had they reached a place of safety than terrific gales again swept the coast, which in their disabled condition they could not possibly have weathered.

" God grant that having been brought so near to eternity and then spared for awhile," wrote one of the party, " our lives may be more entirely devoted to Him and to the work before us. Through all I never felt the least regret, or anything but joy in the thought that I had come."

The voyage over, Mr. Taylor's difficulties were in a sense

begun.   Looking out on that familiar scene—the crowded river, the European houses along the Bund, and the wall of the Chinese city beyond—he realised in a very practical way the responsibilities that had come to him.   Where was he to find accommodation for so large a party that would afford the facilities required ?   Boxes from the hold, more or less soaked with sea water, and all the baggage from the cabins had to be unpacked, dried, and rearranged.   Much must be left in Shanghai for a time, as in addition to personal belongings they had with them household goods from Coborn Street, a considerable quantity of stores, printing and lithographic presses, and a large supply of drugs and medical apparatus.   All these, after careful examination, needed safe dry storage, and the washing machines, mangle, and ironing-stove must be unpacked and set to work, for there was the clothing of more than twenty people to be laundered after a four months' voyage.   Little wonder he was tempted to feel anxious, remembering the difficulty of obtaining even temporary accommodation in the Settlement.[1]

For those were not the days of Missionary Homes and Agencies.   Foreign hotels were few and very costly ; Chinese inns were out of the question for such a party ; and the native boats to which they might have been transferred would not have met the case.   Furnished houses were rarely to be had, even if expense were no consideration, and the hospitality of European residents could not reasonably be counted on.   The missionary community in Shanghai at

[1] It is impossible, in view of the cosmopolitan city of to-day, to imagine how primitive were the conditions in Shanghai as recently as 1866.   A temporary building, since used as a gymnasium, did duty for the Cathedral. The British Consulate, though occupying the same site as at present, was an insignificant structure.   The Garden Bridge, now traversed daily by a ceaseless stream of vehicles, was so narrow that two wheelbarrows could barely pass each other, and pedestrians had to pay a three cash toll.   As to conveyances, the choice lay between sedan-chairs and wheelbarrows, rickshaws not having yet come over from Japan.   One of the Consuls possessed a carriage, and so did the Commissioner of Customs ; but there was little use for them, the Bund scarcely extending beyond the British Settlement, and the Nanking Road soon running off into fields and market-gardens.   Other roads were just tracks and footpaths, save where they neared the river, and the Gardens of to-day were, at low tide, an unsavoury mud bank.   As for the native city, walled in and crowded with a dense population, the less said of it the better, from a European standpoint.

the time consisted of only nine married and three single men ; and who among them would be able, however willing, to receive so many visitors ?   Then again, if the party had to be divided, some in one home and some in another, how was the work to be attended to ?   Altogether the situation was complicated and would have given rise to anxiety, had it not been that, both from the *Lammermuir* and from friends at home, prayer had been going up for months past that the Lord would Himself see and provide.

Meanwhile, unknown to Mr. Taylor, a friend of Ningpo days had moved up to Shanghai, bringing with him the printing-press of the American Presbyterian Mission.   In a semi-foreign house he was living near the Chinese city (East Gate), and with a view to future needs had purchased a disused building intended for a theatre, which formed a convenient warehouse or " go-down " connected with his premises.   Large and empty, this building immediately suggested itself when the *Lammermuir* appeared in the river and he learned that it carried Mr. Taylor's party. How they must need the cheer of a friendly welcome, and some place in which to dispose their belongings !   If nothing better offered, his home was open to them, such as it was, with the " go-down " in addition.   So taking a *sampan* [1] that very afternoon, William Gamble sought out his friends to put at their disposal a bachelor's hospitality.

Almost too good to be true must it have seemed when, three days later, Mr. Taylor returned from Ningpo to remove his family and fellow-workers to the quarters thus provided. Captain Bell had insisted on their remaining on the *Lammermuir* meanwhile ; and though absent so short a time Mr. Taylor had been greatly prospered.   Escorting Miss Rose to her future home, he had been enabled to come into touch with all the senior members of the Mission, save Mr. and Mrs. Stevenson, who were some distance inland. [2]   The church at

[1] The primitive Chinese gondola.
[2] In the great city of Shao-hing-fu with a quarter of a million inhabitants they had succeeded in obtaining a footing, adding thus a fourth station to those already opened by the Mission before the arrival of the *Lammermuir* party.   Living over their little chapel at the junction of three busy streets, hard by one of the water-ways of that Venice of mid-China, they were " feeling very happy and getting on with the language."

Bridge Street, amid their rejoicing, had come to his help in a practical way, for which he was most thankful—sending back with him the evangelist Tsiu, one of the fruits of his own early labours, and a Christian woman as well as two men to help in caring for the new arrivals.

" HE gently clears our way," wrote Mrs. Taylor the following Sunday. " On the morning of this day last week (Sept. 30) we knew not where we should store our goods, and had it not been that Captain Bell arranged for us to stay on board, we should not have known where to lay our heads. That any missionary would be able to receive us all seemed impossible ; and here God had in readiness one who not only can accommodate our party, but whose views concerning missionary work coincide in large measure with Hudson's. All our goods, with the exception of a few boxes not yet brought out of the hold, are safe in Mr. Gamble's ' go-down,' where Hudson and I and four of the young men sleep. The others are in Mr. Gamble's house, where we all take our meals ; and he has kindly promised, though somewhat reluctantly I believe, to allow us to remunerate him for our board."

At the end of the " go-down " the floor of the stage remained, and on this were extemporised sleeping compartments—sheets being pinned together for walls and a step-ladder doing duty as staircase.

" There is no lack of ventilation," wrote one of those billeted there, " the windows being unglazed, square openings, supplemented by plenty of crevices in the roof. The wind makes noises ghostly enough for any romance ; and the rats keep up a perpetual scuffle among our boxes and the loose straw. On windy nights our linen walls are very restless indeed ; but there is not much difficulty in sleeping after a long day's work."

" We had our two stoves put up," recalled another, who with her Swiss training was a competent laundress, " and with washing, mangling, and ironing going on at the same time . . . the warehouse was as busy as a beehive. We often wished friends at home could have looked in upon us, just to see how happy we all were ! It would have rejoiced their hearts to see how lovingly, how kindly the Lord was dealing with His children."

" Missionary work under the most favourable conditions," was Miss Faulding's impression of it all ! " Mr. Taylor does

---

not another foreigner to be found in a long day's journey. Neng-kwei, the basket-maker of Ningpo, was their helper ; for whose story see *Hudson Taylor in Early Years*, pp. 461-2.

manage so nicely for us ; he thoroughly understands how to go about everything."

In the midst of many occupations he had little time for writing, and little thought to give to the criticisms that buzzed about the foreign community. That ladies should be brought out to wear Chinese dress and live in the interior roused indignation in certain quarters. It was freely hinted that Mr. Taylor must be a madman or worse, and that Bedlam would have been a safer destination for himself and his companions than Shanghai. "But he went quietly on," as Mr. Rudland remembered, "saying little or nothing about it ; always letting discourtesies drop out of sight so graciously, without affecting his own friendliness."

One of the few letters Mr. Taylor did manage to write from Shanghai was to his mother.

"The Lord is with us," he said, "and we are all, I trust, enjoying fellowship with Jesus. We have and may expect to have some trials :

But with humble faith to see
Love inscribed upon them all,
This is happiness to me.

Our Father not only *knows*, but *sends* them all in love."

The next stage of their journey was to be a leisurely one, *via* the Grand Canal to Hang-chow, the far-famed capital of the neighbouring province. Here it was hoped they might be enabled to commence operations and, with Mr. Stevenson between them and Ningpo, complete a chain of C.I.M. stations a hundred miles into the interior.[1] At one or other of the cities *en route* Mr. Taylor expected to leave some of the young men with the evangelist. They were to travel by native house-boats, giving regular hours to study, and waiting upon God as to their ultimate location.

To take so large a party inland at all was a step of faith, especially as it included an English nurse and four little children, besides six unmarried ladies. In the whole of China, at that time, there was not *one* unmarried lady

[1] Hang-chow and Ningpo, about a hundred miles apart, form approximately an equilateral triangle, with Shanghai as its apex.

missionary to be found away from the treaty ports; and
the entire staff of such workers, including these new arrivals,
numbered only seventeen. Seventeen missionary women
free to devote their time to schools, hospitals, and evangelisation—it was a mere nothing, even for the ports ! And away
from those few, coast-board cities, scarcely a voice was
raised to tell of Redeeming Love to the women and children
of half the heathen world. " The Lord giveth the word :
the women that publish the tidings are a great host." [1] To
add to their number in China and facilitate their all-important work was one of Mr. Taylor's chief objects in the formation of the Inland Mission, and he was prepared to let
devoted women make the sacrifices necessary and to take
upon himself the responsibility of helping them in every
way possible.

For their protection as well as to lessen difficulties he
considered the wearing of native dress essential, with a
large measure of conformity to Chinese manners and
customs.

" In my judgment," he wrote on this subject, " the adoption
of the Chinese costume would be desirable even were we residing
in the treaty ports ; but for work in the interior such as we contemplate I am satisfied that it is an absolute pre-requisite. No
foreign missionary to the best of my knowledge ever has, in
European costume, carried on such a work ; and my strong conviction is that, at present, no foreign missionary could do so.
He may travel under the protection of his passport almost anywhere ; but quietly to settle among the people, obtaining free
and familiar communication with them, conciliating their prejudices, winning their esteem and confidence, and so living as to
be an example to them of what Chinese Christians should be,
requires the adoption not merely of their costume but of their
habits also to a very considerable extent. Merely to put on their
dress, and act regardless of their thoughts and feelings, is to make
a burlesque of the whole matter, and will probably lead the person
so adopting it to conclude, before long, that it is of very little
value to him. But I have never heard of any one, after a *bona
fide* attempt to become Chinese to the Chinese that he might gain
the Chinese, who either regretted the course taken or wished to
abandon it."

---

[1] Psalm lxviii. 11, R.V.

The grounds upon which this sacrifice was advocated were so important that we venture to give further extracts.[1]

Had our Lord appeared on earth as an angel of light, He would doubtless have inspired far more awe and reverence, and would have gathered even larger multitudes to attend His ministry. But to save man He became man, not merely like man. And further, the immediate objects of His personal ministry being " under the law " (" the lost sheep of the house of Israel ") He likewise was born " under the law," not a mere proselyte but a real Jew ; " for it became Him in all things to be made like unto His brethren." In language, in appearance, in everything not sinful He made Himself one with those He sought to benefit. Had He been born a noble Roman rather than a Jew, He would perhaps, if less loved, have commanded more of a certain kind of respect, and would assuredly have been spared much of the indignity He suffered. This, however, was not His aim : He " emptied Himself." Surely no follower of the meek and lowly Jesus will be likely to conclude that it is " beneath the dignity of a Christian missionary " to seek identification with this great though benighted people, in the hope that he may see them washed, sanctified, justified, in the name of the Lord Jesus and by the Spirit of our God. . . .

I am not alone in the opinion that the foreign dress and carriage of missionaries (to a certain extent affected by some of their pupils and converts), the foreign appearance of chapels, and indeed the foreign air imparted to everything connected with their work has seriously hindered the rapid dissemination of the Truth among the Chinese. And why should such a foreign aspect be given to Christianity ? The Word of God does not require it ; nor, I conceive, could sound reason justify it. It is not the denationalisation but the Christianisation of this people that we seek. We wish to see Chinese Christians raised up—men and women truly Christian, but withal truly Chinese in every right sense of the word. We wish to see churches of such believers presided over by pastors and officers of their own countrymen, worshipping God in the land of their fathers, in their own tongue, and in edifices of a thoroughly native style of architecture. " It is enough that the disciple be as *His Master*." If we really wish to see the Chinese such as we have described, let us as far as possible set before them a true example. Let us in everything not sinful become Chinese, that we may by all means " save

---

[1] The letter, which was a long one, was written to help Mr. Berger in putting the matter before young people at home who were candidates for the Mission.

some." Let us adopt their dress, acquire their language, seek to conform to their habits and approximate to their diet as far as health and constitution will allow. Let us live in their houses, making no unnecessary alteration in external form, and only so far modifying their internal arrangements as health and efficiency for work absolutely require.

This cannot but involve, of course, a certain measure of inconvenience, such as the sacrifice of some accustomed articles of diet, etc. But will any one reflecting on what HE gave up Who left heaven's throne to be cradled in a manger ; Who, having filled all things and wielded omnipotence, became a feeble infant wrapped in swaddling clothes ; Who from being the loved one of the Father—never misjudged, never unappreciated, and receiving the ceaseless adoration of all the hierarchies of heaven—became a despised Nazarene, misunderstood by His most faithful followers, neglected and rejected by men who owed Him their very being and whose salvation He had come to seek, and finally, mocked, spit upon, crucified and slain with thieves and outlaws, will any follower of Christ, reflecting on these things, hesitate to make the trifling sacrifice indicated above ?

We give you credit, dear friends, for being prepared to give up not these little things only, but a thousand times more for Christ's sake. . . . Let there be no reservation. Give yourself up wholly and fully to Him Whose you are and Whom you wish to serve in this work, and there can be no disappointment. But once let the question arise, "Are we called to give up this or that ?" once admit the thought, " I did not expect such and such inconvenience or privation," and your service will cease to be that free and happy one which is most conducive to efficiency and success. " God loveth a cheerful giver."

Mr. Taylor's companions of the *Lammermuir* party being one with him in these convictions, the change into native dress was effected without delay. They did not remain long enough in Shanghai to complete the ladies' outfits, but the young men submitted to the somewhat trying process of shaving the front part of the head and donning the *queue* and loose-fitting garb of the country, Mr. Taylor doing the same. Mrs. Taylor also appeared in Chinese costume at Mr. Gamble's table. To her it meant no little sacrifice. She had not worn it during her previous residence in China, and experience enabled her to realise something of the restrictions it must involve.

" Things which are tolerated in us as foreigners, wearing
foreign dress," she wrote to Mrs. Berger, " could not be allowed
for a moment in native ladies.   I do not at all mean to imply a
doubt as to the desirability of the change ; but the nearer we
come to the Chinese in outward appearance, the more severely
will any breach of propriety according to their standards be
criticised.   Henceforth I must never be guilty, for example, of
taking my husband's arm out of doors !   And in fifty or a hundred
other ways we may, without great watchfulness, shock the
Chinese by what would seem to them grossly immodest and un-
feminine conduct. . . . Pray much for us in respect to this
matter."

To avoid giving unnecessary offence in Shanghai, the
step was not taken until after the meeting in which, at Mr.
Gamble's invitation, a number of missionaries and others
came together to commend the new enterprise to the guidance and blessing of God.   Although Mr. Taylor and his
fellow-workers were regarded none too cordially in certain
quarters, they could not but feel on this occasion a real
brotherliness of sympathy which was most encouraging.[1]
And Mr. Gamble's interest had deepened into the warmest
friendship.   Indeed he was more than reluctant to part from
his adopted family, many though their claims had been upon
his time and resources.   Accompanying them to the river on
Saturday evening, the 20th of October, he hardly knew how
to say good-bye.   The junks on which they were to travel
were moored out in the stream, and all the party had left
the jetty save Mr. Taylor and Rudland.   Busy with helpful
services to the last, Mr. Gamble quietly laid a package on
the seat of the *sampan*, stepped ashore, and was gone amid
the shadows.   It was the roll of dollars he had reluctantly
accepted in payment for their board, and on a slip of paper
he had written, " For the good of the Mission."

[1] It is interesting to recall the names of those who in 1866 formed
the staff of the two British and four American societies at work in
Shanghai : they were the Revs. W. Muirhead and G. Owen (L.M.S.) ; Mr.
Alex. Wylie (B. & F. Bible Society) ; the Revs. E. H. Thomson (Protes.
Epis.) ; M. T. Yates (Southern Baptist) ; W. G. Cunnyngham, J. W. Lam-
buth, J. J. Allen, and M. L. Wood (Meth. Epis., South) ; J. M. Farnham,
J. Wherry (Presby. Board), and Mr. W. Gamble of the Presby. Press.
The kindness of Mr. Farnham and Mr. Gamble established a special sym-
pathy between their mission and the C.I.M. which continues to this day.

It was "the fairest night imaginable," and dropping down-stream in the moonlight the travellers were soon alongside the dear old *Lammermuir*.[1] The sailors saw them coming and were all on deck to meet them. In the forecastle a last, brief service was held. "Yes, we part, but not for ever," was sung on the well-remembered deck. Then with a last look at their cabins, hallowed by sacred memories, and with many a farewell, the missionaries left for their boats. "Whither, pilgrims, are you going?" was struck up by the ship's company.

"But that tells nothing apart from the singing," Miss Blatchley wrote, "of all the associations brought to mind that made many of the voices unsteady. As we pushed off, they stood along the bulwarks and, raising their caps, gave us three hearty English cheers. In the moonlight and stillness we glided round the stern—sailors and midshipmen following on to the poop, where they repeated the cheers and stood looking after us till we passed out of sight." [2]

Four weeks later it was a company thoroughly Chinese as to outward appearances that drew near the famous city of Hang-chow. The gipsy-life so romantic at first had become wearisome enough in their slow-going boats. Happily the days were fine with the crisp freshness of autumn, but the nights were bitterly cold, and it had become an urgent matter to find more adequate shelter. Nowhere on the way, however, had it been possible to rent premises. Again and again, just when it seemed they had succeeded,

[1] To the sorrow of the missionary party, who had continued to hold meetings on board, some of the crew had fallen back into old habits amid the temptations of port life. "Their deep contrition, however," Mr. Taylor was able to write, "encourage us to hope that they are really children of God"; and others, both among the officers and men, gave only cause for rejoicing.

[2] One link with the *Lammermuir* still remained, for Mr. Brunton, formerly the dread of the crew, was with the young men on their boat. "He came a little way up-country with us," continued Miss Blatchley; "and on Sunday, in the beautiful sunset light, Mr. Taylor baptized him in the river."

Hearing from this officer, doubtless, of their being without much in the way of European comforts, Captain Bell sent after them—before they could finally get away—two pots of butter, a barrel of treacle, a cooked ham, a joint of beef, and a cheese! To him the party had given a beautiful Bible and a travelling rug.

negotiations had fallen through, and from place to place they had been obliged to move on, an unbroken party.

Bravely they had kept up their studies and used every opportunity, with the help of their Chinese companions, for making known the Way of Life. But crowded quarters, repeated disappointments, and growing concern with regard to the reception that might be expected at their destination made the journey a trying one, bringing out both the strength and weakness of individual characters. All were suffering from the cold ; several, including the children, were more or less ill ; and the Ningpo servants began to talk about going home for the winter. The boat-people, needless to say, were full of complaints. Far from their accustomed waters, in a district dangerously unsettled through the Rebellion. they too were feeling the stress of anxiety, and were clamouring to be set free to return to Shanghai. Altogether the situation was a critical one, and prayer was the only resource of much-tried hearts.

" We were of ourselves just *helpless*," wrote one of the party, " but we knew that we were being led by the Hand that opens and *no* man shuts ; the Hand that had prepared for us at Shanghai a hospitable roof and storage for our goods ; so we prayed and moved forward, nothing doubting."

It was upon Mr. Taylor the burden pressed most heavily, as he left the boats in an unfrequented place near the city and set out with the evangelist to seek the home it was so necessary to find. When he was gone and they were left in a good deal of suspense, Mrs. Taylor gathered all the party for united prayer. The circumstances affected her in quite a special way, for before long she was to lay in little Gracie's arms the baby-sister for whom the child was daily asking in her prayers. Yet that mother-heart, so tender in its solicitude, was perfectly at rest. " Who will bring me into the strong city ? " had come in her Psalm for that morning, " Who will lead me into Edom ? Wilt not Thou, O God ? . . . Give us help from trouble, for vain is the help of man. Through God we shall do valiantly." Quietly she read the passage now, and none who were present could ever forget the prayer that followed. It changed an hour of painful suspense into one of soul-out-pouring, preparing the young missionaries as nothing else could have done for whatever news Mr. Taylor might bring.

And very soon he came. Before they could have expected it his voice was heard near the boats—and with radiant face he was among them. Yes, all was well. The Lord had indeed gone before. Just as in Shanghai, a home was ready, waiting !

Knowing that a friend of Ningpo days, belonging to the same Mission as Mr. Gamble, had recently moved to Hang-chow, Mr. Taylor called on him first of all to acquaint him with their arrival.

" We have been expecting you," was Mr. Green's kindly welcome, " and I have a message you may be glad to receive."

A young American missionary, it appeared, had just left the city to bring his wife and child from Ningpo to the home he had prepared for them. His house, furnished and ready, would be empty for a week at least, and he had bethought him of Mr. Taylor's party.

" Tell them," he said to Mr. Green, " to go straight to my place when they come. It is at their disposal for the time being."

The house was on a quiet street and could be reached in boats without observation. Mr. Kreyer was not expected back for several days, and all they had to do was to take possession. Well can one imagine the praise meeting that was held then and there, before the boats moved on !

" Who will bring me into the strong city ? Who will lead me into Edom ? Wilt not *Thou*, O God ? "

CHAPTER VIII

O THAT THOU WOULDEST BLESS ME INDEED

1866–1867.   AET. 34–35.

IT was no time for resting on their oars, however.   Under cover of darkness the whole party had entered Hang-chow without causing any excitement, and had taken up their abode in Mr. Kreyer's premises.   But the latter was returning shortly, and the question of a home of their own was urgent.   Where in the great city, still suffering from the ravages of the Tai-ping Rebellion, they were to find quarters large enough for themselves and the work they hoped to do was indeed a problem.   But in this again the Lord had gone before them " to search out a resting-place."

Nothing could have been more suitable, as Mr. Taylor soon discovered, than the very first house to which he was directed.   Large and well built, it had been a Mandarin's residence, but was sadly dilapidated now, and a regular rabbit-warren occupied by a number of families.   The situation was excellent, in a quiet corner, near the city wall and busy streets.   The upper storey offered sleeping accommodation for the whole party, a second staircase making it possible to shut off a separate wing for the young men. This was so manifest an advantage that it decided Mr. Taylor to obtain the premises if possible—the downstairs' rooms being adaptable for guest-halls, chapel and dispensary, printing-press, dining-room, servants' quarters, etc.

Almost with fear and trembling, after hearing the rent demanded, he made an offer which was not accepted.   The landlord, perceiving that the matter was urgent, hoped by prolonged negotiations to drive a better bargain. Sunday, however, intervened—putting a stop as far as the missionaries were concerned to business transactions—and to the surprise of the landlord he saw no more of his would-be tenants. But though they had nothing to say to him apparently, they had much to lay before the Lord. The day was given to prayer, and when on Monday morning his decision was asked it was much more favourable.

" They must have other houses in view," he said to himself. " If I am not careful I shall lose good tenants."

With surprising alacrity, after this, he came to terms, so that by Tuesday evening the necessary documents were signed and sealed. Some of the occupants had already moved out to liberate the upper storey. Five families remained, but there was plenty of room, the landlord urged, for Mr. Taylor's household. Let them only move in, and before long they should have the entire premises. On Wednesday morning accordingly, November 28—the very day Mr. Kreyer was to return—so early that the sleeping city knew nothing of what was happening, the *Lammermuir* party made their way through the silent streets and entered upon a home of their own after six months of travelling and unsettlement.

" Here then for the present," wrote Miss Blatchley, " Mr. Taylor intends us to remain as quietly and as little seen as possible, the study of the language affording sufficient occupation. By the time any of us are ready for work among the people it will be known that a number of foreigners are living in the city, and that no disturbance or mischief has resulted, and we shall gain access to them, *D.V.*, with less difficulty, exciting less suspicion than could otherwise have been the case. We trust also to find an advantage from coming direct to the capital of the province, as a footing gained here will pave our way, to some extent, in less important places." [1]

For already the thought of extension was occupying their minds. So great, indeed, was Mr. Taylor's desire to spread the light, that the very first Sunday in their Hang-

---

[1] A letter to the Hon. Miss Waldegrave, one of many written by Miss Blatchley as Mr. Taylor's secretary.

chow home found him not there at all but away in the neighbouring city of Siao-shan. Messrs. Meadows and Crombie
had come over from Ningpo to see if they could be of service,
and Mr. Taylor was glad to avail himself of their help in this
evangelistic effort. Two days spent in the neighbouring
city, during which they had excellent opportunities for
preaching the Gospel, so convinced them of its importance
as a centre for missionary work that they were thankful to
be enabled to rent a small house before leaving, with a view
to settling out some of the new arrivals as soon as possible.

" Had not the Lord specially helped us, in answer to special
prayer," Mr. Taylor wrote on his return, " we should have failed
both in Hang-chow and in Siao-shan, as we had failed in other
places previously."

His heart beat high with hope, and it is interesting to
notice that he had not been in Hang-chow three weeks before
he was informing Mr. Berger about postal and banking communication with the inland provinces.

" You will be glad to learn," he wrote before the middle of
December, " that facilities for sending letters by native post and
transmitting money through native banks to various points in
the interior are very good. I do not think there will be any
difficulty in remitting money to any province in the empire which
will not be easily overcome. In the same way letters from the
most distant places can be sent to the ports. Such communication is slow and may prove rather expensive, but is tolerably sure.
Thus we see the way opening before us for work in the interior."

Meanwhile there was no lack of work immediately around
him. Happily a spell of milder weather favoured the process
of getting their premises somewhat into order. To the un-
initiated, the latter looked more like a collection of out-
houses and barns, in deplorable condition, than the handsome residence Mr. Taylor assured them it once had been.
In any case, the work of settling-in involved scraping thick
dirt from the floors of the upper rooms—and they were
clean compared with the downstairs quarters.

" It is pretty cold weather," Mr. Taylor wrote on returning
from Siao-shan (Dec. 4), " to be living in a house without

any ceilings and with very few walls and windows. There is a deficiency in the wall of my own bedroom six feet by nine, closed in with a sheet, so that ventilation is decidedly free. But we heed these things very little. Around us are poor dark heathen—large cities without any missionary; populous towns without any missionary; villages without number, all destitute of the means of grace. I do not envy the state of mind that would forget these, or leave them to perish, for fear of a little discomfort. May God make us faithful to Him and to our work."

Well was it that the party were in Chinese dress, for they lived at close quarters for a month or more with the families who shared their rambling abode. Although the house took on by degrees a measure of cleanliness, it had little acquaintance with " foreign " things and ways that could prove disquieting. Knives and forks, together with English crockery and cooking, had been left behind in Shanghai, and the simplest of Chinese furniture was found to meet all requirements. There were the regulation chairs and tables in the guest-hall, for the proper reception of visitors, but for the rest—boards and trestles, wooden benches, and beds consisting of a wooden frame strung with cocoanut fibres sufficed. At meal-times a Chinese company, to all appearances, gathered round the table minus a cloth, set with basins and chopsticks, and the food served was equally familiar to the neighbours who were looking on. Perhaps it was this that disarmed prejudice and made a way for friendly intercourse. There was nothing to be afraid of.

" These people are like ourselves," was the conclusion soon come to. " They eat our rice and wear our dress, and their words we understand."

So from the first one and another began to drop in to Chinese prayers attracted by the singing, and before the new arrivals had been a week in the house one woman was openly interested in the Gospel. Miss Faulding, who had made good progress with the language, was welcomed as a daily visitor in her room and among the other tenants, and the reports that went out proved reassuring to relatives and friends.

" We have been getting the house a little more comfortable," wrote this bright member of the party (Dec. 12), " though

there is plenty still to be done.   Mr. Taylor and the young men
have contrived paper ceilings fixed on wooden frames, which keep
out some of the cold air ; for the upstairs rooms have roofs such
as you find in chapels at home.   They also have papered some of
the walls or wooden partitions between the rooms.   Of course
we are as yet in confusion, but we are getting on and I hope shall
be settled some day.

   " The lodgers are to leave next week ; they occupy principally
the ground floor. . . . I am so glad for them to have been here,
for many come to Chinese prayers and listen attentively.   We
could not have visited out of doors just yet . . . but I read and
talk with these women every day, and they seem to like it.   One
woman I have great hope of.   She has given up burning incense,
and says that since we came she has begun to pray to God.   They
are all employed in making imitation money out of silver paper,
to be burnt for the use of dead relatives—a great trade here.
While I am reading to them, they often take out their pipes and
have a few whiffs, almost choking me with smoke.   Of course I
don't say anything, for every woman seems to smoke.   They ask
plenty of questions about ourselves, and sometimes such things
as, ' Where must we go to worship God ? ' . . . Yesterday we
had a congregation of ten neighbours gathered in by the woman
who is so interested, besides our lodgers and servants."

   Thus the good work began, and before Christmas we read
of attentive audiences of fifty or sixty at the Sunday services.

   " You would be amused at many things we see," Miss Faulding wrote again in February : " a man nursing an immense dog
all through the service ; a woman mending a large man's shoe ;
and another, close by me, giving me a lesson in the approved
style of dressing children's hair, using her thin fingers as a comb.
She evidently thought she could do two things at a time, for she
certainly listened to what was being said."

   With what interest the young missionaries watched
these developments, and how fervently in their noon prayer
meetings they sought the life-giving touch of the Holy
Spirit for one and another who seemed impressed !   Among
these a soldier, for example, reading for the first time a
Gospel and a copy of the book of Acts, gave cause for encouragement.

   " What a difference there was," he remarked, " between

Judas and Paul ! the one a disciple who betrayed his Master ; the other a persecutor who became the most devoted of His followers."

A Buddhist priest, too, hearing Mr. Taylor preach at a street-corner, rejoiced the evangelist, Tsiu, by coming daily with intelligent questions. A third, who dropped in out of curiosity and was welcomed by one of the young men, was so touched by the kindly spirit behind the poor attempt at Chinese that he came again, and soon joined the little group who every morning were to be found in the guest-hall, reading the Scriptures.

" I was going into the city the other day," wrote Mr. Sell as early as the 1st of January, " when a man called out : ' I am coming to worship the true God to-morrow,' referring to our Sunday services. Thus, you see, we are already known and our work talked about."

As the house began to take on a more habitable appearance, two texts in Chinese found a place on the walls of the dining-room :

> " *I must work the works of Him that sent me.*"
> " *Even Christ pleased not Himself.*"

That " *must* " was very real to the missionary household. It was *work*, real earnest, self-sacrificing work, that filled the busy days, crowding chapel and guest-hall with friendly hearers.

With the Chinese New Year, early in February (1867), came golden opportunities. A dispensary had by that time been opened, precursor of all the medical work for which Hang-chow has become famous. With much else upon his hands, it was not easy for Mr. Taylor to attend to scores of patients daily, but there was no other doctor nearer than Ningpo or Shanghai, and his heart went out to the people in their sufferings. From far and near the patients came with every variety of complaint both of body and soul ; and when holiday-makers were added at the New Year season, the doctor and his helpers were overwhelmed with guests.

" How I should have liked some of our home-friends to have been with us to-day," Miss Faulding wrote at this time.[1] " We have had such good services (Sunday) ; at least two hundred present, sitting as quietly as an English audience, and having the Truth so forcibly put before them. Many this afternoon were shut out for want of room. I think we shall soon have to enlarge our borders. One woman who had heard of us from her neighbours came three miles to the service. Some tell us that they have given up burning incense to their idols ; and several, both men and women, say they believe, and are asking for baptism. The medical side of the work is invaluable. I cannot tell you what a thrill of joy one constantly feels at the sight of so many heathen listening to the Gospel. . . . Mr. Taylor's illustrations in preaching are so good and varied, and his words seem to come with a power that would be astonishing did one not know how many are praying that God's blessing may rest upon our work."

" Mr. Taylor has over two hundred patients daily," she continued a fortnight later (March 16). " People bring their wares and stay near our door, in the hope of getting more custom from the numbers that gather here than they could elsewhere. Sedan-chairs with their bearers are generally waiting, to carry those who cannot walk. The evangelist spends most of his time talking to the patients, and Mr. Taylor generally gives a short address. We have some most hopeful inquirers."

When reinforcements arrived from England (February 23), the first sent out after the sailing of the *Lammermuir*, Mr. Taylor was too busy to see anything of them until some hours later. He was standing on a table at the time, preaching to a crowd of patients in the courtyard, and could only call out a hearty welcome as the party entered, escorted by Mr. Meadows. The new arrivals were more than satisfied with this state of affairs, however, and it was not long before John McCarthy was at Mr. Taylor's side, soon to become his principal helper in the medical work. Those were days in which, amid external hardships, his fellow-workers had at any rate the privilege of close and constant association

---

[1] To her mother's care it was due that a complete series of the bright, girlish letters have been preserved that give so natural a picture of daily life at Sin-kai-long (Hang-chow) from the first. Miss Faulding was only twenty-two when she went to China, and her parents, who were old friends of Mr. Taylor's, did much to maintain a prayerful interest in the Mission throughout a large circle.

with the leader who embodied to so remarkable a degree their ideals of missionary service.[1]

"If only Mr. Taylor could be in three or four places at the same time it would be a decided advantage," Miss Faulding continued in May. "He is wanting to visit the governing cities of this province, to look out the most eligible places for stations : he and Mr. Duncan have been on the point of starting several times. Then there is Ningpo where he is needed, and here he is overwhelmed with work. He wants to go to Shao-hing too (Mr. Stevenson's stations) that he may give further help with the colloquial dialect, there is hardly any knowing what his movements may be ; yet he goes on so quietly and calmly always— just leaning upon God and living for others—that it is a blessing merely to witness his life."

All this, needless to say, was a great joy to Mr. Berger and the friends at home. That within six months of their arrival the *Lammermuir* party should not only be settled in the interior, but that they should be cheered with so much of blessing in their rapidly growing work, was a wonderful answer to the prayers that had been going up on their behalf. No less strenuous than their own was the life Mr. and Mrs. Berger were living in the service of the Mission. Already advanced in years, it was not easy for them to turn their quiet home into a Mission-centre, using as offices both dining-room and study ; to encumber the billiard-room with packing-cases ; to receive at their table candidates for China and friends of the missionaries ; to direct wrappers, and send out with their own hands the *Occasional Paper* ; to attend to a large correspondence, keep accounts, transmit money, arrange for the outgoing of new workers, help with their preparations, fit up their cabins, see them off from any port at any hour of the day or night, and correspond with those already on the field. Yet all this they did with the loving interest of a father's and mother's heart. When it became necessary they went further, and adapted a cottage

---

[1] "I think of him as I ever knew him," wrote Mr. McCarthy from Western China thirty-eight years later, "kind, loving, thoughtful of every one but himself, a blessing wherever he went and a strength and comfort to all with whom he came in contact . . . a constant example of all that a missionary ought to be"

on their grounds for the young men candidates and another
for a tutor who gave secretarial help.

"Mr. Aveline and I seldom get more than half an hour's
exercise a day, which is insufficient for health," Mr. Berger wrote
in February 1867. "Still we are very happy and rejoice in the
work."

How he could find time amid the claims of business as
well as these self-imposed tasks to write regularly and freely
to Mr. Taylor as he did is a marvel. He seems never to
have missed a mail. A whole volume of his letters—thin
foreign paper stitched into a leather binding—has been
preserved, covering a period of about two years from the
sailing of the *Lammermuir*. Reflecting the sympathy and
eager interest with which mail after mail was received, this
correspondence deals with varied questions, from important
spiritual principles to details concerning individual workers.
Penned in joy and sorrow, as the tidings from China were
cheering or otherwise, these letters breathe a faith and love
that were unchanging, and form a veritable storehouse of
wisdom, helpfulness, and encouragement.

For all was not, invariably, as Mr. Berger could have
wished, and there were hours of painful exercise of mind
at Saint Hill as well as in Hang-chow. Even on the voyage
out, as we have seen, Mr. Taylor had had cause to regret the
spirit of certain members of the party, and as time went on
their presence became an increasing difficulty. Among the
letters, most of which brought only joy to the home-circle,
were others of a very different nature. Complaints and
criticism awakened Mr. Berger's concern, and plainly
revealed an attitude on the part of some that threatened
the harmony and indeed the very existence of the Mission.
It was only one or two at first, who were not prepared to go
all lengths in wearing native dress and adapting themselves
to their surroundings in accordance with the principles of
the Mission. But their disaffection went so far as to permit
of their carrying exaggerated reports to outsiders, one of
whom, with the best intentions, took them up seriously
and considered them sufficient ground for strenuous opposi-

tion to the work. So prejudiced was he, indeed, by what he heard against Mr. Taylor, that he would not inquire from him, or the members of the Mission who felt with him, as to the charges made. Without letting them even know of the course he was taking, this influential missionary wrote the strongest accusations to Mr. Berger and others, attacking not only the methods of the C.I.M. but Mr. Taylor's fitness for the position he occupied.

Having heard nothing of the other side, these painful letters came as a bolt out of the blue to the friends at Saint Hill. Never suspecting that the disaffected members of the Mission were writing home in a bitter spirit, far less that they had stirred up a comparative stranger to do so, Mr. and Mrs. Taylor were saying nothing to the disparagement of any fellow-worker. They were seeking by prayer and patience to remove difficulties and conquer opposition, determined that none should be prejudiced in Mr. Berger's eyes by any word from them, as long as there was the least hope of improvement. But the restraint was costing them dear in more ways than one. As early as February (1867) Mrs. Taylor had longed to pour out her heart to her beloved friend Mrs. Berger, but refrained in accordance with Mr. Taylor's judgement.

" We yesterday received your loving letters written on the arrival of our first mail from China," she wrote on the second of that month. " They are so sweet to us ; and at a time like this, when Satan seems desiring to have us that he may sift us as wheat, they are peculiarly helpful.

" Oh, if you were here, how your hearts would grieve ! But we must not be surprised, must we, at troubles and *offences* coming, and severe sorrow too ? This work was not undertaken with the expectation that it would be free from difficulties. And *our God* Who has hitherto helped us and has brought us thus far, Who was with us in the typhoon and delivered us from the jaws of death, will surely be with our Mission in the storm, delivering it too from shipwreck.

" But you will be anxious to know what the present sorrow is. In my last letter I mentioned that Mr. and Mrs. —— had gone to Siao-shan, and that Mr. Williamson was there to help make their house comfortable. . . .

" I had written to the middle of the last sentence when my

dear husband desired me not to enter into details by this mail. He intends, I believe, writing to Mr. Berger and showing the letter to the persons concerned, so as to give an opportunity for explanation on the other side.   So, though it does seem hard to be unable to tell you all about this heavy burden, I must obey the injunction, ' Wives, submit yourselves.'   This I think I may mention—we are for the present driven out of Siao-shan."

In defiance of Mr. Taylor's wishes the missionaries in question had gone back to English dress, to the serious detriment of their interests in that inland city.   The Mandarin, who had left them in peace before, then determined upon their ejection.   With his soldiers and underlings he had come upon them suddenly on the evening of January the 28th, and had ordered them to leave the city before morning. To put them in fear he seized the evangelist, Tsiu, whom at great sacrifice Mr. Taylor had spared from Hang-chow, and had him cruelly beaten—six hundred stripes on the back with rods, and a hundred more on the face with a strip of leather. Sorely bruised and shaken, there was nothing for it but for Tsiu to make his way as best he could to the capital ; and he was quickly followed by the rest of the party, who had to be accommodated in Hang-chow while the matter was being adjusted.

Those were months of extreme trial to all the household at *Sin-kai-long*.   Mr. Taylor was overwhelmingly busy with medical work and the throngs of holiday-makers brought by the New Year season.   In a reasonable and patient spirit he sought to draw the ejected missionaries into all that was going on, and to conquer causes of difficulty.   But another influence was at work ; and instead of responding to his efforts they kept apart, openly wearing English dress, refusing to come to the meetings, and seeking to foment opposition to Mr. Taylor's authority and arrangements.   In this, unhappily, they were encouraged by the afore-mentioned missionary, who was just leaving for furlough.   Believing their reports to be true, he felt it his duty not only to write as we have seen, but personally to discredit the new methods of the C.I.M among its supporters.

When one remembers the circumstances, it is easy to see

that there may have been, in the practical working of the Mission, some cause for complaint. At thirty-four years of age there still remains much to learn, and Mr. Taylor's fellow-workers were all younger than himself. " The man who never makes a mistake," as Mr. Spurgeon said, " never makes anything " ; and they were striking out, it will be borne in mind, on a new and confessedly difficult line of things. But oh, how true and deep the longing that filled their hearts to walk before God and be well-pleasing to Him ! If only the older missionary could have known *all*, and used his experience to safeguard where he apprehended danger, how different the result might have been ! As it was, he came very near accomplishing his avowed object, which was nothing less than to put a stop to the entire work.

Under these painful circumstances, Mr. Berger was wonderfully helped, although his letters of that spring and summer show the distress through which he was passing. Taking the course of true friendship, he wrote freely to Mr. Taylor, sending him copies of the correspondence.

" My earnest prayer to God," he said with the first detailed accusations, " is that you may not be further moved by the letter than the Lord would have you be ; and may He give the right spirit and the wisdom that will enable us both to do that which will please Him.

" The difficulties at home are neither few nor slight, but yours are truly mountainous. . . . You need our every sympathy and prayer ; and be sure, my dear Brother, whatever Mr. —— may have penned, you hold the same place in our hearts as before. That God will supply you and me with increasing wisdom and ability for the work to which He has called us, we need neither fear nor doubt. All that is required on our part is to lay aside everything we discover to be either faulty or erroneous, and constantly to be adding to our stock of both wisdom and love. Oh yes ! we will commit this matter to the Lord Who knows that we did our best. He is very pitiful, and will never leave nor forsake us in this our time of trial."

How serious the trial was to be, and how long continued, the writer could not realise at the time.

" Were we not sure," he wrote on May 8, " that God has given us this work to do, I fear we should be disposed to question whether it was right to continue it; but as it has not been entered upon without counting the cost and feeling sure of our calling, we are enabled to cry to the Lord for the needed help in this time of deep trial: and if *we* feel this, *you* must feel both the sorrows and the assurance of God's calling in tenfold force.

"Let us then strengthen our hands in God, by examining ourselves solemnly before Him to ascertain where we are failing, or have failed, when we shall be better fitted to determine where those linked with us have also failed. The Lord graciously enable us to do this in very truth.

"I am in receipt of two letters from ——. . . . May God enable you, my dear Brother, to keep in very close and holy fellowship with Jesus, so that your loving manner may melt them and eventually restore confidence. As you have not stated in what they have gone astray, I feel I cannot enter into details. . . . Whatever you decide upon, I am sure you will act only after much quiet prayer, and I shall not feel hurt in any degree though you may not see with me or be able to carry out your own wishes. . . .

"I have written under very great pressure of various kinds, and beg you will forgive me if I have in any way expressed myself in an unlovely spirit. You know the deep and true affection I have for you and your dear wife, and it will, I trust, never be disturbed."

So courteous in every word and thought! in the long series of his letters there is not one deviation from this humble, Christlike spirit. And in spite of all that he himself was going through, he was steadfastly encouraging.

May 19: That you may be enabled to cast upon God the terrible trial resulting from Mr. ——'s conduct, and from those acting with him, I earnestly pray. Let us not fear, dear Brother, anything but our own failings; and these may we ever be discovering, confessing, and putting away. I quite expect God will appear for us in the right time.

Occasional Paper number eight will contain the cash account for twelve months, and judging from the contributions in the year (£2800, of which I have contributed little more than £100) I think we ought to give unfeigned thanks, take courage, and go forward, though with great caution and prayerfulness of spirit.

May 21: My hope and confidence are in God, and I seek to roll the burden of all upon Him. You and I have our lessons to learn; and if we will learn them, I doubt not God will still further use us in His service.

It seems to me, dear Brother, we must enlarge our field of vision in regard to this work ; that you must not undertake so much of the detail, but a more enlarged oversight ; that you must not have so many immediately depending upon you. . . . Oh what need for wisdom in every step of this work ! . . .

I have now £1700 in hand, and would gladly put £1000 to the Mission if we can employ it wisely.   I wish to continue aiding the work.   So I think you must pray about how we had best proceed.   I merely make suggestions, and you will canvass them with your dear wife and any others whose judgment you value.

June 7 : As regards your headship in China, I consider it is beyond being questioned, and that you must not allow the thought of appealing to me on the part of any ; and I would advise you to act, as I am sure you would, calmly, lovingly, but firmly and unflinchingly for the Lord, in all cases where immediate action is needed.   I think you will see that I must act in the same way in England, respecting candidates for China.

I am exceedingly rejoiced to notice that with the exception of —— none have sympathy with Mr. —— and his doings. . . . The Lord will bring all these things to a calm in due time, I quite think.   He will teach you the best method to adopt, and us at home.   May we only be careful to be found in a teachable spirit.

August 5 : I do trust the many tokens from our Father's hand, though so afflictive, are effecting in us a more quiet and chastened spirit, leading us to *dwell* more " in the secret place of the most High."   I think I can truly say, " None of these things move me."   I am happier than ever, and more sure that the work we have set our hands to is indeed the Lord's work.   May we therefore expect it to prosper.

August 24 : It is not our mistakes but our refusing to correct them when discovered that will prove baneful : of course it would be better not to make mistakes.   We have much to learn in order to carry on this work to the glory of God.

It is to be regretted that Mr. Taylor's part in this correspondence has not been preserved, but the spirit in which both he and Mrs. Taylor met these trials may be judged from letters written by the latter to Mrs. Berger, many of which remain.   From the quiet of her room early in February she wrote—a little daughter five days old lying beside her :

I have been listening to my beloved husband and others playing and singing in the chapel some of our favourite hymns.   One in particular, " Oh for the robes of whiteness, oh for the tearless eye," seemed to take me away in thought to happy Saint Hill, and I was almost tempted to wish myself back in that home of rest and love. But it is not for the soldier on the battlefield, however sorely pressed or wounded, to wish himself back in safety and ease. And then, it was sweet to look forward to

> The no-more weeping, within that land of love;
> The endless joy of keeping the bridal feast above.

Oh, beloved Sister ! if the Lord will only work by us, and set His seal upon our efforts, we will endeavour to rejoice in tribulation.

" Do pray for us very much," she continued a few weeks later (March 19), " for we do so need God's *preserving* grace at the present time. We have come to fight Satan in his very strongholds, and he will not let us alone. What folly were ours, were we here in our own strength ! But greater is He that is for us than all that are against us. One is sometimes tempted to feel overwhelmed with the sense of Satan's power here ; but our God will not fail nor forsake us. I should be very sorry to see discord sown among the sisters of our party, and this is one of the evils I am fearing now. . . .

" What turn Mr. —— matters will take I cannot think. One thing I know, ' the Hope of Israel ' will not forsake us. One is almost tempted to ask, ' Why was —— permitted to come out ? ' Perhaps it was that our Mission might be thoroughly established on right bases early in its history."

April 15 : God can in His all-wise providence utterly frustrate the designs of our great adversary to bring us and our work into disrepute. I feel encouraged, too, by looking back on our own experience in many sad months of the year before our marriage. It was a marvel that *my* mind even was not poisoned against my dear husband ; and we could have no communication with one another, so as to hear the other side.[1] Yet God mercifully kept us from being influenced by the aspersions ; and the remembrance of His past dealings must reassure us now.

> He cannot have taught us to trust in His Name,
> And thus far have brought us, to put us to shame.

And all the while souls were being saved, and the prayer answered with which the *Lammermuir* party had entered the New Year: " O that Thou wouldest bless me indeed, and enlarge my coast, and that Thine hand might be with me,

---

[1] See *Hudson Taylor in Early Years*, pages 420 *et sqq.*

and that Thou wouldest keep me from evil that it may not grieve me." [1] Before the end of March there were twelve candidates for baptism, " a little, green oasis," as Miss Blatchley wrote, " amid the clouding of manifold troubles." The weekly Enquirers' Meeting had to be begun that month, in spite of a wave of popular excitement which resulted in serious danger and persecution, and many of the converts gave evidence of a real change of heart. [2] In May came the first baptisms, amid the joy of which Mrs. Taylor wrote to the friends at Saint Hill :

Perhaps our dear Lord sees that we need sorrows to keep us from being elated at the rich blessing He is giving in our work.

For at the same time the unhappy spirit of the Siao-shan party seemed only to increase, and Mr. Berger's difficulties at home had reached a climax. These complications greatly hindered Mr. Taylor in taking the pioneering journeys necessary if younger workers were to be planted out. All around them, even in that coast-board province, were millions upon millions to whom " no tidings came " of the one, the only Saviour. To these in their sin and need His heart went out, moving those other hearts of the little missionary community with His own constraining love. No fewer than *sixty cities* in that one province were still without preachers of the Gospel, native or foreign, nine of these being capitals of prefectures, or *Fu* cities from which the rest were governed. To open stations of the Mission in these centres was a purpose Mr. Taylor was prayerfully considering. In a journey round the Ningpo district he had taken counsel with his more experienced fellow-workers, finding Mr. Meadows and Mr. Stott ready to move on to places as yet unreached. Two important Fu cities in the east and south — Tai-chow and Wen-chow — were now

---

[1] 1 Chronicles iv. 9, 10.

[2] In February and March, after the riotous disturbance at Siao-shan, matters looked very serious for the missionary community in Hang-chow as well as for the native Christians. A plot to get rid of all foreigners— worked up by so-called " doctors " of the city, who saw their gains imperilled—might easily have been successful but for the prompt action of the local authorities. As it was, the young converts were tested in a very real way, and had practical demonstration of the power of prayer.

allocated to them, Mr. Jackson of the *Lammermuir* party volunteering to accompany Mr. Meadows. This left the north and west more particularly to the Hang-chow workers, several of whom were anxious to get out alone among the people, so as to make more progress with the language.

Freeing himself, therefore, with no little difficulty from headquarters, Mr. Taylor turned his face northward at the end of April, with Duncan, the stalwart Highlander, as a companion. Years before he had had some memorable experiences in the region of the Great Lake, when evangelising with the Rev. William Burns. Little or no progress had been made in that turbulent district since then, and it was with thankfulness the travellers found, even in the *Fu* city of Hu-chow, an open door for the Gospel. Mr. Taylor was not able to remain long, but so much was he impressed with the importance of this centre that he almost decided, a few months later, to make it his own headquarters. Meanwhile it was visited from time to time by his fellow-workers, one earnest convert giving them great joy, and becoming on his own account a real soul-winner.

Into the broad estuary of the Hang-chow river flows the beautiful Tsien-tang from the mountains in the west of the province. To this district Mr. Taylor next turned his attention, when the temporary closing of the dispensary in June afforded him respite from medical claims. Duncan, who was developing gifts as a pioneer, was again his companion, and Mr. McCarthy, the evangelist Tsiu, and a couple of Hang-chow Christians made up the party.

Picture then the flat-bottomed boat with its arched roof of matting in which they took their place among other passengers. It was a cheerful scene—for there was little sleeping, although they did not set out till after dark. The magnificent river, three miles wide, was flooded with moonlight, and a strong favourable wind kept away mosquitoes. Under the bamboo-matting the travellers were lying about in the flicker of little lamps, some eating, some smoking, almost all chatting, the foreigners in Chinese dress being the main subject of conversation. Toward morning, after the approved ablutions in hot water, Mr. Taylor and his companions had prayers together at the front of the boat, the music of "There is a Happy Land" floating out over the water. Having asked the blessing of God, a passage from the Bible was read and explained, their fellow-travellers listening with attention.

Changing into a smaller boat farther up the river, they found themselves crowded in with a strange assortment of passengers. "I had often heard of lying 'heads and tails,'" wrote Mr. McCarthy, who was having his first experience of things purely Chinese, "but now we had to practise it!" Next to Mr. Duncan was an unhappy prisoner with chains around his legs, sentenced to banishment from his own province for murder. Opposite were a couple of opium-smokers with their lighted lamps. Farther on, packed very closely, were five or six Mandarins' runners, a few soldiers, and other people occupying the remaining space.

Rolling up their bedding in the morning, the missionaries again had a brief service, Mr. Taylor speaking from the fifth of Matthew. This opened the way for conversation with one and another as they slowly tracked on all day. Here and there picturesque temples and pagodas stood out against the ever-changing background of magnificent hills. Towns and villages told of a dense population, and every opportunity was taken of preaching in the streets and tea-shops when the boat came to a standstill. Provisions had to be purchased as they went, and Mr. McCarthy retained a lively recollection of Duncan's tall figure in a white summer gown, his shaven head with its platted *queue* protected by a huge straw hat lined with blue calico, in one hand a palm-leaf fan, and in the other a live chicken carried by the legs.

At Yen-chow, a *Fu* city a hundred miles above Hang-chow, a stay of several days was made, and there Mr. McCarthy remained with one of their Chinese helpers, while Mr. Taylor and the others went on. Still farther up the river, they left their boat at a busy suburb of Lan-chi, where Mr. Duncan hoped to stay for a time. A Ningpo man in a tea-shop, hearing them speak his own dialect, was attracted and helped to find a lodging. A teacher also was given in answer to prayer, and in their large upstair rooms the missionaries were kept busy with visitors.

" I left Duncan in what we consider comfortable lodgings for travellers," Mr. Taylor wrote on his return journey : " a roof over his head, more or less leaky of course, but still a roof ; a floor under his feet, and not a floor only but rich accummulations of well-trodden dirt, which could only be partially removed by considerable exertion. Having a shutter at one end of the room, if no window, it would be ungrateful to complain of the absence of both door and window-shutter at the other end—the more so as in event of rain beating in beyond endurance it is easy to nail up a few pieces of matting which lie ready to hand, awaiting such an emergency."

The meagre furnishing of the room, consisting of little but boards and bamboo trestles, had tempted Duncan to the " lavish expenditure of sixpence " for the purchase of a chair, with which, and his travelling rug, pillow, and mosquito netting, he felt well set up.

In a letter to his mother on this journey Mr. Taylor referred to the boards of a boat as harder to lie on than they once were, though he could still pass a night very contentedly if not very comfortably on such a bed. He tells of getting up before daylight wakened the other passengers, for quiet waiting upon God, and of the joy of pouring out his heart for every member of the Mission as the sun rose over the summer land. He gives a little picture too of travelling on after dark, another boat lashed to their own for company, and all the passengers gathered together to hear the message of Redeeming Love.

" I preached to them till I was tired," he wrote, " and I supposed they would be too. After a short prayer, I concluded, but no one moved to go away ; they seemed to want to hear more. So I began again and talked for a long time, and again stopped. Still no one moved. A few leading questions were asked, and once more I spoke to them at great length. At last, wearied out, it was I who, after urging on them the immediate importance of turning to Christ, had to remind them of the lateness of the hour and suggest that it was time to retire."

These were the important things, the things that mattered; and " to realise more steadily," as he expressed it in this letter, " the fulness we possess in Jesus." Trials he expected and did not shrink from, if they might but work out the deeper purposes of God.

" More than a year has elapsed," he had written to Mr. Berger (May 30), " since we parted on the deck of the *Lammermuir*, but both you and I can still say—of the past, ' Ebenezer,' of the present, ' Jehovah-nissi,' and of the future, ' Jehovah-jireh,' thanks be to His grace ! Burdens such as I never before sustained, responsibilities such as I had not hitherto incurred, and sorrows compared with which all my past sorrows were light have been part of my experience. But I trust I have, in some feeble measure, learned more of the blessed truth that

> Sufficient in His arm alone,
> And our defence is sure.

" I have long felt that our mission has a baptism to be baptized with. It may not be past yet. It may be heavier than we can foresee. But if, by grace, we are kept faithful, in the end all will be well."

CHAPTER IX

AND ENLARGE MY COAST

1867–1868. AET. 35–36.

LITTLE reference has hitherto been made to an element that entered largely into Mr. Taylor's experience; he was the tenderest of fathers. His children meant more to him than is usually the case with a very busy man, and his delight in them from their infancy was second only to his sense of responsibility for their training. It had cost him much to bring them to China; and journeys that involved an absence from home of weeks at a time, with no means of communication save by special messenger, were a real test both to him and to those left behind.

" It is an easy thing to sing, ' I all on earth forsake,' " he wrote to his mother on the first of these occasions (January 1867). " It is not very difficult to think, and honestly though ignorantly say, ' I give up *all* to Thee and for Thee.' But God sometimes teaches one that that little word ' all ' is terribly comprehensive. Thank God He has left me much, very much; and above all, He never leaves us."

A tiny sheet of pink notepaper with a flower painted in one corner followed Mr. Taylor on this journey. The single word " Papa " in large round hand on the envelope showed from whom it came, but the worn travel-stained condition of the little missive, as one handles it now, is more eloquent than the loving words :

Dear Papa, I hope God has helped you to do what you wanted, and that you will soon come back. I have a nice bead-mat for you when you come home . . . dear, *dear* Papa.

Carried in her father's pocket-book for many a long year, Gracie's little letter, probably the first she ever wrote, tells of the hard life he led no less than of his tender love for her. She was the eldest of his flock, the precious link with early years when he had first met, loved, and married her mother in Ningpo. Three sons had been given them in England, followed by the baby sister, whose arrival brought special joy to Gracie's heart. But though all were equally dear to their parents, there was about the little maiden of eight years old a peculiar charm. On the *Lammermuir*, the wonderful change in some of the sailors when they came to know and love the Lord Jesus had so impressed her, that she too gave her heart to the Saviour as never before. Her deeply spiritual nature had developed like a flower in the sunshine, under the consciousness of His love, so that toward the end of this first summer in Hang-chow her father could write to the grandparents :

I do wish you had seen her lately. Since her conversion she had become quite another child. Her look was more soft, more sweet, more happy.

That first summer was intensely hot, and when the thermometer stood at 103° indoors it seemed time to seek relief. The children were all suffering, and Mrs. Taylor was so ill that it was with difficulty she could be got out of the city. A boat trip of six miles brought them to the hills, where amid the ruins of a once famous temple accommodation had been found. A couple of sheds, or long narrow buildings, were still habitable, in addition to the hall that held idols, and in the former—the priests being willing to turn an honest penny—the Hang-chow party established themselves. The hills were lovely, though the glory of azaleas, wistaria, and other spring flowers had passed away. Pines, oaks, and elms afforded welcome shade, while mountain streams made music, and as far as eye could see there was one unbroken sweep of higher or lower ranges, canals, and rivers, with the Hang-chow Bay and the open sea beyond. It would have been a paradise as compared with the city, but for the illness of several of the party, and the sorrowful sights and sounds of idol worship close at hand.

As they left their boats the first day and were going up the steep stone path made for pilgrims, little Gracie noticed a man making an idol.

" Oh, papa," she said earnestly, " he doesn't know about Jesus, or he would never do it ! Won't you tell him ? "

Her hand clasped in his, Mr. Taylor did so, the child following with eager interest. Farther on they came to a shady place and sat down to rest. Gracie's thoughts were still full of what had happened, and she seemed relieved when her father suggested that they should pray for the man they had been trying to help.

" We sang a hymn," he recalled when every memory of her was precious, " and then I said, ' Will you pray first ? ' She did so, and never had I heard such a prayer. She had seen the man *making an idol* : her heart was full, and she was talking to God on his behalf. The dear child went on and on, pleading that God would have mercy upon the poor Chinese and would strengthen her father to preach to them. I never was so moved by any prayer. My heart was bowed before God. Words fail me to describe it."

And now, a week later, how dark the shadow that had fallen on that father's heart !

" Beloved brother," he wrote to Mr. Berger on the 15th of August, " I know not how to write or how to refrain. I seem to be writing, almost, from the inner chamber of the King of kings. Surely this is holy ground. I am trying to pen a few lines by the couch on which my darling little Gracie lies dying. Her complaint is hydrocephalus. Dear brother, our flesh and our heart fail, but God is the strength of our heart and our portion for ever.

" It was no vain nor unintelligent act when, knowing this land, its people and climate, I laid my wife and children, with myself, on the altar for this service. And He Whom so unworthily, with much of weakness and failure, yet in simplicity and godly sincerity, we are and have been seeking to serve, and not without some measure of success—He has not left us now."

" Who plucked this flower ? " said the gardener.

" The Master," answered his fellow-workman. And the gardener held his peace.

It was not that there was any questioning of the dealings of God with them or their precious child. But the loss was so great, so overwhelming !

" Except when diverted from it by the duties and necessities of our position," he wrote to his mother in September, " our torn hearts will revert to the one subject, and I know not how to write to you of any other. Our dear little Gracie ! How we miss her sweet voice in the morning, one of the first sounds to greet us when we woke—and through the day and at eventide ! As I take the walks I used to take with her tripping at my side, the thought comes anew like a throb of agony, ' Is it possible that I shall never more feel the pressure of that little hand, never more hear the sweet prattle of those dear lips, never more see the sparkle of those bright eyes ? ' And yet she is not *lost*. I would not have her back again. I am thankful *she* was taken, rather than any of the others, though she was the sunshine of our lives. . . . But she is far holier, far happier than she could ever have been here.

" I think I never saw anything so perfect, so beautiful, as the remains of that dear child. The long, silken eyelashes under the finely arched brows ; the nose, so delicately chiselled ; the mouth, small and sweetly expressive ; the purity of the white features ; the quiet composure of the countenance—all are deeply impressed on heart and memory. Then her sweet little Chinese jacket, and the little hands folded on her bosom, holding a single flower—oh, it was passing fair ! and so hard to close for ever from our sight.[1]

" Pray for us. At times I seem almost overwhelmed with the internal and external trials connected with our work. But He has said, ' I will never leave thee nor forsake thee,' and ' My strength is made perfect in weakness.' So be it."

" He makes no mistakes " was the unshaken conviction of these hearts ; and it was with thankfulness they saw, as their bereavement became known, the chastening effect it was having upon others besides themselves. Tidings of the goodness of God in this respect were no little cheer to Mr. and Mrs. Berger amid their difficulties at home.

" HE is keeping Satan altogether under just now," Miss

[1] Miss Bowyer also wrote from Hang-chow at the time : " I never saw anything so lovely as dear little Gracie the evening after her death (on August 23) : it was the sweetest expression of countenance one could behold on earth."

Blatchley was able to write in October, " and I am sure will never let him work against us so as to prevail. How devoutly grateful we ought to feel for the state of things in the Mission now as compared with a few months ago—when our lute seemed too full of rifts for harmony ever to come back again."

In His own way, as they prayed and trusted, God was bringing it back. In His own way, too, He was leading to fresh developments.

For, meanwhile, the great, waiting land, in all its need and darkness, was not forgotten. Difficulties had been more and trials heavier than had been anticipated, but even as Mr. and Mrs. Taylor gave back the little one they so tenderly loved to Him Whose loan she had been, they consecrated themselves afresh to the task of reaching inland China with the Gospel. At the bedside of their dying child in the temple, Duncan, the steadfast Highlander, Mr. Taylor's chief companion on pioneering journeys, had been keeping watch. Nanking was upon his heart—the famous city twice capital of China, with its ancient wall twenty miles in circumference, and its large population still without any witness for Christ. Duncan was not specially gifted or cultured, but he possessed grit and perseverance and a great love for souls. He it was who had toiled at Chinese with the man at the wash-tub while waiting a better teacher, sitting beside him for hours, repeating sentences as he said them or verses that he read from the Gospels, and winning him to Christ at length by his very earnestness in seeking to make the Saviour known.[1] It was something of a risk, no doubt, to let Duncan go forward in such an undertaking. But he could be spared ; he was a man who, his resolution once formed, never wavered ; and the burden of those souls was on his heart.

The early autumn, therefore, saw this solitary pioneer on

---

[1] " It is a great blessing when God gives one a hunger for souls," Mr. Taylor wrote many years later (November 1902). " A good many of our early workers had it. We get better people now in some ways, better educated and so on, but it is not often you find that real hunger for souls— people willing to live anywhere and endure anything if only souls may be saved. They were very often humble people. If they were to offer to our Mission now, they might not be accepted—George Duncan, for example ! But nothing can take its place, or make up for the lack of it. . . . It is so much more important than any ability."

his way northward, a letter written the day before he reached his destination giving some impression of the spirit he brought to bear upon his task.

Sept. 17, 1867 : On Sunday we had a good deal of rain, and I could not get into the city (Chin-kiang). I had a fine quiet day, did a good deal of reading, and had time for meditation on the Word and the matchless grace of the Lord Jesus. Oh, to be always in a humble, devout, and consecrated spirit, drawing richly from the fountain of infinite grace, being filled with the fulness of " Him that filleth all in all," continually realising that Christ is made unto us " wisdom and righteousness and sanctification and redemption," and that we are " complete in Him." I feel I want this so much ! I have often to say with the Psalmist, " Thou did'st hide Thy face, I was troubled." Nothing can ever substitute for the presence of Christ. " Whatever else may be denied, Thy presence, Lord, be given." I am sure a real Christian cannot be but miserable without it. Other helpers soon fail, apart from Him, and comforts flee. All our springs are in Him. He must be all in all, the paramount object of our soul's affection, or we cannot be happy ourselves or make others happy around us. Oh that I might be satisfied, filled with His fulness ! The ambitious man may take the honours of the world, so I may but have Christ. He shall be enough for my soul ! To hear Him say " I am thy salvation " is more to us than anything the world can give.

Needless to say, the young missionary received no welcome at Nanking. Up and down its long streets he and his Chinese helper searched in vain for any lodging that would take them in. Immediately on hearing of a foreigner's arrival, word had been sent from the Prefect to every hostelry that they were on no account to receive him, and as night fell the outlook was far from cheering. Apparently, however, the priest in charge of the Drum Tower had not been included among possible hosts, and when the weary strangers sought his aid he was not unwilling to render it. He had no proper room, he said, for visitors, but if they liked to sleep in the Drum Tower at night and be out all day, so as not to frighten people who came to worship, he would share with them his accommodation.

It was a miserable place ! Few, very few Europeans would have thought it possible to live there at all.

But " we gladly accepted it," wrote Duncan, " and managed very nicely, though we have rather more rats than I like. At night they want to devour everything ! "

Between the depredations of these marauders and the solemn sound of the drum, beaten at intervals, it was not possible to get much sleep, and at day-dawn they had to roll up their bedding and turn out on the streets of the city. The tall figure of the missionary soon became familiar in the tea-shops and frequented thoroughfares, and the neighbourhood of the Drum Tower must have known him well before he succeeded in finding another residence. A carpenter at last had courage to receive him, dividing off a strip of his single upstairs' room for the use of the foreigner. On the other side of the matting lived the Chinese family, while below was the shop and kitchen, so that the new arrivals had every opportunity for picking up colloquial conversation. After a time Duncan persuaded his landlord to share with him the lower room as well. A slight partition was put up, giving the missionary a long but very narrow street chapel, the first ever opened in Nanking ; and there he sat, like Judson in his *zayat*, receiving and conversing with all who would turn in.

" I am not able to talk much," he wrote, " but God helping me, I will say what I can, and T'ien-fuh (the Chinese evangelist) makes them understand. Oh, to make everything conduce to the gathering in of precious souls and the glory of our Master ! "

Thus was commenced permanent missionary work in the great city that is now one of the strongest centres of the Christian Church in China. Duncan may not have been able to do much ; but he held the fort with quiet courage, and one soul at any rate was saved in that first street chapel.[1] A remarkable answer to prayer, also, was given which it is good to recall.

Soon after his arrival in Nanking Duncan had inquired about banks through which money could be remitted to him,

[1] " This self-denying work was not in vain. One man who first heard him there became interested, convinced, converted. After due probation he was baptized ; and being early removed, left his dying as well as living testimony to the grace of Him Who is mighty to save." See *China's Millions* for September 1875, article by J. Hudson Taylor.

and had sent Mr. Taylor the names of two that had representatives in Hang-chow. But one of these had failed, it
appeared, while the other had left the city. This information was communicated to Duncan as soon as possible, and
he set about seeking other agencies, but without success for
a time. The situation did not disquiet him. He was sure
that the Master Who had sent him there, and was giving him
acceptance with the people, would not fail in some way or
other to provide. Still, his last piece of silver had to be
changed ; the strings of cash disappeared one by one ; and
the cook who was really anxious came and said :

"What shall we do when the money is all gone ? "

"Do ? " was Duncan's quiet reply ; "we will ' trust in
the Lord and do good ' ; so shall we ' dwell in the land,' and
verily we shall be fed."

To go back to Hang-chow himself would have been
possible ; but Duncan well knew that if once he left the city
it would be ten times more difficult to get in again. His
hardly won position was too precious to be endangered.
So he wrote that he would trust in God and hold on.

Matters were in this position when, to Mr. Taylor's relief,
Rudland arrived unexpectedly, ready for any service. He
was more than willing to carry supplies to Nanking, and set
off at once by boat for the ten or twelve days' journey.
Wind and weather, the condition of embankments and the
temper of the boat-people all seemed favourable, until he
came to a place where the water was so low in the Canal that
they could go no farther. Repairs were needed somewhere,
and would be put through in time. Meanwhile the Foreign
teacher must make up his mind to wait !

But this was just what Rudland could not do. So far
he had been wonderfully prospered in answer to prayer, and
though surprised at the hindrance being permitted, he was
sure the Lord had some way of helping him on. All was
explained, however, when he found that by abandoning the
boat and striking off overland he could shorten the journey
by four days. This meant sixty miles on foot, with only
Chinese shoes, or on a springless wheelbarrow ; but eagerly
he pressed on.

And what of Duncan and his companions ? The cook had saved five dollars from his wages, and when his master's supplies came to an end he revealed this little store and begged him to accept it.

" But you know I do not borrow," said Duncan simply.

" No, sir," urged the man, " it is a gift—a gift to the Lord."

That being evidently his intention, Duncan took it thankfully, and they were of one mind in making it go as far as possible. But five dollars, however economically used, will not last indefinitely, and the morning came when there was not enough to provide another meal. It was Saturday too ; and the cook had to stop his master, who was going out to preach as usual, with the question :

" What shall we do *now* ? "

" Do ? " was still the answer ; " we will ' trust in the Lord and do good ' ; so shall we ' dwell in the land,' and verily we shall be fed."

But Chu-meo watched his friend and teacher down the street with a sinking heart. *Verily thou shalt be fed*—it was a promise from God's Word, he knew, and they were fulfilling the conditions ; but would it, would it *prove true*, now they had nothing else to depend upon ?

Twelve miles from the city, that very morning, Rudland, limping painfully along, fell in with a donkey-boy looking for a job.

" Oh, yes, he had heard of the foreigner living in Nanking ! For a few tens of cash he would take this friend to his door."

As the sun set that evening, returning from a long day's work, what was Duncan's surprise to see his faithful servant running with a joyous face to meet him.

" It's all right, it's all right," he cried, panting for breath; " Mr. Rudland—the money—a good supper ! "

" Did I not tell you this morning," he replied, laying a kindly hand on his shoulder, " that it is *always* ' all right ' to trust in the living God ? "

This experience, tidings of which Rudland carried back to Hang-chow, was a great encouragement both to the missionaries and native Christians. There too the Lord was working, and the sorrowful days of summer were giving place to the joy of harvest. To Mr. Taylor's great thankfulness, he had been joined by his old friend Wang Lae-djün of Ningpo, who was by this time an experienced Christian worker. An engagement with another mission had detained him ; but no sooner was he free than he came over to see if he could be of use to those to whom he owed everything spiritually. Twice already baptisms had taken place at Hang-chow, and there was quite a group of believers who needed pastoral care. This Mr. Taylor was little able to give, with all the other claims upon him, and it was with great thankfulness he recognised in Wang Lae-djün the very helper needed.

And now the little church inaugurated in July with nineteen members was growing rapidly under the helpful oversight of its native pastor. Mr. Taylor himself was keeping in close touch with them, preaching on Sundays whenever he could, and seeking to develop a missionary spirit among the Christians. Many glimpses are given in the correspondence of the period of this side of his activities, the more directly missionary work in which he delighted ; but upon these we must not dwell. Of the October baptisms Mrs. Taylor wrote :

When I went down to the afternoon service I saw such a sight as would have rejoiced the hearts of dear friends at home. Our courtyard in front of the main part of the house is a large one, and it was more than filled with a quiet, attentive audience. One hundred and sixty persons were seated. Dear Lae-djün baptized three men and three women, and the service was held there as being more convenient than the chapel.

And this brings us to one of the important discoveries Mr. and Mrs. Taylor were making along the lines of women's work. For the new departure of going to the people in their own homes, dressed as they were, and with nothing that could make them feel the Gospel message to be foreign to their own life and surroundings was justified by results.

" I think if you could see how the people love and trust us you would rejoice," Miss Faulding wrote that autumn. " It does so please them to see us liking to be like themselves in outward things. They express the greatest satisfaction, and are delighted especially that our shoes and style of hair-dressing should be the same as theirs. Instead of having difficulty in getting access to the people, they come here day after day saying,

" ' *Fuh Ku-niang*,[1] we want you to come to our house and teach us about the religion.'

" A woman said to me the other day, ' Do come, my mother wants to hear. . . .'

" I sometimes long that my whole time could be spent in visiting, at others that at least half could be given to the school— for I do so long to see native preachers raised up there, and the boys want training. Then again, we need books so much that if I could spend several hours daily with the teacher I should be glad. The work just seems overwhelming taking this city alone, and how much more so when one looks beyond to provinces full of cities in which there is no missionary ! And look beyond we must.

" My heart does so well up with joy that I am here, and here among the people to a great extent as one of themselves. . . . Nothing could be more encouraging than our position—so almost more than willingly the people listen. I should think when I go out I often speak to more than two hundred persons. . . . Yet I am never treated in any way rudely, but with all kindness. Sometimes, indeed, it is with difficulty I get out of having to smoke a pipe, while tea and lunch I frequently have to take."

Rich and poor alike welcomed this gentle visitor ; and it was not a passing curiosity, for the more she became known the more was she invited into homes of all sorts. Ladies in Mandarins' families sent for her, and she was welcomed even to a Buddhist nunnery, but as of old it was " the common people " who gave most heed to the message.

" I have now been out of each of the city-gates (ten of them)," she wrote after fifteen months in Hang-chow, " and am widely known in every part of the city, but still find it difficult to over-take all the visits I am asked to make. *Fuh Ku-niang* often wishes she could make herself into two or three, or else accomplish two or three times as much as she can in a day. I am very glad I can speak to the people in the Hang-chow dialect ; it pleases

---

[1] *Fuh*, the character chosen as the nearest in sound to Miss Faulding's surname, means *happiness* : " Miss Happiness," a suitable name for the bright-faced girl who was a messenger of life and peace to so many in Hang-chow. and who is lovingly remembered there to this day.

them, and I believe brings the Truth home more than the most fluent Ningpo would do.

"I sat down the other day beside a peasant girl and said, with my hand on hers :

"'If you want to be happy you should worship God. Your rice is the gift of Heaven. It is Heaven that creates and preserves life, is it not ? (Quoting two well-known Chinese proverbs.) I want to tell you about true happiness which the Lord of Heaven will give you, if you worship Him.'

"I had not time to say more before she got up, and standing in the door of her little hut, bowed herself three or four times in worship of Heaven. So simply and eagerly did she express her longing for happiness ! Then she sat down again by my side and listened attentively while I told her of God and heaven and hell, and the wonderful way of salvation.

"As I came home it was raining and not very pleasant, but this and other receptions I had just had made me feel ' Would that others might know the joy of this work, and come and carry the Truth to every Chinese home ! ' "

This spirit won its way, and it was largely due to such visiting that new faces were always to be seen in the chapel at Sin-kai-long.

"I wish you could have been with me the other day," Miss Faulding continued a week later, " as I went to one and another of the straw huts among the ruins. The people had mostly seen or heard of me before, and apologising for their wretched homes (which are wretched indeed !), they received me cordially. As so often happens, my dress met with high approval, which led me to say :

" ' I have come here to be a Hang-chow woman. I eat your rice, wear your dress, speak your words, and I desire your happiness. You see, we are all sisters.'

" This last specially pleased the woman to whom I was speaking.

" ' Ah,' she said, ' you call me your sister ! That is good ! Then I may call you my Great (or Elder) Sister.'

" ' But your years are more than mine.'

" ' Yes,' she replied, taking my hand in hers, ' but you have come to teach us ; so you are my Great Sister.'

" It seemed as if, in finding a little sympathy, new springs in her nature had been touched. Putting her arm round my shoulder as we were leaving, she said :

" ' I *will* come on Sunday ; I *will* come on Sunday.' "

And come they did—men, women, and children, whether
to school or sewing-class, dispensary or public meetings.
The medical work had done much to attract; but Mr.
Taylor as he watched it all could not but be profoundly
impressed with this new line of things, new at any rate in
China.

" No mightier power has been entrusted to us," he wrote that
first autumn, " than the true sympathy that identified itself
with those it seeks to benefit. It carried *the heart* captive; and
to get close to the hearts of the people is our great aim; to win
their confidence and love our daily object.

" In its actual influence on the people at large," he continued
with regard to such work as the ladies were doing, " I am strongly
inclined to consider it the most powerful agency at our disposal."[1]

And fuller experience only justified the conclusion. Yet
of all the innovations connected with the Mission none met
with stronger opposition. The presence of unmarried ladies
in the interior at all was, with many, a sufficient ground for
condemning the whole work, and determined efforts were
made to secure their recall to the coast. It was strongly
stated in letters home that to send unmarried ladies to inland
stations was a waste of life and energy, as there was no opening for their labours. This moved Mrs. Taylor deeply, and
quite early in the summer she had written to Mrs. Berger:

Oh, how can any one who knows the love of Christ look round
upon these groping, perishing heathen and call any expenditure
" a waste " which brings about their conversion! Had we the
right people and suitable accommodation, I believe that twenty
Sisters could easily find work in Hang-chow to-morrow. I feel
pretty sure I could find work for ten Miss Fauldings and ten Miss
Bowyers. The Lord ever keep them as simple and true-hearted
as they are!

I have always found that the great difficulty in the way of
female agency has been location. So few married couples (and I
do not wonder at it, or blame any for it) are prepared to give up
the retirement and privacy which are so pleasant, and to receive
comparative strangers into their family. My dear husband and I
have at times discussed the feasibility of establishing some of

---

[1] From Mr. Taylor's first general letter to friends at home after reaching Hang-chow, dated October 1867.

the Sisters in a house by themselves, and perhaps after a time this might be done. . . . But may *the Lord* direct. It is His work we are doing, and He can and will raise up helpers. Mr. ———'s assertion about their being very little opening, etc., stirs me to hope and pray that God will show his mistake by pouring out a large blessing upon this instrumentality, feeble though it be in itself.

Thus they were grappling with big problems, and obtaining, even then, glimpses of developments to which God was leading in His own way. And in the process He was developing *them*, preparing one and another for the special work that lay before them. How little Rudland, for example, or any one else in those early days, could have foreseen the usefulness for which he was being fitted. Of all the Hangchow party he was the one who seemed, at any rate to himself, least likely to do much in China. He could not get hold of the language ; and the more he tried to study the worse became the headaches, that left him utterly discouraged. But Mr. Taylor was developing as a leader no less than his fellow-workers along other lines.

" I wonder could you spare time to help *me* a little ? " he said to Rudland one day, after prayerfully considering how to meet the difficulty.

" Gladly would I," responded the young man, " but what is there I can do ? "

" Well, I am troubled about the printing-press. The workmen seem to get through so little when left to themselves, and I really have not time to look after them. You managed so well in putting the press together ; do you not think you could superintend it for me now ? "

In vain Rudland protested that he knew nothing about printing.

" If you will just go in and begin at the beginning," said Mr. Taylor, " the men will be pleased to show you how to set up type, etc., and the fact of your being there will keep them to their work."

So Rudland left his books for the cheerful activity of the printing-room. The workmen were glad to have his company and proud to display their superior knowledge.

Listening to their conversation by the hour together, he found himself picking up words and phrases more quickly than he could discover their English equivalents. It was the Gouin system to perfection! and all his spare time he was fain to spend over the dictionary to make out what he had been learning. The headaches were soon conquered, and the lines laid down for a life service, that was to include the translation and printing of almost the entire Scriptures in a dialect spoken by millions to whom the Word of God was thus made accessible.

Resourcefulness was one of the characteristics Mr. Taylor was developing to the advantage of those associated with him. They were learning to know that if anything could be done to meet a case of need he was pretty sure to see it, and not likely to be hindered by difficulties that grit, grace, and gumption could overcome. None who were in Hang-chow at the time would forget his arrival one night, for example, long after the city gates were shut and they had given up hope of seeing him. One of the party was seriously ill, and in Mr. Taylor's absence no medical help was available. A messenger was sent after him, and he turned back from an important journey only to find himself too late to enter the city. Darkness had fallen, and the gates were closed and barred. There seemed nothing for it but to spend the night on the river, while a precious life might be at stake.

But who was this coming up behind him who seemed confident of getting in? A Government messenger with despatches! then the gate would be opened surely? But no: a basket, he saw, was being let down over the wall, in which the messenger was to be drawn up. It was no use asking for a passage in that uncertain craft, but Mr. Taylor's quick eye caught means of steadying it. Hanging from the basket was a rope, which it was the work of a moment to seize as it was ascending. It required pluck and determination, however, to hold on and face the angry guards at the top.

"I gave them two hundred good reasons," said Mr. Taylor on reaching home, "why they should allow me to proceed."

"Two hundred! how had you time?"

" They came out of my cash-bag," was the smiling reply,
" so it did not take very long."

Among all the mercies that crowned the year 1867—the
first complete year for the *Lammermuir* party in China—
none was greater than the answer to the prayer with which
it had opened, " O that Thou wouldest bless me indeed and
enlarge my coast." The stations occupied by the Mission
had doubled in number in that short period.[1] At its commencement, the distance between the most widely separated
had been only four days' journey ; but at its close,
Duncan in Nanking was as much as twenty-four days, by
ordinary means of travel, from Stott in Wen-chow,—a considerably enlarged sphere of labour when one remembers
that, with the exception of Hang-chow, no Protestant
missionaries save those of the C.I.M. were settled anywhere
away from the coast or the treaty ports. And the earnest
spirit at *Sin-kai-long* was just as marked an answer to prayer.

" Oh ! that we may be made capable of bearing much blessing," wrote one of the young workers to Mrs. Berger in November.
" Do pray that we may each be drawn close to the Saviour, and
kept walking with Him in such sweet fellowship that for us to
live may be Christ. Then, what wonders should we see ! . . .
The destitution in the light of eternity is awful. It stares us in
the face. Human effort cannot meet it ; nothing can, short of
divine power. So do pray. Oh ! we need to lay hold upon God
about it. May He make us really in earnest. How can we
trifle, how can we be listless in view of His unfailing promise that
what we ask in faith we shall receive ? . . . Why are we not
Israels ? God grant that we may learn how to pray."

For the great land around them, as well as for their own
spiritual needs, the last day of the year was again set apart
for prayer and fasting. From eleven in the morning till
3 P.M. one meeting lasted,

" without weariness," Miss Blatchley wrote, " God's Holy
Spirit wrapping us round in renewed dedication and truly baptizing us : ' He shall baptize you with the Holy Ghost and with

---

[1] In addition to Siao-shan, which was near Hang-chow, Tai-chow-fu,
Nanking, and Wen-chow had been opened—all important governing cities
and centres of population.

fire.' At 8.30 we again met for united prayer, and still that *power* gathered and increased. Mr. Taylor read the 90th Psalm. We continued in prayer and singing till the year ended, and at twelve partook of the Lord's Supper. A holier time I have never known."

And there was need for such inward strengthening. In spite of success—*because*, indeed, of the footing gained in some places, there was great and increasing opposition in others. From his sick-bed, only a few weeks earlier, Mr. Taylor had been carried to the Governor's *ya-men* to report in person the ill-usage of Mr. McCarthy's helpers, who had been set upon and almost beaten to death in Hu-chow. As soon as he could travel, he had gone direct to the scene of the riot, living himself in a boat within the turbulent city, and giving two weeks of careful, patient effort to smoothing matters over, only to find that for the time being foreigners must retire. No sooner had the new year dawned than Mr. Williamson was driven out of another important city, through attacks on those who had befriended him ; and Mr. Taylor, who was making a tour of the older stations, was overtaken with the tidings that Kin-hwa-fu had had to be given up.

" I went to see the poor fellow in prison," Mr. Williamson wrote of the middleman who by order of the Mandarin had suffered three thousand blows. " His back and legs were severely swollen and bruised. He was shut up in a den with a number of criminals, confined like so many wild beasts in a cage. The weather was very cold, and there seemed every probability of the poor fellow losing his life from the treatment he had received. . . . Next morning the landlord was sent for to the *ya-men*, while the mother and wife of the imprisoned man were threatening to commit suicide, blaming us for bringing all this trouble upon them. The same day, in order to save these poor people from further ill-usage, we left the house . . . returning to Hang-chow."

It was proving harder even than had been anticipated, this pioneering work—yet how Mr. Taylor's heart went out to the Christless multitudes around them ! Crossing the beautiful district of Tai-chow-fu for the first time, he was profoundly impressed with its countless villages and hamlets among the mountains as well as the towns and cities of its populous plains.

"Are there no servants of our common Lord rusting away at home," he wrote to Mr. Berger, "or at least doing work that others would do if they left it, who might be out here among these numberless towns and villages ?

"As we passed the gate of one little town, a coffin was being borne to its last resting-place.

"'Alas !' said the native Christian with me, 'if the Gospel were preached in this place to-day, it would be too late for that poor man.'

"Yes, and for how many more will it be too late ! My thoughts were busied, now with the untold need of the un-occupied provinces, now with the neglected districts of this province, until I was compelled to roll the burden on the Lord, and cry to Him for wisdom to dispose aright of those He may send to help me, and to plead for more native and foreign workers."

Very easily, as one can see, might the whole Mission have become absorbed in that one coast-board province, small though it was among all the provinces of China. But, providentially, door after door was closed. Riots, disturb-ances, sickness, and other troubles hindered developments that would have tended in this direction, and gradually, almost insensibly, Mr. Taylor's own way seemed guided northward.

"If you will not smile at my planning in our dining-room," Mr. Berger had written in a letter that crossed Mr. Taylor's quoted above, "I will tell you my musings concerning your future movements. I fancy you will some day transfer your headquarters to some desirable city or town very near the Yangtze River, perhaps within easy reach of Hang-chow. Thus you would, I suppose, have access to a Consul, and facilities for going to Shanghai and up the river, so as to reach many provinces. The LORD guide you in all things : 'He that believeth shall not make haste.'"

It was not easy after sixteen months in Hang-chow to face the thought of leaving the work that had become so dear to them for "some desirable city near the Yangtze" in which to begin all over again. Fifty baptized believers were gathered already in the little church under Pastor Wang's care, and there were many inquirers. But Mr. and Mrs. McCarthy and Miss Faulding would remain in charge of the station and be quite able to receive and help new workers. Duncan at Nanking was sorely needing relief, and Mrs. Taylor was ready to go either there or anywhere else as the work seemed to require. But much had to be considered as spring came on, and the noon prayer meetings were times of real drawing near to God.

To Mr. and Mrs. Judd, who had recently arrived from home, all this was very memorable.

" It really was building the wall in troublous times," he wrote of those days : " one never knew what friends who were away might be suffering. Scarcely any station was opened without a riot. The noon meetings were solemn hours—often prolonged, because there was so much to pray about. One feels the thrill of them still."

The quiet courage of Mr. and Mrs. Taylor, taking up themselves the pioneering work in which experience was so needed, specially impressed Mrs. Judd.

" One always felt braver when with them," she recalled, " more able to endure hardness. One seemed to catch something of their spirit. Those solemn hours of waiting upon God when we first reached Hang-chow can never be forgotten. The powers of darkness seemed so real, as one stronghold after another was attacked by our small band of workers. But the presence of the Lord was more real, as Mr. Taylor pleaded that ' with all boldness ' we might speak His Word, and that the Name of Jesus might be glorified ; and we were confident that victory would be the Lord's and ours."

But the leader of the Mission, conscious only of weakness in himself, was taken up with Another.

" I am sure you never forget us at the Throne of Grace," he had written to his mother, thinking of what the coming summer might mean to wife and children. " I try to live a day at a time, and even so have enough to do ; but though I *try*, I do not always succeed. Pray for more faith, more love, more wisdom for me. . . . What could *I* do without the promise, ' Lo, *I* am with you alway ' ? "

PART III

TREASURES OF DARKNESS

1868–1870.   AET. 36–38.

What then ?   Why then another pilgrim song ;
    And then a hush of rest divinely granted ;
And then a thirsty stage (ah me, so long !)
    And then a brook, just where it most is wanted.

What then ?   The pitching of the evening tent ;
    And then, perchance, a pillow rough and thorny ;
And then some sweet and tender message sent,
    To cheer the faint one for to-morrow's journey.

What then ?   The wailing of the midnight wind,
    A fev'rish sleep ; a heart opprest and aching ;
And then a little water cruse to find,
    Close by my pillow, ready for my waking.

What then ?   I am not careful to inquire :
    I know there will be tears, and fears, and sorrow ;
And then a loving Saviour drawing nigher,
    And saying, " I will answer for the morrow."

What then ?   For all my sins His pardoning grace,
    For all my wants and woes His loving kindness ;
For darkest shades the shining of God's face ;
    And Christ's own hand to lead me in my blindness.

What then ?   A shadowy valley lone and dim,
    And then a deep and darkly rolling river ;
And then a flood of light—a seraph hymn
    And God's own smile, for ever and for ever.

CHAPTER X

1868.   Aet. 36.

PLEASANT enough for the first few weeks was that spring journey up the Grand Canal.   Hang-chow was left behind on the 10th of April, Mrs. Taylor and the children travelling by house-boat in a measure of comfort.[1]   After long confinement within city walls, the freedom and freshness of the country were delightful.   Extensive mulberry plantations bordered the Canal, with plum, peach, and apricot orchards in bridal array.   Wheat and barley covered the valleys, interspersed with great tracts of peas and beans in flower.   The Canal itself, alive with boat traffic, was an endless interest to the children, while the background of hills refreshed their elders with ever - changing loveliness.   And there were many opportunities for coming into friendly relation with other travellers and the people whose homes they were passing day by day.

The little boys spinning their tops were a great source of interest.

" One man asked if he might take the foreign toy and show it to a Mandarin's lady in a boat close at hand," wrote Miss Blatchley.   " In a few moments the lady invited us to come and see her.   Tea was offered, and the servants were told to boil some eggs for the children.   In the afternoon this lady called upon

---

[1] Mrs. Taylor was accompanied by Miss Blatchley and the children's nurse, Mrs. Bohanan (who had replaced Mary Bell, her sister, now married to Mr. Rudland).   Mr. Taylor followed ten days later, having been detained by illness in the family of one of the American missionaries in Hang-chow.

us in our boat.   We were glad she did, as it gave Mrs. Taylor an opportunity for putting the Gospel clearly before her."

On Sunday they did not travel.   The boat was moored to the shore, and a service held with open doors and windows.

" A few came on board and sat with us," continued the journal.   " A Mandarin's wife living just opposite came across and stayed till the service was over.   Before she left, Mrs. Taylor explained the way of salvation to her more fully.   She seemed to drink in every word.   Our Christian servant called at her house in the afternoon."

At one great city *en route*—Soo-chow—workers of the Mission had recently obtained a settlement, and a stay of three weeks enabled Mr. Taylor, who there caught up the party, to give considerable help in medical and other ways.[1] Beyond this point all was unbroken ground.   Save for Duncan at Nanking and the L.M.S. and Wesleyan workers in the treaty port of Hankow, not a Protestant missionary was resident northward or westward anywhere in the interior.   To join the former in his lonely post was Mr Taylor's intention, unless some more important opening should detain him by the way.

And this was just what happened when Chin-kiang was reached—that busy centre of population and commerce at the junction of the Grand Canal and the mighty flood of the Yangtze.   Being a treaty port, a few foreigners, including the British Consul, were living in the Settlement outside the native city, and in one of the suburbs the L.M.S. had a chapel in charge of a native preacher.   No missionary, however, was to be found nearer than Shanghai, at a distance of twenty-four hours by steamer.   Much impressed with the strategic importance of this place, Mr. Taylor set on foot inquiries with a view to renting premises, and was soon in

---

[1] The charm as well as importance of this place from the Chinese point of view may be judged from their proverb, " Above is Heaven ; below— Hang-chow and Soo-chow."   Mr. Charles Schmidt—formerly an officer under General Gordon in the " Ever-Victorious Force "—had been the first to live and preach Christ in this city.   Converted through the instrumentality of Mr. Meadows, he was a warm friend to the C.I.M., and at his request the Mission had also undertaken work in Soo-chow.   Mr. Henry Cordon had succeeded in renting premises a few weeks previously, in which regular services were now commenced with help from Mr. and Mrs. Taylor.

treaty for a house inside the city, which was ultimately obtained, though not without serious difficulty and danger. Meanwhile, seeing that the negotiations were likely to be prolonged, he continued his journey across the Yangtze and a few miles up the northern section of the Grand Canal.

And now the travellers were nearing the far-famed city of Yang-chow, of which Marco Polo was once Governor. Rich, proud, and exclusive, it contained a population of three hundred and sixty thousand, still without any witness for Christ. Life on the water by this time was losing its charm. Spring had given place to summer, and with the intense heat the rainy season had come on. Day and night it poured incessantly, and the children, cooped up in the leaky boat, where nothing could be kept dry, were exposed to serious risks. Waiting upon God very definitely for guidance, it was with no little thankfulness that Mr. and Mrs. Taylor saw the way open before them much more readily than could have been anticipated. Within the city, their native helpers had come into friendly touch with an inn-keeper able and willing to receive the whole party. The accommodation he offered, moreover, was not on the ground floor—always more or less malarious at such a season—but five rooms forming an upper story which they could have to themselves. This was so unusual from every point of view that they could not but feel it providential, and, thankfully leaving the crowded junks on the Canal, they took possession of their new quarters.

" Were it not that you are old travellers yourselves," Mrs. Taylor wrote to Mrs. Berger (June 18), " I should think it impossible for you to realise our feelings last Monday week, when we exchanged the discomforts of a boat, into every room of which the heavy rain had been leaking, for a suite of apartments in a first-rate Chinese hotel—such a place as my husband who, as you know, has seen a good deal of Chinese travellers' accommodation, never before met with ; and that hotel, too, inside the city of Yang-chow."

" An open door . . . a little strength " and " many adversaries "—it was no new situation for heralds of the Cross, though it was to prove more serious in its outcome than Mr. Taylor at first anticipated. For to begin with, the people seemed friendly. The presence of the mother and children disarmed suspicion. Evidently this foreigner in " civilised " (*i.e.* Chinese) dress was no commercial or political agent, and curiosity attracted many visitors. The inn-keeper, indeed, who had been a little anxious, offered his services as " middleman," if Mr. Taylor wished to rent premises and settle in the city.[1]

It was not easy when matters had reached this point for Mrs. Taylor to leave her family in their temporary quarters and go down alone to Shanghai. But one of the servants was ill with what threatened to be smallpox—a disease very prevalent in the city—and the baby was not vaccinated. She was now their only little daughter, and months of whooping-cough had sadly reduced her strength. There were mission matters in Shanghai that needed attention, and Mr. Duncan's fiancée had to be met and escorted inland. No one could undertake these duties and care for the sick baby as well as Mrs. Taylor, and there seemed no reason why the boys should not be left with Miss Blatchley and the nurse. Under these circumstances, Mr. Taylor concluded that she should take the journey, and saw her off in the middle of June by steamer from Chin-kiang.

In the latter city negotiations about the house were making progress, and he was able to get the deed signed soon after Mrs. Taylor left. Possession was promised in a fortnight, if the Governor granted a favourable proclamation. Applied for by the British Consul this also was promised, " if all were straightforward." Feeling reasonably sure of one home at any rate, Mr. Taylor then sent for the Rudlands, who were waiting at Hang-chow to bring the printing-press and family belongings. " If all were straightforward " covered a good deal, however, in the Mandarin's mind, and left a loophole that unfriendly subordinates were not slow to appreciate. Endless were the difficulties and complications that arose in consequence, fostered by the district official, who proved to be intensely anti-foreign.

[1] In the interests of this kindly host, Mr. Taylor had called upon the local Mandarin, making his presence and purposes known, and had obtained an assurance that there should be no interference.

Meanwhile Mr. and Mrs. Taylor in their separation were facing unexpected troubles. The infection caught by the Chinese helper proved to be measles, and one by one the children at Yang-chow sickened, until all were down with it—the youngest desperately ill with bronchitis as a complication. Mr. Taylor could only be thankful that the baby at any rate might escape, and that her mother was spared some of the anxiety and nursing. When they had parted, it was fully expecting that ten days or a fortnight would see her home again ; but now, every post seemed to bring either business to be attended to in Shanghai, or calls for help from one and another of the stations. Mr. Taylor could not leave Yang-chow under the circumstances, and was obliged to put unwonted responsibilities upon the one he would fain have relieved could he have known her circumstances.

For at the coast Mrs. Taylor all the while was fighting a brave fight for the life of their youngest child. Kindly received by Mr. Gamble, she had had the baby vaccinated without delay, hoping to get through her business and be ready to return as soon as the *Hindustan* should bring Mr. Duncan's expected bride. The vaccination proved effective, but never had she seen a child so ill with it before. Medical help had to be called in, and before long it was evident that the baby was suffering from a severe attack of measles in addition to vaccination and whooping-cough. And Mrs. Taylor herself was far from well.

Even before the letters came from Yang-chow telling of the illness of the boys, her mother's heart had anticipated it, and all that their father would be suffering. Her one comfort was that he would not know about little Maria, or about the distressing home mails she was receiving. For there had been a revival of the painful opposition which had already caused Mr. Berger so much anxiety, and the letters from Saint Hill, while gracious and loving as ever, had much that was painful to communicate. It was under these circumstances that her indomitable spirit shone out, and the faith that made her, as her fellow-workers were not slow to realise, " the backbone of the Mission." Yet she was clinging and sensitive to an unusual degree, depending upon her husband,

and loving him—if that were possible—even more than she was loved.

" The Lord give us a single eye to do His will," she wrote on June 29, after expressing her readiness to go on to Tai-chow, " and then guide us just where He would have us. . . .

" I have received a packet of letters from Hang-chow this morning, enclosing the last mail from home.   I am afraid some of the contents of the latter may distress you, but ' our Father knoweth.'   Let us cast *all* our burdens, and they are many and weighty, upon our omnipotent, all-wise, loving Father.   They are but feathers to Him !   As to Mr. ——'s continued opposition, that too is in God's hands, and surely He will stand by us.

> He cannot have taught us to trust in His Name
> And thus far have brought us to put us to shame.

" Let us remember how He worked for us with regard to Mr. L—— ;   yes, how He has appeared for us again and again. ' Thou hast been my help ; leave me not neither forsake me, O God of my salvation.' "

" Do pray that God will give me wisdom and a clear head," she added with regard to business matters, " as well as singleness of eye."

A few days later the doctor's visit was far from re-assuring.

Perhaps his manner, more than what he actually said, made me feel that possibly we might be called to give up this little one too.   The Lord is our stay, and He will not leave us now.

" My own Treasure," she continued on July 10, " is it that our tender Father is endeavouring to teach us by His present dealings lessons which He *might* take sterner methods to impress ?   Oh ! may He Himself help us to learn them, giving us docile, teachable spirits.   How much we lean upon each other for comfort or counsel we only find out when long separated, and perhaps He is trying to teach us to lean in the same way, and to a yet fuller extent upon Himself—our heavenly Husband Who is so thoroughly competent to undertake for us in every perplexity, difficulty or danger.   Satan sometimes says, ' Yes, He is fully competent in any other difficulty but the present.   You can hardly expect Him to manage this particular matter for you—it is too trivial,' or ' too complex.'   And how ready we are to believe him !—instead of honouring God with unwavering confidence."

It was a comfort to hear about this time that the little patients in Yang-chow were better, though she seemed as far as ever from being able to return to them. The vessel she was awaiting was much overdue, and no word had been received as to its whereabouts. Moreover, as soon as the baby could be left with her Chinese nurse, Mrs. Taylor was expecting to go on to Ningpo at any rate—little realising that it was in Yang-chow she was now needed most.

For the intense heat of summer, combined with many anxieties, had tried Mr. Taylor more than his letters showed. Houses had been offered him in plenty, but just when all seemed propitious the negotiations would break down, and promises of a favourable proclamation " to reassure the people " were unfulfilled, until hope deferred made the heart sick. At last, however, about the middle of July, the proclamation appeared ; the house then in question was at once handed over to them, and the little party moved in, thankful for the greater liberty thus afforded. Six weeks in the inn after two months of boat-life had prepared them to appreciate a home of their own again, if home it could be called with the mother so far away.

But the letter that told the good news brought her strange sinking of heart. A few pencilled lines, written evidently in great weakness—written from Chin-kiang—what could it mean ?

I think I told you we had got the proclamation for Yang-chow. We have not yet got the one for this place—hope to do so to-morrow. But I must return, I am so ill. Would you write Meadows and ask if he can come and help me ? . . . God bless you. Go to Ningpo, darling, if you think well, and may God go with you. If our hearts are to be rendered up a sacrifice, the will of the Lord be done. Soon we shall never part again. . . ."

The words were faint and wavering, as must have been the hand that traced them. Alone in a boat, and so ill ! And she could not know whether he had got back to Yang-chow, or how he was being cared for.

It was Sunday the 26th of July. The up-river steamer would be starting in a few hours that would land her at Chin-kiang the following evening. There was no question in Mrs. Taylor's mind as to whether she ought to go. Mr. McCarthy had come to Shanghai and would wait for the long-delayed

Hindustan. She saw her way to arranging for help at Ningpo, and the baby was well enough to travel. But what about the steamer ? If it had not been Sunday how gladly would she have taken it ! As it was she did not hesitate to let it go without her, although the alternative was a journey by foot-boat of at least two days and nights. With a heart that cried to God she quietly made her preparations, waiting until evening before engaging her boat.

That boatman, surely, had a tale to tell when he came back from taking the foreign lady with her nurse and child to Chin-kiang ! Starting before dawn on Monday morning, they had travelled steadily on *via* the Grand Canal until he was obliged to drop the oar from very weariness. But while he slept they travelled still. Hour after hour by day or night, whenever he was obliged to rest, the lady had taken his place, plying the oar as naturally as she spoke his Ningpo words, caring little for heat or backache if only they could press forward—and all because her husband was ill and she wanted to get to him as quickly as possible. Much as he wondered at the unusual proceeding, the boatman little knew what it was that gave strength to that mother's heart as well as to her fragile form. It was prayer that carried them through, despite heat and weariness—prayer how abundantly answered when upon reaching Yang-chow she found her loved ones an unbroken circle and was able to nurse Mr. Taylor back to his usual health.

Happy though they were to be together again in a home of their own, it was not long that the missionary household was to enjoy even a measure of security. The big wandering premises had from the first been besieged with visitors, so much so that Miss Blatchley had had no choice but to make it a rule that none might come upstairs but the ladies of Mandarins' families. This was before Mrs. Taylor's return, and her presence did but attract more interest. There was much to be done between whiles to make the new home habitable, as well as to prepare at Chin-kiang for the arrival of the Rudlands. Preaching at Yang-chow on Sundays, Mr. Taylor had to go frequently to the other city where the house matter was still unsettled, the Governor withholding

MRS. HUDSON TAYLOR (*née* MARIA DYER).

To face page 144

MRS. HUDSON TAYLOR (*née* J. E. FAULDING).

the proclamation without which the landlord could not be kept to his bargain. It was generally known that the deeds had been signed and the deposit paid over, and the way in which the missionary and his Consul were being worsted was the laugh of tea-house and restaurant.

Nor was this all. Exaggerated reports reaching the neighbouring city naturally suggested in certain circles that the visitors might be treated with as scant courtesy in Yang-chow. Why allow them to make friends and settle down, when by carrying things with a high hand they could be ejected? Upon the strength of the Chin-kiang situation, a meeting was held among the literati and a decision arrived at to stir up trouble. This was done by means of anonymous hand-bills, attributing the most revolting and unnatural crimes to foreigners, especially those whose business it was to propagate " the religion of Jesus." Early in August, the missionaries began to realise the change that was coming over the attitude of the people. Friendly visitors had given place to crowds of the lowest rabble about the door, and a fresh set of posters, quite unfit for translation, was as fuel to the fire.

" On Saturday the 15th," wrote Mr. Reid who had come over from Nanking, " Mr. Taylor received an anonymous letter, advising him to use all possible precautions, as on the following day there was to be a riot. . . . We had but one source of comfort, and that a well-tried one ; and meeting together that evening we poured out our hearts to the Lord, Who did not fail us. Next morning (Sunday) the people assembled at an early hour, and began knocking and battering upon our door . . . until we thought it best to go out and try to pacify them. . . . I think I never felt more the power and value of speaking gently than on that day. Dear Mr. Taylor spoke often to those assembled in a very kind manner ; and while we watched, those inside the house prayed, and God graciously brought us through, confirming to our hearts the promise, ' Lo, I am with you alway.' "

The trouble went on, however, and on the 18th Miss Blatchley wrote :

For the last few days we have been almost in a state of siege. Mr. Taylor, just up from a sick-bed and weak as he is, has hardly dared to leave the gate, Messrs. Reid and Rudland with him :

and on Saturday night Mr. Duncan opportunely arrived. Happily, before the disturbance became very serious, we were able by pressing on the workman to get the many entrances into our wandering premises contracted into one. . . . But our trust is not in the walls we build, which an infuriated mob could easily overthrow . . . but under the shadow of His wings.

The most calumnious hand-bills against us have been posted about the city.   In one of them the Name of Jesus is blasphemed in the vilest terms, and the paper professes to emanate from the god of war, Kwan-ti.   To-day (Tuesday) was placarded as the day for attacking our house and setting it on fire, regardless of native or foreign occupants.   Once or twice the mob has seemed inclined to break in by force, but the disturbance is less than on Sunday.   God is with us, we do not fear. . . . We know that whatever happens will be by His permission, for we have put our-selves into His hands.   He will not leave us.   As I write He is sending thunder and the threatening of rain, which will do more for us, Mr. Taylor was saying, than an army of soldiers.   The Chinese shun rain ; the most important matters they will post-pone on account of it.   May God forgive these poor blind people, and defeat Satan, by making these disturbances the means of more widely diffusing the truth among them.   " *Surely* the wrath of man shall praise Thee ; and the remainder of wrath Thou shalt restrain."   Any attempt to set the place on fire now would be vain indeed, for the rain is coming down in torrents.

After this, it looked as though the worst was over.   In spite of all that had been said against them, the quiet, friendly demeanour of the missionaries was winning its way, and the storm seemed to have spent itself without disaster. From Wednesday to Saturday the wearied household had a little respite, and glad indeed were they that none of them, not even the women and children, had fled from the threaten-ing danger.

But, strange to say, before the close of the week an opportunity occurred for reviving the agitation.   A couple of foreigners from Chin-kiang, wearing not the native costume adopted by Mr. Taylor's party, but undisguised " foreign dress," came up to visit Yang-chow, and were seen in various parts of the city.   This was too good a chance to be lost, and no sooner had they left with the impression that all was quiet, than reports began to be circulated that children were missing in all directions, entrapped by the " foreign devils." The weather was intensely hot, which always predisposes to excitable foregatherings. Children *had* disappeared, so the people believed—twenty-four at least had fallen a prey to the dreaded foreigners. And on their premises, as was well known, vast stores of treasures were accumulated! Boat-loads of goods had been brought in only a few days previously.[1] Courage! Avenge our wrongs! Attack—destroy! Much plunder shall be ours.

Forty-eight hours later, in a boat nearing Chin-kiang, the letter quoted above was bravely finished.

" We have had to flee from Yang-chow," Miss Blatchley continued to Mrs. Berger. " I cannot stop now to describe the last few days, if indeed they are describable—for we must send off our notes, such as we have ready. Next mail must bring further particulars. Meanwhile you will join us in praise to God for saving our lives and limbs, and our *most* valuable property. The rioters sacked every room excepting mine, in which were all our most important papers and the bulk of our money—a considerable sum, three hundred dollars, having reached us from Chinkiang only an hour before the breaking into the house.

" Poor Mr. Reid is the most severely hurt of all ; a brick-bat struck his eye while he was standing ready to catch Mrs. Taylor and me—as we had to escape for our lives by jumping from the verandah roof over the front of the reception hall. Dear Mrs. Taylor hurt her leg very much. I, whose fall was not broken (as Mr. Reid was wounded, and so disabled from helping me), came down on my back on the stones, and it is only by God's great loving-kindness that I have not a broken spine or skull. I have only a wound on my arm, and that the left arm. It is getting very painful, as it is ulcerating, and I am tolerably bruised all over ; but there is so much to be thankful for that this seems as nothing, except that it makes one rather awkward, for I feel so stiff. We have not had time yet to change our blood-stained clothes."

And Mrs. Taylor wrote to the same beloved friend :

[1] But for the difficulties at Chin-kiang there never would have been, humanly speaking, a Yang-chow riot. Arriving there with a large quantity of goods and finding no house available, Mr. and Mrs. Rudland and Miss Desgraz had come on to Yang-chow early in August. Thus three additional foreigners, and all the paraphernalia needed for a printing-press and a second household, had been crowded into Mr. Taylor's premises. No wonder the Yang-chow people were tempted with thoughts of plunder !

I do not know whether I shall be able to give you much idea, by this opportunity, of the perils through which we have passed within the last forty-eight hours. *Our* God has brought us through : may it be to live henceforth more fully to His praise and glory. We have had, so to speak, another typhoon—not of so long duration as the literal one we experienced nearly two years ago, but at least equally dangerous to our lives, and more terrible while it lasted. . . . I believe God will bring His own glory out of this ; and I hope it will tend to the furtherance of the Gospel. . . .—Yours in a present Saviour,   ———

"A *present* Saviour"—how little could the rioters understand the secret of their calmness and strength ! Awed by something, they knew not what, the infuriated mob had been restrained from the worst excesses. Murder, though intended, had been averted again and again ; and both Mr. Taylor, exposed to all the fury of the populace on his way to seek help of the authorities, and those he had to leave, who faced the perils of attack and fire in their besieged dwelling, were alike protected by the wonder-working hand of God.

But they were hours of anguish—anguish for the mother as she gathered her children and the women of the party in the upper room that seemed most sheltered ; anguish for the father, detained at a distance, hearing from the Mandarin's *ya-men* the yells of the rioters bent on destruction.

"After they were gone (Mr. Taylor and Mr. Duncan) we feebler ones could do nothing," wrote Mrs. Taylor, " assembled in my room to plead for God's protection, both for ourselves and for those who faced the fury of the storm without. Mr. Rudland and Mr. Reid were doing their best to keep the crowd from entering our premises. I do not know that the Throne of Grace ever seemed so near to me as that night and the following morning. Not that the closeness of communion with God was greater than at any other time ; but I felt able in an especial manner to lay hold of God's *strength*. And earnestly did we plead with Him to raise as it were a wall of fire around my dear husband and Mr. Duncan, and to give His angels to encamp round about them. I specially needed His sustaining grace to keep me quiet and calm and to give me soundness of judgment, that no rash step might be taken, for naturally all looked to me to say what was to be done."

Outwardly as calm as if there were no danger,[1] Mrs Taylor went through those terrible hours, more than once saving the life of a fellow-worker by her presence of mind and perfect command of the language,[2] her heart, meanwhile, torn with anxiety for the loved one it seemed more than likely they might never see again.

"But for the protection afforded us by the darkness," Mr. Taylor wrote of that desperate effort to summon aid, " we should scarcely have reached the *ya-men* alive. Alarmed by the yells of the people the gate-keepers were just closing the doors as we approached, but the momentary delay gave time for the crowd to close in upon us : the as yet unbarred gates gave way to the pressure, and we were precipitated into the entrance hall. Had the gates been barred, I am convinced that they would not have been opened for us, and we should have been torn to pieces by the enraged mob.

"Once in the *ya-men*, we rushed into the judgment hall, crying ' *Kiu-ming! Kiu-ming!* ' (save life! save life!), a cry the Chinese Mandarin is bound to attend to at any hour of the day or night.

" We were taken to the room of the Chief Secretary, and kept waiting three-quarters of an hour before we had an audience with the Prefect, all the time hearing the yells of the mob a mile or more off, destroying, for aught we knew, not only the property, but possibly the lives of those so dear to us. And at last when we did get an audience, it was almost more than we could bear with composure to be asked as to what we really did with the babies ; whether it was true we had bought them, and how many ; what was the cause of all this rioting ? etc., etc.

" At last I told His Excellency that the real cause of all the trouble was his own neglect in not taking measures when the matter was small and manageable ; that I must now request him first to take steps to repress the riot and save any of our friends who might still be alive, and afterwards make such inquiries as he might wish, or I would not answer for the result.

" ' Ah,' said he, ' very true, very true ! First quiet the people,

---

[1] " In the Yang-chow riot," Mr. Taylor wrote some years later, " when she and the little children were in danger of being massacred at any moment, she was as calm as in her own parlour in London : and I am quite certain that if she could have altered any of the circumstances she would not have done it, so satisfied was she at all times that God's ordering was best."

[2] Mr. Judd recalls that it was " her calmness and the fact that she spoke such beautiful Chinese " that disarmed the man whose hand she stayed in a murderous attack on Mr. Rudland.

and then inquire. Sit still, and I will go to see what can be done.'

" He went out telling us to remain, as the only chance of his effecting anything depended on our keeping out of sight ; for by this time the number of rioters amounted to eight or ten thousand. The natives estimated them at twenty thousand.

" We were kept in this torture of suspense for two hours, when the Prefect returned with the *Ts'ao-fu* (Governor of the military forces of the city, some three thousand men) and told us that all was quiet ; that the *Ts'ao-fu* himself, the *Sheo-pe* (Captain of the soldiers who guard the gates), and two local Mandarins had been to the scene of the disturbance ; that they had seized several of those who were plundering the premises, and would have them punished. He then sent for chairs, and we returned under escort. On the way back we were told that all the foreigners we had left were killed. We had to cry to God to support us, though we hoped this might prove exaggerated or untrue.

" When we reached the house, the scene was such as baffled description. Here, a pile of half-burned reeds showed where one of the attempts to fire the premises had been made ; there, debris of a broken-down wall was lying ; and strewn about everywhere were the remains of boxes and furniture, scattered papers and letters, broken work-boxes, writing-desks, dressing-cases, and surgical instrument cases, smouldering remains of valuable books, etc.—but no trace of inhabitants within."

After a long and agonising search it was with unspeakable thankfulness he learned that some at any rate of the party were hiding in a neighbour's house. The darkness of the night had favoured their escape from their own burning premises. Taken from one room to another as the danger of discovery increased, they had finally been left without a glimmer of light in the innermost apartments.

" Mr. Reid lay groaning with pain," wrote Miss Blatchley, " the poor tired children wanted to sleep and we dared not let them, as at any moment we might have to flee again. Mrs. Taylor was almost fainting from loss of blood ; and I now found that my arm was bleeding from a bad cut, and so painful that I could not move it, while most of us were stiff and sore with bruises."

Then it was that suspense about Mr. Taylor was hardest to bear. In the darkness and silence, the uncertainty as to his fate as well as their own was terrible.

" I cannot attempt to describe to you our feelings," Mrs. Taylor continued to Mrs. Berger. " How my dear husband and Mr. Duncan were faring or had fared we could not tell. Where they were, why they had not yet returned, whether we ourselves would live till morning, or what would become of us we knew not. . . . But God was our stay, and He forsook us not. This confidence He gave me, that He would surely work good for China out of our deep distress.

" At one time we were told that soldiers had arrived from the Governor and were driving the rioters away, but still no tidings of my husband ! Poor Mr. Reid was laid on the floor of an inner room, and nurse with baby (who happily slept) and Mr. and Mrs. Rudland were there too. The older children were with Miss Desgraz, Miss Blatchley, and myself in the outer room. We did our best to keep them quiet and awake, for we did not know at what moment we might have to flee again.

" ' Mamma,' said one of them, ' where shall we sleep to-night as they have burned up our bed ? '

" I assured him that God would give them somewhere to sleep, little thinking it would be—that very night—in their own nursery.

" At last, after a much shorter time than it appeared to us, we heard my dear husband's voice outside the door, which had been barred for greater safety. He had had difficulty in finding us, and on his way back from the *ya-men* had heard various reports as to what had happened during his long detention. Some said we were all killed, others that we had fled, and his heart sickened on nearing the house as he distinguished a smell that proved to be fur-lined garments burning. . . . He told us that the rioters had all been driven out, and he thought we might venture back to our own rooms (which had *not* been burned down) . . . for there would be a guard around the premises. How our hearts went up to God in thanksgiving that He had spared us to each other ! . . . A short time before we heard my husband's voice, I had felt encouraged to hope that help was at hand, by the fact that my own strength was rapidly ebbing away from loss of blood. I was anxious not to let any one know how much I was hurt, as I felt it would alarm them, and it seemed most important that all should keep calm.

" It was after midnight when we returned. My heart was too full for me to pay much heed to the scene of ruin through which we passed, but at the foot of the stairs my eye fell on a bead mat worked for me by our little Gracie before leaving England. The sight of it at that moment seemed to speak of our Father's love and tenderness in a way that perhaps it would be difficult for another to understand." (It was a year that very day since their little daughter had been taken Home from the temple at Pen-shan.) "I asked some one to pick it up and give it to me. We found the floor of my room strewn with clothes, etc., which had been turned out of boxes in the search for gold and silver. The leaves of my poor Bible, which I had been unable to take with me, were scattered about in every direction. Kind, loving hands collected them for me. Some, I was told, were found downstairs, and not a leaf is missing.

"For the remainder of the night we were in quiet, though for some of us there was no sleep. Early in the morning the guard retired, and as there was no relay the people began to come in again to plunder, for now there were many entrances. Again my husband had to go to the *ya-men*, and again commenced a season of anxiety similar to though in some respects more trying than the night before. Once more my room became our sanctuary . . . till, just when it seemed as if in another minute the crowd would be upstairs, the alarm was given that the Mandarin had come, and his soldiery soon dispersed the people.

"In the afternoon of that day we left the city . . . under an escort of soldiers to see us safely to the Yangtze. I have been much struck by the way in which God used these men—who would have been quite as ready to take our lives as to protect them—for His people's help. As we passed out of the city in chairs, Miss Blatchley heard some of the people say derisively, 'Come again! Come again!'

"'Yes,' I thought, 'GOD will bring us back again, little as you expect it.'"

CHAPTER XI

THE DARKEST HOUR

1868–1869. AET. 36–37.

IT was *thankfulness* more than anything else that filled the hearts of that little company, wounded and suffering as they were, on the boats that took them to Chin-kiang. The Mandarins had insisted on their leaving for a time, that the house might be repaired and the people quietened, and with no thought of compensation, still less of revenge, the missionaries looked forward to a speedy return. Homeless and despoiled of almost everything, they rejoiced in having been counted worthy to suffer " for the sake of the Name," and their hearts were cheered as they recalled the protecting care of God. Had not their lives been spared as by a miracle ? Were not the children well and happy ? And even the money and more important Mission papers were safe, though the room in which they lay had been open to the rioters.

Upon reaching Chin-kiang, homeless and in urgent need of succour, great was the kindness received from the foreign residents. Though the community was small, they managed to put up all the refugees, Mr. and Mrs. Taylor taking a room on the ground floor which, being damp, they considered undesirable for others. Here, in the midst of debris from the riot they set to work at once on the business and correspondence of the Mission, having nine or ten stations and many fellow-workers to think of as well as the party with them.

" *How* you are, *where* you are, and in what circumstances, we know not ! " wrote Mr. McCarthy from Hang-chow. " We can only seek to lay hold on the living God, in believing prayer, and commit you all to His safe keeping. How precious is His Word now, how powerful, how suitable ! May you indeed find it so. Oh, may you find that ' out of the eater came forth meat, and out of the strong, sweetness.' The Lord will not forsake you ; He *cannot.* . . . Let nothing turn *us* from *His* purpose to bless China through our feeble means. . . . ' Who is sufficient for these things ? ' No one but He Who has said, ' Lo, I am with you alway.' In His Name, for His sake, take courage ; the darkest hour is just before the dawn."

It was a dark hour indeed that was coming upon the leader of the Mission, a period so painful in some of its aspects that even the sufferings of the riot seemed little in comparison. To begin with, the troubles at Yang-chow were made public in a way Mr. Taylor would least have desired. A resident at Chin-kiang, with the kindest intentions, wrote stirring accounts to the Shanghai papers, and public feeling demanded that action, prompt and decisive, should be taken by the British authorities. This brought the Consul-General, Mr. M. H. Medhurst, and later on the Ambassador himself, Sir Rutherford Alcock, into the matter. A gunboat was sent up to Chin-kiang, and there was much coming and going of British officers and blue-jackets. All this so impressed the authorities, that they seemed about to recognise their treaty obligations and yield to the not unreasonable demands of Mr. Medhurst, when—the gunboat going down-river on account of the illness of her commander—they changed their tactics and became openly overbearing. Long and difficult negotiations were the result, and it was not until a flotilla of gunboats anchored off Nanking, and war seemed imminent, that the Viceroy gave way and put matters right.

These proceedings, it need hardly be said, caused grave concern to Mr. Taylor. While grateful for Mr. Medhurst's desire to help, how much rather would he have gone back at his own risk to live down unfriendliness and opposition by patient continuance in well-doing. Detained in Chin-kiang week after week, he saw the difficulty grow only more serious, and meanwhile was faced with distressing complications of another sort in his own circle. For the painful spirit persisted in by certain members of the Mission had reached a climax. A little group of five, having gone back from its principles, after causing endless trouble, were themselves unhappy in association with it. One of these had now to be dismissed for conduct " utterly inconsistent with the position of a Christian missionary."[1] For more than two years Mr. and Mrs. Taylor had done everything in their power to help this particular brother and his wife to live and work happily in the Mission. The suffering they had endured from discourtesy, disloyalty, and untrustworthiness could never be told, and not the least part of it was to see the harmful influence exerted upon others. In severing their connection with the C.I.M. Mr. Taylor realised that he might be opening the door for the retirement of three ladies who from the first had been their confidantes—and so it proved, to the relief of all who had been associated with them, and who had marvelled at Mr. Taylor's patience in bearing so long.[2] But the sorrow of his heart was very real over the loss of these workers, and he was conscious of the questions to which it must give rise among the friends of the Mission at home.

A letter to Mr. Berger written even before the Yang-chow riot showed how the true character of the work was more and more unfolding itself to his mind. With Mrs. Taylor away in Shanghai, bearing so bravely her share of the burdens, it had meant much to him when he wrote (July 3) :

It is most important that married missionaries should be *double* missionaries—not half or a quarter or eight-part missionaries. Might we not with advantage say to our candidates:

---

[1] Quoted from Mr. Taylor's letter of dismissal, September 12, 1868 : a letter that cost him untold sorrow, and was only written " after many weeks cf anxious, prayerful thought."

[2] Writing of a missionary candidate at home who had manifestly mistaken his calling, Mrs. Taylor said :

" One thing seems very clear from Mr. M.'s letter, namely, that he is not likely to be one who would work happily in the C.I.M. And oh, we will be thankful to God when He makes this plain *in England*, and thus prevents persons from coming out who might work sorrow in our midst. Not that I would repine at the past or the present. The Lord was entreated to guide about those who should come out, and if He has suffered some to come who have caused us untold sorrow, may we not regard this as part of the storms that are to make our young Mission strike its roots deeper into the soil ? "

" Our work is a peculiar one. We aim at the interior, where the whole of your society will be Chinese. If you wish for luxury and freedom from care . . . *do not join us*. Unless you intend your wife to be a true missionary, not merely a wife, home-maker, and friend, *do not join us*. She must be able to read and be master of at least one Gospel in colloquial Chinese before you marry. A person of ordinary ability may accomplish this in six months, but if she needs longer there is the more reason to wait until she has reached this point before you marry. She must be prepared to be happy among the Chinese when the duties of your calling require, as they often will, your temporary absence from home. You, too, must master the initial difficulties of the language and open up a station, if none be allotted to you, before you marry. With diligence and God's blessing you may hope to do this in a year or so. If these conditions seem too hard, these sacrifices too great to make for perishing China, *do not join our Mission*. These are small things to some of the crosses you may be permitted to bear for your dear Master ! "

China is not to be won for Christ by self-seeking, ease-loving men and women. Those not prepared for labour, self-denial, and many discouragements will be poor helpers in the work. In short, the men and women we need are those who will put Jesus, China, souls first and foremost in everything and at all times : life itself must be secondary—nay, even those more precious than life. Of *such* men, of *such* women, do not fear to send us too many. Their price is far above rubies.

The riot and all that grew out of it did but emphasise these considerations and deepen Mr. Taylor's thankfulness for many of the fellow-workers already given him. He rejoiced in the devotion to Christ which had led them to cast in their lot with such a Mission ; in their love for the Chinese and willingness to live in close touch with them, and in the practical way they were adapting themselves to their sur-roundings. It could not but be obvious to him, as it was to them, how helpful Mrs. Taylor's quiet, unconscious influence was in this direction. Happy the younger workers like Mr. and Mrs. Judd—first to volunteer for Yang-chow after the riot—who on their arrival in China had early been moulded by her strong though gracious personality.

"How impressed I was," recalled Mr. Judd in this connec-tion, " with her calm, holy, happy appearance, as well as her Christian carriage ! She, with Mr. McCarthy and a native helper, had come seven days' journey from Hang-chow to meet our party. She gave us the warmest welcome and every assistance possible, but it was evident that she had no mercy on fastidiousness as to food or any other matters. As soon as we were settled on our boats (in Chinese dress, of course) dinner was served, and Mrs. Taylor politely handed me a pair of chopsticks and a basin containing soup with some sort of little turn-overs floating in it.

" ' Will you take puppy-dumplings, Mr. Judd ? ' she said with a smile.

" Immediately, all I had heard about the Chinese eating dogs, etc., rushed into my mind. But I dare not question the contents of a dish handed me by such a lady ! Making the best of it, therefore, I began to eat—and found nothing worse than little bits of pork nicely covered with dough."

Mrs. Judd also, who was scarcely more than a bride, had reason to remember that journey. Dismayed she may well have been to see, as night drew on, cockroaches creeping out of crevices in the boat ! She had always had a horror of these creatures, and felt she could not endure to have them crawling over her in the night.

" Oh, Mrs. Taylor," she exclaimed, " I really cannot go to bed with all these cockroaches about ! "

With another new arrival she prepared a light by which to sit up all night, keeping watch against their unwelcome visitors. But Mrs. Taylor quietly said :

" Dear child, if God spares you to work in China, you will have many nights like this, and you will not be able to afford to lose your sleep. Can you not lie down quietly, and trust Him to keep you ? I should advise you to."

Ashamed, and longing for such control over her feelings, the young missionary watched Mrs. Taylor go to rest, and after a real conflict did the same and had a good night's sleep.

" This may seem a trivial circumstance," she recalled long after, " but many a night when threatened by sterner foes and far greater dangers, I looked back on that simple lesson of trust and was strengthened."

Mrs. Taylor's one desire now, in spite of all that had happened at Yang-chow and her own immediate expectations, was to return to that city and win a way to darkened hearts for the saving love of Christ. Such a development seemed very improbable, for Mr. Medhurst was involved in what looked like endless difficulties. Even the premises in Chin-kiang rented weeks before the riot could not be obtained, and the C.I.M. party had to crowd into two little foreign houses in the Settlement for which a high rental was demanded. All September and October the weary negotiations went on, until finally in November, Sir Rutherford Alcock sent five gunboats up the river to Nanking.

Mr. Taylor all the while, in spite of a suffering illness, was planning and attempting fresh efforts for the evangelisation of districts yet unreached. His certainly was no ease-loving spirit. As soon as strength permitted he was away on a pioneering journey, with Williamson as his companion, to Tsing-kiang-pu, a city a hundred miles north of Yang-chow, which he hoped might form a base from which to reach the northern provinces. Honan was on his heart, and distant Shan-si, and at the same time he was meditating advance toward western China. His old friend Mr. Wylie had just returned from an extensive journey in the interests of the Bible Society, and, eager to learn all he could of conditions in the interior, Mr. Taylor had gone down to Shanghai to see him. All that he heard of the great province of Sze-chwan, in which Mr. Wylie had been severely handled, made him long to go himself without delay to commence more permanent work.[1] Nothing deterred by the Yang-chow difficulties, the same spirit was animating many of the members of the Mission, and Mr. Meadows had left his home and work to others that he might lead an advance into the first inland province westward from Chin-kiang—An-hwei with its twenty millions, among whom there was not a single Protestant missionary.[2]

All this increased the thankfulness with which the news

---

[1] In February 1869 Miss Faulding wrote to her mother : " Mr. Taylor longs to go forward now more than ever, and is hoping that the end of this year may find him in Sze-chwan."

[2] " Many of our number are much stirred up to press into the interior," Mr. Taylor wrote from Chin-kiang about the middle of September, " and our recent disasters, if such I may call them, only make us the more determined to go on, leaning on the Almighty Power of our Captain. Pray for us. We need much grace. You cannot conceive the many daily calls there are for patience, for forbearance, for tact in dealing with the many cases of difficulty, of misunderstanding that arise among so many persons

was at last received of an amicable settlement of the Yang-chow matter. Patience and determination had conquered— or was it the unceasing prayer that had reinforced Mr. Medhurst's efforts ? His reasonable demands were all conceded, even to the placing of a stone tablet at the entrance to the Yang-chow house, stating that the foreigners were there with the full recognition of the authorities. Quite a function was arranged to reinstate the party ; and on November 18 Mr. Taylor was able to write from Yang-chow once more, with a grateful heart, " the result of this case will probably be greatly to facilitate work in the interior."

But it was the family life and friendly spirit of the missionaries that disarmed suspicion and gradually won its way among the people. They could not but be touched when the children were brought back after all that had taken place, and when it appeared that Mrs. Taylor had not hesitated to return under conditions which made peace and quietness specially desirable.

" In this again," she wrote to her beloved friend at Saint Hill, " God has given me the desire of my heart. For I felt that if safety to my infant permitted, I would rather it were born in this city, in this house, in this very room than in any other place —your own beautiful home in which I have been so tenderly cared for, the comforts and luxuries of which I know well how to appreciate, not excepted."

So it was there the happy event took place, calling forth the congratulations of their Chinese neighbours on the arrival of a fourth son ! This in itself could not fail to make a favourable impression, as did also the perfect recovery of all who had suffered injury in the riot. The landlord of the inn (a Mr. P'eng) and two others who had befriended the missionaries in that terrible experience were by this time candidates for baptism ; and when before the end of the year the Chin-kiang house was also in their possession, Mr.

---

of different nationality and language and temperament. Pray the Lord ever to give me the single eye, the clear judgment, the wise and gentle manner, the patient forbearing spirit, the unwavering purpose, the unshaken faith, the Christ-like love that are needed for the efficient discharge of my duties. And ask Him to send us sufficient means and suitable helpers for the great work which we have as yet barely commenced."

Taylor might well write: " Once again we raise our Ebenezer —' Hitherto hath the Lord helped us.' "

But the Yang-chow difficulties were far from ended with this satisfactory settlement. " The devil's growl," as Mr. Spurgeon called it, had yet to come, and an angry growl it was, that upset not a few friends of the Mission. For the action of the Consular authorities gave rise to a storm of indignation at home. Missionaries were making trouble as usual, demanding the support of gunboats in their ill-judged crusade against ancestral worship. The country would be involved in war before the Government had even time to consider the matter! It seems almost incredible as one looks back upon it, that so much misrepresentation could have found its way into the daily papers, and that for a period of four or five months Mr. Taylor and his doings could so largely have occupied the public mind. China, of course, was farther off then than now, and there was far less understanding of its problems. But, even so, the attention the subject evoked and the prejudice displayed were extraordinary. From the " connected narrative " in the *Times* of December 1, " explaining " the whole situation, to the discussion in the House of Lords on March 9— in which, after a heated declamation, the Duke of Somerset urged that all British missionaries should be recalled from China—the matter seems hardly to have been absent from the public mind. The vigorous attitude enjoined upon the British Representative at Peking by a former Government was utterly repudiated now, and there was not much to choose between the accusations heaped upon the Consular authorities and upon the missionaries.[1] But Mr. Taylor it

[1] In a long letter to Mrs. Berger, explaining all the circumstances that attended the riot, Mrs. Taylor said (February 11, 1869) : " As to the harsh judgings of the world or the more painful misunderstandings of Christian brethren, I *generally* feel that the best plan is to go on with our work and leave God to vindicate our cause. But it is right that you should know intimately how we have acted, and why. I would suggest, however, that it would be undesirable to *print* the fact that Mr. Medhurst, and through him Sir Rutherford Alcock, took up the matter without application from us. The new Ministry at home censures those out here for the policy which the late Ministry enjoined upon them. It would be ungenerous and ungrateful were we to render their position still more difficult by throwing all the onus, as it were, on them.

was, all through, who had brought the country to the verge of war by his irresponsible conduct. Needless to say, the brunt of all this fell upon Mr. Berger.

" The excitement, indeed I may almost say storm, seems bursting over us now," he wrote on December 17. " The *Times* is very severe, and incorrect in some things. Whether to reply to the false statements I scarcely know. . . . At present the Yang-chow outrage is the all-absorbing subject. Our letters to-day, I think, number from twenty to thirty."

December 31 : The —— Editor is so unscrupulous and unfair, and I am so unable to say how, or how far, you called upon the Consul in the matter,[1] that I greatly question the wisdom of replying at all. God is a refuge for us, " A very present help in time of trouble." Though we have much trial and perplexity in various ways, God has greatly blessed His Word to me, so that my joy abounds over all the sorrows.

January 13, 1869 : It rejoices our hearts that you are again at Yang-chow. The late riots have led to such an immense increase of correspondence and claims upon me, that I must guard against breaking down entirely.

January 28 : Through Christ, I am kept in great peace and quiet of soul, though the storm has raged terribly of late. Gleams of brightness are not withheld . . . so do not be cast down, dear Brother. Hope in God, Who will never leave nor forsake those who seek to please Him.

February 25 : We are just back from Bristol, where we spent a happy and profitable week, and found many dear friends who remembered and inquired most affectionately after you and Mrs. Taylor. The sympathy expressed for you and those with you in the late trial was great and very sweet ; and none spoke more warmly of you than dear Mr. Müller. . . .

I asked for his opinion respecting the appeal to the British

" Perhaps one secret of our matter being taken up so warmly was that it was looked upon as a climax to a series of provocations which the English had suffered from the Chinese ; and the representatives of our Government were, I believe, not sorry to have an opportunity of, and good ground for, settling off a number of ' old counts.' "

Government officials and merchants, as well as missionaries, suffered in the same way at this time, in districts as widely separated as Swatow, Formosa, and the Yangtze valley. See an able article in the *Scotsman* for April 12, 1869, entitled : " The Late Disturbances in China."

[1] The only appeal of any kind that Mr. Taylor had made to the Consular authorities had been a verbal message on August 22, and a pencilled note the following morning—when the riot was beginning all over again after that awful night of suspense and anguish—*simply informing them of the situation.*

Consul, and you would have rejoiced to have heard him repudiate the spirit of judging you, or of fault-finding. He said he would never have spoken to me on the subject, had I not asked him for his judgment : after which he said that, had poor George Müller been in such circumstances, he cannot tell what he might have done ; still he thought the more excellent way would have been to trust in God. . . . That we must not set up what *we* think the more excellent way, as a rule for others, he quite agreed with me. . . . Finally, Mr. Müller only allowed me, upon my request, to refer to his opinion with the understanding that it was that we might help each other in serving the Lord, and not in any spirit of fault-finding or condemning you.

March 11 : The Yang-chow matter is before the House of Lords, and I hope to send you a copy of the *Times* ere long. You can scarcely imagine what an effect the matter has produced in the country. Thank God I can say, " None of these things move me." I believe He has called us to this work, and it is not for us to run away from it, or allow difficulties to overcome us. . . . Be of good courage, the battle is the Lord's.

March 24 : I have not had a moment in which to look at the accounts sent me in your last two letters ; indeed I have never been so pressed before, both in my business and the affairs of the Mission. Still I hope in God, and believe He will bring us safely out of this tremendous storm. What to do for the best, I know not.

April 8 : I think I can say I never felt prayer to be so real as I do now. God has graciously given me more faith, and I feel greatly helped heavenward.

One result of all these difficulties was, not unnaturally, a falling off in the income of the Mission, so that for the first time Mr. Taylor was faced with serious shortness of funds in China. This would have been much more the case if the Lord had not laid it upon the heart and put it into the power of Mr. George Müller largely to increase his gifts. He had been sending regularly to several members of the Mission sometimes as much as twenty-five pounds a quarter ; and now, within a day or two of the Yang-chow riot (long before he heard of it), he wrote to Mr. Berger asking for the names of others who were thoroughly satisfactory in their work whom he might add to his list. Mr. Berger sent him six names from which to choose, and his choice was to take them all. This was not only a substantial help, it was a great encouragement, for it meant added sympathy and prayer on the part of one who knew the way to the Throne. And more and more Mr. Taylor was feeling the need of just such fellowship.

" I am in strange ups and downs," wrote the saintly Rutherford, " and seven times a day I lose ground : I am put often to swimming, and again my feet are set on the rock that is higher than myself. . . . I have seen my abominable vileness ; and if I were known, there is none in this kingdom would ask how I do." [1]

Little as those nearest to him could have supposed it, this was very much Mr. Taylor's own experience. " Emptied " as he was " from vessel to vessel," constantly under pressure of strain and stress, his spiritual life had hardly kept pace with the demands upon it. Outwardly it may not have seemed so.

" Our hearts were much drawn to Mr. Taylor," said one of the fellow-workers constantly with him, " by seeing his gentle, humble, tender spirit under the administrative trials of those early years."

" I have known him under all circumstances," wrote another before the Yang-chow riot, " and I feel that if you could see him daily you would indeed admire his self-abnegation, humility and never-flagging earnestness. Very few in his case would have shown the forbearing, loving spirit he has shown. . . . No one knows how much he has felt our troubles, nor how he had suffered from depression. If he were not in the habit of casting his burdens on the Lord, he must have sunk under them. Grace, not natural temperament, has supported him."

But " the heart knoweth its own bitterness," and the load Hudson Taylor was carrying was almost more than he could bear. It was not the work with all its difficulty and trial : when consciously in communion with the Lord these seemed light. It was not shortness of funds, nor anxiety about those dearest to him. It was just—himself : the unsatisfied longing of his heart ; the inward struggle to abide in Christ ; the frequent failure and disappointment. So bitter was this experience that even when it was left far

[1] Letter to Lady Boyd from Aberdeen, May 1, 1637.

behind he could never forget it. This it was that made him always sympathetic with younger workers in their spiritual conflicts, quick to see and make the most of every opportunity to help them. Fellowship with God was to him a great reality, a great necessity. He had known much of it ; much too of the terrible void of losing it. " Like a diver under water without air, or a fireman on a burning building with an empty hose," he found himself face to face with heathenism and all the claims that pressed upon him, but alas ! too often out of touch with Christ. Had he been responsible for himself only this would have been bad enough, but with all the demands upon him it was unbearable— especially in view of the subject to which his thoughts in common with those of his fellow-workers were being directed.

For just at this time the pages of the *Revival* (now the *Christian*) were largely occupied with a genuine holiness movement destined, in the providence of God, to lead to the Keswick Convention with its world-wide influences for good. Finding its way to all the stations of the Mission, this paper was bringing the subject of a deeper spiritual life prominently before its readers, and not a few, like Mr. Taylor himself, were hungering for a fuller experience of the possibilities it set forth, which they saw to be in accordance with the Word of God. It was the life of habitual victory over sin, the life that is in deep reality " Not I, but Christ " for which their hearts longed. All through the summer and autumn of 1868 these articles were appearing, one series entitled " The Way of Holiness " being specially helpful.

" Surely the words ' Christ liveth in me,' ' For me to live is Christ,' cannot mean less than habitual victory over sin," said the writer. " None are so manifestly, pitiably weak as the ' little children ' of the Kingdom when without the presence of Christ ; but none so strong as those who abandon self to Him, that He may live in them, perfecting His strength in their weakness. . . . *You* have failed, not Christ. I feel confident that the point of your failure is in not having committed, unreservedly, everything to Him, in perfect self-abandonment.

" The Holy Spirit never creates hungerings and thirstings

after righteousness, but in order that Christ may fill the longing soul.

"Faith in Jesus crucified is the way of peace to the sinner ; so faith in Jesus risen is the way of daily salvation to the saint.

"You cannot be your own Saviour, either in whole or in part.

" ' *Purifying their hearts by faith* ' : how my soul leaped up at those words, seeing in a moment the possibility of deliverance ! ' If then it is *by faith*,' I exclaimed, ' I will trust Jesus for a pure heart, and now ! ' . . .

"Can we trust Jesus too fully for everything His Word sets before us ?

" ' Who gave Himself for us that He might redeem us from all iniquity, and purify unto Himself a peculiar people (peculiarly His own) zealous of good works.' When is this redemption ? Now. From what ? From all iniquity. What else does His sacrifice propose ? To purify you unto Himself. When ought you to receive this redemption ? Now. And this purification ? Equally now, and with the same simple faith.[1]

" ' The Lord gives me to drink of His love as out of a river,' Thomas Walsh testified. ' I laid me down but could not sleep, through a deep and comfortable sense of the love of Christ. His Spirit rested on me, and made my heart flame with love to my God, my all. It never entered into my soul to conceive of thus loving Him with all the heart, until He revealed it to me by His Spirit. The fire of divine love burned incessantly in my soul.' "

To know *that* redemption, that love, in fuller measure was Mr. Taylor's deepest longing ; but oh, how different were the actual experiences of his soul ! With the growth of the Mission his way seemed ever more beset with inward and outward perplexity, and with a need for the exercise of faith and grace which he had not faith and grace to meet. Sometimes he was buoyed up by hope, sometimes almost in despair.

Life was too busy as a rule for his correspondence to reveal much of the crisis through which he was passing, but early in 1869 he found himself alone on a journey which gave opportunity for one of the old-time letters to his mother Leaving Mr. Judd in charge at Yang-chow and Mr. Rudland

[1] Titus ii. 14 in Weymouth's translation reads : " Who gave Himself for us, to purchase our *freedom from all iniquity*, and purify for Himself a people who should be specially His own, zealous for doing good works."

at Chin-kiang, he had brought his family to Ningpo for the time being, while he went to and fro among the older stations of the Mission. Danger of riots detained him in Tai-chow-fu for a month, while the city was full of students for the yearly examination. Both there and in Wen-chow, where Mr. Stott had weathered persistent storms of opposition, the work was already bearing fruit, and Mr. Taylor had the joy of baptizing the first believers. In a more recently opened station, Ning-hai, he found five candidates for baptism and a general willingness to hear the Gospel, where thirteen months previously there had been neither convert nor preacher. His heart had been so burdened about the place on his former visit that he had definitely prayed that the Gospel might be brought there before long, and now it was cheering to see the answer. But while, writing from that very city, he gave his parents the good news, it was their help he sought in those personal matters of which he could hardly have spoken so freely to any other.

" I have often asked you to remember me in prayer," he said (Mar. 13, 1869), " and when I have done so there has been much *need* of it. That need has never been greater than at the present time. Envied by some, despised by many, hated perhaps by others ; often blamed for things I never heard of, or had nothing to do with ; an innovator on what have become established rules of missionary practice ; an opponent of mighty systems of heathen error and superstition ; working without precedent in many respects, and with few experienced helpers ; often sick in body, as well as perplexed in mind and embarrassed by circumstances ; had not the Lord been specially gracious to me, had not my mind been sustained by the conviction that the work is His, and that He is with me in what it is no empty figure to call ' the thick of the conflict,' I must have fainted and broken down. But the battle *is* the Lord's : and He will conquer. We may fail, do fail continually ; but He never fails. Still I need your prayers more than ever before.

" My own position becomes continually more and more responsible, and my need greater of special grace to fill it ; but I have continually to mourn that I follow at such a distance and learn so slowly to imitate my precious Master. I cannot tell you how I am buffeted sometimes by temptation. I never knew how bad a heart I had. Yet I do know that I love God and love His work, and desire to serve Him only and in all things.

And I value above all things that precious Saviour in Whom alone I can be accepted. Often I am tempted to think that one so full of sin cannot be a child of God at all ; but I try to throw it back, and rejoice all the more in the preciousness of Jesus, and in the riches of that grace that has made us ' accepted in the Beloved.' Beloved He *is* of God ; beloved He *ought* to be of us. But oh, how short I fall here again ! May God help me to love Him more and serve Him better. Do pray for me. Pray that the Lord will keep me from sin, will sanctify me wholly, will use me more largely in His service."

CHAPTER XII

THE EXCHANGED LIFE

1869. AET. 37.

In the old home at Hang-chow Mr. McCarthy was sitting writing. The glory of a great sunrise was upon him—the light whose inward dawning makes all things new. To tell his beloved friend and leader about it was his longing, for he knew from his own experience something of the exercise of mind through which Mr. Taylor was passing. But where to begin, how to put it into words he knew not, and the day was full of pressing duties.

" I do wish I could have a talk with you *now*," he wrote, " about the way of Holiness. At the time you were speaking to me about it, it was the subject of all others occupying my thoughts—not from anything I had read, not from what my brother had written even, so much as from a consciousness of failure ; a constant falling short of that which I felt should be aimed at ; an unrest ; a perpetual striving to find some way by which I might continuously enjoy that communion, that fellowship at times so real, but more often so visionary, so far off ! . . . Do you know, dear brother, I now think that this striving, effort, longing, hoping for better days to come, is not the true way to happiness, holiness or usefulness : better, no doubt far better, than being satisfied with our poor attainments, but not the best way after all. I have been struck with a passage from a book of yours left here, entitled *Christ is All*. It says :

" The Lord Jesus received is holiness begun ; the Lord Jesus cherished is holiness advancing ; the Lord Jesus *counted upon as never absent* would be holiness complete.

" This (grace of faith) is the chain which binds the soul to Christ, and makes the Saviour and the sinner one. . . .

A channel is now formed by which Christ's fulness plenteously flows down. The barren branch becomes a portion of the fruitful stem. . . . One life reigns throughout the whole.

" Believer, you mourn your shortcomings ; you find the hated monster, sin, still striving for the mastery. Evil is present when you would do good. Help is laid up for you in Christ. Seek clearer interest in Him. They who *most* deeply feel that they have died in Christ, and paid in Him sin's penalties, ascend to highest heights of godly life. He is most holy who has most of Christ within, and joys most fully in the finished work. It is defective faith which clogs the feet, and causes many a fall.

" This last sentence I think I now fully endorse. To *let* my loving Saviour work in me *His will*, my sanctification is what I would live for by His grace. Abiding, not striving nor struggling ; looking off unto Him ; trusting Him for present power ; trusting Him to subdue all inward corruption ; resting in the love of an almighty Saviour, in the conscious joy of a *complete* salvation, a salvation ' from all sin ' (this is *His* Word) ; willing that His will should truly be supreme—this is not new, and yet 'tis *new to me*. I feel as though the first dawning of a glorious day had risen upon me. I hail it with trembling, yet with trust. I seem to have got to the edge only, but of a sea which is boundless ; to have sipped only, but of that which fully satisfies. Christ literally *all* seems to me now the power, the *only* power for service ; the only ground for unchanging joy. May He lead us into the realisation of His unfathomable fulness."

August 21 : How then to have our faith increased ? Only by thinking of all that Jesus *is*, and all He is *for us* : His life, His death, His work, He Himself as revealed to us in the Word, to be the subject of our constant thoughts. Not a striving to have faith, or to increase our faith, but a looking off to the Faithful One seems all we need ; a resting in the Loved One entirely, for time and for eternity. It does not appear to me as anything new, only formerly misapprehended.

Life was, if anything, specially full and busy for Mr. Taylor at this time. He had returned from his journey round the older stations to an endless succession of duties that kept him on the move between Yang-chow and Chin-kiang. Both were in a sense the headquarters of the Mission, and the growing church in the former and the demands of the printing-press in the latter filled every moment that could be spared from account keeping, correspondence, and

directorial matters.   There had recently been baptisms in
Yang-chow, and Mr. Judd was glad of all the help Mr.
Taylor could give in caring for the young converts.   The
heat of summer had told upon all the party, and Mr. Taylor
himself had been laid aside by severe illness in the middle
of August.   Now, early in September, he was recovering,
and trying to overtake the work that had accumulated.
The Cordons had come over from Soo-chow to consult him
about their movements ; the Duncans were on their way
from Nanking for special conference ; others were coming
and going on various matters, and there was a good deal of
proof-reading on hand.   Mrs. Judd also was dangerously ill,
and required Mr. Taylor's attention as a doctor.   It was no
time, surely, for an outstanding crisis in spiritual things !

Yet, oh, how deep the heart-hunger, in and through all
else !   *That* did not diminish.   It seemed to increase, rather,
with all the need there was to minister to others.   Leaving
a full house in Chin-kiang, Mr. Taylor had run up to Yang-
chow to see his patient, and was returning now alone by a
little boat chosen less for comfort than for speed.   It was
early in the morning, and he was eager to be in Chin-kiang,
where Mrs. Taylor was, in time for breakfast, so as not to
lose a moment of the day for work.   Coming down the
Grand Canal and crossing the Yangtze (two miles wide) he
had quiet for thought—thought and prayer.   Were it not
recorded in his own words it would be difficult to believe,
certainly impossible to imagine, such conflict, suffering,
almost despair in spiritual things in one who had long and
truly known the Lord.   Ah, was it not that very fact that
made it possible ?   Nearness to Christ had been to him so
real and blessed that any distance was unbearable.   So
deeply did he love that any clouding of the Master's face was
felt, and felt at once with anguish of heart.   It is the bride
who mourns the absence of the bridegroom, not one who has
been a stranger to His love.

Reaching the little crowded house at Chin-kiang, Mr.
Taylor made his way as soon as possible to his room to
attend to correspondence.   There, amid a pile of letters, was
one from Mr. McCarthy.   We do not know if he was alone

as he read it : we do not know just how the miracle was wrought. But—" as I read, I saw it all. I looked to Jesus ; and when I saw, oh how joy flowed ! "

It was Saturday the 4th of September ; the house was full, and others were coming ; somehow they must be put up and kept over Sunday, for this great joy could not but be shared.[1] As soon as he could break away from his glad thanksgivings, Mr. Taylor went out, a new man in a new world, to tell what the Lord had done for his soul. He took the letters, Mr. McCarthy's and one from Miss Faulding in the same strain, and, gathering the household together in the sitting-room upstairs, told out what his whole life was telling from that time onward to the glorious end. Other hearts were moved and blessed ; the streams began to flow. From that little crowded home in Chin-kiang city they flowed on and out, and are flowing still—" rivers of living water." For " whosoever drinketh of the water that I shall give him," Jesus said, " shall never thirst ; but the water that I shall give him shall be in him a well of water springing up into everlasting life."

And he did more than tell. Pressed though he was with business matters, his correspondence took on a new tone. Here is one of the first letters written with that tide of joy and life more abundant sweeping through his soul. Books and medicines were needed from Yang-chow, and in sending for them Mr. Taylor gave directions so detailed that all needless trouble would be spared. The pencilled lines on half a sheet of notepaper show that he was very busy—but how at leisure in spirit !

CHIN-KIANG, *September* 6, 1869.

MY DEAR SISTER—We had a very happy day here yesterday. I was *so* happy ! A letter from Mr. McCarthy on this subject

---

[1] September 4 saw the following entry in Miss Blatchley's journal : " Mr. Taylor here (Chin-kiang) by about breakfast-time. He had met the Duncans, and they came back with him. Soon after, the Cordons also arrived. . . . All are to stay over Sunday for special prayer *re* holiness. Mr. McCarthy's letter on the subject, awaiting Mr. Taylor, God used for a channel of blessing to him. He too has now received the *rest* of soul that Jesus gave to me some little time ago. Mr. McCarthy and Jennie (Miss Faulding) both seem to have obtained it, as also had Miss Desgraz before we returned from the South. Others too, the Rudlands, Cordons, Duncans, Judds, and Miss Bowyer have had their minds much exercised on the same subject—how to attain holiness of heart and life."

has been blessed to several of us. He and Miss Faulding also seem so happy ! He says : " I feel as though the first glimmer of the dawn of a glorious day had risen upon me. I hail it with trembling, yet with trust."

The part specially helpful to me is : " How then to have our faith increased ? Only by thinking of all that Jesus *is*, and all He is *for us* : His life, His death, His work, He Himself as revealed to us in the Word, to be the subject of our constant thoughts. *Not* a striving to have faith, or to increase our faith, *but* a looking off to the Faithful One seems *all* we need."

Here, I feel, is the secret : not asking how I am to get sap *out* of the vine *into* myself, but remembering that Jesus *is* the Vine—the root, stem, branches, twigs, leaves, flowers, fruit, all indeed. Aye, and far more too ! He is the soil and sunshine, air and rain—more than we can ask, think, or desire. Let us not then want to get anything out of Him, but rejoice in being *ourselves in Him*—one with Him, and, consequently, with *all* His fulness. Not seeking for faith to bring holiness, but rejoicing in the *fact* of perfect holiness in Christ, let us realise that—inseparably one with Him—this holiness *is* ours, and accepting the fact, find it so indeed. But I must stop.

Returning to Yang-chow to see his patient, Mr. Taylor became the bearer of his own glad tidings.

"When I went to welcome him," recalled Mr. Judd, " he was so full of joy that he scarcely knew how to speak to me. He did not even say, ' How do you do ? ' but walking up and down the room with his hands behind him, exclaimed :
" ' Oh, Mr. Judd, God has made me a new man ! God has made me a new man ! ' "

That midnight conversation and the change that had come over his beloved leader greatly impressed the younger missionary. He too had seen these things theoretically, as so many do, without really apprehending them.

" I have not got to *make* myself a branch," he could never forget Mr. Taylor saying. " The Lord Jesus tells me I *am* a branch. I am *part of Him*, and have just to believe it and act upon it. If I go to the bank in Shanghai, having an account, and ask for fifty dollars, the clerk cannot refuse it to my outstretched hand and say that it belongs to Mr. Taylor. What belongs to Mr. Taylor my hand may take. It is a member of my body. And I am a member of Christ, and may take all I need of His fulness. I have seen it long enough in the Bible, but I *believe* it now as a living reality."

Simple as it was, the new point of view changed everything.

"He was a joyous man now," added Mr. Judd, "a bright, happy Christian. He had been a toiling, burdened one before, with latterly not much rest of soul. It was resting in Jesus now, and letting Him do the work—which makes all the difference! Whenever he spoke in meetings, after that, a new power seemed to flow from him, and in the practical things of life a new peace possessed him. Troubles did not worry him as before. He cast everything on God in a new way, and gave more time to prayer. Instead of working late at night, he began to go to bed earlier, rising at five in the morning to give two hours before the work of the day began to Bible study and prayer. Thus his own soul was fed, and from him flowed the living water to others."

Six weeks after these experiences, when Mr. Taylor was rejoicing in the abiding fulness of this new life, a letter reached him from England that specially touched his heart. It was from his sister, Mrs. Broomhall, the intimate friend and correspondent of his early years, who now with a growing family round her was sore pressed, as he had been himself, by outward responsibilities and inward conflict rather than rest in spiritual things. With a great longing to help one so dear to him, Mr. Taylor took up his pen to reply. As he wrote, the whole story of his own extremity and deliverance was poured out in a letter so precious that it is given in full, despite the risk of some repetition :

October 17, 1869 : So many thanks for your long, dear letter. . . . I do not think you have written me such a letter since we have been in China. I know it is with you as with me —you *cannot*, not you *will* not. Mind and body will not bear more than a certain amount of strain, or do more than a certain amount of work. As to work, mine was never so plentiful, so responsible, or so difficult ; but the weight and strain are all *gone*. The last month or more has been perhaps, the happiest of my life ; and I long to tell you a little of what the Lord has done for my soul. I do not know how far I may be able to make myself intelligible about it, for there is nothing new or strange or wonderful—and yet, all is new! In a word, "Whereas once I was blind, now I see."

Perhaps I shall make myself more clear if I go back a little. Well, dearie, my mind has been greatly exercised for six or eight months past, feeling the need personally, and for our Mission, of more holiness, life, power in our souls. But personal need stood first and was the greatest. I felt the ingratitude, the danger, the sin of not living nearer to God. I prayed, agonised, fasted, strove, made resolutions, read the Word more diligently, sought more time for retirement and meditation—but all was without effect. Every day, almost every hour, the consciousness of sin oppressed me. I knew that if I could only abide in Christ all would be well, but I *could not*. I began the day with prayer, determined not to take my eye from Him for a moment; but pressure of duties, sometimes very trying, constant interruptions apt to be so wearing, often caused me to forget Him. Then one's nerves get so fretted in this climate that temptations to irritability, hard thoughts, and sometimes unkind words are all the more difficult to control. Each day brought its register of sin and failure, of lack of power. To will was indeed present with me, but how to perform I found not.

Then came the question, " Is there *no* rescue ? Must it be thus to the end—constant conflict and, instead of victory, too often defeat ? " How, too, could I preach with sincerity that to those who receive Jesus, " to them gave He power to become the sons of God " (*i.e.* God-like) when it was not so in my own experience ? Instead of growing stronger, I seemed to be getting weaker and to have less power against sin ; and no wonder, for faith and even hope were getting very low. I hated myself ; I hated my sin ; and yet I gained no strength against it. I felt I *was* a child of God : His Spirit in my heart would cry, in spite of all, " Abba, Father " : but to rise to my privileges as a child, I was utterly powerless. I thought that holiness, practical holiness, was to be gradually attained by a diligent use of the means of grace. I felt that there was nothing I so much desired in this world, nothing I so much needed. But so far from in any measure attaining it, the more I pursued and strove after it, the more it eluded my grasp ; till hope itself almost died out, and I began to think that, perhaps to make heaven the sweeter, God would not give it down here. I do not think I was striving to attain it in my own strength. I knew I was powerless. I told the Lord so, and asked Him to give me help and strength ; and sometimes I almost believed He would keep and uphold me. But on looking back in the evening, alas ! there was but sin and failure to confess and mourn before God.

I would not give you the impression that this was the daily experience of all those long, weary months. It was a too frequent state of soul; that toward which I was tending, and which almost ended in despair. And yet never did Christ seem more precious—a Saviour who *could* and *would* save such a sinner ! . . . And sometimes there were seasons not only of peace but of joy in the Lord. But they were transitory, and at best there was a sad lack of power. Oh, how good the Lord was in bringing this conflict to an end !

All the time I felt assured that there was in Christ all I needed, but the practical question was how to get it *out*. He was rich, truly, but I was poor ; He strong, but I weak. I knew full well that there was in the root, the stem, abundant fatness ; but how to get it into my puny little branch was the question. As gradually the light was dawning on me, I saw that faith was the only pre-requisite, was the hand to lay hold on His fulness and make it my own. *But I had not this faith.* I strove for it, but it would not come ; tried to exercise it, but in vain. Seeing more and more the wondrous supply of grace laid up in Jesus, the fulness of our precious Saviour—my helplessness and guilt seemed to increase. Sins committed appeared but as trifles compared with the sin of unbelief which was their cause, which could not or would not take God at His word, but rather made Him a liar ! Unbelief was, I felt, *the* damning sin of the world— yet I indulged in it. I prayed for faith, but it came not. What was I to do ?

When my agony of soul was at its height, a sentence in a letter from dear McCarthy was used to remove the scales from my eyes, and the Spirit of God revealed the truth of *our oneness* with *Jesus* as I had never known it before. McCarthy, who had been much exercised by the same sense of failure, but saw the light before I did, wrote (I quote from memory) :

" But how to get faith strengthened ? Not by striving after faith, but by resting on the Faithful One."

As I read I saw it all ! " If we believe *not*, He abideth faithful." I looked to Jesus and saw (and when I saw, oh, how joy flowed !) that He had said, " *I* will never leave *you*." " Ah, *there* is rest ! " I thought. " I have striven in vain to rest in Him. I'll strive no more. For has *He* not promised to abide with me—never to leave me, never to fail me ? " And, dearie, *He never will* !

But this was not all He showed me, nor one half. As I thought of the Vine and the branches, what light the blessed Spirit poured direct into my soul ! How great seemed my mistake in having wished to get the sap, the fulness *out* of Him. I saw not only that Jesus would never leave me, but that I was a member of His body, of His flesh and of His bones. The vine now I see, is not the root merely, but all—root, stem, branches, twigs, leaves, flowers, fruit : and Jesus is not only that : He is soil and sunshine, air and showers, and ten thousand times more than we have ever dreamed, wished for, or needed. Oh, the joy of seeing this truth ! I do pray that the eyes of your under- standing may be enlightened, that you may know and enjoy the riches freely given us in Christ.

Oh, my dear sister, it is a wonderful thing to be really one with a risen and exalted Saviour ; to be a member of Christ ! Think what it involves. Can Christ be rich and I poor ? Can your right hand be rich and the left poor ? or your head be well fed while your body starves ? Again, think of its bearing on prayer. Could a bank clerk say to a customer, " It was only your hand wrote that cheque, not you," or, " I cannot pay this sum to your hand, but only to yourself " ? No more can your prayers, or mine, be discredited *if offered in the Name of Jesus* (*i.e.* not in our own name, or for the sake of Jesus merely, but on the ground that we are His, His members) so long as we keep within the extent of Christ's credit—a tolerably wide limit ! If we ask anything unscriptural or not in accordance with the will of God, Christ Himself could not do that ; but, " If we ask anything according to His will, He heareth us, and . . . we know that we have the petitions that we desire of Him."

The sweetest part, if one may speak of one part being sweeter than another, is the *rest* which full identification with Christ brings. I am no longer anxious about anything, as I realise this ; for He, I know, is able to carry out *His will*, and His will is mine. It makes no matter where He places me, or how. That is rather for Him to consider than for me ; for in the easiest positions He must give me His grace, and in the most difficult His grace is sufficient. It little matters to my servant whether I send him to buy a few cash worth of things, or the most expensive articles. In either case he looks to me for the money, and brings me his purchases. So, if God place me in great perplexity, must He not give me much guidance ; in positions of great difficulty, much grace ; in circumstances of great pressure and trial, much strength ? No fear that His resources will be unequal to the emergency ! And His resources are mine, for *He* is mine, and is with me and dwells in me. All this springs from the believer's oneness with Christ. And since Christ has thus dwelt in my heart by faith, how happy I have been ! I wish I could tell you, instead of writing about it.

I am no better than before (may I not say, in a sense, I do not wish to be, nor am I striving to be) ; but I am dead and buried with Christ—aye, and risen too and ascended ; and now

Christ lives in me, and "the life that I now live in the flesh, I
live by the faith of the Son of God, Who loved me, and gave
Himself for me." I now *believe* I am dead to sin. God reckons
me so, and tells me to reckon myself so. He knows best. All
my past experience may have shown that it *was* not so ; but I
dare not say it *is* not now, when He says it is. I feel and know
that old things have passed away. I am as capable of sinning
as ever, but Christ is realised as present as never before. He
cannot sin ; and He can keep me from sinning. I cannot say
(I am sorry to have to confess it) that since I have seen this
light I have not sinned ; but I do feel there was no need to
have done so. And further—walking more in the light, my
conscience has been more tender ; sin has been instantly seen,
confessed, pardoned ; and peace and joy (with humility) instantly
restored : with one exception, when for several hours peace
and joy did not return—from want, as I had to learn, of full
confession, and from some attempt to justify self.

Faith, I now see, is "the *substance* of things hoped for," and
not mere shadow. It is not *less* than sight, but *more*. Sight
only shows the outward forms of things ; faith gives the substance. You can *rest* on substance, *feed* on substance. Christ
dwelling in the heart by faith (*i.e.* His Word of Promise credited)
is *power* indeed, is *life* indeed. And Christ and sin will not dwell
together ; nor can we have His presence with love of the world,
or carefulness about "many things."

And now I must close. I have not said half I would, nor *as*
I would had I more time. May God give you to lay hold on these
blessed truths. Do not let us continue to say, in *effect*, "Who
shall ascend into heaven, that is to bring Christ down from above."
In other words, do not let us consider Him as afar off, when God
has made us *one with Him*, members of His very body. Nor
should we look upon this experience, these truths, as for the
few. They are the birthright of every child of God, and no one
can dispense with them without dishonour to our Lord. The
only power for deliverance from sin or for true service is CHRIST.

And it was blessing that stood the test as the busy days
went by. Well might Mr. Taylor have said with George
Müller of Bristol at this time : "If I had strength to work
twenty-four hours every day I could not half accomplish
what is ready for my hands and feet and head and heart."
With him, too, he could have added : "Yet with all this, I
consider my first business to be, and my most important
business every day, to get blessing in my own soul—for my

own soul to be happy in the Lord, and then to work, and to work with all diligence." A few extracts from the correspondence of one fortnight will show how many and varied were Mr. Taylor's occupations, and that the joy of the Lord was indeed his strength. " Now He makes me happy all day long," he had written to Mr. Berger a little earlier, " makes my work light, and gives me joy in seeing Him blessing others. How can I but rejoice ! I have no fear now of our work being too heavy for Him, either out here or in the home department."

To Mr. Reid at Nanking, Oct. 18 : " My heart warms towards you as I sit down to write. Business is very pressing, but it does not hinder my joy in the Lord. . . . I enclose the first six pages of your valuable little book, and am buying Chinese type to print it."

Same day, to Mr. Cordon : " My soul is so happy in the Lord ! and as I think of the blessing He gave me on the happy day when we all met here together, I know not how sufficiently to thank and praise Him. Truly Jesus is the great need of our souls. And He is the great gift of our Father's love—Who gave Him *for* us, and makes us one *with* Him in resurrection life and power. . . . The mission funds are lower than they were before."

From Yang-chow, Oct. 27 : " Our work here is very encouraging at present. We cannot too much thank God for this. Five persons have been baptized . . . eight others are about ready to be received, and several more will, I trust, follow after a little time. It is the Provincial Examination at present, and the daily congregations are large and attentive. . . . I quite think we shall see great things here, for we are one with Jesus."

To Mr. Jackson at Tai-chow-fu, Oct. 30 : " I would ask you to remember funds in prayer : they are lower than they have ever been. Yet we are not and have not been forsaken, or lacking really : and we assuredly shall not be, if we have faith as a grain of mustard seed. . . . The precious truths we talked over together (at Ningpo) make me happy all the day. I hope you find it so too."

Postscript to a letter to An-king, Oct. 31 : " It occurs to me to add that some of the members of the Mission may be unaware of the amount of labour involved in serving them. It is a *real pleasure*, but it is none the less onerous. For instance, I have to write to Mr. Müller to thank him for your cheque ; to Mr. Lord asking him kindly to sell it as he gets a better price than the Shanghai Banks will give ; then to enter it in his account and in my cash account ; then to send the amount to Mr. Hart, with a note requesting him kindly to forward it. Of course, I must also advise you of it, but this may not involve special writing. I thank God for permitting me to be a hewer of wood and drawer of water in His glorious work, and do cheerfully what little I can to help, only regretting the impossibility of doing *all* that all wish. Just now I have seven different portions of Old and New Testament (whole books) and long tracts sent me in several dialects, with requests to revise them. This, if possible at all, is the work of weeks if not months. Yet I am praying for guidance as to whether I may not have to leave to-night for one of our most distant stations, on account of a case of sickness."

It was a serious test in November when tidings came of an uprising in An-king, the newly opened station which was their farthest point inland. Mr. Taylor was on a journey at the time, and out of reach of letters, and the first he heard of it was a rumour that Mr. and Mrs. Meadows and Mr. Williamson had all been killed.

" What shall we say ? " he wrote in suspense that would have been anguish, as he travelled with all haste to Chin-kiang. " ' Father, glorify Thy Name," though the flesh is weak and trembles. Jesus is our strength ; and what we cannot do or bear *He* can both do and bear in us. . . . We are not our own, nor is the work ours. He Whose we are and Whom we serve will not prove unequal to the emergency."

To his relief he found that the report had been exaggerated. The riot was indeed a serious affair, but the missionaries had escaped with their lives, even the little children being uninjured. Judging by the troubles that had grown out of the Yang-chow riot, however, this might be far from the end of the matter. Already adverse criticism at home had resulted in a lessening of funds, so that in four months —May to September—less had been received by *a thousand pounds* than in the corresponding period of the previous year. This would have caused Mr. Taylor considerable anxiety, especially in view of the new complications, but for the reality of the blessing that had come to him.

" You will have heard from other quarters," he wrote to Mr. Berger in December, " of An-king affairs. The Lord has

kept my soul in peace about the whole thing. From the first I
could not but see that the opponents of missions, especially those
opposed to us, might make an unfavourable use of it. But the
Lord reigns. We are serving Him, He knows at what cost and
in Whose strength. He will not leave His own work. . . .

"I see no objection to your referring to the state of funds
in writing to various members of the Mission ; you would not
seek to depress their spirit, but rather to turn them from man
to God, the almighty, unfailing One.

"Oh! dear Brother, *the one thing* we need is to be brought
into more vivid realisation of our nearness to, oneness with Him.
Almost all our difficulties would have been either obviated or
better met had we had this more truly in our hearts. Difficulties
greater and more serious than I have ever had *crowd* around me.
The last few months have been of unparalleled pressure and
constant movement ; but I have enjoyed more leisure of soul
and rest of spirit than ever before, and more joy in the Lord.
If satisfied with His will and way, *there is rest.*

"Should there be another typhoon over the An-king riot
do not be cast down. The Lord will strengthen you and us by
His own might to bear much more than this. . . . When Jew
and Roman combined to oppose, God carried through His
cause ; and He will still carry it through."

To his mother he wrote also :

I am more happy in the Lord than I have ever been, and
enjoy more leisure of soul, casting more fully every burden on
Him Who alone is able to bear all. To be content with God's
will and way is rest. Things may not be in many respects as
I would wish them ; but if *God* permits them to be so, or so orders
them, *I* may well be content. Mine is to obey, His to direct.
Hence I am not only able to bear up against the new trial at
An-king but to be *fully* satisfied about it, not to wish it otherwise, but to thank God for it. " Even so, Father, for so it seemed
good in *Thy* sight." Still, you will pray much for us all, will
you not ? [1]

Christmas that year was a very happy season, spent by

[1] Written in a boat, near Yang-chow, December 4, 1869. By the
blessing of God the missionaries were not only reinstated at An-king without special difficulty, but the station became the centre from which a widespread work was carried on in districts never before reached by the Gospel ;
and when Yang-chow developed into a receiving home for the women of
the Mission, where they could have special help in the study of the language,
An-king came to fill the same important rôle for the men. Both are to
this day training homes of the Mission.

Mr. and Mrs. Taylor with their family in Yang-chow. That its festivities did not centre around roast beef and plum pudding may be judged from the recollections of Mr. C. T. Fishe, who had recently arrived from home.

" I was very young at the time," he wrote, " and was much touched by Mr. Taylor's amiability. He was very kind to me. I helped him in his dispensary and medical work, and was with him a good deal whenever he was in Yang-chow. He guided my studies, and was keen on the aspirates. He was, of course, exceedingly busy, and appeared quite a young and lively man. He loved playing with his children, and did not seem burdened with care. He was fond of music and singing, and used to play the harmonium for the Chinese on Sunday evenings for an hour at a time, and have them sing hymns. . . .

" His favourite theme in those days was the fifteenth chapter of John. We had many helpful times of prayer and study. He seemed to be growing much in spiritual things, and that passage was his special delight. The noon prayer meeting was held daily. *Times of Refreshing* was our favourite hymn-book, and we often sang ' Praise the Saviour ' and ' Immanuel's Land.' "

As to the household arrangements :

" They lived exclusively on Chinese food," he continued, " and I well remember the difficulty we had in hunting up a knife, fork and spoon when a foreigner unskilled in the use of chopsticks came to Yang-chow. Condensed milk was not yet on the market, and they used few if any foreign stores. There was one luxury, however—a big barrel of treacle that had recently come out on the *Lammermuir*. This was eaten with rice and much appreciated."

That they were feeling the shortness of funds and doing all they could to lessen personal expenses, so as to be able to help their fellow-workers, is evident from a letter written at the end of December in which Mr. Taylor said :

I am thankful to be able to send you seventy-five dollars for your own use, and the same sum for the school. You must husband the latter to the utmost. More than a thousand pounds less have been contributed during the first half of this (financial) year than last year. I do not keep a cook now. I find it cheaper to get cooked food brought in from outside at a dollar a head per month. Miss Faulding's school at Hang-chow costs her a trifle more than this, with a cook in the house. Let us pray in faith for funds, that we may not have to diminish our work.

To diminish one's comforts seemed to him of small account ; but " to diminish our work "—well, thank God, that was something he never had to do. Four shillings a head per month for board expenses, and food brought in ready cooked from an eating-house, might be regarded by some as " missionary hardship." But they were thoroughly happy in their Chinese surroundings, living very much in touch with the people and very near the Lord.

And then, on New Year's Eve, a beautiful thing happened —a token for good reached them that was as cheering as it was unexpected.

" My dear Brother," Mr. George Müller had written in October, " the work of the Lord in China is more and more laid on my heart, and hence I have been longing and praying to be able to assist it more and more with means, as well as with prayer. Of late I have especially had a desire to help all the dear brethren and sisters with you with pecuniary means. This I desired especially that they might see that I was interested in them all. This my desire the Lord has fulfilled, and I now send you a cheque for £10 for Miss Blatchley, £10 for Miss Bowyer, £10 for Miss Desgraz, £25 for Mr. Harvey, £25 for Mr. C. T. Fishe, £25 for Mr. Reid, £25 for Mr. Jackson, £25 for Mr. Stott, £25 for Mr. Ed. Fishe, £25 for Mr. Rudland, £25 for Mr. Cordon. Be pleased to convey these cheques to each, with the request to acknowledge the receipt of the amount.

" Likewise I enclose a letter for all the dear brethren and sisters connected with the China Inland Mission. May I ask you, dear Brother, to let it be read by all who are now with you ; and would you kindly have it copied out for those who are not with you, to send it to them with their money. I feel how I burden you ; but I think it would be a service to the Lord to let the dear brethren and sisters see, individually, how interested I am in them."

The eleven cheques enclosed were for all the members of the Mission to whom Mr. Müller had not previously been ministering. Writing by the same mail Mr. Berger said :

Mr. Müller, after due consideration, has requested the names of *all* the brethren and sisters connected with the C.I.M., as he thinks it well to send help as he is able to each one, unless we know of anything to hinder. . . . Surely the Lord knew our funds were sinking, and thus put it into the heart of His honoured servant to help.[1]

But it was not money only ; it was the loving sympathy of such a man of God, and the prayerful interest with which his gifts were followed that made them so precious.

" My chief object," he wrote in his letter to the missionaries, " is to tell you that I love you in the Lord ; that I feel deeply interested about the Lord's work in China, and that I pray daily for you. I thought it might be a little encouragement to you in your difficulties, trials, hardships and disappointments to hear of one more who felt for you and who remembered you before the Lord. But were it otherwise, had you even no one to care for you, or did you at least seem to be in a position as if no one cared for you, you will always have the Lord to be with you. Remember Paul's case at Rome (2 Tim. iv. 16-18). On Him then reckon, to Him look, on Him depend ; and be assured, if you walk with Him and look to Him, and expect help from Him, He will never fail you. An older brother who has known the Lord forty-four years, who writes this, says to you for your encouragement that He has never failed him. In the greatest difficulties, in the heaviest trials, in the deepest poverty and necessities, He has never failed me ; but, because I was enabled by His grace to trust in Him, He has always appeared for my help. I delight in speaking well of His Name."

---

[1] Mr. Müller's gifts for the next few years amounted to nearly £2000 annually. In 1870 he sent Mr. Taylor £1940. He was now largely assisting twenty-one missionaries, who with twelve wives constituted the entire staff of the Mission—thirty-three, including Mr. and Mrs. Taylor.

CHAPTER XIII

JESUS DOES SATISFY

1869–1870. AET. 37–38.

To Mrs. Taylor the new life that had come to her husband and many of their fellow-workers was a joy not unmixed with wonder. The experiences they were finding as something new and further had long been her secret of victory and peace. "It was just resting in Jesus," as she expressed it, "and letting Him do the work"—a little sentence, but one that really lived out made her life the strength to the mission that Mr. Taylor had often realised it to be. And now husband and wife were one in a new way, and helpers of each other's faith. During their first separation after that time of blessing, he wrote from Hang-chow (November 9, 1869):

It is a bright, sunny morning, but the sunshine without is as nothing to the sunshine within. He has taught me something of what is meant by " Rejoice in the Lord " ; and rejoice I must, and rejoice I do. I want you too to have fellowship, partnership in this joy. It is not that I have anything new to tell you, but I am feeling it all anew. I have hitherto used the words " Rejoice in the Lord " as meaning in our oneness with Him, or in the measure of His grace imparted to us or working in us. Of course it is not this. At other times it has been more the thought of rejoicing in fellowship with Him—in that which gives Him joy, or which is ensured to us in Him. . . . Yet, clearly, it is not this either. I now see it is *not* in what He is to me, *not* in what He is working, or has worked, or may work in, for or by me, but *in Himself* I am to rejoice ; in what He is and has in Himself absolutely.

And this, it appears to me, is the only possible or even legitimate ground for constant, unchanging, full joy. We cannot but rejoice, when our oneness with Him is realised, in His preciousness, grace, love, holiness, indeed in all His perfections. He is " the same, yesterday, and to-day and for ever." If our joy be in His keeping down sin in us, a fall or two destroys that ; if it be in His working in or through us, we may not be conscious of the measure in which He is doing so, and may be puffed up or cast down without due reason ; but if it be in Him as *He is*, this cannot change or fluctuate. . . . Ah, my darling, what ground for changeless joy we have in JESUS !

The beauty of their life together was specially seen at Yang-chow, which was more home to them than any of the other stations. There the children were left with Miss Blatchley when Mr. and Mrs. Taylor were away on journeys, and there they had the joy of reunion, and happy fellowship with their colleagues Mr. and Mrs. Judd.

" The Lord is greatly working in this city," Miss Blatchley wrote at the end of 1869. " The converts here are different from any others we have known in China. There is such life, warmth, *earnestness* about them."

Noticing that Mr. Judd was suffering in health at this time, Mr. Taylor wished to secure his getting more exercise. Duncan, who was something of a farmer, was going up the Grand Canal on an evangelistic journey, and it was quite natural to ask him to purchase and bring back a nice little horse for riding if he came across one. Mr. Taylor was away when the horse arrived, but knowing it to be his intention to ride it, Mr. Judd obtained a good native saddle, bridle, etc., and kept the animal exercised. This was just what Mr. Taylor wished. Too busy on his return to go out himself, he asked Mr. Judd kindly to continue " doing good deeds " in this way, and when leaving again charged him to remember that the horse needed exercise.

" Did Mr. Taylor never ride it ? " we asked on hearing the story.

" No, never ! he was far too busy. But he was careful to pay its expenses. It was simply his way of providing horse exercise for one who could not otherwise have taken it.

And it did me a world of good. I exercised that pony not a little, going to villages to preach, and had some remarkable experiences with it. But he was just like that, all through. In doing kindnesses, he would scarcely let you know, much less feel, that you were under any obligation. And Mrs. Taylor was just the same, loving, unselfish, thoughtful of others."

" Was she really kept free from care amid the practical concerns of everyday life ? "

" Wonderfully so ! I never saw her worried."

" Not with Chinese servants, or with the children ? "

" Not with servants, children, or anything else ! I never recall any part of her conduct, in the few years I was privileged to know her, without seeing her face shining with the brightness that comes from the Holy Spirit's anointing."

" How does the branch bear fruit ? " asked Mrs. Harriet Beecher Stowe in her little booklet on *How to live on Christ*. " Not by incessant effort for sunshine and air ; not by vain struggles for those vivifying influences which give beauty to the blossom, and verdure to the leaf : it simply abides in the vine, in silent and undisturbed union, and blossoms and fruit appear as of spontaneous growth.

" How, then, shall a Christian bear fruit ? By efforts and struggles to obtain that which is freely given ; by meditations on watchfulness, on prayer, on action, on temptation, and on dangers ? No : there must be a full concentration of the thoughts and affections on CHRIST ; a complete surrender of the whole being to Him ; a constant looking to Him for grace. Christians in whom these dispositions are once firmly fixed go on calmly as the infant borne in the arms of its mother. Christ reminds them of every duty in its time and place, reproves them for every error, counsels them in every difficulty, excites them to every needful activity. In spiritual as in temporal matters they take no thought for the morrow ; for they know that Christ will be as accessible to-morrow as to-day, and that time imposes no barrier on His love. Their hope and trust rest solely on what He is willing and able to do for them ; on nothing that they suppose themselves able and willing to do for Him. Their talisman for every temptation and sorrow is their oft-repeated child-like surrender of their whole being to Him."

Nothing could more truly describe the experience into

which Mr. Taylor was being brought, and which Mrs. Taylor so fully shared with him.[1]

That such blessing should be tested by increasing trials is not to be wondered at. Inwardly and outwardly the period upon which they were entering was to be one of unprecedented distress. In the work they were to experience the power of the adversary as never before, while in personal matters new and deep sorrows awaited them. But for the preparation of heart which unconsciously to themselves had thus been made, things would have gone very differently both with Mr. Taylor and with the Mission.

> The shadow of a cross falls deep and broad ;
> With Thee I enter, tremblingly, the shade :—
> Whence this new light which brightens round me, Lord ?
> " The fellowship of suffering," He said.[2]

To begin with, the time had come for breaking up that happy family life which meant so much to Mr. and Mrs. Taylor. They dared not risk another summer for their elder children in China, and the delicate health of Samuel, who was only five years old, made it clear that he should go with his brothers and sister. This meant separation from four of their little flock, leaving only the baby born after the Yang-chow riot to ease the aching loneliness. For some time it was a question as to whether the mother should not go herself, but the necessity for this seemed obviated when Miss Blatchley volunteered to take her place in caring for the children. To part from her was almost like giving up a daughter, so devoted had she been in sharing all their experiences. But she truly loved the children, and Mr. Taylor was ready to forgo her secretarial help in order that Mrs. Taylor might remain in China. Plan as he might, they could not see far ahead, and could only trust the little party to a care infinitely wiser and more tender than their own.

" God will provide. Oh, He is a Father ! " Mr. Taylor wrote in this connection. " My precious Mother, you can enter some-

---

[1] The booklet quoted above was one they specially valued. Mr. Taylor sent one to every member of the Mission at this time. It had appeared in full as an article in *The Revival*.
[2] Lines written by Miss Blatchley a few months later.

what into our feelings as this dark cloud draws near.   Sometimes it seems, for awhile, to take all one's strength and heart away, but God does and will help us.   It is so good of Him to have given us to know more than we ever have known of His heart, His love, His gift, His joy, before calling us to take this step.   We know as we did not that we can do all things through Christ our Strengthener, and would not faint nor be ungrateful.   And there are many mercies connected with this trial.   Dear Miss Blatchley's love and self-sacrifice we can never repay.   Next to ourselves, the children love her and she them.   She knows just what our wishes are regarding them, in sickness and in health.   I am sure you will do what you can to help her . . . and you will specially pray for my dear Maria.   When all the bustle of preparation and the excitement of departure are over, then will come the trying time of reaction.   But the Lord, Whose work calls for the separation, can and will support her."

Very painful it was, as the time drew near, to see the parting begin to tell upon the child about whom they were most concerned.   Or was it only that his chronic trouble had increased, and that with care the voyage would set him up again ?   Taking the opportunity of a decided improvement, the family set out from Yang-chow, accompanied by Mr. Harvey and Mr. Fishe.   The boats were delayed in starting, and hardly had they got clear of the city when the little invalid showed signs of a relapse.   All night long they watched beside him, doing everything that could be done under the circumstances.   But at dawn the following morning he fell into a deep sleep, and from the turbid waters of the Yangtze passed without pain or fear to the Better Land.

Before a driving storm the parents crossed the river, there more than two miles wide, to lay their treasure in the little cemetery at Chin-kiang, and then went on with the others to Shanghai.   A few weeks later, after taking them all on board the French mail which was to sail at dawn the following morning, Mr. Taylor wrote at midnight : [1]

" I have seen them awake, for the last time in China . . ." (He was returning to fetch Mrs. Taylor who was still on board.) " Two of our little ones we have no anxiety about ; they rest

---

[1] To Mr. Berger, March 22, 1870.

in Jesus' bosom. And now, dear Brother, though the tears will not be stayed, I do thank God for permitting one so unworthy to take any part in this great work, and do not regret having engaged and being engaged in it. It is *His* work, not mine nor yours : and yet it is ours—not because we are engaged in it, but because we are His, and one with Him Whose work it is."

This was the reality that sustained, and more than sustained them. Never had there been a more troubled summer in China than that on which they were entering.

" Politically, we are facing a crisis," Mr. Taylor had written some weeks earlier. " If our Government continues their present, I had almost said *mad* policy, war must result. In the meantime our position is becoming always more embarrassing. . . . You can scarcely judge how intricate our path seems at times." [1]

And yet in the midst of it all, with a longing for their little ones that was indescribable, they never had had more rest and joy in God.

" I could not but admire and wonder at the grace that so sustained and comforted the fondest of mothers," Mr. Taylor wrote as he recalled it afterwards. " The secret was that *Jesus* was *satisfying* the deep thirst of heart and soul."

Mrs. Taylor was at her best that summer, borne up, it would seem, on the very tempest of troubles that raged about them. Sickness was rife in the Mission, and before they could reach Chin-kiang after parting from the children, news came to them of Mrs. Judd's being there and at the point of death. After days and nights of nursing, Mr. Judd was almost too weary to bear up, when in the courtyard below he heard sounds of an unexpected arrival. Who could it be at that hour of night, and where had they come from ? No steamer had passed up-river, and native boats would not be travelling after dark. Besides it was a wheelbarrow that had been trundled in. A long day's journey on that spring-less vehicle a woman had come alone, and soon he saw the face of all others he could have longed to see. He had thought them far away, but Mr. Taylor, who could not leave the boat on account of another patient, had consented to Mrs. Taylor's pressing on alone to give what help she could.

[1] To Mr. Berger, February 11, 1870.

" Suffering though she was at the time and worn with hard
travelling," he recalled, " she insisted on my going to bed and
that she would undertake the nursing. Nothing would induce
her to rest.

" ' No,' she said, ' you have quite enough to bear, without
sitting up any more at night. Go to bed, for I shall stay with
your wife whether you do or not.'

" Never can I forget the firmness and love with which it
was said, her face shining meanwhile with the tenderness of Him
in Whom it was her joy and strength to abide."

Nothing but prayer brought the patient through, just as
nothing but prayer saved the situation in many an hour of
extremity that summer.

" We had previously known something of trial in one station
or another," Mr. Taylor wrote to the friends of the Mission,
" but now in all simultaneously, or nearly so, a wide-spread
excitement shook the very foundations of native society. It is
impossible to describe the alarm and consternation of the Chinese,
when first they believed that native magicians were bewitching
them, or their indignation and anger when told that these in-
sidious foes were the agents of foreigners. It is well known how
in Tien-tsin they rose and barbarously murdered the Romish
Sisters of Charity, the priests, and even the French Consul.
What then restrained them in the interior, where our brothers
were alone, far from any protecting human power ? Nothing
but *the mighty hand of God*, in answer to united, constant prayer,
offered in the all-prevailing name of JESUS. And this same power
kept *us* satisfied with Jesus—with His presence, His love, His
providence."

It is easy to read, but only those who have passed through
like experiences can have any idea of the strain involved.
The heat of the summer was excessive, which added to the
unrest of the native population. Ladies and children had
to be removed from several of the stations, and for a time it
seemed as though the Chinese Government might insist on
their leaving the country altogether. This necessitated
much correspondence with officials, both native and foreign,
and constant letters of advice and sympathy to the workers
most in peril. The accommodation of the little house at Chin-
kiang was taxed to its utmost, and so great was the excitement, even there, that no other premises could be obtained.

" Old times seem to be coming round again," Mr. Taylor wrote to Miss Blatchley in June (referring to the Yang-chow riot), " but with this difference, that our anxieties are not as before confined to one place."

By this time it looked as though all the river-stations might have to be given up. Mr. and Mrs. Taylor were making their home at Chin-kiang, to be more in the centre of things, he sleeping on the floor in sitting-room or passage that she might share their bedroom with other ladies.

" One difficulty follows another very fast," he wrote to Hang-chow at the end of the month ; "but God reigns, not chance. At Nanking the excitement has been frightful. . . . Our people have met with no insult, even on the streets, but had the Roman Catholic place been sacked, they could hardly have escaped scot-free. We need to pray for them, for the three months' Examination have barely commenced (bringing tens of thousands of scholars to the city).

" Here the rumours are, I hope, passing away, but at Yang-chow they are very bad. . . . Pray much for us. My heart is calm, but my head is sorely tried by the constant succession of one difficulty upon another. I do not think we shall have to abandon this house (Chin-kiang)."

Yet the troubles of the time were not allowed to inter-fere with as much work among the people as was possible. Mrs. Taylor, especially, with fewer household and family cares, was seeking to help the little church at Chin-kiang. In the hottest days of June she wrote to Miss Blatchley :

We have been holding classes on Sundays and two or three evenings in the week, having two objects specially in view : first, to interest the natives, those who can read, in searching the Scriptures, and those who cannot, in learning to do so ; and secondly, to set an example to the younger members of the Mission, who know pretty well that we have no lack of work. It may be a practical proof to them of the importance we attach to securing that the Christians and other natives about us learn to read and understand for themselves the Word of God.

The joy that had come to Mr. Taylor in a deeper appre-hension of living, present oneness with Christ seems in no-wise to have been hindered by the troubles of the time. The pages of his letter-book reveal, in fact, not so much the endless difficulties as the full tide of blessing that carried him through all. Though no detail is overlooked in the business part of the correspondence, letter after letter is taken up with that which was far more important. To Miss Desgraz, for example, he wrote in the middle of June after a careful letter about Yang-chow affairs :

And now, my dear Sister, I have the very passage for you, and God has so blessed it to my own soul ! John vii. 37-39 : " If any man thirst, let him come unto Me and drink." Who does not thirst ? Who has not mind-thirsts or heart-thirsts, soul-thirsts or body-thirsts ? Well, no matter which, or whether I have them all—" Come unto ME and " remain thirsty ? Ah, no ! " Come unto ME and *drink*."

What, can Jesus meet my need ? Yes, and more than meet it. No matter how intricate my path, how difficult my service no matter how sad my bereavement, how far away my loved ones, no matter how helpless I am, how hopeless I am, how deep are my soul-yearnings—JESUS can meet all, all, and more than *meet*. He not only promises me rest (Matt. xi. 28-30)—ah, how welcome *that* would be were it all, and *what* an all that one word embraces ! He not only promises me drink to alleviat my thirst. No, better than that !

" He who trusts me in this matter (who believeth on ME— takes me at my word) out of him shall *flow* . . ."

Can it be so ? Can the dry and thirsty one not only be refreshed, the parched soil moistened, the arid places cooled, but the land be so saturated, that springs well up, streams flow down from it ? Even so ! And not mere mountain torrents, full while the rains last, then dry again . . . but " out of his belly shall flow rivers "—rivers like the mighty Yangtze, ever deep, ever full. In times of drought brooks may fail, often do ; canals may be pumped dry, often are ; but the Yangtze *never*. Always a mighty stream ; always flowing, deep and irresistible !

" ' Come unto me and *drink*,' he wrote in another June letter. " Not, come and take a hasty draught ; not, come and slightly alleviate, or for a short time remove one's thirst. No ! ' *drink*,' or ' *be drinking* ' constantly, habitually. The cause of thirst may be irremediable. One coming, one drinking may refresh and comfort ; but we are to be ever coming, ever drinking. No fear of emptying the fountain or exhausting the river ! "

How sorely the lesson would be needed by his own heart, in days that were drawing near, he little knew when writing ; but the blessed Reality did not fail him.

One of the beautiful things of this summer was the corre-spondence between Mrs. Taylor and Mrs. Berger, which was growing, if anything, more helpful. Though four years had elapsed since they parted on the *Lammermuir*, there was rarely a mail that did not carry letters between them. Ninety-one of Mrs. Berger's letters remain, revealing a love and tenderness that are imperishable. And what labours, too, they disclose ; what a life of prayer in the interests of the Mission ! With all the duties of her position and the claim of hospitality, it is a mystery how Mrs. Berger could accomplish so much. If her husband was head of the home department, she certainly was its heart and hands ; though her work was done so quietly that a visitor might have thought she was hardly busy at all. The results were felt, however, in every station of the Mission. Like Mr. Müller in his Orphan Homes, this devoted friend carried all its workers on her heart. She not only loved and prayed for them, she thought about each one individually, making notes as to their probable needs. Her shopping expeditions to London were well prepared for in this way, and it came to be a common experience in China that Mrs. Berger's parcels brought answers to prayer in many a welcome form.

More precious than her gifts, however, was the spirit of this ministry, of which glimpses may be obtained in her letters to Mrs. Taylor.

" Oh, that our hearts were larger, more loving, more sym-pathising," she wrote after the Yang-chow riot, " and our heads wiser, so that you might get some little help through us ! "

He will love you through all, and be to you what you most need in every trying hour.

He and you have had dealings in secret, and therefore He can, use you in His service and make you a blessing in various ways.

Ah, beloved sister, we *say* little to either of you, but much do we ponder and pray over your accumulation of sorrows. You are living, dying for Him Who lived and died for you. I look forward to the day when my eyes shall see the smile of love He will give you. Even now you have the consciousness of His approval, and does it not suffice ?

Who can teach like God ? And do we not need to get alone with Him if we would be filled with the sunshine of heaven, and

so become useful to those around us ? Does not our strength
to meet difficulties, perplexities, annoyances, sorrows of the way,
largely depend on our having been much alone with Him ?

> The heart that trusts forever sings,
> And feels as light as it had wings ;
> A well of joy within it springs :
> Come good or ill,
> Whate'er to-day to-morrow brings,
> It is His will.

It was not easy to be much alone that summer, yet the
loving sympathy that flowed out in constant help to others
told of much inward fellowship with God. After a wakeful
night in the middle of June, partly through the illness from
which she was suffering and partly on account of the great
heat, Mrs. Taylor managed, for example, to pen the following note to Mrs. Rudland, who had just lost a much-loved
child.

MY DEAR MARY—I cannot write much, but I send a line to
tell you that our hearts grieve and our eyes weep for you. May
you be enabled to realise your precious little one as safely nestling
in Jesu's own arms, for that more than anything else will help
to assuage the bitterness of the painful separation. " Them
which sleep in Jesus will God bring with Him." They will be
restored to us ; they will be ours again—ours for ever. And
then we shall be able to understand why they were taken from
us here. *Then* we shall be able to say from the depth of our
hearts, " Our Jesus has done all things well." Meanwhile let
us *believe* this. By His grace we will not doubt either His *love*
or His *wisdom*. Let us cling to Him when His waves and His
billows go over us.

Prayer was her very life at this time. It had long meant
much to her, but with a consciousness of failing strength it
came to be in a new sense her refuge.

" It often comforts me about the children," Miss Blatchley
wrote some months later, " to remember how much she prayed
for them. I have seen her at night, when she thought all were
sleeping, with head bowed, kneeling for a long, long time on the
bare floor. And when I picture her so, I always feel that she
was praying most especially for you and the dear children."

Far away were those little ones now, and she longed

with all a mother's longing to know of their being safely sheltered somewhere in England. With thankfulness amid the trials of that hot season she thought of Saint Hill—the cool green walks and pleasant lake, the lawns around the house and the atmosphere of love within—and pictured the little travellers as welcomed to Mrs. Berger's motherly heart. Her own heart was filled with love and joy in receiving, meanwhile, a new gift from God. Born on the 7th of July, this little one was her fifth son, and called forth all the pent-up love of his parents' hearts.

"How graciously the Lord has dealt with me and mine," Mr. Taylor wrote home to Barnsley. "How tenderly did He bring my loved one through the hour of trial, and give us our last-born, our Noel. How I thanked Him as I stroked the soft, silky hair, and nestled the little one in my bosom ! And how she loved him, when with a father's joy and pride I brought him to her for her first kiss, and together we gave him to the Lord."

But an attack of cholera had greatly prostrated the mother, and lack of natural nourishment told upon the child. When a Chinese nurse could be found, it was too late to save the little life, and after one brief week on earth he went back to the Home above, in which his mother was so soon to join him.

"Though excessively prostrate in body," Mr. Taylor wrote in the same letter, "the deep peace of soul, the realisation of the Lord's own presence, and the joy in His holy will with which she was filled, and in which I was permitted to share, I can find no words to describe."

She chose herself the hymns to be sung at the little grave, one of which, "O holy Saviour, Friend unseen," seemed specially to dwell in her mind.

> Though faith and hope are often tried,
> We ask not, need not, aught beside ;
> So safe, so calm, so satisfied,
>   The souls that cling to Thee.
>
> They fear not Satan nor the grave,
> They know Thee near, and strong to save ;
> Nor fear to cross e'en Jordan's wave,
>   While still they cling to Thee.

Weak as she was, it had not yet occurred to them that for her too the end was near. The deep mutual love that bound their hearts in one seemed to preclude the thought of separation. And she was only thirty-three. There was no pain up to the very last, though she was weary, very weary. A letter from Mrs. Berger had been received two days previously, telling of the safe arrival at Saint Hill of Miss Blatchley and the children. Every detail of the welcome and arrangements for their well-being filled her heart with joy. She knew not how to be thankful enough, and seemed to have no desire or thought but just to praise the Lord for His goodness. Many and many a time had Mrs. Berger's letters reached their destination at the needed moment ; many and many a time had her loving heart anticipated the circumstances in which they would be received, but never more so than with this letter.

"And now farewell, precious Friend," she wrote. "The Lord throw around you His everlasting arms."

It was in those arms she was resting.

At daybreak on Saturday the 23rd of July, she was sleeping quietly, and Mr. Taylor left her a few moments to prepare some food. While he was doing so she awoke, and serious symptoms called him to her side.

"By this time it was dawn," he wrote, "and the sunlight revealed what the candle had hidden—the deathlike hue of her countenance. Even my love could no longer deny, not her danger, but that she was actually dying. As soon as I was sufficiently composed, I said :

"' My darling, do you know that you are dying ? '

"' Dying ! ' she replied. ' Do you think so ? What makes you think so ? '

"I said, ' I can see it, darling. Your strength is giving way.'

"' Can it be so ? I feel no pain, only weariness.'

"' Yes, you are going Home. You will soon be with Jesus.'

"My precious wife thought of my being left alone at a time of so much trial, with no companion like herself, with whom I had been wont to bring every difficulty to the Throne of Grace.

"' I am so sorry,' she said, and paused as if half correcting herself for the feeling.

" ' You are not sorry to go to be with Jesus ? '

" Never shall I forget the look with which she answered, ' Oh, no ! It is not that. You know, darling, that for ten years past there has not been a cloud between me and my Saviour. I cannot be sorry to go to Him ; but it does grieve me to leave you alone at such a time. Yet . . . He will be with you and meet all your need.' "

.   .   .   .

But little was said after that. A few loving messages to those at home, a few last words about the children, and she seemed to fall asleep or drift into unconsciousness of earthly things. The summer sun rose higher and higher over the city, the hills, and the river. The busy hum of life came up around them from many a court and street. But within one Chinese dwelling, in an upper room from which the blue of God's own heaven could be seen, there was the hush of a wonderful peace.

" I never witnessed such a scene," wrote Mrs. Duncan, a few days later. " As dear Mrs. Taylor was breathing her last, Mr. Taylor knelt down—his heart so full—and committed her to the Lord ; thanking Him for having given her, and for the twelve and a half years of happiness they had had together ; thanking Him, too, for taking her to His own blessed presence, and solemnly dedicating himself anew to His service."

It was just after 9 A.M. when the quiet breathing ceased, and they knew she was " with Christ, which is far better."

CHAPTER XIV

SHALL NEVER THIRST

1870–1871. AET. 38–39.

" My thirsty days are all past," Hudson Taylor had felt and said and written that very summer, rejoicing as never before in the Saviour's promise, " He that cometh to Me shall never hunger ; and he that believeth on Me shall never thirst." Would it prove true *now*—now that the joy of life on its human side was gone, and there was nothing left but aching loneliness and silence ? Would it prove true now —when, under the pressure of continued difficulty on every hand, health began to give way, and, sleepless at night, he found himself scarcely able to face the suffering not to speak of the labours of each new day ? If ever the reality of the power of Christ to meet the heart's deepest need was put to the test of experience it was in this life, swept clean of all that had been its earthly comfort—wife, children, home, health to a large extent—and left amid the responsibilities of such a Mission and such a crisis, far away in China.

Hastening to his side with stricken hearts, Mr. and Mrs. Judd, who had been at the coast for her convalescence, found the baby they had left in Mrs. Taylor's care so well and bonnie that his mother hardly knew him, but the one who had nursed him back to health laid with her own little one beneath the sod.

" I need not tell you how we loved her," Mr. Judd wrote to friends at home. " Our hearts are full to overflowing, but we feel unable to speak to dear Mr. Taylor about her. He is evidently so happy in the Lord Jesus that he needs no words of ours. God is at this time his refuge and strength, and for some months past has been teaching him more and more of His own fulness, thus preparing him for the stroke."

A few days only before his great bereavement, when there was no thought of immediate danger, Mr. Taylor had written to his mother at home (July 11):

I find increasing comfort in the thought that all things are really in our Father's hand and under His governance. He cannot but do what is best.

> God nothing does nor suffers to be done,
> But we would do the same, could we but see
> Through all the events of things as well as He.

And now, on August 4, he continued:

I have just been reading over my last letter to you, and my views are not changed, though chastened and deepened. From my inmost soul I delight in the knowledge that God does or deliberately permits *all* things, and causes all things to work together for good to those who love Him.

He and He only knew what my dear wife was to me. He knew how the light of my eyes and the joy of my heart were in her. On the last day of her life (we had *no* idea that it would prove the last) our hearts were mutually delighted by the never-old story of each other's love, as they were every day, nearly; and almost her last act was, with one arm round my neck, to place her hand upon my head, and, as I believe, for her lips had lost their cunning, to implore a blessing on me. But He saw that it was good to take her; good indeed for her, and in His love He took her painlessly; and not less good for me who must henceforth toil and suffer alone—yet not alone, for God is nearer to me than ever. And now I have to tell *Him* all my sorrows and difficulties, as I used to tell dear Maria; and as she cannot join me in intercession, to rest in the knowledge of Jesus' intercession; to walk a little less by feeling, a little less by sight, a little more by faith.

To Mr. Berger he had written some days previously:

And now, dear brother, what shall I say of the Lord's dealings with me and mine? I know not! My heart is overwhelmed with gratitude and praise. My eyes flow with tears of mingled joy and sorrow. When I think of my loss, my heart—nigh to breaking—rises in thankfulness to Him Who has spared *her* such sorrow and made her so unspeakably happy. My tears

are more tears of joy than of grief. But most of all I joy in
God through our Lord Jesus Christ—in His works, His ways,
His providence, in Himself. He is giving me to prove (to know
by trial) " What is that good and acceptable and perfect will
of God." I do rejoice in that will. It is acceptable to me ; it
is perfect ; it is love in action. And soon, in that same sweet
will, we shall be reunited to part no more. " Father, I will
that they also whom Thou hast given me be with me where I am."

It was only to be expected that as the days wore on there
should be some measure of reaction, specially when illness
came and long wakeful nights.

" How lonesome," he recalled, " were the weary hours when
confined to my room. How I missed my dear wife and the
little pattering footsteps of the children far away in England !
Then it was I understood why the Lord had made that passage
so real to me, ' Whosoever drinketh of the water that I shall
give him *shall never* thirst.' Twenty times a day, perhaps, as
I felt the heart-thirst coming back, I cried to Him :
" ' Lord, you promised ! You promised me that I should
never thirst.'
" And whether I called by day or night, how quickly He
always came and satisfied my sorrowing heart ! So much so
that I often wondered whether it were possible that my loved
one who had been taken could be enjoying more of His presence
than I was in my lonely chamber.[1] He had literally fulfilled
the prayer :

> Lord Jesus, make Thyself to me
>   A living, bright Reality ;
> More present to faith's vision keen
>   Than any outward object seen ;
> More dear, more intimately nigh,
> Than e'en the sweetest earthly tie."

.   .   .   .

What more can be added to experiences so sacred ?
Were it not that the correspondence of the period is too
precious to be passed over, one would hesitate to dwell upon
the intimacies of this stricken soul with its God. But letters
remain that have a message, surely, for such days as ours.
Let them tell their own story.

[1] " To *know*," he added in connection with the promise above quoted
(John iv. 14), " that ' shall ' means *shall*, that ' never ' means *never*, and
that ' thirst ' means *any unsatisfied need* may be one of the greatest revelations God ever made to our souls."

To Mr. Berger, August 14 :

It is Sunday evening. I am writing from Mr. White's bungalow. The cool air, the mellow, autumnal beauty of the scene,
the magnificent Yangtze—with Silver Island, beautifully wooded,
reposing, as it were, on its bosom—combine to make one feel as
if it were a vision of dreamland rather than actual reality. And
my feelings accord. But a few months ago my home was full,
now so silent and lonely—Samuel, Noel, my precious wife, with
Jesus ; the elder children far, far away, and even little T'ien-pao
in Yang-chow. Often, of late years, has duty called me from
my loved ones, but I have returned, and so warm has been the
welcome ! Now I am alone. Can it be that there is no return
from this journey, no home-gathering to look forward to ! Is
it real, and not a sorrowful dream, that those dearest to me lie
beneath the cold sod ? Ah, it is indeed true ! But not more
so, than that there is a home-coming awaiting me which no
parting shall break into, no tears mar. . . . Love gave the blow
that for a little while makes the desert more dreary, but heaven
more home-like. " I go to prepare a place for you " : and is
not our part of the preparation the peopling it with those we
love ?

And the same loving Hand that makes heaven more home-
like is the while loosening the ties that bind us to this world,
thus helping our earth-cleaving spirits to sit looser, awaiting
our own summons, whether personally to be " present with the
Lord," or at " the glorious appearing of our great God and
Saviour." " Even so, come, Lord Jesus," come quickly ! But
if He tarry—if for the rescue, the salvation of some still scattered
upon the mountains He can wait the full joy of having all His
loved ones gathered to Himself—surely we, too, should be
content, nay, thankful, a little longer to bear the cross and unfurl
the banner of salvation. Poor China, how great her need ! Let
us seek to occupy a little longer.

I have been very ill since I last wrote to you, through a
severe attack of dysentery. My strength does not return rapidly.
I feel like a little child. . . . But with the weakness of a child
I have *the rest of a child*. I know my Father reigns : this meets
all questions of every kind. I have heard to-day that war has
broken out in Europe, between France and Prussia ; that it is
rumoured that England joins the former and Russia the latter.
If so fearful doings may be expected ; but, " the Lord reigneth."

To Miss Blatchley, in July and August :

Nearly three weeks have passed since my last letter to you :
a little lifetime it has been. . . . I cannot describe to you my

feelings ; I do not understand them myself. I feel like a person stunned with a blow, or recovering from a faint, and as yet but partially conscious. But I would not have it otherwise, no, not a hair's breadth, for the world. My Father has ordered it so—therefore I know it *is*, it must be best, and I thank Him for so ordering it. I feel utterly crushed, and yet " strong in the Lord and in the power of His might." Oft-times my heart is nigh to breaking . . . but withal, I had almost said, I never knew what peace and happiness were before—so much have I enjoyed in the very sorrow. . . .

I think I sent you a few weeks ago a copy of some notes on John vii. 37 : precious thoughts they have been to me, and needed and true. I now see more and deeper meaning in them than then. And this I know : only a thirsty man knows the value of water, and only a thirsty soul the value of the Living Water.

I could not have believed it possible that He could *so* have helped and comforted my poor heart.

Thursday, Friday, and Saturday were all spent in bed, and part of yesterday—ague and affection of the liver this time. It throws me back very much, but the Lord's will be done. Yesterday . . . in the cold stage of the ague, I was shaking until the bed shook under me ; but I enjoyed such a vivid realisation that I was altogether the Lord's, purchased not with silver and gold—that I had not a particle of property, so to speak, in myself—that it filled my heart to overflowing. I felt, if He wanted me to shake, I could shake *for Him* ; if to burn with fever, I could welcome it for His sake.

> Come joy or come sorrow, whatever befall,
> His presence and love (*more* than) make up for it all.

By the end of the month (August) the youngest of Mr. Taylor's children, the motherless baby alone left to him of his family, was hanging between life and death. As the only hope of saving him, his father took him with Mrs. Duncan's kind help to Ningpo and the island of Pu-du. A fortnight spent there, however, proved an anxious time, and to his parents in Barnsley Mr. Taylor wrote (September 25) :

T'ien-pao has not improved so much as I had hoped. May the Lord help me to be patient and trustful. Long-continued anxiety and weariness from want of rest, sorrow from repeated bereavements and trouble in the work, from the state of China and the timidity of the workers, and other trials from without and within do make one feel the need of a strong arm to lean upon —aye, and a tender one too. And here, thank God, our great need is just met. " As one whom his mother comforteth," so He comforts us. Strengthened by His power, though troubled on every side, we are not forsaken, nor left to doubt either the wisdom or love of Him Who is at the helm.

There was much sickness in the Mission at this time. Mr. Meadows lay ill at Kiu-kiang, too far away for Mr. Taylor to reach him, and the Crombies near at hand were so seriously run down that arrangements had to be made for their leaving at once for England. While seeing them off at Shanghai, it became evident that Mrs. Crombie could not with safety be left. There was no doctor on board, and the Captain offered Mr. Taylor a free passage to Hongkong, in the hope that by the time they reached there she might be out of danger. He had no choice but to go, for the patient was in too serious a condition to be removed from the ship. The result was that all the month of October was taken up with the double journey. To set out at a moment's notice, leaving his sick child in the care of friends at Ningpo, was far from easy ; but it proved the means of saving Mrs. Crombie's life, and gave Mr. Taylor the change and comparative rest he sorely needed. It afforded an opportunity, too, of sending home gifts to his children—the little daughter of three years old and the boys of eight and nine, who were constantly on his heart.

" You do not know how often Papa thinks of his darlings," he wrote from Hongkong (Oct. 16), " and how often he looks at your photographs, till the tears fill his eyes. Sometimes he almost fears lest he should feel discontented when he thinks how far away you are from him : but, then, dear Jesus, Who never leaves him, says : ' Don't be afraid. I will keep your heart satisfied. You know it was your Father in heaven who took them to England, and who took Mamma to her little Noel, Samuel, and Gracie in the Better Land.' Then I thank Him, and feel so glad that Jesus will live in my heart and keep it right for me.

" I wish you, my precious children, knew what it was to give your hearts to Jesus to keep every day. I used to try to keep my own heart right, but it would be always going wrong ; and

so at last I had to give up trying myself, and accept Jesus' offer
to keep it for me.   Don't you think that is the best way ?   Perhaps
sometimes you think :   ' I will try not to be selfish, or unkind,
or disobedient.'

    " And yet, though you really try, you do not always succeed.
But Jesus says, ' You should trust that to Me.   I would keep that
little heart, if you could trust Me with it.'   And He would too.

    " Once I used to try to think very much and very often
about Jesus, but I often forgot Him : now I trust Jesus to keep my
heart remembering Him, and He does so.   This is the best way.
Ask dear Miss Blatchley to tell you more about this way, and pray
God to make it plain to you, and to help *you* so to trust Jesus."

    To Miss Blatchley he wrote regularly, showing how fully
he realised the responsibility of her charge and the importance of discipline in dealing with the children.   Yet his
heart craved tenderness for them too, and keenly felt their
share in his great loss.

    " You will love them all the more," he had written in August,
" now that they can never again know a mother's care.   God
will help you to bear with them, and to try to correct them by
lovingly pointing out the right way rather than by too frequent
reproof—' Don't do this or that.'   This I feel is where I most
failed with them ; and now, there is only you to make up for
my deficiencies."

    And in a later letter :

    Do try to keep their confidence and love.   Do try so to sym-
pathise that they may learn to bring their troubles to you, assured
of your willing ear and help ; so that they may tell you their
faults and even their sins.   If you can, by God's help, get this, the
boys are safe from many a snare they might otherwise be led into.

    To keep their confidence and love himself, even at so
great a distance, he toiled many an hour long after body and
mind craved rest.   Returning to Shanghai, for example,
amid other letters penned in his comfortless third-class
quarters were the following :

    MY DARLING TREASURES—It is not very long since my last
letter, but I want to write again.   I wonder if you will try to
write me a little answer ? . . . I have been thinking to-night—
if Jesus makes me so happy by always keeping near me, and
talking to me every minute or two though I cannot see Him,

how happy darling Mamma must be! I am so glad for her to be with Him . . . I shall be so glad to go to her when Jesus thinks it best. But I hope He will help me to be equally willing to live with Him here, so long as He has any work for me to do for Him and for poor China.

Now, my darling children, I want you to love Jesus very much, and to *know* that *He* really does love you very much. Don't you think your far-off, dear Papa would be very pleased to see you and talk to you, and to take you on his knee and kiss you? You know he would! Well, Jesus will always be *far more pleased* when you think of Him with loving thoughts, and speak to Him with loving words. Don't think of Him as some dreadful Being. Think of Him as very good and very great, able to do everything, but as very gentle and very kind. When you wake, say to Him, either aloud or in your hearts:

"Good morning, dear Jesus. I am so glad you have been by me all night, and have taken care of me. Teach me how much you love me. Take care of my heart: make it think good thoughts. Take care of my lips: only let them speak kind, good words. Help me always to know what is right and to do it."

He likes us to talk to Him. When I am walking alone, I often talk aloud to Him. At other times I talk to Him in my heart. Do not forget, my darling children, that He is *always* with you. Awake or asleep, at home or elsewhere, He is *really* with you though you cannot see Him. So I hope you will try not to grieve so constant and kind a Friend.

And to Miss Blatchley :

I have written again to the dear children. I do long for them to learn early, and, once for all, the precious truths which have come so late to me concerning oneness with and the indwelling of Christ. These do not seem to me more difficult of apprehension than the truths about redemption. Both need the teaching of the Spirit, nothing more. May God help you to live Christ before these little ones, and to minister Him to them. How wonderfully He has led and taught us, has He not? How little I believed the rest and peace I now enjoy *possible* down here. It is heaven begun below, is it not? May we ever enjoy it! Compared with this union with Christ, heaven or earth are unimportant accidents. . . .

Try to explain these most sweet and practical yet simple truths to the children, and to draw out their desire for these things. . . . "Out of the mouths of babes and sucklings Thou hast perfected praise." In all your intercourse with friends of the Mission, seek to deepen their realisation of the value of Christ, and of our union with Him. Should you succeed in interesting them in China or in the Mission, your efforts may end there ; but if you minister blessing to their souls, they will the better enter into Christ's command and purposes toward China, and will be more likely to become helpers in prayer, and not less so pecuniarily. After all, what we want is not money but power. . . . Doubtless it is in answer to many prayers that my own soul has been so sustained under sore trial. Seek prayer for us, and we shall have all things : let it be lacking, and our very blessings may become a snare.

"Oh ! it is joy to feel Jesus living in you," he wrote on the same journey to his sister, Mrs. Walker ; "to find your heart all taken up by Him ; to be reminded of His love by *His* seeking communion with you at all times, not by your painful attempts to abide in Him. He is our life, our strength, our salvation ; He is our wisdom and righteousness, our sanctification and redemption ; He is our power for service and fruit-bearing, and His bosom is our resting-place now and for ever."

To Mr. Berger he wrote on October 13 :

Ah ! my dear brother, what a wonderful expression is that, "In Christ Jesus." And what a wonderful *fact* is our being in Christ Jesus and He in us. Day by day I am learning a little and a little more of it, and it is so sweet, so practical, so simple, so all-sufficient ! And yet no truth makes one feel so utterly childlike. It is like playing in the shallows of a boundless ocean. . . . Oh, the unsearchable riches of His fulness ! and all is ours—for He is ours and we are His.

Hastening to Ningpo on his return, in the hope of being able to take his youngest child with him to Chin-kiang, he found him desperately ill with croup, and scarcely expected to live. This was a sore trial. But Mission affairs were urgent, after an absence of a month or more, and as soon as there was decided improvement, leaving him in the care of Dr. Parker, Mr. Taylor pressed on to Hang-chow and the neighbouring stations. Long were those visits remembered with gratitude to God.

"He came to us full of the Spirit," wrote Mr. Cordon of Soo-chow, "and, though he has lately experienced such deep sorrow, spoke only of the wisdom and goodness of the Lord."

Both there and with Mr. and Mrs. Stevenson at Shao-
hing he had much spiritual fellowship, rejoicing especially
in the progress of the work at the latter station.

At Hang-chow also there was much to encourage. The
church was prospering under the faithful ministry of Pastor
Wang, and seven evangelists were at work in the surrounding districts. Detained there by medical duty, it was a
refreshment to Mr. Taylor to see something of old friends,
including Mr. and Mrs. McCarthy and Miss Faulding, who
had been almost a member of his own family from the time
of their sailing for China. Four years of steady work in
Hang-chow had developed in her rare sweetness of character
and depth of spiritual experience. Though still only twenty-
seven, she was a most efficient missionary, a force for good
and for God widely felt in that heathen city. Her schools,
for which, in faith, she had assumed entire financial responsibility, were prospering both as regards numbers and results.
Several of the boys had committed to memory the entire
New Testament, with the exception of two Gospels, and not
a few had become earnest Christians and gave promise of
future usefulness.[1]

And there it was home letters found him—the first from
England after tidings of Mr. Taylor's sorrow had been
received. Nothing could exceed the tenderness of Mr. and
Mrs. Berger's sympathy, or their sense of the loss the Mission
had sustained.

"The contents of your letter dated Chin-kiang, July 30,"
wrote Mr. Berger, "have so stunned us that I feel even now,
after two or three days' knowledge of the facts, quite unfit for
writing, especially to yourself ; still, you so well understand
this feeling that I need not hesitate.

"Oh ! that I could transport myself and my dear wife to
your side, to share in close fellowship your deep sorrow. For,
however much you may be able to realise that the Lord has
done it, and even to acquiesce in His will, the grief inseparable
from the loss of one so deeply and deservedly loved must be
most poignant, and probably your later feelings of desolation

---

[1] One of these married, a few years later, the daughter of Wang Lae-
djün, becoming his co-pastor in Hang-chow, and is still (1918) in charge
of the Sin-kai-long Church.

will be keener than those that immediately followed your bereavement.

" The blank would be too painful, but for the loving fellowship of Jesus : but it is just here one finds the glimmer of light and hope rising in the mind. He will not, cannot fail to pour in oil and wine to the wounded heart. ' In all our afflictions He was afflicted ' ; and if we were reconciled by His death, when enemies, how much more shall we be saved, cared for and ministered to as His own, seeing ' He ever liveth.'

" Jehovah wounds and He heals. He even kills and makes alive ; and may we not say advisedly, He afflicts for our profit. Out of this, the deepest sorrow and trial you have ever been called to pass through, shall surely flow some inconceivable blessing. It may unfold slowly, like the bud ; but our Father never takes away to leave us poor."

While still in Hang-chow—home of so many memories— Mr. Taylor replied to these beloved friends, seeking to reassure them with regard to his experiences. To Mr. Berger, November 18 :

Many, many thanks for your loving sympathy in my bereavement—I cannot properly say loss. I feel it an inexpressible gain. She is not lost. She does not love me less now, nor do I love her less, or less rejoice in her. And I do from day to day and every day so delight in the love of Jesus, *satisfy* my thirsty heart when *most* desolate from His fulness, feed and rest in green pastures in the recognition that *His* will has been done and is being done, as no words can express. He only knows what her absence is to me. Twelve years and a half of such unbroken spiritual fellowship, united labour, mutual satisfaction and love, fall to the lot of very few. . . . But were the blank less, I should know less of His power and sustaining love.

And to Mrs. Berger the same day :

No language can express what He has been and is to me. *Never* does He leave me ; constantly does He cheer me with His love. He who once wept at the grave of Lazarus often now weeps in and with me. He who once on earth rejoiced in spirit and said, " Even so, Father, for so it seemed good in Thy sight," daily, hourly, rejoices in spirit in me, and says so still. His own rest, His own peace, His own joy He gives me. He kisses me with the kisses of His love, which are better than wine. Often I find myself wondering whether it is possible for her, who is taken, to have more joy in His presence than He has given me.

If He has taken her to heaven, He has also brought heaven here to me, for He *is* heaven. There is no night, no gloom, in His presence. In His presence there is " fullness of joy."

At times He does suffer me to realise all that was, but is not now. At times I can almost hear again the sweet voice of my Gracie ; feel the presence of little Samuel's head on my bosom. And Noel and his mother—how sweet the recollection, and yet how it makes the heart ache ! . . . And then, He who will soon come and wipe away every tear comes and takes all bitterness from them . . . and fills my heart with deep, true, unutterable gladness. I have not to seek Him now ; He never leaves me. At night He smooths my pillow ; in the morning He wakes my heart to His love. " I will be with thee all day long : thou shalt not be alone, nor lonely." I never was so happy, dear Mrs. Berger, I know you sympathise, and I feel I must tell you of His love. It is of JESUS I would speak :

> He brings a poor, vile sinner
> Into His house of wine.

Meanwhile there was no lessening of the pressure of outward difficulties. Politically, the aspect of affairs had for months been darker than Mr. Taylor had ever known it in China. The Tien-tsin massacre in which twenty-one foreigners had lost their lives, including the French Consul and Sisters of Mercy, was still unsettled, and the Chinese authorities, knowing that Europe was involved in war, took no steps to allay anti-foreign feeling.

" In the event of any riot now," Mr. Taylor had written in October, " not only a few plunderers are to be feared : all the people are roused. . . . Unless something is done about the Tien-tsin murders before long, I fear you will learn of even more serious troubles. The Chinese generally are satisfied that only consciousness of guilt, and weakness, have prevented vengeance from reaching the perpetrators of those crimes : in other words, that foreigners do really eat children, etc., and are now unable to defend themselves. . . . But the Lord reigns." [1]

---

[1] " Never in my lifetime has any year witnessed such events as has the year 1870," Mr. Berger had gone on to say in the letter of July 30, quoted above, " whether in relation to our mission or the world at large. Rome is now I suppose the capital of free Italy. France lies humiliated to a degree. The Pope's temporal power is no more. China seems to be rising to expel foreigners, the heralds of the Cross among them. And personally we have suffered the loss of the most devoted labourer for China's millions that could be found, as well as of a beloved friend. ' Be still and know that I am God,' is a word appropriate at such a juncture. May we all have grace to give heed to it."

It was scarcely to be wondered at that the long strain of excitement and danger should tell on the nerves, and even the spiritual life of lonely missionaries ; but it was no little sorrow to Mr. Taylor when an inland station was abandoned that might have been held, and when some dear fellow-workers seemed to fail in faith and courage. He knew the weakness of his own heart too well to be harsh toward others, and sought as far as in him lay to strengthen their hands in God. The last day of the year was set apart as usual for prayer and fasting, in arranging for which Mr. Taylor wrote to the members of the Mission :

The present year (1870) has been in many ways remarkable. Perhaps every one of our number has been more or less face to face with danger, perplexity and distress ; but out of it all the Lord has delivered us. And some of us, who have drunk of the cup of the Man of Sorrows more deeply than ever before, can testify that it has been a most blessed year to our souls, and can give God thanks for it. Personally, it has been alike the most sorrowful and the most blessed year of my life, and I doubt not that others have to a greater or lesser extent had the same experience. We have put to the proof, His faithfulness, His power to support in trouble and to give patience under affliction, as well as to deliver from danger. And should greater dangers await us, should deeper sorrows come than any we have yet felt, it is to be hoped that they will be met in a strengthened confidence in our God.

We have had great cause for thankfulness in one respect : we have been so placed as to show the native Christians that *our* position as well as theirs has been, and may be again, one of danger. And they have been helped, doubtless, to look from " foreign power " to God Himself for protection, by the facts that (1) the former has been felt to be uncertain and unreliable, both with regard to themselves and to us, and (2) that we have been kept in calmness and joy in our various positions of duty. If in any measure we have failed to improve for their good this opportunity, or have failed to rest for ourselves in God's power to sustain in or protect from danger, as He sees best, let us humbly confess this and all conscious failure to our faithful, covenant-keeping God. . . .

I trust we are all fully satisfied that we are God's servants, sent by *Him* to the various posts we occupy, and that we are doing His work in them. He set before us the open doors into which we have entered, and in past times of excitement He has

preserved us in them. We did not come to China because
missionary work here was either safe or easy, but because *He*
had called us. We did not enter upon our present positions
under a guarantee of human protection, but relying on the
promise of *His* presence. The accidents of ease or difficulty,
of *apparent* safety or danger, of man's approbation or disapproval,
in no wise affect our duty. Should circumstances arise involving
us in what may seem special danger, I trust we shall have grace
to manifest the reality and depth of our trust in Him, and by
our faithfulness to our charge *prove* that we are followers of the
Good Shepherd who did not flee from death itself. . . . But,
if we would manifest this calmness *then*, we must seek the needed
grace *now*. It is too late to look for arms and begin to drill
when in presence of the foe.

With regard to funds Mr. Taylor continued:

I need not remind you of the liberal help which, in our need,
the Lord has sent us direct from certain donors, nor of the blessed
fact that He abideth faithful, and cannot deny Himself. If
we are really trusting *in Him* and seeking *from Him*, we cannot
be put to shame: if not, perhaps the sooner we find the unsound-
ness of any other foundation, the better. The Mission funds,
or the donors, are a poor substitute for the living God.

So great was the pressure on Mr. Taylor at this time that
he wrote early in December that he had never known anything like it, save just before leaving England with the
Lammermuir Party. Missing the efficient help of both Mrs.
Taylor and Miss Blatchley, he was overwhelmed with correspondence, accounts and all manner of detail in addition to
the general direction of the work. But for Mr. C. T. Fishe,
who had now been twelve months in China, he could not
have got through at all, and it was with thankfulness he
saw his way at the close of the year to appointing him
Secretary to the Mission on the field.

Well was it that such help came when it did, for Mr.
Taylor had borne all and more than he had strength for
physically. Flooded though his soul had been with joy in
the Lord, the poor body had suffered, and he had to learn
more than ever before of the close and often humbling connection between the one and the other. A badly deranged
liver made him sleepless and brought on painful physical

depression. This was increased by lung-trouble which caused not only pain but serious difficulty in breathing. And time did not lessen the desolation. After the home-life in which he had delighted, it was a change indeed to be one of a bachelor household. But Mr. and Mrs. Rudland had been called to Tai-chow-fu ; Mrs. Duncan had rejoined her husband at Nanking ; and with his youngest child still in Ningpo, Mr. Taylor had only one or two young men for his companions. His suffering condition made him the more conscious of outward loneliness.

" Well, it is but one day at a time," he wrote to Mr. Berger at the close of the year. " To-day, by His grace, we can bear to-day's burden ; to-morrow we may be with Him where there is no burden ; or, if otherwise, He will be with us, and in His presence there is ' fullness of joy,' this world's tribulation not-withstanding."

This experience continued for some time, so that six weeks later he was writing of " days of sorrow and nights of heaviness," but of his one unfailing Refuge also, as " wonder-fully near, wonderfully real." [1] And in it all he was proving the sustaining power of the Word of God.

" ' In due season we shall reap if we faint not '—this has been to me the word in season I know not how often," he wrote to Mr. Berger early in the New Year. " And the best of God's precious Word is that the more nourishment and savour we get out of it, the more we find in it. It does not fail nor weary us with sameness, however often we come to it."

Passages which already had meant much to him unfolded new depth and meaning, and in the very darkness permitted

---

[1] To Mr. and Mrs. Grattan Guinness he had written in January (1871) thanking them for no little help afforded to Miss Blatchley and his children while in Paris, and saying as to his own experiences :

" I need not tell you of the difficulties and dangers, the pressure daily changing, and the sickness and sorrows of the past year. I think I may say that in the aggregate they have equalled, if not exceeded, those of the sixteen previous years of my missionary labour. Be this as it may, the Lord had previously taught me practically, as I never knew it before, our *present, real* oneness with Christ ; and with the exception of the past two months, it has been the happiest, the most joyous year of my life. For the last two months my liver has been so deranged that I have rather realised the Lord Jesus as my *refuge* than as my abounding joy ; but none the less precious are the blessings I receive in Him. Oh, my dear Brother ! in this dark, dark land, one does need a *deep* assurance of the presence of Jesus."

for a time, he was making more his own treasures which
through coming years he was to pour out for others.   Thus
to Mr. Müller, who in the recent death of his wife had lost
his chief friend and helper, he wrote in March (1871) :

You *do* know, beloved Brother, what the cup is that I am
daily called to drink—yes, many times every day.   You *know*
that it does not become less bitter, nor is the lack of help less
felt as days run on into weeks and weeks into months.   And you
know too how His grace can make one glad to have *such* a cup
from His hand, or any other cup He may be pleased to give.
Yet the flesh is weak ; and your sympathy and prayers I do
prize and thank you for.   They tell me of Him Who, when the
poor and needy seek water and *there is none*—no, not one drop—
opens rivers in high places and fountains in the midst of the
valleys.

It was under these circumstances he came to see fresh
power and beauty in the promises from our Lord's own lips
which had already been made so vital in his experience.
" Whosoever drinketh of the water that I shall give him,"
stood out in letters of light as he saw the full bearing of the
original.   The force of *continuous habit* expressed by the
present tense of Greek verbs flooded the passage with new
meaning, over against his long-continued and increasing
need.

" Do not let us change the Saviour's words," he often said
in later years.   " It is not ' Whosoever has drunk,' but ' Whosoever drinketh.'   It is not of one isolated draught He speaks,
or even of many, but of the continuous habit of the soul.   Thus
in John vi. 35 the full meaning is, ' He who is habitually coming
to me shall by no means hunger, and he who is believing on me
shall by no means thirst.'   The habit of coming in faith to Him
is incompatible with unmet hunger and thirst."

" It seems to me," he had written to a friend at the time,
" that where many of us err is in leaving our drinking in the
past, while our thirst continues present.   What we need is *to
be drinking*—yes, thankful for the occasion which drives us to
drink ever more deeply of the Living Water."

PART IV

THE GOD OF THE IMPOSSIBLE

1871–1877. Aet. 39–45.

Far up in the Alpine hollows, year by year, God works one of His marvels. The snow patches lie there, frozen into ice at their edges from the strife of sunny days and frosty nights ; and through that ice-crust come, unscathed, flowers in full bloom.

Back in the days of the bygone summer, the little soldanella plant spread its leaves wide and flat on the ground to drink in the sun-rays, and it kept them stored in the root through the winter. Then spring came, and stirred its pulses even below the snow-shroud. And as it sprouted, warmth was given out in such strange measure that it thawed a little dome in the snow above its head. Higher and higher it grew, and always above it rose the bell of air, till the flower-bud formed safely within it ; and at last the icy covering of the air-bell gave way, and let the blossom through into the sunshine, the crystalline texture of its mauve petals sparkling like the snow itself, as if it bore the traces of the fight through which it had come.

And the fragile thing rings an echo in our hearts that none of the jewel-like flowers nestled in the warm turf on the slopes below could waken. We love to see the impossible done. And so does God.

You do not test the resources of God till you try the impossible.—F. B. Meyer.

God loves with a great love the man whose heart is bursting with a passion for the impossible.—William Booth.

From *The Glory of the Impossible* by L. Lilias Trotter.

CHAPTER XV

THOU REMAINEST

1872. AET. 40.

MARCH winds, tossing the big elms at Saint Hill and sweeping round the house that had so warmly welcomed Mr. Taylor on his return from China, did but make the fireside more home-like when at length he had time to sit down quietly and talk over with Mr. and Mrs. Berger all that was on their hearts. Six years almost had elapsed since the outgoing of the "Lammermuir Party," years of wonderful progress considering the initial difficulties. The mission which up to that time had had but two stations and seven members, now numbered more than thirty foreign and fifty native workers, in thirteen central stations at an average distance of a hundred miles apart. Nothing could have exceeded, as we have seen, the devotion with which Mr. and Mrs. Berger had watched over its interests, giving their time and substance, their home, *themselves* indeed to its service. And now, all that must change. The love and prayers would continue, but to younger hands must be committed the task that had proved too much for their strength. Saint Hill was to be sold, its beloved owners finding it needful to winter abroad, and to them no less than to Mr. Taylor the parting was painful, and the position full of problems. For who was to take their place, and bear all the responsibility of the home-work of the mission? Who would edit its *Occasional Paper*, test and train its candidates, carry on its correspondence, keep in touch with its friends, and do all the thousand and one things they had done without expense to its funds, prompted by a love that felt it never could do enough ? Such co-operation could no more be replaced than parental care in a family, and the need for the change had come so suddenly that Mr. Taylor had no plans in view. The work in China was now a large one, entailing an expenditure of about three hundred pounds a month. His own health was much impaired by those six strenuous years, and rest of mind and body would have been grateful in view especially of a speedy return to the front. But the home base could not be neglected. Unequal as he felt to the task, there was nothing for it but to take up the entire responsibility himself, looking to the Lord to liberate him when and as He should see fit. " Thou remainest " was a certainty that meant much to Hudson Taylor in those days.

" My path is far from easy," he had written in February. " I never was more happy in Jesus, and I am very sure He will not fail us ; but never from the time of the foundation of the Mission have we been so utterly cast upon God. It is well doubtless that it should be so. Difficulties afford a platform upon which He can show Himself. Without them we could never know how tender, faithful and almighty our God is. How much we may and ought to trust Him ! " [1]

" The change about Mr. and Mrs. Berger's retiring has tried me a good deal," he wrote a little later to the same correspondent. " I love them so dearly ! And it seems another link severed with the past in which my precious departed one (who is seldom absent from my thoughts) had a part. But His word is, ' Behold, I make all things new.' "

The week spent at Saint Hill in March enabled Mr. Taylor to go through all the accounts of the mission, the balance handed over by Mr. Berger being £336 : 1 : 9. It is interesting to note that the first entry in the cash-book after this transaction was a gift of fifty pounds from the retiring Home Director. To the friends of the mission Mr. Berger wrote that same day (March 19, 1872) :

It is difficult to describe the feelings with which I commence

---

[1] To Miss Desgraz at Yang-chow, written from Salisbury at 5 A.M. on a wintry morning, February 8, 1872.

this letter. . . . You will gather from the notice on the face of this Number [1] that the management of the home department of this Mission is about to pass into other hands. Failing strength on the part of myself and my dear wife, combined with increasing claims, unmistakably indicate the necessity for this step. Our sympathies for the work are as warm as ever, and we would fain hope that our future efforts in China's behalf, if they should be of a less active nature, may not prove less serviceable.

My relation with dear Mr. Taylor has been one of unbroken and harmonious fellowship, to which I shall ever look back with feelings of satisfaction and gratitude. Mr. Taylor purposes taking the management of the home department upon himself *pro tem*, to which I think there can be no objection, as none of the funds subscribed for the Mission are ever appropriated to his private use. It is sincerely to be hoped that in taking this responsibility he will not overtax his powers, and that ere long he may succeed in finding efficient and permanent helpers. . . .

Writing to his parents, a few weeks later, Mr. Taylor used note-paper bearing the modest heading,

China Inland Mission,
6 Pyrland Road,
Newington Green, N.

It was a far cry from Saint Hill to a little suburban street on the outskirts of London, such as Pyrland Road was in those days ; and the change from Mr. Berger's library to the small back bedroom which had to do duty as study and office in one was equally complete. But how dear and sacred to many a heart is every remembrance of number six and the adjacent houses—numbers four and two—acquired as need arose. For more than twenty years the entire home-work of the Mission was carried on from this centre, a few steps only from its present quarters. The weekly prayer-meeting was held in the downstairs rooms, two of which could be thrown together ; and many a devoted band of missionaries, including " the Seventy " and " the Hundred," were sent forth from these doors, from which no suitable candidate for work in China was ever turned away. But we are running far ahead of the small beginnings of 1872, when Mr. Taylor was himself the whole executive of the

[1] The letter appeared in *Occasional Paper*, No. 29.

Mission, and it is well to be recalled by one who cherishes a vivid memory of those early days.

In the busy world of London, a bright lad full of life and spirits had given his heart to the Lord, and his life also, for whatever service He might appoint. Hearing an address from Mr. Meadows, recently returned from China, he had a strong desire to learn more about the Inland Mission, little thinking that he would one day be its chief sinologue as well as one of its most useful workers.[1]

" After a good deal of thought and prayer," he wrote, " I determined to seek an interview with Mr. Taylor ; and in company with a friend started out one Saturday afternoon for the north of London, to find Pyrland Road, where the headquarters of the Mission were located. When we reached the place, we found that but half the street was built, and away to the north stretched open fields. Traces of this state of things still exist in the name ' Green Lanes ' borne by a busy street close by. . . . The house we sought was number six, and on reaching it we were shown into the room where the meeting was to be held. Strictly speaking it was two rooms, divided by folding doors, but these were thrown open and the two rooms turned into one. A large harmonium stood at one side, and various Chinese articles were arranged in other parts of the room, but beyond this there was little either of furniture or decoration. A large text, ' My God shall supply all your need,' faced the door by which we entered, and as I was not accustomed to seeing texts hung on walls in that way, decidedly impressed me. Between a dozen and twenty people were present, including the late Miss Blatchley.

" Mr. Taylor opened the meeting by giving out a hymn, and seating himself at the harmonium led the singing. His appearance did not impress me. He was slightly built, and spoke in a gentle voice. Like most young men, I suppose I associated power with noise, and looked for great physical presence in a leader. But when he said, ' Let us pray,' and proceeded to lead the meeting in prayer, my ideas underwent a change. I had never heard any one pray like that. There was a simplicity, a tenderness, a boldness, a power that hushed

---

[1] The name of Mr. F. W. Baller is well known to students of Chinese, who are indebted to him for many valuable helps, including his Primer and Dictionary. A member of the Mandarin Bible Revision Committee, his work is now chiefly literary ; but it is interesting to recall that long before he became distinguished in this realm he was among the early pioneers of the Mission whose itinerations did so much to open inland China to the Gospel.

and subdued one, and made it clear that God had admitted him into the inner circle of His friendship. He spoke with God face to face, as a man talketh with his friend. Such praying was evidently the outcome of long tarrying in the secret place, and was as a dew from the Lord. I have heard many men pray in public since then, but the prayers of Mr. Taylor and the prayers of Mr. Spurgeon stand all by themselves. Who that heard could ever forget them? It was the experience of a lifetime to hear Mr. Spurgeon pray, taking as it were the great congregation of six thousand people by the hand, and leading them into the Holy Place; and to hear Mr. Taylor plead for China was to know something of what is meant by ' the effectual, fervent prayer of a righteous man.'

" The meeting lasted from four to six o'clock, but seemed one of the shortest prayer-meetings I had ever attended. Most present took part audibly. There were no long, awkward pauses; but the Spirit of the Lord, the Spirit of liberty, was manifestly present. The meeting over, tea was served, giving an opportunity for friendly intercourse. I introduced myself to Mr. Taylor, who asked me to stay till others were gone, when he would see me alone. This he did, taking me upstairs to a room on the first floor. He was the soul of kindness—drawing me out, making me feel quite at home, and encouraging the hope that I might one day see China and labour there. This was more indeed than I had anticipated when I set out to seek him. My idea was that perchance I might some day go as a helper to a missionary: to be a missionary myself seemed too great an honour. . . . Seeing I was young, scarcely twenty, Mr. Taylor gave me some good advice as to what to do until the Lord's way should be made plain. The interview over, I went home with a light heart, filled with gratitude to God for His goodness in thus encouraging me to hope in Him."

Longing to press forward with the great task before the Mission, it must have been difficult indeed for Mr. Taylor to curb himself to the routine of office work as the days and weeks went by. He was not in haste to rush into new arrangements, having no indication as to what might be the mind of the Lord. But when prayer for the right helpers seemed to bring no answer, and the work to be done kept him busy morning, noon and night, it would have been so easy to be impatient or discouraged! But in the dark days of 1870 he had learned some deep lessons about waiting for, as well as waiting upon God.

" Beloved Brother," he had written in this connection to one with him in China, " you are passing through a time of trial —or to change the word to bring out the meaning more clearly, a time of testing, proving. The Lord make you to stand the test, and when proved enable you to approve yourself before God and man as a labourer who needeth not to be ashamed. I ought to be able to sympathise with you, and I am. . . . This year has been by far the most painful of my life, but also by far the most blessed. In all these trials I have had the assured confidence that the work is His, not mine ; that He had permitted, or ordered, the very things which my short-sightedness would fain have removed or prevented ; that He *could* terminate our difficulties at any moment, and sooner or later *would* terminate them, if that should be for His glory. . . .

" Then again, it is no small comfort to me to know that God has called me to my work, putting me where I am and as I am. I have not sought the position, and I dare not leave it. He knows why He places me here—whether to do, or learn, or suffer. ' *He that believeth shall not make haste.*'   That is no easy lesson for you or me to learn ; but I honestly think ten years would be well spent, and we should have our full value for them, if we thoroughly learned it in them. . . . Moses seems to have been taken aside for forty years to learn it. . . . Meanwhile let us beware alike of the haste of the impatient, impetuous flesh, and of its disappointment and weariness."

The deepened current of Mr. Taylor's own life could not but be felt throughout the circle of the Mission. His chief reason for settling in North London had been to be in touch with " Mildmay " and all it stood for—the far-reaching institutions founded by the Rev. W. Pennefather, Vicar of the parish, whose ministry he greatly valued. The annual Conference convened by him for Christians of all denominations was still the only one of its kind in England, and made the neighbourhood a gathering ground for spiritually-minded people to whom oneness in Christ was more than minor differences. Mr. Taylor had been in touch with the Conference from its early days at Barnet, and now that he was a near neighbour Mr. Pennefather soon discovered qualities that fitted him to take a leading place among its speakers. The meetings of 1872 were largely attended, visitors coming from the Continent as well as from all parts of the United Kingdom to be present. Two thousand five hundred people crowded the great hall daily, and among the ministers on the platform were D. L. Moody, and the leaders of the movement for Scriptural holiness which had already brought so much blessing through the pages of *The Revival*. It was a surprise to Mr. Taylor, and doubtless to many who heard him, that a missionary, comparatively young and little known, should be asked to give the opening address, but the promise he had learned to claim was fulfilled that day in his experience as never before—" from him shall flow rivers of living water."

Not the great meetings, however, or that address so full of blessing, made the deepest impression on the young visitor from Barnstaple who was staying at Pyrland Road. Memorable as they were, she was more interested and even more helped by the family life she was sharing day by day. The place at Mr. Taylor's side that had been so empty was now taken by one fitted in every way to be a help and comfort. It had been his loved one's wish for his own sake, as well as that of the children and the Mission, that Mr. Taylor should marry again, and very unexpectedly his thoughts had been turned in that direction. Miss Faulding, the life by God's blessing of the women's work in Hang-chow, had been obliged to come home on furlough, and travelling by the same steamer—other arrangements having fallen through at the last moment—Mr. Taylor found the regard he had long felt for her developing into something more than friendship. The marriage had not been long delayed, and he was thankful for the children to see as much of her as possible before she returned with him to China. But though it was the home of a bride, the arrangements at Pyrland Road were just as simple as at Coborn Street in the early days, and Mr. and Mrs. Taylor were carefully economising in order to add to the funds of the Mission.

Miss Soltau, who had come up from Barnstaple with the earnest desire to give her life to China, was in no way deterred by the real self-sacrifice she saw at the heart of things. Hudson Taylor valued and sought after among the leaders of the Conference, and Hudson Taylor in the little office and daily prayer-meeting of the mission house hard by, might seem to be living two very different lives; but the reality of the one explained to her the growing influence of the other, and carried home many a lesson.

"I remember dear Mr. Taylor's exhortation," she wrote long after, "to keep silent to all around and let our wants be known to the Lord only. One day when we had had a small breakfast and there was scarcely anything for dinner, I was so thrilled to hear him singing the children's hymn:

> Jesus loves me, this I know,
> For the Bible tells me so.

Then he called us all together to praise the Lord for His changeless love, to tell our needs and claim the promises—and before the day was over we were rejoicing in His gracious answers."

Far from discouraged by the shortness of funds after Mr. Berger's retirement, Mr. Taylor was praying and planning more definitely than ever for advance to the unreached interior of China. During the week of the Conference a few special friends were at Pyrland Road between the meetings, and standing before the large map in the sitting-room their hearts were moved by the thought—How are these Christless millions to be reached? Miss Soltau was of the number, and well remembered Mr. Taylor saying:

"Have you faith to join me in laying hold upon God for eighteen men to go two and two to those unoccupied provinces?"

They knew what he meant, and then and there covenanted with one another to pray daily in definite faith for this, until the Lord should bring it to pass. Then all joined hands, and Mr. Taylor led in a prayer never to be forgotten.

It was about this time that, from unexpected quarters, guidance began to come as to the future management of the home side of the Mission. It was but natural that Mr. Taylor had, perhaps unconsciously, been looking for helpers who, like Mr. and Mrs. Berger, could assume the whole responsibility. But none such were forthcoming. The burden, meanwhile, of directing the work in China from a distance, as well as attending to all that had to be done at home, was very heavy. He was toiling far beyond his strength. " The thing thou doest is not good," wrote two old friends, business men in London ; " thou wilt surely wear thyself away ; . . . thou art not able to perform it thyself alone." They urged the advice of Jethro—to divide among a number such responsibility as could be delegated, offering themselves a measure of help with correspondence, account-keeping, etc.

At Greenwich also, one evening in July, the matter was brought up still more definitely. Mr. Taylor was visiting Mr. and Mrs. Richard Hill, who would gladly have given themselves to the work of the Mission had family claims permitted. As it was, Mr. Hill suggested the formation of a Council of Christian friends, not to take any responsibility with regard to the management of affairs on the field, but to divide among themselves the home work of the Mission, thus setting Mr. Taylor free to return to China.

This suggestion, reinforced by Mr. Hill's offer to become Hon. Secretary to such a Council, proved a seed thought. The more Mr. Taylor considered it, the more he saw that it was simply an enlargement of the plan upon which the C.I.M. had been worked from the beginning. A Council, not a Committee of Management, could undertake many of Mr. Berger's former responsibilities. Mr. Taylor was purposing to leave Miss Blatchley in charge of his children at Pyrland Road. Intimately acquainted with the work both at home and in China, she would be of the greatest assistance to the Council, and would be able to keep up the prayer-meeting and provide a centre for returning missionaries. Passing through her hands the daily correspondence could be attended to, and only necessary letters forwarded to the Secretary, while the Council would deal with candidates and with funds, keeping in touch with the friends of the Mission through its *Occasional Paper*. After some weeks of thought and prayer, therefore, he wrote to Mr. Hill on the 1st of August :

Could you take tea with us on Tuesday next about 6 P.M. and spend the evening ? I would ask one or two friends interested in the work, and Mr. George and Mr. Henry Soltau, to join us, and we might have some quiet prayer and conversation about the Mission and those whose co-operation it would be well to seek ; after which, perhaps, we might see our way to further action more clearly. It seems to me that a little time thus spent would be helpful, before asking many either to meet or to join us in the proposed Council.

Quietly, thus, the way opened. The meeting was held and the Council practically formed that night (August 6, 1872), which in the goodness of God has so faithfully stood behind the work for more than five-and-forty years.[1]

It was not a large balance Mr. Taylor was able to hand over to the Secretaries when he set out for China a couple of months later. A little over twenty-one pounds was all they had in hand ; but there was no debt, and with all the promises of God for the future as in the past they were without carefulness. With regard to the new arrangements, Mr. Taylor wrote to the friends of the Mission :

We trust none will think that because the form of the home-work is changed the character of the work itself is altered. Now that the Mission has grown, more workers are needed at home, as abroad. But the principles of action will be the same. We shall seek pecuniary aid from God by prayer, as heretofore. He will put it into the hearts of those He sees fit to use to act as His channels. When there is money in hand, it will be remitted to China ; when there is none, none will be sent ; and we shall not draw upon home, so that there can be no going into debt. Should our faith be tried, as it has been before, He will prove Himself faithful, as He has ever done ; nay, should our faith fail, His faithfulness will not—for it is written, " If we believe not, yet He abideth faithful."

Candidates for the Mission, he was glad to be able to announce, would have the benefit of practical training in London, in connection with the Lamb and Flag Schools and Mission carried on by Mr. George Soltau. Love radiated from that centre amid the slums of Clerkenwell—warm,

---

[1] At the first regular meeting of the Council, October 4, 1872, Mr. Henry Soltau was appointed to act as joint Honorary Secretary with Mr. Richard Hill. The remaining members were Messrs. John Challice, William Hall, Joseph Weatherley, and George Soltau. The late Mr. Theodore Howard, for thirty-five years the Home Director of the Mission, and Mr. William Sharp, now the senior member of the Council, joined a little later—the former in 1872 and the latter in 1877.

practical Christian love, drawing young and old, men, women, and children, to the Source whence it came. This was the power Mr. Taylor longed to see at work all over China, and he was thankful that those who wished to join the C.I.M. should be tested and trained in such an atmosphere. On this important subject he continued :

One thing, and one only, will carry men through all, and make and keep them successful ; the LOVE OF CHRIST, constraining and sustaining, is the only adequate power. Not *our* love *to* Christ, nor, perhaps, even Christ's love to us personally ; rather His love to poor, ruined sinners *in* us. Many waters will not quench that love, nor floods drown it. That love will seek the wandering sheep *until* they are found ; and if, when found, they are but wayward, wandering sheep still, will yet love and care for them. Oh, beloved friends, pray that *this* love may be in us, abide in us, dwell richly in us all who are already on the field, and in those who join us. But this love will not be put into any one by a journey to China. If it be not there already, a change from a more to a less favourable sphere is not likely to produce or develop it. Our aim, therefore, must be to ascertain as far as possible whether it exists, and is combined with the needful grace, ability, perseverance and tact, and is operative here in England in those who desire to go out.

In the work itself our aim will be, as heretofore, to encourage as much as possible the gifts of the native Christians, and to lead them on to an ever-deepening knowledge of and love for the Word of God, so that as soon as possible they may be able to stand alone. We shall seek, by God's help, to plant the standard of the cross in new and unoccupied regions ; to get as near to the people, and to be as accessible to them as possible, that our *lives* may commend the Gospel to the heathen whom we endeavour by word to instruct : and *you* will seek grace and wisdom from God, that it may really be so. Pray that we may daily follow Him Who took our nature that He might raise us to be partakers of the Divine nature. Pray that this principle of becoming one with the people, of willingly taking the lowest place, may be deeply inwrought in our souls and expressed in our deportment.

CHAPTER XVI

THINGS WILL SOON LOOK UP

1872–1873. AET. 40–41.

AFTER an absence from China of a year and three months, Mr. Taylor was prepared to find matters needing a good deal of attention. It had not been possible to leave any one in charge of the whole work, none of the members of the Mission having sufficient experience to fit them for such a position. Mr. C. T. Fishe, who had received and forwarded remittances and given much help in business matters, had been laid aside by a long, most serious illness, and others too had been incapacitated in a similar way. That there would be much to see to and put in order on his arrival Mr. Taylor well knew, and the voyage had been made the most of for preparation of spirit, soul and body. And now the yellow waters of the Yangtze were around them as they lay at anchor, waiting for the fog to clear before they could proceed up the river to Shanghai. Embracing the opportunity for letters, Mr. Taylor wrote to his mother that November day (1872) :

I should tremble indeed, had we not God to look to, at the prospect of being so soon face to face with the difficulties of the work. Even as it is, I can scarcely help feeling oppressed : "Lord, increase *my* faith." Do pray earnestly for me. One more unworthy there could not be. And oh, how I feel my utter incapacity to carry on the work aright ! May the mighty God of Jacob ever be my help. . . . I can form no conception as to what our course may be, or whether it will take us N., S., E., or W. I never felt so fully and utterly cast on the Lord : but in due time He *will* lead us on

Met by Mr. Fishe on arrival, the travellers learned that although there was cause in the southern stations especially for encouragement, the need for Mr. Taylor's presence was even greater than they had anticipated. Duncan of Nanking had been obliged, through failing health, to relinquish the post he had so bravely held, and even then was on his way home, as it proved, to die. The absence of the Judds on furlough, and Mr. Fishe's illness, had left the work in the Yangtze valley with little supervision, and it was important to send some one to take charge without delay. Transferring themselves and their belongings to a native boat, Mr. and Mrs. Taylor set out forthwith for Hang-chow. Warm was the welcome that awaited them in the old home from Mr. and Mrs. McCarthy and the members of the church, many of whom owed their spiritual life, under God, to the one who returned to them now as a bride. Mr. McCarthy's six years in China qualified him for larger responsibilities, and leaving Hang-chow to Pastor Wang, with help from Mr. and Mrs. Taylor, he willingly undertook the difficult work on the Yangtze (in An-hwei).

And now commenced for the leader of the Mission an experience such as he had never known before to anything like the same extent. Not only were certain stations undermanned through the absence of senior workers, sickness and trial of various sorts had told on those who remained, while native leaders had grown cold, some having even lapsed into open sin. The tidings that came to him were to a large extent discouraging, and as he began to move from place to place Mr. Taylor found plenty of cause for humiliation before God.

" I do not attempt to tell you how beset with difficulty the work is on every hand," he wrote to his mother early in the New Year (1873). " But I know you ever pray for me. And the difficulties afford opportunities for learning God's faithfulness, which otherwise we should not have. It gives me great comfort to remember that the work is *His* ; that He knows how best to carry it on, and is infinitely more interested in it than we are. His Word shall not return unto Him void : we will preach it then, and leave results with Him. . . .

" Poor Yang-chow, it is not what it once was ! I hear sad

accounts of some of the members. But they are to be more
pitied than blamed, for they have not been fed or watched over
as young Christians need. May the Lord help me to seek out
and bring back some of the wanderers."

In the wintry weather with snow deep on the ground,
he set to work at once, leaving Mrs. Taylor at Hang-chow
for a time. Lonely indeed must it have seemed to open the
empty house at Chin-kiang, his once happy home, and
gather the Christians together for little services with no
companion but the evangelist. It was just by getting into
close touch with the native helpers, however, that he hoped
to cheer and strengthen them, and for this he laid himself
out in centre after centre.

" I have invited the Church members and enquirers to dine
with me to-morrow (Sunday) after the morning service," he
wrote to Mrs. Taylor, who would so gladly have been with him.
" I want them all to meet together. May the Lord give us His
blessing. Though things are very sadly, they are not hopeless ;
they will soon look *up*, with God's blessing, if looked after." [1]

That was his practical, reasonable conviction : the work
would soon look up, with God's blessing, if looked after.
In this confidence he went on, prayerfully and patiently,
taking up himself the hardest places, and depending on the
quickening power of the Spirit of God. Joined by Mrs.
Taylor, he spent three months at Nanking, giving much
time to direct missionary work.

" Every night we collect large numbers by means of pictures
and magic-lantern slides," he wrote to Mr. Berger from this
centre, " and preach to them Jesus. . . . We had fully five
hundred in the chapel last night. Some did not stay long,
others were there nearly three hours. It was considerably after
10 P.M. before we could close the chapel. May the Lord bless
our stay here to souls. . . . Every afternoon, women come to
see and hear."

This was followed by a similar sojourn at Yang-chow
and Chin-kiang, before he went on up-river to the newer
stations.[2]

[1] A letter dated Chin-kiang, January 18, 1873.
[2] It was with great interest he visited Mr. Cardwell at this time, and
learned from his own lips something of the pioneering work in which he

" If you are ever drinking at the Fountain," he had written to Miss Blatchley as the New Year opened, " what will your cup be running over with ?   Jesus, Jesus, Jesus ! "

That it was so in his own case is manifest. Amid much that was difficult and disappointing, amid cold, discomfort, weariness, it was a full cup he carried in this sense, and the overflow was just what was needed. It was so real and unmistakable, the joy of his heart in the Lord ! and it did good like a medicine wherever he went. Most people need encouraging, not preaching at or an attitude of condemnation, and tired missionaries no less than Chinese converts responded to a loving spirit full of joy in an all-sufficient Saviour.

So the visits accomplished their object, and were continued until Mr. Taylor had been, once at any rate, to every station and almost every out-station in the Mission. Not content with this, he sought out the native workers in each place, so that the evangelists, colporteurs, teachers, and Biblewomen, almost without exception, came under his influence. It was, in measure, as with the prince of missionaries :

We were gentle among you, even as a nurse cherisheth her children ; [1] so being affectionately desirous of you, we were willing to have imparted unto you not the Gospel of God only, but also our own souls, because ye were dear unto us. . . . We exhorted and comforted and charged every one of you, as a father doth his children, that ye would walk worthy of God, who hath called you unto His kingdom and glory. . . . For what is our hope, or joy, or crown of rejoicing ?   Are not even

---

was engaged in the beautiful province of Kiang-si. All round the Poyang Lake he had travelled, and up the four main rivers on which the important cities were found. In scores of these, besides populous towns and villages, he had preached the Gospel, selling 15,500 Scripture portions and tracts. Throughout the whole of these journeys, steadily pursued for a year and a half (1871–72), he had not met a single missionary or native preacher, nor come across a mission station or a convert—for in the whole great province with its twenty millions he was the only evangelist outside the treaty port of Kiu-kiang. Well might Mr. Taylor say, " The importance of such journeys is very great, and the need of these districts truly appalling."

[1] Or as Weymouth renders it : " Gentle as a mother, when she tenderly nurses her own children."

ye, in the presence of our Lord Jesus Christ at His coming ? For ye are our glory and joy."

But it was work that cost, carried on under special difficulties, for Mr. Taylor had all his correspondence and directorial duties to attend to at the same time. It meant constant travelling, through summer heat as well as winter cold, and involved long separations from Mrs. Taylor, who could not always accompany him. At times they were together in stations that needed an extended visit ; or she would stay on where there was sickness, to give help in nursing or among the women. How glad they were of his medical knowledge in those days ! for it gave opportunity for really serving their fellow-workers as well as the native Christians. Needless to say it added to Mr. Taylor's burdens, as when he reached a distant station on the Yangtze to find eighty-nine letters awaiting him, and took time to send, the very next day, a page or more of medical directions about "A-liang's baby "—A-liang being a valued helper at Chin-kiang. But whether it meant longer letters or extra journeys, or the strain of nursing and medical responsibility, he was thankful for any and every way in which he could help. Capacity for usefulness, the power really to serve others, was the privilege he desired most.

And such an outpouring of heart and life could not but tell.

" The Lord is prospering us," he was able to write to his parents in July ; " and the work is steadily growing, especially in that most important department, *native help*. The helpers themselves need much help, much care and instruction ; but they are becoming more efficient as well as more numerous, and the future hope for China lies, doubtless, in *them*. I look on foreign missionaries as the scaffolding round a rising building ; the sooner it can be dispensed with the better—or rather, the sooner it can be transferred to other places, to serve the same temporary purpose.

" As to difficulties and sorrows, their name is legion. Some spring from the nature of the work, some from the nature of the workers. Here Paul and Barnabas cannot see eye to eye ; there Peter so acts as to need public rebuke ; while elsewhere exhortation is needed to restore a wanderer or quicken one growing cold. . . . But it is the Lord's work, and we go on from day to day. HE is competent to meet all matters that may arise, as and when they crop up." [1]

Sorely was this faith needed when, after nine months in the Yangtze valley, Mr. Taylor turned his attention to the southern stations, in the province of Che-kiang. Not that the work was discouraging; on the contrary, there was much to cheer in some directions. But it was there the unexpected tidings reached him of the complete breakdown of Miss Blatchley's health. Apart altogether from sorrow in the thought of her removal was the serious question as to how her place was to be filled. Gifted, devoted, and with some experience, matters had tended more and more to come into her hands. Not only was she keeping the mission-house going, and the weekly prayer-meeting; she was editing and sending out the *Occasional Paper*, dealing with correspondence to a considerable extent, and caring for the children she had received as a sacred charge from their mother, the friend she had supremely loved. All this made it difficult indeed to see how her place could be filled; and Mr. Taylor, unable for the present to return home, could do nothing.

It seemed the last drop in a full cup; for already, in addition to the burdens upon him in China, he was tried and perplexed by the irregularity as well as diminution of supplies from home. It was but natural that Mr. Berger's retirement should continue to be felt in these and other ways. The work had grown up in his hands. To the friends and supporters of the Mission he seemed almost as

---

[1] " I feel, Darling," Mrs. Taylor wrote in one of their long partings (Nov. 10, '73), " that we *must* lean fully and constantly on Jesus if we are to get on at all, and I have been seeking to do it, and in believing prayer to bring our many needs to Him. I have written down the names of our foreign and native helpers, that I may be able to plead for them all daily. If we would have power for what Jesus calls us to do, we must not expend it in bearing burdens that He would have us cast on Him, must we ? And there is abundant supply, with Him, for all this work, for all we need, isn't there ? It's unbelief that saps our strength and makes everything look dark; and yet He reigns, and we are one with Him, and He is making everything happen for the very best; and so we ought always to rejoice *in Him*, and rest, though it is not always easy. We must triumph with God, and then we shall succeed with men, and be made blessings to them. You know these things, and can put them much better than I can, but still it does us good to remind one another, doesn't it ? "

much a part of it as Mr. Taylor himself.   His extensive business had given him a familiarity with financial and practical matters that was invaluable, and the needs of the workers in China were upon his heart day and night.   This could not be so to the same extent with other friends, no matter how interested and anxious to help.   The members of the C.I.M. Council, moreover, were all new to their responsibilities.   They did what they could, with no little sacrifice and devotion, but they had experience to gain.

Meanwhile it was in China that the difficulties of the situation were most acutely felt.   Mr. Taylor did what was possible by correspondence ;   and irregularities that could not be dealt with in that way had just to be taken to the Lord in faith and prayer.   Small though the Mission was in those days comparatively, there were fifty buildings to be kept up and a hundred workers provided for, including missionaries' wives and native helpers.   There were all the children besides, in families and schools, making fully a hundred and seventy mouths to feed daily.   Travelling expenses were also a serious item, with a work extending to five provinces and furloughs involving the expensive journey to England.   Altogether, Mr. Taylor's estimate of a hundred pounds a week as a working average could not be considered extravagant.   Indeed it was only with most careful planning and economy that the work could be carried on vigorously upon that sum.

But there were many weeks and even months in which little or nothing was forwarded to him for the general purposes of the Mission.   Funds were not coming in plenti-fully at home, and many gifts—such as those of Mr. Müller and Mr. Berger—were sent to the workers direct or to Mr. Taylor for transmission.   This left but little for the general fund, from which home expenses had to be met as well as the current outlay for all but specially supported workers in China.

" When I arrived, I found it needful at once to dispose of the money I had brought," he wrote in his second letter to Mr. Hill,[1] " and we are asking the Lord to incline His stewards to

---

[1] Hang-chow, December 16, 1872.

send you funds, for our present supplies will soon be exhausted. What a comfort it is to know that though supplies may be exhausted our Supplier never can be so!"

"The exchange keeps against us," he mentioned a month later, "and there seems every likelihood of its remaining so for the present. We can only accept things as they are. 'The Lord will provide' whether the exchange be high or low."

And the Lord did provide, right through that year of testing (1873)—a period that would have been one of "constant and wearing anxiety from this cause alone, but for the privilege, the precious resource," as Mr. Taylor put it, "of casting the daily, hourly burdens on Him as they arose. As it was, His love made it one of much peace."

"May God make this year a year of much blessing to you," he wrote to a young worker who had recently joined the Mission.[1] "Do not be afraid of His training school. He both knows His scholars, as to what they are, and He knows for what service they are to be fitted. A jeweller will take more pains over a gem than over a piece of glass; but the one he takes most pains over is longest under discipline and most severely dealt with. Once *finished*, however, the burnish never tarnishes, the brightness never dims. So with us. If we are purified, at times, as in a furnace, it is not merely for earthly service, it is for eternity. May you so appreciate the plans of the Master that you can triumphantly glory in the love that subjects you to such discipline, though the discipline itself be sharp and to the flesh hard to bear. . . .

"Will you pray often for me? do pray earnestly. No one knows the many difficulties of my path and the deep needs I have which the Lord alone can meet. Ask, too, for funds for the many expenses of the Mission. I have had none at all, now, for some week or two past—but the Lord will provide. Our profession of looking to and of confidence in Him must not be a vain one, then it will not be put to shame."

And now, in addition to this long-continued shortness of funds and all the other difficulties of the work, had come the keen personal sorrow of Miss Blatchley's illness. Concern about his children, too, was very real. Who was caring for them, or how they would be provided for if their almost mother were taken, he did not know. And before he and

[1] Miss Emmeline Turner: a letter dated Nanking, March 19, 1873.

Mrs. Taylor could be with them again, many months *must* elapse.

" No words can express my sorrow," he wrote to his mother —a few pencilled lines as he travelled over the mountains to Feng-hwa—" for what I fear will be the end of this attack of illness. I feel it selfish to sorrow for what will be infinite gain to one so ready for the change : but, ' Jesus wept,' and He is unchanged, and can sympathise still in our grief and pain in bereavement. This has been long foreseen, but I did not expect it so suddenly. I thought the disease was so far quiescent that dear *Ai-mei* [1] might be spared till we once more visited England, and that ours might have been the privilege of ministering to her as long as human ministry could avail. The Lord seems to see it best otherwise, and we *will* trust Him. He cannot err, nor fail to do the kindest, the best thing every way—for her, for us, for ours. He will show His care for His own work."

Reaching Ningpo a few days later, it was an added pain to learn, by cablegram, that Miss Blatchley was hoping against hope for his immediate return, that she might be able to resign her charges direct into his hands. How he longed to go to her and to the children ! The difficulty as to funds alone would have made it impossible, however, for it was only by being on the spot he could divide the small supplies coming to him in such a way as to meet the most urgent needs as they arose. It meant much that he could say in the very next letter to his mother (December 2, '73) :

The words, " God, my exceeding joy," have been constantly in my heart of late. He is making me in this deep sorrow to rejoice in Himself " with joy unspeakable and full of glory "; making me trust Him, rest in Him, and *feel* an " Even so, Father " to it all.

To a fellow-worker in special trial he had written some months previously :

The one thing we need is to *know* God better. Not in ourselves, not in our prospects, not in heaven itself are we to rejoice, but in the Lord. If we *know* Him, then we rejoice in what He gives not because we like it, if pleasing, not because we think it will work good, if trying, but because it is *His* gift, *His* order-

---

[1] " Beloved Younger-sister," the Chinese equivalent of Emily, Miss Blatchley's Christian name.

ing; and the like in what He withholds or takes away. Oh, to know Him! Well might Paul, who had caught a glimpse of His glory, count " all things " as dung and dross compared with this most precious knowledge! *This* makes the weak strong, the poor rich, the empty full; this makes suffering happiness, and turns tears into diamonds like the sunshine turns dew into pearls. This makes us fearless, invincible.

If we *know* God, then when full of joy we can thank our Heavenly Father, the Giver of all; when we feel no joy we can thank Him for that, for it is our Father's ordering. When we are with those we love, we can thank Him; when we yearn for those we love, we can thank Him. The hunger that helps us to feel our need, the thirst that helps us to drink, we can thank Him for; for what are food or drink without appetite, or Christ to a self-contented, circumstance-contented soul? Oh to *know* Him! How good, how great, how glorious—our God and Father, our God and Saviour, our God and Sanctifier—to know Him!

Pray on and labour on. Don't be afraid of the toil; don't be afraid of the cross: they will *pay well.*

And now the year that had seen so much of trial in his own experience was to end in thanksgiving. " Don't be afraid of the toil; don't be afraid of the cross," he had written: " they will pay well "; and pay they did, in just the way he would most have desired.

Upon reaching Shao-hing early in December, he found Mr. Stevenson away visiting his out-stations. In a mountainous district seventy or eighty miles to the south, he was witnessing a remarkable work of the Spirit, and Mr. Taylor was only too glad to join him. Up the beautiful river he went, recalling the first time he had come over that way on a lonely journey from Tai-chow. Crossing the watershed, he had found just over on the Shao-hing side a populous district which interested him deeply. First one city and then another was visited, surrounded by numerous towns and villages accessible from this mountain stream, in none of which the gospel of the grace of God was being made known. From the steps of the principal temple in Cheng-hsien, he had looked down on the grey-roofed city at his feet, and had counted thirty or more towns and villages at no great distance. With a straitened heart he had realised something of what it meant that parents and children, old and young, in all those homes, should be living, dying, without God. To the crowd that gathered round him he had preached long and earnestly ; and when from sheer weariness he could make himself heard no longer, he had gone on farther up the hill to pour out his heart in prayer to God.

And now those prayers were being answered. Often had he thought of them, when following Mr. Stevenson's early efforts to settle an evangelist in the district. For some time they had met with nothing but opposition and discouragement, but now a very different day had dawned, largely through the conversion of one remarkable man in Cheng-hsien.

A leading Confucianist, proud of his learning and position, this Mr. Nying would have been the last to have anything to do with the foreigner who came from time to time to preach strange doctrines in his city. But he was interested in Western science, and happened to have some translation of a work upon the subject which he did not fully understand. Taking advantage, therefore, of one of Mr. Stevenson's visits, he strolled along to the mission-house, and entered into conversation with the evangelist. Soon he was introduced to the young missionary, who talked with him of the matters about which he wished to inquire. Then turning to the New Testament lying on the table, Mr. Stevenson quite naturally went on :

" Have you also in your library the books of the Christian religion ? "

" I have," replied the scholar ; " but, to be quite candid, I do not find them as interesting as your works on science."

This led to a conversation in which it appeared that Mr. Nying was sceptical as to the existence of God or the soul, and considered prayer manifestly absurd.

" If there *were* a Supreme Being," he urged, " He would be far too great and distant to take any notice of our little affairs."

Patiently the missionary sought to bring him to a better point of view, but without success ; and at length, seeing that argument was useless, he availed himself of a simple illustration.

" ' Water and fire are opposing elements,' we say, ' and can never combine. Water extinguishes fire, and fire evaporates water.' Very well, so much for our argument ! But while we are talking, my servant has put on the kettle, and see, here is water raised to the boiling point, ready to make you a cup of tea.

" You say there is no God, and that even if there were He would never condescend to listen to our prayers : but believe me, if you go home to-night and take up that New Testament, and before opening it humbly and earnestly ask the God of Heaven to give you His Holy Spirit that you may understand it aright, that book will be a new book to you and will soon mean more than any other book in the world. Put it to the proof ; and whether you pray for yourself or not, I will pray for you."

More impressed than he cared to show, the scholar went home.

" Well, here is a strange thing," he thought. "Absurd as it seems, the foreigner was in earnest ; and so concerned is he about a man he never saw or heard of till to-day that he will *pray* for me—and I do not pray for myself."

That night when alone, Mr. Nying took up the book in question with a feeling almost of amusement. How could any intelligent person imagine that a few words addressed to some unknown Being, who might or might not exist, would turn a dull book into an interesting one, or make any change in one's outlook upon life ? Yet, incredulous as he was, he somehow wanted to put it to the test.

" O God, if there be a God," he found himself saying, " save my soul, if I have a soul. Give me Thy Holy Spirit, and help me to understand this book."

Once and again as evening wore on, Mrs. Nying looked into the room, to find her husband engrossed in study. At length she ventured to remonstrate, reminding him of the lateness of the hour.

" Do not wait for me," was his reply ; " I have important matters in hand." And he went on reading.

The book had become a new book indeed, and hour after hour as he turned the pages a new spirit was taking possession of him. But for days he dared not confess the change to those nearest to him. His wife came of an aristocratic family, and he thought much of her and of their children. He knew that as a Christian he would be despised if not cast out by their relatives, and that rather than endure such humiliation she would probably leave him. Yet his heart burned within him. The wonderful Saviour of whom he read was becoming real to him as he could never have believed it possible. The words He had spoken long ago were living and powerful still. Nying felt that they searched him through and through, and brought not only a new consciousness of sin, but peace and healing. And oh, the joy that began to well up within him !

"When the children are in bed," he said to his wife at length, "there is something I should like to tell you."

It was a desperate resort, for he had no idea what to say or how to begin. But it committed him to some sort of confession of his faith in Christ, though he trembled to think how she would receive it.

Silently they sat on either side of the table when evening came, and he *could* not open the subject.

"Is there not something you wanted to say to me ?" she inquired.

Then it all came out, he knew not how ! and she listened with growing wonder. The true and living God—not any of the idols in the temples ; a way by which sins might be forgiven ; a Saviour Who could fill the heart with joy and peace : to his surprise she seemed to be following eagerly.

"Have you really found Him ?" she broke in before long. "Oh, I have so wanted to know ! For there *must* be a living God. Who else could have heard my cry for help, long, long ago ?"

It was when the Tai-ping rebels had come to the city in which her parents lived, burning and pillaging everything. Their home had been ravaged, like the rest. Many people were killed ; many committed suicide ; and she, helpless and terror-stricken, had crept into a wardrobe to hide.

She heard the soldiers ransacking the house, and coming nearer and nearer.

" Oh, Heavenly Grandfather," she cried in her heart, " *save me* ! "

None but the true and living God could have answered that prayer. The idols in the temples were helpless to protect *themselves*, even, from the terrible marauders. But though they had been in the very room, they had passed over the hiding-place where she was crouching, scarcely daring to breathe. And, ever since, she had so longed to know about *Him*—the wonderful God Who had saved her.

With what joy and thankfulness her husband assured her not only that there *was* such a Being—supremely great and good—but that He had spoken, had made Himself known to men ! Did ever the story of Redeeming Love seem more precious, or heart rejoice to tell it forth more than that of the once proud Confucianist as he began to preach Christ in his home and city ? So fervent was his spirit that it disconcerted those who thought to laugh him out of his new-fangled notions.

" You must control that disciple of yours," said the local Mandarin to the Chancellor of the University. " He is disgracing us by actually preaching the foreign doctrine on the streets. When I remonstrated with him he even began to preach to *me* ! and said he was so full of the ' Good News,' as he calls it, that he could not keep it in."

" I will soon bring him to reason," was the confident reply. " Leave him to me ! "

But the Chancellor fared no better than the Mayor, and was fain to beat a hasty retreat. Loving his Bible, and helped by visits to Shao-hing, Mr. Nying soon became a preacher of much power. Among the first converts he had the joy of winning was a man who had been the terror of the neighbourhood. Nothing was too bad or too heartless for Lao Kuen ! What power had turned the lion into a lamb the villagers could not tell, but the old father whom he had formerly treated with cruelty and neglect could testify to the reality of the change, and, like his son, was soon a believer in Jesus.

In ever-widening circles the blessing spread, till it reached the keeper of a gambling-den and house of ill-fame in a neighbouring town. His conversion was even more notable than the others, for it banished the gaming-tables, emptied his house of bad characters, and turned his best and largest room into a chapel. It was his own idea to have it cleaned and whitewashed before offering it, free of cost, as a place of worship.

These and others formed the group of converts of whose baptism Mr. Stevenson had written. Ten altogether had followed Mr. Nying in confessing Christ, and there were not a few interested enquirers. Upon Mr. Taylor's arrival in the city they began to drop in, until he found himself surrounded by this bright, earnest company of believers. And oh the rejoicing, the greetings and conversations, the singing and prayers ! It was a little bit of heaven below— a precious foretaste of the hundredfold reward.

An afternoon meeting was held in Mr. Nying's house, at which his wife and daughter were present, and in the evening the Christians met again in the chapel.

" I could have wept for joy," Mr. Taylor wrote, " to hear what grace had done for one and another of those present ; and most of them could tell of some relative or friend of whose conversion they had good hope. . . . I have never seen anything like it in China."

CHAPTER XVII

NOT DISOBEDIENT UNTO THE HEAVENLY VISION

1873–1874. Aet. 41–42.

It would be little cause for wonder if, amid joy and encouragement such as we have just recorded, Mr. Taylor's heart had gone out in quickened longing after the multitudes yet unreached; but the really significant thing is that he had never lost the vision. Amid all that had gone before of trial and disappointment, amid all that was yet awaiting him of counter-attack on the part of the enemy and searching tests of faith, the vision never left him. It did but become, if anything, more commanding. To one of the Secretaries of the Mission he had written soon after landing:

I do so hope to see some of the destitute provinces evangelised shortly. I long for it by day and pray for it by night. Can He care less?

And to Miss Blatchley (January 1, 1873):

I want you to pray daily that God will direct us as to which provinces we should attempt, and how. We have the almighty God with us; the all-wise Counsellor to guide; the indwelling Spirit to give efficacy to the preached Word. Ask for me more simple trust in Him, and boldness to attempt great things. . . . Try to get friends to promise and seriously endeavour to pray *daily* about the opening up of new provinces to the Gospel. Christ *must* speedily be proclaimed in them: how and by whom we must ask Him.

Subsequent letters breathe the same spirit, though they necessarily touch upon financial difficulties and local problems.

Pray hard; trust undoubtingly; expect great things from God. If we have a few men of the right stamp we shall soon see more than one unoccupied province entered.

But the long year wore on, and little in the way of men or means was forthcoming.

Under these circumstances it was but natural that Mr. Taylor should value more than ever the co-operation of Chinese fellow-workers. He was giving himself, as we have seen, to encouraging the native leaders, and was full of plans for developing and using them to the utmost.

" I am aiming at such organisation of our forces as will enable us to do more work with fewer foreign missionaries," he wrote to his parents in April. " I *hope* I may be able, ere the year closes, to commence a college for the more thorough training of our native helpers. Long desired, there seems more probability of our attaining this than heretofore."

To place two native helpers in each governing city of a district, with colporteurs in centres of less importance, all under the supervision of an experienced missionary, was the plan kept steadily in view, beginning with the capitals of provinces and departments. Nothing if not orderly, his mind worked along these lines, pending special indications of divine guidance. These being given, he was ready at any time to throw his best men into positions of seemingly less strategic value, if only it were evident that the Spirit of God was at work. Apart from such indications, the above plan was adhered to as closely as possible. It was essential, therefore, to develop the Chinese workers, as well as obtain missionaries of the right kind. Men of faith, with a personal knowledge of God as the Hearer and Answerer of prayer; men of stamina to rough it, and to live as he did in closest contact with the people, were the missionary helpers he longed and prayed for.

" We are going on into the interior," he wrote to a member of the Council somewhat later. " There is great difficulty in conveying much luggage, and the sight of it, in many places, would ensure robbery. If any one is not prepared to rough it, he had better stay at home at once."

And to another: " The only persons wanted here are those

who will rejoice to work—really to labour, not to dream their lives away ; to deny themselves ; to *suffer* in order to *save*. Of such men and women there is room for any number, and God will support any number : they are His jewels, and *He* values and cares for them.

Hastening to Shanghai to meet Mr. Judd with reinforcements, Mr. Taylor's mind was full of these things, and he was not altogether sorry for the lack of a receiving home, though it involved some inconveniences. It was his purpose to secure such a home on this visit, for the Mission was growing so large as to need a business centre at the coast.[1] But in the meanwhile he put up at a native inn, glad of the opportunity of seeing in a natural way what the young men who accompanied Mr. Judd were made of.

Early that November morning the new arrivals had set out to enquire for Mr. Taylor. From friends of Mr. Judd's they learned that the leader of the Mission was in Shanghai, and had probably gone down to the steamer to meet them. They turned back therefore, and on the way Mr. Judd exclaimed, " There is Mr. Taylor ! "

" We looked," wrote one of his companions, " but could only see a Chinaman on a wheelbarrow. The barrow stopped and the figure advanced toward us. It was a good thing that there was some one to do the introducing, for we should never have recognised Mr. Taylor. The weather was cold, and he had on a wadded gown and jacket. Over his head he wore a wind-hood with side pieces which fitted close to the face, leaving nothing but a medallion-shaped opening for nose, eyes and mouth. In his hand he grasped a huge Chinese umbrella, which he carried in true native style, handle foremost. In his wadded clothes he looked almost as broad as he was long, and to our foreign eyes was the oddest figure we had ever seen. He said he had made arrangements for the ladies and Mr. Judd to stay with friends in the French Settlement, and, turning to Henry Taylor and myself, added :

---

[1] Some distance down Broadway in the American Settlement, five little native shops were taken, almost opposite the old Sailors' Home. The open fronts were built up, and the whole connected with a long upstairs passage. Such was the first C.I.M. Home in Shanghai, arranged for by Mr. Taylor in November, and occupied by Mr. and Mrs. Edward Fishe before the close of 1873.

" ' After we have been to the vessel, perhaps you will accompany me to my hotel.' "

Little realising what was in store for them, the young men cheerfully agreed.

" It may be as well to say, for the sake of those who do not know Shanghai," Mr. Baller continued, " that it is divided into three Settlements, all situated on the banks of the Woo-sung River, and separated from each other by creeks. The English Settlement lies in the centre, between the Soo-chow Creek and a muddy ditch called the Yang-king-pang. On the north is the American Settlement, and on the south the French. Running parallel with the river is a broad boulevard called The Bund, edged by a strip of well-kept lawn (and beautiful Public Gardens now). Following Mr. Taylor along The Bund, we traversed its entire length, then crossed a bridge into the French Settlement, and so on and on to the point where it tails off into the suburbs of the Chinese city. Lines of junks lie along the river here, and trade and bustle are the order of the day. Here, too, are heaps of malodorous refuse, fish, vegetables, muck from the streets, filth of all sorts, while stenches, massive and unrelieved, assail the fastidious foreigner. . . .

" Turning up a side street at right angles to The Bund, Mr. Taylor threaded his way among the crowds till he stopped at the door of a native post office. Passing through the front part of the office, he led the way to a small door secured by a Chinese lock. This he opened and invited us to follow him up the stair. It was pitch dark and very narrow, but we stumbled up till we came to a door which he entered. We followed him, and found ourselves in the ' hotel.' It consisted of a room about twelve feet square, innocent of any adornment, and containing a square table, a small skin-covered box, and a native food-basket. Along one side was a raised dais, on which, if I remember aright, was spread a native coverlet. A window opened out on to the street, but it had paper of a grimy hue instead of glass, and did not count for much in the way of illumination.

" Mr. Taylor very courteously asked us to be seated, and after making enquiries as to our voyage, produced a Bible. He read the 17th chapter of the Gospel by John, and asked what we thought was the meaning of the words, ' That the love wherewith Thou hast loved me may be in them, and I in them.' I do not remember what we said, but I was distinctly impressed with the fact that he asked us. . . . Reading over, we knelt down and had prayer together, when he commended us to the Lord who had brought us to China."

So far so good : but Mr. Taylor was beginning to feel confidence in the mettle of these young missionaries, and was minded to introduce them himself, as far as possible, to things Chinese. Rather than return to the Settlement for breakfast, therefore, he decided to take them to a native restaurant. They had been out since 5 A.M., and it was now almost nine, so that they were equal to the occasion as far as appetite was concerned. But first he enquired whether they would care to wash their hands.

We replied in the affirmative ; but as there was no trace either of washstand, soap, towel or basin, we wondered how the ablutions were to be performed. Mr. Taylor went to the door and called out something in Chinese, whereupon a man appeared who was, we understood, his servant. He went to the basket in the corner and fished out of its depths a wooden basin and what looked like a pocket-handkerchief. Leaving the latter on the table he descended to the street, and going to a hot-water shop bought enough hot water to fill the basin. On his return he placed it on the table, and, taking the rag, which was, we noticed, woven with a large mesh, he dipped it in the water, and wringing it out handed it to Mr. Taylor. We watched him use it with considerable interest. By the time he had gone over the area that needed cleansing, the cloth was nearly cold. This meant another dip, another and drier squeeze, and a renewed application to face and hands, this time more in the way of polishing than cleansing. The mystery was solved. Here was plain living and high thinking ; here was *multum in parvo* ; here was economy and cleanliness combined. Sponge, soap, towel—all were included in the magic cloth ! We followed suit, and found the operation very refreshing, partly from its novelty and partly from its effects. And no compunction of conscience that we were running up a hotel bill by living in luxury, troubled us. . . . We began to realise that we were in a land where money could be made to go a long way.

"Now," said Mr. Taylor, "let us go and have breakfast."

Nothing loath we sallied forth, Mr. Taylor leading the way, and this time dived into the recesses of an adjoining street, far from the foreign quarter. After enquiry in one or two native cook-shops as to whether they had a certain kind of vegetable, Mr. Taylor finally led us into one and invited us to be seated. Four narrow forms were placed around a table. The cooking was being carried on in the front part of the shop, while customers sat at a number of square tables in the back. Our table had once been new, and probably had once been clean, but it must have been many years before we were born. However, what it lacked in purity it made up in polish. . . . A pair of chop-sticks was brought and placed before each of us, after having been carefully wiped on the shady cloth which dangled over the shoulder of our attendant. Happily for me and my com-panion, we had acquired some skill in the use of these implements while crossing the Pacific. We had often fraternised with the Chinese passengers, imitating them in the use of chop-sticks till we could take up a bean without dropping it. But for this, the fable of the Stork and the Fox would have had an illustra-tion in our case that morning.

At last the supreme moment arrived, and the waiter brought in four basins of piled-up rice and placed them before us. This was followed by several basins of hot vegetables, and a large basin of chunks of fat pork, *the pièce de résistance* of the meal. Mr. Taylor's servant, true to the courteous instincts of his race, fearing that in our inexperience we should not make a good meal, chose out the fattest and largest lumps and laid them in triumph, with a winsome smile, intended to hearten us to the task, on the top of our basins. It had some interest for us the first few times ; but after steadily going through four or five pieces in succession, it began to pall, and we had to appeal to Mr. Taylor to ask him to desist. He, good man, took our feeble protest against any more chunks to be the natural outcome of a polite training, and was rather grieved when we declined any longer to feed upon the fat of the land.

Such was our first meeting with Mr. Taylor in China, such our reception, such our first toilet and meal. Things have greatly altered since then, but I would gladly forgo all the improvements, if I could have the experiences of that morning over again. Our leader and director showed us how to do it by his own example, and stamped us at once, in all the freshness of our early zeal, with his own stamp. Hence we took to Chinese dress, Chinese food, Chinese ways as a duck to water. Personally, I can never be thankful enough for that experience. I have been in many dirtier inns since then, in many parts of China, and have had far rougher accommodation than that of Mr. Taylor's " hotel," but the remembrance of his example has made things easy and silenced murmuring.

Leaving the young men at Nanking to their studies, in charge of Mr. and Mrs. Judd, Mr. Taylor hastened back to the patients he was caring for and the stations he was visiting in Che-kiang. The twelve millions of that province, small though it was among the provinces of China, lay heavily on his heart. Far from overlooking, in his growing concern for the interior, needs more immediately around him near the coast, he was stirred with sorrow and shame over the great, waiting fields so easily accessible, that yet had no labourers. Writing to Mr. Hill from one of the southern stations in January (1874) he said :

The work is now greatly extending, and I hope will yet do so. . . . If the Lord spare me, and permit me to labour here a year or two more, I trust there will be no county left in this province in which we have not preached Christ, either by located or itinerant labours. At present there are many such. . . . Of the sixty-three Hsien cities in this province (each governing a county) fifteen have workers for Christ resident in them. Ten have been opened by us, five by others ; forty-eight remain un-opened. In one of them I have just rented a house ; to another I hope to send a couple of men to-morrow. If they succeed in obtaining an opening, there will still be four *Fus* and forty-six *Hsiens—fifty cities in all* to be possessed for Christ. And in the meantime, how many precious souls will have passed beyond the reach of the Gospel ! The Lord help us to be faithful. The claims of my family at home on the one hand, and the claims of the perishing heathen here on the other, cast me in an agony upon the Lord :—" Lord, what wilt *Thou* have me to do ? " [1]

The position was indeed a perplexing one. Miss Blatchley's serious illness, as we have seen, deprived the home-work of her invaluable services. To relieve her of the care of house and children, he had already sent home one of his best helpers ; but Miss Desgraz, who was sorely needing furlough, could not assume the many responsi-bilities Miss Blatchley had been obliged to lay down. And

[1] From Tai-chow Mrs. Taylor had written a few weeks earlier (November 17, 1873) : " When I think of your responsibilities and burdens which I am not with you to share, my heart would sink if I did not feel that Jesus is with you, loving you so tenderly and ready to meet each need of every moment, and abundantly to bless you. I am asking Him continually to uphold, strengthen and guide you, to refresh you with His unspeakable love, and to give you richly every blessing. I am very, very happy in Jesus. My joy and rest were never so full before. He has taken *all* my cares away. *We have Jesus,* and He is ready always to do for us every good thing. I must tell you more of the burdens I have been bearing, and the way God has been leading me when you come. As far as I know the reasons for and against going to England, they seem to me stronger for remaining here : the Lord will guide."

there was no one else who could, in his own absence. Fourteen months of patient, plodding work in China had done
much to improve the situation he had found on arrival,
but matters were still critical in several stations, and he
longed to secure not only improvement but advance. Then
again the state of funds was increasingly serious, and though
this indicated a need for his presence in England it made
it almost impossible for him to leave the workers on the
field. Never had they been so long and severely tried, and
it was only by keeping in closest touch with every station
that he could tell how to pray and to help. And all the while
his sense of responsibility deepened for the multitudes
around him, so dark, so needy, so accessible !

" Last week I was at Tai-ping," he continued, in his letter
of January 26, to Mr. Hill, " one of the unopened cities I have
referred to. . . . My heart was greatly moved by the *crowds*
that literally *filled* the streets for two or three miles, so that we
could hardly walk—for it was market-day. . . . We did but
little preaching, as we were seeking a place for permanent work,
but I was constrained to retire to the city wall and cry to God
to have mercy on the people, to open their hearts and give us
an entrance among them.

" Without any seeking on our part we were brought into
touch with at least four anxious souls. An old man found me
out, I know not how, and followed me to our boat. I asked him
in, and enquired his name.

" ' My name is Dzing,' he replied. ' But the question which
distresses me, and to which I can find no answer, is—What am
I to do with my sins ? Our scholars tell us that there is no
future state, but I find it hard to believe them.'

" ' Do not believe any such thing,' I replied, ' for there is an
endless future before every one of us. One must either burn
for ever in hell-fire, or rejoice for ever in heavenly bliss.'

" ' Then what *can* I do ; what am I to do with my sins ? '

" How easy it would have been at home to say, ' Believe on
the Lord Jesus Christ and thou shalt be saved ' ; but this would
have had no meaning to him. He had never heard the words
Jesus Christ, nor would he have had any idea as to their import.

" ' Some say,' he went on, ' live on vegetable food alone
(a popular method of fasting, supposed to be highly meritorious
in China, as sparing animal life, and tending to keep under the
body). ' Should I live on a vegetarian or a mixed diet ? '

" ' There is no merit in the one or sin in the other,' I replied. ' Both affect the stomach, not the heart.'

" ' Ah, so it has always seemed to me ! It seems to leave the question of sin untouched. Oh, Sir ! I lie on my bed and think. I sit alone in the day-time, and think. I think and think and think again : but I cannot tell what is to be done with my sins. I am seventy-two years of age. I cannot expect to finish another decade. To-day knows not to-morrow's lot, as the saying is ; and if true of all, how much more so of me. Can *you* tell me what is to be done about my sins ? '

" ' I can indeed,' was my reply. ' It is to answer this very question I have come so many thousand miles. Listen—and I will explain just what you want and need to know.'

" Gladly then I told him of a living, loving God—our Father in heaven ; pointing to various proofs of His fatherly love and care.

" ' Yes ! ' he interrupted, ' and what are we to do to recompense such favour, such goodness ? I do not see how it is to be recompensed. Our scholars say that if we worship Heaven and Earth and the idols at the end of the year, it is enough. But that does not satisfy me.'

" ' And you do not yet know half there is to give thanks for.'

" I then went on to speak of sin and its consequences, of God's pity, and the incarnation and death of Christ as a substitute— the innocent for the guilty, that He might bring us to God.

" ' Ah ! ' he exclaimed, ' and what can we do to recompense *such* grace ? '

" ' Nothing,' I replied, ' absolutely nothing but *receive it* freely, as God's free gift—just as we do the sunlight, wind and rain.'

" The poor old man told me of all the idols he worshipped, and was quite overwhelmed to think that in doing so he was sinning against the true and living God. It takes time for the mind to grasp such a total reversal of all it has believed for well-nigh seventy years. When my companions returned he listened again to the wonderful story of the Cross, and left us soothed and comforted—yet evidently bewildered—to think over all he had heard, more than glad to know that we had rented a house and hoped soon to have Christian colporteurs resident in the city.''

Little wonder such an experience brought to a crisis the exercise of mind through which Mr. Taylor had been passing. Two women in the same city, and a young man, had shown similar earnestness in learning from his native

companions the Way of Life. Multitudes from the surrounding towns and villages would come on market-days
to the little " Gospel Hall," and there the enquirers would
be taught until they in their turn could become teachers of
others. Just the same work needed doing in all the fifty
cities throughout the province that still remained without
the message of salvation. And oh, the great Beyond !
Must he hold his hand, and refrain from going forward as
the way opened, on account of financial straitness, or the
needs that seemed to call him home ? All the winter he had
been definitely waiting upon God, and specially since Mr.
Judd's return with reinforcements, to know " whether He
would have us prepare to work in some of the new provinces
or not, and also whether we should occupy more stations in
Che-kiang ? " His mind was increasingly assured that they
ought to do both ; that God's resources were equal to the
occasion, and that they must lay hold of His strength and
" honour Him with a *full* trust."

How definite was the step of faith to which Mr. Taylor
was led at this juncture has only come to light while these
pages are being written. In a Bible in the possession of his
son in London,[1] an unsuspected record was found—just a
few pencilled lines that obviously had a close connection
with his visit to Tai-ping and conversation with the old man
on the boat. It was written the day after the letter to Mr.
Hill just quoted, when his mind was still full of what he
had seen and heard.

Tai-chow, January 27, 1874 : Asked God for fifty or a hundred
additional native evangelists, and as many foreign superintendents
as may be needed, to open up the four *Fus* and forty-eight Hsiens
still unoccupied in Che-kiang ; also for the men to break into
the nine unoccupied provinces. Asked in the Name of Jesus.
I thank Thee, Lord Jesus, for the promise whereon Thou hast
given me to rest. Give me all needed strength of body, wisdom
of mind, grace of soul to do this Thy so great work. Amen.

It was not until many years later, when Mr. Taylor
could look back over all the way in which the Lord had led

---

[1] The Bible, a leather-bound Bagster, had been a gift from Mrs. Taylor
on his first birthday after their marriage, and was his constant companion
at this time. It was given by him to his third son, Mr. C. E. Taylor.

him, that he was impressed with the fact that every important advance in the development of the Mission had sprung from or been directly connected with times of sickness or suffering which had cast him in a special way upon God. It was to be so now ; as though a deeper preparedness of spirit were needed, before he could be trusted with the answer to this prayer.

There was quite enough, as far as outward experiences went, to account for the serious illness that overtook him before he could get back to his temporary quarters at Feng-hwa. In the depth of winter he had been almost incessantly on the road for weeks past, bearing an unusual strain even for him, physically and mentally. So persistent had been the calls upon him, that he had scarcely seen Mrs. Taylor for three months. Ten weeks out of twelve had been spent apart, though they were planning as well as longing to meet. About the middle of December they had found one another at last, in the empty mission-house at Feng-hwa, and had actually had the joy of being alone together, strange to say, for the first time ! The little honeymoon was soon broken into, however, by a call for help in serious illness. Two days' journey away, the Crombies were threatened with the loss of their only remaining children. This meant hard travelling over mountain passes deep in snow ; and before he could return a messenger had come in haste from a more distant station with news of a whole family down with small-pox.

Only waiting until the coolie could arrive with his belongings, whom he had out-distanced in his eagerness to be with his loved one again, Mr. Taylor set out once more to cross the mountains. It was a desperate business facing January storms on those heights, more than one of which could only be scaled by steps literally cut in the rock. Anxieties pressed sorely upon him with regard to Miss Blatchley and his children at home, as well as in connection with the shortness of funds in China.

" Well, the Lord reigns," he had written to his mother from a wretched inn on the road. " Trials cannot rob me of this unchanging source of joy and strength."

But the overtaxed physical powers at length gave way, and his patients were no sooner convalescent than Mr. Taylor himself went down with fever, and was so ill as to be hardly able to get back to Feng-hwa. The interval, from the time when they were out of danger until he could safely leave them, he had employed in the evangelistic journey which brought him in touch with old Dzing, and led to the definite prayer recorded above.

And now, how unpromising seemed the sequel to that step of faith ! Week after week he lay in helplessness and suffering, able to do nothing but wait upon the Lord. Of all that in His providence was drawing near, Hudson Taylor was unconscious. He only knew that God had given him to see something of the purposes of His heart ; that he was sharing in some measure the compassions of Christ for the lost and perishing, and that the love of which he felt the yearnings was His Own infinite love. That that love, that purpose, would find a way to bless, he could not doubt. So he just prayed on—holding in faith to the heavenly vision ; ready to go forward when and as the Lord should open the way. Never had advance seemed less possible. But in the Bible beside him was the record of that transaction of his soul with God, and in his heart was the conviction that even for the inland provinces—the Western Branch of the mission he longed to plant, as a stepping-stone to the far interior—God's time had almost come.

And then, as he lay there slowly recovering, a letter was put into his hands that had been two months on its way from England. It was from an unknown friend, a Mrs. Grace of Wycombe, Buckinghamshire, who had only recently become interested in the Mission.

" My dear Sir," the somewhat trembling hand had written early in December, " *I bless God*, in two months I hope to place at the disposal of your Council, for *further* extension of Inland China Mission work, £800. Please remember, for *fresh* provinces. . . . I think your receipt-form beautiful—' The LORD our Banner : the LORD will provide.' If faith is put forth and praise sent up, I am sure that Jehovah of Hosts will honour it."

Eight hundred pounds for " fresh provinces," for

" further extension " of inland work—hardly could the convalescent believe he read aright ! Could any one have penned those words who did not know the exercise of soul he had been passing through all those months ? The very secrets of his heart seemed to look back at him from that sheet of foreign note-paper. Even before the prayer recorded in his Bible, the letter had been sent off ; and now, just when it was most needed, it had reached him with its wonderful confirmation.

From his sick-room back to the Yangtze valley was the next step, and those spring days witnessed a happy gathering at Chin-kiang. There, as in almost all the stations, new life had come to the little company of believers. Young converts were being received into the Church, and native leaders were growing in grace and usefulness.[1] Older missionaries were more hopeful, amid the needs of their great districts, and the young men, who had made good progress with the language, were eager for pioneering work. As many as could leave their stations came to meet Mr. Taylor for a week of prayer and conference, before he and Mr. Judd set out to seek, up the great river, a home for the new Western Branch.

[1] To his parents, Mr. Taylor wrote in April : " To seven new counties we have been enabled to carry the Gospel since I reached China, and in nearly as many others fresh towns have been opened up. The Hang-chow Church has sent out its first missionary, *chosen by themselves and supported by their own gifts.*" He added in May : " Mr. Stevenson has blessing in all his stations, and has baptized eight since I was with him. Wang Lae-djun is also prospered. Recently he has baptized the first converts in three out-stations. Mr. Crombie writes of blessing in Feng-hwa and Ning-hai ; and we are meeting with encouragement in the northern stations.
To Mr. Hill he gave further details (May 29) : " We have the joy of cheering reports as to spiritual progress from all the stations nearly. Mr. Stott writes that the work has not been so encouraging at Wen-chow for a year and a half or two years. Mr. Rudland tells of another, the seventeenth candidate for baptism at Dien-tsi (when an idol temple had been given for a place of worship). . . . Four persons were baptized here (Chin-kiang) yesterday, and we had good meetings. One of these is a native of Hunan, one of the unoccupied provinces which has long been on our hearts. (' His soul seems all on fire for the conversion of his own people,' Mr. Taylor added in a later letter.) Is it not good of God so to encourage us when we are sorely tried for want of funds ? "
And in June Mr. Taylor reported five or six enquirers at Tai-ping— where he had met the old man who did not know what to do with his sins— and baptisms also from several other stations.

It was not any improvement in the state of funds that accounted for the new note of joy and confidence.

" I feel no anxiety," Mr. Taylor wrote to his mother on the 1st of May, " though for a month past I have not had a dollar in hand for the general purposes of the Mission. The Lord will provide."

Quoting again the hymn they were singing daily at the Conference—" In some way or other, the Lord will provide " —he wrote to Miss Blatchley a little later :

I am sure that if we will but wait, the Lord *will* provide. . . . We go shortly, that is, Mr. Judd and myself, to see if we can procure headquarters at Wu-chang from which to open up Western China, as the Lord may enable us. We are urged on to make this effort now, though so weak-handed, both by the needs of the unopened provinces and by our having funds for commencing work in them, while we have none for the general work. . . . I cannot conceive how we shall be helped through next month, though I fully expect we shall be. The Lord cannot and will not fail us.

To Mrs. Taylor he had written during April, " The balance in hand yesterday was sixty-seven cents ! The Lord reigns : herein is our joy and confidence." And to Mr. Baller he added, when the balance was still lower, " We have this, and all the promises of God."

" Twenty-five cents *plus* all the promises of God," wrote the latter, recalling the experience, " why, one felt as rich as Croesus ! and sang—

> I would not change my blest estate
> For all the earth holds good or great ;
> And while my faith can keep its hold,
> I envy not the sinner's gold.

One thing that concerned Mr. Taylor more at this time than shortness of supplies was the fear lest, in their desire to help, friends at home should be tempted to make appeals in meetings, or even more personally, for funds. To one and another he wrote very earnestly on the subject, begging that this might not be done. The trial through which they were passing was no reason, to his mind, for changing the basis on which they had been led to found the Mission. In acknowledging one of Mr. George Müller's generous contributions [1] he had written early in April :

The work generally is *very* cheering, and we feel happier than ever in the Lord and in His service. Our faith never was so much tried : His faithfulness never so much experienced.

And this position was to him far more safe and blessed, as long as the trial was permitted, than the alternative of going into debt or making appeals to man. How truly this was the case may be seen from the following letter to a member of the Council, written just after the Conference at Chin-kiang (April 24) :

I am truly sorry that you should be distressed at not having funds to send me. May I not say, " Be careful for nothing." We should use *all* care to economise what God does send us ; but when that is done bear no care about real or apparent lack. After living on *God's faithfulness* for many years, I can testify that times of want have ever been times of special blessing, or have led to them. I do beg that never any appeal for funds be put forward, save to God in prayer. When our work becomes a begging work, it dies. God is faithful, must be so. " The LORD is my Shepherd, I shall not want." He has said : " Take *no* thought (anxiety) for your life, what ye shall eat, or what ye shall drink, nor yet for your body, what ye shall put on. But seek first (to promote) the kingdom of God, and (to fulfil) His righteousness, and *all these things shall be added unto you.*"
" Obedience is better than sacrifice, and to hearken than the fat of rams." It is doubting, beloved Brother, not trusting that is tempting the Lord.

At this very time, it is interesting to notice, Mr. and Mrs. Taylor were themselves giving largely to the work in various ways. A considerable proportion of all they received for their own use was passed on to fellow-workers, and a property yielding an income of four hundred pounds a year, which had recently come to Mrs. Taylor from a relative, was joyfully set apart for the Lord's service. The intimate friend to whom Mr. Taylor was writing had questioned the wisdom of this course, which led to one of the

---

[1] Most opportunely had this help arrived at the beginning of the quarter (gifts of £325 in all)—ten cheques for members of the Mission, including one of £30 for himself.

few references he ever made to the subject.   Anxious that
their position should not be misunderstood, he continued in
this letter :

As to the property my dear wife has given to the Lord for
His service, I most cordially agreed with her in the step, and
do so now.   I believe that in so doing she has made hers for
ever that which was her Master's, and only entrusted to her so
to use.   It is not a modern question, this of principal or interest,
endowment or voluntary support, and we cannot expect *all* to
see alike on the subject.   We might capitalise the annual income
of the Mission, and use only the interest ; but I fear the income
would soon be small, and the work not very extensive.

But you may, I think, be mistaken as to our thought and
intention, as well as with regard to the nature of the property.
The whole cannot be realised, half of it being reserved to provide
annuities. . . . At present all we have is about four hundred
pounds of annual interest, payable in varying quarterly sums.
We do not propose to put either principal or interest into the
General Fund (though we might be led to do so), but to use it,
equally avoiding stint or lavishness, as the Lord may direct,
for special purposes not met by the General Fund.   We are
neither of us inexperienced, unacquainted with the value of
money, or unaccustomed either to its want or possession.   There
are few more cool and calculating, perhaps, than we are ; but
in all our calculations we calculate on God's faithfulness, or seek
to do so.   Hitherto we have not been put to shame, nor have I
any anxiety or fear lest we should be in the future.

Never has our work entailed such real trial or so much exercise
of faith.   The sickness of our beloved sister, Miss Blatchley,
and her strong desire to see me ; the needs of our dear children ;
the state of the funds ; the changes required in the work to
admit of some going home, others coming out, and of further
expansion, and many other things not easily expressed in writing
would be crushing anxieties if we were to bear them.   But the
Lord bears us and them too, and makes our hearts so very glad
in Himself—not Himself plus a bank balance—that I have never
known greater freedom from anxiety and care.

The other week when I reached Shanghai, I was in great and
immediate need.   The mails were both in—no remittance ! and
the folios showed no balances at home.   I cast the burden on
the Lord.   Next morning on waking I felt inclined to trouble,
but the Lord gave me a word, " I know their sorrows, and I am
come down to deliver. . . . *Certainly* I will be with thee " ; and
before 6 A.M. I was as sure that help was at hand as when, near

noon, I received a letter from Mr. Müller which had been to Ningpo, and was thus delayed in reaching me, and which contained more than three hundred pounds.

My need now is great and urgent ; God is greater and more near : and because *He is*, and is *what He is*, all must be, all is, all will be well. Oh, my dear Brother, the joy of knowing the LIVING GOD, of seeing the LIVING GOD, of resting on the LIVING GOD in our very special and peculiar circumstances ! I am but His agent. He will look after His own honour, provide for His own servants, and supply all our need according to His own riches—you helping by your prayers and work of faith and labour of love. As to whether He will make the widow's oil and meal go a long way, or send her more—it is merely a question of detail ; the result is sure. The righteous shall not be forsaken, nor his seed beg their bread. In Christ, *all* the promises are Yea and Amen.

CHAPTER XVIII

OUT OF WEAKNESS WERE MADE STRONG

1874-1875. AET. 42-43.

IT was a memorable day for Hudson Taylor when he set out with his like-minded companion to follow the mighty Yangtze, if not to its upper waters, at any rate to its confluence with the tributary Han, where the metropolis of mid-China formed the farthest outpost of Protestant missions. Six hundred miles from the coast, this great centre of culture and commerce lay far beyond any inland station he had yet visited ; but northward, westward, southward of it stretched the nine unopened provinces, from the tropical jungles of Burma to the barren steppes of Mongolia and the snowy ramparts of Tibet. Vast was that waiting world, and vast the longings with which Hudson Taylor turned his face—as he had long turned his heart—toward its silent appeal.

" My soul yearns, oh ! how intensely," he wrote at this time (June 1874), " for the evangelisation of the hundred and eighty millions of these unoccupied provinces. Oh, that I had a hundred lives to give or spend for their good ! "

Meanwhile in England very different were the experiences of those most closely connected with the work. Tenderly cared for by Miss Soltau, Mrs. Duncan, and others, Miss Blatchley still lingered, but it was in great weakness and suffering ; and the ebb-tide of her life seemed to leave the cause she had so faithfully served almost stranded.

" I seem to see her now," wrote Miss Soltau, " her lovely face so wan, lying on the sofa, with the tears running down her cheeks as she prayed for every missionary at every station. Oh, the burden on that loving heart of the great work ! And so conscious was she that she was leaving it before long for the Better Land. One Saturday Miss Pillans Smith might be with us, and another, dear Mrs. Duncan. For many weeks I do not think we ever numbered ten ; and never shall I forget the feeling of desolation and helplessness when we two would find ourselves alone—as if no one in the wide world cared for the little band of toilers in far-off China ! "

It had been to Mr. Taylor, as we have seen, a keen sorrow that he could not hasten home when first he heard of this illness, to relieve the beloved friend to whom he and his, as well as the Mission, owed so much. But month after month had gone by, and it was not until he had seen Mr. Judd in possession of suitable quarters at Wu-chang [1] that the way began to open for his return to England. But even before he could leave China, the one he so hoped to succour had set out on a longer journey. For her all need of human help was past.

" Dear, much-loved Emily ! " wrote Miss Soltau. " Our loss only those can estimate who really knew her. . . . Yet, not for one moment would I recall that tender heart from its joy in His embrace. . . . Very lovely have been the last two years, . . . such growth in grace, such sweet rest in the Lord, such loving tenderness to all around ! It was a great privilege to be with her."

. . . . . .

" The most glorious triumphs of Christ are spiritual," we quote from the pen of the Rev. H. Grattan Guinness,[2] " and His

---

[1] Not that the house first rented proved to be the permanent headquarters of the Western Branch of the C.I.M. No fewer than twelve different arrangements had to be made—twelve houses found and rented, if not occupied for longer or shorter periods—before the missionaries were allowed to settle in that proud, anti-foreign capital of two provinces. Across the river in the treaty port of Hankow, it might have been easier to obtain premises ; but the London Missionary Society and the Wesleyan Mission were already there, represented by able and devoted workers. Time after time, as they faced their seemingly endless difficulties, Mr. and Mrs. Judd found, in common with all the pioneers of the Mission, that a day set apart for prayer and fasting turned the tide, and brought deliverance as well as blessing.

[2] In their newly founded East London Institute for Home and Foreign Missions, Mr. and Mrs. Guinness were even then preparing not a few of the pioneers destined to open up inland China. Messrs. Baller and Henry

noblest work is that wrought in the secret of the soul. Not the conquest of kingdoms, but *self-conquest*; not the renunciation of anything external merely, but *self-renunciation*; not the consecration of substance, but *self-consecration* in the service of GOD and man—these are the hardest deeds to accomplish, and the most divine attainments. They shine with the peculiar light of Calvary.

" Emily Blatchley, though unknown to the world, was a true heroine, and an instance of this noble, Christ-like self-sacrifice for the good of others. Her memory is fragrant, for her life was consecrated to Christ and the salvation of the heathen. For his sake she took care of a little flock, the children of the Rev. J. Hudson Taylor of the China Inland Mission. She tended them in health and in sickness, at home and abroad, for years ; and as long as health permitted was their only teacher. This she did to help forward the evangelisation of China, by setting Mr. and Mrs. Taylor as free as possible for directly missionary work. Not content with caring for Mr. Taylor's children, she became a Secretary of the Mission. She wrote in its interest thousands of letters ; she kept its accounts ; she edited its *Occasional Papers* ; she helped to bear its burdens ; she worked long hours, and often far into the night. She not only toiled with head and hand, but with her heart too, for she prayed for the Mission. She daily remembered its missionaries by name at the Throne of Grace, and pleaded continually its cause with God. She suffered too. She ' endured hardness ' when in China and on long journeys, putting up with much discomfort. She ministered to her fellow-missionaries, and nursed them when they were sick. She bore the trial of her faith and that of love as well, for in the cause of missions she sacrificed her heart's affections. And all this she did in a quiet, unpretending way, and with a calm perseverance which continued to the end of life. None could have given more to the work of God among the heathen than she did, for she gave all she had—*herself*. Blessed be God for the grace bestowed upon her, and for the everlasting rest into which she has entered : for the grace which caused her to toil for Jesus, and then to sleep in Him.

" Faithful friend of a feeble but heroic Mission, would that all its helpers were like-minded with thee ! Would that all those who have ministered to it of their substance had as constant a memory of its wants as thine ! The China Inland Mission has

---

Taylor, already in China, proved to be the first of a thousand and more young workers who from Harley House, Bow, went out to the ends of the earth, including all Mr. and Mrs. Guinness's own children.

no eloquent advocate of its claims. It has no denomination for its support. It has no great names on which to rely. It is, therefore, cast the more on God, and on the faithful love and help of the comparatively few who can appreciate the simplicity, faith, and devotedness which characterise its work in the interest of China's millions. But let those few remember that it is no small honour to be enabled to recognise and minister to the Master when He appears in the garments of poverty and weakness.

"Friends of the China Inland Mission, a precious helper has just been removed from our midst ; let us close our ranks and seek to fill the gap. That Mission now needs our help more than ever ; let us prove ourselves worthy of the occasion. Let us help the work *afresh* ; and let us *persevere* in helping it. Here, around this newly opened grave, let our interest in this work revive ; and help Thou, O Lord ! Is not Thy Name inscribed upon its banner ? Is not its song Ebenezer, and its hope Jehovah-jireh ? Bless, then, this Mission, and let the little one become a thousand for Thy glory's sake." [1]

.   .   .   .

Strange and sorrowful was the home-coming in October, to find Miss Blatchley's place empty, the children scattered, the Saturday prayer meeting discontinued, and the work almost at a standstill. But, even then, the lowest ebb had not been reached. When on his way up the Yangtze some months previously, a fall had severely shaken Mr. Taylor. The steamer by which he and Mr. Judd travelled was McBain's smallest cargo-boat, and the gangway down to " between decks " was little more than a ladder. Slipping on one of the top steps, Mr. Taylor had fallen heavily to the bottom, coming down upon his heels, and a sprained ankle had been only a small part of the damage. Extreme pain in the back disabled him for several days, and even when the ankle was well he still needed the help of crutches. Concussion of the spine often develops slowly ; and it was not until he had been at home a week or two that the rush of London life, with constant travelling by train and omnibus, began to tell. Then came gradual paralysis of the lower

---

[1] Miss Blatchley entered into rest on Sunday morning July 26, 1874, and was buried in Highgate Cemetery. The above appreciation—a wreath of tender thoughts to lay upon her grave—appeared in The *Christian* a few days later.

limbs, and the doctor's verdict that consigned him to absolute
rest in bed. Stricken down in the prime of his days, he
could only lie in that upstairs room conscious of all there
was to be done, of all that was not being attended to—lie
there and rejoice in God.

Yes, rejoice in God ! With desires and hopes as limitless
as the needs that pressed upon his heart ; with the prayer
he had prayed, and the answers God had given ; with
opportunities opening in China, and a wave of spiritual
blessing reviving the churches at home that he longed to
see turned into missionary channels ;[1] with the " sentence
of death " in himself, and only the faintest hope that he
would ever stand or walk again, the deepest thing of all was
that unquestioning acceptance of the will of God, as wise,
as kind, as best. Certain it is that from that quiet room,
that room of suffering, sprang all the larger growth of the
China Inland Mission.

A little bed with four posts was now the sphere to which
Hudson Taylor found himself restricted—he who had hoped
to do so much on this visit to England. Were not the
receiving-home in Shanghai and the chain of river-stations
ready for the pioneers ? was not money in hand for their
initial expenses ? was not the home department calling for
entire reorganisation ? If ever strenuous, active effort had
been needed, it was surely at this juncture : and a little bed

---

[1] Just as the launching of the Mission had coincided with an epoch
of spiritual revival in the home churches (see p. 48), so now the commencement of its larger growth synchronised with a remarkable movement for
the deepening of spiritual life. Messrs. Moody and Sankey were in the
midst of their first great missions in London, crowding among other places
the Agricultural Hall, with its seating capacity of twenty thousand. Dr.
Boardman's memorable book *The Higher Christian Life* was being widely
read, and conferences on the lines of " Keswick," which indeed grew out
of them, were drawing together Christians of all denominations. Notable
among these was the Brighton Convention of this summer (ten days in
June 1875), when audiences of two to three thousand filled the Corn
Exchange, and rivers of blessing were opened in many hearts that were
to flow to the ends of the earth. From the deep experience through
which he had himself been brought in China, Mr. Taylor was able to enter
into the spirit and purpose of these gatherings in no ordinary way. He
was sufficiently recovered to be one of the speakers at the Brighton Convention, and his life-long connection with " Keswick " may thus be said
to have dated from its very inception.

with four posts was his prison, shall we say, or opportunity?
Between the posts at the foot of the bed hung a map—though
he hardly needed it—a map of China. And round about
him day and night was the Presence to which he had fullest
access in the Name of Jesus.

" I will give thee a place of access among these that
stand by " (Zech. iii. 7). Might not they all have had it?
We at any rate all " have our access by one Spirit unto the
Father " (Eph. ii. 18). That Hudson Taylor not only had
it but *used it* made all the difference.

Long after, when the prayers that went up from that
bed of pain had been more than answered, and the workers
of the Mission were preaching Christ far and wide throughout inland China, a well-known leader of the Scottish Church
said to Mr. Taylor:

" You must often be conscious of the wonderful way
God has prospered you in the C.I.M. I doubt if any man
living has had a greater honour."

" I do not look upon it in that way," was the quiet
answer. Then turning to his friend in the carriage he said
earnestly: " Do you know I sometimes think that God
must have been looking for some one small enough and
weak enough for Him to use, so that all the glory might be
His, and that He found me." [1]

.   .   .   .   .   .

The outlook did not brighten as the year drew to a close.
Mr. Taylor was less and less able to move, even in bed, and
at last could only turn from side to side with the help of a
rope firmly fixed above him. At first he had managed to
write a little, but now could not even hold a pen, and circumstances deprived him of Mrs. Taylor's help for the time
being. Then it was, with the dawn of 1875, that a little
paper found its way into the Christian press entitled:

" APPEAL FOR PRAYER
On behalf of more than a hundred and fifty millions of
Chinese."

[1] Dr. Elder Cumming mentioned this incident to the writers as having
taken place when he and Mr. Taylor were driving together to the funeral
of the venerable Dr. Somerville of Glasgow.

It briefly stated the facts with regard to the nine un-opened provinces ; that friends of the C.I.M. had long been praying for men to go as pioneer evangelists to these regions ; that recently four thousand pounds had been given for the purpose ; and that among the converts in the older stations of the Mission were some from the far interior, who were earnestly desiring to carry the Gospel to the districts from which they had come.

" Our present, pressing need," it continued, " is of more missionaries to lead the way. Will each of your Christian readers at once raise his heart to God, and spend one minute in earnest prayer that God will raise up, this year, eighteen suitable men to devote themselves to this work ? "

It did not say that the leader of the Mission was to all appearances a hopeless invalid. It did not refer to the fact that the four thousand pounds recently given had come from his wife and himself, part of their capital, the whole of which they had consecrated to the work of God. It did not mention that for two and a half years they and others had been praying daily for the eighteen evangelists, praying in faith. But those who read the appeal felt the influence of these things and much besides, and were moved as men are not moved by sayings and doings that have not their roots deep in God.

So before long Mr. Taylor's correspondence was largely increased, as was also his joy in dealing with it—or in seeing, rather, how the Lord dealt with it and with all else that concerned him.

" The Mission had no paid helpers," he wrote of this time, " but God led volunteers, without pre-arrangement, to come in from day to day to write from dictation, and thus letters were answered. If one who called in the morning could not stay long enough to answer all, another was sure to come, and perhaps one or two might look in in the afternoon. Occasionally, a young friend who was employed in the city would come after business hours and do any needful bookkeeping, or finish letters not already dealt with. So it was day by day. One of the happiest periods of my life was that period of forced inactivity, when one could do nothing but ' rejoice in the Lord ' and ' wait patiently for Him,' and see Him meeting all one's need. Never were my letters, before or since, kept so regularly and promptly answered.

" And the eighteen men asked of God began to come. There was first some correspondence ; then they came to see me in my room. Soon I had a class studying Chinese at my bedside. In due time the Lord sent them forth,[1] and then the dear friends at Mildmay began to pray for my restoration. The Lord blessed the means used and I was raised up. One reason for my being laid aside was gone. Had I been well and able to move about, some might have thought that *my* urgent appeals rather than God's working had sent the eighteen men to China. But utterly laid aside, able only to dictate a request for prayer, the answer to our prayers was the more apparent."

When he was so far recovered that the physicians wished him to sit up for an hour or two daily, he could scarcely find time to do so, as several letters record. Every moment was taken up with interviews, with correspondence through his willing helpers, and with care for the work in China. The weekly prayer meeting was now held in his room, and the Council gathered from time to time at his bedside.

" I am just venturing to do a little myself," he wrote to Miss Turner at the end of February. " I sit up in an easy chair for two hours some days. I cannot write much, but just pen a few lines to let you know that you are not forgotten. . . .

" Three months in bed is a long time. It would have been very weary, but that the Lord Jesus has made it very happy. Some nights when I have never slept at all, I have had much happy time to think of you all and to pray for you."

And to another friend in China a couple of months later :

You will be glad to hear that at last I am recovering. My back is gaining strength, and after nearly five months in bed I am now

---

[1] It had been quite a problem as to how arrangements were to be made for the outgoing of party after party with the leader of the Mission a helpless invalid ; but in this too the Lord provided unexpected and most efficient help. Mr. Taylor had prayed much about it, and rejoiced to find that a warm friend from Glasgow, whom he had last met on the steamer at the time of his accident, was passing through London. Mr. Thomas Weir, from his connection with China shipping and his love for the Mission, was the one person whose advice Mr. Taylor would most have welcomed ; and when it proved that he could give the matter personal attention it was a cause for great thankfulness. The economical arrangement Mr. Weir made at that time with the Directors of the Castle Line continued to work well for a number of years.

able to get up and down stairs. . . . I believe that God has enabled me to do more for China during this long illness than I might have done had I been well. Much thought, much prayer, and some effort in the way of writing by dictation have brought my intense desire for the evangelisation of all the unreached provinces visibly nearer.

By this time a marked change had come over the spirit of the scene at Pyrland Road. Instead of a deserted house, many were coming and going. The first party of the Eighteen had already sailed, and candidates overflowed all the accommodation available for their reception. Another house, indeed, had to be taken for this purpose, for in answer to the " Appeal for Prayer " published in January, no fewer than sixty offers of service were received during the year. How important Mr. Taylor felt it that no hasty decisions should be made, may be judged from the following letter used in his correspondence with candidates at this period. If their response to this faithful statement of the case warranted the hope that they would work happily in the Mission, they were invited to spend a longer or shorter time at Pyrland Road for personal acquaintance.

" While thankful for any educational advantages that candidates may have enjoyed," he wrote, " we attach far greater importance to spiritual qualifications. We desire men who believe that there is a God and that He is both intelligent and faithful, and who therefore trust Him ; who believe that He is the Rewarder of those who diligently seek Him, and are therefore *men of prayer*. We desire men who believe the Bible to be the Word of God, and who, accepting the declaration ' All power is given unto me,' are prepared to carry out to the best of their ability the command, ' Go . . . teach all nations,' relying on Him who possesses ' all power ' and has promised to be with His messengers ' always,' rather than on foreign gun-boats though they possess some power ; men who are prepared, therefore, to go to the remotest parts of the interior of China, expecting to find His arm a sufficient strength and stay. We desire men who believe in eternity and live for it ; who believe in its momentous issues whether to the saved or to the lost, and therefore cannot but seek to pluck the ignorant and the guilty as brands from the burning.

" The Mission is supported by donations, not subscriptions. We have, therefore, no guaranteed income, and can only minister to our missionaries as we ourselves are ministered to by God. We do not send men to China as our agents. But men who believe that God has called them to the work, who go there to labour for God, and can therefore trust Him Whose they are and Whom they serve to supply their temporal needs, we gladly co-operate with—providing, if needful, outfit and passage money, and such a measure of support as circumstances call for and we are enabled to supply. As may be seen from the last *Occasional Paper* (No. 39), our faith is sometimes tried ; but God always proves Himself faithful, and at the right time and in the right way supplies all our need.

" One-third of the human family are in China, needing the Gospel. Twelve millions there are passing beyond the reach of that Gospel every year. If you want hard work and little appreciation ; if you value God's approval more than you fear man's disapprobation ; if you are prepared to take joyfully the spoiling of your goods, and seal your testimony, if need be, with your blood ; if you can pity and love the poor Chinese in all their mental and moral degradation, as well as literal filth and impurity, you may count on a harvest of souls now and a crown of glory hereafter ' that fadeth not away,' and on the Master's ' *Well done.*'

" You would find that, in connection with the China Inland Mission, it is no question of ' making the most of both worlds.' The men, the only men who will be happy with us, are those who have this world under their feet : and I do venture to say that such men will find a happiness they never dreamed of or thought possible down here. For to those who count ' all things ' but dross and dung for ' the excellency of the knowledge of Christ Jesus our Lord,' He does manifest Himself in such sort that they are not inclined to rue their bargain. If, after prayerfully considering the matter, you still feel drawn to engage in such work, I shall be only too glad to hear from you again."

Young men and women who came to Pyrland Road on probation, encouraged rather than daunted by the spirit of the above letter, soon found occasion to rejoice in God as the Hearer and Answerer of prayer. Such, for example, was the experience in May that followed the sailing of Mr. George King for China. It had been difficult to spare him ; for, busy though he was in the city during the day, he had been one of Mr. Taylor's most faithful helpers both before and after office hours.

" Perhaps the Lord will lessen the amount of correspondence for a time," said the latter, " unless He sends us unexpected help."

The correspondence lessened. Mr. King sailed on the 15th, and for a week or two the work was so far reduced as to continue manageable.

On the morning of the 25th, however, when the household gathered for noonday prayer, Mr. Taylor called attention to the fact that this lessening of correspondence had involved a lessening of contributions also.

" Let us ask the Lord," he suggested, " to remind some of His wealthy stewards of the needs of the work."

Casting up the amounts received from the 4th to the 24th of the month, he found that they came to a little over sixty-eight pounds.

" This is nearly £235 *less* than our average expenditure in China for three weeks," he added. " Let us bring the matter to the Lord in prayer."

The answer was not long delayed. That very evening the postman brought a letter which was found to contain a cheque to be entered " From the sale of plate," and the sum thus realised and sent to the Mission was £235 : 7 : 9. Little wonder that prayer was turned to praise at the next noon hour, or that Mr. Taylor in telling the facts could not help exclaiming, " Trust in Him at all times, and you will never be disappointed ! " [1]

Quite as remarkable was another experience that soon followed. It was early in June, and Mr. Taylor was returning from Brighton, where he had taken part in a memorable Convention on Scriptural Holiness. Waiting for his train at the station, he was accosted by a Russian nobleman who had been attending the meetings, and who on learning that Mr. Taylor was going to London suggested that they should find seats together.

" But I am travelling third class," said the missionary.

" My ticket admits of my doing the same," was the courteous reply. And they seem to have found a carriage

---

[1] " What a life of praise and joy and rest," he wrote a few weeks later, " we should all lead, did we but fully believe in God's wisdom and love, and, gladly acquiescing in His will and way, cast every care on Him in trustful prayer."—*China's Millions* for August 1875.

alone together, for presently Count Bobrinsky took out his
pocket-book with the words :

" Allow me to give you a trifle toward your work in
China."

Glancing at the bank-note as he received it, Mr. Taylor
felt there must be some mistake—it was for no less than
fifty pounds.

" Did you not mean to give me five pounds ? " he said
at once. " Please let me return this note : it is for fifty."

" I cannot take it back," replied the other, no less surprised. " It was five pounds I meant to give, but God
must have intended you to have fifty; I cannot take it
back."

Impressed with the incident, Mr. Taylor reached Pyrland
Road to find a prayer meeting going on. A remittance was
about to be sent to China, and the money in hand was short
by £49 : 11s. of the sum it was felt would be required. This
deficiency was not accepted as inevitable. On the contrary,
it called together those who knew of it for special prayer.
£49 : 11s. was being asked for in simple faith, and there
upon the office table Mr. Taylor laid his precious bank-note
for fifty pounds. Could it have come more directly from
the Heavenly Father's hand ? " Whoso is wise and will
observe these things, even they shall understand the loving-
kindness of the Lord."

No less encouraging to faith was the widespread interest
aroused in a new departure connected with the outgoing of
the Eighteen. Even the Council, meeting at Mr. Taylor's
bedside, had been startled by his revival of a plan to which
in earlier years he had given much consideration—that of
obtaining access to Western China (the far inland provinces)
by way of Burma and the Irrawaddy. At that time it had
been abandoned as premature, but now unexpected developments brought it again to mind. The British Government,
seeking to develop trade with Western China, was about to
send an exploring party to the mountainous region lying
beyond Bhamo on the upper waters of the Irrawaddy.
Only a hundred miles, traversed by frequent caravans,

separated that frontier town from the Chinese province of Yün-nan; and Mr. Taylor was surprised to find, in an unknown visitor shown up to his room one day, a traveller who had himself taken the journey. Conversation with this gentleman assured him that Bhamo, with its large resident as well as floating population of Chinese, would be an admirable centre from which to reach the western provinces. Remarkably enough, Mr. Stevenson, who had shared Mr. Taylor's interest in the matter ten years previously, was again in England. So important did it seem to obtain direct access to those great regions not for trade only but for the Gospel, that he was willing to forgo the joy of returning to his own stations for the time being, that he might establish a branch of the Mission at Bhamo, D.V., for this purpose. This was the proposal that startled the Council, coming at a time when there seemed little hope of Mr. Taylor's ever being more than an invalid. But so earnestly did he plead the cause upon his heart that they were not only brought to his point of view, but one of the Hon. Secretaries, Mr. Henry Soltau, himself volunteered to accompany Mr. Stevenson in his difficult if not hazardous undertaking.

Farewell meetings, in many places addressed by Mr. Stevenson and Mr. Soltau, called forth a volume of prayer, and brought the Mission and its objects once more into prominence.[1] Very readable letters telling of their voyage to Burma and progress up the beautiful Irrawaddy to Mandalay, the capital of the despotic native king, and his remarkable friendliness in granting them an interview and permission to reside at Bhamo, where there were at that time no foreigners, deepened the interest. And with this may be connected a characteristic move on Mr. Taylor's part, by which he was enabled to make the most of these communications. For the spring of this year (March 1875)

---

[1] To one of the missionaries in China Mr. Taylor wrote at the end of February: " You will have heard that Mr. Stevenson sails, D.V., March 30, for Bhamo—via Rangoon, Burma—to open a new mission there, before returning to Shao-hing. Pray much for this mission to Western China. It is giving a wonderful impetus to interest in the whole work."

saw the last number of the little quarterly, which had told the story of God's gracious dealings with the Mission from its commencement. New wine must have new bottles, and all the life and blessing that had come with the appeal for the Eighteen needed more adequate representation. This Mr. Taylor saw ; and though it meant taking upon himself, in his poor health, the burden of an illustrated monthly, he sought strength for this also as part of the service to which his life was given.

But it was a great undertaking ; for those were not the days of illustrated papers such as we have now, and *China's Millions* when it appeared was quite an innovation.[1] Its up-to-date articles and pictures, when Burma was occupying a good deal of public attention ; its Chinese stories brightly translated for young people, and full-page texts with floral designs for children to colour on Sundays ; its news of pioneer journeys, and of conversions and progress in the older stations ; and above all its spiritually helpful articles from Mr. Taylor's pen came to be looked for by friends old and new.

" I vividly recall," wrote one of the young candidates, himself the Editor of the *Life of Faith* in later years, " Mr. Taylor's intense and eager interest in the first proof."

Another, whose abounding energy placed him in the van as a pioneer in the unopened provinces, told of the joy with which Mr. Taylor received the first completed number.

" I sold six the day it came out to a bookseller near Bow Station," was his lively recollection, " and disposed of many outside Moody and Sankey's great hall near by. The newsboys did not get hold of the title very well—they used to shout, ' *Chinese Millions*, a penny ! ' "

The work involved in addressing and wrapping copies for the post was recalled by yet another—first of the pioneers to settle in the province of Kwei-chow, and subsequently the valued Treasurer of the Mission in China.

We thought it a fine paper in those days. It was a great

---

[1] To Mrs. Hudson Taylor the Mission was indebted for this title, its first form being, *China's Millions and Our Work among Them.*

business sending it out to everybody ! There was no publication department then, or for long after ; no department, indeed,
of any kind outside Mr. Taylor's busy room.

So wonderfully was the health of the latter restored in
answer to prayer, that he was able for an astonishing amount
of work. A brief holiday taken in August to join his children
in Guernsey was spent almost entirely in writing. Though
longing to share with them the delights of that beautiful
coast, he only managed to get out once during his stay of a
fortnight ; but the letters he despatched to China and elsewhere were worth their weight in gold.

" I am thankful to be able to send you ninety dollars," he
wrote to one of the younger members of the Mission.[1] " The
Lord does provide, *does* He not ? How blessed it is to trust in
Him ! It is far happier to *want*, trusting Him, than to be richly
supplied, leaning on supplies rather than on the Supplier. I find
this life happier every year, though not less trying to faith.

" You will find the dear native helpers improve on acquaintance, I trust. *They* need our energy and faith to help them ;
we, divine life and power. Read the Word with much prayer
with them, dear Brother. Hold much holy communion with
our Lord. Feed on the living Word ; and when you find it
marrow and fatness to your soul, tell them what *you* are *finding
there*. Oh ! you will find it a blessed and holy service ; a
fruitful and happy calling. You will not be kept long sowing
thus before you are rejoicing over the first-fruits of the harvest."

Work as he might, however, he could not write personally
to *all* the members of the Mission, though all were so truly
upon his heart. He had to content himself with a circular
letter sent off on his return to London, in which he sought
to share with them some of the precious lessons learned in
weakness and suffering.

" It is nearly twelve months," he wrote on the 26th of August,
" since I sailed from China, and ten since I reached England. Few
have been the letters I have written to you, but every day of
this time you have been on my heart. Usually not once nor
twice daily but oftentimes have you and your circumstances,
sphere of labour and surroundings, as far as known to me, been

---

[1] From a letter to Mr. (afterwards Dr.) Douthwaite, who was taking
up settled work in Chü-chow Fu, near the Kiang-si border of Che-kiang.

remembered and commended to God. I wish it were possible to write to each one of you more frequently and at length; but I take comfort in the thought that you all know me, and know that I am at work for you and for China to the full extent of my ability. May God bless you all and each of those dear to you; bless and prosper the work He has given you, and in due time make it manifest that HE has been working in and through you.

"When I came home, I hoped to have done much for China. God soon put that out of the question, as you know, and for many long months there was little I could do but pray. And what has been the result? Far more has been done *by God*, far more is being done, far more will be done *by Him* than my most sanguine hopes ventured to anticipate.

"And shall we learn no lesson from this? Shall we not each one of us determine to labour more *in prayer*; to cultivate more intimate communion with God by His help; thinking less of our working and more of *His* working, that He may in very deed be glorified in and through us? If we can and will do this, I am quite sure that ere long there will be *abundant* evidence of it in the improved state of our congregations and churches, in the preparedness of the people for the message, and in the power with which it is delivered. More souls will be saved; the believers will lead more holy lives, and our own knowledge of God and joy in Him will be multiplied. Surely we ought to lead beautiful lives, glorious lives, if we are really with Him Who is Chiefest among Ten Thousand, the Altogether Lovely! 'The people that do *know their God* shall be strong and do exploits.'"

CHAPTER XIX

THE FAITHFULNESS OF GOD

1875–1876. Aet. 43–44.

"There are commonly three stages in work for God," Mr. Taylor would sometimes say: "first *impossible*, then *difficult*, then *done*." The project of reaching the nine unopened provinces with the Gospel had not yet passed beyond the first stage. It was still, to all appearances, impossible. Despite the stipulations of the Treaty of Tientsin, ratified as early as 1860, the interior was inaccessible as ever. Passports, besides being practically unobtainable, meant little or nothing of protection, and the European who would venture far from the beaten track had to take his life in his hand. As an evidence of the almost insurmountable obstacles, one has but to recall that after nearly seventy years of work in China, Protestant missions were still confined to few, very few centres—*thirty-nine stations* only being occupied by the representatives of all societies.

"To some it may seem almost incredible," Mr. Taylor wrote in an early number of *China's Millions*, "that outside the thirty-nine places named on the page opposite there is not one Protestant missionary to be found in any of the thousands of Chinese cities, in any of the tens of thousands of large towns, or in any of the hundreds of thousands of villages, with their millions of perishing inhabitants. Yet such, alas, is the case."

And, strangely enough, even since the appeal for the Eighteen the situation had become decidedly more difficult. For the British exploring party sent to open up communication with Western China had met with tragic disaster. On

276

the mountainous frontier of Yün-nan, a member of the expedition, Mr. Augustus Margary, had been treacherously murdered with the connivance of the Chinese authorities, and the latter would give neither apology nor the reparation international justice required. As month by month the negotiations were prolonged at Peking, relations became increasingly strained in high places, which meant that foreigners were in added disfavour all over China. It certainly was not the moment, as far as human probabilities were concerned, for anything like advance. And yet the appeal for eighteen pioneers had gone out ; the men were being given ; and, " assuredly gathering " that the Lord's time had come, faith was strong in many hearts.

In the first issue of *China's Millions* (July 1875) Mr. Taylor had written on this subject :

It was nine years on the 26th of May since the *Lammermuir* party sailed for China. . . . We have needed all the time since then to gain experience and to gather round us a staff of native workers, through whose aid we are occupying some fifty stations and out-stations in five provinces. We believe, however, that the time has come for doing more fully what the Master commanded us ; and by His grace we intend to do it—not *to try*, for we see no scriptural authority for trying. " Try " is a word constantly on the lips of unbelievers. " We must do what we can," they say ; and too often the same attitude is taken up by the child of God. In our experience, to try has usually meant *to fail*. The Lord's word in reference to His various commands is not " Do your best," but *"Do it"* ; that is, do the thing commanded. We are therefore making arrangements for commencing work in each of these nine provinces—without haste, for " he that believeth shall not make haste," but also without unnecessary delay. . . . " If ye be willing and obedient, ye shall eat of the good of the land." " Whatsoever He saith unto you, do it."

Among the " treasures of darkness " that had come to Mr. Taylor in 1870 had been a new conception of the scope and meaning of faith, upon which a flood of light had been thrown by a passage in his Greek Testament. A letter to Mrs. Berger toward the close of that year of bereavement (November 18) showed that he had already made the discovery which was to be a mine of wealth through all his later life, but gave no clue as to how it had come about. It was just in his usual reading, as he often related, that he was struck with the words, " *Ekete pistin Theou.*" How strangely new they seemed ! " Have (or hold) the faithfulness of God " : surely it was a passage he had never seen before ? Turning to the corresponding words in English he read (Mark xi. 22) : " Have faith in God." Ah, *that* was familiar enough ; and something within him whispered, " the old difficulty ! " How gladly would he have and increase in faith in God, if only he knew how ! But *this* seemed entirely different. It laid the emphasis on another side of the matter in a way he found surprisingly helpful. It was not " have " in your own heart and mind, however you can get it, " faith in God," but simply " hold fast, count upon *His faithfulness* " ; and different indeed he saw the one to be from the other.[1] Not my faith but God's faithfulness—what a rest it was !

And now, just five years later, the subject was filling his mind as he faced the seemingly impossible situation before the Mission. He knew that the impossibility was only seeming, and for his editorials in the new magazine had chosen the title " China for Christ." In the fourth of these papers, which dwelt upon the definite plan before the Mission for evangelising all the inland provinces, he wrote (November 1875) :

Want of trust is at the root of almost all our sins and all our weaknesses ; and how shall we escape it but by looking to Him and observing His faithfulness ? . . . The man who holds God's faithfulness will not be foolhardy or reckless, but he will be ready for every emergency. The man who holds God's faithfulness will dare to obey Him, however impolitic it may appear.

---

[1] As to the correctness of this modified translation, Mr. Taylor noted : " For the rendering ' God's faithfulness,' see Rom. iii. 3, where ' the faith of God ' evidently means His faithfulness. The verb translated ' hold,' is thus rendered in Matt. xxi. 26, ' all *hold* John as a prophet.' In the corresponding passage in Mark xi. 32, it is rendered ' *count* ' ; and in that in Luke xx. 6, a different Greek verb is used, which well illustrates the meaning, ' They be *persuaded* that John was a prophet.' Let us see that in theory we hold that God is faithful ; that in daily life we count upon it ; and that at all times and under all circumstances we are fully persuaded of this blessed truth."

Abraham held God's faithfulness and offered up Isaac, " accounting that God was able to raise him from the dead." Moses held God's faithfulness and led the millions of Israel into the waste, howling wilderness. Joshua knew Israel well, and was ignorant neither of the fortifications of the Canaanites nor of their martial prowess, but he held God's faithfulness and led Israel across the Jordan. . . . The Apostles held God's faithfulness, and were not daunted by the hatred of the Jews or the hostility of the heathen. . . . " And what shall I more say ? for the time would fail me to tell " of those who, holding God's faithfulness, had faith, and by it " subdued kingdoms, wrought righteousness, obtained promises . . . out of weakness were made strong, waxed valiant in fight, turned to flight the armies of the aliens ? "

Satan, too, has his creed : Doubt God's Faithfulness. " Hath God said ? Are you not mistaken as to His commands ? He could not really mean just that. You take an extreme view, give too literal a meaning to the words." . . . How constantly, and, alas, how successfully are such arguments used to prevent whole-hearted trust in God, whole-hearted consecration to God ! . . . How many estimate difficulties in the light of their own resources, and thus attempt little and often fail in the little they attempt ! All God's giants have been weak men, who did great things for God because they reckoned on His being with them. . . .

Oh ! beloved friends, if there is a living God, faithful and true, let us hold His faithfulness. . . . Holding His faithfulness, we may go into every province of China. Holding His faithfulness, we may face with calm and sober but confident assurance of victory every difficulty and danger ; we may count on grace for the work, on pecuniary aid, on needful facilities, and on ultimate success. Let us not give Him a partial trust, but daily, hourly serve Him, counting on *His faithfulness*.

For ten years this had been, in the main, the attitude of the Mission, when in the spring of 1876 the first anniversary services were held to report progress. Mr. Taylor was by this time well enough to move about with the help of a strong walking-stick, and the new, young, earnest life that had come into the work with the outgoing pioneers was felt by all its friends and supporters. No more striking evidence could have been given of the place it was coming to hold in the sympathies of the Lord's people than the large and representative gatherings that filled the Mildmay Conference Hall. But remarkable as were the meetings, how little could the speakers really tell of all that had filled those first ten years—all that had been experienced of the love and faithfulness of God ! Statistics are not without their meaning, however, and it was with joy Mr. Taylor pointed out on the large map twenty-eight stations in five provinces in which churches had been gathered—six hundred converts having been baptized from the beginning. Of these, more than seventy were devoting their lives to making known the Gospel, and in them lay the chief hope of the future, specially as regarded the evangelisation of the unreached interior. Sixty-eight missionaries had been sent to China, of whom fifty-two were still connected with the Mission. Means for their support had never failed—though that also which is "more precious than gold" had not been lacking—"the *trial* of your faith." Without a collection or an appeal of any kind for funds, fifty-two thousand pounds had been received, and the Mission was not and never had been in debt.[1]

How much of prayer and practical self-denial lay behind these facts the Report did not reveal, but the candidates at Pyrland Road could have supplied some details not lacking in interest. Preparing, themselves, to face danger and sacrifice in the work to which the Lord was calling them, it meant everything to have the encouragement of their leader's example. In him they found faith, not as a finished product to be obtained they knew not how, but as a practical, growing experience. They could *see* his faith lay hold upon God more and more, see him daily pay the price of spiritual power and fruitfulness.

"It was a great delight to be with him in those days," said Mr. Broumton. "He used to call Easton and me to his room for long talks about China, giving us advice as to how to go about our pioneering journeys, with many an illustration from his own experience. His interest in the outgoing of the Eighteen was intense."

---

[1] "We have never had to leave an open door unentered from lack of funds," said Mr. Taylor's Report on this occasion ; "and although the last penny had not unfrequently been spent, none of our native agents or foreign missionaries have ever lacked the promised 'daily bread.' Times of trial have always been times of blessing, and needed supplies have never failed " or come too late.

Of his first visit to Pyrland Road, while Mr. Taylor was still an invalid, another wrote : [1]

Who that has known it can ever forget his bright, winning greeting ? It captivated you in a moment. He led me to his study, which was also the " office " of the Mission. It was the back room on the ground floor, and could be entered from the front sitting-room by large folding doors. Shall I say I was shocked, or surprised, or both ? At any rate I had an absolutely novel experience. The room was largely occupied with packing-cases and some rough shelves set along one of the walls. Near the window, which looked out on the dreary back-gardens, was a writing-table littered with papers. In front of the fireplace where a fender is usually found was a low, narrow, iron bedstead, neatly covered with a rug—Mr. Taylor's chief resting-place by night and by day. I hardly think there was a scrap of carpet on the floor, and certainly not a single piece of furniture that suggested the slightest regard for comfort or appearances.

Mr. Taylor offered no word of apology or explanation, but lay down on his iron bedstead and eagerly plunged into a conversation, which was, for me, one of life's golden hours. Every idea I had hitherto cherished of a " great man " was completely shattered : the high, imposing airs, and all the trappings were conspicuously absent ; but Christ's ideal of greatness was then and there so securely set in my heart, that it has remained through all the years, up to this moment. I strongly suspect that, by his unconscious influence, Mr. Hudson Taylor did more than any other man of his day to compel Christian people to revise their ideas of greatness. . . .

I mention these details because they throw light upon some of the important principles upon which Mr. Taylor based his life and service. He profoundly realised that if the millions of China were to be evangelised, there would have to be a vast increase in self-denial and self-sacrifice upon the part of Christians at home. But how could he ask and urge others to do what he was not practising himself ? So he deliberately stripped his life, on all sides, of every appearance of self-consideration and self-indulgence. . . .

And it was just the same in China ; but there an additional principle came into action. He would not ask those who worked with him to face hardships he himself was not willing to endure. He never used his position as Director of the Mission to purchase for himself the least advantage or ease. He made it his, under

[1] The Rev. C. G. Moore, for many years a member of the China Inland Mission.

all circumstances, to live in that spirit and practice of self-sacrifice which he expected to find in his brethren on the field. However hard his lot might be in China, every missionary knew that Mr. Taylor had suffered in the same way, and was ready to do so again. No man could suspect, at any time, that while he himself was bearing the cross, his leader, under more favourable circumstances, was shirking it. Herein was one explanation of the remarkable and affectionate attachment to Mr. Taylor on the part of so many in the Mission.

And now he was going back—back to China to speed the pioneers, as he fully hoped and expected, on their far inland journeys. A gracious answer to the prayers of many years had made this possible, in the coming of his beloved sister and her husband, Mr. and Mrs. B. Broomhall, into the home department of the work. Long before the Mission came into existence he had written to them from China (June 1860) :

I have not given up hope of seeing you . . . I believe you will yet come. I believe you will be sent by God. And a happy work you will find it. We have only the Lord to look to for means, for health, for encouragement—and we need no other. He gives us all ; and He best knows what we need.

How real was the faith involved in joining the Mission, when at length the way opened, may be judged from the fact that they had by that time a family of ten growing boys and girls. But this was perhaps one of their chief qualifications. What hearts are so large and what hands so free for others as those filled with love and service in which self has no part. Number 2 Pyrland Road, which became the home of Mr. and Mrs. Broomhall, soon radiated an atmosphere of helpfulness, spiritually and in other ways, that made it for many a long year the best loved centre of the Mission. Number 6 was still Mr. Taylor's home, but the two were practically thrown into one, the intervening house being occupied for offices and candidates. Mr. Taylor's little back room was now exchanged for a more cheerful study, and a Secretary was installed in the person of Mr. William Soltau, who took over much of his work. Barely waiting to see these arrangements completed, however, and to give time for the preparation of the party of eight who sailed with him, Mr. Taylor set out early in September (1876), notwithstanding the war-cloud that hung heavily over the eastern horizon.

For the negotiations that had dragged on so long at Peking had come at last to a stalemate. Nothing would induce the Chinese Government to give satisfaction of any sort for the murder of Mr. Margary; and the British Ambassador, having exhausted diplomatic resources, was on the point of retiring to the coast to put the matter into the hands of the Admiral. It seemed impossible that war could be averted, and there were many among the friends of the Mission who strongly advised against Mr. Taylor's going out.

" You will all have to return," they said. " And as to sending off pioneers to the more distant provinces, it is simply out of the question."

It was indeed a critical juncture. After years of prayer and preparation, evangelists for the unentered provinces had been given; had gone to China, and having acquired some knowledge of the language were ready to set forth. Could it be that the iron gate of the last ward—having opened thus far—was again to close, leaving the prayer of faith unanswered? Mr. Taylor did not think so. Indeed he felt as sure that God's time had come, as he was that the men had been given. He was fully aware that in event of war, not the pioneers only, but *all* his fellow-workers might have to leave their inland stations. That matters could not look more threatening was obvious. Even before he sailed, though this he may not have heard, Mr. Thomas Wade had actually left Peking to make way for the commencement of hostilities. Every effort had failed, and a war that might close the country entirely to missionary effort was all but begun.

But no, *prayer* had not failed. In the third-class cabin of the French Mail, as in the prayer meetings at Pyrland Road, fervent supplication was going up to God that He would overrule the crisis for the furtherance of His own great ends. With Him it is never too late. At the last moment, utterly improbable as it seemed, a change came over the Peking Foreign Office. More alive to the situation than his fellows, the Viceroy Li Hung-chang hurried to the coast, overtaking the British Ambassador just in time to reopen negotiations ; and there, at Chefoo, was signed the memorable Convention which threw open the door of access at last to the remotest parts of China. This was the news that awaited Mr. Taylor on his arrival in Shanghai, the agreement having been signed within a week of his leaving England ; and already three parties of the Eighteen had set out and were well on their way to the interior.

" Just as our brethren were ready," he wrote, " not too soon and not too late the long-closed door opened to them of its own accord."

CHAPTER XX

THE GATES OF THE WEST

1876–1877. Aet. 44–45.

AND what were the provisions of that notable Convention signed at Chefoo on September 13, 1876 ? As concerned the pioneers simply these : that foreigners were at liberty to travel in any part of the Emperor's dominions ; that they did so under his protection, and were to be received with respect and in no wise hindered on their journeys. Imperial proclamations were to be posted in every city, giving publicity to these arrangements ; and for a period of two years British officials might be sent inland, specially to see that this clause was carried out. As a matter of fact, representatives of the C.I.M. were the first, and for years almost the only foreigners, to avail themselves of this great opportunity. Far and wide they travelled, crossing and recrossing all the provinces of the interior, and penetrating even into eastern Tibet. Thirty thousand miles were thus traversed in the next eighteen months, Scriptures and tracts being everywhere sold or distributed, and friendly relations almost uninterruptedly maintained. At first, indeed, the missionaries were supposed to be Government agents, and their arrival spread dismay in the official breast. For there had been no unseemly haste in issuing the proclamations ; and more than one Mandarin hit upon the happy expedient of entertaining the visitors with elaborate hospitality, while the city was hurriedly placarded with the belated documents.[1]

[1] From the distant city of Si-an-fu, capital of Shen-si, Mr. Easton wrote on his first journey (Dec. 20, 1876) : " At every city and village of

It must not be supposed, however, that the pioneers had a bed of roses. Though the attitude of the Government was favourable for the time being, the prejudices of the literati were unchanged, and the difficulties of travel, great and small, remained the same. Wonderful were those journeys with their new experiences, their launching out into the unknown, their fervent love for souls, their brave endurance, manifold perils, and the exercise of young hearts cast upon God! Fain would we follow the footsteps of the evangelists, see with their eyes, hear with their ears, live over again experiences so well worth while, both for time and for eternity. The openness of the people and their response in spiritual things was what impressed them most. Whether it were Mr. Judd in Hu-nan, Henry Taylor in Ho-nan, or Easton and Parker on their way to the far north-west, all found the same willingness to listen, with here and there a deep heart-hunger in some who were seekers after truth.

" As we spoke of Jesus and His sufferings for our sin," Henry Taylor wrote on his journey to Ho-nan, " we saw tears stealing down some faces. The women go in, heart and soul, for idolatry, as you know, but still find their hearts unsatisfied and their minds in a maze."

Fifty-six days were spent, even on this first journey, in carts and inns, on foot and wheelbarrow, passing from city to city through the southern part of the province, where roads were roughest and accommodation poorest, and where little food was obtainable beyond steamed bread and rice, or coarse home-made vermicelli. Starting at earliest dawn, they often travelled on till dark, preaching by the wayside or in crowded streets, everywhere telling the glad tidings of Redeeming Love.[1]

In the city and district of Ju-ning several earnest inquirers were met with—Wang, the young school-master;

any size, a large proclamation from the Peking Foreign Office makes it easy for us to travel. At Shen-chow we first noticed it; the officials putting it out after our arrival, and being very polite to us."

[1] This journey and another taken in 1875—a few months only after the murder of Margary—show that the pioneers who were *ready* did not wait for the Chefoo Convention, or any other Government assistance, thankful though they were for the new Treaty when it came.

Hu, the devout vegetarian ; the medicine vendor who had no cure for a corrupt heart ; the old scholar, who humbly knelt, the first time he ever heard of Jesus, to ask that his sins might be laid upon the divine Sacrifice, and who seemed astonished that any one could be indifferent to the good news about *such* a Saviour ; and a Mr. Mu, also a man of letters, in whose heart there was an evident work of the Spirit of God. Several of these came daily to read and pray with the missionary and his Chinese companion, and Mr. Mu was urgent in his desire to be baptized. Only the promise that they would come again in a few months, *D.V.*, prevailed upon him to wait until he could learn more of what it really meant to be a Christian.

Later journeys, while they brought encouragement in finding this man and others steadfast in the faith, brought also perils from which only the hand of God could have delivered. Convinced that he should shorten his visit to the provincial capital (Kai-feng) on one occasion, Henry Taylor left a day or two earlier than he had intended. Not until months later did he learn that that very day a crowd of students had come to the inn, and, not finding him, had torn down the sign-board, and would have set fire to the place had not the authorities intervened. They had bound themselves by an oath to kill the foreigner, and had been lying in wait in different parts of the city. When he did not appear they went in search of him, and their rage on learning that he was already far away knew no bounds.

Short of money on another occasion, he sent his helper to Hankow for silver, waiting his return in an inn. To his surprise a proclamation presently appeared, forbidding any one on pain of the severest punishment to sell anything to the foreigner. This, of course, included food, which the landlord of the inn dared no longer supply. Not knowing what to do, Henry Taylor was praying alone in his room one night when he heard a stealthy movement at the shutter. With some trepidation, for robbers are commonly armed in Ho-nan, he went to the window and saw a man apparently trying to get in. Before he could give the alarm the stranger beckoned to him to be silent. Fumbling in his girdle he produced a little loaf of bread, then another and another, six in all, something like large steamed dumplings. These he handed in through the window, and without a word disappeared in the darkness.

Next night he came again, and the same scene was transacted.

"Not want, not want!" he whispered emphatically, when the missionary offered the few cash he had left.

He dared not stay for conversation, but was faithful in his visits until supplies came, and Mr. Taylor was able to leave for the coast.

Many a story could the pioneers have told of answers to prayer almost equally remarkable ; of friendliness among all classes, as well as the old, bitter opposition ; of opened hearts here and there, and access to regions never before visited by foreigners. Interested inquirers were met with again and again in remote places, and letters were received telling of baptisms in the clear water of some mountain stream, and even of little gatherings for the Breaking of Bread. The principle on which these itinerations were carried out was that of a widespread dissemination of saving truth, to be followed by settled work as the way should open. Thoughts wholly strange and new need time to filter into the mind of a community as of an individual. By coming back again and again, impressions could be deepened and interest followed up. The aim was, meanwhile, to gather information, and look for indications as to where to settle. For permanent localised work was the object kept in view : only, not a station first, and a church (or no church) after-wards ; but, if possible, signs of a real work of the Holy Spirit to begin with—mission-house and chapel to follow as they were needed. To this end itineration had to be patiently pursued ; and even when inquirers were gathered and a district seemed full of promise, it was often long before it was possible to settle. In Ho-nan, as we have seen, there was much to indicate the Ju-ning district as suitable for permanent work. Some thirty people were found on the return of the evangelists, who seemed truly to have accepted the Gospel. While still homeless save for their room in an inn, Henry Taylor and his companions baptized two of these—a man named Wang, and Mr. Mu, through whose preaching most of the others had been interested. At length a house was rented, in a little city at the foot of the hills, and six happy weeks spent among the people.[1] Then the literati stirred up trouble. For days the place was in an uproar and the missionaries' lives were in danger ; and few letters are more pathetic than the pencilled lines that tell of their finally having to withdraw and give up the premises.

Well was it, then, that the leader of the Mission was within reach, able to advise and comfort. No one had passed through more of such trials than he, and it was on purpose to guide the pioneers and strengthen their hands in God that he had returned to China.

For himself, little that he had planned was to be accomplished during the first few months after his arrival. A chill caught in the China Sea led to serious illness. He was able to go up-river as far as Chin-kiang, but there had to learn many a lesson of patience, as he found himself needed at nearly every station in the Mission, and unable to do more than pray and help by correspondence.

" It is difficult to realise," he wrote to Mrs. Taylor in November, " that I cannot run about as I once did " ; and in another letter, " the weakness that prevents overwork may be the greatest blessing to me."

Yet overwork seemed almost inevitable ; for Mr. C. T. Fishe, in broken health, had gone home on furlough, and there was no one else to take his place as Secretary to the Mission in China. This meant long hours daily at office work, besides Mr. Taylor's directorial duties and the oft-recurring claims of *China's Millions*, of which he was Editor.

[1] At Kio-shan Hsien, near which in " a beautiful mountain stream " the baptisms had taken place. As the first-fruits of Ho-nan, it is interesting to record that these converts were baptized on April 1, 1876, by Mr. Henry Taylor, Mr. G. W. Clarke, and the Evangelist Yao, who accompanied them. " We returned to our inn," wrote Mr. Clarke, " and after instructing them from several portions of Scripture on the Lord's Supper, partook of it with them for the first time."

" We have never been so long separated," he wrote again when the worst of his illness was past, " but He Who has helped us day by day for more than two months, *will* help us till He gives us the joy of reunion. . . . The Lord be with you and comfort your heart with His love. May you find it *better* than mine."

> Oh ! it is good to soar
>   The winds and waves above,
> To Him Whose purpose I adore,
>   Whose providence I love ;
> And in His mighty will to find
> The joy and freedom of the mind.

Thus it was that Henry Taylor returning sorrowfully from Ho-nan, George Nicoll, homeless through a riot at I-chang, and other troubled spirits could be sure of finding not only counsel and help at Chin-kiang but a heart of tender sympathy, exercised with the sorrows of many, yet free from anxious care.

Despite absence from home and loved ones, and the limitations of ill-health which he was feeling keenly, Mr. Taylor was enabled so to cast his burdens on the Lord that, as he wrote to Mr. Hill in February (1877), he " could not but rejoice seven days a week." Whenever work permitted, he was in the habit of turning to a little harmonium for refreshment, playing and singing many a favourite hymn, but always coming back to—

> Jesus, I am resting, resting, in the joy of what Thou art ;
> I am finding out the greatness of Thy loving heart.

Some around him could hardly understand this joy and rest, especially when fellow-workers were in danger. A budget of letters arriving on one occasion, as Mr. Nicoll relates, brought news of serious rioting in two different stations. Standing at his desk to read them, Mr. Taylor mentioned what was happening and that immediate help was necessary. Feeling that he might wish to be alone, the younger man was about to withdraw, when, to his surprise, some one began to whistle. It was the soft refrain of the same well-loved hymn :

> *Jesus, I am resting, resting, in the joy of what Thou art* . . .

Turning back, Mr. Nicoll could not help exclaiming, "How *can* you whistle, when our friends are in such danger!"

"Would you have me anxious and troubled?" was the long-remembered answer. "That would not help them, and would certainly incapacitate me for my work. I have just to roll the burden on the Lord."

Day and night that was his secret, "just to roll the burden on the Lord." Frequently those who were wakeful in the little house at Chin-kiang might hear, at two or three o'clock in the morning, the soft refrain of Mr. Taylor's favourite hymn. He had learned that, for him, only one life was possible—just that blessed life of resting and rejoicing in the Lord under all circumstances, while HE dealt with the difficulties inward and outward, great and small.

Second only to his longing for the evangelisation of the inland provinces was the desire that possessed Mr. Taylor at this time for unity and blessing in the forthcoming Conference of missionaries to be held in Shanghai. Never had opportunities been greater, or the need for spiritual power more urgent, that they might be used aright. Mr. Taylor longed to see advance on a wide front—not in the C.I.M. only, but on the part of all societies—and a strong, united appeal to the home churches for adequate reinforcements. To bring this about, as he realised, nothing less than a wonderful answer to prayer could avail; for party spirit was running high over the difficult "term question," [1] and many missionaries were holding aloof from the Conference altogether, feeling that it would be an occasion for controversy if not strife. And yet China was open from end to end as never before. Five hundred missionaries, all told, formed the little company to whom was entrusted the stupendous task of its evangelisation. How great their need of power—the real power of the Holy Spirit poured out, as at Pentecost, upon united, expectant hearts!

There were still some months before the Conference,

[1] The perplexing question, that is, as to what Chinese term should be adopted as the nearest and most unambiguous equivalent for the Scriptural idea of GOD.

convened for May (1877), and this interval Mr. Taylor was seeking to make the most of.

" There is one very important matter to pray about," he wrote to Mrs. Taylor in February—" the forthcoming conference. It *will* be *a power* : shall it be for good or evil ? This rests much with us, through the use of believing prayer. Unless there is a great outpouring of God's Holy Spirit, very much harm may result : very much has already resulted from preliminary discussions. . . . Nor are *we* likely to pass without attack if some have their way. But our God is an *almighty* Saviour, and my hope is in Him. If His Spirit be poured out, evil will be kept in check ; and if we ask for it, will it not indeed be so ? Let us pray, then, much for this—pray daily for this . . . that division and discord may not prevail instead of unity and love."

But Mr. Taylor not only prayed ; he did all that in him lay to promote the unity he felt to be of such importance, and to remove misunderstandings. It was hardly to be wondered at, as he was the first to recognise, that the C.I.M. should have come in for a large share of criticism. Its aims and methods never had been popular, and its new departure in the direction of widespread evangelisation was of the nature of an experiment. Because the pioneers were for the most part young, at the beginning only of their missionary life, it was argued that it could not be right to use them in work so difficult and important. Undoubtedly they *were* ignorant and inexperienced as compared with older missionaries, especially with the able men to be found in the foremost ranks of other societies. No one would have been more thankful than Mr. Taylor to have seen such workers take the field. But they were all needed, more than needed in their actual posts. There was no suggestion that some or any of *them* should be set free, though China was accessible at last, from end to end, to preachers of the Gospel. Was, then, no one to go because they could not send the best ? Mr. Taylor had good reason to believe that these young workers had been given in answer to prayer, and that the hand of God was in the coincidence of their being ready, on the spot, when the Gates of the West were thrown open. He was doing all he could to liberate experienced missionaries, and was thankful to have reliable Chinese Christians to send with the younger evangelists. Experience, he well knew, would be one of the great gains that would come to them as they pursued their task ; and meanwhile, if they were not burdened with much knowledge, which often spells discouragement, they had the health and hopefulness of youth ; the buoyancy of body, mind, and spirit which is in itself so great a gift. If only their critics, and they were many, could come nearer—could meet and know the men in question, and hear from their own lips of the wonderful opportunities God was giving—objections, he had no doubt, would give place to sympathy. But how was this to be brought to pass ?

A leader less humble, perhaps, less truly taught of God, might have brushed aside unfriendly criticism, absorbing himself in what he felt to be his own work. But years of self-effacing discipline had not been in vain. Now that the opportunity prayed for through half a lifetime had come, the grace to use it wisely and to the glory of God was not withheld. Keenly as Mr. Taylor felt the attitude of opposition, he knew that those whose views differed most widely from his own might have just as sincere a desire for the advancement of the Kingdom of God. He had grasped, moreover, something of the real, indissoluble oneness of the body of Christ : that it is not that the eye *should not* say to the hand, " I have no need of thee "—it *cannot.* " If the foot shall say, because I am not the hand, I am not of the body ; is it *therefore not of the body* ? " On the contrary, whatever it may say or feel, of the body it is and must remain. The bearing of this principle upon the position of the C.I.M. he saw with increasing clearness. As a hand, this pioneering effort might reach out a certain distance beyond the rest of the body ; but if it would go further, *the body must go too* : there could be no other way. A large part, and not the easiest part of his work as he was learning, must consist in the humble, patient endeavour to carry his brethren with him in any new departure to which he was constrained of God. How much easier it would have been to go on alone, independently, he may have felt. But where is there room for independence in a living organism, every part of which is bound up with the whole ?

These thoughts in mind, Mr. Taylor went on from Chin-kiang, as soon as he was able, to the new centre of the Mission at Wu-chang. Mr. Judd had just set out with one of the pioneers for the far-off capital of Kwei-chow, and his place had to be filled. There were problems also to consider as to how to keep in touch with distant workers, so as to reach them regularly with supplies. For several weeks Mr. Taylor had the benefit of experienced help, while Mr. McCarthy was preparing for what proved to be one of the most remarkable journeys ever taken in Western China.[1] Difficult as it was to spare him, Mr. Taylor rejoiced in the project almost as much as if he were going himself, and many were the hours of consultation and prayer they had over the whole forward movement.

Remembering their own spiritual difficulties, they felt the importance of providing help for younger workers whose strenuous life exposed them to so much of trial and temptation. The thought of calling together as many of the pioneers as possible for a week of conference had long been in Mr. Taylor's mind, and in sending off recent parties he had arranged that they should return for books and money at a given time. And now as he considered the matter with Mr. McCarthy, they saw in such a reunion the possibility of just the *rapprochement* needed with workers of other societies. For the missionary community in Hankow, across the river, was considerable, and if united meetings could be

---

[1] Without saying anything of their hopes in this connection, Mr. Taylor and he made plans for a walk *right across China*—from the Yangtze to the Irrawaddy ; which Mr. McCarthy was enabled to accomplish in seven months, taking time to preach the Gospel fully in many places, and opening Chung-king, the first Mission-station in the province of Sze-chwan with its population of nearly seventy millions. The only foreigner met with on this long journey—on which he was accompanied by the faithful soldier-evangelist Yang Ts'üen-ling—was Mr. Broumton, alone in the city of Kwei-yang ; until at Bhamo Messrs. Stevenson and Soltau welcomed the wayworn travellers. This journey laid the needs of *the women* so deeply on Mr. McCarthy's heart that he was used to stir up many to pray and labour for their salvation, and much of his subsequent useful-ness was connected with the development of Women's Work in the inland provinces.

arranged, much might be done to promote mutual understanding, and prepare the way for the larger Conference in
Shanghai.

The response this suggestion met with from the London
and Wesleyan Missions was so encouraging that Mr. Taylor
could not but feel that, already, prayer was being answered ;
and he determined to seek opportunities for closer intercourse, especially with those whom he knew to be critical
toward the C.I.M. This was not easy, on account of the
great pressure of work upon him, nor was it a line of things
his sensitive spirit would have chosen. But, as he had
written to Mrs. Taylor soon after reaching Wu-chang :

It is our Father Who orders *all*—these experiences included.
I feel more and more that it is with *Him* we have to do : not so
much with men, or things, but with Him. And herein lies our
power to do and suffer patiently, perseveringly. We *can* take
rebuffs, sorrows, disappointments from His hand, though we might
resent them from one another. And joys are doubly joys when
received from Him.

In this spirit he was glad rather than otherwise to find
himself delayed in Hankow one evening until it was too late
to recross the river. Before he could reach the other side
the city-gates would be shut, and without bedding, etc., he
could not very well go to an inn. It was necessary, therefore, to seek hospitality ; and this Mr. Taylor did by calling
upon a missionary with whom he was but slightly acquainted,
and who took a very unfavourable view both of himself and
the C.I.M. Quite simply he explained the circumstances,
asking whether it would be convenient to put him up for
the night. Christian courtesy admitted but one reply, and
the sense of having done a kindness opened the way for
friendly intercourse. Mr. Taylor being as good a listener as
he was a talker, his host found himself drawn into helpful
conversation, even upon spiritual things. A cordial friendship resulted ; the missionary in question taking an early
opportunity of letting it be known that he had had " no idea
Mr. Taylor was so good a man."

Down the Yangtze more or less the same experience was
repeated, as Mr. Taylor visited the river stations with a view

to making arrangements for Mr. McCarthy's district.[1] Where missionaries of other societies were to be found, he took time to see something of their work, enjoying a Sunday especially with the Rev. David Hill at Wu-sueh. At Kiu-kiang he had a good deal of intercourse with the American missionaries, putting up apparently in native quarters.[2]

" The wind is strong and cold," he wrote to Mrs. Taylor during this visit (Feb. 24). " I am writing by a little window in a dark attic. The chair is not a foot high, yet I can touch the tiles as I sit. The hail-stones that came through the roof in the night, my ' boy ' swept up into a heap this morning, a foot and a half square and one or two inches thick. I was writing with numbed fingers till 3 A.M., and out to breakfast at eight. Nature does not enjoy these things ; but my heart rejoices in my Father's arrangements, and I cannot keep the words of ' *What a Friend we have in Jesus,*' and the music too, from welling up within—cannot and do not want to, for it is all *true,* is it not ? "

" I have written to *The Missionary Recorder,*" he continued a few days later, " asking special prayer for the outpouring of God's Spirit, not only at the Conference but before ; that we may all go up filled with the Spirit, and not merely *hoping* for a blessing." . . .

A day or two later, out on the wind-swept river, he was thinking and praying over the needs of the province he had just touched in passing (Kiang-si).

" It is stiff soil," he wrote, " and none but fully consecrated men will accomplish much. Comfort-seeking, etc., won't do there. *Cross-loving* men are needed. Where are they to be found ? Alas—where ! Oh, may God make you and me of this spirit ! and may our only prayer be, ' Lord, what wilt Thou have *me* to do ? ' I feel so ashamed that you and the dear children should affect me more than millions here who are perishing—while we are sure of eternity together. The good Lord forgive us, or me rather. . . .

" There are such openings in China as there never have been and as are not likely to recur. Just while the effect of the

---

[1] To Mr. and Mrs. Edward Pearse, who joined him at An-king, this chain of stations was committed, the importance of the work being seen in the fact that the converts baptized on this journey (March 1877) represented no fewer than six provinces.

[2] The C.I.M. house was closed, Mr. and Mrs. Cardwell being at home on furlough.

Imperial proclamations lasts (and this will largely be over in a very few months) we can do in weeks what would have taken months or years before. I see God's hand in bringing me here just now, on this and many other grounds."

Meanwhile the long-closed gates were opening indeed. In the north and far north-west, the pioneers held on their way; Mr. McCarthy was already nearing the western province of Sze-chwan, larger than the whole of France and far more populous; Judd and Broumton had been prospered in renting premises in the capital of Kwei-chow,[1] eight hundred miles south-west of the nearest mission station; while from Bhamo Messrs. Stevenson and Soltau had made extended journeys into the Kah-chen hills, from which two or three hours' descent would have brought them into Chinese territory.[2] To his beloved friend Mr. Berger, so long one with him in prayer for these very developments, Mr. Taylor had recently written:[3]

It will afford you no small joy to know that our prayers are so far answered that work is begun in six of the nine provinces. You will have heard that Stevenson and Soltau are not permitted at present to enter Yün-nan. I trust the delay will only be temporary, and that the way may ultimately be all the more open. It is such a rest to know and feel that God knows how to carry on His own work. . . .

My heart is unspeakably glad that He led my dear wife and myself to use our means in aid of this and other similar work in needy lands, and to separate for a season in furtherance of His cause. Can we be mistaken in trusting Him to do what He so easily can—to supply the men and means needed for carrying on His own work, and extending it? My glad heart says, " No," little as I know Him: and what is more, His word says, " He that spared not His own Son, but delivered Him up for us all, how shall He not, with Him also, freely give us all things? "

---

[1] Thus was opened in February 1877 the first *permanent* Mission-station in any of the nine hitherto unoccupied provinces. Kwei-yang is still a centre of the C.I.M. in that province, in which it has now ten stations, 57 out-stations, and 6330 communicants.

[2] It was a sore trial to Mr. Stevenson and Mr. Soltau to be withheld from carrying out the purpose with which they had gone to Bhamo, not through any difficulty with the Burman or Chinese authorities, but through the attitude of the Indian Government, which declined to grant the pass-ports needed to cross into Chinese territory. News of this unexpected difficulty reached Mr. Taylor in the Yangtze valley, in February 1877.

[3] On the s.s. *Kiang-yung*, travelling up to Wu-chang, January 6, 1877.

Thus with thankfulness and expectation Mr. Taylor returned to Wu-chang to meet the pioneers as they gathered for their little conference. From the far inland provinces they came, as well as from the river stations—seventeen C.I.M. workers in all, to be joined by a dozen or more of the Hankow missionaries. The chief responsibility for the meetings rested upon Mr. Taylor ; and as always in times of special need, a day was set apart for prayer and fasting. He and his fellow-workers were one in the longing for an outpouring of divine blessing that should sweep away all coldness and deadness in their own hearts, all criticism and misunderstanding ; an enduement with " power from on high " for the great work to be done.

Wonderful in the days that followed was the answer to these prayers. In Mr. Judd's garden-house on the hill-side, and the L.M.S. chapel across the river, the presence of God was consciously felt. " Take time to be holy " was the burden of Dr. Griffith John's message, followed by practical talks from Mr. Taylor and others on the real problems, the inward, spiritual problems, of missionary life. Much time was given to prayer, especially for the unopened provinces ; and the story the young evangelists had to tell, simple though it was, called forth deepest sympathy. The hopefulness of these inexperienced workers, their enthusiasm and genuine confidence in GOD as able and willing to do the impossible, were contagious as well as cheering.

" I thank God for Mr. Taylor ; I thank God for the C.I.M. ; I thank God for my younger brethren," Dr. John said earnestly at the closing meeting, adding that he was sure he was but expressing the feeling of all the Hankow missionaries.

Three weeks later came the Shanghai General Conference, and Mr. Taylor having sent off the pioneers, strengthened and encouraged, turned to the difficult task awaiting him at the coast. The paper he had to read was upon " Itineration Far and Near, as an Evangelising Agency," and while it was the subject of all others nearest his heart, he well knew that next only to the " term question " it would probably call forth differences of opinion, if not bitterness of feeling. " *Jesus, I am resting, resting,*" was the hymn he most often

asked for in the little crowded house where the C.I.M.
contingent gathered ; [1] and despite the seriousness of the
issues involved, his mind was kept in peace.

And once again prayer was answered and the seemingly
impossible brought to pass. The " term question," which
had threatened to prove so serious a difficulty, was by general
consent excluded from the deliberations ; and Mr. Taylor's
paper, as *The Celestial Empire* recorded, " secured the
deepest interest of his audience." [2]   From Dr. John's
opening address with its searching, powerful appeal for a life
in the Holy Spirit, to the call of the united conference " to
the Mission Boards, Colleges and Churches of the World "
for men and women to meet the great opportunity, all was
cause for thanksgiving—" a gathering fraught with blessing
to the people of China," as Mr. Taylor wrote, " the most
important step China missions have yet taken." The
parting, after two weeks of fellowship (May 10-24) was
" like the breaking-up of a family never more to meet on
earth." No discordant note remained. Even the Chinese
dress of Mr. Taylor and his fellow-workers had ceased to
offend, and the forward movement they represented had
passed into the confidence and prayerful sympathy of most
if not all present.

[1] The C.I.M. Headquarters in Shanghai had been moved by this time
to 7 Seward Road, Hongkew, Mr. and Mrs. Cranston generously acting
as house-father and house-mother. While paying for the rooms they
occupied, they undertook all the Mission business that had to be transacted in that port, and boarded the missionaries as they came and went.
In spirit they were almost members of the Mission, and with Mr. and Mrs.
Thos. Weir, also residents in Shanghai, were, and still are, among its most
valued friends.

[2] " God greatly helped me this afternoon with my paper," he wrote
himself ; " the feeling, now, is very kind toward us."—To Mrs. Taylor,
May 12, 1877.

PART V

BURIED LIVES: MUCH FRUIT

1878–1881. AET. 46-49.

Hearken, O daughter, and consider . . . forget also thine own people and thy father's house ; so shall the king greatly desire thy beauty : for He is thy Lord and worship thou Him.—Ps. xlv. 10, 11.

If the world were mine, and all its store,
    And were it of crystal gold,
Could I reign on its throne for evermore
    From the ancient days of old,
An empress noble and fair as day,
    Oh gladly might it be—
That I might cast it all away :
    Christ, only Christ for me !
                    Matilda of Hefta, 13th century.

The LORD giveth the word ; the women that publish the tidings are a great host.—Ps. lxviii. 11, R.V.

CHAPTER XXI

" FOR JESUS' SAKE "

1877–1879. AET. 45–47.

SERIOUS tidings were already reaching Mr. Taylor, before
the Shanghai Conference, of the long-continued drought in
the northern provinces. Failure of the wheat and other
crops, year after year, had brought a vast population to the
verge of famine, and letters from two of the pioneers on
their second visit to Shan-si were full of the impending
calamity. Realising in measure what the situation meant,
and the opportunity it afforded for practising as well as
preaching the Gospel, Mr. Taylor was anxious to do as much
as possible to supply Messrs. Turner and James with funds
for famine relief. They were the only Protestant missionaries in all the stricken area, and their letters published in
China's Millions could not fail to awaken sympathy. But
the assistance would have to be long-continued, and on this
ground alone Mr. Taylor saw that his return to England
should be as speedy as possible.

The forty weeks of his expected absence from home were
nearing an end, but not so the work to be done in China.
None of the older centres of the Mission had yet been visited ;
and keen as he was about the pioneering, the settled stations
with their little churches were ever on his heart. In his
poor state of health it was no easy matter to face the intense
heat of summer in visits to the Che-kiang stations, with all
that was involved of work and arduous travelling. He had
fully expected to get through before the Shanghai Conference ; but now that important occasion had come and

gone, and he seemed little nearer the return to England that was in many ways so urgent.

" Sometimes it does seem hard," he had written to Mrs. Taylor early in May, " to be so long away from you. But when I think of One Who spent thirty-three years away from His heaven, and finished them on Calvary, I feel ashamed of my own selfishness."

And while the Conference was going on :

I do like our absence from one another, for Jesus' sake, to cost us something—to be a real sacrifice. May His worthy and loving heart accept it.

Much exhausted after the Conference, and suffering from neuralgia though he was, he set out therefore on a thorough visitation of the Che-kiang stations,[1] accompanied most of the way by a travelling-companion whose presence proved specially helpful among the women.

Miss Elizabeth Wilson, whom he was escorting to Wen-chow, had by this time been more than a year in China. Though scarcely beyond middle-age, and full of energy and brightness, her silvery hair brought her the advantage of being considered " old," among a people with whom such an appellation is an honour, and her coming to China at all was rather a wonder to other foreigners. But Mr. Taylor knew the whole story. He had met her long before, as a girl on a visit to London, and had learned of her earnest desire to give her life to missionary work. But at that time she was needed in her Westmorland home, and when her sister married and her parents became invalids the cherished hope had to be hidden in her heart.

" Years went on," as Mr. Taylor said in speaking of her subsequent usefulness in China, " and this loving daughter never

---

[1] Mr. Taylor not only visited on this journey (May to October 1877) all the stations *and out-stations* of the Mission in Che-kiang, with one exception (illness at Wen-chow obliging him to hurry past Hwang-yen) ; he crossed over from Wen-chow to Chü-chow-fu on the Tsien-tang river, staying at Chu-chow (the district now occupied by the Barmen Mission), at Yung-kang, Kin-hwa-fu and Lan-chi on the way. In all this region there was then *no resident missionary*. At Chü-chow-fu, under Mr. Douth-waite's care, he met the first converts from Yü-shan, in the neighbouring province of Kiang-si (see pp. 334, 335). Thence he returned down the Tsien-tang river to Hang-chow.

let her parents suspect that she was making any sacrifice on the one hand, yet never recalled the gift she had given to the Lord for missionary service on the other. When five years had gone by, she began to feel, ' If I am delayed much longer, the language will be hard to learn.' But she waited God's time.

"Ten, twenty, thirty years passed away ere the Lord set her free; but the vow of twenty was as fresh in her heart at fifty as when first it had been offered. Within three weeks of the death of her surviving parent, she wrote to our headquarters in London of her desire to spend the remainder of her days in missionary work in China." [1]

Very interesting it was, now, to see the welcome with which the Christian women received this unexpected visitor, especially in stations where they had no lady missionary. With their Romanised New Testaments wrapped in coloured handkerchiefs (the precious book it had cost Mr. Taylor and others years of labour to provide) they walked miles on tiny feet to meet the travellers, and begged in place after place that the " Elder Sister " might stay among them, that they as well as the men might have some one to teach them the things of God.

From Miss Wilson's recollections of this journey we learn of the exceeding love with which Mr. Taylor was received in many places, especially among the mountain people of what had been Mr. Stevenson's out-stations. Simple as they were, and poor, they entertained him with generous hospitality, so that the inns in which he had often sojourned knew him no more, on that route at any rate. To some of the villages he was carried in the primitive mountain-chair, hanging from a single pole, the Christians themselves being his bearers and resolutely refusing payment.

It was a sorrow to miss, in this beautiful district, one who had been called Home since Mr. Taylor's last visit three and a half years previously. Then, the scholar Nying had been, under God, the inspiration of the work ; now, his place

---

[1] Miss Wilson, a sister of the well-known Convener of the Keswick Convention, Mr. Robert Wilson, went out as a self-supporting worker with the last party of the Eighteen (1876), and remained twelve years in China. " Whether she will be strong enough to go back, as she so much desires, I do not know," Mr. Taylor wrote after her return (1888), " but I do know that her life there has been an immense blessing."

was empty. The truth he had so faithfully proclaimed was still bearing fruit, however, in many a life, sometimes in strangely unexpected ways. There was the cotton-weaver of Cheng-hsien, for example, saved through the preaching of Tao-hsing (himself one of Nying's children in the faith), saved through a hole in the wall, amid ridicule and laughter, but blessedly saved! It was a joy to Miss Wilson as well as Mr. Taylor to meet this man and hear his story.

He was just a poor orphan lad, the slave and drudge of the family who had adopted him. Hearing unusual sounds of merriment one day from the adjoining house, he left his work and went to a little opening he knew of, where a knot had dropped out of the wooden partition, to see what was going on. The son of the neighbouring family had just returned from the city and was telling his experiences. He was making fun, it appeared, of some one he had heard talking to a crowd. It was the well-known gambler, Tao-hsing, who had " eaten the foreign religion " and whose life had become so changed.[1] He was telling the matchless story of the Prodigal Son, telling it out of a full heart. Travestied as it was in the reproduction, it still appealed to the dejected, lonely listener, as nothing else that he had ever heard. Could it be that there was a God—a Father in heaven—Who loved like that !

" Oh, go on, go on ! " he cried almost without knowing it when the recital ended. " Let us hear more of those good words."

Astonishment and laughter on the other side of the partition drove him from his vantage-ground, but only to send him in search of his neighbour, from whom he learned where the wonderful teaching could be heard. And once he had grasped the heavenly message, nothing would induce him to turn away from the Saviour Whom, not having seen, he loved. Called up one night during the following winter, he was told by the people with whom he lived that they would stand it no longer. He must give up his employment, his home, the affianced bride for whom he was working—

[1] For the conversion of the gambler see p. 242.

give up everything and be thrust, penniless, into the streets —or have done with this new-fangled religion.

What, give up Christ ? It was a terrible ordeal, for the people were very angry. But he was kept amid all the excitement, and enabled to tell them unhesitatingly that nothing could alter his choice. Then and there he found himself hustled out into the darkness ; heard the door barred behind him, and felt the driving sleet beat upon his shelterless head. There was no refuge but in God.

" A week or two later," Mr. Taylor wrote, " the family found they could not manage without him. After trying in vain to induce him to turn from the Lord, they took him back ; and when we were there, there was hope of the conversion of several members of that household. Truly the Gospel is still ' the power of God unto salvation ' ; we have no need to be ashamed of it, or fear for its success ! "

Farther south over the mountains, Miss Wilson had the new experience of being entertained in more than one village temple, cleared of idols, which had been given by its owner for Christian worship. Eleven baptisms took place in the temple at Dien-tsi during their visit, quite a company of church members and inquirers assembling for the feast Mr. Taylor provided.

Then, too, she remembered his never-ending labours on boats, in sedan-chairs and in the stations to which they came—always the little white skin box that held his papers ; always the letters to be answered, articles to be written for *China's Millions*, or Mission business to attend to. It was the element of fervent, unfailing prayer for his fellow-workers, however, which impressed Miss Wilson most. No less than three times daily he was in the habit of waiting upon God on their behalf, once at least mentioning by name every member of the Mission, though they already numbered seventy apart from Chinese helpers.

Much though there was to encourage in connection with this five months' journey, there were also little churches that greatly needed quickening, and missionaries who were in poor health and tried in spirit. And these places, Miss Wilson noticed, were not passed over hurriedly. Even when much of discomfort was involved, Mr. Taylor would stay on, doing all he could to help—relieving the workers in charge by conducting daily meetings, getting into touch with the Christians and accompanying the missionary to his out-stations. At one centre where there was sickness the house was so full that, Miss Wilson being accommodated, no room could be found for Mr. Taylor. But the family were greatly needing help, and though it was the hottest part of summer he remained for three weeks, sleeping on the verandah at night, and doing without any place to himself through the day.

By this time he had in mind a plan for helping the little churches, which he longed to see carried out. Why should there not be a Chinese conference for native leaders much on the same lines as the united meetings recently held in Shanghai ? Such a gathering had never at that time been thought of, much less attempted, but Mr. Taylor saw the stimulus and encouragement it might afford.

" Pray very much for a blessing on our Ningpo Conference," he wrote to Mrs. Taylor when arrangements were in train. " The brethren and natives all greatly need quickening, *and I do.* This hot weather seems to relax soul as well as body."

Who has not felt it ? But he could not go on and leave things in a low state spiritually. He would give all the time, take all the trouble and responsibility of arranging the meetings, *in faith* that God would make them just the blessing needed. And when at last his visits were completed and he was in the midst of preparations for the return to England—taking with him a difficult party to care for : one sick mother, one newly widowed, and several ailing children—he left everything to come himself and take part in the Conference, as if it were the only concern upon his mind.

And that first Union Conference of native pastors and evangelists, it is good to record, exceeded even his expectations. Three English and three American societies were represented, the delegates coming from all parts of the province, and the meetings were entirely in Chinese.

" It was one of the most interesting conferences I have ever
attended," Mr. Taylor wrote, " and we were both surprised and
delighted at the ability displayed by our native brethren. . . .
When it is remembered that all these men were themselves, but
a few years ago, in heathen darkness, we cannot but feel encouraged, and look for yet greater things in the future. . . .
May God hasten the time when such meetings shall be held in
every province of the Chinese Empire."

Joyful was the reunion just before Christmas when Mr.
Taylor reached home after this fourth visit to China. He
had been away almost sixteen months, and the little ones
of two and three years old could not remember him. The
elder brothers and sister were fast growing up, and an
adopted daughter had been added to the family, the doubly-
orphaned child of Duncan, the pioneer missionary of Nanking. Seven children filled the little home to overflowing,
and made the Christmas season full of gladness to the
father's heart.

Not that he had much time to spend with them. After
visiting almost every station in the Mission, and meeting
every fellow-worker with one exception,[1] Mr. Taylor had
come home deeply impressed with the need for immediate
reinforcements. Twenty-four men and at least six women
were urgently wanted, and for that number he was praying—
thirty new workers to go out if possible in the following year
(1878). Among the candidates awaiting his arrival, several
were ready to go forward, and Mr. Taylor was soon absorbed
in farewell meetings, which brought him in contact with
many friends.

" I am praying for an increase of £5000 a year in our income,"
he wrote to a senior member of the Mission in February, " and
for £2000 extra for outfits and passages. Will you daily join
in this prayer ? We are daily remembering you all by name
before the Lord. May you be filled with the Spirit, and all
around you be blessed from the overflow. ' My cup runneth

[1] The one member of the Mission he had not met on this visit to China
was Mr. Broumton, holding the fort alone in the distant province of Kwei-
chow—the only Protestant missionary south of the Yangtze, at that time,
in the western half of China.

over ' : GOD puts these words in our mouth ; *we* must not con-
tradict them."

Meanwhile grievous news was coming, mail by mail, of
the terrible famine in North China. In January it was
estimated that six million people were starving, and the
united efforts of the Chinese Government and of the foreign
Relief Committee were wholly inadequate to cope with the
disaster. In public meetings and through the press, Mr.
Taylor was making known the facts, with the result that
funds were coming to the C.I.M. freely for use in relief work.
But more than money was needed. Not only were tens of
thousands dying of starvation ; thousands more were being
sold into slavery—girls and young women literally taken
away in droves by cruel traffickers from the south. Children
were perishing in multitudes who might be gathered into
orphanages and saved for time and eternity, and everywhere
the poor suffering women were accessible as never before.
Surely the time had come when missionary *women*, as well
as men, should be found at the front in the newly opened
provinces of inland China !

But where was the woman who could take the lead ?
To go to that famine-stricken region, two or three weeks'
journey from the coast, was no easy matter. Some one with
experience was needed ; some one with a knowledge of the
language, fitted to help and care for younger workers. In
China there was no one in the C.I.M. circle free and suitable ; and at home ? Ah, that was where light began to
come for Mr. Taylor—but at such a cost !

Yes, there was one who undoubtedly combined the
qualifications necessary. Experienced, prayerful, devoted,
with a knowledge of the language and the confidence of her
fellow-workers, Mrs. Taylor could give just the help required.
But how could she be spared from home ? How could he
let her go so soon after their long parting ? And if the
sacrifice was great for him, who shall say what it meant to
the mother's heart ? At first, indeed, she could not see it
to be called for. Her husband in poor health and overwhelmed with work surely needed her, to say nothing of the
children Could it be right to leave him, even if the family

were provided for ? The struggle, if not long, was desperately hard ; but for her, as for him, only one issue was possible. A little worn brown note-book tells the rest ; and it is the same wonderful story that every truly Christian heart has known, of God's own Word meeting the inward need, the need so deep as to be voiceless even to Him, but none the less understood.

Point by point all her difficulties were met, her questions answered, until she knew beyond a doubt that it was God Himself Who had need of her out there in China. And, even then, His tender care went further. HE knew the inward shrinking, the hours of testing that must come.

" I felt like Gideon," Mrs. Taylor wrote, " that my strength in China would be, ' Have not I commanded thee ? ' and I wanted some fleeces to confirm my faith, and as a token for those who would have me remain at home. I asked God to give me, in the first place, money to purchase certain requisites for outfit, as we had none to spare ; and further, to give me liberally, as much as fifty pounds, so that there might be money in hand when I went away."

The very next afternoon (Thursday) a friend called to see Mrs. Taylor, and before leaving said :

" Will you accept a little gift for your own use, to get anything you may need for the journey ? "

And the sum put into her hand was ten pounds—just the allowance made by the Mission at that time towards the cost of outfit.

No one knew, not even Mr. Taylor, about the fleeces ; and with a wondering heart she waited. Several days passed without bringing the further answer to her prayer. Perhaps the Lord was withholding it that she might trust Him without so much confirmation ?

" Yesterday (Sunday)," she continued, in a letter to Mr. Taylor's mother, " I felt He would provide at the right time, and was very happy—realising that He is my Helper, and that in going I should learn more of Him and find His strength made perfect in my utter weakness."

Glancing next morning over the letters to see if there was one that might contain a gift for themselves, she came to the conclusion that there was not, and opened first a letter from Barnsley, thankful that Mr. Taylor's parents approved the step they were taking. And lo, from his father was enclosed a cheque for fifty pounds ! Overwhelmed with joy and thankfulness, she ran to Mr. Taylor's study : but he was not alone.

" When I returned " (for she was called away), " he was reading your letter, and considering how the Lord would have the money applied. He knew we needed it, but never takes anything for ourselves that is left optional.

" ' Oh,' I said, ' that fifty pounds is mine ! I have a claim on it that you do not know of.' And I told him all the circumstances.

" So we accept it with warmest thanks to you, and with gratitude to God. I had said to the Lord : ' Fifty pounds just now would be worth more than a fortune to me at another time. It would be a guarantee of all other needs being met.' I feel it is such tender consideration for my weakness to send it ; and you and dear father may be assured, when I am far away, that the memory of this gift will be a continual strength and help to me."

Meanwhile, Mrs. Broomhall, who was away from home at the time, had heard of the proposed step, and was deeply moved. With the care of the Mission-house and candidates, as well as her own family of four boys and six girls, it would have been easy and true to think that her hands were full. But hers was the love that " never faileth," and in a busy, practical life she knew the secret of so waiting upon God as to have her strength daily renewed.

" If Jenny is called to go to China," she said without hesitation, " I am called to care for her children."

Nothing could have given Mrs. Taylor greater comfort ; for with such loving supervision close at hand, even the little ones could remain with their father, and the home-life be carried on as usual. But there was yet more that the Lord had it in His heart to provide. The very day before Mrs. Taylor left England, accompanied by several new workers,[1] a letter came to hand from an old friend expressing warm

---

[1] The party, which included Adam Dorward, J. H. Riley, and S. R. Clarke, men of notable usefulness in later years, sailed on the 2nd of May 1878.

sympathy with the object she had in view. It contained a gift toward the Orphanage she hoped to found ; and to her surprise on looking at the cheque, it proved to be for *a thousand pounds.*

"Please enter it anonymously," he wrote. "It does not represent any superabundance of wealth, as my business affairs will miss it. But if you, for Christ's sake, can separate, I cannot give less than this." [1]

It was a great step forward when, the heat of summer over, Mrs. Hudson Taylor set out from Shanghai to go to the inland province of Shan-si. Two younger ladies accompanied her—Miss Horne and Miss Crickmay—and they travelled under the experienced escort of Mr. Baller. Never before had foreign women attempted to go so far inland, and with their work in the famine-stricken region, a little light began to shine for the women and children of that vast waiting world—the hundred and eighty millions of the far interior. When the news reached Mr. Taylor by cablegram—

"I cannot tell you how my heart and prayers go with you all," he wrote. "*The Lord be glorified in this movement.* . . . I do thank God for giving me such a wife as alone could satisfy my heart—one to whom the Lord Jesus is more than husband ; to whom His work is more than love and enjoyment here. I *know* He is blessing and will bless our dear children ; I *know* He is blessing and will bless you ; I *know* He is blessing and will bless me too, and the work. And I am glad to think I am not selfishly, for my own help or enjoyment, depriving you of the eternal fruit of what you are now sowing. What will not the harvest be ! "

For himself, meanwhile, the sacrifice involved was very real. As long as Mrs. Broomhall could come in and out freely from her home next door, he did not feel the burden of family care ; but when his own children developed whooping-cough, calling for the isolation of his household, more

[1] The day after Mrs. Taylor had sailed, the one who was missing her most sorely wrote : "Your dear Mother has borne up bravely, and says she is 'proud of you.' I, darling, am *grateful* for the grace which has taken you from me, and which I *count on* to sustain you all the way. HE will not fail me either, or the work He has given us to do. We *will* trust Him—in all and for all."

responsibility naturally fell to his share. In addition to
very full days of work, Mr. Taylor had many an anxious
night of watching by little bedsides from which the mother
was absent. No " mere man " could have done more, or
done it better, and it bound the children to him in a way that
made it well worth while ; but it was a tax on time and
strength, of which he had little enough to spare.

" I took Ernie down to Barnet," he wrote when they were
getting better. " He enjoyed himself famously," in the home
of Mrs. Taylor's parents, " and I am somewhat better for it too.
I enjoyed the quiet and the hayfield, and putting him to bed
at night, and praying with him and dressing him, etc. He
clung to me so tenderly."

The answer to the petition in which many were uniting
for thirty new workers in the current year was at the same
time bringing added burdens. At the Annual Meetings
(May 27) Mr. Taylor was able to tell of many candidates,
some of whom seemed of unusual promise, but of a balance
in hand, all obligations being met, of only *twenty-nine pounds*.
The money Mrs. Taylor had given, with his hearty concurrence, for pioneering work in the inland provinces (£4000)
had carried them through the two years since the Chefoo
Convention. But the extensive itinerations of that period—
involving thirty thousand miles of travel—had exhausted
it, and the income of the Mission had not yet correspondingly
increased.

" With current income not equal by so large a sum to the
expenses of the work," Mr. Taylor said on that occasion, " the
question might well be asked, ' Is the project of sending out
twenty or thirty additional labourers at all a prudent one, even
if men and women who appear suitable are found ? '
" Well, we have looked the thing in the face, dear friends,
and this is the conclusion we have come to : with the current
income of the Mission we have nothing to do, but with GOD we
have everything to do. *We* are not going to send out twenty or
thirty new missionaries, or one ; but we are asking GOD to send
twenty or thirty. If *He* sends twenty or thirty devoted mis
sionaries, He is just as able to supply them as He has proved
faithful and loving in supplying those who have gone hitherto
. . . Up to the present, God has carried us safely through.

As for the future—if by His grace He will only keep us, individually, *faithful to Him*, that ensures everything." [1]

That he was deeply feeling the responsibility of leadership in a mission which had already grown beyond the desires and hopes with which it was founded, is evident from a letter to Mrs. Taylor of a few weeks later.

" I have been praying very much this morning," he wrote on June 14, " for a wise and understanding spirit, and for largeness of heart, and organising capacity. The Lord make me equal to increasing claims."

Very thankful must she have been to hear of a break that came soon after, an unexpected holiday—the first he had taken, apart from sea voyages, during the twelve years since the formation of the Mission. At the invitation of the Hon. Miss Waldegrave and Lady Beauchamp, who generously met the expense, he joined their family party in the Engadine for two or three weeks. It was the first time he had been in Switzerland, and many letters tell of the delight with which he drank in the beauty of lake, mountain, and Alpine flowers, and the glacier air which seemed to give him new life. With true consideration, his friends left him free to attend to correspondence or wander as he would in the pine forests on the mountain side. Even there Mission matters followed him—as many as twenty-five letters being received one day, most of which required answers. Comparative leisure enabled him to write freely to Mrs. Taylor, among others, whose absence he was specially feeling amid those beautiful scenes.

" Every day I look at the little Bible marker you gave me, with the words ' For Jesus' sake,' " he wrote from Sils Maria (Aug. 27), " and I am thankful for the reminder. It is not for

---

[1] How real were Mr. Taylor's convictions on this point may be judged from the unstudied expression of his feelings in a letter to Mrs. Taylor of September 20 :

" Nothing is coming in for the general fund scarcely ; but this is usual at this time of year. We must all get nearer to God ; we must all abide in Christ ; our lives must be more up to our principles and privileges, and all will be well. Let us trust for all, and we shall find all. God *can* bless *each* member of the Mission ; let us ask it in faith, and *expect it*. Nothing else, nothing less can satisfy Him ; nothing less must satisfy us."

your pleasure or mine that we are separated, nor for money-making, nor for our children's sake. It is not even for China, or the missionaries or the Mission : no—*for Jesus' sake.* HE is worthy ! And He is blessing you, and is making the people I meet so kind to me, one and all."

When they reached Pontresina, it was the glaciers that attracted him most. With an umbrella for the sun (China fashion), a few biscuits in his pocket and a Bible as his sole companion, he would spend most of the day on or near them.

" The effect of the air on the system is wonderful," he continued. " I could not possibly have conceived it. It seems to go direct to the seat of weakness, and carry healing. . . . I have been thinking to-day, darling, that all this refreshment, all this kindness, is the answer of God to *your* prayers for me ; and the thought has given added pleasure to all I have enjoyed."

Entering into every detail of her life in that famine-stricken region of North China, he wrote of the comfort it was to think of her as " a weak instrument in Almighty hands."

" Keep loving and patient with all," he said in another letter, " especially with any who *try* your patience, if it be tried."

And every letter was full of longing to be with her once more—to help forward the work, especially in the inland provinces.

Many were the problems thought out and prayed over in those mountain solitudes. A critical time had come, he could not help feeling, in the history of the Mission. Prayer had been wonderfully answered, and the whole interior opened up to the work of evangelists ; but now the more responsible step had to be taken of sending women inland, to follow up what had been begun. In praying for the first twenty-four " willing, skilful labourers " on the sands at Brighton, he had hardly contemplated this. The pioneer missionaries would marry ; it was well they should. The converts, many of them, would be women. There would be families to care for—their own and those of the Christians. If it had caused an outcry when *men* were sent to face the loneliness and dangers of life in the far interior, what would happen when he encouraged single ladies, or even young married women, to do the same ?   Then there were questions connected with the home organisation of the growing work.

But most of all it was with the Lord Himself those hours of soul-refreshing silence were occupied.   On coming down from the glacier heights to the level of the lakes once more, he wrote to a Swiss member of the Mission (from Lausanne, September 13) :

May God keep you, and not only keep you—*fill* you more and more, and keep you running over with the living waters. The one thing, I judge, to bear in mind is that it has " pleased the Father that *in Him* should all the fulness dwell." Apart from Him we have nothing, are nothing, cannot bring forth any fruit to God. He will not give some of His riches to you and some to me, to use and live on away from Himself. But *in* Him *all* is ours. With Him there is a constant feast for us. To know Christ as the Bridegroom is most blessed ; to be not betrothed, and having occasional visits, but married. " I *am* with you alway," " I will *never* leave thee," " I will not fail thee, nor forsake thee "—such are now His messages of love to us.

Upon the many meetings that awaited Mr. Taylor's return to England in September we must not dwell, nor upon the remarkable answers to prayer that facilitated the out-going of all the thirty asked for and given in 1878. Twenty-eight new missionaries actually sailed before the close of the year, and several others were accepted to follow shortly. Not one really suitable candidate was declined for lack of funds, though some had to be told that there was not a penny in hand to send them out. But again and again the Lord's provision came ear-marked, so to speak, to meet the special need.[1]

---

[1] The very day one October party sailed, for example, Mr. Taylor wrote to two young men of much promise, accepting them for work in Shan-si. Although he had nothing, as he frankly told them, toward the expense of passages and outfits, he invited them to come to London with a view to an early departure. These communications were posted at 5.15 P.M., and by the nine o'clock delivery, that same evening, a letter was received from Lord Radstock (then in Stockholm) enclosing, among other gifts, the sum of one hundred pounds *to send two new workers to the famine-stricken province of Shan-si*. Thus, even before the young men could set out in faith for London, the money needed was in hand and the way open for them to go forward.

And in matters more perplexing than finance, help was given that cleared the way for Mr. Taylor's return to China. The Council was strengthened by the addition of Mr. William Sharp—now its senior member ; and Mr. McCarthy, who was finding important openings for deputation work, undertook the sub-editing of *China's Millions*. More important still was the acceptance of the post of Home Director by Mr. Theodore Howard—Chairman of the Council and a life-long friend of the Mission. The appointment of Mr. B. Broomhall as General Secretary recognised the invaluable service he had rendered at Pyrland Road for the last three years ; while Mrs. Broomhall continued to care for the outgoing and returning missionaries and the seventeen children.

There were still circumstances that called for prayer, and no lack of difficulties to be met both in England and in China.

" I do not expect an easy time of it," Mr. Taylor wrote home to Mr. Broomhall from Hongkong, " and but for the precious truth, ' My strength is made perfect in weakness,' I should be almost afraid to arrive in my present weak state. I am very glad that our fast-day, May 26th, is near, and shall look for a large outpouring of spiritual blessing in connection with it. God is with us ; let us only walk humbly with Him and all will be brought round. You will pray for me, will you not ? The all-important thing is to improve the character of the work, and to deepen the piety, devotion, and success of the workers ; to remove stones of stumbling, if possible ; to oil the wheels where they stick ; to amend whatever is defective and supplement as far as may be what is lacking ; no easy matter where suitable men are wanting, or only in course of formation. That I may be used of God, at least, in some measure, to bring these things about is my hope ; but I shall need your prayers ; for *God's* wisdom, *God's* grace, *God's* strength alone can suffice : but they will suffice."

CHAPTER XXII

HE GOETH BEFORE THEM

1879–1880. Aet. 47–48.

MRS. HUDSON TAYLOR had come to Shanghai. All the way from Shan-si she had travelled upon an uncertainty—yet sure in her own mind that she was being led of God. Was her husband on his way to China ? Was he ill and needing her urgently, as she had seen in that curiously vivid dream ? And how could she help him best ?

A thousand miles away from the port at which he would land, she had felt painfully out of reach ; and though he had suggested joining her there, to see something of the northern provinces, she knew how unlikely it was that he would be able to escape from claims nearer the coast. The work she had undertaken for the famine orphans was well established, and her companions were now able to carry it on. Two of the missionaries at the capital (Tai-yuan-fu) had been joined by their wives, so that there was no longer the same need for her presence. And that dream, fitting in with other elements of guidance, had decided her to cross the mountains and return to Shanghai, that she might be at hand in case of need.

It led also to definite and earnest prayer for Mr. Taylor, which was sorely needed. For he *was* on his way out, as we have seen, and in the Indian Ocean had become so seriously ill that a Singapore doctor doubted whether he could reach Hongkong alive. He decided to go on, however ; and the news that reached him in the latter port of Mrs. Taylor's being actually in Shanghai, when he had thought her far away and inaccessible, was so cheering that it helped him over the rest of the voyage. Her letters too were encouraging.

" I have been spreading before the Lord," she had written soon after reaching Shanghai,[1] " some of the numerous difficulties that await you, and thinking of them with something of rejoicing. What a platform there will be for our God to work and triumph on ; and how clearly we shall see His hand ! May He keep you without care, and bring you up like Jehoshaphat, your mouth filled with songs of praise in prospect of certain victories. . . . Oh, the resources of the grace you have to draw upon ! ' According to His riches in glory,' . . . ' According to your need.' Surely, to need much grace and therefore to have much given is not a thing to be troubled about, is it ?

" Don't you think that if we set ourselves not to allow any pressure to rob us of communion with the Lord, we may live lives of hourly triumph, the echo of which will come back to us from every part of the Mission ? I have been feeling these last months that of all our work the most important is that unseen —upon the mount of intercession. *Our* faith must gain the victory for the fellow-workers God has given us. They fight the seen, and we must fight the unseen battle : and dare we claim less than constant victory when it is for *Him*, and we come in His Name ? "

Met by Mr. Weir with his private launch, Mr. Taylor was carried without fatigue to the very door of the Mission-house, then on the Soo-chow Creek, where he found quite a party awaiting him. Each one had special needs or problems to be dealt with ; and Mr. and Mrs. Dalziel, in charge of the home and business department, were keeping open house for seamen, among whom an encouraging work was going on. This thoroughly suited the earnest band Mr. Taylor had brought with him, several of whom decided to give their first night in China to prayer and praise. They gathered in a room next to Mr. Taylor's, and had a memorable time, full of liberty and blessing, never realising that to the invalid on the other side of the partition it meant hours of wakefulness and pain. Nothing would have induced Mr. Taylor to stop them, however ; he rejoiced far too much in their

---

[1] A letter dated March 18, 1879.

fervent spirit, but it proved scarcely the best preparation, in his own case, for the busy days that followed.

At first, in the joy of reunion, he was full of plans for visiting the stations and helping the new missionaries who had been sent out (thirty-four in number) during his recent visit to England. But the strain of all that had to be attended to was more than he could bear, and within a fortnight he was so ill that again life itself was hanging in the balance. The physician consulted had little hope, unless he could at once be removed to a more bracing climate. Summer was coming on, and it was useless to attempt to remain anywhere in the Yangtze valley. The northern port of Chefoo, with its freedom and freshness, he recommended as the best available refuge : but how to get there was the difficulty.

It was an anxious journey, from the Monday evening when they went on board, through the long hours of Tuesday —moving slowly in a damp sea-mist, while the fog-horn droned its melancholy sound—and especially that second night when Mrs. Taylor was almost at her wits' end. All the milk she had brought for the invalid had curdled, in spite of being boiled and put in the ice-chest, and some things he might have fancied she reproached herself for having failed to bring. He was so low that he could hardly take anything, and she feared he would be too weak to be moved from the steamer when Chefoo was reached. Weary though she was she dared not sleep, for Mr. Taylor could do nothing for himself, and from time to time was very faint.

" In my distress I cried to God to help me," she wrote to Miss Desgraz at Chin-kiang. " I asked Him either to enable Mr. Taylor to take the food we had, or to show me what I could get for him, or to make him better without anything—as He had said, ' Man doth not live by bread alone.' I pleaded too that the fog might clear away, and that God who loved His own child would undertake for him, as the responsibility was too great for me to bear. I thought of ' God is a refuge and strength, a very present help in trouble,' and ' Yea, though I walk through the valley of the shadow of death, I will fear no evil, for Thou art with me.' ' He doeth all things well ' came to my mind with comfort, and ' All the way my Saviour leads me.' Then I

Y

turned to Mr. Taylor and was able to prevail upon him to take a little food. In the night he had a cupful of arrowroot, and next day was decidedly better. . . . That afternoon I went on deck, and fell in with an officer with whom I was able to have some earnest talk about spiritual things. I began about the improvement in the weather, and he said : ' Yes, it was remarkable ! About 9.30 the fog cleared right away, and we had a splendid, moonlight night.'

" It was between 9 and 9.30 that I had been praying about it, before going to rest."

Next morning she could not but feel a little anxious as they neared Chefoo. The vessel was only staying an hour, to discharge passengers and cargo, and there had been no time to make arrangements as to where to take the patient on landing. Eagerly she looked out for the Customs House officer, a kindly Christian man whose acquaintance she had made on her recent journey from Shan-si ; but when his boat came alongside Mr. Ballard was not on board. The illness that kept him at home deprived her of a helping hand when one was most needed ; and for the moment it seemed desolate to transfer their belongings to a native *sampan* and take Mr. Taylor ashore, ill as he was, with no idea where to go. Had it not been for the fog, however, their vessel would have come in some hours earlier, and they would have had to land in the middle of a cold night. So the morning sunshine was a token of the loving care of One Who had gone before them, and to Whom their every need was known.

Lying there in the little boat while his companions went in search of quarters,[1] how far was Mr. Taylor from imagining all that his illness and forlorn arrival were to mean of help and comfort for his fellow-labourers ! He had come to China full of hope for extension, especially in the field of Women's Work. The success that had attended Mrs. Taylor's efforts proved that the interior was no less accessible to women missionaries than to men ; and having sent his own wife first, he felt the more free to encourage others in

[1] Mr. and Mrs. Taylor were accompanied on this journey by Mr. J. J. Coulthard, one of the party just arrived from England who was much with them this summer, acting as Mr. Taylor's secretary ; and who afterwards became his son-in-law.

following her example. But it was a great task that lay before him, a great responsibility, calling for all he could give of time and strength. Did it not mean coming into personal touch with the new workers, as well as gathering up the threads at all the older stations, that he might know where reinforcements were most needed and who could best be spared for the forward movement? And here he was, laid aside, able to do nothing; and though happily he did not know it, long months were to elapse ere he would leave that silent shore again.

That silent, waiting shore—how much of help it was to afford in the practical problem of reaching the far interior with the Gospel! Scattered homes, missionary homes, centres of light and love among the people—yes, that was what he longed to see all over inland China. And what about the little children sent in love to such homes; sent to be not only their parents' joy and comfort, but an incalculable help in the work to which their lives were given? What about the need that must arise in the not distant future for a more favourable climate for those little ones than inland cities could afford, and for mental and physical training that should not separate them wholly from the influence of parents who must remain in China? What about the need of those parents, and others throughout the Mission, for rest and refreshment from time to time, and for a health resort in cases of illness like his own? All this Mr. Taylor could foresee but dimly, nor did he then imagine the extensive and complete equipment of buildings that was to arise on that far sweep of shore—the hospital, sanitarium, schools of the Mission; the bright, breezy centre of young life from which incalculable influences for good were to flow, on and on through long years and to the ends of the earth. But the Lord knew, the Lord foresaw, the Lord planned it all. And was He not beginning, even then, to answer the countless prayers with which each of those young lives would be received and surrounded, though for love of Christ the parents might have little they could do for their children but pray. Such sacrifices mean much to the infinite Father-heart.

In the home of Mr. Ballard, meanwhile, Mrs. Taylor had met with a cordial welcome. His illness proved only a passing indisposition, and he and his wife were given to hospitality. They were young, newly married people, and had room for visitors, so the missionary party soon found themselves received into a real home, as paying guests.

" Under the shadow of a high cliff and quite on the sea-shore," was Mrs. Taylor's description of their new surroundings.

" Mr. Taylor bore the moving better than I expected," she continued to Miss Desgraz, " though in his weak state, of course, he felt it. When, however, we had been a little while here, the sense of rest among kind people, in such a pleasant spot, seemed to refresh him, and every hour since has done him good. It is so quiet about here, with only Mr. and Mrs. Ballard. Mr. Taylor can sit on the verandah and drink in the sea-air—looking out on the hills all round the bay, and on the junks and steamers. The sea-weed smells so refreshing ! Has not God been good to us ? "

The summer that followed proved exceptionally trying. Few could remember a hotter season in China. Work such as Mr. Taylor had planned, down in the Yangtze valley, would in all probability have cost his life ; and the illness of one and another made him long to share with them the very real benefit he was deriving from Chefoo. Several of the newly-arrived young missionaries were sent for first of all, and an unused building known as " The Bungalow " was called into requisition. With three small rooms and an empty warehouse or " go-down " it possessed possibilities, and was soon occupied by a student party. But, for them, it was found possible to rent premises over at the Bluff—the fine headland with its purely Chinese villages, across the bay. And this arrangement was made none too soon ; for even before the young men could vacate it, the Bungalow was needed for other occupants.

Far away in Wu-chang, Mr. and Mrs. Judd were breaking down under the strain of their work and the overpowering heat, and it seemed as though they and their family would be obliged to return to England. " Come up here if you can," wrote Mr. Taylor, telling them how wonderfully Chefoo was answering in his own case ; but he had to pray that their way might be opened, as he had no money to send them just then for travelling. Under these circumstances, Mr. Judd was glad of an opportunity to sell the furniture they would no longer need ; and with the proceeds took his suffering wife and five little boys down the Yangtze and up to the northern port, at which a warm welcome awaited them.

To see those children playing on the beach was as much joy, almost, to Mr. Taylor as to their own parents, and he longed to bring the same relief to other fellow-workers and their families. But nothing was to be had in the way of accommodation, save The Bungalow, in which Mr. and Mrs. Judd were ingeniously making the best of circumstances. Boxes and packing-cases they turned into chairs and tables, in default of better, spreading their Chinese bedding on the floor at night.

" There was no furniture to be had in Chefoo in those days," wrote Mr. Judd, " save one kind of chair made of willow. It was altogether a new place ; besides which, we had no money for anything except necessaries. Seeing a number of Chinese houses at no great distance however, I went over, and found a shopman selling off his shelves very reasonably. These I bought, and adapted to our requirements. Some of them did for beds, like berths on a ship, and didn't our boys enjoy them ! I can truly say we lacked nothing—though it was a case of picnicking on the floor at first, which we did very willingly."

When things had got thus far, Mr. Taylor was so much better that he felt he must go down to Chin-kiang to see about certain rather surprising developments. For while he had been laid aside, unable to do anything in the matter most upon his heart, the Lord Himself had been working. His time had come, indeed, for opening the door of faith to the long-waiting womanhood of the recently entered provinces. Cost what it might, the Gospel must be carried to them too " according to the commandment of the eternal God " ; and He had His messengers ready. Providentially, it was the pioneers themselves who broke the ice. After repeated journeys, the far interior did not seem to them so very different from inland districts near the coast. Prospered in obtaining houses, they were quite at home among the people, and saw the advantage of having some settled stations. What more natural than that they should wish to be married, and take the first foreign women to those outlying regions as their own home-makers and fellow-missionaries ? To this Mr. Taylor, who had himself led the way, could raise no objection. Thus when he came down in August to the Yangtze valley, one young couple had already started for the far north-west, and others were preparing for similar journeys.

Meeting a terrific gale on the way from Chefoo to Shang-hai, the steamer by which Mr. Taylor travelled had come very near shipwreck. It was one of the worst typhoons recorded on that stormy coast, and for some time even Mr. Taylor felt doubtful as to the issue. He knew the vessel was not a strong one, and while earnestly praying for deliverance and the lives of all on board, blew up his swimming-belt and put it on, to be ready for the worst. And then, great calmness came to him in the assurance that his prayers, definitely offered in the Name of Jesus, would be answered.

" I took off my swimming belt," he wrote next day (Aug. 1), " turned the bedding over and found the under side moderately dry, and taking off my wettest things lay down in the others. . . . I had a good night—a much more quiet and restful one than the night before. It was *a little before one* that I felt God had answered prayer. The Captain put the ship's head round, I learn, and ran before the wind for some hours. But what interests me most is to hear from one of the officers to-day that the barometer, which had been very low, began to rise *soon after* 1 A.M. I had asked that if it were His will, the Lord would shorten the storm. . . . It was of course some time later before it perceptibly abated. To God be all the thanks and praise. Will He not go on to help in all things ? "

A busy month was spent in Shanghai and Chin-kiang, with visits to Yang-chow, where Mr. Taylor was altering the old premises to fit them for more aggressive work.

" It does seem so homelike," he wrote of the latter place : " how I should like to settle there for the remainder of my days and be a missionary again ! "

In letter after letter to Mrs. Taylor he spoke of being so thankful he had come ; of seeing the Lord's hand manifestly working in the removal of difficulties and the solution of problems ; of his purpose to go on to Hankow, despite the fresh heat-wave that could not last long, etc. Then came a break in the correspondence, and for the fourth time in as many months it looked as though his work were to be cut short, his earthly service ended. Dysentery returned with the overpowering heat, and very near the spot where his loved ones lay sleeping Hudson Taylor came once more to the borderland.

But the life that had not yet attained its widest usefulness was still prolonged. Nursing him day and night with the utmost devotion, Rudland managed to get the patient down to Shanghai and on board the coasting steamer, and indeed would not leave him till he was safely back in Chefoo once more. And there again the bracing air did wonders, and Mr. Taylor was lured into spending much time out of doors by a new project that almost thrust itself upon him.

Delighting day by day in that long sweep of sandy shore, he and his fellow-workers could not but see how much it would mean to the Mission to have a sanitarium there, and some day, perhaps, a school for missionaries' children. But they knew from experience the difficulty of obtaining land in China, and that when property has to be acquired peace is more than likely to be destroyed. They contented themselves, therefore, with looking longingly at the hills, where a retired spot with nicely rising ground offered an attractive situation. How well it would suit them—with its fresh-water stream running down to the shore ! But, for the time being, they could only pray. They did not often go over there even, knowing how prices are apt to go up if any interest is shown in a possible purchase. But one day Mr. Taylor was walking over the ground with Mr. Judd when a farmer came up and asked, to their surprise, if they wanted to buy land. They had just been saying, as a matter of fact, what an admirable site that bean-field would afford, if only they could get it.

" Do you want land ? " repeated the man, seeing their hesitation.

With little apparent interest they indicated that they might be prepared to buy some.

" Then will you buy mine ? " was the next surprise.

He was offering that very bean-field ; and at no un-reasonable price, as they soon discovered.

" Then and there the bargain was struck," recalled Mr. Judd. " I never knew a piece of business settled so easily. The money was paid and we got the field, with a gully and fresh water running down beside it. Then neighbouring farmers were willing to sell theirs as well ; and we bought all we wanted at a remarkably fair price. Now, of course, it is much more valuable."

The land given thus in answer to prayer, it was a question of how to utilise it at the least possible expense for the purpose of a sanitarium. Stones, brick and timber, if brought from a distance, would cost a good deal, and locally little or nothing was obtainable.

" Let us quarry our own stone," said Mr. Taylor, " and make bricks as we require them." He was his own archi-tect, and Mr. Judd's account of the whole proceeding—original and enterprising as it was—is not lacking in interest.

Neither Mr. Taylor nor I had any experience in house-build-ing. We employed men to quarry stone out of the gully, and made most of our bricks from the surface soil, which did well for that purpose. Then it occurred to us to make use of a ship called the *Christian* which had been wrecked in the bay. It had been built chiefly of oak and Norwegian pine, which served our purpose splendidly. We bought a large part of the wreck, using the deck for rafters and the oak for heavy beams. A Shanghai newspaper remarked, I remember, that the *Christian* had ceased going to sea, and had joined the C.I.M.

From another wreck, the *Ada*, we were able to buy teak, which made the floors. The cabin-fittings from that wreck came in most usefully. There was a splendid sideboard. We bought doors, locks, cupboards, everything we liked to take, at two dollars a hundredweight.[1] We squared the doors as well as we could, got keys for many of the locks, and they answered

---

[1] The dollar was 3s. 9d. that summer.

all right. The worst of the teak was the holes that the bolts had left. We filled them up, but the filling was very apt to come out, leaving openings in inconvenient places. I do not say that the house was well built, but it was wonderfully good considering our lack of experience. There were five rooms upstairs and about as many down, with outhouse and lean-to rooms besides. It was marvellously cheap ; and the Europeans in the Settlement were amazed at the rapidity with which it was put up. They could hardly believe their eyes when they saw it finished !

All this meant a new lease of life to Mr. Taylor. The complete change of occupation and long hours spent in the open air did wonders for him physically.

" How you would like to go out to the ground and see the operations," Mrs. Taylor wrote in November. " It is quite a busy scene. Builders, brickmakers, stonemasons and carpenters all have their matting tents, while others you might find occupied by Mr. Judd and Mr. Coulthard, or Mr. Taylor and Mr. Hunt. Looking well after the men is necessary to save expense and mistakes. The young men are finding it a capital school for the language, and are looking twice as robust as when they came out. The Gospel is explained to the workmen daily, at an enlarged sort of family prayers, and on Sundays they rest, at half pay, and one or two services are held for them. The young men find it an excellent opportunity for living Christ as well as speaking of Him, for patience is often exceedingly tried. The front of the house will face the sea, from which it is five minutes' walk, and the back looks on the hills. . . . It is so bracing and pleasant here. Mr. Judd is hardly like the same person."

It long stood, that simple, first construction in which began the justly famous Chefoo Schools of to-day. Two of Mr. Judd's sons, now valued members of the Mission, were the first pupils ; and Lao Chao, converted among the workmen on the building, grew into the trusted head-servant of a large staff of helpers. For gradually, hospital and private houses, school after school and the new sanitarium have sprung up, transforming those sunny slopes, that silent shore into a scene of delightful activity. There, with its competent teachers, every one of whom is a full member of the Mission, the C.I.M. cares for its children from Kindergarten up to College years, giving them a thorough, Christian education, and at the same time cherishing family relationships ; brothers and sisters meeting from the various schools, and parents coming from time to time to rest in the sanitarium.

Far in the future, however, were these developments as the year 1879 drew to a close. Busily occupied though he was, Mr. Taylor had still in mind the special purpose with which he had come to China ; and leaving Mr. Judd in charge of building operations he set out, as soon as health was re-established, for the advance post of the Mission at Wu-chang. The young couples who had left for the interior some months previously were now in their distant homes, beginning work for the first time among the women of the western and north-western provinces. What that work would mean, Mr. Taylor largely realised, and how great would be the need for sisterly help and companionship. Never in all the history of the Mission had he been called to take a step which cast him more in faith upon the living God. What, send women—unmarried women, young and defenceless—into all the dangers and privations, the hardship and loneliness of life in the far interior of China?   Let them take those perilous journeys of weeks and months at a time, and condemn them to isolation in crowded cities, hundreds of miles from any other foreigner? The responsibility was great indeed, and keenly he felt it. He was but a servant, however, not the Master. And if women were waiting to go at the Master's call, surely the time had come to help them rather than hinder.

Travelling by mule-litter with Mr. Coulthard from Chefoo to the Grand Canal, Mr. Taylor had leisure for thought and prayer over the situation. Three and a half weeks brought them to Chin-kiang, by roughest roads, with inns so poor that they even had to share their accommodation with the mules at night, when those voracious animals fell to eating the straw pillows on which their fellow-travellers were sleeping. Disturbed as might be their rest, however, and chilly as were their comfortless quarters that Christmas

season,[1] the younger missionary never failed to see, if he
woke early enough, the little candle burning that told of
Mr. Taylor's quiet hour over the Word of God.

And it all came about so naturally, when at length
Mr. Taylor reached Wu-chang. A number of C.I.M. people
were there, for various reasons, with Mr. and Mrs. Baller
in charge. Daily they met for Bible reading and prayer,
the needs of the lonely workers at the distant outposts
burdening their hearts. A thousand miles up the Yangtze,
Mr. and Mrs. Nicoll had just reached Chung-king, where she
was the only foreign woman in the great province of Sze-
chwan. For hard as it had been to part, Mr. and Mrs.
George Clark had gone on further—another seventeen days'
journey to the capital of Kwei-chow, where Mr. Broumton
was holding the fort alone. This latter post was very
distant, very isolated and Mr. Trench, on his next evangelistic journey, was to call in and see the little party. Yes,
he could act as escort, if there were ladies willing and ready
to go. And there were. Mrs. William McCarthy, newly
widowed, whose husband had been designated to that very
province, only asked to give her life to what was to have
been their united task; and Miss Kidd, beloved by the
Chinese no less than her fellow-workers, was more than
willing to accompany her. So the week of meetings was
followed by one of busy preparation.

"Such a venture of faith as it was!" said Mr. Coulthard,
looking back with more understanding than he or any of the
young missionaries could have had at the time. "The last
meeting to commend them to God was deeply solemn. Mr.
Taylor no doubt felt it as we could not. We never thought of
danger; but he realised what might be involved, and his heart
was moved accordingly."

For the route decided upon lay across Hu-nan, turbulent
and anti-foreign; and in addition to the Chinese Christian
woman who had volunteered to accompany the ladies,
Mr. Baller was to be spared to reinforce the party. This

---

[1] The journey occupied from December 9 to January 3 (1880), when
they rejoined Mrs. Taylor at Chin-kiang, the latter having gone round by
sea.

practically exhausted the resources of the station, and when a call came for the help of ladies in quite another direction, no foreign escort was available.　Mrs. Taylor had just come up-river, with a young worker who had already been two years in China.　Miss Fausset, with true courage, was ready to go at once to the help of Mrs. King ; but it meant a three months' journey by house-boat, without coming to a single place at which there were foreigners, and there was no one save Miss Wilson to accompany her.

Then it was that advancing years and silvery hair came to their own in a new way ; for Miss Wilson's venerable appearance, from the Chinese point of view, made it possible for the ladies to travel without foreign escort, and they were quite prepared to undertake the journey with the Lord alone as their Protector.　It is easy to write the words, easier still to read them with passing interest ; but only those who have known from experience what such journeys meant in the early days can at all appreciate the situation. Mr. Taylor knew ; yet he encouraged these brave women, and assumed the responsibility of letting them go.

Not lightly, however, or at little cost did he go through with this matter.　No one of experience being left in the Mission-house, he engaged the boat himself and made all arrangements, even to packing food-baskets and rolling up their bedding with his own hands.　Delayed after they had gone on board, he spent the first night with them among the crowded shipping at the mouth of the Han—sharing the only available cabin with Miss Wilson's protégé, a leper lad rescued at Yang-chow, who had become an earnest Christian and proved invaluable as a helper.

" I complained," wrote Miss Fausset, " about the unpleasant odour of his bedding," forgetting the hundred and one other things about which she did *not* complain, " and the worst of it was discarded next day.　But Mr. Taylor had slept in the same compartment with the poor fellow all night."

Seeing that the vegetable oil, which was all they had been able to procure for cooking, made their food unpalatable, Mr. Taylor went ashore next morning and was gone some time.

" When he returned," Miss Fausset continued, " he was carrying a basket on his arm (having no servant with him) in which were sweet potatoes, eggs and lard. One never could have thought a little lard capable of doing so much good, or making so enduring an impression ! "

When the boatmen really started (March 1, 1880) Mr. Taylor still remained on board till they got well out on the Han ; then after a helpful time of prayer, while the attention of the ladies was occupied, he slipped into his little *sampan* and was gone. Never were travellers more faithfully escorted than by his prayers. Day and night he went with them in spirit, as they had the comfort of knowing, and Miss Fausset could never forget the earnestness with which he said on meeting her again :

" I have prayed for you thousands of times."

As news began to come from distant stations in which these and other pioneers were winning their way to the homes and hearts of the people, Mr. Taylor rejoiced with new, unutterable joy.

" I cannot tell you how glad my heart is," he wrote to his mother in July, " to see the work extending and consolidating in the remote parts of China. It is worth living for and worth dying for."

CHAPTER XXIII

WOMEN WHICH LABOURED WITH ME IN THE GOSPEL

1880–1881. AET. 48–49.

BACK in the terrible days of the Tai-ping Rebellion, Captain Yü of the Imperial army was stationed for a short time in Ningpo, one of the famous cities of his own province. While there, he fell in with preachers of " the Jesus Doctrine," and learned something of the teachings of Christianity. Naturally a thoughtful, religious man, he could not but be impressed, but the little he had heard left him with no clear knowledge of the way of salvation. Fifteen long years went by without bringing him further light ; but he was seeking, groping after the truth, and doing all in his power to win and help others to win " the favour of Heaven."

Among a sect of reformed Buddhists strongly opposed to idolatry he had found kindred spirits, and was giving all his time to going from place to place as their accredited agent, though without remuneration. His preaching was necessarily rather negative than positive—denouncing the folly and sin of idol-worship, and proclaiming the existence of one true, supreme Ruler of the universe, the only God who should be worshipped, but of Whom he could tell his hearers practically nothing.

He was growing an old man before, in an inland city (Kin-hwa-fu), he met another foreign missionary. Dr. Douthwaite had come over from his station on the Tsientang river, and with Pastor Wang Lae-djün was preaching daily in a newly opened Gospel hall. Here the devout Buddhist heard in all its fulness the glad tidings of salvation—heard, believed, and found himself a new creature in Christ Jesus. After his baptism a year later (1876) he went down to Chü-chow-fu to be under Dr. Douthwaite's care, for medical treatment, and the latter was rejoiced to see how much progress he had made in knowledge of the Word of God.

"I well remember how, after we had been reading the Scriptures and praying together," he wrote, "Yü earnestly entreated me to let him go out as a preacher of the Gospel.

"'I have led hundreds on the wrong road,' he said, 'and now I want to turn them to the Way of Truth. Let me go. I ask no wages; I do not want your money. I only want to serve the Lord Jesus.'"

Three weeks later this ardent missionary, sent out with the prayers of the little church at Chü-chow-fu, returned with his first convert. He had crossed the watershed between Che-kiang and the adjacent province of Kiang-si, and in the beautiful district of Yü-shan had visited some of his former disciples. One of these it was who accompanied him now—a cheery farmer, also named Yü, who was himself to become an earnest soul-winner.

"He seemed to be just boiling over with joy," recalled Dr. Douthwaite. "As soon as he saw me he fell down on his knees, bumped his head on the floor, and said how grateful he was that I had come to that city.

"'For forty years I have been seeking the Truth,' he said, 'and now I have found it!'

"He was one of the many in China who are dissatisfied with all they have, and are groping in the dark for something that can really meet the heart's need. Well, this man earnestly requested to be at once baptized.

"'Oh,' I replied, 'we cannot go so fast! We must know a little of you and your antecedents.'

"'No,' he urged, 'let me be baptized *now*. I am an old man, and have come three days' journey. I may never be able to travel so far again. I believe everything you have told me about the Lord Jesus. There is no reason why I should not be baptized to-day.'

"On further enquiry, I myself could see none; so I baptized him and he went away rejoicing.

"But he did come back, bringing with him six or seven

neighbours to whom he had been preaching the Glad Tidings (Feb. 1877). They, too, definitely expressed their faith in Christ, saying that from what they had heard they were convinced that idolatry was false and sinful, and were prepared to give it up. After a few months' testing, I had the joy of receiving them too into the church."

The ex-Captain meanwhile, continuing his labours, had been led to another man from the same district whose heart the Lord opened. Travelling to Yü-shan one day, carrying his few belongings, he had joined company with a stranger who soon became interested in his conversation. Perceiving the old " Teacher " to be a good man, Farmer Tung insisted on relieving him of his bundle of bedding, etc., as they tramped along together mile after mile. So fully did the story of the life, death and resurrection of Christ meet the young man's need, that from that day he too was not only a believer in Jesus but a preacher of the Gospel. On visiting his village (Ta-yang) some months later, Dr. Douthwaite was surprised to find the courtyard of the house filled with an orderly assembly of people waiting as if for a meeting. Stools, chairs, baskets, inverted buckets, whatever could be used as a seat had been requisitioned, and the company consisted of women as well as men—all eagerly expectant. They were waiting, he found, for him to address them ; and on asking how such an audience had been gathered at short notice, he was still more interested to learn that had he *not* been coming the meeting would have been held just the same. It was their custom to come together every evening in Farmer Tung's house or courtyard, to sing hymns and pray and read from the Word of God ; and in villages far and near, for miles around, the Good News had been made known.[1]

[1] " During the year which followed this visit to Ta-yang, Dr. Douthwaite baptized fifteen converts from that village, and an equal number from other villages in the same district—all the fruit of the labours of Captain Yü and Farmer Tung. In this obscure village, on the eastern border of Kiang-si, the first Christian Church in the Kwang-sin River district was organised. Subsequently a house was rented in the city of Yü-shan, which was made the centre of missionary effort in that district, and preaching-halls were soon opened in other places " (from *The Jubilee Story* of the C.I.M., by Marshall Broomhall, p. 138).

But what has this story, interesting as it may be, to do with our subject—the opening up of Women's Work in the inland provinces ? Simply, that in this beautiful district and through the earnestness of these young converts, God was preparing for a remarkable development of that work ; just as, at Chefoo, He was making unexpected provision for future needs. The schools as we see them to-day, with their numerous activities and advantages, were not primarily of Mr. Taylor's planning ; nor was the chain of ladies' stations that now extends from Yü-shan all down the Kwang-sin River. With its native pastor and evangelists, its churches, schools, teachers, and scores of unpaid workers ; with more than three thousand five hundred believers baptized from the commencement, and thirty foreign missionaries *all of whom are women*, that chain of stations is unique in China and perhaps in any mission-field. It has afforded a singular demonstration of what God can do in using the weak things of the world to accomplish His purposes ; and by its con-firmation of Mr. Taylor's convictions and the lines on which he and his fellow-workers were acting, it has inspired and strengthened similar efforts in many other places.

But all this was as yet undreamed of in the summer of 1880. Mr. Taylor only knew that God was leading ; and after taking the momentous step of sending single women inland, even without foreign escort, he set out himself for the older stations of the mission, little thinking that this journey was to be a link in the chain of such happenings. Thoroughly to investigate the work in Che-kiang was his object ; and the tact and sympathy with which he went about it greatly impressed his young companion, Mr. Coulthard.

" At some of the stations there would be many difficulties," he said in this connection, " but it was wonderful how they disappeared in the course of a visit from Mr. Taylor. Some said he was able to get his own way through personal magnetism, but I saw how he prayed about everything, and was so wise in not being influenced by the prejudices of others. His love and genuine interest were unmistakable. Was there a child in the station—his heart went out to it, and the little one would be sure to respond, opening the way for friendly intercourse with the parents. And his talks over the Bible were so helpful. He had meetings too with the Chinese—just the ordinary Sunday and week-day services, but full of blessing. It was all very simple, but real; and difficulties were invariably settled."

Together they were keeping up as they journeyed the administrative work of the Mission — answering letters, sending out remittances, corresponding with the home department, and doing most of the preparation of *China's Millions.* After six weeks of such travelling, they struck across from Tai-chow-fu by a mountainous route never before taken by foreigners to what had been Dr. Douthwaite's station.[1] There, several years previously (1877), Mr. Taylor had met some of the early converts brought in through the labours of the ex-Buddhist, Captain Yü. The progress of the work interested him deeply, and he decided to cross into the neighbouring province, and return to the Yangtze by way of the Kwang-sin River.

Upon his visits to Farmer Tung and the newly opened out-station at Yü-shan we must not dwell; but in the light of those lives touched with the love of Christ, the darkness of all that lay around them and beyond was felt the more. Three native evangelists on that long stretch of river, and nothing else in all the million-peopled province, save the work in and near Kiu-kiang—it was a state of things to burden a spirit less alive to its responsibilities than Mr. Taylor's. Upon reaching Chefoo a few weeks later,

"None can be more anxious than myself," he wrote, "to see Women's Work commenced in the interior of the various provinces. This has long been the consuming desire of my heart."[2]

Did the vision come to him—as he passed those very cities day after day, which were to witness the loving, self-sacrificing labours of girls then free and happy in far-off Christian homes: the vision of lives laid down for Jesus' sake, quietly put into the upbuilding of that kingdom which

[1] Failure of health had obliged Dr. and Mrs. Douthwaite to remove to more favourable surroundings (at Wen-chow), and before long led to their finding the sphere for which they were ideally suited, in the rapidly growing C.I.M. colony at Chefoo.

[2] From a letter to Mr. Sowerby, then a young missionary at Hwei-chow, An-hwei, October 26, 1880.

is " righteousness, joy, and peace " in human hearts, into the comforting of sorrows and the lightening of darkness he could but deeply feel as he passed on ?   Whether he saw it or not, there was One who knew why Hudson Taylor had been brought to the Kwang-sin River ; One who knew where to find the treasures of love, ready to be outpoured in His service from many a woman's heart.

And all the while in distant provinces, hundreds of miles farther north and west, a beginning was being made. Strange and new as was the presence of foreign ladies in the great inland cities they now called home, it was no more so than the experiences that were coming to them. Full of interest were the letters Mr. Taylor was receiving, though the pre-occupations they told of left little time for writing.

" We have had a busy time since our arrival," wrote Mr. Nicoll from the metropolis of Western China.[1] " As soon as it was known that my wife had come, the women flocked to see her. . . . Since the Chinese New Year we have been quite besieged. With the exception of yesterday and to-day, when it has been raining, we have had from two to five hundred daily."

And the interest did not pass away with the festive season.

" For nearly two months past," Mrs. Nicoll wrote somewhat later, " I have daily seen some hundreds of women. Our house has been like a fair. Men also have come to hear the Gospel in as large numbers. They are spoken to in the front part of the house ; the women I see in the guest-hall and the yard before it, for the room is soon filled. . . . Often while getting one crowd out at the front-door another has found its way in at the back."

How much she needed help may be imagined ; for, without a Christian woman anywhere within reach, the only person she could fall back upon was a member of their household who, being an old man, was tolerated among the guests in the inner courtyard. As the summer wore on she had to get up at three o'clock in the morning to obtain quiet for Bible study or letters. The busy day that followed rarely brought opportunity for rest ; and more than once

[1] Chung-king, in Sze-chwan : a letter dated February 1880.

she fainted from weariness in the midst of her visitors, returning to consciousness to find the women fanning her, full of affection and concern.[1]

Among many well-to-do women who were her friends was one elderly lady who cared for her like a mother. From time to time, knowing how weary she must be, this lady would send round her sedan-chair with an urgent request for Mrs. Nicoll to return in it immediately. If she succeeded thus in getting her away from the Mission-house, she would put her on the most comfortable bed in her own apartment, send out all the younger women, and sit down herself to fan her until the tired missionary was fast asleep. Then she would prepare an inviting meal and on no account let her go home until she had taken a good dinner.

That was the surprise, the unexpected encouragement that everywhere awaited these first women who went—the people were glad to see them, were eager, often, to hear their message, and showed not only natural curiosity and interest, but real heart sympathy. Crossing the desperately anti-foreign province of Hu-nan, for example, on its western border where few if any European travellers had ever been seen, Miss Kidd could write of friendly women wanting to detain them.[2]

---

[1] Mr. Henry Soltau, in giving an account of his visit to Chung-king (Jan. 1881) says : " At the service on Sunday I was much struck with the number of women present, all of whom remained to the close, and afterwards, when the men had left, had a service by themselves with Mrs. Nicoll and the old Cantonese Christian. This work among the women is a most important portion of the mission here. They pay great respect to Mrs. Nicoll and really seem to have an affection for her, while she is deeply interested in them, finding more work to do than she can compass. I could not help feeling what an honour I should regard it had I one of my own sisters labouring in such a field as this. Mrs. Nicoll has access to the homes of the rich and poor. Some of the women I have seen have been dressed in the most handsomely embroidered silks and satins and come in chairs. Mrs. Nicoll helps the women with a few medicines. And she is the only foreign lady in all this province of twenty-one million people !— the first Christian woman who has ever lived and worked among the women of Sze-chwan." It is now known that there are from sixty to seventy millions in this province.

[2] " We set out on our journey with considerable fear and trembling," Mr. Baller recalled. " We did not know what might happen. . . . We found, however, contrary to our expectations, that the people received us with a great deal of kindness. There is a very large floating population in Hu-nan, and many of the boats on the Tung-ting lake are manned by

" Why do you go to Kwei-chow ? " they said in several places : " we too want happiness and peace. Stay here and be our teachers."

" All the way along," wrote Miss Kidd, " except at large cities, Mrs. M'Carthy and I have been able either to go ashore and visit the women ourselves, or to invite them on board our boat to see us. I do like these Hu-nan women so much ! They have been very kind, most willing to receive us, and ready to listen to what we have to say. . . . It was a great boon having our native sister with us. Of course, as the women had never seen foreigners before, they were a little afraid at first ; but she would speak to them and tell them all about us and what we had come to do, and soon they would draw near, take us by the hand and invite us to their homes. Once indoors, we would soon be surrounded by quite a crowd of them.

" At one village a little incident occurred that amused me a good deal. We had anchored for the night, and some women invited us to go ashore. Mrs. M'Carthy had toothache, so I went alone. A woman about half my size, with a baby in her arms, took hold of one of my hands and a girl of about fifteen took the other and led me along the street, telling me not to be afraid, they would take care of me ! At the house, such a number came to see me, and some of them seemed to understand the Gospel very well. The same woman with her baby led me back to the boat. May the Lord bless her, kind soul ! "

And their experiences on reaching Kwei-yang were no less encouraging.

" We find the people most friendly," Mrs. M'Carthy wrote during the following summer, " and we go in and out without the least inconvenience. As we walk about, we get many invitations to sit down and drink tea. We are always having our names called out, as is the manner of the Chinese, and many a face brightens when we come in sight."

With Miss Wilson and Miss Fausset it was just the same

---

women and worked by them. These women came round our boat as soon as we anchored, and our sisters had not the slightest difficulty in preaching the Gospel to them ; and instead of being hostile, they were highly delighted to see the foreign ladies. They stroked their hands and stroked their cheeks and said : ' Dear me, what beautiful white skins you have ! How much powder you must use ! ' They complimented them on their good looks, and enquired what they had come for. This our sisters were not slow to explain. They sang Chinese hymns to the women, with which they were delighted."

in their distant northern province.   Arrived in Han-chung-fu
they found Mr. and Mrs. King in the midst of an absorbing
work.   God had a people in that place, and it was all the
missionaries could do to keep up with developments that
before long gave them an unusually bright little church of
over thirty baptized believers.   One of these, an elderly
woman who seemed all on fire with love to Christ, never
wearied of accompanying Miss Wilson to the surrounding
villages.

" Nothing could be kinder than our reception everywhere,"
Miss Wilson wrote in October 1880.   " I am as well as ever I
was, and the old lady, my companion, is radiant.   If we should
not be back by Tuesday, do not be anxious, for she takes me on
to one place after another."

Their experiences were pretty strenuous, however,
" eating and sleeping with the people, and walking and
talking all day."

" We sit down on the dry path outside a hamlet," she continued on her return to Han-chung, " and soon the women come
round us, and ask us probably to a house, in front of which they
bring out low benches and sit down to listen very attentively.
. . . Then after giving our message we pass on, not accepting
their kindly proffered pipes, and sit down again where we see
people working in the fields.   They leave their ploughs or pulling
up of cotton-plants, and come to see and I think to hear, for
they get to know our object.   Scarcely any can read.   I do so
want them to have preaching nearer than twelve miles off, and
hope Hwang may go to the market-town.   He is anxious to do
so, and could sell books and be better for the change, as he is
always ailing—feet and hands sorely lessened through his leprosy.
But God uses his weakness to keep him accessible in one place,
and at liberty for talking to any who may come to hear.   He
has a sweet Christian experience, and perhaps, had he not this
thorn in the flesh, might be exalted, for several have been led
to Christ through him.

" While we were in the villages the people were so hospitable,
asking us to meals whenever they were having them, and not
willing to take any money.   An old couple near our first village,
when I was too tired to walk back, brought me out food to
where I was resting, and would have me sleep at their house.
A huge, round, flat basket, filled with straw, made us a comfortable and roomy bed.   My companion had gone back and brought

a wadded quilt and everything she could think I might want, on her back, dear old creature ! We managed without these etceteras on our two days' expedition. . . . My bed one night was quite luxuriously soft, on cotton-plant leaves, stored for fuel, which made a sort of eiderdown coverlet as well. . . . The people sat round the door in the dusk, listening to the old woman, and asking all about foreigners. Several young men had heard the preaching in the city, so were prepared to think well of our message. We were led step by step in such pleasant paths that we want to go again, hoping that other hamlets too may be equally accessible. Our experience next time may not be the same ; but we have precious seed to sow on whatever ground, and some will spring up we must expect ; for has not the Lord Jesus shed His blood for these, and will He not call out of this province a people for His Name, and send us to seek them ? "

A few weeks later, when Miss Wilson had been about six months in Han-chung-fu, Mr. and Mrs. Parker came up, on their way to a still more needy and distant sphere. They were bound for Kan-su, the farthest north-west of all the provinces, which, with its Mohammedan and Chinese population of ten millions, had but one solitary witness for Christ. Up there in his loneliness, Mr. Easton was longing for their coming, and though it meant another ten days' journey, over rough roads and mountain ranges, Miss Wilson could not let the little bride go on alone. To be her helper and companion, this brave lady set out again to face the unknown—riding on the top of her baggage on one of the pack animals, and accompanied by her faithful attendant the leper Hwang.

It was the depth of winter when they reached Tsin-chow, but hardly had they settled in their new home before the work began to take on a more encouraging aspect. Even the timid Tibetans were attracted by the fame of "the foreign doctor," and the friendliness of all classes was remarkable. Five months only after their arrival Mr. Parker wrote (June 2, 1881) :

The wife of a Tao-ist priest had an ulcerated neck reaching from ear to ear, a disease very common in this district and believed by the people to be incurable. My wife visited her, and she began to mend very rapidly under her treatment. The news spread quickly, and for three weeks Mrs. Parker went into

the city daily to visit the sick. Most of the women patients have
long been sufferers, their ailments are constitutional, or the
result of poor, indigestible food ; but many have been much
relieved, and to Chinese eyes several remarkable cures have
taken place. For several days I sat in the reception-room,
making promises of calls and giving medicines from sunrise to
sunset. The wife of the chief Mahommedan *A-hung* we have
staying in our house, to be attended to. She has a gathered arm
of two years' standing. People are beginning to come in from
the country. I doubt whether there is a lane or courtyard in
the city where a visit from my wife or Miss Wilson would not be
welcomed. . . . Three candidates are waiting to be baptized."

Thus at point after point in the far interior, prayer was
being answered and the seemingly impossible brought to
pass.[1] "Do love the Chinese women," Mr. Taylor had
said to Miss Wilson when she first went out. "Whatever
is your best time in the day, give that to communion with
God ; and *do love the Chinese women.*" This was the power
that was telling now on hearts that were learning through
human love, unknown before, the wonder of the Love that
" passeth knowledge."

"What is this strange, warm feeling we have when we
come here to you ? " said a group of visitors to one of the
first women missionaries in Ho-nan. "We never feel it
anywhere else. In our own mothers' homes we do not feel
it. Here our hearts are *k'uan-ch'ao*—broad and peaceful.
What is it warms them so ? We have never felt it before."

But such service was not without its cost. While there
was much to encourage—for by the end of 1880 the pioneers
were rejoicing in sixty or seventy converts gathered into little
churches in the far inland provinces—there was much also
to call for faith and patience and the spirit of those who

[1] Shortly before Mrs. Hudson Taylor had left home (May 1878) to lead
in this pioneer movement, a special Prayer Union had been formed in
England " to seek blessing upon the one hundred and twenty-five millions
of heathen women in China." Daily prayer for those labouring among
them was the condition of membership ; and who shall say how much
the safety, happiness, and success of the first women workers to go to the
far inland provinces was due to the united, definite prayer focussed thus
upon their labours ? The circular setting forth the objects of the Union
was headed with the promise : " If two of you shall agree on earth as
touching anything that they shall ask, it shall be done for them of my
Father which is in Heaven " (Matt. xviii. 19).

overcame " by the blood of the Lamb " and " loved not their lives unto the death." First to go to the women of western China, Emily King was the first also to be called to higher service. But before her brief course ended—the one precious opportunity in which she had given her all—she had the joy of seeing no fewer than eighteen women baptized on confession of their faith in Jesus. Dying of typhus fever in her far-off home (May 1881), this it was that raised her above the sorrow of leaving her husband desolate, and their little one but five weeks old without a mother. The Man of Sorrows was seeing of " the travail of His soul " among those for whom He had waited so long ! And she was satisfied.

This it was that strengthened the mother's heart by a little lonely grave, when in that same month of May Mrs. George Clarke went on from Kwei-chow, in which she had been the only woman missionary, to the still more distant and difficult province of Yün-nan. The sisters who had come to her help were able by that time to carry on the work ; and the precious child who had filled her hands as well as her heart had been taken to a safer, better Land.

" The Lord has been leading us by a painful path," the father wrote. " Doubtless He saw best to take our dear boy to Himself, to send us to Yün-nan ; for if he had been spared we should not have thought of leaving Kwei-chow. Now, where is the married couple who can go as well as we ? "

Forty days' journey westward lay the city in which a house was waiting ; and Yün-nan with its twelve millions was without a resident missionary, or any one at all to bring to its women and children the glad tidings of a Saviour's love. Kneeling beside that little grave, the mother conse-crated herself afresh to God for this work, and went on to the loneliness and privations she knew so well, to do in a second great province of western China what she had already been doing in Kwei-chow. And though only two and a half years later she too was called to her reward, the fruit of that life, the answer to her many prayers lives on.

" I seem to have done so little," she said to her husband toward the end. " I seem to have done less than any woman in China."

It was two years and more since she had seen a sister-missionary, or had had any one save her husband to share the prayers and tears over what, in those days and for long after, was a hard and fruitless field. But faith rose above discouragement.

" Others will come after us," she said when her brave task was nearly done.   " Others will come after us——"

.   .   .   .   .   .

The harvest is white to the reaping now, in that province where her life was the first to be laid down.   From the snow-capped mountains that reminded her of her own Switzerland, on which she loved to watch the sunset glow, the long neglected tribespeople are coming, coming in their hundreds to the Saviour she so truly loved and served.   More than eight thousand baptized believers form the present member-ship of a church in Yün-nan and Kwei-chow that is growing beyond the power to overtake it of those who long and pray for fellow-workers, called of God, to garner the precious sheaves.   Who will come while still the Master tarries, and share both in the present toil and in the endless joy of Harvest home ?

PART VI

THE RISING TIDE

1881–1887. AET. 49–55.

"We have lost the eternal youthfulness of Christianity and have aged into calculating manhood. We seldom pray in earnest for the extraordinary, the limitless, the glorious. We seldom pray with real confidence for any good to the realisation of which we cannot imagine a way. And yet we suppose ourselves to believe in an infinite Father."—ANONYMOUS, Edinburgh, 1910.

"For many years it has been my practice in travelling among the nations to make a study of the sources of the spiritual movements which are doing most to vitalise and transform individuals and communities. At times it has been difficult to discover the hidden spring, but invariably where I have had the time and patience to do so, I have found it in an intercessory prayer-life of great reality."
—JOHN R. MOTT.

"Believe me," said Coleridge to his nephew two years before his death, "to pray with all your heart and strength, with the reason and the will, to believe vividly that God will listen to your voice through Christ, and verily do the thing He pleaseth thereupon,—this is the last, the greatest achievement of the Christian's warfare upon earth. Teach us to pray, Lord."—Coleridge's *Table Talk*.

CHAPTER XXIV

1881. AET. 49.

" ARE the itinerations of the C.I.M. really valuable from a missionary point of view ? Are they not unproductive and aimless wanderings ? Can we hope for much good from the journeys themselves, and will they lead to more definite and settled work ? " Such were some of the questions Mr. Taylor felt it desirable to answer in a paper for *China's Millions* early in 1881. It was now four and a half years since the Chefoo Convention had thrown open the gates of the west, and pioneer journeys had been made in all the then unoccupied provinces. Was it too early to discern the trend of the movement, or to speak of spiritual results ? It was surely not little to be able to point, even then, to seventy baptized believers in those regions hitherto destitute of the Gospel, and to settled work in no fewer than six important centres in five provinces, in all of which women missionaries were to be found as well as men. When one records the name of Pastor Hsi as among those first converts, it will be seen how well worth while were the labours that had brought such a man out of darkness into God's marvellous light.[1]

---

[1] It is interesting, in view of Pastor Hsi's subsequent usefulness, to quote Mr. Turner's reference to his baptism, with that of several others at Ping-yang Fu, in November 1880. Mr. David Hill, who had been the means of his conversion, had by that time returned to his regular work in the Yangtze valley. " On Saturday the 27th, five of our native brethren were baptized. . . . Hsi Liao-chuh, aged forty-five, a native of a village thirty *li* (10 miles) from here, is a man of great ability and influence. He came to us at the beginning of the year. He had read Christian books, and he soon broke off his opium, demolished his idols, and accepted Christ

He was already receiving opium-smokers into his home, to cure them of their craving and lead them to Christ, and was one of those whose faithfulness under persecution and zeal in making known the one and only Saviour filled Mr. Taylor's heart with joy, and led him to ask in his turn the question, " While the Lord so cheers us in our work, shall we hesitate to continue, nay to go forward ? "

But Mr. Taylor's was not the only pen that by this time was found to advocate the line of things he and his fellow-workers had felt led to adopt.

" They are opening up the country," wrote Alex. Wylie of the L.M.S., as early as 1880, " and this is what we want. Other missionaries are doing a good work, but they are not doing *this* work."

And one of Her Majesty's Consuls included, in the same year, the following statement in his official Report from Hankow :

Always on the move, the missionaries of this society have travelled throughout the country, taking hardship and privation as the natural incidents of their profession, and, never attempting to force themselves anywhere, they have made friends everywhere ; and, while labouring in their special field as ministers of the Gospel, have accustomed the Chinese to the presence of foreigners among them, and in great measure dispelled the fear of the barbarian which has been the main difficulty with which we have had to contend.

Not only do the bachelor members of the Mission visit places supposed to be inaccessible to foreigners, but those who are married take their wives with them and settle down with the goodwill of the people in districts far removed from official influence, and get on as comfortably and securely as their brethren of the older missions under the shadow of the Consular flag and within range of a gunboat's guns ; and, while aiding the foreign merchant by obtaining information regarding the unknown interior of the country, and strengthening our relations by

as his Saviour. He is a man of quick temperament, and his conversion was rapid and full of joy. He is serving the Lord in his own neighbourhood. . . . Last evening these dear brethren were formally received into Christian fellowship, and the newly formed church—the first Protestant Church of Shan-si—gathered around the table of our Lord." For the subsequent life of this man of God see *Pastor Hsi : one of China's Christians*, published by the China Inland Mission and Messrs. Morgan & Scott.

increasing our intimacy with the people, this Mission has, at the same time, shown the true way of spreading Christianity in China.

Spreading the knowledge of the Truth—this was indeed the aim kept in view ; and though it meant deliberately forgoing the more rapid ingathering to be expected from concentrating upon older work, Mr. Taylor held firmly to the principle, " There is that scattereth and yet increaseth." To realise how extensive and thorough-going were the labours of the pioneers, one must look a little beyond the summer of 1881, though even then there was abundant cause for encouragement. In the midst of his six years of almost uninterrupted travelling—journeys arduous beyond description, in which he traversed every province in China (except Hu-nan) and even entered Mongolia and Tibet— James Cameron had reached the mountainous regions of northern Shan-si, within and without the Great Wall. There, joining forces with other brethren, he was engaged in the systematic visitation of *every city* not only in that province but in the neighbouring one of Shen-si, beyond the Yellow River, and in the eastern part of Kan-su. Patiently and persistently, in face of untold hardship, they pressed their way through wintry snows and summer heat to the remotest corners of those far-reaching plains and valleys, missing out only two places of minor importance that were practically inaccessible on account of the rainy season.

Meanwhile, in the far South, equally faithful work was being done. Even before Cameron had passed through on his first extensive journey, John M'Carthy had traversed on foot the three south-western provinces, preaching every-where as he went. George Clarke and Edward Fishe, at the same time, were evangelising in Kwang-si—still farther south, and until then wholly unreached. To this province the latter had been designated ; but fever contracted on their first journey cut short the service he hoped to render, and his companion had the sorrow of laying him in a far-off grave. Still the good work went on, and in the year that followed (1878) Kwang-si was visited again and again. When Mr. Clarke married and brought his bride to Kwei-yang, Broumton, who had hitherto held the fort alone, was set free to travel, and visited with others nearly every city in eastern Yün-nan. The western part of the province fell to the eager pioneers, J. W. Stevenson and Henry Soltau, when at last they were permitted to cross the hills from Burma, and unite the advance guards of the mission coming from east and west. Mr. Taylor was at Wu-chang when they reached the Yangtze in the spring of 1881—the first Europeans to travel from the Burman frontier right through to Shanghai.

It was a time of notable happenings, that month of March at Wu-chang ; for then Mr. Taylor saw off another large party, including ladies, to cross the turbulent province of Hu-nan to Western China, and hardly had they started before Adam Dorward appeared, fresh from five and a half months of pioneering in that very region. Hu-nan was graven on his heart, and he had just commenced the self-sacrificing labours that for eight years he continued almost without intermission, giving his life at last in hope of the blessed results we see to-day. Little wonder that a crying need began to be felt, rising out of these developments—the need for reinforcements to follow up such labours and enter many a widely opened door !

This then was the state of things when Mrs. Taylor was obliged to return to England, after more than three years' absence (October 1881), and Mr. Taylor set out from Chefoo, now his headquarters, for conference with several of the pioneers at Wu-chang. The summer had been one of intense heat and no little trial on account of sickness and shortness of funds.

" Unless one could really cast the burden on the Lord," Mr. Taylor had written to Mr. Theodore Howard, " and feel that the responsibility of providing for His servants is *His*, one would be much concerned at the present aspect of things."

And to a fellow missionary :

When shall we get through our difficulties ? Funds seem dropping lower and lower. We need much prayer. But God cannot fail us : let us trust and not be afraid.

Those who were with him at Chefoo that summer noticed how much time he spent in prayer.

" What would you do," he said quite simply to Mr. and Mrs. Nicoll one day, " if you had a large family and nothing to give them to eat ? That is almost my situation at present."

Many were the occasions, also, when he called the household together for special thanksgiving. For if not in one way, then in another, the daily needs were met and Mr. Taylor was enabled to send out sufficient if not ample supplies.

" The amounts received these two months are very low," he had written to Dr. Harold Schofield in May, " and but for God's goodness in giving us more contributions in China than ever before in the same time, I should have much less to distribute. Is it not blessed to see how His watchful care provides, now in this way, now in that ; now giving more here and less at home, then more at home and less here. . . . Any way, it is all like Him, blessed ; and we are blessed to be in His loving hands."

Accompanying himself on the harmonium, Mr. Taylor used often to sing at this time some little verses which, simple as they were, meant much in his experience :

> By the poor widow's oil and meal
>   Elijah was sustained ;
> Though small the store, it lasted long,
>   For God that store maintained.
>
> It seemed as if, from day to day,
>   They were to eat and die ;
> But God, though in a hidden way,
>   Prolonged the small supply.
>
> Then let not fears your mind dismay ;
>   Remember God has said,
> " The cruse and barrel shall not fail :
>   My people shall be fed."

That summer was memorable also for the personal sorrow it brought to Mr. and Mrs. Taylor in the death of both their beloved mothers within a few weeks of each other. In the midst of much sickness and trial of various kinds this bereavement was specially felt, and made the parting all the harder in October, when Mrs. Taylor's return to England could no longer be delayed. The three years she had been in China had brought her so fully into the work that for Mr. Taylor it meant losing his right-hand helper. But it was clearly her duty to return to home responsibilities, and he could not be free for months to come.

" God is helping us very much," he wrote ten days after she had left, " and not less by our trials than by our joys. I am sure you have been longing for me, as I for you. At the right time, by the right way the Lord will bring us together again. Let us seek to live all the more with Him, to find Him a satisfying portion."

Travelling up the Yangtze in November, he was more than ever confirmed in a position of quiet trust in the Lord, and in the conviction—tested in many ways—that in the main the Mission was on the right lines before Him.

" You are ploughing the Mediterranean, I hope," he wrote on November 21, " and will soon see Naples. I am waiting here (on the landing-stage at An-king) for a steamer to Wu-chang. I need not, cannot tell you how much I miss you, but God is making me feel how rich we are in His presence and love. . . . He is helping me to rejoice in our adverse circumstances, in our poverty, in the retirements from our Mission. All these difficulties are only platforms for the manifestation of His grace, power and love."

And from Wu-chang four days later, when the Conference had begun : [1]

I am very busy at work here. . . . God is giving us a happy time of fellowship together, and is *confirming us in the principles on which we are acting.*

---

[1] There had been little or no prearrangement about these meetings. As Mr. Taylor came up-river, he brought with him one and another who seemed to need refreshment, and Mr. Coulthard's bachelor housekeeping was taxed to the utmost. Dorward was there from Hu-nan, Parrott and Pigott from the north, Trench and Miss Kidd from the far south-west, and other workers from Central China. Just a family-party they seemed —overjoyed to have Mr. Taylor all to themselves, quite unconscious of what was to be the outcome. A spirit of prayer prevailed ; and in their daily Bible Readings, morning and evening, Mr. Taylor was seeking to establish these younger workers in the Scriptural principles on which the Mission was based.

That one little sentence, taken in connection with the crisis to which they had come, lets in a flood of light upon the important sequel to those days of fellowship at Wu-chang. For unconsciously, perhaps, to the younger members of the Mission, it *was* a crisis, and more was hanging in the balance than Mr. Taylor himself could realise. After years of prayer and patient, persevering effort, a position of un- paralleled opportunity had been reached. Inland China lay open before them. At all the settled stations in the far north, south, and west, reinforcements were needed, whole provinces as large as kingdoms in Europe being at last accessible to resident as well as itinerant missionary work. Not to advance would be to retreat from the position of faith taken up at the beginning. It would be to look at difficulties rather than at the living God. True, funds were low—had been for years, and the workers coming out from home were few, while several retirements had taken place in China. Difficulties were formidable ; and it was easy to say, " All these things are indications that for the present no further extension is possible." But *not* to go forward would be to cripple and hinder the work ; to throw away oppor- tunities God had given, and to close, before long, stations that had been opened at great cost. This, surely, could not be His way for the evangelisation of inland China.

What then was to be done ? What answer must be given to the pioneers who were writing and eagerly looking for help ? There are several different ways of working for God, as Mr. Taylor reminded the little company.

One is to make the best plans we can, and carry them out to the best of our ability. This may be better than working without plan, but it is by no means the best way of serving our Master. Or, having carefully laid our plans and determined to carry them through, we may ask God to help us, and to prosper us in connection with them. Yet another way of working is to begin with God ; to ask His plans, and to offer ourselves to Him to carry out His purposes.

This then was the attitude taken up. Day by day the needs of the whole work were laid before the Lord, guidance being sought as to His will in connection with them.

" Going about it in this way," Mr. Taylor continued, " we leave the responsibility with the Great Designer, and find His service one of sweet restfulness. We have no responsibility save to follow as we are led ; and we serve One Who is able both to design and to execute, and Whose work never fails."

It was only gradually it came to them—for it seemed too big a thing for faith to grasp. Walking over the Serpent Hill in the midst of Wu-chang, Mr. Taylor was counting up with one of his fellow-workers how many men and women it would really take to meet the most pressing claims. Station after station was considered, their thoughts quickened meanwhile by the scene outspread before them—the homes of no fewer than two million people being gathered at that confluence of the mighty Yangtze with the Han. Thus it was the thought dawned, overwhelming almost in its greatness. Fifty to sixty new workers ? Why, the entire membership of the Mission was barely a hundred ! But fifty or sixty, at the lowest computation, would be all too few. " *Other seventy also*," came to Mr. Taylor's mind : " the Lord appointed other seventy also, and sent them. . . ."

But it seemed too much to ask ; not in view of the great, waiting field, but in view of wholly insufficient resources. Just then, as they walked, Mr. Parrott's foot struck against something hard in the grass.

" See," he said, stooping to pick up a string of cash, " see what I have found ! If we have to come to the hills for it, GOD is well able to give us all the money needed ! "

But they did not run away with the new idea all at once. Several prayer meetings and quiet consultations were held before they came to feel liberty and confidence in asking the Lord for seventy new fellow-workers.

" I quite believe that Mr. Taylor prayed the prayer of faith to-night," wrote Mr. Parrott of one of those meetings ; and of another, " There was a great spirit of expectancy."

This was the spirit, indeed, that characterised the whole transaction—definite expectation that God would answer definite prayer in the Name of Jesus.

" If only we could meet again," said one, " and have a

united praise meeting when the last of the Seventy has reached China ! "

Three years had been agreed upon as the period in which the answer should be looked for, as it would hardly be possible to receive and arrange for so many new workers in a shorter time.

" We shall be widely scattered then," said another with a practical turn of mind. " But why not have the praise meeting now ?   Why not give thanks for the Seventy before we separate ? "

This happy suggestion commending itself to all, the meeting was held, and those who had joined in the prayer joined in the thanksgiving also, with which the answer was received—in faith.

CHAPTER XXV

DEEPER DOWN

1882. AET. 50.

FIRED with new faith and refreshed with spiritual blessing, the little party scattered from Wu-chang. What a message was theirs to take and send throughout the Mission !

"The Lord has been with us indeed," Mr. Taylor wrote on his way down river. "We have been guided, I believe of Him, to ask for 'other Seventy also,' and if He tarry He will send them I am sure. I am now on my way to Chin-kiang, where I hope to have some meetings for spiritual blessing. . . .

"God is faithful, and expects us to walk by faith. . . . We have our definite lines of working : we must not leave them, nor grow weary in them. If any leave us on account of them, they, not we, are the losers. . . . God remains faithful. Do not be cast down if you meet with difficulties at home. All things are working together for good, as in due time we shall see. Pray much for me. . . . Satan is a terrible reality, so is the flesh ; but more is He Who is within us. If God be for us, who, what can overcome us ? "[1]

---

[1] This letter to Mrs. Taylor was written, as it happened, on the very day of her arrival in England, December 1, 1881. Tidings of a fresh bereavement awaited her, for Mr. Taylor's father had passed away a few weeks previously.

"My dear and honoured father," he wrote on hearing of it, " has been taken Home, painlessly and without a moment's warning. None was needed : to him, to die was gain. I realised very thankfully that the long, dreary winter we had dreaded for him, alone—without my dear mother, for fifty years his companion—would not distress him now ; but I could not help a feeling of desolation at the thought of no more Father's or Mother's welcome ; no old home to go to, should I return to England again. But it dawned on me that not only are they both at rest, in the presence of the Lord Jesus, but they are *reunited*, freed from infirmity and imperfection for ever : and then the old home feeling came back to my

358

The meetings at Chin-kiang early in December were fully as encouraging as those at Wu-chang had been. All the members of the Mission present agreed to pray daily for the Seventy until they should be given. When Mr. Taylor left, several of the young men went down with him to the steamer.

" We had prayer in his cabin," Mr. Parrott wrote. " Five of us prayed for the Seventy, and Mr. Taylor promised to tele-graph home and ask them to receive and send out this number, if we would continue praying. . . . Certainly the Lord is reviv-ing us : other missionaries at Chin-kiang have also been present in our meetings."

From that time on it was a constant joy to Mr. Taylor to see how the prayer for reinforcements was taken up throughout the Mission. No one knew better than he did what it meant to his fellow-workers to be not willing only, but earnestly desirous that the staff of the Mission should be so largely increased, when funds were and had long been low. But he knew too that it is a safe thing to launch out upon a course of obedience, no matter what testings may be involved.

" I do feel more and more the blessedness of real trust in God," he wrote to Dr. Harold Schofield before the close of the year (Dec. 23). " Faith, He tries, but sustains : and when our faithfulness fails, His remains unshaken. ' He cannot deny Himself.'

" I have asked Mr. Pigott to hand you some silver which he took back with him to Shan-si : I enclose receipts. It comes as the answer to more than usual prayer ; may I not hope that a more than usual blessing will rest on it ? It is not the much or the little that is all-important. The handful of meal in the widow's barrel might last longer than a store on which God's blessing did not rest. I do feel that our adorable Master has made us so *rich* in Himself, has so given us the *wealth* of His own heart's love and all that that includes and implies, that we can do without any one else, or anything else, as He may see best. It is yet true that ' man doth not live by bread alone ' ; and equally true that yearning human hearts are not to be satisfied with earthly love alone. How many have to feel, if not say,

heart—only centred there, where I would have it, instead of down here. It has made me so happy ! "

' Whoso drinketh of this water shall thirst again ' I   But we can sing,

> . . . Thy love so pure and changeless,
>   satisfies my heart :
> Satisfies its deepest longings ; meets,
>   supplies its every need ;
> Compasses me round with blessing :
>   Thine is love indeed.

" The Lord Jesus, this year of very peculiar trial from almost every quarter, does make my heart well up and overflow with His love. He knows what our separations and other incidents of service mean, and He so wonderfully makes all loss gain, as many seem unable to understand. Excuse my running on in this way. My glad heart seems as if it must have vent, even among figures and remittances."

A few days later, in the scene of his early labours at Ningpo (January 1882), Mr. Taylor was drafting an appeal to the home churches which in due course was signed by seventy-seven members of the Mission in China.   The sense of responsibility that lay behind it, as well as its quiet confidence in God may be judged from the following extracts :

Souls on every hand are perishing for lack of knowledge ; more than a thousand every hour are passing away into death and darkness. . . . Provinces in China compare in area with kingdoms in Europe, and average between ten and twenty millions in population. One province has no missionary ; one has only one, an unmarried missionary ; in each of two other provinces there is only one missionary and his wife resident ; and none are sufficiently supplied with labourers. Can we leave matters thus without incurring the sin of blood-guiltiness ?

After requesting prayer for more workers " in connection with every Protestant missionary society on both sides of the Atlantic," the needs of the C.I.M. were specially referred to.

A careful survey of the spiritual work to which we ourselves are called . . . has led us to feel the importance of immediate and large reinforcements, and many of us are daily pleading with God in agreed prayer for forty-two additional men and twenty-eight additional women, called and sent out by God, to assist us in carrying on and extending the work already committed to our charge. We ask our brothers and sisters in Christ at home to join us in praying the Lord of the Harvest to thrust out this " other seventy also." We are not anxious as to the means for sending them forth or sustaining them. *He* has told us to look to the birds and flowers, and to take no thought for these things, but to seek first the kingdom of God and His righteousness, and that all these things shall be added unto us. But we *are* concerned that only men and women called of God, fully consecrated to Him, and counting everything precious as dross and dung " for the excellency of the knowledge of Christ Jesus my Lord," should come out to join us ; and we would add to this appeal a word of caution and encouragement, to any who may feel drawn to offer themselves for this blessed work. Of *caution*, urging such to count the cost ; to wait prayerfully on God ; to ask themselves whether they *will* really trust Him for *everything*, wherever He may call them to go. Mere romantic feeling will soon die out amid the toilsome labour and constant discomforts and trials of inland work, and will not be worth much when severe illness arises and perhaps all the money is gone. Faith in the living God alone gives joy and rest in such circumstances. But a word also of *encouragement*, for we ourselves have proved God's faithfulness and the blessedness of dependence on Him. He is supplying and ever has supplied all our need. And if not seldom we have fellowship in poverty with Him Who for our sakes became poor, shall we not rejoice if the Day prove that we have been, like the great missionary Apostle, " poor, yet making many rich; having nothing, yet possessing all things " ? He makes us very happy in His service, and those of us who have children desire nothing better for them, should the Lord tarry, than that they may be called to similar work and similar joys.[1]

What should we not expect from 1882 after this beginning, with the prayer for the Seventy being taken up in such a spirit throughout the Mission ? Should we not confidently look for a rising tide of spiritual blessing both at home and in China, and that Mr. Taylor especially, as representing the movement, should be led on from strength to strength ? Perhaps a deeper knowledge not only of the " acts " but of the " ways " of God would modify such expectations, and lessen the surprise with which one finds the reality to have

[1] Shortly before this was written, Mr. Taylor had welcomed his eldest son to China, Mr. Herbert Taylor, who for thirty-six years has continued in faithful labours—first in the Chefoo Schools, and subsequently in evangelistic and pastoral work.

been very different.   For in England as in China, difficulties
did not lessen.   Working to the limit of his powers, Mr.
Broomhall was not able to report any decided increase
either of funds or of service.   Eleven new workers were sent
out, but three only of the number were men, when five times
as many had been hoped for.   So great was the trial as to
shortness of supplies that Mr. Taylor could scarcely wonder
at the retirement of one and another from the Mission
whom he knew to be loosely attached to its principles.
Government posts were to be had at a salary of fifty pounds
a month, in which it was easy to think that exceptional
opportunities for usefulness would be found.   And, most
sorrowful of all, as he moved from place to place the work
in some important stations seemed to be going back rather
than forward.

Faith was thus thrown into the crucible in many ways,
and the reality behind outward seeming, both as to Mr.
Taylor's own position and that of others, was tested as
never before.   Weaknesses were brought out with startling
clearness—need of spiritual power, of organisation, of leaders
of more calibre.   With answered prayer on the one hand as
to the opening up of inland China, and a growing faith for
large reinforcements on the other, they were forced to a
realisation of the utter inadequacy of existing arrangements
to carry on the work even as it was.   And in and through
it all, Mr. Taylor himself was assailed by such depression,
loneliness and forebodings, due in part to illness, that one
stands amazed at the record merely—the little that could
be put into letters of those long painful months.

Yet the soul was sustained upon its inward way.   Wonderful indeed is the conflict, the dimly-seen midnight wrestling
of this man of prayer with his God.   Much he had known
already of Him Whose larger blessing he so deeply craved.
Did it seem in the darkness as if all were failing him ?
Strengthened and upheld by the Hand that seemed against
him, he was yet to prove the faithfulness of Him to Whom
he clung with the heart-cry, " Show me now Thy Name."

> Wilt Thou not yet to me reveal
> Thy new, unutterable name ?

Tell me, I still beseech Thee, tell ;
 To know it now resolved I am :
Wrestling, I will not let Thee go,
 Till I Thy name, Thy nature know.

What though my shrinking flesh complain,
 And murmur to contend so long ?
I rise superior to my pain,
 When I am weak, then I am strong ;
And when my all of strength shall fail,
 I shall with the God-Man prevail.

Yield to me now : for I am weak,
 But confident in self-despair ;
Speak to my heart, in blessings speak,
 Be conquered by my instant prayer ;
Speak, or Thou never hence shalt move,
 And tell me if Thy name is Love.

'Tis Love ! 'tis Love ! Thou diedst for me !
 I hear Thy whisper in my heart ;
The morning breaks, the shadows flee,
 Pure, universal Love Thou art ;
To me, to all, Thy mercies move :
 Thy nature and Thy name is Love.

My prayer hath power with God ; the grace
 Unspeakable I now receive ;
Through faith I see Thee face to face,
 I see Thee face to face, and live !
In vain I have not wept and strove :
 Thy nature and Thy name is Love.

I know Thee, Saviour, who Thou art,
 Jesus, the feeble sinner's Friend ;
Nor wilt Thou with the night depart,
 But stay and love me to the end ;
Thy mercies never shall remove :
 Thy nature and Thy name is Love.[1]

. . . .

Thus it was that Hudson Taylor held on—hard pressed
in faith and circumstances, sustained, borne down at times,
but strengthened. Thus it was that he was brought out
victorious.

[1] From Wesley's noble hymn commencing, "Come, O Thou Traveller
unknown," familiar to Hudson Taylor from childhood.

"Were not my hope in God, I should be terribly discouraged by my recent visits," he wrote on February 13. "But the Lord reigneth." [1]

Feb. 17 : I do trust that good may result from these visits. They cost me a good deal, physically and mentally, and do not effect nearly as much as I could wish.

Feb. 21 : May the Lord have mercy upon us, and purge out from among us every false and vain thing, and make us pure and holy before Him in love. . . . These things almost break my heart. I do not know what to do, sometimes. But if I grieve over . . . want of Christlike devotion, what must He feel Who shed His blood for souls ? Blessed Jesus ! how unworthy of Thee *I* am. Make *me* more like Thyself.

June 16 : There are many and serious difficulties to be met, but the Lord is at our right hand, and we shall not be moved by them if He uphold us.

> All the way my Saviour leads me,
> What have I to ask beside ?

July 7 : Travelling by foot-boat. I do live in your love, during this long, long separation. If the Lord do not come first, it will end ; but oh, the end seems so far off ! And you are, perhaps, longing for me, I will not say as much, but in the same way. I am so glad we can both say " *All* for Jesus " ; and He fully knows how much that " all " means sometimes, does He not ? May He be gracious to us, and keep our hearts full of His *manifested* love and conscious presence, and then we shall not faint nor be weary by the way.

July 22 : Chefoo. I do believe God is doing and will do *great* things for us. As to health, I never was better.

July 31 : 4 A.M. . . . I have had a trying time here, and it is not altogether past yet. One is very much tempted to say or to think, Satan is too much for us, and thus to dishonour our almighty Saviour. . . . By *God's* help, I do manage to get things through.

Aug. 7 : I feel sure that if we are only simple in faith and loyal in service, God will teach us much that at present we have little practical knowledge of. . . . Here, we all feel that blessing is not far off. . . . If I were to tell you the mercies we have had of late, the interpositions of God's hand, it would be a long letter ! and " yet there's more to follow." I feel sure God *will* do, *is* doing, great things for us. Let us open wide our mouths and enlarge our hearts, for He is faithful.

---

[1] This and the following quotations are all from letters to Mrs. Taylor.

September and October were specially trying months; since the formation of the Mission, Mr. Taylor had never been more overwhelmed. But for the reality of that inward sustaining, he *must* have broken down physically, if not in faith and courage. As it was, he was consciously shaken, though not " moved."

" Pray especially for guidance in the organisation of the work," he wrote on October 21, " and for men of calibre to carry it on. . . . Abundant spiritual power and some considerable capacity in leadership are just now great desiderata. If I could be free from all but the spiritual oversight, I might do good for some time to come."

Nov. 23 : Sometimes I venture to indulge the hope that I shall be able to get away in January, and reach you early in March. It seems too good to be true, and I feel afraid to build upon it ; for, if hindered, the disappointment will be so great. If I really do know my heart, my first wish is to do God's will in the matter ; but you and the dear children do draw so, that I am often afraid lest my motives in wishing to go home quickly are not so purely for the furtherance of God's work as I could wish. Oh, how graciously God has ordered it that we are " *accepted in the Beloved,*" " Complete in Him " !

Dec. 5 : I would not withhold anything from the Lord Jesus. I do want to *finish* the work He has given me to do. . . . But I think that ere long He will restore us to one another, and I hope the days of our parting may then be ended, and no more such lengthened separations be our lot.

Dec. 30 : Shanghai. To-morrow (Sunday) I preach at the Masonic Hall—the last morning sermon of 1882, as I preached the first.[1] May God give me the message. I am glad to serve Him here. It is heavy and constant labour, but very happy. . . . My path will not be easy, with regard to leaving. So little is coming in at home. . . . The Lord *will* provide, no doubt ; but it seems as if I must be near, to pray and to divide as closely as possible. Well . . . I am praying for guidance, and He will give it. Many enjoy our meetings. They little

---

[1] The " Shanghai Free Christian Church " was by this time well established, and had been meeting in the Masonic Hall for twelve months. Mr. Taylor was so much interested in its beginnings and preached for them so frequently that he was practically its first Pastor. He was succeeded by Messrs. Pearse, Judd, and other members of the Mission, for longer or shorter periods. Notes of many of Mr. Taylor's sermons are preserved, showing how faithfully he gave himself to this ministry.

know what they cost you and me. Is anything of value in Christ's service which costs little ?

> Upon the cross of Jesus, mine eye at times can see
> The very dying form of One Who suffered there for me.

How light our burdens, how small our love, compared with that ! "

Yet there were gleams of brightness, all the more welcome for the shadows, and some outstanding experiences that told of a deepening work of God. Memorable among these was the Conference at An-king in June, when Mr. Taylor spoke on a subject that was filling his heart. To some it may seem strange that the Scripture from which he derived most of the " power of endurance and encouragement " [1] he so sorely needed at this time was the Song of Solomon ; but those who have been brought by the King into " His chambers " in the treasure-house of its inspired pages will know the matchless revelation they contain of " the love that passeth knowledge " and the response it seeks from its own. This was Mr. Taylor's theme at the Conference, and much of the most helpful ministry of his later years may be traced to the same source. [2]

" I have gone through the Canticles in the way of exposition during this visit," he wrote to Mrs. Taylor from An-king, " and the Lord has wonderfully opened His heart to us all. We have also dwelt on some of the distinctive principles of our position and work, I think with great profit."

And a few days later :

I wish I could give you any adequate idea of the blessing we have had in An-king. . . . So long as God gives us such times as these, we will not be cast down, however great the difficulties and trials by the way.

---

[1] A literal rendering of Romans xv. 4. See *The New Testament in Modern Speech*—Dr. Weymouth.

[2] It is worthy of notice that just as Mr. Taylor's first insight into the spiritual teaching of the Song of Solomon was obtained in the period of trial and testing that preceded his first marriage (see *Hudson Taylor in Early Years*, p. 426), so now in heart-loneliness and prolonged separation from home and loved ones it became as never before his "garden of delights." In *Union and Communion* (price 1s. from the Offices of the C.I.M.) will be found the line of thought which made him to many the most practically helpful expositor of this book.

It was chiefly for an outpouring of a spirit of prayer that this Conference was memorable, and for the manifest presence and power of the Holy Ghost. Seven months had now elapsed since in a similar gathering the decision had been reached to ask in faith for seventy new fellow-workers, and to this little company on their knees at An-king came a wonderful confirmation of their convictions as to that purpose.

" We have had a day of united fasting and prayer to-day," Mr. Taylor wrote on June 30, " and a wonderful time of blessing it has been. The Holy Spirit seemed so to fill us this morning that several of us felt as if we could not *bear* any more."

And to another correspondent :

I wish it were possible to give you *any idea* of the wonderful time of blessing we have had at An-king. They are a band of fully consecrated workers there, and were ready for blessing. . . . We arranged on my arrival for two meetings each day, 7-9 A.M. and P.M., and often went beyond these hours ; and some of the stronger ones spent a large part of several nights in prayer. On the morning of our fast-day the Holy Spirit seemed so to fill several of us that *each* felt (as we found in private conversation afterwards) that we could not bear any more and *live.*

Mr. Parrott wrote of one meeting in which prayer with thanksgiving, especially for the Seventy, continued without intermission for almost two hours ; and one cannot but trace the rising tide of spiritual blessing that began to make itself felt, to the waiting upon God of this and of other special meetings toward the close of the year.

Meanwhile, Mr. Taylor had paid another visit to the district in which he had found a few months previously so much to discourage. Then he had written of his efforts being all or " nearly all in vain, so far as this part of the work is concerned." Now, baptized afresh with a spirit of love, he was enabled to find his way to hearts that had seemed closed against him, and a work of grace was the result, that was not only to save valuable workers from being lost to the Mission, but was to set them in its front rank as regards fruitfulness in soul-winning.

It was at Chefoo that the later months of the year were spent and some of its most important work accomplished ; [1] and there Mr. Taylor begun to see his way at length to returning to England. There, too, faith was encouraged by definite answers to prayer in the matter of funds. Early in October, for example, they were looking with special expectancy for the home remittance, autumn journeys having to be provided for those who were going up country, to whom Mr. Taylor would have been glad to entrust extra supplies for their own and other stations.

"We were at table," he recalled, "when we received our letters (the home mail) ; and when on opening one of them I found, instead of seven or eight hundred pounds for the month's supplies, only £96 : 9 : 5, my feelings I shall not soon forget !

"I closed the envelope again, and seeking my room, knelt down and spread the letter before the Lord, asking Him what *was* to be done with less than ninety-seven pounds—a sum it was impossible to distribute over seventy stations in which were eighty or ninety missionaries, including their wives, not to speak of about a hundred native helpers, and more than that number of native children to be fed and clothed in our schools. Having first rolled the burden on the Lord, I then mentioned the matter to others of our own Mission in Chefoo, and we unitedly looked to Him to come to our aid ; but no hint as to our circumstances was allowed to reach any one outside.

"Soon the answers began to come—kind gifts from local friends who little knew the peculiar value of their donations, and help in other ways, until the needs of the month were all met without our having been burdened with anxious thought even for an hour. We had similar experiences in November and again in December ; and on each occasion, after spreading the letter before the Lord and leaving the burden with Him, we were ' helped.' Thus the Lord made our hearts sing for joy, and provided through local contributions in China for the needs of the work as never before nor since."

---

[1] One outgrowth of the manifold testings of this year was the increasing attention given to the question of organisation within the Mission, about which several circular letters were sent to all the stations. One of them, dated August 12, 1882, gave permanence to the arrangement by which Mr. Coulthard had for some time been acting as Mr. Taylor's representative at Wu-chang, especially in financial matters for the western and north-western provinces, and Mr. Parrott as Corresponding Secretary dealing with letters that did not need the Director's personal attention.

Encouraged in this way to remember that it was the Lord to Whom they must look, and not to friends in England, the little circle at Chefoo were the more prepared for Mr. Taylor's suggestion that they should unite in asking some definite " token for good " of the same sort to strengthen faith at home. Letters received had shown how really concerned were some of the workers and friends of the Mission as to the appeal for the Seventy. It had been kept in the background as much as possible, just because it seemed too great an advance to contemplate at such a time ; and Mr. Taylor, who by no means ignored the difficulty, felt it laid on his heart to ask the Lord to put His seal upon the matter in a way that could not be mistaken. It was at one of the daily prayer meetings at Chefoo, on or about the first of February (1883), and the few who were present were conscious of much liberty in laying their request before God.

" We knew that our Father loves to please His children," Mr. Taylor wrote in recalling this experience, " what father does not ? And we asked Him lovingly to please us, as well as to encourage timid ones at home, by leading some one of His wealthy stewards to make room for a large blessing for himself and his family by giving liberally to this special object."

A few days later Mr. Taylor sailed for England, and it was not until they stopped at Aden that he learned the sequel. No account of that special prayer-meeting had been written home, nor could a letter of that date have reached London until the end of March. But at Pyrland Road, Mr. Broomhall had the great and unexpected joy of receiving— *on the second of February*—a sum of three thousand pounds for work in China, contributed by friends whose confidence he enjoyed in a special way.

Nor was this all. On landing at Marseilles, Mr. Taylor took the opportunity of visiting Mr. and Mrs. Berger at Cannes.

" The April *China's Millions* there came to hand," he wrote, " and I found in the list of donations this three thousand pounds, acknowledged under the date of February 2, with the text, ' Ask of ME, and I will give thee the heathen for thine inherit-

ance, and the uttermost parts of the earth for thy possession,'
as follows :

Father	. .	. £1000
Mother	. .	. 1000
Mary	. .	. 200
Rosie	. .	. 200
Bertie	. .	. 200
Amy	. .	. 200
Henry	. .	. 200
		£3000

" It was most striking to see how literally God had fulfilled
our prayer, and led His faithful steward to *make room for a
large blessing for himself and his family*. Never before was a
donation sent to us in such a way, and never since, save on one
occasion, a year and five months later, when a donation for the
same fund is entered thus in *China's Millions* :

Father	. .	. £200
Mother	. .	. 200
Mary	. .	. 100
Rosie	. .	. 100
Bertie	. .	. 100
Amy	. .	. 100
Henry	. .	. 100
Baby	. .	. 100
		£1000

" A beautiful instance, this, of a father who seeks that each
member of his family should have ' treasure in heaven.' "

CHAPTER XXVI

ABOVE ALL THAT YE ASK

1883–1884. AET. 51–52.

PARIS and Easter-tide : how little had either Mr. or Mrs. Taylor in their long separation imagined such a setting for the reunion that came at length ! Even the day or two spent at Cannes had seemed long when the traveller learned who was coming to meet him. Before leaving China he had been much impressed with the prophecy of Zephaniah, especially the closing chapter with its wonderful revelation of the heart of God : " The Lord thy God in the midst of thee is mighty ; He will save, He will rejoice over thee with joy ; He will rest (or " be silent ") in His love, He will joy over thee with singing."

" The whole passage had been made a great blessing to me," he said, " but it was not until I reached Paris that I learned the full preciousness of this clause. For there I was met by my beloved wife (after a separation of fifteen months), and as we sat side by side in the cab, though she had so much to say and I had too, I could only take her hand and be silent—the joy was too deep for words. Then it came home to me : if all this of earthly affection is but the type, what must it be when He is ' silent in His love ' ? And that love is drawn out by our trust. Oh, it is such a pity to hinder ! "

Reaching home at the end of March, Mr. Taylor was in good time for spring and summer meetings, and soon had cause to notice the new position accorded to the Mission in the esteem of the Christian public. The eight years of Mr. Broomhall's unwearied labours had told especially in the

direction which was his forte—that of inspiring confidence
and making friends. Then, too, the achievements of the
pioneers, women as well as men, in effecting a settled residence in almost all the inland provinces had called forth
thanksgiving to God. In many parts of the country people
were wanting to hear how the seemingly impossible had been
brought to pass ; how, without appeals for money or even
collections, the work had been sustained ; and how in the
most distant parts of China little groups of converts were
being gathered. Meetings, therefore—meetings in all directions—soon claimed the leader of the Mission—the un-
obtrusive man so sure of his great God !

The correspondence of the next two years, the period of
Mr. Taylor's stay in England, is deeply interesting from this
point of view. To him who had never sought it had come
the loving appreciation of high and low, rich and poor, old
and young, to a remarkable degree.

" If you are not dead yet," was the charming communication
of a child at Cambridge to whom " Hudson Taylor " was a household word, " I want to send you the money I have saved up to
help the little boys and girls of China to love Jesus."

" Will you do me the kindness," urged Canon Wilberforce
of Southampton, " to give a Bible reading in my house to about
sixty people . . . and spend the night with us ? *Please* do us
this favour, in the Master's name."

" Much love to you in the Lord," wrote Lord Radstock from
the Continent. " You are a great help to us in England by
strengthening our faith."

From Dr. Andrew Bonar came a hundred pounds,
forwarded from an unknown Presbyterian friend " who
cares for the land of Sinim." Spurgeon sent his characteristic invitations to the Tabernacle, and Miss Macpherson to
Bethnal Green.

" My heart is still in the glorious work," wrote Mr. Berger,
with a cheque for £500. " Most heartily do I join you in praying for seventy more labourers—but do not stop at seventy !
Surely we shall see greater things than these, if we are empty
of self and only seeking God's glory and the salvation of souls."

There are letters from the nobleman inviting Mr. Taylor
to his castle, and from the old family servant, sending a gift

for China after his departure.   And there are letters, above all, telling of blessing received in the meetings, not through Mr. Taylor's addresses only, but through his personality and spirit.

" It was the man himself we were drawn to," wrote one of the new friends of this year (the Rev. J. J. Luce of Gloucester). " It was what he *was* that gave such sweet, undying force to what he did. . . . Behind it all was a wealth of faith and knowledge of God, and of experience in His ways, that made you feel a dwarf indeed in comparison.

" Never can I forget a meeting in our schoolroom one summer evening (June 1883).   It was an after-meeting at the close of a Convention for the Deepening of Spiritual Life, and a group of young men gathered round him while he told in the simplest way the story of his student days, and of his preparation for the work in China to which the Lord had called him.   The effect on my own spirit, and I think upon others too, was overwhelming. I felt as though I had never yet given up anything for Christ, never yet learned to trust the Lord. . . . I was so moved that I had to ask Mr. Taylor to stop : my heart was broken. . . . We were only twelve all told on that occasion, but three went to China as a result." [1]

" To me, 1883 was a place of great darkness," wrote a godly woman occupying a position of influence, " and the foundations of faith were shaken.   I did not speak to any one of what I was passing through, for I knew everything, as I thought, in theory."

Constrained by the duties of her position to attend a conference of which her husband was Convener, she expected nothing but weariness from the missionary meeting, to which she went conscious of " intense soul-hunger, underneath rebellion and unbelief."

" As Mr. Taylor began to speak," she continued, " a great calm and stillness came over me—a fresh revelation of God's coming down to meet human need.   The fountains of my inmost being were broken up . . . I saw a little of what consecration really meant ; and as I began to yield myself to God, fresh hope, light and gladness came into my life—streams that have been flowing ever since."

---

[1] And Mr. Luce himself, who wished he could have gone to China, became not only one of Mr. Taylor's best-loved friends, but a member of the London Council and a true prayer helper in the Mission ; a ministry continued to this day.

Many conferences that summer and autumn gave Mr. Taylor access to representative audiences ; opportunities he did not fail to make use of, though in a way all his own.

" When he was speaking," Mr. Luce recalled, " you could be quite sure that, whatever else he might say, he would make no plea for funds. Often I used to hear him explain, almost apologetically, that his great desire was that no funds should be diverted from other societies to the China Inland Mission ; and that it was for this reason he had taken up lines of working which he hoped would preclude interference with other organisations. Nothing gave him more genuine pleasure than to speak well of other missions. . . .

" Oh, the self-emptied spirit, the dignified way in which his life of faith was lived out, the reality of it all ! Instead of wanting to get anything out of you, he was always ready to give to you. His heart and mind were full of *that*. Some people seem to be asking all the time, though they may not do so in actual words : he—never."

At the Salisbury Conference Canon Thwaites was impressed with Mr. Taylor's humility more than anything else—" or the way, rather, in which God clothed him with humility." Yet there was *power* in his addresses, especially in the missionary meeting, a power of the Holy Spirit which " was intense, almost awful " ; and of the praise meeting with which the Conference ended, Mrs. Thwaites hardly knew how to write. No reference was made on that occasion to the Inland Mission, but it was for *China* that lives were consecrated and money flowed in. In spite of there being no collection, people emptied their purses, stripped themselves of their jewels, handed over watches, chains, rings and the like, and gave their lives to God for His service.

Fifteen or sixteen offers for the mission-field were the result, and a whole jewelry case was sent in next day. People had received so much that they felt they could give anything.

So fully were Mr. Taylor's time and strength occupied in these ways that it is amazing to find how much he was doing all the while of correspondence and his own special work in the Mission. From a pair of substantial manuscript books lying before us, we might conclude that he had been wholly engrossed in directorial duties, instead of being almost continuously engaged in meetings. One of these volumes contains a list of his China letters—when received, when answered, with a line as to their contents—and the other is filled in the same way with particulars about home correspondence. From this source alone one learns of two thousand six hundred letters attended to by Mr. Taylor personally (Mrs. Taylor often acting as his amanuensis) during a period of ten months, fully taken up with travelling and meetings. Little wonder he began to need a private secretary.

Much prayerful thought was being given also to a subject second to none in its importance, that of organisation within the Mission, on the China side of things especially. In frequent meetings with the Council and in private conversations, Mr. Taylor was seeking light upon how to prepare for the larger growth that was coming, and after five months at home—busy though he was with Summer Conferences—he sent out a carefully considered letter to all the members of the Mission, stating what was proposed and asking their judgement.[1]

Meanwhile, out in China the need for reinforcements was increasingly felt. Five only had been sent out in the first quarter of the year, but fifteen sailed in the months that

---

[1] " It is important to secure that no contingency shall alter the character of the Mission," Mr. Taylor wrote (Aug. 24, 1883), " or throw us off those lines which God has so signally owned and blessed from the commencement. But our home arrangement of assisting the Director by a Council may be introduced into the China work ; the members of that Council may themselves be Superintendents of districts, in which capacity they may in their turn be assisted by district Councils of our missionaries. In all this no new principle will be introduced, yet our work will be rendered capable of indefinite expansion while maintaining its original character. Many local matters can thus be locally considered and attended to without delay, and local as well as general developments will be facilitated. I have hitherto had the opportunity of conferring only with those of our number who might be within reach, and that at irregular intervals. The plan I now propose will, through the district Superintendents, bring me into conference with all our missionaries of experience, and will secure an increasingly effective supervision of the whole work. It will also make apparent what has all along been the case—that all important measures are adopted only after full conference with those best qualified to throw light upon them. . . . I shall be glad to hear from you how these suggestions strike you, and how far they commend themselves to your mind."

followed,[1] and many fresh candidates were in touch with the Mission.

"We look anxiously for news of the coming Seventy," wrote Mr. Easton from the north-western province of Shen-si, "and trust that warm-hearted, earnest brothers may join us here."

And from Tai-yuan-fu, the capital of the adjoining province, Dr. Schofield sent a special plea :

We are praying daily for the seventy new labourers, and I hope that at least four of them will come to this province. There are now three or four towns within a day or two's journey, in each of which we have old patients—three of them double cataract cases who can see well. Some of them are not only grateful, but were seemingly interested in the Gospel while with us. These openings I long to see followed up.

He did not say how deeply he was burdened for the whole, great, waiting land, with its teeming millions ; how stealing time from work and rest he was giving himself to prayer, day by day, that men of God might be raised up for its evangelisation ; how labouring beyond his strength he was becoming known not only as the wonder-working doctor, who could restore sight to the blind and almost raise the dead, but as the man with a message, the unwearied preacher with the heart of love.

To the crowded dispensary there came a patient with virulent diphtheria. The doctor did what he could, but having no isolation ward was reluctantly compelled to refuse the poor man admission. Returning later, however, he managed to elude the gate-keeper, and crept into a small room near the entrance, in which before morning he died. Hearing to his concern that a patient had passed away, the doctor hastened to the spot. The odour in the room was overpowering, and a glance revealed the danger to which he and others were exposed. In the prime of his manhood, after only three years in China—the three happiest years of

---

[1] The first to sail after Mr. Taylor's return was Mr. Marcus Wood, now and for many years the beloved Secretary of the Mission in England, with whom Mr. J. N. Hayward, for many years Treasurer in Shanghai, has recently been associated.

his life, as he had written more than once—Harold Schofield's work on earth was done.

But why recall it now ? What had it to do with the
special developments of 1883 ? Only this—that Schofield
died *praying*. During all the later months of his life, full
as they were of splendid service, his chief pre-occupation
had been prayer. For this he would leave wife and children,
denying himself rest and recreation, and making time at
any cost for waiting upon God. It was China that was on
his heart—and the sleeping Church at home. And the
petition he urged with special fervency was that God would
touch the young life of our universities, and raise up men of
gifts and education for His work among the heathen. There
was no Student Christian Federation in those days, no
Volunteer Movement in any of the Colleges. Himself a
distinguished prizeman, who had taken more than £1400
in scholarships, he knew well the value of thorough mental
training ; and remembering all that had been said in his
own case about " sacrifice of brilliant prospects," he prayed
for a new spirit to come over Christian thinking, more in
harmony with His Who " made Himself of no reputation "
that dying souls might live.

It was the 1st of August when Harold Schofield, stricken
with a malignant fever, laid down his life in the work he so
truly loved. But the prayers of those last months had not
been in vain. News of his death, though cabled to England,
did not reach Mr. Taylor immediately, but *that very day* a
letter came to him in the north of England that one cannot
but connect with Dr. Schofield's prayers. It was from a
young officer in the Royal Artillery who had for some time
been thinking of offering himself, he said, for the work of
the China Inland Mission. He asked an interview with
Mr. Taylor, signing the name that, little as either of them
could suppose it, was in due course to replace his own.
D. E. Hoste writing from Sandown Fort in July, Stanley
P. Smith coming up from Trinity College and his exploits
on the river, these and the others who joined them making
the well-known " Cambridge Seven," whose going out
awakened a new spirit indeed throughout the universities

of the United Kingdom and America, and through them of the world—what were they but the answer to those sacred pleadings in which a believing heart had entered into fellowship with God ?

" I have sometimes thought," wrote the author of *The Evangelisation of the World*, " that in those prayers the greatest work of Harold Schofield's life was accomplished : that, having prayed thus, he had ' finished the work ' God had given him to do, and so was taken to his eternal reward." [1]

But if 1883 was memorable, with its many causes for encouragement, what shall be said of 1884, and the movement into which these young men came ?   It was a rising tide indeed of spiritual power and blessing ; a year of intense activity, in which Mr. Taylor seemed to do the work of ten ; a year of incessant meetings, and the flowing in of sympathy and gifts as never before ; a year of harvest in the matter of new friends and workers ; and above all a year of close and constant dependence upon God.   It was the last of the three years in which the Seventy were to be given, according to the faith that had received them from the Lord ; and given they were in royal fashion—most of the large party that sailed toward the end of October being over and above the number.[2]   Forty-six in all were sent out during the twelve months ; and it was not only the number but the calibre of the workers that was remarkable.   Often must Mr. Taylor have been reminded of the prayer going up from many hearts that the Seventy might be *God-sends* as well as God-sent to China.

And here attention may well be drawn to some of the outside influences that contributed to the developments of

[1] Published a year or two later (1885) under the title *A Missionary Band*, this remarkable work by Mr. B. Broomhall had a large circulation, and powerfully influenced the founders of the Student Volunteer Movement which came into existence a few months later, and which Dr. A. T. Pierson characterised as " the epiphany of youth."   Apart from the Bible, Dr. Robert Speer has stated, no books so influenced his career as *The Evangelisation of the World* and Blaikie's *Personal Life of Livingstone*.

[2] This was Miss Murray's party, which, proceeding at once to Yangchow, formed the nucleus of the present invaluable Training Home for the study of the language (still under Miss Murray's care), and included the little band who were used of God to inaugurate the now fruitful and extensive work on the Kwang-sin River.

this wonderful year and the years that followed, chief among which was the second visit of Messrs. Moody and Sankey to the United Kingdom. The foundations of the C.I.M. were laid, as we have seen, at a time when the spiritual life of the churches had been marvellously quickened by the Great Revival of 1859. Moody's first visit in 1873 had brought to the front again the supreme duty of soul-winning, preparing the way for many a forward movement, including the appeal for the Eighteen and the opening up of inland China ; and now, when a fresh advance was to be made in missionary enterprise, the heart of Christian England was being stirred to its depths by a practical, overwhelming demonstration of the power of the Gospel. Who shall say how much the world-wide work of foreign missions owes to these devoted evangelists ?

Then there was a book, equally simple and God-honouring. Published many years before, *China's Spiritual Need and Claims* had about it a living power. Edition after edition had been called for, and always the same deep spiritual influence seemed to flow from its pages. Steeped in prayer from the first, it had been used of God continually to call forth consecration in His service ; and now enlarged and brought up to date it was to have a new lease of life in the attractive edition of 1884.

" That was the book that did the work," said Mr. Stevenson, who was just home from Burma. " At a single meeting five pounds' worth would be purchased. Many new friends were attached to the Mission as a result, and a constant stream of gifts flowed in.

" It was a time of remarkable progress. Everywhere we had splendid openings, and neither labour nor forethought were spared in making the most of them. It was a new thing to be able to tell of China open from end to end, and the big map we carried with us made it all so real. M'Carthy's walk across China was of unique interest, and I too had travelled overland from Bhamo to Shanghai. Nobody else had such a story to tell in those days, just as no other mission had settled stations far in the interior. The outgoing of party after party introduced us to many new circles, and within the Mission itself all was hope and courage."

But still it was in prayer the work was really done. Quietly, at the back of everything, the spiritual life was maintained at the heart of the Mission. Never had the daily and weekly prayer meetings been more full of power. When Miss Murray's party came up from Glasgow, for example, on their way to China, it was no easy matter to accommodate all who gathered on Saturday afternoon. Many old friends were present, including the beloved Reginald Radcliffe, aglow with holy enthusiasm. From stirring scenes up north Mr. McCarthy had come, and with him Messrs. Hoste and Stanley Smith. Nothing of excitement followed them, however; the presence of God and the sense of responsibility were too deep for that.

" We had a glorious meeting," wrote Mrs. Taylor of this occasion (Oct. 18). " Such power I think I never felt before. It seemed as though the world were being moved in that little room."

In the midst of these experiences Mr. and Mrs. Taylor were facing another long separation. The outgoing of so many new workers urgently called for his presence in China, and she could not be spared from home. He too seemed needed in England—never more so, with doors opening on every hand, candidates applying and friends ready to help. Yet it was in China the fight had to be fought and the new recruits got into line. So the parting had to come, and Hudson Taylor went forward in the spirit of Livingstone's entry in his journal for one of his last, lonely birthdays in central Africa : " My Jesus, my King, my Life, my All— again I dedicate my whole self to Thee."

Sending Mr. McCarthy on ahead to deal with the most pressing matters, and leaving Mr. Stevenson to stand by Mr. Broomhall and the Council for a while at home, Mr. Taylor was preparing to set out early in January with a party of young men, including Messrs. Hoste, Stanley Smith, and Cassels, when the unexpected happened, and God's purposes broke in upon these well-laid plans with an over-flowing fulness that carried all before it.

It came about very naturally, and apart altogether from

design or effort. In his *History of the Church Missionary Society*, Mr. Eugene Stock speaks of " the extraordinary interest aroused in the autumn of 1884 by the announcement that the captain of the Cambridge Eleven and the stroke oar of the Cambridge boat were going out as missionaries." When the news reached Edinburgh it deeply stirred a group of medical students who for some months had been burdened about the indifference to spiritual things in the university, especially among their fellow-medicals. A series of remarkable meetings had just been held at Oxford and Cambridge in which Mr. Taylor and several of the outgoing party had won the sympathies of the undergraduates for foreign missions as never before. But they were too much occupied with preparations for an early departure to be able to follow up even such promising openings. Then it was that, providentially, Reginald Radcliffe came upon the scene—that fervent evangelist whose parish was the world and whose aim nothing less than that the Gospel should be preached " to every creature." Loving Scotland with a special love, he longed to bring the outgoing band into touch with her university life, and on obtaining Mr. Taylor's permission wrote to Professor Simpson to suggest that Studd and Stanley Smith should visit Edinburgh.[1]

Coming just at the time when those medical students were earnestly seeking guidance as to how to bring the claims of Christ before their fellows, the suggestion was hailed with thankfulness.

" Many had heard of Stanley Smith," wrote Professor Charteris, " and to every one who knew anything of cricket the name of Studd was familiar. And so the word went round

---

[1] By this time Messrs. D. E. Hoste and Stanley P. Smith (stroke of the Cambridge Eight a couple of years previously) and the Rev. W. W. Cassels of St. John's, Cambridge (late curate of All Souls, South Lambeth, and now Bishop in Western China) had been joined by Mr. C. T. Studd, ex-captain of the Cambridge Eleven. A little later Mr. Montagu Beauchamp, nephew of Lord Radstock, also a university oar, and Messrs. C. P. and A. T. Polhill, sons of a late M.P. for Bedford (" the former an officer in the 2nd Dragoon Guards, and the latter a Ridley Hall Theological student, and both of them prominent Eton and Cambridge cricketers ") made up the party to seven—a strong team from the university man's point of view.

our class rooms, ' Let us go and give the athlete missionaries a welcome ! '

" The men gathered—about a thousand, and the two missionaries spoke, well supported by Mr. Landale who is home from China, and others. Smith would have made his mark as an orator anywhere ; he has unusual powers of thought, imagination, and utterance, and a colder man than he would have been roused by the audience to whom he was invited to tell how the ' love of CHRIST constrained ' him to give up all home prospects and go to far-off China to preach the Gospel. Studd has not the gifts of an orator, but he never went more straight at the mark in the cricket-field than he did in his manly narrative of the way God had led him for years, from stage to stage of the Christian life, until he was ready to forsake father and mother, home and friends, because of his love for his Redeemer.

" The students were spellbound. Those two speakers were so manly—types indeed of handsome, healthy manhood—were so happy, spoke in such unconventional style, that when they had done hundreds of students, who had little thought of such a thing when they came into the hall, crowded round them to grasp their hand, followed them to the train by which they were going right off to London, and were on the platform saying " God speed you," when the train steamed away."

But that was not to be the end of it. During their campaign with Mr. Radcliffe the latter had seen the possibilities of such work, and had unfolded a plan for further meetings. Invitations had been urgent to return to Scotland, especially from Edinburgh students, and in spite of the early date fixed for the sailing of the party it was hoped that Mr. Taylor might accompany them.

" Could you come," wrote Mr. Stanley Smith to the beloved leader of the Mission ; " and if not, may we go ? "

By this time it was becoming clear to Mr. Taylor that the hand of God was in the movement, and greatly must he have longed to make the most of his share in it. He had been very conscious of the power of the Holy Spirit with those of the seven who had helped him in his meetings, and had seen the influence of their joyous consecration not over students only, but over leaders of Christian life and thought.[1]

[1] " The visit of Messrs. Stanley Smith and Studd to Melbourne Hall (Leicester) will always mark an epoch in my own life," wrote the Rev.

The whole thing was beginning to stand out before him : the uniqueness of the opportunity and of the band of fellow-workers who had been given him ; the evident purpose of the Lord of the Harvest to use them along lines that had always been his own ideal—through the deepening of spiritual life among His people, to thrust out many fresh labourers into His harvest. How his heart was in it all ; how he would have rejoiced to stay and help ! But, for him, duty clearly pointed in another direction.

Thus then it was arranged : Mr. Taylor going on ahead to get through important matters awaiting his attention in Shanghai, and Mr. Radcliffe undertaking, with Mr. Broomhall and others, the campaign that was to be so far-reaching in its results. One notable meeting Mr. Taylor had at Exeter Hall, when all the outgoing party were present—a meeting which in measure prepared him for Mr. Eugene Stock's comment :

The influence of such a band of men going to China was irresistible. No such event had occurred before ; and no event of the century had done so much to arouse the minds of Christian men to the tremendous claims of the Field, and the nobility of the missionary vocation.[1]

F. B. Meyer. " Before that time my Christian life had been spasmodic and fitful ; now flaming up with enthusiasm, and then pacing weariedly over leagues of grey ashes and cold cinders. I saw that these young men had something which I had not, but which was within them a constant source of rest and strength and joy. And never shall I forget a scene at 7 A.M. in the grey November morning, as daylight was flickering into the bedroom, paling the guttered candles, which from a very early hour had been lighting up the page of Scripture, and revealing the figures of the devoted Bible-students, who wore the old cricketing or boating costume of earlier days, to render them less sensible of the raw, damp climate. The talk then held was one of the formative influences of my life."

[1] " The gift of such a band to the China Inland Mission—truly it was a gift from God," continued the Editorial Secretary of the C.M.S., " was a just reward to Mr. Hudson Taylor and his colleagues for the genuine unselfishness with which they had always pleaded the cause of China and the world, and not of their own particular organisation, and for the deep spirituality which had always marked their meetings. And that spirituality marked most emphatically the densely crowded meetings in different places at which these seven men said farewell. They told, modestly and yet fearlessly, of the Lord's goodness to them, and of the joy of serving Him ; and they appealed to young men, not for their Mission, but for their Divine Master. No such missionary meeting had ever been known as the final gathering at Exeter Hall on February 4, 1885. We have be-

But it was not in public gatherings that these men were knit to their leader and the Mission with which they had cast in their lot. It was behind the scenes in quiet hours the work was done, and chiefly in times of prayer at Pyrland Road, as on the last day of 1884. There was no disguising on these occasions the poverty, as far as material resources were concerned, of the Mission that had closed its latest balance sheet with only ten pounds in hand—" ten pounds and all the promises of God." But how small a matter this seemed with the presence of the Lord Himself so consciously felt ! It never had been Mr. Taylor's way to minimise the trials that awaited young workers in China, especially if they desired to identify themselves with the people along the lines of the C.I.M. Speaking of himself in the third person, one of the Cambridge Party recalled :

Mr. Taylor was careful to set before him the real character of life and work in inland China, telling him quite plainly that it involved isolation, privation, exposure to the hostility of the people and the contempt of his own countrymen, and also many trials of faith, patience and constancy.

" Mr. Hoste went away deeply impressed with the character of the man with whom he had been speaking," was the young officer's only comment, " and with his heart more than ever set upon becoming a missionary in China."

Very memorable to such a spirit was that New Year's Eve spent in prayer and fasting. When Mr. Taylor left London three weeks later, some of the party were again in Scotland, rejoicing to tell of all the wealth they were finding in deeper fellowship with Christ, which so far outweighed anything of worldly advantage they were laying down. And in a blinding snow-storm, as he crossed France alone, the traveller's heart was full of praise for news received only that morning from the northern capital :

" Two thousand students last night—wonderful times ! It is the Lord."

come familiar since then with meetings more or less of the same type, but it was a new thing then. In many ways the Church Missionary Society owes a deep debt of gratitude to the China Inland Mission and the Cambridge Seven. The Lord Himself spoke through them ; and it was by His grace that the Society had ears to hear." (From *The History of the Church Missionary Society*, vol. iii. p. 285.)

CHAPTER XXVII

THE PRICE OF PROGRESS

1885–1886. AET. 53–54.

Who, that one moment has the least descried Him,
  Dimly and faintly, hidden and afar,
Doth not despise all excellence beside Him,
  Pleasures and powers that are not and that are.

Aye, amid all men bear himself thereafter
  Smit with a solemn and a sweet surprise,
Dumb to their scorn and turning on their laughter
  Only the dominance of earnest eyes.

Yes, thro' life, death, thro' sorrow and thro' sinning,
  He shall suffice me, for He hath sufficed :
Christ is the end, for Christ was the beginning,
  Christ the beginning, for the end is Christ.

Myers.

How little the Church yet knows of her glorious Lord, that
missionary work can ever be counted sacrifice ! To be His
ambassadors, His witnesses, His fellow-workers, to share in
some measure " the fellowship of His sufferings," that we
may " know Him and the power of His resurrection " and
in some deeper, fuller sense " win Christ "—how can it but
be *gain*, infinite and eternal ?

Long had this been the attitude of Mr. Taylor's heart,
and that it was so still comes out very simply in a letter
written as he was crossing France. He had been making
the most of an empty side of a carriage when, at Lyons,
additional travellers entered in the middle of the night.
He judged them to be a newly married couple, on account

of their evident youth, and at first felt disposed to regret the loss of space to lie down, for he was very weary.

"But they taught me a lesson, I trust," he wrote to the loved one left behind. "The French lady seemed simply to adore her husband. There was something about their ways one could not describe, which told how fully they were all in all to each other. Her eyes followed his every movement. If she touched him, there was something indescribable in the touch. They were oblivious of every one else. She wished for something at a station : he almost flew to procure it—and what thanks her eyes gave him ! Some smiled. But I said to myself, ' How infinitely more worthy is my Lord of adoring love than this young husband can be ! How much more He loves me ! He has *died* for me ; He lives for me ; He delights to give me the desires of my heart. Do I love Him so ? Cannot I take my eyes off Him ? Is He really all in all to me ? Am I oblivious of all others, because of His presence and love ? Is it joy to leave all—you, my precious one, included—to please Him ?

"Oh, Darling ! that love did me good, and does still. The pain of parting is very real, but Jesus is very real, too. He will be a satisfying portion to you during my absence, and to me in your absence. Let us be thankful that *our* honeymoon has lasted so many years, and will last. But most of all, let us seek to be more to our Lord, to find more in our Lord, as time passes on. We shall never be alone, shall we ? "

Nearing Shanghai some weeks later, the sense of responsibility in connection with all that lay before him was very great. An absence of two years, at a time of unparalleled growth and extension in the Mission, meant that many problems would await him for which he had neither wisdom nor strength.

"Soon we shall be in the midst of the battle," he wrote from the China Sea (Feb. 28, '85) ; "but the Lord our God in the midst of us is mighty, so we will trust and not be afraid. ' He will save ' : He will save all the time, in everything."

Meanwhile, in Edinburgh, the movement begun among the students was not only growing in popularity, it was taking on a deeper tone.

"Students, like other young men," wrote Dr. Moxey of this second visit, " are apt to regard professedly religious people of their own age as wanting in manliness, unfit for the river or cricket-field, and only good for psalm-singing and pulling a long face. But the big, muscular hands and long arms of the ex-captain of the Cambridge Eight, stretched out in entreaty, while he eloquently told out the old story of Redeeming Love, capsized their theory ; and when Mr. C. T. Studd, whose name is to them familiar as perhaps the greatest gentleman bowler in England, supplemented his brother athlete's words by quiet but intense and burning utterances of personal testimony to the love and power of a personal Saviour, opposition and criticism were alike disarmed, and professors and students together were seen in tears, to be followed in the after-meeting by the glorious sight of professors dealing with students, and students with one another."

" We had a wonderful time," wrote one of the undergraduates. " I should think three-fourths of that meeting waited to an after-meeting, and the great hall was covered with men anxious about their souls. Christians were stimulated all round, and many I believe came that night to an out-and-out decision for God.

" The following evening we met again in the Free Assembly Hall, and again had times of great blessing. To the men whom God had so signally used we said, ' Can you not possibly come back ? '

" They said, ' Well, we are going to the West. We are to pass this way again on Friday, and if you can arrange it shall be glad to meet your students again, then.'

" We met in the same hall, and I think that I never saw a meeting like that. We had obtained a special lease of the hall. We ought to have left by half-past ten, but got permission to remain till midnight ; and up to that hour the floor was covered with men anxiously inquiring, ' What must I do to be saved ? ' " [1]

The precious days of January (1885) were hastening on, and it yet remained to pay farewell visits to Oxford and Cambridge.

" I want to recommend to you my Master," said Studd in his last address to the men of his own university. " I have had many ways of pleasure in my time, and have tasted most of the delights this world can give ; but I can tell you that these pleasures are as nothing compared with my present joy. I

---

[1] " We were then unable to stop," continued the same writer. " Professor Drummond took up the meetings. Every Sunday evening the Oddfellows' Hall was crowded with students, and each address was followed by an after-meeting. Many students during that never-to-be-forgotten winter session (1884–1885) were converted."

had formerly as much love for cricket as any man could have ; but when the Lord Jesus came into my heart I found that I had something infinitely better. My heart was no longer set on the game : I wanted to win souls, to serve and please Him."

"What a priceless testimony is this to spiritual realities," commented the Master of Pembroke.[1] "What a victory is scored to faith ! for however eccentric his conduct may be thought, plainly he has demonstrated that there are unseen powers that sway a man's heart much more forcibly than any motives of the world. We who can recollect the strong man, how great he would rise up with his bat, with what force he would hurl his ball, how grand an ovation he would receive as captain of the victorious eleven after some international contest, who know how such a man is sought out, caressed and idolised, can in some measure estimate his sacrifice, or rather the new force that has laid hold of him. For he was not leading a sinful life, but simply says that a stronger fascination has come over him, and he submits like a captive to it, with his eyes open, rationally and willingly, and in the new service finds a satisfaction far excelling the old."

It was this hidden power, this spring of inward joy that was so attractive, and multitudes everywhere wanted to see and hear for themselves. From Exeter Hall in London (headquarters of the Y.M.C.A.) came an urgent request for one last meeting, and the departure of the missionaries was delayed another day to make it possible. Fresh from the moving scenes at Oxford and Cambridge the whole party came up to London for this last farewell, and the great hall was densely crowded.

"It was a sight to stir the blood," wrote a correspondent of *The Nonconformist*, "and a striking testimony to the power of the uplifted Christ to draw to Himself not the weak, the emotional, the illiterate only, but all that is noblest in strength and finest in culture."

"I could not but ponder," said a thoughtful observer in *The Record*, "what were the main reasons for the might of a movement which has drawn to it man after man of a very noble type, and of just the qualities most influential in the young Cambridge world. My main reasons, after all, reduced themselves to one —the uncompromising spirituality and unworldliness of the programme of the Mission, responded to by hearts which have

---

[1] The Rev. C. E. Searle, D.D.

truly laid all at the Lord's feet, and whose delight is in the most open confession of His Name and its power upon themselves. I venture to pronounce it inconceivable, impossible, that such a meeting should have been held in connection with any missionary enterprise of mixed aims, or in which such great truths as personal conversion, present peace and joy in believing, the present sanctifying power of the Spirit, the absolute necessity among the heathen of faith in Christ for salvation, and the loss of the soul as the alternative, were ignored, or treated with hesitation. Nor could such a profound interest possibly be called out, did the work not demand of the workers very real and manifest self-sacrifice and acts of faith." [1]

All this was a great joy to Mr. Taylor and those with him in China ; so also were the meetings he had arranged for the Cambridge Band at various ports on the way out, and others in Shanghai, Peking and elsewhere on arrival. To get the young men into work studying the language was important however, so meetings were curtailed, and they

[1] Three months later (May 1885) an Edinburgh student came up to the Annual Meetings of the C.I.M. in London to tell of further developments :

" The story with which I have to deal," he said, " is that of a movement, perhaps the most wonderful that ever had place in the history of university students, certainly the strangest that ever took place in the history of Scottish universities. I have to tell you how our great Edinburgh University and the allied medical schools, with between three and four thousand students, have been shaken to their very depths ; how the work has spread to all the other universities of Scotland ; and how, already, as the students of these universities have gone far and wide, the work is spreading in all its depth and reality throughout the whole country, I might almost say, throughout the world. . . .

" The present work has been carried forward by the very best men in our university. Some of our best-known professors and assistant professors . . . have been actively engaged in it. And among the students it has not been any one set, but our best intellects, our medallists, our scholars, our bursars, our prize-men—these have been among the most prominent in carrying forward this work. As to results, as I said before, we cannot estimate them. I believe that the number of conversions, even in our own university, is to be counted by hundreds and not by scores. And, as one result, scores of men have given themselves to missionary work, and have entered on medical courses in preparation for it. . . . I have just to ask you to praise God with me, and with Edinburgh University, for sending among us those two missionaries-elect of the China Inland Mission, Studd and Stanley Smith."

In the following year, a similar work of grace commenced among university men in North America, from which developed the Student Volunteer Movement and ultimately the World's Student Christian Federation. And, back of it all, one remembers Harold Schofield's prayers.

were soon on their way, in Chinese dress, to the interior—
northward to Shan-si and westward to Han-chung-fu.

For himself, Mr. Taylor was not expecting to be long
detained in China, there being much of importance to require
his presence at home.   He hoped to give effect, on this sixth
visit, to the plans for organisation that had been maturing
in his mind, and to see something of the work in the interior,
especially in the province of Shan-si.   The time had come
when superintendents were needed to afford help and
guidance to the largely increased number of recruits, and
some one who could be associated with himself as Deputy
Director, in view of his necessary absences from the field.
A China Council also was desirable, to assist the Director or
his Deputy, as the London Council had long helped Mr.
Taylor at home ; and it was important to establish training
centres for the study of the language, in which new arrivals,
men and women respectively, could have experienced help
in preparing for their life-work.

Seen in the light of subsequent developments it was to
be expected that the great adversary would leave no stone
unturned to hinder and if possible frustrate these purposes.
" Our wrestling is not against flesh and blood, but against
the principalities, against the powers, against the world-
rulers of this darkness, against the spiritual hosts of wicked-
ness in the heavenly places."   Wonderful things had been
happening in connection with the Mission, wonderful things
were yet to happen, and the enemy seems to have been
prepared at every point to oppose and hinder.   Month after
month went by, and at the close of 1885, Mr. Taylor wrote :

A year ago I thought to be back in England ere December
was out, but I seem to be as far from it as on landing.   Not
that nothing has been done !   A great deal, thank God, has
been accomplished, and not a little suffered—but He knows all
about that.   Such a hand-to-hand conflict with the powers of
darkness as I have seldom known has been no small part of
the work of the year ; but " hitherto the Lord hath helped us " :
and He *will* perfect that which concerns us, whatever that perfecting may mean or involve.

" Borne on a great wave of fervent enthusiasm," as Mr.

Eugene Stock expressed it, the work had been swept into a new place in the sympathy and confidence of the Lord's people. "The Mission has become popular," Mr. Broomhall was writing from England; but out in China, Hudson Taylor had to fathom the other side of that experience.

"There must be a good deal more effected by pain," he wrote to Mrs. Taylor a few weeks after landing, "than we know of at present. It seems essentially connected with fruitfulness, natural and spiritual."

To no one else could he unburden his heart; and as the separation lengthened, many were the revealing passages in his letters.

Oct. 15: Great trial, great blessing are very present. My only rest is in God. But He is more than ever all to me, and I am resting in Him.

Nov. 1: I have it much impressed on my heart to plead mightily for a special outpouring of the Holy Spirit on those who cause most concern. This is what they need; this would put all right, and nothing else will. So long as the motto practically is "Not Christ but I," our best organisation will never give the victory over the world, the flesh and the devil. The motto *must* be changed.

Nov. 9: "It is three weeks to-day since I was out of doors," he continued after an illness due to overstrain. "Satan is so busy just now! there is trial on every hand" . . . mentioning no fewer than seven causes of special anxiety. "In the midst of it all God is revealing Himself. The work is wonderfully advancing, and those who will have it are getting showers of blessing."

Nov. 11: I am sure you will pray hard for us. The conflict is heavy indeed. Satan harasses on all sides; but the Lord reigneth, and shall triumph gloriously. . . . It is easy enough to fancy we are weaned children when we don't mind much the thing we miss; but at other times and about other things we are less in danger of making this mistake.

Nov. 14: I believe we are on the eve of great blessing, perhaps of great trial too. The Lord our God in the midst of us is "mighty to save"; let us trust Him. Flesh and heart often fail: let them fail! He faileth not. Pray very much, pray constantly, for Satan rages against us. But God uses this most diligent though unwitting of His servants to refine and purify His people and to bring in the greatest blessings—witness the Cross.

The winter months were the most painful, and Mr. Taylor was anticipating what it would mean to be without the comfort even of letters on the long journey he expected to take after the Chinese New Year.

" I am wondering how you will bear the three months' fasting from letters while I am inland," he wrote in January 1886. " I shall feel it dreadfully, but it has to be gone through. The Lord help and comfort you. . . . There is much to distress. Your absence is a great and ever-present trial, and there is all the ordinary and extraordinary conflict. But the encouragements are also wonderful—no other word approaches the truth —and half of them cannot be told in writing. No one dreams of the mighty work going on in connection with our Mission. Other Missions too, doubtless, are being greatly used. I look for a wonderful year.

" Sometimes I feel almost crushed by one thing and another . . . but the wonderful progress, the wonderful love of most of our people, the effect that is being produced at home and abroad is worth the crushing of a score of us. And if you and I be the sacrifices (among others) shall we regret it—I do not say complain ? Nay more, shall we not be willing, glad, *eager* to win at any cost (and God only knows how great it is) such real, abiding blessings ? "

And a couple of months later (March 10), when once again his plans had all been broken up :

I do so comfort myself with that hymn :

> What grace, O Lord, and beauty shone
>   Around Thy steps below !
> What patient love was seen in all
>   Thy life and death of woe !
>
> Thy foes might hate, despise, revile,
>   Thy friends unfaithful prove ;
> Unwearied in forgiveness still,
>   Thy heart could only love.
>
> Oh give us hearts to love like Thee,
>   Like Thee, O Lord, to grieve
> Far more for others' sins than all
>   The wrongs that we receive.

Darling, we must not pick our crosses, nor be dissatisfied with the training and discipline. Soon it will all be past and our

separations over for ever. We cannot expect lightly to assault
Satan's domain ; if we do, we shall be corrected.

As to the progress that was being made, it is difficult now
that the organisation of the Mission is so complete to realise
what it meant to work it all out, when men were only gradually growing in fitness for various posts, and any delegation
of Mr. Taylor's authority was apt to be regarded with
misgivings if not opposed through misunderstanding. The
family feeling in the Mission had been very precious to its
early workers, who were accustomed to dealing with Mr.
Taylor direct about every matter in which advice and help
were needed. Much more of difficulty lay in the way of
associating others with himself in these responsibilities than
even he anticipated ; but the appointment of Superintendents for a number of provinces, arrangements for
receiving new arrivals in suitable training homes where help
could be given them with the language, and the better
ordering of business and financial matters in Shanghai were
part of the outcome of his labours in 1885.[1]

Twice had serious illness called him to Yang-chow during
the year, twice had a life of incalculable value to the Mission
hung in the balance. In answer to prayer, Miss Murray
had been raised up, and the plan Mr. Taylor unfolded even
when it seemed that she might never work again had been
brought to fruition.

"Lord, I am so weak and ill," was all she could say at
first, "why does Mr. Taylor speak of these things now ? "

But the long convalescence was brightened by a sense
of call to much-needed service ; and the Mother of the
women's training home—the heart that has poured itself

[1] As early as 1870, Mr. Taylor had sought to develop helpers upon
whom he might devolve responsibility in the supervision of the work ;
but as he wrote to Mr. McCarthy at that time, " such a position has to
be *gained*, and the ability is only in and from the Lord."

A year later he wrote again (Jan. 18, 1871) : " I wish you to feel
responsible before the Lord for seeking to help the brethren in all these
stations. Really help them ; really feel responsibility about them ; really
pray much for them, and as far as possible with them. Feel and evince a
deep interest in all their out-stations and work generally. And above all,
do not let them dream you are taking a higher place than their own :
leave God to show that in due time. You are really their head as you
become their servant and helper."

out ever since in love and blessing reaching to every part of the Mission—came out of that illness ready for the appointed task.

At An-king also, steps had been taken to improve and consolidate the work, that it might become a helpful training centre for young men during their first months in China. In Mr. W. Cooper, the wise and prayerful leader was recognised for the post of Superintendent of the province and Pastor of the An-king church, while in Mr. Baller, shortly afterwards associated with him, the students had from the first an ideal teacher and friend.[1]

The older work in the province of Che-kiang was next organised, Mr. Meadows (the senior member of the Mission) being appointed Superintendent, with Mr. Williamson of the *Lammermuir* party as his helper. But it was not until the close of the year that Mr. Taylor saw with thankfulness who was to be his own Deputy. With an exceptional record of varied and useful service behind him, Mr. Stevenson had returned to China, landing on Christmas Eve after an absence of ten and a half years. All that time, in Burma and elsewhere, he had often longed to be at work again in his old sphere. But the Guiding Hand had been preparing him for wider usefulness ; and so real a blessing had come to him, spiritually, that he was ready to be a helper of many.[2]

" The Rev. J. W. Stevenson has, I am thankful to say, accepted the position of Director's Deputy," Mr. Taylor wrote in March (1886) to the members of the Mission. " He will assist, *D.V.*, by visiting for me many places I cannot reach ; will represent me in my absence from China, and deal with all questions brought before him by the Superintendents requiring immediate determination.

" I feel sure you will all share with me in thankfulness to God for this appointment, and feel that it is one of the most

---

[1] A week spent at that station in November 1885, when the training home was decided upon, enabled Mr. Taylor to hold a conference in which he went over the *Principles and Practice of the C.I.M.* signed by the members of the Mission before leaving England. The addresses embodied in the *Retrospect*—which has since, in many editions, attained so wide a circulation—were originally given in those meetings, to the refreshment of all present.

[2] " Ever since the Keswick Convention," he had written before leaving England, " my cup has been running over."

important steps in advance that we have recently been able to make. I should ask your special prayers for Mr. Stevenson, that he may be spiritually sustained, and that divine wisdom and grace may be given him for the weighty responsibilities of his post ; and also that you will remember each of the Superintendents in your prayers, that they may be blessed, and helped in the discharge of their duties. Without full spiritual power, no experience or ability will avail for the important and momentous work they have undertaken." [1]

One thing that had tried Mr. Taylor a good deal all through 1885 had been the frustration, again and again, of his purpose to visit the northern provinces. Reasons of importance seemed to require his presence in Shan-si without delay, yet endless complications detained him at Shanghai or called in other directions. More than once he had been on the point of starting ; and it was not until the time really came—twelve months and more after it had been expected—that he began to see how wisely even the hindrances had been . planned. But for Miss Murray's illness combined with other delays, he would not have taken a journey, for example, which proved of great importance. Far up the Tsien-tang river was a station he found himself obliged to visit, and by crossing the watershed into the neighbouring province of Kiang-si it would take little longer to return by the Po-yang Lake than the other way. Both the Tsien-tang and the Kwang-sin rivers were

---

[1] Shortly afterwards Mr. J. F. Broumton, prevented by unavoidable circumstances from returning to his former sphere in Kwei-chow, consented to take up the account-keeping and statistics of the Mission. " The first cash-book I had handed to me," he recalled, " and the only one in use at that time, was an ordinary threepenny account book [preferred, until then, for convenience in travelling]—very different from the large ledgers we use now ! I took over the accounts from Mr. Taylor himself, and arranged with him about carrying on the work at Wu-chang rather than in Shanghai. It was midnight on the 1st of May (1886) before the transfer was made and we set off for the steamer. Everything had to be balanced up to the cent. Mr. Taylor was very particular about details." Five and a half years at Wu-chang, followed by eleven years in Shanghai as Treasurer, so demonstrated Mr. Broumton's ability and devotion to his arduous task that more than once Mr. Taylor wrote of him with thankfulness as second to none in his value to the Mission.

Mr. J. E. Cardwell in the business department and Miss Mary Black in charge of the Mission-house (Yuen-ming-yuen Buildings) were also much associated with Mr. Taylor at this time.

of exceptional beauty at that season, and hoping that the complete change of boat-life would help to re-establish Miss Murray's health, he arranged for several of the Yang-chow party to accompany him.

Thus, then, the months of May and June (1886) brought to that long-waiting district the loving hearts and earnest, prayerful lives that were to become its channels of divine blessing. Six years had passed since Mr. Taylor on his previous visit had met the converts gathered in through the labours of Captain Yü in the neighbourhood of Yü-shan. The little out-stations he had visited then among the hills and down the river were out-stations still, and had rarely seen even a passing missionary. But one great difference he noticed that was suggestive. For a young worker, a girl of only twenty, had recently come over from what had been Dr. Douthwaite's station, to take a few days' holidays in that beautiful region. Cared for by the evangelist and his wife, she had spent a week in the county town of Chang-shan, sharing their home and sleeping in an attic to which she climbed by a ladder-like stair. But neither this nor any other consideration could keep visitors away, and from morning till night her room was besieged with women and children. Warm-hearted Agnes Gibson welcomed them all, and spent her much-needed " holiday " in telling the old, old story, which had never seemed more precious.

The result was that when he came this second time Mr. Taylor found a marked change in the Sunday services. On his previous visit the Christians had been all and only men ; and so bitter was the opposition of their women-folk that they had even rented a room for themselves, where they might read and pray undisturbed. Now, however, the women were as much in evidence as the men, and a deputation of the latter waited upon him to point the moral.

" We want a missionary of our own," they said, " and we want *a lady*. If one visit of a week could bring about such a change, what might not be accomplished if we had a Lady-Teacher all the time ? " [1]

---

[1] So much were they in earnest that they were ready, at their own expense, to put down a board floor and make other alterations in the

This was unanswerable ; and it was moreover the very development Mr. Taylor had long desired to see. As he travelled with the Misses Murray and their young companions down the Kwang-sin river, passing city after city in which no voice was raised to tell of the love of Jesus ; as he saw the welcome with which these gentle visitors were received, not only by little groups of Christians in lonely out-stations but by the people everywhere, he realised with thankfulness that the time had come, and that the Lord had sent His own messengers.[1] It was no easy work that lay before them, and no light responsibility he assumed in consenting to let them undertake it. But with their hearts drawn out in prayer for place after place—cities like Ho-kow with its eighty thousand, or I-yang, for which they had a memorable time of waiting upon God, he could do no other. Going forward therefore in faith, he arranged for the Misses Mackintosh, Gibson and Gray to return with an older worker, and settle down among the native Christians, making the evangelisation of this populous region their life-work. And if the step cost him more, far more, than his fellow-travellers could realise, never was confidence in God more fully justified than by the result.[2]

Mission-house (toward which they had put aside ten dollars) if only Mr. Taylor would send them a teacher of their own. This he could not at the moment arrange for, though ladies were appointed to the district soon after. The station in question (Chang-shan) has now for many years been occupied by Miss Marie Guex from Vevey and her sister Madame Just, Swiss members of the Mission.

[1] " As to Miss Mackintosh, Miss Gibson and Miss Gray," he wrote at the time, " they read the Mandarin Testament as fluently as English, and with few mistakes. They have been wonderfully prospered both in their studies and work. It would do you good to see them among a group of Chinese women."

[2] Within the first year of Women's Work on the Kwang-sin river forty-two additional converts were baptized, and within four years the Yü-shan Church alone had grown from about thirty to one hundred and eight members. At the present time, in a complete chain of ten central stations and sixty out-stations, there are over two thousand two hundred communicants and a large number of enquirers, pupils in schools, etc., cared for by native leaders—ladies being still the only foreign missionaries.

As early as 1868, Mr. Taylor had written to Miss Faulding, upon leaving Hang-chow : " I do not know when I may be able to return, and it will not do for Church affairs to wait for me. You cannot take a Pastor's place in name, but you must help (Wang) Lae-djun to act in matters of receiving and excluding as far as you can. You can speak privately to

Returning to Shanghai after six weeks' absence Mr. Taylor found himself faced by a serious problem. He arrived, as it happened, on the very last day of an option obtained upon a building site in the Settlement that he greatly desired to purchase for future use. It was a valuable plot of land, two acres in extent, admirably situated for the purposes of the Mission, but the price was almost £2500. Real estate could not but increase in value in such a locality, and other offers were being made for this particular property. It seemed providential that the last stages of Mr. Taylor's journey had been remarkably prospered, so that he had reached Shanghai earlier than could have been expected. But though he was in time, he had not money in hand to justify the purchase. If lost, the opportunity would never recur ; yet what was to be done ?

One thing at any rate was possible : the whole matter could be laid before the Lord in definite, united prayer. If it were of Him for the Mission to have and use that plot of land, He could bring it about, however unlikely it might seem. The clear duty was to refer the problem to Him, in the confident expectation that He would deal with it in the way that was best. This then they did at the noon prayer meeting (June 14) when no outsiders were present ; and then and there the answer was given.

Among the party just arrived from home was one who had been interested in China through Mr. McCarthy's meetings in Scotland two years previously. Large business

---

candidates, and can be present at Church meetings, and might even, through others, suggest questions to be asked of those desiring baptism. Then after the meeting you can talk privately with Lae-djun about them, and suggest who you think he might receive next time they meet. Thus he may have the help he needs, and there will be nothing that any one could regard as unseemly." Upon these lines the Kwang-sin river work has prospered by the blessing of God.

In reply to a letter from Dr. Happer of Canton, Mr. Taylor wrote in July 1890 : " The principal reasons to my mind for the safety and comfort of Women's Work among the Chinese are, firstly, that the ladies walk with God, and the ' beauty of holiness ' upon them gives a dignity before which lewdness cannot live ; and secondly, that they are really entrusted to the care of the Lord Himself as their Escort, when commended to Him for their work. And He is faithful to the trust, and does keep those who are committed to Him. We expect Him to do it, and He does not disappoint us."

responsibilities rested upon him at that time, and it was not until he could see how these were to be cared for that he felt free to join the Inland Mission. Unexpected delays in his coming out had coincided with delays in Mr. Taylor's northern journey, so that the two met in Shanghai on the very day in question, met one might almost say in that prayer-meeting. The outcome was a gift sufficient to cover the purchase of the entire property, followed (though that was a later thought) by the still larger gift of all the buildings necessary to make it the most complete and serviceable of headquarters. It was a wonderful provision, a wonderful answer to prayer, and a wonderful anticipation of the enlargement in the Mission that was at hand.

Two days later Mr. Taylor set out on his northern journey, tidings from Mr. Stevenson who had preceded him filling his heart with thankfulness.

" Praise for twenty years of blessing from our gracious Father ! " the latter had written from Han-chung-fu on the anniversary of the sailing of the *Lammermuir* (May 26). " The struggles and victories of all these years are part and parcel of your spiritual fibre. May the third decade witness mighty outgoings of power through the Mission that shall astonish fainthearted Christians and be a source of strength to all wholehearted followers of our risen Saviour.

" Well, dear Mr. Taylor, I am so overflowing with joy that I can scarcely trust myself to write. He has done great things for us up here—glory to His Name ! I do bless Him for the peace and joy that fill my soul, and also for the floods that have come down upon my beloved Brothers and Sisters at present in Han-chung. We had the full tide last night, and found it hard work to break up such a glory-time as had never been witnessed in Han-chung before. . . . The Lord has given us a wonderful manifestation of Himself these last few days. But we are all satisfied that there are infinite stores yet at our disposal of grace and power. . . . I do wish you could have been with us last night, and have witnessed the deep, overflowing joy, and heard the glad, full surrender of all present to Christ. I do not think you would have slept much for delight. As long as we keep banded together in love and consecration, as is happily the case here, there need be no doubt regarding our success in China—*none*.

" The blessing at the meetings with the native Christians . . .

was like a heavenly breeze filling us with great delight and bright hope for the future.   There are quite a number of characteristic converts here—some of them with most decided convictions and dauntless courage and enterprise for the Lord.   It is truly refreshing to find, so far in the interior, a band of men and women so simple and devoted. . . . I never was so hopeful as I am to-day with regard to the Gospel in this land."

CHAPTER XXVIII

DAYS OF BLESSING

1886. AET. 54.

IT had come at last—the opportunity so long looked forward to ! For seven years Mr. Taylor had been planning to visit Shan-si. Once he had even set out, only to be recalled by claims at the coast. But now, the better organisation of the Mission permitting an absence of several months from Shanghai, he hoped to strengthen the work not in Shan-si only but in other regions lying farther inland. For many desires were on his heart in connection with this journey. Each station to be visited had its problems, but greatest of all was the question how to evangelise the vast population to which the missionaries now had access. To bring help and encouragement to these lonely toilers was his chief object, and to confer with them about the organisation of the native church, which in some places was growing rapidly. It was also his hope to establish a Church of England district in the great western province of Sze-chwan, a matter which had long been under consideration. In the Rev. W. W. Cassels the Mission had for the first time one qualified to take the lead in such an enterprise, and Sze-chwan with its sixty-eight millions had as yet only two centres in which Protestant missionaries were to be found. Mr. Cassels with others of the Cambridge party had been gaining experience in Shan-si, where they were eagerly awaiting Mr. Taylor's coming, and he was looking forward with no less pleasure to seeing them in the midst of their work.

But first of all the desired province had to be reached,

over the vast plains of Chih-li and the mountain passes
beyond.   Such travelling was strange to Mr. Taylor, hitherto
accustomed to the endless water-ways of central and southern
China.   Springless carts and northern roads, consisting of
unmade tracks over sun-baked or rain-flooded country;
rivers to be crossed without bridge or ferry, and dangerous
passes braved in litters swinging from the backs of mules
very prone to stumble; these by day, and big, noisy inns
at night, together with northern speech, food, and manners,
all made large demands upon strength and patience.   While
a native junk on canal or river may leave much to be desired,
it is at any rate a shelter you can call your own; but to
exchange the weariness of a cart in which you have been
jolted and shaken for hours for a brick-bed shared with
others in a close not to say filthy room, the minor occupants
of which may be numbered by hundreds if not thousands,
is quite another matter.

To Mr. Taylor and his companions the journey was
memorable for its discomforts.   Setting out toward the end
of June, they found the heat intense.   Flies swarmed everywhere; food was difficult to obtain; and at night the younger
men, new to such conditions, were thoroughly "played out,"
and often too tired to unpack their provisions or forage for
a meal.   More than once they were roused after hours of
slumber by Mr. Taylor's cheery invitation to come and share
his "midnight chicken," prepared as likely as not with his
own hands.[1]

Two weeks even of such experiences soon passed, however, and great was the contrast when the hospitable home
of Dr. and Mrs. Edwards was reached.   There in the capital
of the province (Tai-yuan-fu) most of the Shan-si missionaries were gathered to meet him, including five of the
Cambridge band, who had now been fifteen months in China.

---

[1] Who that ever travelled with him could forget his unfailing care
and thought for others, and the practical way in which he could turn his
hand to anything.   Cooking was quite in his line.   "All the way Mr.
Taylor prepared food for me," recalled Miss Murray of the journey down
the Kwang-sin river, when she was recovering from her serious illness.
"He used to make omelets in the back of the boat.   We would hear him
beating up the eggs.   He managed to get the things somehow!"

Had Mr. Taylor been able, as he had planned, to follow them to their sphere of labour a year or so previously, he would have found them far less ready for his visit than they were now. Then, only two C.I.M. stations existed in the province, and in the southernmost of these they were beginning, under Mr. Baller's tuition, the study of the language. Now, with considerable fluency in Chinese, they had come up, each from their own centre, full of the problems that press upon young missionaries in the midst of a large and growing work.[1]

For the district in which they found themselves was that of Mr. Hsi, the ex-Confucian scholar, and his friends Chang and Ch'ü of the Buddhist temple and little city of Ta-ning among the Western Hills. On either side of the Fen river these men, full of their first love and zeal, were sounding out the glad tidings of salvation far and wide. Seventy-two baptisms at the Spring Gatherings, a few months earlier, had doubled the membership of the Ping-yang church, and made the need for wise and careful supervision all the more apparent. The time had come for setting apart some of the Chinese leaders as deacons and elders in the village gatherings, and for recognising the God-appointed ministry of Hsi and others who were doing pastoral work. But before going on to the native conference at which these ordinations were to take place, Mr. Taylor was thankful for the quiet days in the capital for united waiting upon God.

Days of Blessing [2]—how truly the title of the book in which a record of these meetings has been preserved expresses what they were in reality ! As one turns the pages, the fragrance of the Lord's own presence cannot but be felt. HE never could be hid ; and from first to last it was His fulness that rejoiced those waiting hearts. Face to face with the overwhelming need around them and the insufficiency within, it was good to remember, as Mr. Taylor put it, that it is not a question of the supply at all but of

[1] With help from Mr. Baller, four new stations had been opened (1885–1886) by Messrs. Hoste, Cassels, Beauchamp and Stanley Smith, in the following order — Kü-wo, Si-chow, Ta-ning, and Hung-tung. In the extreme north of the province Kwei-hwa-ting and Ta-tung-fu had also been occupied by members of the C.I.M.

[2] Edited by Mr. (now Sir) Montagu Beauchamp.

the Supplier. " He (the Lord Jesus) is enough for Shan-si, from the Great Wall to Ho-nan. We have a grander Saviour than we realise ! "

Upon the main theme of the conference—*Christ our All-Sufficiency for personal life and godliness, as well as for all the exigencies of our service*—we must not dwell. Never was Mr. Taylor more helpful, more at his best, than in drawing upon the treasures of the Word of God,[1] and on his own experience, for the encouragement of fellow-workers. But the subject is too full for these pages. Some echoes, merely, of the conference may be gathered from suggestions made by Mr. Taylor as to the relation of the missionary to his work :

How can we secure the development of strong, healthy, Christlike native Christians unless we are living strong, healthy, Christlike lives ourselves ?

Very few have been long in connection with missions without hearing a great deal of the faults and failures of the native Christians. Is it not the case that their faults and failures are very much the reflection of our own ?

What the spiritual children will be depends on what the spiritual father is. . . . The stream will never rise higher than its source, but it will not fall far short of it, circumstances permitting. The hardness of heart which is a hindrance to the Gospel is not that of the hearers ; it is the hardness of this heart of mine.

---

[1] Speaking of the Lord Jesus as our Sufficiency, Mr. Taylor said : " It is well to remind ourselves of the close connection that exists between the written Word of God and the incarnate Word of God. We shall never enjoy the one apart from the other. It is through God's own revelation in the written Word that we really see and know the Word Who was made flesh, and Who rose from the dead. It is through the written Word we shall feed on Him, not through our own speculations. It is important that we bear in mind that as the Incarnate Word is a Divine Person, so is the written Word a Divine Message ; and as we may rest all our soul's interests on Jesus Christ, so we may rest all our soul's weight on the Word of God. To be unsettled on the question of inspiration is to be overcome by temptation, and to be unable to accomplish God's work. The connection between full faith in God's will as revealed in His written Word and in the Incarnate Word is so close and intimate, that you can no more separate them than you can separate between body and soul, or soul and spirit. Begin to separate them, and to study theology *instead* of the Word of God (rather than as a mere aid in gaining a fuller grasp of it) and if it does not make you weaker rather than stronger you will be fortunate indeed. No ! Take God's Word as it stands, and God's Christ as He reveals Himself to us, and enjoy all in Him " (*Days of Blessing,* p. 55).

When God's grace is triumphant in my soul, and I can look a Chinaman in the face and say, " God is able to save *you*, where and as you are," that is when I have power. How else are you going to deal with a man under the craving for opium ? The cause of want of success is very often that we are only half saved ourselves. If we are fully saved and confess it, we shall see results.

On the need for *contact*, close and real, not only with the Lord Himself but with those whose good we seek, Mr. Taylor dwelt with insistence. A very thin film between surfaces will prevent their union ; and so also in things of the spirit. There must be heart-contact with the Chinese, and personal contact too, he urged, if our lives are to be invested to the utmost profit.

I do like to look at *every* practical question in connection with Christ. The Incarnation shows that, provided we keep from sin, we cannot go too far in meeting this people and getting to know them, getting to be one with them, getting into sympathy with them.

There is wonderful instruction in the way in which the Lord Jesus wrought His works of mercy. He *touched* the leper and the blind when He healed them. . . . The woman felt that if she only touched the hem of His garment she would be sure to be healed ; and the Saviour felt that virtue had gone out of Him. If we keep so far from the people that they cannot even touch the hem of our garment, how will virtue go out of us ? Sometimes they are not clean, and we are tempted to draw our skirts together ; but I believe there is no blessing when this is the case. The Lord Jesus became a curse for us, and in that way delivered us from the curse. There is power in drawing near to this people. A poor woman in Cheng-tu, when she heard of Mrs. Riley's death said : " What a loss to us ! *She used to take hold of my hand* and comfort me so." If you put your hand on the shoulder of a man, there is power in it. Any Christian, full of the Holy Ghost, may often impart blessing thus. Contact is a real power that we may use for God.

For consistent lives he pleaded, telling lives, lives not out of sight. We are to *manifest* the truth, as well as preach it (2 Cor. iv. 2. Cp. Acts xx. 26-35).

We tell this people that the world is vain ; let our lives *manifest* that it is so. We tell them that our Home is above, that all these things are transitory; does our dwelling look like it ? Oh, to live consistent lives ! The life of the Apostle was thoroughly consistent. . . . No one could feel that *his* home was here : all saw that it was up there.

But it is no use living lives such as *would* emphasise our teaching, if our lives are out of sight and our teaching only is in evidence. Must we not seek to make our lives as open as our teaching ? This is no easy matter. The man who lives two or three miles away from the chapel, and merely goes and preaches to his audience is often disappointed. . . . What wisdom we need to live lives that do emphasise our teaching, and to see that our lives are so ordered that those who receive the teaching may catch the emphasis too.

Hard missionaries are not of much use : they are not like the Master. He is never hard. It is better to be trusting and gentle and sympathising, even if often taken in, rather than sharp and hard. The converts of Paul saw that the Apostle deemed it a small thing to die for them. To the Philippians he wrote : " Yea, and if I be offered—my blood poured out as a drink-offering—upon the sacrifice and service of your faith, I joy and rejoice with you all."

It is not preaching only that will do what needs to be done . . . Our life must be one of visible self-sacrifice. There is much sacrifice in our lives of which the Chinese cannot know. God knows all about it, and we can well afford to wait His declaration of it and His award. There is much we have left for the sake of the Chinese which they have never seen. That will not suffice. They must *see self-sacrifice* in things they cannot but understand.[1]

---

[1] It was remarkable that in that city (Tai-yuan-fu) where the blood of martyrs was to be so freely shed, Mr. Taylor should dwell upon the necessity for sacrifice, and the certainty not only that persecution must come, but that it would be overruled for blessing.

" Paul was in bonds in Rome, and we might have imagined that his position was one that would have deterred the brethren. But what does he tell us ? That they waxed confident through his bonds. So far from his sufferings taking courage out of the believers, when they found what a little thing a chain was to an Apostle, they felt, ' We can preach with good courage ! What is it, after all, if only Christ is in us ? ' Christ living, Christ reigning, made the Apostle so superior to these things that it encouraged others to go forward, though at the risk of the same trials. . . .

" There is no better way of proving to the world that the devil's power is not so great after all than by letting him have his fling, and showing in the midst of it what a triumph over him the believer has in Christ. Just as Jesus, by dying, conquered him who had the power of death, so frail, feeble martyrs, many of them women, were able to show that all the power of Pagan Rome could do *nothing* against those who were filled

With all his desire that the gifts of the native church should be developed, Mr. Taylor was keenly conscious of the danger of allowing education, medical work, or any other auxiliary to usurp the foremost place.

Let us feel that everything that is human, everything outside the sufficiency of Christ, is only helpful in the measure in which it enables us to bring the soul to Him. . . . If our medical missions draw people to us, and we can present to them the Christ of God, medical missions are a blessing; but to substitute medicine for the preaching of the Gospel would be a profound mistake. If we put schools or education in the place of spiritual power to change the heart, it will be a profound mistake. If we get the idea that people are going to be converted by some educational *process*, instead of by a regenerative re-creation, it will be a profound mistake. If we put our trust in money or learning or eloquence, or in anything but the living God, it will be a profound mistake. Let all our auxiliaries be auxiliaries—means of bringing Christ and the soul into contact —then we may be truly thankful for them all. . . . Let us exalt the glorious Gospel in our hearts, and believe that *it* is the power of God unto salvation. Let everything else *sit at its feet.* . . . We shall never be discouraged if we realise that in CHRIST is our Sufficiency.

What is the object of being apprenticed to a builder but to learn to build ? What is the outcome of being joined to a Saviour if we do not learn to save ? Though we might ourselves be saved, should we be His *disciples* indeed ?

In its practical influence on Christian character, Mr. Taylor felt that the truth of the Second Coming—the personal return of the Lord Himself to reign upon earth— was of paramount importance.

You will often read in missionary reports that the people

---

with Christ. Hence there were many conversions in the very arena . . . and the blood of the martyrs proved itself to be indeed the seed of the Church. . . . Their foes thought they had succeeded ; it was even announced in their edicts that Christianity was defunct ; but it was paganism that tottered.

" We need not be afraid of persecution. *It is coming ; it is sure to come.* Only let us have such success as to make the people fear the abolition of their customs, and we shall see severe persecution. But are we to fear lest the Gospel should triumph sufficiently to bring such results about ? Or are we to feel that, when it does come, it will bring to us the very conditions that will ensure still greater success ? " (*Days of Blessing*, pp. 41-43.)

have turned to God from idols, to serve the living and true God, but not in one out of ten do you hear anything about their waiting for His Son from heaven (I Thess. i. 9). I believe that the ignorance of the native Christians generally of the fact that Christ is coming again, and that the present state of things is to be utterly overthrown, is one reason for the selfishness and worldliness to be found in some branches of the Church in China.

Well do I remember the effect, when God was pleased to open my own heart to this great truth that the Lord Jesus was coming again, and that He might come *at any time*. I had not many books, but it sent me to see if I could give a good account of *all* I had, and also of the contents of my little wardrobe. The result was that some of the books disappeared before long, and some of the clothing too. It was an immense spiritual blessing to me. When I go home from China, and can make time to go through my house from attic to basement with my dear wife, to review our things in the light of His speedy return, I always find it a profitable spiritual exercise to see what we can do without. It is important to remember that we are stewards who have to give an account of everything that we *retain* ; and unless we can give a good reason for the retention, shall we not be ashamed when the Master comes ? And since He may come any day, is it not well to be ready every day ? I do not know of any truth that has been a greater blessing to me through life than this.

Very practical, too, was his attitude as to the fulness laid up for us in Christ.

God is willing to give us all we need, as we need it. He does not equip for life-service *all at once*. He does not expect us to toil along, burdened with next year's provisions on our back. There are fresh supplies on the way, fresh light, fresh power, fresh revelations as circumstances require.

Oh, to be *filled* with the knowledge of God's will ! to be so filled with the presence of the Lord Jesus, so *one with Him*, that His life may flow through our veins ; that He may borrow our lips to speak His messages, borrow our faces to look His looks of patience and love, our hands to do His service and our feet to tread His weary journeys. The dear Master can never be weary again by the side of any well, but *we* may be weary by the side of many for Him.

Whatever the sufficiency of Christ is for *us*, there is the same sufficiency in Him for our native converts.

In times of discouragement it is a great help to remember that the Lord's work is not *our* work for the Lord, but the Lord's own work through us and others. " HE will not fail, nor be discouraged."

Refreshed in spirit, it was time for the workers from the south of the province to hasten back to their stations after this week of meetings. The rainy season had set in, and it would be all they could do to make final arrangements for the native conferences before Mr. Taylor's arrival at Hung-tung. Mr. Stevenson was there already, having come over from the neighbouring province of Shen-si to join Mr. Taylor in this part of his programme. Finding the missionaries absent, he had spent several weeks among the Chinese Christians, glad of the opportunity for coming into close touch with the leaders and their work. To him as to Mr. Taylor it was a new experience to find, in these northerners, men of such vigorous independence of character, and he was not slow to see how much it meant for the future of the native church.

But it was more than energy and initiative that impressed him, about Mr. Hsi especially. During the five or six weeks spent in his district Mr. Stevenson travelled with him, visited his home and Refuges, listened with delight to his preaching, and saw him among the church members, to whom he was a shepherd indeed.

" I was profoundly interested," he recalled. " His spirituality and earnestness ; his prayer and fastings ; the intensity of his purpose—nothing in the world but the *one thing*—and his ability as a practical leader were most remarkable. I had never seen such influence over others ! He was so strong that all seemed to yield to him, and yet humble too. I was specially struck by the way people came to consult him. He had everybody's burdens to bear, and was always ready to advise and pray with those who needed help.

" His knowledge and use of Scripture also impressed me. One sermon on the temptation of Christ that he preached was very striking. Familiar passages seemed to unfold new meaning under his touch and in the light of his spiritual experience. God was to him a tremendous reality. Constantly and in everything he dealt with God. In a very real way he dealt with Satan too. His conflicts with the evil one at times were such that he would give himself for days to fasting and prayer. Even when travelling, I have known him fast a whole day over some difficult matter that needed clearing up.   That was always his resource—*fast and pray*."

That such gifts and grace should be taken full advantage of in the organisation of the church was evident, and Mr. Stevenson was ready to confirm the judgement of the local missionaries by which Mr. Taylor had largely to be guided in the steps to be taken at the conference.   It had been easier to set out for Hung-tung than to get there.   Held up by the rain in that loess region, Mr. Taylor and his companions had had exciting experiences in some of the deep gullies worn in the friable soil.   A hundred feet below the surface, in places, the road was sometimes a quagmire, sometimes a rushing torrent, and turbulent streams among the hills had to be crossed.   Two weeks of such travelling brought them to their destination, however, on July 30, to find the Hung-tung Christians assembled in force for the conference.

What it was to Mr. Taylor to meet these men and see for himself the inspiring work of which he had heard may be better imagined than described.   When one thinks of all that it had meant to him of faith and toil and prayer—all that he had done and suffered that inland China might have the Gospel—one can understand that to be welcomed by such a company of believers on his first visit to the far interior would be one of the most moving experiences of his life.   With Mr. Hsi he was impressed no less than Mr. Stevenson had been, and it was a wonderful meeting, that first day of the conference, when they took the Sunday morning service between them (August 1).

" There cannot have been fewer than three hundred listeners in the court," wrote Mr. Stanley Smith.   " It made our hearts glad to think of Mr. Taylor's joy as he saw those earnest worshippers, and in that sight *some* outcome of years of prayer that has known no ceasing, of labour that has known no respite : above all, it raised our hearts to Him Who in that gathering was seeing further of the travail of His soul and being satisfied."

It was not easy to get Mr. Hsi to accept the position to which Mr. Taylor, as leader of the Mission, wished to appoint him.   But for Mr. Stevenson's influence he would probably have held back, so deep was his sense of unworthiness. But the latter was sufficiently intimate with him for Mr. Hsi to feel that he really understood the local problems as well as his own limitations ; and when the Deputy Director led him to see that Mr. Taylor was but confirming what was manifestly a divine appointment, he could no longer demur. From that Saturday until the Ordination Service of the following Monday he gave himself to fasting and prayer, literally touching no food ; and the sense of the presence of God with him was deeply solemnising.

" Mr. Hudson Taylor, inviting the brethren working in the district to unite with him in the laying on of hands," Mr. Stanley Smith recorded, " after a few words of fervent prayer, set him apart to be a watcher over and feeder of the sheep of God. Mr. Hsi was ordained pastor of no particular district. He has done such an extensive work, and been so owned of God, that it was thought best that he should be free to go anywhere for the work of God in these parts, knowing well how he would be welcomed by all the churches. Mr. Song was then set apart as native Pastor of the Ping-yang church."

The appointment of two elders followed and of sixteen deacons, after which over seventy baptized believers united in the Communion Service led by Pastor Hsi.

One day's journey farther south—at Ping-yang-fu—another conference was held, attended by as many of the Ta-ning Christians as could come down from the mountains. It was a busy season for farming folk, and unusually heavy rains had made travelling in such regions almost impossible, but a warm-hearted company responded to the invitation of their beloved missionary, Mr. Cassels, to meet " the Venerable Chief Pastor," whose children in the faith they also were. Tenderly he spoke to them of the deeper lessons of his own life, and how, through its sorest trials, he had learned what the Lord Jesus Christ can be to those who simply trust Him. The ordination of Ch'ü, the fervent and scholarly evangelist of the Ta-ning district, and the appointment of five deacons, fitly closed the meetings, after which Mr. Taylor had to turn his face westward for the long journey to Han-chung-fu.

A brief visit first to Pastor Hsi's home, ten miles across the plain, gave him the opportunity of seeing more of this remarkable man and the Opium Refuge work for which he was responsible. Accompanied by quite a party, Mr. Taylor arrived in the cool of the day.[1] Everything was beautifully arranged for their coming, the guest hall being fitted up as a state chamber, and the courtyard on which it opened covered with an awning that it might do duty as a chapel. Here the principal meetings were held, the joy on all faces reflecting the golden characters of welcome above the guest hall, shining out from their crimson background—" *Ta Hsi Nien*," or " Year of Great Happiness."

Interesting as it all was, perhaps the best part of the visit to Mr. Taylor was the account he heard of the opening of a Refuge in one of the cities he had passed on his journey through the province. The place had long been on Pastor Hsi's heart, though he little anticipated the way in which his desire to commence work there was to be granted. Having no means in hand that he could use for the purpose, he prayed the more earnestly day by day at family worship that the Gospel might be given to the Christless population of Hwo-chow.

" We have prayed very often for that city," his wife said at length, " is it not time to *do* something there ? "

" Gladly would I," responded her husband, " but money is lacking. I have nothing to use for the purpose, and renting houses is expensive."

"How much would it require ? " was her next question. And on hearing his reply she went away and said no more about it.

But she too could not forget Hwo-chow ; and next morning it was an unadorned little figure that came up and laid some packages on the table after family worship.

" I think," she said, " that God has answered our prayers about that city."

Missing something in her appearance as well as surprised

---

[1] Dr. Edwards and Messrs. Stevenson, Stanley Smith, and Beauchamp were with him, as well as his son, Mr. Herbert Taylor, who had been his companion all the way from Shanghai.

at her words, Pastor Hsi opened one of the packets, to find
nothing less than all her jewelry—the gold and silver
ornaments, bracelets, rings, and even hair-pins so indispensable to a Chinese lady and that form her marriage dower.

" You cannot surely mean," he began, " you cannot do
without——"

" Yes, I can," she said joyfully. " I can do without
these : *let Hwo-chow have the Gospel.*"

And with the money they had brought, the Refuge had
been opened and a good work begun.[1]

" But do you not miss your beautiful things ? " said Mr.
Taylor, turning to his hostess.

" Miss them ! " she replied, almost with surprise. "Why,
I have *Jesus* : is not He enough? "

Little wonder it was hard to part from friends like these,
and from the fellow-missionaries he was leaving behind to
share with them the great work developing in all that part
of the province. Messrs. Studd and Beauchamp were going
on with Mr. Taylor to take part in opening up the Church
of England district he hoped to arrange for in Sze-chwan.
Mr. Cassels was to follow shortly ; but Messrs. Hoste and
Stanley Smith were remaining in south Shan-si, and for
them the parting was hardest.

" Their first stage was by moonlight," wrote the latter,
" and we accompanied them out some way. A few last words
of helpful counsel, a few last words of mutual love, a few last
words in solemn stillness as with hands locked in his we each
received his parting blessing, and the visit to Shan-si, so long
expected, so long deferred, but now so blessed in its outcome,
was over."

To fruitful fields ready for the reaper they went back,
but on beyond there was no sign of harvest. Out-distancing
his companions, all but Mr. Beauchamp, that he might save
a mail at Han-chung, Mr. Taylor pressed forward ; but even
so, twenty-four travelling days were occupied on the journey,
in which not a single Mission station was passed, because in
all that populous region there was none.

[1] For the remarkable sequel see Miss Cable's *The Fulfilment of a Dream*,
published by Messrs. Morgan & Scott and the China Inland Mission.

It was strenuous travelling, for which Mr. Beauchamp's athletic training stood him in good stead. With a couple of pack animals they were able to carry a few necessaries, Mr. Taylor riding most of the way, for his companion preferred to walk.

" Our great difficulty was in getting anything to eat," Mr. Beauchamp recalled, when the overpowering heat by day obliged them to travel at night, " and we constantly lost our way for want of some one to direct us. At first Mr. Taylor was greatly troubled that I should carry him across rivers, and also that I was unable to get much sleep ; but having once overruled his objection I carried him many a time. With Mr. Taylor on my shoulder and a Chinaman on either side to weigh us down, we were able to cross in safety some strong streams, waist deep.

" Night travelling was one of the hardest experiences I ever had, because I could not sleep by day. Occasionally, when I did drop off, I would wake to find that Mr. Taylor had been looking after me, rigging up mosquito-netting to keep the flies away. Walking at night, I have been so sleepy that even the motion could not keep me awake, and have fallen right down while plodding on—the tumble rousing one for the time being !

" The inns being closed at night, we used often to lie down by the roadside, when the animals had to be fed. Our own fare consisted chiefly of rice and millet. Occasionally we were able to purchase a chicken, eggs, cucumbers, or a little fruit. But we did not stop at regular stages, and as it was the rainy season nothing was brought out for sale in the places through which we passed. With so much rain, we often got soaked through. The way we managed was to take off our garments one by one and dry them in front of the fire. On one occasion this so offended the ' Kitchen God ' that Mr. Taylor had to come and make peace. Of course we carried no bedding, though Mr. Taylor always had two pillows, one for the head and one for the thigh, and we each carried a plaid. The medicine-chest sometimes came in useful as an extra pillow."

Again and again it seemed as if they must be stopped by the rain, but in answer to definite prayer help was given at every point.

" I remember coming to one river," continued Mr. Beauchamp, " where there were a few houses and people who made a harvest by carrying travellers over. They met us saying the river was impassable, nevertheless for a thousand cash apiece they would take us across. This was outrageous : so I went into the water which was rising by inches, the rain being a perfect deluge. When the men saw we were not to be deterred, they came and gave some help, glad to be paid a fair price for their work. After we were over, the water rose by feet. Had we been half an hour later, no crossing would have been possible. The river was by that time a wild, raging torrent.

" On the farther side there was a small village, but no inn. To go on was impossible. Stay we must, though the only shelter we could find was apparently a pig-sty. So we turned the occupant out, borrowed a few forms, took the doors off their hinges to lie on, and rolling ourselves in our plaids prepared to pass the night as comfortably as circumstances would admit. We were only masters of the situation for a short time, however ; for the pig came back, charged the make-shift door, which at once fell in, and settled down to share the apartment with us. After reflection, I concluded that it was too cold to turn out on the chance of ignominious defeat at the hands of the enemy.

" Next day was still cold—high mountains instead of the Si-an plain, drenching rain instead of burning sun. The road was washed away in places, but still Mr. Taylor would push on. Where the river side was impassable, we had to clamber up steep banks as best we could, and follow crumbling tracks on the mountains. Nothing would stop him, though he often begged me to remain behind. We had several narrow escapes from landslips—the path giving way behind us and rolling stones and earth into the stream. We had no fear of robbers ; and the wolves, though we saw them, did not attack us. We went forty-eight to fifty miles one day ; and the last three stages we made into two, not to miss the mail at Han-chung."

Mr. Taylor's cheerfulness and power of endurance greatly impressed his fellow-traveller. Hearing him singing on one occasion when they were very hungry, and catching the words " We thank Thee, Lord, for this our food," Mr. Beau-champ could not but inquire where the food was.

" It cannot be far away," was the smiling reply. " Our Father knows we are hungry and will send our breakfast soon : but *you* will have to wait and say your grace when it comes, while *I* shall be ready to begin at once ! "

And so it proved ; for just ahead they met a man with ready-cooked rice to sell, which made an excellent meal.

But the soul never went hungry. A box of matches, a

foreign candle, and his Bible in four small volumes were included in Mr. Taylor's travelling kit whatever else had to be left behind.

" He would invariably get his quiet time an hour before dawn," Mr. Beauchamp wrote, " and then possibly sleep again. . . . When I woke to feed the animals I always found him reading the Bible by the light of his candle. No matter what the surroundings or the noise in those dirty inns, he never neglected this. He used to pray on such journeys lying down, for he usually spent long times in prayer, and to kneel would have been too exhausting."

Kept thus in touch with unfailing springs, the travellers reached Han-chung-fu to bring as well as find a blessing. Much as Mr. Stevenson's report had led him to expect of the converts in this centre, Mr. Taylor was not disappointed. In the intervals of attending to a heavy mail, he saw a good deal of Dr. Wilson's medical work and of the schools and native helpers. The earnest spirit of the Christians greatly rejoiced him, especially in view of their interest in the adjacent province of Sze-chwan, from which not a few of them had come as emigrants. Their keen desire to carry the message of salvation back to their own people encouraged the hope Mr. Taylor entertained—that of seeing eastern Sze-chwan, as yet almost entirely destitute of the Gospel, opened up by the Church of England workers of the Mission.[1]

For the moment, the outlook was not encouraging. A serious riot had taken place at Chung-king—one of the only

---

[1] With regard to the denominational position of the Mission, Mr. Taylor had written as early as 1866 (a few weeks only after the arrival of the *Lammermuir* party) in reply to an inquiry from the Rev. W. Muirhead of the L.M.S., Shanghai :

" Those already associated with me represent all the leading denominations of our native land—Episcopal, Presbyterian, Congregational, Methodist, Baptist and Paedobaptist. Besides these, two are or have been connected with the ' Brethren ' so called. It is intended that those whose view of discipline correspond shall work together, and thus all difficulty on that score will be avoided. Each one is perfectly at liberty to teach his own views on these minor points to his own converts ; the one great object we have in view being to bring heathen from darkness to light, from the power of Satan to God. We all hold alike the great fundamentals of our faith, and in the presence of *heathenism* can leave the discussion of discipline while together, and act as before God when in separate stations."

two centres in Sze-chwan at which Protestant missionaries were working—and easy as it would have been for Mr. Taylor to enter the province from Han-chung, he might have found it impracticable to leave again without delay by the Yangtze. Tidings received from the coast had made it clear that he must return to Shanghai as soon as possible. Mission affairs required his presence, and he was still a month's journey from civilisation in the shape of a foreign steamer. But though he had to leave the actual pioneering in Sze-chwan to others, he could at any rate help in opening the way by definite waiting upon God. A day was set apart therefore for fasting and prayer, when Mr. Taylor united with the Han-chung circle in seeking the guidance of the Holy Spirit and a fresh baptism of love and power upon those who were to go forward. Very conscious were the missionaries, so soon to be scattered, of access to God in the all-prevailing name of Jesus, and the answer to their prayers was apparent not only in the occupation of Eastern Sze-chwan before the close of the year, but in a quickened sense of responsibility which led to extension in other directions also.

We may almost feel ourselves one with that little group, far in the heart of China, through the recollections jotted down at the time of one of the last meetings before Mr. Taylor left. In the twilight of a summer evening they had gathered in Dr. Wilson's courtyard. Lamps were lighted under the broad eaves of the open guest-hall, and beyond were the shining stars.

Mr. Taylor's subject was Phil. iii. : that what we give up for Christ we gain, and what we keep back is our real loss. We seemed to lose sight of the speaker and to hear only the voice of the Holy Spirit. It was a time of humbling and confession, nearly every one was broken down. . . . I cannot tell you what it was to sit there and hear Mr. Taylor tell of the hundreds of towns and cities he had passed, and not a single Christian in any of them ! Vividly he described all this and the condition of the people : and there were we, comfortably settled down, taking for granted perhaps that we had obeyed our Master's command, practically forgetting that Han-chung-fu was not the world, and that people even in the villages at hand might never hear of Christ unless we set ourselves to go to them.   The way in which he spoke of eternity—life eternal or death eternal —must have moved the coldest heart.   One sentence I specially remember :

"Let us make earth a little less homelike, and souls more precious.   Jesus is coming again, and so soon !   Will He find us really obeying His last command ? "

CHAPTER XXIX

THE HUNDRED

1886–1887. Aet. 54–55.

PROFOUNDLY impressed by all he had seen of the accessibility and need of the northern provinces, Mr Taylor had come by boat a thousand miles down the Han, bringing with him the little daughter of one of the Han-chung missionaries, whose parents saw that nothing but a change of climate could save her life. Only five years old, little Annie could speak no English, though, when not too shy, she could prattle away in Chinese prettily enough. Strange to say, she was never shy with Mr. Taylor. It had been hard for the mother to part with her, frail as she was from months of illness ; but once on the boat in Mr. Taylor's care she wonderfully brightened up. It speaks much for the confidence with which fellow-workers regarded him that Mr. and Mrs. Pearse had no hesitation about the arrangement, save on the ground of giving Mr. Taylor trouble. They knew there would be no woman in the party, and that for a month or six weeks he would be the only one to see to little Annie's food and clothing, as well as to care for her by day and night. They were quite satisfied that the child would not suffer, however, though even they might have been surprised at the comfort Mr. Taylor found in her companionship.

" My little charge is wonderfully improving," he wrote to Mrs. Taylor on the journey, " and is quite good and cheerful. She clings to me very lovingly, and it is sweet to feel little arms around one's neck once more."

Hard as it was to be so long absent from home and

loved ones, the way was not yet clear for Mr. Taylor's return to England. Nearly two years had passed since he had come out in advance of the Cambridge Party, but great as had been the progress in many directions, the recently developed organisation needed strengthening before he could think of leaving China.

" Oh, how weary I have been with the hundreds of letters ! " he wrote to Mrs. Taylor some weeks after his return to the coast. " How many questions have had to be taken to the Lord ! The way is now becoming somewhat clearer."

The year was drawing to a close (1886), and the chief object before him was the formation of a Council of experienced workers to help Mr. Stevenson in his new capacity as Deputy Director. The latter had also returned from his inland journey, full of enthusiasm over what he had seen in the northern provinces. He had spent several weeks with Pastor Hsi after Mr. Taylor had left, visiting widely scattered groups of converts, and was more than ever impressed with the vitality and possibilities of the work. His heart was overflowing with joy in the Lord, the joy that is our strength, and coming freshly into responsibilities Mr. Taylor had been bearing for years he brought with him no little accession of hope and courage.

" We all saw visions at that time," he himself recalled. " Those were days of heaven upon earth : nothing seemed difficult."

In this spirit, then, the Superintendents of the various provinces gathered for their first meeting, at An-king, in the middle of November. Several were detained in their own stations, and one or two were at home on furlough, but a little group of leaders, including Mr. McCarthy, spent from two to three weeks with Mr. Taylor and Mr. Stevenson. Before the Council was convened at all, a whole week was given to waiting upon God with prayer and fasting (the latter on alternate days), so that it was with prepared hearts they came to the consideration of the questions before them.

Upon the conclusions of that Council Meeting, important as they were, we must not dwell in detail. A little grey

book, embodying the chief results, soon found its way to all
the stations of the Mission—a little book breathing the spirit
of the Master, as well as packed full of wise and helpful
suggestions. There were instructions for special officers,
the Treasurer, the Secretary in China, and the Superintendents ; instructions for senior and junior missionaries,
lady evangelists and probationers, all based upon a thorough
understanding of conditions in China. A course of study in
the language, carefully prepared by Mr. Stevenson, Mr.
Baller, and others, was adopted for use in the Training
Homes ; and the Principles and Practice of the mission were
restated and somewhat amplified for younger workers.[1]

" It is hoped that all our friends will have seen from the
foregoing," Mr. Taylor wrote in a concluding letter, " that what
is sought is to relieve and help each one, and only to conduce
to that harmonious co-operation without which the working of
a large and scattered Mission would be impossible. Those at
a distance must be helped by those near, and this can only be
done as those near know the extent to which they can depend
on the co-operation of those at a distance.
" The principle of godly rule is a most important one, for it
equally affects us all. It is this—the seeking to help, not to
lord ; to keep from wrong paths and lead into right paths, for
the glory of God and the good of those guided, not for the gratifica-
tion of the ruler. *Such rule always leads the ruler to the Cross*,
and saves the ruled at the cost of the ruler. . . . Let us all
drink into this spirit, then lording on the one hand and bondage
on the other will be alike impossible. . . . When the heart is
right it loves godly rule, and finds freedom in obedience."

But there is something more important than the Grey
Book which must be traced to the meetings of this first
China Council, and that is the spirit of faith and expectancy
which launched the mission at this time upon new testings

---

[1] It is difficult in these days to realise how young the Mission still
was. It had been founded little more than twenty years, and while several
scores of its members had been out more than five years, by far the larger
number were new-comers. Out of a total of a hundred and eighty-seven
no fewer than a hundred and ten were junior missionaries or probationers,
which meant that they were young in years as well as in experience. It
was clearly desirable, therefore, to formulate for their benefit much that
had been learned at great cost by those to whom they looked for help
and guidance.

of the faithfulness of God. Up in Shan-si it had begun, when Mr. Stevenson had written from the capital:

We are greatly encouraged out here, and are asking and receiving definite blessings for this hungry and thirsty land. We are fully expecting at least one hundred fresh labourers to arrive in China in 1887.[1]

It was the first suggestion of the Hundred. Ardent as he was and full of confidence in God, he kept the matter to the front on his return to Shanghai and in the Council Meetings, but Mr. Taylor seems at first to have shared the general impression that this was going rather too fast. A hundred new workers in one year, when the entire staff of the Mission was less than twice that number—why, even if the men and women were forthcoming, think of the additional expenditure involved!

" Yes," urged the Deputy Director, unperturbed, " but with needs so great how can we ask for less ? "

That was difficult to answer ; for fifty central stations and many out-stations in which resident missionaries were needed, not to speak of China open from end to end, made a hundred new workers even in one year seem but a small number.

And so, little by little, they were led on, until, in the Council Meetings, such was the atmosphere of faith and prayer that the thought could strike root. Begun with God, it could not fail to be taken up by hearts so truly waiting upon Him ; and before leaving An-king Mr. Taylor was writing home quite naturally :

We are praying for one hundred new missionaries in 1887. The Lord help in the selection and provide the means.

A little later at Ta-ku-tang, amid the quiet of lake and mountains, he was working at accounts, etc., with a view to leaving for England as soon as possible, when an incident occurred that fanned expectancy to a flame. Mr. Taylor was dictating to his secretary, walking up and down the room as was his wont, when he repeated in one of his letters what he had written above : " We are praying for and

[1] In a letter to Mrs. Hudson Taylor from Tai-yuan-fu, Sept. 16, 1886.

expecting a hundred new missionaries to come out in 1887."
Did he really mean it ? Mr. Stevenson saw the secretary,
a young man who was himself to be one of the Hundred,
look up with an incredulous smile. "If the Lord should
open windows in heaven," that look seemed to say, "then
might this thing be." Mr. Taylor saw it too, and immediately caught fire.

"After that, he went beyond me altogether," recalled Mr.
Stevenson. "Never shall I forget the conviction with which
he said :
"'If you showed me a photograph of the whole hundred,
taken in China, I could not be more sure than I am now.'
"Then I sent out a little slip throughout the Mission : 'Will
you put down your name to pray for the Hundred ? ' and cabled
to London, with Mr. Taylor's permission : 'Praying for a hundred
new missionaries in 1887.'"

Thus the step was taken, and the Mission committed to a
programme that might well have startled even its nearest
friends. Yet it was in no spirit of rashness or merely human
energy. Far too deeply had Mr. Taylor learned the lessons
of experience to embark upon such an enterprise without
the assurance that he was being led of God, without much
forethought as well as faith, and the determination to see it
through by unremitting toil no less than unceasing prayer.

"The accepting and sending out of the Hundred," he wrote
to Mrs. Taylor early in December, " will require no small amount
of work, but the Lord will give strength ; and no little wisdom,
but the Lord will guide. There is all-sufficiency in Him, is there
not ? . . . We are ready to receive say fifty at once, and shall
be ready for others shortly, *D.V.* We sing a little prayer at
each meal :

> Oh send the hundred workers, Lord,
>   Those of Thy heart and mind and choice,
> To tell Thy love both far and wide—
>   So shall we praise Thee and rejoice :
> And above the rest this note shall swell,
> My Jesus hath done all things well."

To an inner circle of friends he also wrote in December :

Will you help us in prayer as often as you can ? This movement will involve great responsibility and much toil, time, and

expense. Some of us are hoping that His "exceeding abundantly" may mean fifty or sixty more missionaries besides the hundred for whom we are asking. Now I need not say that that must mean a good deal more than praying. Much correspondence about the candidates will be needed ; much prayer and thought about which of them to accept and which to decline. The labour of arranging for and attending farewell meetings, to secure the prayers of at least six congregations for each party that comes out, will be great. Outfits and passages for a hundred people will come to £5500, and travelling expenses for many of them from distant parts of Great Britain and Ireland, as well as the cost of board in London, will materially add to this sum. The money, much of it, will come to our office at Pyrland Road in small gifts, each calling for a letter of thanks, which will involve additional help in correspondence, etc. So we shall have much need of Divine guidance, help, and strength, all of which He will supply, but for which He will be enquired of.

Am I wrong then in asking your prayers for myself and for those who will be associated with me in this important work ? As I look forward in faith and think of the " willing, skilful " men and women who are coming—of the barren fields they will help to till, of the souls they will be the means of saving, and above all of the joy of our Redeemer in this movement and its widespread issues—my heart is very glad, and I think yours will be too.

It was this vision, this spirit of joy that upheld him through all the wonderful and strenuous days of 1887. But what a year it was ! Preceded by two days of prayer because one was not enough,[1] it ended with the last party of the Hundred on their way to China—all the work accomplished, all expenses met—and with a fulness of blessing that was spreading and to spread in ever-widening circles.

The story of the Hundred has often been told—it belongs to no one mission or land. We know how, with growing courage, Mr. Taylor and those associated with him were led to pray for ten thousand pounds of additional income, as necessary to meet the increased expenses ; and that it might be given in large gifts, so that the home staff should not be

---

[1] " To-morrow and the day after we give to waiting on God for blessing," he wrote to Mrs. Taylor on December 29. " We need two days at least, this year. We have much to praise for, much to expect ; but Satan will be busy, and we must be prepared by living near to God, by putting on the whole armour of God."

overwhelmed with correspondence. We know that no fewer than six hundred men and women offered themselves to the Mission that year for service in China; that one hundred and two, to be exact, were sent out; and that not ten but eleven thousand pounds of extra income was received, no appeal having been made for financial help. And we know, most wonderful perhaps of all, how definite prayer was answered as to the very form in which the money came; the whole being received in just *eleven gifts*, involving little or no extra work to the office staff of the Mission. But such a story bears retelling, especially from Mr. Taylor's letters, to the glory not of man or methods, but of GOD.

" We want workers, not loiterers," was one of the first things he wrote after his return to England, and what an example he set by his own unparalleled labours throughout the year! Everywhere the friends of the Mission had heard of the prayer and expectation with which he had come home, and invitations to speak in meetings poured in from many parts of Great Britain and Ireland. With brief intervals for correspondence and Council Meetings, Mr. Taylor was travelling and speaking all the time. Yet he seemed to be interviewing candidates all the time; writing letters—China letters, home letters, endless letters—all the time; giving himself to prayer, and well he might; prayer and Bible study for the feeding of his own soul and of the multitudes to whom he ministered; prayer over all the problems of the work and the needs of every member of the Mission.

The number of letters he wrote during the year would be incredible, but for the details as to each one recorded in his correspondence index. They averaged thirteen or fourteen for every day of the twelve months, Sundays excepted; and as he often had two, three, and four meetings a day, as well as travelling, it is no wonder one comes upon pages that tell of thirty or forty letters written within twenty-four hours. And these were not business notes, or mainly to do with his programme of meetings. They were many of them long, thoughtful letters to Mr. Stevenson about the direction of affairs in China; answers to correspondence sent on to him from the field, which required careful consideration; and replies to people who consulted him about spiritual and other difficulties, having been helped through the meetings.

Three visits to Ireland and four to Scotland, an extensive campaign with his beloved friend, Mr. Reginald Radcliff, and Mr. George Clarke, on the subject of World Evangelisation, and attendance at no fewer than *twenty* conventions for the deepening of spiritual life, in most of which Mr. Taylor spoke repeatedly, were but part of his outward activities. Besides these there were farewell meetings in churches of all denominations, as party after party went out, and frequent addresses in drawing-rooms or from the pulpit to the circles the young missionaries represented. Then how much it meant merely to interview the candidates! So busy was the Council with those who came before them in London, that they had occasionally to meet twice and three times a week, to get through the work.

"We were in Glasgow last week," wrote Mrs. Taylor in March, "holding one, two, or three meetings every day; and my husband had conversations with forty candidates."

And in Edinburgh, at the very time she was writing, he was dealing with twenty more. At one meeting in the Scottish capital, so deep was the interest that a hundred and twenty people definitely offered themselves for foreign missionary work, to go or stay as God might lead; and at the close of a conference in the south of England, half the audience that had filled the Corn Exchange accompanied Mr. Taylor to the station, singing missionary hymns and in other ways expressing sympathy.

At Pyrland Road, meanwhile, Mr. and Mrs. Broomhall were no less busy and encouraged. Invited to breakfast with a friend in London early in the year, Mr. Broomhall found himself one of several guests who had at heart the interests of the kingdom of God. Conversation turning on the C.I.M., Mr. Broomhall took from his pocket a letter which had touched him deeply. It was from a poor widow in Scotland who, with only a few shillings a week to live upon, frequently sent gifts for the work in China. She could do without meat, she said, but the heathen could not do without the Gospel. Very real was the self-denial that lay behind the simple words, and very real the prayers with which the modest gifts were accompanied. This it was, doubtless, that led to results from that letter far beyond anything the writer can have asked or thought.

At the close of the meal, the host said that all he had ever given to the work of God (and he had given much) had never cost him a mutton-chop. His interest had been chiefly in home missions, but he wanted now to forward the evangelisation of China. And to Mr. Broomhall's surprise, he then and there promised five hundred pounds for the work of the C.I.M. A little further conversation round the table led to similar promises from three of the guests, while another who had been unable to come, upon hearing what had transpired, made up the sum to two thousand five hundred pounds. Just as in connection with the Seventy, the Lord was encouraging the home leaders of the mission, giving them practical evidence that the prayer daily ascending in China from so many hearts was in line with His purpose.

And they must surely have needed such encouragement ; for the strain of the year at Pyrland Road was unremitting and very heavy. No one rejoiced more in the forward movement and all it meant for dark hearts and lives in China than the Mother of the mission-house, upon whom came the burden of receiving and caring for the candidates. How it was ever done in that little home, with seven or eight of her own children still in the family circle, remains a mystery. Nothing but the early morning hour, when Mrs. Broomhall found her strength daily renewed in fellowship with God, could have carried her through, making her life the blessing it was to all who came and went. The noon meeting that gathered the busy household for prayer she never failed to make the most of, and who shall say how much the spirit thus maintained had to do with the rising tide of blessing ?

Great was the joy when on Mr. Taylor's birthday, just before the Annual Meetings,[1] a cable from Shanghai brought

---

[1] Mr. Taylor completed his fifty-fifth year on May 21, 1887, and the 26th of the same month brought the anniversary of the sailing of the *Lammermuir*, twenty-one years previously.

news of large ingatherings. In Pastor Hsi's district two hundred and twenty-six had been baptized at the spring conference, which proved a time of great encouragement. A letter also from Mr. Berger came as a token for good, bringing a gift of five hundred pounds—the second or third he had given—toward the outgoing Hundred.

" I hope this note will reach you on the morning of the 26th," he wrote. " You will be very full of praise to God, I am sure, for all He has condescended to do through the China Inland Mission during the past twenty-one years. May all the glory be given to Him to Whom alone it is due.

" Let me share again in the prosperity of the blessed work by sending £500 toward the amount necessary for sending out the hundred or more labourers this year. ' To the Lord '—not the tithes only, but ourselves, our all! The exchange is altogether in our favour : our all, a little handful, versus God's all, illimitable riches of every kind! May grace be poured into your lips and heart on Thursday in an especial manner."

No wonder Mr. Taylor began his address at the Anniversary Meetings by recalling the quaint saying of a wellknown coloured evangelist : " When God does anything, He does it handsome "! That very morning another cable had been received from China, announcing a donation of a thousand pounds toward the expenses of the Hundred— fifty-four of whom were already either sent out or accepted. Up to that time all who were ready among the accepted candidates had gone forward, and Mr. Taylor could with confidence say :

God is, in this matter of funds, giving us signs that He is working with us ; that this work is pleasing to Him, and that therefore He is prospering it. He will give the whole Hundred, and He will provide for them.

Speaking of the twenty-one years of " goodness and mercy " they were that day commemorating, and of the way in which financial needs had been supplied, he continued :

The Lord is always faithful. . . . People say, " Lord, increase our faith." Did not the Lord rebuke His disciples for that prayer ? It is not great faith you need, He said in effect, but faith in a great God. Though your faith were small as a grain of mustard-seed, it would suffice to remove mountains. We need a faith that rests on a great God, and expects Him to keep His own word and to do just as He has promised.

Now, we have been led to pray for a hundred new workers this year. We have the sure word, " Whatsoever ye shall ask in My name, I will do it, that the Father may be glorified in the Son." Resting on this promise, it would not have added to our confidence one whit if, when we began to pray in November, my dear brother-in-law, Mr. Broomhall, had sent me out a printed list of a hundred accepted candidates. We had been spending some days in fasting and prayer for guidance and blessing before the thought was suggested to our minds. We began the matter aright, with God, and we are quite sure that we shall end aright. It is a great joy to know that thirty-one of the Hundred are already in China, but it is a greater joy to know that more than a hundred of our workers in China are banded together in daily pleading with God to send out the whole Hundred.

And by the Hundred we mean one of God's " handsome " hundreds ! . . . Whether He will give His " exceeding abundantly " by sending us more than a literal hundred, or whether by stirring up other branches of the Church to send many hundreds, which I should greatly prefer, or by awakening missionary enthusiasm all over the Church and blessing the whole world through it, I do not know. I hope that He will answer prayer in all these ways ; but sure I am that God will do it " handsome." . . .

I do want you, dear Friends, to realise this principle of working with God and asking Him for everything. If the work is at the command of God, then we can go to Him in full confidence for workers ; and when God gives the workers, we can go to Him for means to supply their needs. We always accept a suitable worker, whether we have funds or not. Then we often say, " Now, dear Friend, your first work will be to join us in praying for money to send you to China."

As soon as there is money enough, the time of the year and other circumstances being suitable, the friend goes out. We do not wait until there is a remittance in hand to give him when he gets there. The Lord will provide in the meanwhile, and the money will be wired to China in time to supply his wants. . . . Let us see to it that we keep God before our eyes ; that we walk in His ways, and seek to please and glorify Him in everything, great and small. Depend upon it, God's work, done in God's way, will never lack God's supplies. . . .[1]

---

[1] " I am far more afraid of unconsecrated money than of no money

And now, if this principle of taking everything to God and accepting everything from God is a true one—and I think the experience of the China Inland Mission proves that it is—ought we not to bring it to bear more and more in daily life ? The Lord's will is that His people should be an unburdened people, fully supplied, strong, healthy and happy. . . . Shall we not determine to be " careful for nothing, but in everything by prayer and supplication with thanksgiving " bring those things that would become burdens or anxieties to God in prayer, and live in His perfect peace ?

It can well be understood that this simple dealing with realities sent a thrill to the heart of the home churches wherever the prayer for the Hundred became known. To many it seemed to shed new light upon the problems of life, and to reveal a new, almost undreamed-of power in dealing with them.

" I have not known what anxiety is since the Lord taught me that the work is His," was Mr. Taylor's testimony wherever he went. " My great business in life is to please God. Walking with Him in the light, I never feel a burden."

" I have had conversations with three people," wrote a friend from Ireland, " all of them Christians, who seem to have received a new thought at your meetings—as if God really *means what He says* when He gives us His promises. If you could return to Waterford and have, say, two evening meetings for preaching the Gospel, and two mid-day meetings to persuade Christians that God does mean all He says in His promises, I believe it would do eternal good."

This was the burden of his message everywhere, backed by a quiet simplicity and joy in the Lord which could not but carry conviction.

" I must close and have a sleep, or I shall fail at the meeting to-night in brightness," he wrote to Mrs. Taylor from Scotland. " I do want to *shine* for Jesus, Jesus only ! ".

And shine he did, though the pressure of work was tremendous.

---

at all," Mr. Taylor said again a few weeks later. " The Lord did not tell His disciples to carry loads of provisions into the wilderness. There was a lad there with five barley loaves and two fishes : it was enough. The Lord wants His people to be, not rich, but in full fellowship with Him Who is rich. Why, as Christians, we are all children of a King ! "

" It was a mighty message last night," Mrs. Taylor heard from her husband's secretary on the same visit. " Many were broken down, to be lifted up of God. After a precious exposition of Zeph. iii., Mr. Taylor spoke very simply and very straight to the heart on ' Trusting God.' He did not finish till close on 9 P.M., but you could have heard any ordinary clock tick most of the time." [1]

" The rush of work is very great," Mr. Taylor wrote himself at midsummer. " Well, praise the Lord, He helps me through day by day, and fills one's heart with blessing and one's lips with praise."

In China, meanwhile, the arrival of party after party was causing no little thanksgiving. The new organisation was working well, the training homes especially proving of incalculable value. Miss Murray at Yang-chow and Mr. Baller at An-king were bringing helpful, encouraging influences to bear on the new arrivals, caring for their health and spiritual life, as well as facilitating their studies. The advice they were able to give from personal observation was invaluable also to Mr. Stevenson, when the time came for allocating young workers to their future stations.

It was about the beginning of November, when Mr. Taylor had the joy of announcing to the friends of the Mission that their prayers were fully answered—all the Hundred having been given and the funds supplied for their passages to China. Many were still volunteering, while Mr. Taylor's third visit to Ireland and his fourth to Scotland were planned but not yet carried out. In all these later meetings, therefore, he had to tell of the response of a faithful God to the prayers of His believing people, and of the way in which His " exceeding abundantly " was being given.[2] Of this he wrote to Mr. Stevenson :

Nov. 11 : . . . Our meetings are evidently a blessing to the Church of God, the most grateful testimonies to spiritual refresh-

---

[1] Fifteen hundred people were present on that occasion in the Town Hall at Motherwell, near Glasgow.

[2] One of the valuable workers over and above the Hundred, given to the Mission toward the close of this year, was the Rev. E. O. Williams, Vicar of St. Stephen's, Leeds. He and Mrs. Williams gladly gave up their important sphere, to go with their young children to the far west of China —the district the Rev. W. Cassels was opening up, in which were millions destitute of the Word of Life.

ment being given at almost every place we visit. New candidates continue to come forward, and I see we cannot get one hundred without getting two from the Lord. Many of those who cannot possibly go this year will be ready to do so before long.

And a month later :

Dec. 8 : . . . With the sailing of the ladies to-day, eighty-eight have left us for China : fourteen others sail on the 15th and 29th respectively.[1]

You must continue very earnestly in prayer, and secure the prayers of our friends generally, that God will magnify His Name and adequately sustain the work with funds. Nothing is clearer to me than that in obtaining a hundred for this year we have obtained at least a second hundred. To send them out and sustain them will require *another* ten thousand pounds of additional income ; and in times like these it is a tremendous rise from a little over twenty to forty thousand pounds annually. One is so glad that God has Himself asked the question, " Is anything too hard for the Lord ? " But we must not forget that He will " be enquired of by the house of Israel, to do it for them." If we get less prayerful about funds, we shall soon get sorely tried about funds. Thank God, there is no need to be less prayerful. We can well afford to be more prayerful, and to God be the glory.[2]

Every day I feel more and more thankful to God for giving you to us, and for giving you such general acceptance. No human prescience or wisdom is sufficient for your position ; but so long as you continue to seek His guidance in every matter, and in the midst of the pressure of work take time to be holy,

---

[1] " Six times that number offered," wrote Mr. Eugene Stock in the *History of the Church Missionary Society*, " but the Council, faithful to its principles, declined to lower the standard, and rejected five-sixths of the applicants ; yet the exact number of one hundred—not ninety-nine nor a hundred and one, but one hundred—actually sailed within the year. (This did not include two Associates.—ED.) Still more significant of God's blessing is the fact that, seven years later, seventy-eight of the Hundred were still on the C.I.M. staff ; and of the remainder, five had died, and most of the others were still labouring in China, though in other connections. Does the whole history of Missions afford quite a parallel to this ? "

[2] In his New Year's greeting to the members of the now greatly enlarged Mission (Jan. 1888) Mr. Taylor said in this connection : " Let us never forget that, if we make no appeal to man, we need very, very definitely to continue our appeal to God. A God-given, God-guided, spiritual impulse is expressed in every donation we receive ; and this, which makes our work peculiarly blessed, will always keep us peculiarly dependent upon Him. How can we sufficiently praise Him for this happy position, this necessity of trustfulness ? "

and time to pray for the workers, the Lord will continue to use and bless you.

Two days before the close of the year Mr. Taylor returned to London, the great work accomplished which, though wrought in faith and deep heart-rest, had taxed both him and those associated with him to the utmost.

" I have assured the friends," he wrote in his last letter of the year to Mr. Stevenson, " that there will be a big Hallelujah when they, the crowning party of the Hundred, reach Shanghai ! It is not more than we expected God to do for us, but it is very blessed ; and to see that God does answer, in great things as well as small, the prayers of those who put their trust in Him will strengthen the faith of multitudes."

Twelve months previously a veteran missionary in Shanghai had said to Mr. Taylor, then on the point of leaving for home :

" I am delighted to hear that you are praying for large reinforcements. You will not get a hundred, of course, within the year ; but you will get many more than if you did not ask for them."

Thanking him for his kindly interest Mr. Taylor replied : " *We* have the joy beforehand ; but I feel sure that, if spared, you will share it in welcoming the last of the Hundred to China."

And so it proved. For among those who gathered to receive that last party with thanksgiving, no one was more sympathetic than the white-headed saint who a few weeks later was called to his reward.

PART VII

WIDER MINISTRY

1888–1895. Aet. 56–63.

" Among the different ways of helping in the present world crisis, there is none which will compare in vital importance with that of wielding the force of prayer. More important than the most earnest thinking upon a problem, more important than a personal interview to influence an individual, more important than addressing and swaying an audience—far more important than these and all other forms of activity is the act of coming into vital communion with God. Those who spend enough time in actual communion with God to become really conscious of their absolute dependence on Him, shall change the mere energy of the flesh for the power of God. . . .

" It is indeed true that he that saveth his time from prayer shall lose it. And he that loseth his time, for communion with God, shall find it again in added blessing and power and fruitfulness."—JOHN R. MOTT.

" Wishes, cares, anxieties prepare the heart for prayer, but are not prayer until they are converted into direct address, supplication, and cry unto God."—ADOLPH SAPHIR.

" The promises are not given to our *wants*, but to our petitions."
—WHATELEY.

CHAPTER XXX

FEW KNOW WHAT IS BETWIXT CHRIST AND ME

1887–1888. AET. 55–56.

AMONG many visitors to Pyrland Road toward the close of the year of the Hundred came one who in a special way was to be identified with the enlargement of Mr. Taylor's influence and the sphere of the Mission. Finding Mr. Taylor still away in Scotland, he took a room near by, and quietly gave himself to studying the work of which he had heard enough to bring him across the Atlantic. In spite of the pressure of those days, Mr. and Mrs. Broomhall welcomed the young stranger almost as a member of their household, giving him every opportunity to become acquainted with the inner life of the Mission, and all he saw did but deepen, by the blessing of God, the desire with which he had come. Of this he was writing to Mr. Taylor in the middle of December (1887):

About five months ago I began correspondence with Mr. Broomhall from America, my home, concerning going to China. As the result of that correspondence I am now at Pyrland Road, and have been here long enough to satisfy myself concerning the spiritual standing of the China Inland Mission, and to confirm my own desire of connecting myself with it. . . . But I came to London with a larger purpose in view. . . . It has been laid on my heart for many months past to talk with you and Mr. Broomhall about the establishment of an American Council that might work as a feeder of men and money for China, on the same principles of faith that have made the China Inland Mission so favourably known. Meeting Mr. Forman in Glasgow I found that he, too, had been praying for something of the same kind for a long time, and that Mr. Wilder, his companion, had also had the matter laid on his heart.

From his meetings in Scotland, bringing to a successful issue the work of that memorable year, Mr. Taylor returned just as simple, quiet, natural as ever, to banish in a moment any apprehension his visitor had felt as to the interview. A little note from Glasgow, " fragrant with the love of Christ," had prepared the way for what proved an important conversation.

" Fear did indeed vanish on that occasion," wrote Mr. Henry W. Frost, " for I found him at leisure from himself, and most gentle and kind. From that hour my heart was knit to this beloved servant of God in unalterable devotion."

But though their intercourse resulted in an abiding friendship, it seemed to the one who was building much upon it to have failed in its object. His interest in the Mission was warmly appreciated and his desire to work with it welcomed, but Mr. Taylor could not see his way to the establishment of an American branch. It would be, he suggested, far better for Mr. Frost to start a fresh organisation, on the lines of the C.I.M. if he pleased, but something that would be native in its inception and development ; for a transplanted mission, like a transplanted tree, would have difficulty in striking root in the new soil. Needless to say this was a great disappointment.

" On reaching my lodgings," the visitor recalled, " I had one of the most sorrowful experiences of my life. At the threshold of my room, Satan seemed to meet me and envelop me in darkness. . . . I had come over three thousand miles only to receive to my request the answer, No. But this was not the worst of it. I had had positive assurance that the Lord had Himself guided me in my prayer, and had led me to take the long journey and make the request that had been made ; but now I felt I could never again be sure whether my prayers were or were not of God, or whether I was or was not being guided of Him."

Only those who have passed through similar experiences can know what such a test of faith meant, and how real was the victory when the one so tried was enabled to trust where he could not understand. This restored "something of soul-rest," and Mr. Frost went back to America leaving the issues with the Lord.

But the matter did not end there. Mr. Frost had learned that Mr. Taylor was returning to China before long, and that if invited to do so he might travel by way of America. This he made known to the Conveners of the Bible Study Conference at Niagara - on - the - Lake and to Mr. D. L. Moody, whose summer gatherings at Northfield were already a centre of much blessing, with the result that invitations began to reach Mr. Taylor to visit the great new world.

Meanwhile, in England, the latter was unremitting in his labours. The widespread interest aroused by the outgoing of the Hundred brought more openings for meetings than he could possibly accept, and very stimulating to faith were the facts he had to tell.

" What a wonderful year it has been, both for you and me ! " he wrote to Mr. Stevenson early in 1888. " Satan will surely leave no stone unturned to hinder, and we must not be surprised at troublesome difficulties coming up : but greater is He Who is for us than all who can be against us."

The certainty of opposition, definite and determined, from the powers of darkness seems to have been much before him, and the question of funds for the largely increased work was one that could not be ignored. But with regard to both the one and the other, his mind was kept in peace.

" God has moved," he said at the Annual Meetings (May '88) ; " are we also moving ? Are we ready to go on with Him . . . ready to be filled with the Holy Spirit ? Oh, this is what we need, need supremely, need more than ever. I have not much anxiety about our income. I do not believe that our Heavenly Father will ever forget His children. I am a very poor father, but it is not my habit to forget my children. God is a very, very good Father. It is not His habit to forget His children. But suppose He should not work in the way He has done, by sending in tens of thousands of pounds ? Well, then, we can do without it. We cannot do without Him, but we can do without any ' it ' in the world. If only we have the Lord, that is sufficient."

"I do not wonder," he had written to Mr. Stevenson in January, "that Satan has been trying you sorely. I should wonder, and almost be afraid, if he did not. It is not likely that he will let work like this pass without showing himself as an opposer. But let us believe, as Mr. Radcliffe reminds us, that when the enemy comes in one way, he will have to flee seven. Difficulties are sure to increase, but the power of the Lord is unlimited. When He asks you or me where we shall buy bread, or how we shall solve this or that problem, it is only to prove us. He always knows what He will do ; and if we wait His time, He will show us also."

It was a summer day toward the end of June when the s.s. *Etruria* put out to sea, carrying among her "Intermediate" passengers, Mr. Taylor, his son, and a secretary. Mr. and Mrs. Radcliffe also were of the party, though not in that semi-steerage accommodation. Outward discomfort mattered little to Mr. Taylor ; but he was finding, almost with surprise, that parting from those he loved best did not become any easier.[1] A long while might elapse before he could return, and the very uncertainty was painful.

"As I walked the deck last night," he wrote to Mrs. Taylor from Queenstown, "I found myself singing softly, ' Jesus, I am resting, resting in the joy of what Thou art '—such a comfort when feeling desolate, and feeling your desolation ! No one comforts like He does."

"Few know what is betwixt Christ and me," wrote the saintly Rutherford ; and little can his fellow-passengers on that Atlantic voyage have realised what lay behind the quiet exterior of the missionary on his way for the seventh time to China. Yet the sweetness was felt, and the power ; and by no one more than the young American who was on the New York landing stage to meet them. For there was about Mr. Frost's spiritual nature a quality that responded in an unusual way to much of which he could be, as yet, but dimly conscious in the life of Hudson Taylor.

It was with joy at any rate that he received the party, including Mr. and Mrs. Reginald Radcliffe, and escorted

[1] His second son, Howard, who was travelling with him, though an accepted member of the Mission, had to go back from America to complete his appointments at the London Hospital as House-Surgeon, Physician, etc.

them to his father's home in Madison Avenue, where there was ample accommodation and the warmest of welcomes. How gracious was the hospitality that encompassed them, the visitors could not at the time fully realise. Unfamiliar with American ways, it was but natural that some mistakes should be made which no one would have regretted more than they, had they been conscious of them. Such, for example, was the almost unconscious act of putting their boots outside the bedroom doors at night, where they were found shining with an irreproachable polish next morning— none of the visitors suspecting the discovery Mr. Frost had made of his father facing this formidable array of English " footwear " in the bathroom, where together they spent no little labour upon them before retiring.[1]

Of the three months that followed it is difficult to write, not for lack of information but because of the very fulness of the records and the importance of events that took place. For who could have foreseen that, arriving in America in July, little known and with no thought but to take part in a few conferences on his way to China, Mr. Taylor would leave again in October, widely loved and trusted, laden with gifts, followed by prayer, and taking with him a band of young workers chosen out of more than forty who had offered their lives for service in the Mission ? If the going out of the Hundred in the preceding year had been a striking evidence of the hand of God working with him, what shall be said of this unexpected movement, deeply affecting Christian life in the Eastern States and Canada, and rousing Toronto, from which the party finally set out, to an enthusiasm rarely equalled ?

" Sunday night, Sept. 23, 1888, saw the greatest and most enthusiastic gathering ever held in Toronto up to that time," wrote one who was present. " The place was the Y.M.C.A.,

---

[1] Mr. Taylor discovered before Mr. Radcliffe, as it happened, that boots and shoes in America are usually attended to by those to whom they belong—a little polishing outfit forming part of one's personal equipment. Having provided himself in this way, it was with real enjoyment he would slip along, when travelling alone with Mr. Radcliffe, and fetch the boots the latter put outside his door, and after cleaning them to perfection, as quietly put them back again.

the hour 8.30 P.M., just after the evening services in the churches. One might say that the cream of Toronto's religious life was gathered there, to hear the Rev. J. Hudson Taylor and the men and women accepted by him for work in China. The power of God was manifest in a wonderful way, and as a result a great and abiding impetus was given to foreign missions."

And the wonder of it all was that it was so unpremeditated !

" I had not the remotest idea in coming to America," Mr. Taylor himself recalled, " that anything specially bearing upon the work of the China Inland Mission would grow out of it. I was glad to come when my way was providentially opened. I wanted to see Mr. Moody, and had heard of over two thousand students wishful to consecrate their lives to God's service abroad.[1] The American societies, I thought, are not quite in a position to take up these two thousand, and perhaps if we tell them about God's faithfulness they will find it written in their Bibles not ' be sent,' but ' go.' I believe in verbal inspiration, and that God could have said ' be sent ' if He had wished it, instead of ' go.' I hoped I might be able to encourage some to ' go.' "

As to bringing forward the work of the Mission with a view to developing an American branch, nothing was further from his thoughts. Had he not told Mr. Frost only a few months earlier that he had no guidance in that direction, sending him back from England perplexed and disappointed ? And if it was not in Mr. Taylor's purpose, still less was it anticipated by those to whom his personality and message came as so new a force that summer at Northfield. The Student Conference was in full swing when he and his companions arrived, and, met by Mr. Moody himself, were driven out to his beautiful home in the middle of the night. It was a strangely new experience to the English

[1] The Student Volunteer Movement, only called into being two summers before, had already attained remarkable proportions—over two thousand undergraduates having signed the declaration : " I am willing and desirous, God permitting, to become a foreign missionary." To Mr. Taylor it must have been no little encouragement to learn of the connection of all this with the China Inland Mission. " The story . . . of the Cambridge band, particularly the account of the visits of a deputation of these students to other British universities, with their missionary message, made a profound impression on us," wrote one of the early leaders. " *Here really was the germ thought of the Student Volunteer Movement*" (Charles K. Ober).

visitors, and one full of interest.   Four hundred men from ninety different colleges filled the Seminary buildings, and overflowed in tents on the far-reaching campus backed by hills and woods.   The afternoon was kept entirely free for recreation.

" Delegates should come fully equipped for bathing, tennis, baseball, football, hill-climbing and all other outdoor exercises," ran the official invitation.   " They should also bring their own reference Bibles and a good supply of note-books."

Morning and evening the spacious auditorium was filled for devotional meetings and Bible study—the open doors admitting birds as well as breezes, and the summer dress of the students giving a rainbow effect in the blending of soft colours.[1]

It was an inspiring assembly, including many pastors, professors, Y.M.C.A. secretaries, and leading philanthropists. The corps of speakers was able and representative, and Mr. Moody, who presided, was at his best.   But it was in the young men themselves the inspiration lay—such power, such possibilities !   Mr. Taylor could not but be moved by such an audience, and to him the students seem to have been attracted in a special way.

" With the exception of my own father," said Mr. Robert Wilder many years later, " Mr. Taylor was the man who was the greatest spiritual help to me.   When he came to Northfield and appealed on behalf of China, the hearts of the delegates burned within them.   And he not only made the needs of the mission-field very real ; he showed us the possibilities of the Christian life.   The students loved to hear him expound the Word of God.   He was a master of his Bible, and his sympathy and naturalness attracted men to him.   His addresses were so much appreciated that Mr. Moody had to announce extra meetings to be held by him in the afternoons—so many of the students were anxious to hear more from the veteran missionary. . . . Eternity alone can reveal the results of that life, and the effect of his words upon our Student Movement.

" One of the founders of the S.V.M., the Rev. J. N. Forman,

---

[1] An unstarched white or coloured shirt and collar, a tie, a belt and light-coloured trousers is the summer costume of the American student, completed with a " sweater," or coat, when warmth is needed.   This is *en règle* for Sundays even at Student Conferences.

has written to me from India : ' One of the greatest blessings of my life came to me through, not from, the Rev. J. Hudson Taylor.' ' Through, not from,' that was how we all felt. He was a channel—open, clean, and so closely connected with the Fountain of Living Waters that all who came in contact with him were refreshed.

" And what impressed us undergraduates was not merely the spirituality of Mr. Taylor, it was his common sense. One asked him the question : ' Are you always conscious of abiding in Christ ? '

" ' While sleeping last night,' he replied, ' did I cease to abide in your house because I was unconscious of the fact ? We should never be conscious of *not* abiding in Christ.'. . .

" When asked, ' How is it that you can address so many meetings ? ' he said to us : ' Every morning I feed upon the Word of God, then I pass on through the day messages that have first helped me in my own soul.'

" ' You can work without praying, but it is a bad plan,' was another of his sayings, ' but you cannot pray in earnest without working.' And ' Do not be so busy with work for Christ that you have no strength left for praying. True prayer requires strength.'. . .

" It was not, however, the words only of Mr. Taylor that helped us, it was the life of the man. He bore about with him the fragrance of Jesus Christ."

And this was the impression wherever he went. Even children felt it.

" To-day is our little boy's fifth birthday," wrote a minister many weeks after Mr. Taylor had stayed in his home. " All the children constantly mention you, and often pray for you."

" It seemed to me," recalled Mr. W. E. Blackstone of Chicago, " that it was the almost visible presence of God in him that made his plain and simple words so powerful."

" A servant of the Lord whose light we had not heretofore seen," was the impression made at the Niagara Conference, where " his presence and words were so blessed as to make the occasion one of the most memorable in the lifetime of many a Christian worker." [1]

But though deeply thankful for such opportunities, it was not until Mr. Taylor had been nearly a month in America that it began to dawn upon him that there was a larger

---

[1] The Rev. W. J. Erdman, D.D., Secretary to the Conference.

purpose concerning this visit than any he had in view. His increasingly full programme had brought him, a few days previously, to Niagara-on-the-Lake, in fulfilment of an engagement made before leaving England. It was the opening of the above-mentioned Conference, and Mr. Taylor found himself in the midst of " a great gathering of deeply taught Christians."

" The premillennial Advent is prominent," he wrote, " and the Word of God is honoured."

A special feature of the Conference, which was under the presidency of Dr. James Brookes of St. Louis, was the large number of ministers present, Canadian as well as American, of various denominations. Mr. Taylor was only able to speak twice, having to pass on to Chicago for other meetings, but the impression made was profound. Personal love to the Lord Jesus as typified in the Song of Solomon, and faith in God (or the faithfulness of God, rather, upon which faith is to lay hold) were his subjects, and he scarcely made any reference to China or the Mission.

" One of the leading evangelists present," Mr. Frost tells us, " confessed that the addresses had come to him almost as a revelation, and many others shared this feeling. . . . Hearts and lives were brought into an altogether new relationship to God and Christ, and not a few, in the joyfulness of full surrender, quietly but finally offered themselves to the Lord for His service anywhere and everywhere."

But of this and subsequent happenings Mr. Taylor knew nothing. His visit to Chicago ended, he had come east again to Attica, a lovely village in the state of New York, where Mr. Frost, senior, and his son had their summer homes. The son was expected on the midnight train from Niagara, and Mr. Taylor was at the station to meet him—eager to hear more of the Conference, but little thinking of the news he had to bring.

For unexpected developments had taken place at the Niagara meetings after Mr. Taylor's departure. Disappointed at not hearing more from him on the subject of foreign missions, the Conference all the more welcomed the addresses of Mr. Radcliffe and Mr. Robert Wilder, for which the way had been well prepared. Burning words were spoken by the veteran evangelist and the young volunteer on the responsibility of each succeeding generation of believers to obey the great command, " Go ye into all the world and preach the Gospel to every creature." He had learned, Mr. Wilder told them, the secret of how to work for the Lord *twenty-four hours a day*, and to keep on doing so all the year round. It was a lady who had made the discovery. When asked how it was possible—

" I work twelve hours here," she replied, " and when I have to rest, my representative in India begins her day, and works the other twelve."

" We want many from the Niagara Conference to work twenty-four hours a day like this," he urged. " Christian friends, you who cannot go, why not have your own representatives on the foreign field ? "

This was a new idea, but seemed so reasonable that Mr. Radcliffe was kept busy answering questions as to how much it would take to support a worker in the China Inland Mission. Two hundred and fifty dollars a year (£50) he thought would suffice,[1] and a meeting was appointed to see what was to be the practical outcome. Dr. W. J. Erdman was in the Chair, but the occasion was not one for much direction or control.

" After singing and prayer," he wrote, " the Secretary, who had in mind the general guidance of the meeting, suddenly found himself entirely emptied of every idea and preference, and the Spirit of the Lord came upon the believers present. The rest of the hour was filled with voluntary praises, prayers and consecration of young men and women to service in the foreign field. It was a meeting never to be forgotten, and money for the China Inland Mission came in without advertisement or urging on the part of any."

But even this experience was surpassed next day when the Conference reassembled.

" As I reached the Pavilion," wrote Mr. Frost, to whom gifts

---

[1] This proved inadequate, however, as it made no allowance for incidental and travelling expenses, house rent, and the like.

and pledges of money sufficient for the support of two missionaries had been given the previous evening, " I found that people had become intoxicated with the joy of giving, and that they were seeking another opportunity for making free-will offerings for the Lord's work in China.   A number were standing up, pledging themselves to give a certain amount toward the support of a missionary, and some were saying that they wanted to work twenty-four hours a day by having a missionary all to themselves.   Again promises and money came flowing in, until, this time, I had scarcely a place to put them.   There I stood in the midst of the assembly—without ever wishing it or thinking such a thing could be—suddenly transformed into an impromptu Treasurer of the China Inland Mission.   And afterwards, upon counting what had been given, I found enough to support not two missionaries but actually *eight*, for a whole year, in inland China."

Returning to his room that summer morning Mr. Frost could not but remember the sorrowful experience through which he had passed in London, when he had wondered whether he could ever know that prayer was really answered, or be assured of the guidance of God again.   The faith that had sustained him then was being exchanged for sight, and as he poured out his heart in wondering thankfulness he realised how safe and good it is " not only to wait upon God, but also to wait for Him."

This then was the story he had to tell, when upon reaching Attica at midnight he found Mr. Taylor on the platform to meet him.

" I kept my secret, however," he continued, " until we reached my father's house and Mr. Taylor's bedroom.   Then, fully and joyously, I described to him how after his departure from Niagara the Spirit had swept over the Conference ; how the offerings had been given and put into my hands to pass on to him ; and how they had been found to amount to a sum sufficient to support *eight* missionaries for a year in China.

" Quietly he listened, and with such a serious look that I confess, for once in my life, I was disappointed in Mr. Taylor.   Instead of being glad, he seemed burdened.   If I remember rightly, he did just say, ' Praise the Lord,' or ' Thank God,' but beyond this there was nothing to indicate that he accepted the news as good news, as I had anticipated.   For a few minutes he stood apparently lost in thought, and then said :

" ' I think we had better pray.'

" Upon this we knelt beside the bed, and he began to ask what the Lord meant by all that had taken place.   It was only as he went on pleading for light that I commenced to understand what was in Mr. Taylor's mind.   He had realised at once that this was a very marked providence, and that God had probably brought him to America for other purposes than simply to give a few addresses on his way to China.   He had inquired from me how the money was to be used, and I had replied that it was designated, by preference, for the support of North American workers.   From this he saw that the obligation was laid upon him of appealing for missionaries from North America —a heavy responsibility, in view of all that it involved. . . . It was becoming clear to him, as to me, that my visit to London and appeal for a branch of the Mission to be established on this continent had been more providential than was at first recognised."

Unexpectedly a crisis had arisen, fraught, as Mr. Taylor could not but see, with far-reaching results.   He was glad to be returning to Northfield shortly for the General Conference, when he would have the opportunity of consulting Mr. Moody and other friends.   For the problem that faced him, after little more than three weeks in America, was no simple one, and as yet the man at his side, young and retiring as he was, had not been recognised as the providential solution.

" God is with us," he wrote to Mrs. Taylor before leaving for Buffalo next morning (July 26).   " Money for a year's support of several new missionaries is either given or promised, and great issues are likely to result from our visit.   There never was more need for prayer than at present.   May the Lord guide in all things."

" I think we must have an American branch of the Mission," he was writing to Mr. Stevenson from Ocean Grove a few days later.   " Do not be surprised if I should bring reinforcements with me."

The conclusion to which Mr. Taylor was thus being led was strongly confirmed on his return to Northfield.   Mr. Moody advised his appealing at once for workers, and introduced him to some of his own students who were feeling called to China.   But even then it was with fear and trembling he went forward.   The Mission had always been interdenominational, but there had been no thought of its becoming international, and twenty-one years of experience had made its leader cautious.[1] But once his mind was made up, the appeal was a strong one.

" To have missionaries and no money would be no trouble to me," was the way he put it ; " for the Lord is bound to take care of His own : He does not want me to assume His responsibility. But to have money and no missionaries is very serious indeed.   And I do not think it will be kind of you dear friends in America to put this burden upon us, and not to send some from among yourselves to use the money.   We have the dollars, but where are the people ? "

One by one, in ways we must not attempt to detail, prepared men and women responded to the call, until Mr. Taylor was assured that it was indeed the Lord's purpose for him to take on a band to China.   When the first three were accepted, he began to be relieved about the funds in hand.   Their passages had been promised independently, but their support for the first year would use a considerable part of the money contributed at Niagara " if things went smoothly." But from this point of view, things did not go at all smoothly.   Parents, friends, or the churches to which they belonged claimed the privilege of sustaining these workers.   When as many as eight had been accepted, the original fund was still untouched, and the further they went the less chance there seemed of getting to an end of it. Consecrated money, Mr. Taylor remarked, was something like the consecrated loaves and fishes, there was no using it up.

But all the while, out of sight, there was a quiet force of prayer at work that went far to account for the wonderful things that were happening.   Mr. Taylor and his party were so carried forward on a tide of interest and enthusiasm that it was all they could do to keep up with their programme, and prolonged seasons of prayer—save for his early morning

[1] " I never felt more timid," he said a year later, " about anything in my life."

hour—were impossible. But in the retirement of that country home at Attica a man was on his knees, prevailing with God.

For, strange to say, Mr. Henry W. Frost was not much in evidence at the meetings. A serious illness that threatened the life of his father kept him from travelling, and when not required in the sick room he had more leisure than usual for thought and prayer. He saw, with the clearness of a listening soul, the way in which things were tending. Money continued to come to him for the support of missionaries in China, and in the middle of August he sent out a circular letter to the contributors asking "many and fervent prayers" that the right persons might be chosen, and that some might be ready to sail without delay, that the opportunity of Mr. Taylor's escort might not be lost. To the latter he wrote also, putting his home and services unreservedly at his disposal for the purpose of becoming better acquainted with candidates.

"This quiet at home is most blessed in one respect," he added (Aug. 27). "I have much opportunity for prayer, and I do praise God for it. I am sure it is what He wants just now, and I do count it a great privilege to tell Him of all our hopes and fears at this critical time. It makes me realise the force of that definition of prayer that one has given, 'Prayer is the attitude of a needy and helpless soul whose only refuge is in God': for I feel our need and I feel our helplessness; yet I feel at the same time what a great and sure refuge we have in our God. Praise His holy Name, He has made us 'prisoners *in* Christ' (Eph. iv. 1, Gk.), and from this vantage-ground we may ask what we will!

"Please very specially remember the C.I.M.'s relation to America. I dare not seek to influence you, yet I ask most earnestly that you will consider the question, Will it not be well to establish a branch here? I have much to say to you upon this, if you are led to listen to it."

Meanwhile Mr. Taylor, as he moved about, was growingly impressed with the spirit and enterprise of American Christians, and with the interest in China awakened among them.

"We had a magnificent meeting last night," he wrote from Lockport on the 14th of August. "Things are working marvellously: the hand of God is everywhere apparent."

A week later, in Hamilton, he found a band of young people who seemed prepared in a special way for his message. From the Secretary of the Y.M.C.A. he learned that they were united in earnest prayer that seven of their number might be privileged to go as missionaries to China. Among the appreciative notices of Mr. Taylor's meetings was one long article in the leading paper that ended somewhat abruptly, as though the editorial scissors had been at work. Another pen, too, than the writer's seemed to have added a closing sentence.

" The venerable gentleman," it said, " concluded a long, most interesting address, by informing the audience that the members of the China Inland Mission depended upon chance providences for a scanty subsistence."

Notwithstanding this disquieting assertion, Mr. Taylor's visit was largely occupied in interviews with candidates for the work, and among the party that sailed with him a few weeks later were four young women and three men from the Hamilton Christian Associations, the Secretary himself following by way of Europe. Such events could not but move the churches, and recall to mind the earnest request of the Rev. John McLaurin, who had arranged the Canadian meetings : " Pray, *pray* that God will make this visit a great blessing to our dear Canada."

Time fails to tell of the growing interest, the abiding impression and the many friendships made as Mr. Taylor moved from place to place.

" I was only a little girl," recalled a Southern lady, " when my mother took me to hear him at Dr. Brookes' Church in St. Louis, but years after I heard Dr. Brookes tell of the wonderful influence of that visit, and how during his stay Mr. Taylor rose regularly about 4 A.M. and spent the early hours with Him Who was the source of his great power.

" Only to-day Mrs. Brookes gave me the details of an incident her sainted husband loved to tell. It was necessary for Mr. Taylor to leave their home early, to get a train for Springfield (Ill.), where he was to speak that day. There was some unaccountable delay in the arrival of the carriage to convey him to the depôt, and Dr. Brookes was much worried, but Mr. Taylor was perfectly calm. When they reached the station the train had left, and there seemed no possible way for him to keep his appointment.   But he quietly told Dr. Brookes :

" ' My Father manages the trains, and I'll be there.'

" Upon inquiry of the agent they found a train leaving St. Louis in another direction, which crossed a line going to Springfield ; but the train on the other line always left ten minutes before this train arrived, as they were opposing roads.   Without a moment's hesitation Mr. Taylor said he would go that way, in spite of the fact that the agent told him they never made connections there.   For almost the first time in the history of that road the St. Louis train arrived ahead of the other, and Mr. Taylor was able to keep his appointment at Springfield.

" When he was leaving next day for Rochester, N.Y., a Mr. Wilson accompanied him to the station.   He felt it impressed upon him that Mr. Taylor did not have sufficient money for the tickets (a matter of about eight pounds), and upon inquiry found this to be the case.

" ' Why did you not tell us ? ' asked Mr. Wilson, who had decided the night before to take the tickets and had come provided.

" ' My Father knew,' was the quiet answer ; ' it was not necessary to speak to any of His children about it.'

" Many of us who heard of these experiences had learned to bring the greater things of life to our Heavenly Father, but the simple, child-like trust of this godly man taught us to come to our Heavenly Father with the smaller details as well.   ' Casting *all* your care (anxiety) upon Him, for He careth for you.' "

By the middle of September Mr. Frost's prayers seemed more than answered.   The number of applicants to join the Mission had risen to over forty, out-distancing even his faith and expectations.   Hundreds of letters had poured in, and Mr. Taylor was wholly unable to cope with the correspondence necessary for completing the cases of candidates.[1]   It was with thankfulness, therefore, he fell back on Mr. Frost's suggestion of a reunion of the outgoing party at Attica, when he might be able to hand over much of the work that remained to his willing hands.

" It is very kind of you to choose Attica as a gathering place," wrote the latter.   " There will be no difficulty in caring for almost any number likely to be invited.   Besides my mother's

---

[1] Eight hundred and twenty-six letters were received by Mr. Taylor between July 1, when he arrived in New York, and October 5, when he sailed from Vancouver.

home and our own, we will be permitted to send guests to three other homes in the village, or if that is not convenient, some of us can put up at the Hotel at very reasonable rates. You may invite freely therefore, and anticipate a comfortable entertainment for all who come. . . .

" You will be glad to know that your letter . . . was a direct answer to many prayers. I have been praying specifically for two things : first, that you might return here, and second, that there might be a series of farewell meetings of just such a nature as you have suggested. Besides these, I have been asking for other things which your letter touches upon. I cannot tell you how it burdens my heart with a sense of unworthiness to find the Almighty God so ready to listen to my cries and so quick to answer them. Please pray for me that I may walk more worthy of such a Father."

Surely not the least remarkable of the converging providences by which Mr. Taylor was led to go forward in these matters was the generous, devoted co-operation of Mr. Frost, and the way in which he was ready to assume whatever of responsibility Mr. Taylor had to devolve.[1]

[1] In this connection, an incident that happened in Toronto could not but confirm Mr. Taylor's assurance that he was being guided of God. Prayerful consideration of the circumstances had led him and Mr. Frost to the conclusion that it would be well to secure the help of a few leading, godly men, as a temporary Council, until, after consultation with friends in London and Shanghai, more permanent arrangements could be made. As most of the young missionaries were from Canada, Toronto seemed the centre indicated, and the valuable help of Mr. Sandham of the Christian Institute, who was editor also of a religious paper, opened the way for such an arrangement. With wide, interdenominational connections, he very kindly undertook the responsibility of Hon. Secretary in Canada, Mr. Frost occupying a similar position in the States. But time was short in which to arrange for a Council.

In an upper room at the Institute Mr. Taylor was in conference with Messrs. Frost and Sandham, the day after the farewell meetings which moved Toronto so profoundly (Sept. 25). The names of several suitable persons had been mentioned who might be asked to join a provisional Council, and among them Dr. Parsons, Mr. Gooderham and Mr. Nasmith, all of that city. It was with regret Mr. Taylor found that he could not arrange for interviews, to put the matter before them in person. He had to leave that very day for Montreal, and was about to request Mr. Sandham to act for him, when a knock was heard at the door. Great was the surprise of those within when the visitor proved to be one of the gentlemen in question. Hardly had Mr. Taylor explained to him the circumstances, and received his assurance of willing co-operation however, before another knock came, and a second of the three appeared. He, too, was glad to serve on the Council, and they were all feeling impressed with the hand of God in the matter, when yet another visitor came seeking Mr. Sandham.

Then came the farewell meetings—the best part in some ways of all that American visit. For the sacrifice was very real that the outgoing missionaries and their families were making, and the love of Christ so overflowed their hearts that few could see or hear them unmoved.

" You have often seen, dear Mrs. Taylor," wrote Mrs. Reginald Radcliffe, whose presence in the party was no little help, " how God has sustained His children when leaving home and loved ones, but I do not suppose even you have ever witnessed such joy as beamed on the faces of the thirteen who left Toronto on the 26th of September." (With another who joined them farther west, they were fourteen in all—eight young women and six men.)

" I believe Toronto and even Canada," she continued, " will long remember those two nights—the farewell and the departure of the missionaries. At the farewell on Sunday night the Y.M.C.A. Hall was so full that an overflow meeting had to be held, and hundreds went away unable to get in. On Monday Mr. Taylor had to leave for Montreal, but it was arranged for the missionary party and their friends to meet at Dr. Parson's church at nine the following evening, to take the Lord's Supper together, going from the church to the station. It was said that from five hundred to a thousand people were at the station, singing and cheering. Finally my husband led in prayer, the great concourse repeating the words aloud after him . . . and slowly the train moved away. As we returned the members of the Y.M.C.A. walked four abreast, singing hymns, up the streets of Toronto."

Very different from these stirring scenes was the memory that lingered in Mr. Taylor's heart with special sweetness. It was in Mr. Frost's home town of Attica the incident had taken place, at one of the first farewell meetings. The father of a dear girl in the party, Miss Susie Parker, had come over from Pittsfield, Mass., and was sitting near the platform. Seeing a wonderful light on his face, Mr. Taylor invited him to say a few words.

It did seem almost too wonderful to be true when the third of the friends entered whom Mr. Taylor had desired to meet before leaving—especially when it transpired that two of the three had not been in the building for months and had no idea that he was there. " They were indeed sent by the Lord," was Mr. Frost's comment, " and we were never disappointed in the choice He had made "

" He told us with a father's feelings," Mr. Taylor loved to recall, " what his daughter had been in the home, to him and to her mother ; what she had been in the mission-hall in which he worked, and something of what it meant to part with her now.

" ' But I could only feel,' he said, ' that I have nothing too precious for my Lord Jesus. He has asked for my very best ; and I give, with all my heart, my very best to Him.'

"That sentence was the richest thing I got in America, and has been an untold blessing to me ever since. Sometimes when pressed with correspondence the hour has come for united prayer, and the thought has arisen, ought I not to go on with this or that matter ?   Then it has come back to me—' *Nothing too precious for my Lord Jesus.*' The correspondence has been left to be cared for afterwards, and one has had the joy of fellowship unhindered. Sometimes waking in the morning, very weary, the hour has come for hallowed communion with the Lord alone ; and there is no time like the early morning for getting the harp in tune for the music of the day. Then it has come again— ' *Nothing too precious for my Lord Jesus,*' and one has risen to find that there is no being tired with Him. That thought also has been a real help to me when leaving my loved ones in England : indeed, I could never tell how many hundreds of times God has given me a blessing through those words."

CHAPTER XXXI

THE CROSS DOES NOT GET COMFORTABLE

1888–1889. AET. 56–57.

CROSSING the Rocky Mountains by Canadian Pacific was a wonderful experience to Mr. Taylor. The greatness of the country as it unrolled before him was in keeping with the greatness of the possibilities he had felt among Canadian as well as American Christians for the rapid, world-wide extension of the kingdom of God. Wonderful, too, was it to have with him the party so unexpectedly given for China and the Inland Mission.

"We are so happy and united," he wrote to Mrs. Taylor *en route.* "You would enjoy knowing the dear young workers God has given us, in the fresh bloom of consecration and love. May it never wear off.

"Every day I feel more thankful for each member of our band. . . . The little difficulties of travel only bring out character more clearly, and show how good God's choice has been.

"You can have little idea how mightily the Spirit of God has been and is working."

The voyage across the Pacific was made the most of for helpful talks and Bible readings with his companions, in which he sought to prepare them for all that lay ahead. The consciousness was much with him, already referred to in letters to Mr. Stevenson, of the certainty of opposition from the powers of evil. For years the Mission had been carried forward on a wave of unparalleled success. During the period of the Seventy its membership had doubled, as we have seen, and since then it had more than doubled again, without the addition of this latest party. And what opportunities for enlargement did not their coming suggest ? But experience had taught him that for every time of prosperity and blessing one of special trial was in store, though even he can hardly have anticipated how long and testing the conflict now before them was to prove.

At Yokohama it began, even before they came in sight of China. For there news was received of the death from hydrophobia of Herbert Norris, the beloved Head of the Chefoo School, who in protecting his boys from a mad dog had himself been bitten ; and that also of Adam Dorward, the devoted pioneer of Hu-nan and a member of the China Council. To one of Mr. Taylor's tender affections, who could so well appreciate the loss that had befallen the Mission, the news was a blow indeed.

" I am almost overwhelmed," he wrote to Mrs. Taylor that October day. " ' My soul is even as a weaned child.' I want to be alone with God and quiet before Him. May He bless you . . . and all at home. May He make us more holy ; more fit for His service *here* as *there*."

Meanwhile further sorrow had been permitted, and on landing in Shanghai Mr. Taylor learned not only of the death of a young worker of much promise, but that in the Home to which he was taking his fellow-travellers another was even then nearing the end of life's journey. Three men within a month, and now this woman of a gracious spirit, who had only come out in the Hundred ! It was a time of heart-searching before God, to see why the hand of His protection had been in measure withdrawn, and a time also in which the cheer of the American Party was sorely needed.

> Jesus, Saviour, pilot me
> Over life's tempestuous sea

was a new hymn in those days, and one they often sang together.

> As a mother stills her child
> Thou canst hush the tempest wild.
> Boist'rous waves obey Thy will,
> When Thou say'st to them, " Be still."
> Wondrous Sovereign of the sea—
> Jesus, Saviour, pilot me.

Times without number during the months that followed did that prayer go up from storm-stressed hearts in the mission-house at Shanghai, where Mr. Taylor was detained by apparently endless troubles. He had come out, as Mr. Stevenson remarked, " full of faith and hope," to do much in the way of consolidation. America had greatly encouraged him. His visit there had been providentially timed to coincide with a stage in the Mission's development when its material basis must take more adequate form. The purely native houses of earlier days had to be superseded, in the ports at any rate, by adequate receiving homes and business centres. All over the field young workers were getting into harness, and still larger reinforcements were expected.

" God is with us of a truth," he had written to Mr. Stevenson from Montreal, " and will give us to see far greater things. I hope after conference with you to be able to look forward to a speedy doubling of our staff. Nothing less I am satisfied should be aimed at, even in the near future ; and I trust that that doubling will only anticipate a doubling again. There ought to be no difficulty in getting at least three hundred good workers from the States and Canada. . . ."

There was scarcely a grey head in the Mission in those days, and under Mr. Stevenson's enthusiastic leadership in China " everything seemed possible." Was there a danger, perhaps, of growing too fast for the spiritual well-being of the work or the faith of its supporters ?

" It was a dark and trying time that winter," recalled the Deputy Director. " There had been so much success, such rapid extension. We were going ahead full sail set, before a favourable breeze. Ballast was needed, though at the time we could not see it, and the prolonged sickness and trial that surrounded us seemed mysterious indeed."

Never was day of fasting and prayer more timely than that which ushered in 1889. New Year's Eve had been set apart, according to the custom of the Mission, for thus waiting upon God, and when it came the need was found to be more urgent, even, than had been anticipated. For only the day before the accumulated trials of previous weeks had been surpassed by the arrival of the saddest party ever received from England. On the voyage out one of the new workers had had a shock which resulted in temporary insanity, and on landing, her condition was that of acute mania. No asylums were to be found in China, even in the foreign Settlements, and she had to be cared for in the already crowded premises the Mission was renting in Shanghai. At the same time another bright, beautiful girl was stricken down at an inland station with black small-pox, and the life of both seemed to hang in the balance. Few among the younger Missionaries was more loved and valued than Maggie M'Kee, and it was with the keenest sorrow Mr. Taylor heard of her death after six days of suffering. Meanwhile a telegram had been received from Hongkong telling of the serious illness of Mr. William Cooper of the China Council. After furlough, he was returning to the province of An-hwei, in which his experience and ripeness of Christian character were greatly needed, but double pneumonia had supervened upon illness by the way, and it was doubtful whether he could live to reach Shanghai.

"We are passing through wave after wave of trial," Mr. Taylor wrote on January 11. "Each day has its full quota. God seems daily to be saying, ' Can you say, " even so, Father," to *that* ? ' But He sustains and will sustain the spirit, however much the flesh may fail. Our house has been a hospital ; it is now an asylum. All that this means the Lord only knows. . . . The night and day strain are almost unbearable. . . . But I know the Lord's ways are all right, and I would not have them otherwise."

"There is absolutely nothing to be done," he added a week later, "but to bear the trial, while using proper means, and wait on God. There are no asylums, and she could not be taken to sea. So whatever time and care the case claims must be given, and it must be pleasing to the Lord for us to be so occupied. . . . He makes no mistakes. He can make none. Even now we accept with thankfulness His dealings, and soon with joy shall see the deep purposes of wisdom and love, wrought out by all that is so mysterious at present."

But more serious than these troubles in China were anxieties that pressed upon him from another quarter. Friends of the Mission in England, it appeared, including some of the London Council, were concerned about the steps taken in America. Not having been on the spot, they were unable as yet to realise the guidance given or the value of the work developed. It was natural, perhaps, that they should fear lest responsibilities taken up quickly should be as quickly forgotten ; and, moreover, no one had as yet fore- seen the adaptability of the Mission, on account of its special form of government, to relations of an international char- acter. The principle of control on the field—the direction of the work not from a distance but by experienced leaders in China—could not but constitute Shanghai the headquarters of the Mission rather than London, making it possible for Mr. Taylor or his representatives there to work with auxiliary Councils in any part of the world, just as with the original Council at home. This natural application of one of the cardinal principles of the Mission came as a surprise, however, to those who had hitherto never dreamed of such develop- ments. Even the necessity for the China Council had hardly yet been fully conceded ; and that it should come to occupy a central position, with affiliations in America and perhaps elsewhere, practically independent of the mother-country, was no little cause for concern. So hazardous did it appear, indeed, to the best interests of the work, that some felt they might have to resign from the Council rather than consent to it, even though this would involve for Mr. Taylor as well as themselves the severance of relations among the oldest and most valued they possessed.

Needless to say, the position was a critical one, and caused the leader of the Mission deep concern. More sure he could not be as to the guidance given in America. Step by step he had been led, almost compelled, to accept the party that had accompanied him, and to appoint as Secretaries and provisional Council those who had been so remarkably provided. Go back upon it he could not, without going back upon what he had assuredly gathered to have been the will of God. But how go forward at such a cost ?

" As to the American question," he wrote to a leading member of the Council in February, " I shall be glad of your views when you have time to write them, but without a visit to America it is difficult fully to understand the matter. I should have been as fearful as you are, if I had not been there. . . . I purposely made all the arrangements tentative, pending my return to England and having the opportunity for full conference about them. . . . My increasing desire is to please God. So far as I know my own heart, this is my only wish in the matter. . . .

> I thirst for Thee, O God, for Thee.
> Oh draw me nearer, nearer still !
> For evermore Thine own to be,
> My will all lost in Thy sweet will.
> As pants the hart for cooling streams,
> So pants my soul, O God, for Thee ;
> As sends the sun its cheering beams,
> So let Thy Spirit shine in me."

But it was in letters to Mrs. Taylor that the manifold anxieties he was passing through found most expression.

"The Lord is sending a very flood of trials," he wrote in January. "No doubt they are all needed. We might be lifted up, perhaps, or lose spiritual life and power, if success were unaccompanied by discipline."

And in February :

Satan is simply raging. He sees his kingdom attacked all over the land, and the conflict is awful. But that our Commander is All-mighty, I should faint. I think I never knew anything like it, though we have passed through some trying times before.

Satan often says, "All these things are against you " ; but God's Word is true and says the opposite.

"I am more and more desirous to do God's will ; to be pleasing to Him, and that at all costs.

It was not all dark, however, for in January (1889) Mr. Taylor was able to write of the spiritual life of the Mission as "higher than ever before," and that "glad tidings of souls won for Christ and very real progress in many directions cheer us amid our trials." In March the pressure was again so great that in asking for renewed earnestness in prayer at home he said : "It seems as if every native Christian and helper as well as missionary were being assailed." Yet, in the midst of it all, he and many of his fellow-workers were learning deeper lessons of the sustaining power of God.

" The cross does not get comfortable," is one revealing sentence in a letter of this winter, " but it bears sweet fruit." How truly it was so in Mr. Taylor's experience may be gathered from the recollections of one who was much with him at the time.

" I never went through such a distressful period," said Mr. Stevenson of 1888–89 ; " everything seemed crowded into those terrible months. I do not know what we should have done without Mr. Taylor ; but oh, the look on his face at times ! The special day of fasting and prayer (a second) was a great help. We never found it to fail. In all our troubles, in all our forward movements, in times of need, whether as to funds or spiritual blessing, we always had recourse to fasting and prayer, and with a quick response.

" One thing that deeply touched me at this time was Mr. Taylor's evident and intense longing to walk uprightly before God. He would go all lengths to do the right thing and put away misunderstandings. Early this spring, when our troubles were at their height, he was burdened about the lack of cordiality between ourselves and two former members of the Mission who were still in Shanghai. The trouble had arisen during one of Mr. Taylor's absences in England, but he could not leave it with simply—

" ' They were wrong, and we did what we could at the time.'

" He wrote a note saying he would be glad to call upon them and talk matters over, greatly desiring that any bitterness of feeling might be removed. On the 4th of March, I remember, he spent a long evening with them, going over the whole story. It must have been very painful, for their attitude was far from conciliatory, but it ended right. He was able to have prayer with them, and friendship was restored.

" Oh, his was a life that stood looking into—searching through and through ! Get a man like Mr. Taylor, and you could start *any* mission to-morrow. It was most wonderful—his life. I never knew any other so consistent ; and I watched him year in and year out, and had exceptional opportunities for doing so. He walked with God ; his life bore the light all through. And he was so gracious and accessible ! Day or night, literally at all hours, he was ready to help in sickness or any trouble. For self-denial and practical consecration, one could not but feel, he stood alone."

A sheet of notepaper bearing a few lines in Mr. Taylor's writing reveals, perhaps, more than anything else the secret of his inward life at this time. Found between the pages of his diary, it brightens the record with unexpected radiance. From the brief entries in the book itself one learns little ; but that well-worn paper, used evidently as a marker and moved on from day to day, what does it not reveal ?

> LORD JESUS, make Thyself to me
> A living, bright Reality :
> More present to faith's vision keen
> Than any outward object seen ;
> More dear, more intimately nigh
> Than e'en the sweetest earthly tie.

Was it not the answer to this daily prayer that made endurance possible ? " Strengthened by His Spirit with power penetrating to your inmost being . . . that Christ may make His home in your hearts through faith " [1]—is it not the very experience for times of trouble ?

" I have been greatly distressed," he wrote to Mrs. Taylor in March, " but all that is passed now. God has spoken, and my heart is at rest. . . . I see no light as to the future of home arrangements ; but I see God, the living God ; and I love Him all the more for this trial—and *trust*."

Mar. 12 : The Lord bless and guide us. This is the greatest trial we have yet had : it will bring the greatest blessing. Now the Lord has taken the burden off my shoulders, and He is going to order the whole thing. It is His work, not mine.

Mar. 27 : As for the C.I.M., it never was so truly the Lord's own work, and He alone is all-sufficient—sufficient for the heartache and the sorrow, as well as for the service.

April 5 : Our hope must be in God; He is equal to all emergencies.

---

[1] Eph. iii. 16, 17, in Weymouth's version : *The New Testament in Modern Speech.*

CHAPTER XXXII

WITH WINGS AS EAGLES

1889. AET. 57.

IT was with confidence in God, though with a deep sense of the gravity of the situation, that Mr. Taylor prepared for leaving China when it became evident that home difficulties could not be settled by correspondence. Very little of all he had hoped to do on this visit had been accomplished ; but the mental patient was recovering, and plans for the large new premises in Shanghai, to which he had been devoting much attention, were finished and in the builder's hands. Mission house, prayer meeting hall, business quarters, and residences for the permanent staff were all to be erected on the site obtained some years previously, and so thoroughly had the details been gone into that Mr. Taylor knew by heart the measurement of every door and window : his interest being only exceeded by thankfulness that the buildings, extensive as they necessarily were, would be no charge upon the funds of the Mission.

Facing the difficulties that awaited him, Mr. Taylor wrote to a member of the London Council before leaving :

Pray that in the reorganisation of our home work we may have much divine guidance, and that the issue of this great trial may be greater blessing all round. " All things work together for good to them that love God " : we all do this and with all our hearts, whatever else we fail in, do we not ? So the issue is sure.

It was in no spirit of self-confidence, however, that he

went forward, as may be seen from a letter to Mr. Stevenson when nearing Aden :

It is so solemn to feel that one may go out . . . as Samson did, unconscious that the Lord has left one, to win defeat and captivity and blindness. May the Lord keep me and keep you very near Himself. All our service will be worse than useless without that. The solemnity of our position as the representatives of such blessed truths as we teach makes me tremble. But the Lord will surely, for His own Name's sake, keep us.

The voyage by French Mail, though specially trying, afforded opportunity for waiting upon God. The heat was excessive, and a couple of hundred soldiers taken on board at Saigon did not add to the comfort or quiet of the third-class quarters. But the solitary English traveller was living less in outward things than in unseen realities.

" One is lonely in the midst of a crowd on this steamer," he wrote to Mrs. Taylor from the Red Sea (May 9). " There are fewer than usual who understand English . . . If our love makes us long so for the glad day of our reunion, how much more must our Master look forward to the completion of His blood-bought Bride and the day of His espousals ! Would that we were all more alive to His longings, more in earnest to do all that in us lies to hasten the day of His desire. One can well understand the glad ' shout ' with which He will come to claim His Bride, when His ' long patience ' is past. Oh, for more likeness to Him, more of His patience, more fellowship in His sufferings ! My Darling, I am so little like Him ! "

A very real sense of his own insufficiency led Mr. Taylor to rejoice at this time as never before in the wonderful deliverance given to the Apostle Paul, not from but *in* his infirmities. On the passage, " My grace is sufficient for thee," he had written shortly before leaving China :

When the pressure was greatest and his own weakness most felt, the Apostle knew himself to be in the very position to be made an instrument of blessing to many, and to be most abundantly sustained himself. . . . And was not this a better answer to Paul's prayers than the mere removing of his " thorn " would have been ? The latter course would have left him open to similar trouble whenever the next distress came ; but God's method at once and for ever delivered him from all oppression

of present and future trials.   Hence he triumphantly exclaimed :
' Most gladly will I rather glory (or rejoice) in my weaknesses,
that the strength of Christ may overshadow and cover me." . . .

Ah, who would not wish to share the Apostle's thorn in the
flesh, if thereby he might be brought in reality into the experience
of his deliverance from the oppression of all weakness, all injury,
all necessity, all persecution, all distress, and might henceforth
know that the very hour and time of weakness was the very
hour and time of truest strength ?

That it was so in this serious crisis is evident from the
joy with which Mr. Taylor wrote to Mr. Stevenson of
answered prayer in connection with the difficulties that had
called him home.   From the very day of his arrival (May 21)
he found that God Himself had been working to make a
continuance of happy relations possible,[1] and when the
annual meetings were held a week or two later, they proved
a time of remarkable blessing :

" I think that all may now be put right," he wrote to Mr.
Stevenson at the end of the month, " and that great good will
result from our great trial."

And a few weeks later :

July 4 : It is impossible not to see in these things the good
hand of our God in answer to many prayers.   I do not think
things have been so cordial for years.   In all this there is abundant
cause for gratitude and praise.

Thus the storm - clouds began to roll away, leaving
behind them clearer vision and hearts more ready for the
larger purposes of God.   The development of the home work
in several important directions was one immediate result.
A Deed of Incorporation for the safeguarding of mission
property was drawn up.   The Council was strengthened by
the addition of Mr. Robert Scott as Treasurer and several
new members.   An Auxiliary Council was formed in Glasgow,
to deal with Scottish candidates, and a Ladies' Council in
London, of which Miss Soltau was appointed Secretary with
entire charge of a department for the help and training of
women-workers.

---

[1] " Many thanks for your good wishes for my birthday," Mr. Taylor
wrote to Mr. Stevenson some weeks later.   " I reached England on that
day, and found the stone already rolled away."

In the midst of these and other arrangements, and with invitations for meetings pressing upon him, it was not easy for Mr. Taylor to cross the Atlantic again for the Niagara and Northfield Conferences. But a visit to America seemed necessary, to strengthen the relations between the oldest and newest departments of the work, and, armed with a cordial letter of welcome to the Toronto Council from the Council in London, he set out early in July. Of the quickened hopes stirring within him, and the way in which he was pressing on to know more of the wonder-working power of God, some impression may be gained from a letter to Mrs. Taylor before leaving Queenstown Harbour (July 6) :

I am hoping to give special time to prayer and Bible-study on the voyage. Darling, I do want our whole life to be an ascending plane—not resting in anything we have learned or felt or attained, but a pressing on and up. . . . God has been faithful to us, as far as we have gone out on His promises and have trusted His faithfulness ; but how little we have done so ! How small, after all, have been our prayers and expectations, seeing we have such a God to do with.

What would a great Sovereign think of a proposal to add one hundred soldiers in the course of a year to his army of invasion in a country like China ? We must get on to a higher plane of thought altogether, and of prayer, if we are to walk worthy of God and deal in any sensible way with the world's crying need. Let us ask in faith for such workers for every department as shall be fit and able to deal worthily with their work at home, in America, in China, and for such an enduement of power as shall make the feeblest mighty and the strong as the angels (messengers) of God. Is it too much to expect of Him, too much to ask for His glory ? May God save us from limiting the Holy One of Israel. May He open our eyes to see *Himself*, and help us to go forward on the strength of His ' Have not I sent thee ? "

We go working on, feeling our weakness and personal need ; feeling the weakness and poverty of the Church and the un-reality or at least extreme shallowness of its consecration ; feeling the power of the one, united front of the world, the flesh and the devil. Do we not want more really to meditate on GOD ; to gaze on Him ; to take in what we are even now competent to take in of His greatness, His resources, His assurances and promises ? Dwelling thus on Him, should we not be enabled to grasp more of the heights and depths of His character and purposes, and be more ready and able to do *His* will ? May He,

Darling, in our separation, become all the more to us, that we may first be more to Him, and then through Him to our work and to each other.

In the little town of Attica two other hearts had been learning similar lessons, hearts united in an equally deep bond of love. Circumstances had changed a good deal for Mr. and Mrs. Frost since Mr. Taylor's previous visit, but their home seemed, if anything, more attractive than before. The marriage gift of his father, it had been beautified by the addition of panelled wooden ceilings, to replace the plaster ones which had fallen in the lower rooms, a detail that was to have a good deal to do with the direction of their lives at this time. With every comfort in their surroundings, a large circle of friends and nothing but happiness in their children, there seemed little of earthly good left to desire. But an unseen Hand was stirring up this nest, and Mr. Taylor's second visit found them in the midst of strange experiences.

For their income, which had hitherto been amply sufficient, had suddenly been cut off through the failure of a flourishing business. At his father's express desire, Mr. Frost had given up his own business some years previously, to devote himself entirely to evangelistic work. The father was well able to supply the needs of the family, and rejoiced to have fellowship in this way in his son's service for the Lord. But now, to his sorrow, this was no longer possible. To have gone back into secular employment would have greatly curtailed Mr. Henry W. Frost's usefulness as an evangelist, and would have necessitated his giving up much active participation in the work of the C.I.M. This he could not feel to be the will of God, after all the way in which he and Mr. Taylor had been led, and it practically came to be, as he expressed it, a question—" Which father are you really trusting ? "

Outside the immediate family no one knew of their position, and both Mr. and Mrs. Frost saw it to be a special opportunity for putting to the test not their faith only but the definite promises of God. A few months previously they had determined never, under any circumstances, to go into debt. Amid the apparent comfort of their surroundings, therefore, and with wide margins of credit in the stores of the little town, they found themselves directly dependent upon their Heavenly Father even for daily bread. How searching as well as precious were the experiences through which they were learning more of His infinite faithfulness is a story to itself that we may not enter upon here. Suffice it to say that their joy in God was growing deeper and their desire to be wholly engaged in His service stronger, although they little anticipated the sacrifice that would be involved.

Great was the encouragement to Mr. Frost, as to Mr. Taylor, of the welcome with which they were received at the Niagara Conference of this summer. The interest in China seemed deeper and the sympathy for the Inland Mission stronger than the previous year. The gifts of 1888 for the support of American workers were largely exceeded, and many new friendships were formed and old ones strengthened.

" The warm welcomes I have had," Mr. Taylor wrote before leaving, " and the assurances from one and another that great and permanent blessings have resulted from my former visit are very cheering. It does seem so wonderful that God can use even me. May He do so more and more, for His own glory."

Mr. Taylor's chief object in coming over being the settlement of the work upon a permanent basis, he gave much time to meetings with the Council and intercourse with its individual members. The number of the latter was increased, and Mr. Sandham finding it necessary, on account of many engagements, to retire from the position he had held, Mr. Frost was invited to assume the sole responsibility as Treasurer and Secretary, making his home in Toronto.

So this was what it had all been leading to ! In view of recent experiences, he was himself prepared for a life of faith with regard to temporal supplies ; but he knew that Mrs. Frost would feel giving up their lovely home very keenly, on account of the children.

" One day as I was in the parlour, resting," he wrote of this critical time, " my wife, unknown to me, was waiting upon God in her own room for guidance. While thus engaged she was led to open her Bible and to read in the book of Haggai ; and she had not read long in this portion of Scripture before she had the light for which she had been so earnestly seeking. A moment later I heard her coming to me across the library and hall. She stepped to my side, and without a word laid her open Bible on my knee, pointing as she did so to the fourth verse of the first chapter of Haggai. I looked at the words indicated and read as follows :

" ' Is it a time for you, O ye, to dwell in your ceiled houses and this house lie waste ? '

" It was not necessary that my wife should say anything to explain her meaning ; the lesson was self-evident. One look in her face showed me that the Lord had won the victory for her, and one look at the ceiling overhead settled the question finally for myself. From that hour, though it was not an easy thing to do, we were united in our desire to give up our home, in order that we might have part in the building of that spiritual house, the temple of Christ's body, which we knew the Lord was waiting to see completed."

Gladly would Mr. Taylor have made it possible for the step to be taken without financial difficulty ; but while he could give them enough for the actual move, there was little over. The contributions at Niagara and in other centres, while amounting to thousands of dollars, were almost all designated for individual missionaries, and could not be drawn upon. About fifty pounds given to Mr. Taylor for his own use he felt free to pass on, but " beyond this " he said quite frankly, " I can promise you nothing. You will have to look to the Lord for supplies, as we do in England and in China."

" I confess," was Mr. Frost's very natural recollection, " that Mr. Taylor's words did not at first suggest an inviting prospect. To move my family and belongings, to take a home in a strange city, to invite a large number of candidates into that home, to supply their needs and our own and to carry on the work of the Mission with little more than two hundred and fifty dollars was certainly not a promising arrangement from an earthly stand-point. But recent experiences . . . had given me to understand that there was a factor in the case not to be left out, and which being reckoned upon altered the proposition. That factor was the Lord Himself. Two hundred and fifty dollars was anything but a large sum with which to begin such an undertaking ; but two hundred and fifty dollars *with the Lord* was all that we could need. Thus, so far as finances were concerned, I soon felt prepared to accept Mr. Taylor's offer."

Could he have foreseen the many and wonderful answers to prayer that were to bring to the American branch of the Mission over half a million dollars within the next seventeen years, and place at his disposal property to the value of forty thousand more, he might have gone forward with less fear and trembling. But then, would there have been the same faith and prayerfulness, the constant, close dependence upon God which have made Mr. Frost so great a strength to the Mission ? Would the Home in Toronto have become the centre of blessing it has been, and the object-lesson to very many whose hearts turn to it with gratitude from China and other lands, of what God can do and be in the lives of those who trust Him without reserve ? [1]

All this was in the future, however, and it was with concern Mr. Frost saw the days and weeks slip by of Mr. Taylor's too short visit. Much helpful fellowship they had together as they travelled from place to place, Mr. Taylor addressing over forty meetings in eighteen different centres during the five weeks he was in America. Four days at Northfield completed the programme, and brought the Mission again before many friends of the previous summer. Mr. Moody's interest was so much deepened that he offered the beautiful and spacious " Northfield Hotel " during the winter, as a training home for the candidates of the Mission, undertaking to give himself a course of one month's Bible lessons, while Dr. A. T. Pierson would give another.

Cheered and strengthened by many tokens for good, Mr. Taylor left America in August, to carry out a full programme of meetings, which included a visit to Sweden before the close of the year. So pressing and constant were his engagements that he found it difficult to obtain the time needed for remembering all his fellow-workers daily before God. Well he knew that to relax prayer was to open the way for the enemy to come in like a flood ; and as he travelled from

[1] To-day the American branch of the C.I.M. is represented by a hundred and fifteen missionaries, working in fifty-seven stations in thirteen of the eighteen provinces.

place to place he literally had to buy up every opportunity for this unseen but important work.

" What line of thought will you be taking to-night ? " asked one who was to speak at the same meeting, after they had travelled together for an hour or two.

" I can hardly tell," was Mr. Taylor's reply. " I have not yet had time to think about it."

" Not time ! " exclaimed the other. " Why, what have you been doing but rest ever since we came into this carriage ? "

" I do not know about resting," was the quiet answer ; " but I do know that since we left Edinburgh I have prayed by name for every member of the China Inland Mission."

This sort of preoccupation did not make him unmindful of the interests of those from whom he received hospitality, however, as may be judged from many a letter.

" I can never forget your fatherly kindness to me," wrote Mrs. Colville of his stay in Motherwell this autumn (near Glasgow). " Often the very memory of your visit refreshes me. There was such a sweet fragrance of Christ in all your words and actions that, praise God, the house is still filled with the odour of the ointment, and whenever your name is mentioned our hearts go out in love. I hope you are well : I know you are happy, for you walk in the light of His countenance."

This was the attractive power felt in Scotland just as in America, the unconscious influence that had had not a little to do with the interest in Sweden which had now grown to considerable proportions. Meeting a young stranger from that country one busy day in Paternoster Row, Mr. Taylor had gone out of his way to show him courtesy. They met again in Exeter Hall—an important occasion connected with the outgoing of the Seventy (1883), when Mr. Taylor might have passed the Swedish visitor with a greeting. But—

" We had a conversation after the meeting," the latter recalled, " and Mr. Taylor talked to me in a very kind way, by which my heart was drawn out to him. He seemed to be full of love."

Further intercourse at Pyrland Road deepened the interest, and when Mr. Holmgren returned to Örebro it was as a staunch friend of the Inland Mission. First as editor of a religious weekly, then as Pastor of one of the leading churches in Stockholm, he did all that in him lay to awaken Swedish Christians to a sense of responsibility for the un-evangelised millions of China, among whom they as yet had no representatives. Eric Folke, an Upsala graduate, deeply conscious of a call from God to that great field, could find no Swedish society to send him there. Going inde-pendently, he was welcomed at the C.I.M. in Shanghai, and passed on to its training home at An-king for the study of the language. Six months later he wrote to Mr. Holmgren of his desire to work in association with the Inland Mission, and a Committee was formed in Stockholm to facilitate the going out of others to join him.

For some time this representative group of friends had been urging Mr. Taylor to visit Sweden, where his name was well known through Mr. Holmgren's paper and his own writings. Tied for time as he was by the second General Missionary Conference in Shanghai, at which he had promised to preach the opening sermon, it was not easy to spare a month for this purpose ; but the Committee was needing advice as to their work in China, for which Mr. Taylor felt in measure responsible, as it was to be carried on in close affiliation with the C.I.M.

The whole thing was coming about so naturally that he can hardly have realised the widening that was taking place in his personal ministry and the connections of the Mission, which was yet to be linked with deeply prayerful movements in many Continental centres as well as in America and Australasia. With the Niagara Conference of the previous year the new movement had begun, and to the present summer may be traced the larger vision, the inward mounting up " with wings as eagles," which was to lead to much of the outward development. For Mr. Taylor himself was growing with the growing work. After the recent difficulties which had so tested and strengthened faith in God, he was full of longing, as we have seen, " to grasp more of the heights and depths of His character and purposes, and be more ready and able to do His will." And now, even before he could pay his promised visit to Sweden, a fuller revelation of that will had come.

Conscious of a new call from God, a new urgency about the work to which his life was given, Mr. Taylor was ready for the important openings his northern journey afforded. New to him was the welcome of Swedish Christians, which exceeded in its warmth and hospitality anything he had previously known ; and new to them was the spirit of the man with so great a burden for China's perishing millions.[1]

" We seldom address fewer than two to five thousand people daily," he wrote toward the close of the visit, in which he was again accompanied by his second son. " Even in small places we have large audiences. Hundreds could not get in last night : and some had come thirty miles to the meeting. May great and lasting blessing be the result."

The eagerness with which many of the poorer people called out or pressed forward in those crowded assemblies, to make their little gifts, greatly touched the visitors.

One dear old sailor who did not look as if he had much to spare, put into the collecting plate his snuff-box—snuff and all ! We were told that it had probably been his companion for thirty or forty years. It was made of a shell, and had a heavy silver top and lid. It sold that night for twenty crowns.

In another place a lady who had been much moved in the meeting came up and putting a beautiful watch into my hand began to speak in English. But her emotion prevented her completing the sentence in any but her own language :

" It is for *Herren Jesu*," she said—repeating several times in Swedish, " The Lord Jesus, the Lord Jesus, the dear Lord Jesus."

In the homes of the wealthy and in centres of learning the same interest was found.

" At Upsala the venerable Dean Torin was at three of my meetings," Mr. Taylor continued in the home-letters for which he made time whatever came. " Professor Rudin, one of the greatest preachers in Sweden, was at all four, and at Howard's, too, which was for students in the university. I had over two

---

[1] Mr. Taylor spent most of November in Sweden and Denmark— passing on to Norway, and returning via Hamburg and Rotterdam early in December 1889.

thousand hearers, morning and evening. . . . Many said they would never forget us, and I do think China will be remembered as never before. . . . I must have addressed fifty or sixty thousand persons since landing, and I doubt not many are saying in their hearts, ' Here am I, send me.' The kindness, hospitality, of the Swedes exceeds all I have ever seen—and I have seen a good deal."

To Mr. Taylor it came just as naturally to be received with gracious kindness by the Queen as to travel third-class on the railways—which he did in spite of many a friendly remonstrance. Of this interesting experience he wrote to Mrs. Taylor :

One of the Ladies in Waiting came to the hotel at which we were staying and took me in a royal carriage to the palace, five miles out of Stockholm. Very shortly after our arrival the Queen entered, and as I moved toward her she came over quite simply and shook hands. She conversed a little about China, and then asked for a Bible reading. Two Ladies in Waiting and two nurses from the Queen's own hospital were present. I took 1 Kings x. 1-13, afterwards showing Her Majesty our map of China, which led to further conversation about the Mission. The Queen ordered coffee and sandwiches to be brought in, and afterwards shook hands very warmly and retired.

In Sweden as elsewhere it was the spirit of the man that added weight to what was said. Seen through the eyes of Mr. Holmgren, who travelled with them, this was if anything the more eloquent message.

" Everywhere the people were drawn to Mr. Taylor," recalled this helpful friend. " He showed much love and affection, which also was returned. It was a joy to see how the children gathered round him in the families we visited, although they could not understand what he said. He spoke very friendly to them and patted their heads, telling them some nice stories.

" Mr. Hudson Taylor felt much gladdened by his visit to Sweden. He gained many friends ; and still to-day when his name is mentioned before those who heard him, their faces are lit up with joy. He also was very simple and without pretensions. On leaving Linköping, for example, he was specially tired. He had had several meetings the day before, and had risen early in the morning. There had already been a meeting at eleven o'clock, and at six there should be another in a town sixty miles away. On the way to the station, Dr. Howard Taylor said to his father :

" ' You are very tired now. Let me take the second-class ticket.'

" In a so gentle way Mr. Taylor answered : ' Well, it is the Lord's money, you know ; we had better be very careful about it.'

" Which answer made a great impression on me. I have many times since heard this word repeat itself in my ears : ' It is the Lord's money : we had better be very careful about it.'

" Lastly, I may mention an incident which also made a great impression upon my mind, and which shows his trust in God. The Committee had intended to meet Mr. Taylor's expenses and those of his son for their journey by taking collections at the meetings. When I met them in Gothenburg I told Mr. Taylor this. Then he looked at me, and with a smiling face said :

" ' Well, I have a rich Father, you know. I will ask Him about it. But I do not think this thought is quite according to His will. He is sure to provide for me ; and I feel that what is gathered by collections ought to be used for the Swedish Mission.'

" I felt very much touched, and if I had had money I should gladly have paid all the expenses of his travels in Sweden. But as to his trust that these would be provided, I said to myself, ' That is all very well in England ; but in Sweden it is not the same.'

" I parted from Mr. Taylor at Christiania. He crossed for England and I returned to Stockholm. In his first letter he said :

" ' A few days after we had come to England I received a letter from some one in Sweden, I do not know from whom. A cheque was enclosed for fifty pounds, and the writer said that this money was to meet my expenses and those of my son for our journey in Sweden, and if anything was left over I might use it as I liked. If you know who has sent it, please give them my warm thanks.'

" I did not know at all from whom it was ; but I felt very much ashamed and humiliated for my unbelief. At the same time I could not restrain my thanksgivings to the Lord for His faithfulness, and that His power is *just the same* in Sweden as in England."

The burden on Mr. Taylor's heart all through this Swedish visit, if burden it could be called, was the deeper apprehension that had come to him of the meaning of the divine command, " Go ye into all the world, and preach the Gospel to every creature." For more than forty years that command had controlled his life, responded to with un-questioning obedience. What had he not done and suffered; how had he not helped and inspired others in seeking to carry it out! Surely if there were a man anywhere who might feel that he had discharged his responsibility in this matter it was Hudson Taylor.

And yet, that quiet Sunday by the sea, how new the conception that had dawned upon him of the Master's meaning in those long-familiar words! It was Mrs. Taylor's birthday (October 6) and they were spending it in her father's home at Hastings. Did it recall that other memorable Sunday, on the sands at Brighton, when he had met the crisis of his life, and had yielded himself to God for the evangelisation of inland China?

What he saw now, in the light of the Holy Spirit's teaching, was a meaning so great, so comprehensive, in those few simple words—among the last that fell from the ascending Saviour's lips—that it seemed as if he heard them for the first time.

" I confess with shame," he wrote a few months later, " that until that moment the question, What did our Lord *really mean* by His command, ' Preach the Gospel to every creature,' had never been raised by me. I had laboured for many years, as have many others, to carry the Gospel further afield; had laid plans for reaching every unreached province and many smaller districts in China, without realising the plain meaning of our Saviour's words."

" *To Every Creature?* " And the total number of Protestant communicants in that great land was only forty thousand. Double the number, treble it, to include adherents, and suppose each one to be a messenger to eight of his fellow-countrymen—even so, only *one million* would be reached. " *To every creature* ": the words burned into his very soul. But how far was the Church, how far had he been himself from taking them literally, as intended to be acted upon! He saw it now, however; and with Hudson Taylor there was but one course—to obey.

" How are we going to treat the Lord Jesus Christ with reference to this command? " he wrote that very day. " Shall

we definitely drop the title Lord as applied to Him, and take
the ground that we are quite willing to recognise Him as our
Saviour, so far as the penalty of sin is concerned, but are not
prepared to own ourselves ' bought with a price,' or Him as having
any claim to our unquestioning obedience ?   Shall we say that
we are our own masters, willing to yield something as His due,
who bought us with His blood, provided He does not ask too
much ?   Our lives, our loved ones, our possessions are our own,
not His : we will give Him what we think fit, and obey any of
His requirements that do not demand too great a sacrifice ?
To be taken to heaven by Jesus Christ we are more than willing,
but we will not have this Man to *reign* over us ?

" The heart of every Christian will undoubtedly reject the
proposition, so formulated ; but have not countless lives in each
generation been lived as though it were proper ground to take ?
How few of the Lord's people have practically recognised the
truth that Christ is either *Lord of all*, or is *not Lord at all* !   If
we can judge God's Word, instead of being judged by that Word ;
if we can give to God as much or as little as we like, then *we*
are lords and He is the indebted one, to be grateful for our dole
and obliged by our compliance with His wishes.   If, on the other
hand, He is Lord, let us treat Him as such.   ' Why call ye Me,
Lord, Lord, and do not the things which I say ? ' "

So, all unexpectedly, he came to the widest outlook of
his life, the purpose that was to dominate the closing decade
of its active service.   With hair fast turning grey and fifty-
seven years of experience behind him, he met the new sense
of responsibility with the old faith and confidence.   Oh,
the fresh appeal of the old incentives ; the uprising of soul
before the old ideals ; the faithfulness to early vision, to
the first calling ; the undimmed power of the one, the ever-
supreme Love !   It is all there—all the purpose of youth
without abatement, without compromise, despite the stern
realities of four and twenty years of the grinding-mill as
leader of the Inland Mission.   It was fine, fine flour now,
but none of it was lost.   " None other Name," none other
sufficiency !   Christ and Him crucified the one the only
remedy for the sin and need of the world ; God, changeless,
inexhaustible, behind His commands and promises ; divine,
constraining love, the motive-power—it is all there, first as
last and last as first.

CHAPTER XXXIII

TO EVERY CREATURE

1889–1890. AET. 57–58.

Not a mere human project but *a divine command* was what Mr. Taylor saw in the words, " To Every Creature," that autumn day by the sea. They came to him with all the urgency of a royal mandate that brooks no delay. It was a question of duty, and no time was to be lost. " If we begin at once," he realised afresh with straitened heart, " millions will have passed away ere we can reach them."

But begin what ? Begin a definite, systematic effort to do just as the Master said—to carry the glad tidings of salvation to every man, woman and child throughout the whole of China. Was not that His order ? Did He not intend it to be obeyed ? Nothing if not practical, Mr. Taylor set himself forthwith to consider, not whether the attempt should be made, but simply—*how* ? And as he thought and prayed he came to see, first of all, that *it could be done*. There was no impossibility about the matter. Armies of scores of thousands could be sent to the ends of the earth for the sake of material conquest, and the Church had at her command resources fully equal to the obligations laid upon her.

Very simply it occurred to him, about the vast population to be reached : a million is a thousand thousands ; given a thousand evangelists, each one teaching two hundred and fifty people daily, and in a thousand days two hundred and fifty millions would have the offer of divine mercy. Surely a task that could, at this rate, be accomplished in little over *three years* should not be thought of as chimerical or beyond the resources of the Christian Church ! [1]

Many objections, he knew, could be raised to this calculation. To begin with some might think it impossible for an individual worker to reach as many as two hundred and fifty people daily ; or that, if they could, such an offer of the Gospel would accomplish little. Mr. Taylor could not but remember, however, the work he had himself done in early years, and especially the many months spent with the Rev. William Burns in thorough systematic evangelisation in districts in which there were no settled missionaries. They had not found it difficult to reach five hundred to one thousand people daily—preaching in all the streets of a given town or city, and entering every shop with books and tracts. As night came on they would repair to a previously announced tea-shop, where interested hearers could meet them for conversation, and any who wished to learn more were invited to their boats for further talk and prayer. How he had loved the work ; how often he longed to be in it still ! And as to results, he in common with many others could recall, among the brightest converts they had ever known, not a few who had truly given their hearts to Christ the first time they ever heard of Redeeming Love.

His calculation, moreover, did not take into account the help to be given by the missionaries already in China—of whom there were considerably over a thousand—nor the immense and invaluable contribution to be made by native Christians. Forty thousand church members, not to speak of enquirers, would make the proposition a very different thing from what it could be without them. He had seen enough already, even in the newly opened provinces, to know that Chinese Christians were ready to lead as well as follow in such an enterprise.

It might be said, however, that our Lord's injunction was not only to " preach the Gospel to every creature," but also to baptize and instruct—" teaching them to observe all

---

[1] Mr. Taylor at that time estimated the population of China at 250 millions, but pointed out that if, as some supposed, it reached 400 millions, the work on the scale indicated would only take five years instead of three.

things whatsoever I have commanded you "—hence the schools, settled churches and much besides, in which the large majority of missionaries were engaged. This Mr. Taylor recognised ; and none can have longed more than he to see such agencies multiplied. It was not the suspension or neglect of any existing work he was considering, but the great unmet need *beyond*. "There is that scattereth and yet increaseth," was a principle he had found deeply true in this connection ; and, after all, a thousand additional workers could not give themselves for five years to a wide-spread evangelistic campaign throughout the whole of China, without fitting themselves all the more fully for the settled work that was sure to follow.

Thus it was that in the December *China's Millions* an earnest, practical paper entitled "To Every Creature" made its appearance, outcome of the deep soul-exercise of that October day. Its plea was for immediate action, first in the realm in which every believer may have power, the realm of prayer. What part the C.I.M. might take in the forward movement Mr. Taylor did not attempt to determine. It was the united, simultaneous action of all the societies that alone could put one thousand evangelists in the field without delay. His recent visits to America satisfied him that on that side of the water fully half the required number could be found.

"Even if the Churches were unwilling," he wrote, " to take it up, are there not five hundred Christian workers in Europe who might go out at their own charges ? But shall we suppose that the Episcopalians of England, and the Presbyterians of Scotland and Ireland, have not each among them one hundred men and women fit for this glorious enterprise ? That the Methodists of the United Kingdom could not supply another hundred, and that Congregationalist and Baptist Churches could not each provide a similar contingent ? We may feel well assured that the United States and Canada would not be behind, and thus the one thousand evangelists might easily be forthcoming. How shall a project like this be translated into practice ? First, by *earnest*, believing prayer. This was our Saviour's plan, and it has been left on record for our guidance : ' The harvest truly is plenteous, but the labourers are few ; *pray ye therefore* the

Lord of the harvest that He will send forth labourers into His harvest.' When we sought for the C.I.M. the Seventy and the Hundred in prayer, and accepted them in faith, we received them in due course from His mighty, loving hand." [1]

Upon the practical suggestions of this and subsequent papers as to how the work could be done we must not dwell. Thorough division of the field, method, and co-operation were his chief points, and that the fullest use should be made of the Chinese Christians. It was no question, as he showed, of merely one offer of the Gospel, in passing, to those who had never heard. A village of a thousand might only detain the evangelists two days (working in pairs), or a neighbouring town twice as long ; but many such towns and villages would keep them in a given district for months, and interested inquirers would not lack opportunities for learning the Way of Life more perfectly. " If one offer of the Gospel is insufficient," he urged in this connection, " what shall we think of *none* ? "

But it was not the Master's *command* only that was occupying Mr. Taylor's thought, it was the Master's *example*. From the first, the feeding of the four thousand recorded in Matthew had been before his mind. No sooner had the words of Christ, " To every creature," come home to him with power than the question had arisen, almost in spite of himself, " From whence can a man satisfy these with bread here in the wilderness ? " The more he thought upon it the more he saw the whole situation in that one incident— the whole problem *and* its solution. Travelling out to China for the second General Missionary Conference, he was thankful not only for the opportunity the gathering would afford for bringing forward the matter about which he was burdened, but also for such a message. What better subject could he take for his opening sermon than the Lord Himself

---

[1] " We cannot take hold of this thing in earnest," was his conviction, " without getting more than a thousand ; and oh, the enlargement, the enrichment that would come in the train of such a movement ! Could China be blessed alone ? Would not the whole world necessarily share in the blessing ? For we could not be blessed on the field without our home churches being brought into it ; and if they were filled with spiritual life, every land would be thought of and cared for. The Church is well able to evangelise the whole world and to do it with rapidity."

face to face with that needy multitude—the *heart* of Jesus and His *sufficiency* ?

He always did preach his sermons first of all to himself, and this was no exception.

" I am so glad of your prayers for spiritual blessing for me," he wrote to Mrs. Taylor from Colombo (April 10) : " this is the one thing I want and need and must have. . . . How constantly we are all in danger of seeking our own ! Darling, I feel I have been forgetting self-denial in the true sense ; hence my unwillingness to be separated from you : and this, I fear, has brought me under a cloud. In one sense, God and His work have been first ; in another, they have not been so as they should. I have not knowingly neglected the work ; but I left you unwillingly instead of joyfully. . . . I do want to be whole-hearted in God's service. May He work this in me."

A little later he could write of being " refreshed and encouraged " (April 23), and that he had been helped by the preparation of his Conference sermon. He could tell in measure how the Redeemer's heart was going out in yearning compassion over the millions in China who were " as sheep having no shepherd," because of the reflected longing in his own soul ; and what else could have strengthened and comforted as did that sacred fellowship ?

" I am so glad it was a *great* multitude," he wrote in the draft of his discourse, " so great that the disciples thought it simply impossible to feed them. Yet the multitude were in real need, and the need too was immediate. It must either be met at once or not at all. . . . Let us notice that in these circumstances the presence of the disciples alone would not have sufficed. They might perhaps have said, ' Poor things ! ' They might have regretted that they had not more bread with them ; but they would have left the multitude hungry. But JESUS was there ; and *His presence* secured the carrying out of His compassionate purpose. All were fed, all were filled, all went away satisfied and strengthened ; and the disciples were not only reproved and instructed, but were enriched also."

It was with special joy Mr. Taylor dwelt on the fact of the multitude being no difficulty, nor yet the smallness of supplies. When all that the disciples had was placed at His disposal, the Master made it suffice and more than suffice. As for the disciples, they were much like ourselves.

They were slow to learn, they had little faith, they were easily appalled and discouraged—but they were near to JESUS. They were within sound of His voice, ready to obey His call and to listen to what He had to say.   And our blessed Master did not scold nor despise them, nor dispense with their services. He lovingly led them on and used them ; and He showed Himself so truly one with them that He would do nothing without them. . . . And can it be true that " this same Jesus," now seated on His Father's throne, is so wonderfully one with us, and with our brothers and sisters in this land, that He will do nothing without us ?   That He, " the true Vine," will bear no fruit save through us, His branches, down here ?   Oh, my brethren, can we dwell on these thoughts without our hearts burning within us ?   Gracious Saviour, is Thy wondrous love still the same, Thy wondrous power still the same, to work through such poor, unworthy instruments as we are ?   Then may I not speak for all and say, " We do now present ourselves afresh to Thee, to be filled and taught by Thy Spirit, and to be, at any cost, used of Thee for the salvation of this great people."

It was for consecration he pleaded, full consecration of all we have and are to Him Who has given Himself without reserve to us.

Now are we all, to-day, in just this relation to Christ ?   Are we before Him in unreserved consecration ?   I do not say in strong faith, I do not say in profound intelligence, I do not say in extraordinary natural or spiritual attainments, but I do say in *unreserved consecration.*   We do not know what it may mean, what it may involve, but we do not need to know.   He knows, that is enough.   We cannot love ourselves as He loves us ; we cannot care for ourselves as He cares for us.   Oh, let us trust Him fully, and now if never before, now afresh if often before, take Jesus as our Master and Lord, and with unreserved consecration give over to Him ourselves, our possessions, our loved ones, our *all*.   He is infinitely worthy ; and He will infinitely make up to us all we give to Him.   For in return for our little all, He will give us Himself and His great all.

And then, in face of the unmet need, Jesus gave thanks. He was thankful for the disciples' sake that they had given their all ; thankful for the people's sake that they were to be fed ; thankful that the Father heard His prayers always, and was now to be glorified through His Son.   " Are we always thankful for our difficulties ? " Mr. Taylor questioned. " Do we see in them the wisdom and love of God, and an excuse, as it were, all the more to claim His power and help ? "

" I do not know that we are told anywhere in the Bible to try to do anything," he continued. " ' We must try to do the best we can,' is a very common expression ; but I remember some years ago, after a remark of that kind, looking carefully through the New Testament to see under what circumstances the disciples were told to *try* to do anything. I did not expect to find many instances, but I was surprised not to find any. Then I went through the Old Testament, very carefully, and I could not find that the Lord had ever told Old Testament believers to try to do anything. There were many commands that appeared impossible to obey, but they were all definite commands : and I think we all need to set ourselves, not to try to obey our Lord as far as we can, but simply *to obey* Him."

When face to face with his audience at last—that responsible body of men and women representing all the Protestant societies at work in China—his heart overflowed the bounds of his written address.

" If as an organised Conference," he urged with conviction, " we were to set ourselves to obey the command of the Lord to the full, we should have such an outpouring of the Spirit, such a Pentecost as the world has not seen since the Holy Spirit was outpoured in Jerusalem. God gives His Spirit *not* to those who long for Him, not to those who pray for Him, not to those who desire to be filled always—but He *does* give His Holy Spirit ' to them that *obey* Him.' If as an act of obedience we were to determine that every district, every town, every village, every hamlet in this land should hear the Gospel, and that speedily, and were to set about doing it, I believe that the Spirit would come down in such mighty power that we should find supplies springing up we know not how. We should find the fire spreading from missionary to flock, and our native fellow-workers and the whole Church of God would be blessed. God gives His Holy Spirit to them that obey Him. Let us see to it that we really apprehend what His command to us is, now in the day of our opportunity—this day of the remarkable openness of the country, when there are so many facilities, when God has put steam and telegraph at the command of His people for the quick carrying out of His purposes.

" As to wealth, there is no end to His resources. Poverty

in His hands is the greatest wealth. A handful of meal blessed by the Lord is quite sufficient to accomplish any purpose the Lord chooses to accomplish with it. It is not a question of resources at all to those who are following the Master, doing what He has for them to do. . . . Let us just obey and cease to reason : and He Who cares for us and for the multitude *to-day* will make no mistake, and will not change to-morrow."

CHAPTER XXXIV

THE COMING THOUSAND

1890–1891.   AET. 58–59.

THE Conference appealed for the Thousand—a thousand men within the next five years, for all forms of missionary work in China.   Taken by representative leaders of American and Continental as well as English Societies, this united action could not but have weight with all sections of the Church at home on either side of the Atlantic.

" We make this appeal," they wrote, " on behalf of three hundred millions of unevangelised heathen ; we make it with the earnestness of our whole hearts, as men overwhelmed with the magnitude and responsibility of the work before us ; we make it with unwavering faith in the power of the risen Saviour to call men into His vineyard, and to open the hearts of those who are His stewards to send out and support them, and we shall not cease to cry mightily to Him that He will do this thing, and that our eyes may see it."

To Mr. Taylor, who was Chairman of the Committee appointed to report the outcome, this step was cause for profound thankfulness.   It was not all he had hoped for, but it went a long way in that direction.   To one who was with him alone just after the opening service, he spoke more freely than he could in public.   His sermon had deeply moved the Conference, though what would be the practical result remained to be seen.

" I believe that the Lord would have us appeal for the Thousand," he said earnestly.   " I believe that if we asked for them for the C.I.M., He would give them.   But," he added with the quietness of a God-subdued spirit, " I believe that He would have *all* His servants in China share both in the prayer and in the blessing."

Meanwhile, in other scenes and unexpected ways, the hand of God was working. Simultaneously, though independently of each other, four ministers in Melbourne had been much exercised about China's spiritual need and claims. It was the very time, strange to say, when Mr. Taylor was writing the papers afterwards published in his little pamphlet " To Every Creature "—the close of 1889. To each of them came the conviction that Australian Christians ought to be doing something toward the evangelisation of the greatest heathen country in the world, and the heathen country nearest their own shores. Of the four, two were Episcopalians, the Rev. H. B. Macartney and his curate, the Rev. C. H. Parsons ; one was a Presbyterian, the Rev. W. Lockhart Morton, and one a Baptist, the Rev. Alfred Bird. After some weeks, when they discovered that the burden was one they shared in common, the friends met together for prayer, and it was not long before they found that the Lord was calling one of their number to give his own life to the work. His place could be filled at home, but few were thinking of the greater need beyond.

Missions to the New Hebrides and New Guinea, as well as in some parts of India, were receiving the support of Australian Christians at this time, but partly in consequence of racial prejudice against the Chinese in their midst, nothing was being done for the vast and populous land from which they came. Yet it was evident that these merchants, market-gardeners, and laundry-men represented a strong, sagacious people, capable of wonderful response to the redeeming love of Christ. Thus when the curate at Caulfield, near Melbourne, desired to go as a missionary to China, it was necessary to seek a connection with one of the societies in the old country. This led to a correspondence with the Inland Mission ; to the acceptance of Mr. Parsons, and his sailing for Shanghai shortly before the Conference which had brought Mr. Taylor from England, and to the earnest desire on the part of his friends in Victoria that a local Council should be formed, to work in connection with the C.I.M. as did the Councils in Toronto and elsewhere.

Nor was this all—for in the neighbouring island of Tasmania similar results had been arrived at, though in a different way. A young missionary who had gone out from England as an Associate of the Mission was obliged, through failing health, to return to Launceston about the time that Mr. Taylor was writing the above-mentioned papers. There in the home of her mother, Mrs. Henry Reed of Mount Pleasant, and in the church built in her father's memory, of which Mr. George Soltau was then pastor, her influence was telling in a remarkable way. China in all its need was the burden on her heart, and as she spoke of it in meetings, with the love and zeal of one who was following in the footsteps of the Master, many were moved with the same spirit. The result was that gifts began to flow in and offers of service, so that just as Mr. Parsons set out from Melbourne to urge the formation of a branch of the Mission in Victoria, Mr. George Soltau was writing to the same effect, conveying Mrs. Henry Reed's desire as well as his own that their old friend, Mr. Hudson Taylor, would visit the Colonies and form a Council for carrying on the work.

Before an answer could be received to these invitations, still further developments had taken place. Mr. Alfred Bird, on a visit to Tasmania, had been welcomed under Mrs. Reed's hospitable roof, and there had met her daughter from China and learned the above circumstances. This was news indeed to carry back to his friends in Melbourne, who heartily endorsed his invitation to Miss Mary Reed and her sister to come over for a campaign of meetings. A missionary from China was a novelty in those days, especially one who had lived in the interior, wearing native dress and working at her own charges. Drawing-rooms, churches, and college halls were thrown open, and the sisters found themselves overwhelmed with work, which resulted in many gifts and candidates for the Mission.

To Mr. Taylor, in the midst of the Conference, all this was full of encouragement. If in China they were being led to ask great things for the Lord's work, He was certainly showing, under the Southern Cross, that He could open up fresh channels of supply. The new headquarters of the Mission also, to which he had been welcomed on landing, encouraged thoughts of development. Commenced as he was leaving China little more than a year previously, these ample premises were completed just in time for his return, and to receive the members of the Mission, eighty of whom gathered for the Conference and for the C.I.M. meetings which followed. The opening of the hall for prayer and public services, and the wedding that took place a few days later, when the generous donor of land and buildings married a fellow-member of the Mission—all the bridal party being in Chinese dress—attracted many friends, and called attention to the wonderful provision the Lord had made for the needs of the growing work.

Upon the C.I.M. Conference we must not dwell, nor upon the subsequent Council Meetings, when for three weeks the leaders of the Mission were occupied with problems of the work and with preparation for future developments. A cable to Melbourne authorising the formation of the proposed Council had put matters in train for Mr. Taylor's visit to the Australian states, and by the end of July he found himself free to set out.[1]

" In the midst of much joy and much sorrow," he wrote to Mr. Theodore Howard before leaving, " the presence of our dear Lord has been a constant feast and a deep rest. The Lord has immense blessing in store for us."

Travelling native passage to Hongkong to save expense, Mr. Taylor and his companions—Mr. Montagu Beauchamp and a secretary—could hardly feel as if they had left China. For they still wore Chinese dress, and, crowded between decks with many fellow-passengers, they had all they could

---

[1] The Australian Council, formed on the 22nd of May 1890, two days after the close of the Shanghai Conference, consisted of a representative group of ministers and laymen : the Revs. H. B. Macartney (Chairman), S. Chapman, Alfred Bird (Hon. Secretary), W. Lockhart Morton, D. O'Donnell, and George Soltau ; the Hon. James Campbell, Dr. Simpson Flett, and Mr. Philip Kitchen (Treasurer). At their first session they had the names of eight candidates for the Mission before them.

do to endure the heat of those August days. The change to a native inn on the quay in Chinatown, Hongkong, while waiting for a steamer to take them on to Sydney, was all the more welcome.

" They put us in an upper storey," wrote Mr. Beauchamp of this experience, " so we had the full benefit of the harbour with all its shipping, the shrieking whistles of countless steam-launches being thrown into the bargain. We had Chinese meals and paid by the day—a dollar and a half covering everything for the party. They gave us a room to ourselves. It was absolute clover ! "

When Port Darwin was reached, the Superintendent of the Steamship Company determined to transfer these " steerage passengers " to the almost empty first-class quarters. Knowing that Mr. Taylor would not consent to such an arrangement, he took advantage of their being detained ashore by a meeting to send word to the Captain to move their belongings, and on returning to the ship at night they were informed that so many Chinese were coming on board that they could no longer be accommodated in the fore-cabin. In great comfort, therefore, they finished the journey : at Thursday Island, even Mr. Beauchamp discarding his Chinese garments for more conventional attire. Hardly had he done so when, in the course of a stroll ashore, he met a friend who would have had difficulty in recognising him a few hours previously. In a pleasant bungalow in that remote spot, he saw, or thought he saw, no less a personage than Henry Drummond. Not feeling quite sure, he mentioned his name aloud in passing, when the Professor looked up quickly, and their surprise and pleasure were mutual.[1]

Of the full weeks that followed the arrival of the party much might be said did limits of space permit ; for open doors awaited them on every hand, and friends old and new

[1] Crossing the Gulf of Carpentaria, Mr. Taylor had noted in his journal that it was a gulf so large that the whole of Ireland might lie upon its waters and be out of sight of land. Many of the islands passed before reaching Australia appealed to him both by their great natural beauty and spiritual darkness. The fine mountains of Celebes and the hills of Timor, wooded down to the water's edge, made a picture not soon to be forgotten. Of the latter he wrote . " It is thirty-six years since I saw this island before, and still *nothing is being done for the souls of its people.*"

were generous with help and sympathy. As it is, however, the story of outward activities must be curtailed for details of greater significance. " Do not speak to me," was said by a thoughtful observer in another connection : " what you *are* thunders so loud that I cannot hear what you say." What message, in this sense, had Mr. Taylor's quiet, steadfast, God-impressed life for the go-ahead world of the Colonies ?

Beginning in Melbourne, where at first the meetings were not large, Mr. Taylor had time to become personally acquainted with the members of the Council, and both there and in Tasmania it was noticed how he laid himself out to help these and other friends in the duties they had undertaken. Of a meeting in the drawing-room at Mount Pleasant to consider the important question of candidates, one who took part in it wrote :

Never can I forget how helpfully Mr. Taylor led us on to see the needs, so that we suggested the rules to be made and the line to be taken by the Council, wholly unaware at the moment of how he was guiding our thought. But that was characteristic of Mr. Taylor ! the grace of our Lord Jesus Christ so overflowing, that those who listened were for the time being scarcely conscious of the wisdom and power behind his words.

The same friend remembered accompanying Mr. Taylor to a meeting in Launceston, when he stopped in the middle of the street, and, looking up, said without any introduction :

" There should be only one circumstance to us in life, and that Circumstance—God."

" What a genius he had for giving utterance to telling sentences," she recalled, " which, like nails driven by a skilful hand, *remain*. I do not think I ever met him without carrying away some such word ; and many of them have spoken comfort to my heart again and again, and to others, as I have passed them on."

His simplicity and the naturalness of all he said and did impressed many. As the meetings became better known, large buildings were filled with eager hearers ; but he was still the same, and as free from self-consciousness as a child. One occasion was long remembered in Melbourne, when a large Presbyterian Church was crowded, the Moderator himself occupying the Chair. In eloquent, well-chosen phrases he enlarged upon what had been accomplished in China through Mr. Taylor's instrumentality, finally introducing him to the audience as " our illustrious guest."

Quietly Mr. Taylor stood for a moment, " the light of God on his face," as one who was present recalled, and then began his address by saying in a way that won all hearts : " Dear friends, I am the little servant of an illustrious Master."

Children were drawn to him, just as in Sweden, and indeed wherever he went. After a meeting in Government House, Hobart, where he was cordially welcomed by Sir Robert and Lady Hamilton, it was just like him to return with pleasure to the nursery of the home in which he was entertained, a few miles out of the city.

" He was just beautiful with little ones," wrote his hostess, Mrs. Fagg, formerly of Singapore. " He took each child in our home, and kneeling with them apart, presented them one by one to his Heavenly Father for definite blessing. . . . Two of those children are now engaged in missionary work, one in India and one in China."

It was the latter, little Edith, only three years old at the time of Mr. Taylor's visit, who remembered him with special affection. A year or two later, when she achieved the triumph of knitting a doll's garment, nothing would do but that it must be sent to China, to Mr. Taylor—" 'Cause I love him so ! "

But it was on those of ripe experience that he made the most impression, and the deeper the spiritual life the more it responded to his own. Thus his host in Melbourne for a fortnight, the Rev. H. B. Macartney, wrote :

He was an object lesson in quietness. He drew from the Bank of Heaven every farthing of his daily income—" My peace I give unto you." Whatever did not agitate the Saviour, or ruffle *His* spirit was not to agitate him. The serenity of the Lord Jesus concerning any matter and at its most critical moment, this was his ideal and practical possession. He knew nothing of rush or hurry, of quivering nerves or vexation of spirit. He knew there was a peace passing all understanding, and that he could not do without it.

Now I was altogether different.   Mine is a peculiarly nervous disposition, and with a busy life I found myself in a tremor all day long.   I did not enjoy the Lord as I knew I ought.   Nervous agitation possessed me as long as there was anything to be done. The greatest loss of my life was the loss of the light of the Lord's presence and fellowship during writing hours.   The daily mail robbed me of His delightful society.

" I am in the study, you are in the big spare room," I said to Mr. Taylor at length.   " You are occupied with millions, I with tens.   Your letters are pressingly important, mine of comparatively little moment.   Yet I am worried and distressed, while you are always calm.   Do tell me what makes the difference."

" My dear Macartney," he replied, " the peace you speak of is in my case more than a delightful privilege, it is a necessity."

He said most emphatically, " I could not possibly get through the work I have to do without the peace of God ' which passeth all understanding ' keeping my heart and mind."

That was my chief experience of Mr. Taylor : Are you in a hurry, flurried, distressed ?   Look up !   See the Man in the Glory !   Let the face of Jesus shine upon you—the face of the Lord Jesus Christ.   Is He worried, troubled, distressed ?   There is no wrinkle on His brow, no least shade of anxiety.   Yet the affairs are His as much as yours.

" Keswick teaching " as it is called was not new to me at that time.   I had received those glorious truths and was preaching them to others.   But here was *the real thing*—an embodiment of " Keswick teaching " such as I had never hoped to see. This impressed me profoundly :—here is a man almost sixty years of age, bearing tremendous burdens, yet absolutely calm and unruffled.   Oh, the pile of letters !   any one of which might contain news of death, of shortness of funds, of riots or serious trouble.   Yet all were opened, read and answered with the same tranquillity—Christ his reason for peace, his power for calm. Dwelling in Christ he partook of His very being and resources, in the midst of and concerning the very matters in question. And he did this by an act of faith as simple as it was continuous.

Yet he was delightfully free and natural.   I can find no words to describe it save the Scriptural expression " *in God*." He was " in God " all the time, and God in him.   It was that true " abiding " of John xv.   But oh, the *lover-like* attitude that underlay it !   He had in relation to Christ a most bountiful experience of the Song of Solomon.   It was a wonderful combination—the strength and tenderness of one who, amid stern preoccupation, like that of a judge on the bench, carried in his heart the light and love of home.

It was this element of delight in God that made him so responsive to the beauty of His works, from the greatest to the least. Behind our house lay an extensive field " in Chancery " all overgrown with epacrid, heather and Australian wild flowers. Oh, his enjoyment of it ! He would go out after his letters had been sent to the post and wander over the common, standing in the midst of that blaze of colour and beauty with the rapture of a child. " All things were made by *Him* " : this was the secret of his unfailing joy in them.

The influence of Mr. Taylor's public utterances may be judged from the result of the meetings.

" Funds are coming in, and many promising candidates offer," he wrote two months after landing. " Fifty-seven was the number I last heard mentioned."

More than sixty applied to join the Mission before the time came for Mr. Taylor's return to China, and many others were profoundly influenced who found their life-work in India and elsewhere. Such, for example, was the young evangelist who felt quite annoyed when he saw in the local paper an announcement of Mr. Taylor's Hobart meetings. He had no sympathy at that time, no patience even, with those who advocated foreign missions ; being convinced, through certain preconceptions, that the whole idea was mistaken and unscriptural. Mr. Reeve was an earnest Bible student, however, and when drawn to the meetings in spite of himself the first thing he noticed was that the speaker, whatever might be his vagaries, was certainly dealing faithfully with the Word of God. Indeed as he listened, Charles Reeve felt that he had never heard the Bible more truly and helpfully expounded, though the conclusions he could not escape ran counter to his strongest convictions up to that hour. For it was on the back seat of that hall, as Mr. Taylor's earnest voice went on, that the call of God came to him, and the Poona and Indian Village Mission of to-day, with its band of devoted workers, is the outcome.

The best of the meetings were naturally the last, when

Mr. Taylor was surrounded by the bright young volunteers who were returning with him to China. He had had no hesitation in letting it be known that he was praying for a hundred fellow-workers from Australasia, and the large number who had already come forward awakened the deepest interest. When the Council arranged for a day of prayer and conference for ministers only, to meet Mr. Taylor and Mr. Beauchamp, no fewer than forty attended ; and the same evening the Melbourne Town Hall witnessed an enthusiastic gathering of three thousand people to bid farewell to the party.

" Many souls have been saved and blessed through these meetings," Mr. Taylor was able to write to Mr. Stevenson. " God is stirring the hearts of His people here ; and if we had more time, we might look for a hundred workers from these Colonies and New Zealand before very long. As it is, I believe the Lord will do great things for China."

Four young men, Miss Mary Reed, and seven other ladies composed the party which was to sail with Mr. Taylor in October. But the vessel was delayed owing to a strike of dock labourers, and an invitation for meetings in Queensland, which he had had to decline, recurred to Mr. Taylor's mind. He little knew how much prayer there had been behind that invitation, or the outgoings of heart with which the Queensland vicar and his wife thought of great, dark China, far away. Their home was attractive, the living one of the best in the Colony, and their work congenial. But the appeal of the Shanghai Conference had reached them, and Mr. Southey noted that ordained men were specially asked for. His health was not very robust, and with three young children to think of, it might well have seemed that he was doing all he could, by earnestly forwarding the cause of missions at home. But this did not satisfy his conscience before God.

" I cannot help feeling," he wrote to Mr. Taylor when he heard that the latter was really coming, " that some of the Ipswich ministers ought to go to the heathen. In a town of eight or nine thousand inhabitants—of whom not quite two-thirds are Protestants—there are nine Protestant churches with ten ministers; and not one of the churches is ever really full. It is not from any wish to change that I write this. I am only anxious to do my Father's will. I am perfectly willing to stay in Queensland if it is His will, and I am willing if it be His will to go to the heathen. There is plenty to do here. Spiritual religion in all the churches is at a sadly low ebb, and there is but little missionary zeal. . . . So that I may truly say that there is work for a child of God here; but it does seem that there is more among the heathen."

Few experiences ever touched Mr. Taylor more deeply than the visit to this happy, delightful home, which the parents were so ready to forsake for the love that is stronger than any earthly tie. Mr. Southey, when he met him that early summer morning,[1] was for a moment disappointed. He had heard and thought so much about the veteran missionary, that he unconsciously expected some one of imposing appearance; and when a single passenger alighted from the express and came toward him, he could hardly believe it was the visitor expected.

"On reaching home," he wrote some years later, "I mentioned this feeling of disappointment to my wife, adding, however, ' I am sure he is a good man.'

"But she was of quicker discernment than I, and after a little chat with our guest came and said, ' Look at the light in his face.'

"And truly Mr. Taylor did have the light of God in his face. So constantly did he look up to God, and so deep was his communion with God, that his very face seemed to have upon it a heavenly light. He had not been many hours in the house before the first sense of disappointment gave place to a deep reverence and love, and I realised as never before what the grace of God could do. Often and often had I longed to go to Keswick, but now God in His love had sent Keswick to me, and I was permitted not to listen to beautiful teaching, but to see the beauty of a life lived in abiding fellowship with the Lord Jesus. In the house he was all that a guest should be, kind, courteous, considerate, gracious. He at once fell into the routine of the household, was punctual at the meal table, studied to give the minimum of trouble, and was swift to notice and to express his thanks for every little service rendered. We could not help noticing the utter lack of self-assertion about him, and his true because

---

[1] Christmas being midsummer, of course, in that southern world.

unconscious humility. About the Lord and His grace and faith-fulness he spoke freely ; about himself and his service he said nothing. Only by questioning did we learn anything of his own labours or experiences, but when he was thus drawn out, how much he had to tell !

"While he was with us the question of our going to China was discussed, and though from the very first he seemed to feel that our offer was of the Lord, yet he took pains to set before us the whole facts of the case. The climate, the discomforts, the absence of medical help, the necessity of parting from the children, etc., were fully gone into. He certainly did not lead us out by withholding from us the real facts ; and more than once after walking up and down our garden, which seemed to have a great charm for him, he said to my wife, ' You won't have a garden like this in China ! ' "

But the refuge in God that they would have, and the certainty of His sustaining grace, was confirmed to them by all they saw of their visitor, and had not a little to do with the step of faith which gave to China two of its truest helpers and to the Mission, ultimately, its beloved Home Director for Australia and New Zealand.

Wonderful were the developments of that winter, both before and after Mr. Taylor's return to China. Arriving on Sunday the 21st of December, he had the joy of finding Mrs. Taylor awaiting him. Arrangements had at last been possible to free her from home responsibilities, and she had long felt that her place was at his side. Unable to be at the last Saturday prayer meeting before leaving Pyrland Road, she had written to the friends to whom she had been in the habit of giving recent news from China :

I had wanted to ask you—when some one else rises to read the letters—to lift your hearts to God for me, and say : " Make her a blessing to her husband : make her a blessing wherever she goes."

We may visit many stations. In a few weeks I hope to join the Shanghai prayer meeting, and I want to cheer them on. May I tell them that you are more in earnest for blessing than ever ? If the Gospel is to be given " To every creature," much will depend on you, dear friends. You must take hold upon God for this. You must uphold our hands in believing, fervent prayer. The work is yours as well as ours, and so will the reward be. The Lord unite your hearts in one, and bow them before Himself in compassion for the lost. Oh, that we could have heart breakings at home over the state of the world! Dr. Pierson says, " Prayer has turned every great crisis in the kingdom of God." It is a solemn question for each one of us, " What are my prayers really effecting ? " Do we know that we *have* the petitions that we desire of Him ?

I want to carry fresh inspiration to the Training Home at Anking, and to the Sisters in Yang-chow. Will you pray that to every place we are allowed to visit, my beloved husband and I may be taken in the power of the Spirit ? The enemy's tactics are to divide, to discourage, to deaden. Let us realise our one-ness in Christ ; let us be strong and of a good courage, and seek zealously and continuously the quickening influences of the Holy Spirit. God grant that the Saturday prayer meeting, which has brought such blessing in the past, may this winter be more than ever a meeting-place with God. We praise for what has been done ; but when we look at what needs to be done, when we think of what might be done, we must humble ourselves before God. Time is short, opportunity great : let us be downright in earnest.

Absent nine years from China, Mrs. Taylor saw great changes, great advance on every hand, and her presence seemed to double Mr. Taylor's capacity for work and happiness in it. And there was need of all he could do and be that winter, to keep pace with the unprecedented growth of the Mission. Great had been the joy in 1887 when a hundred new workers had come out within twelve months ; but now, in *half* that time, *a hundred and thirty-one* were received in Shanghai for the C.I.M. alone. Sixty-six of them, indeed, arrived in little over three weeks—a new thing on any mission field! And the sources of supply were no less remarkable than the numbers.[1]

[1] The analysis of these arrivals was as follows : from October 19 to December 25, 1890, nine parties reached Shanghai from Europe, Canada, and Australia, numbering in all fifty-three new workers. From January 1 to April 12, 1891, seven parties from Europe, the United States, Canada, and Australia were received, adding seventy-eight new workers, the last party being that of Mr. Southey.

The sixty-six who arrived in little over three weeks were the Scandinavian thirty-five on February 17, followed by nine from England on February 21, four from Canada on February 26, three from Australia on the 7th of March, and the second detachment of the Scandinavian party,

Far away in northern Europe, the little pamphlet "To Every Creature" had fallen into the hands of a devoted evangelist, the Rev. F. Franson—Swedish by birth but a naturalised American—who had worked for seven years with D. L. Moody. Always keen about foreign missions, its appeal for absolute loyalty to the Lord Jesus Christ and unquestioning obedience to His great command fired a soul whose zeal could not but move others. Twice had Franson been in prison for his uncompromising earnestness in preaching the Gospel; and now, with a burning heart, he carried this new crusade throughout the region where he then was, which happened to be northern Germany. Wonderfully used of God, he was the means of widespread blessing, and meeting in Barmen with kindred spirits—Messrs. Polnick, Paas, and others—it was there the missionary interest specially developed. The China Alliance Mission was the result, and wishing to work on the lines of the C.I.M. its leaders entered into correspondence with Mr. Taylor. It was not long before its first representatives sailed for China as associates of the Inland Mission; but Franson, by that time, had entered upon another campaign, among the Scandinavian churches in America.

Well known throughout the States, he had no lack of openings, and he proceeded on the plan, as he wrote to Mr. Taylor, of encouraging the Lord's people "to give support each church to one missionary."

"This plan has proved to be a very good one," he continued. "I have succeeded very well. Not only have this party their support secured, but another expedition of some ten will leave Omaha twelve days later than this one. We arrange it so that we do not send any who has not been used of God to blessing for souls. . . . A good many have offered themselves but have been refused, some on the ground of insufficient health, some on the ground of incapability for mission work. A very great interest has been created all over America among Scandinavians, through my personal visits and the visits of these missionaries."

Chosen men and women of devoted spirit, their intention

which arrived on March 10, proved to number fifteen—five more than had been expected. Well was it that the new C.I.M. Home in Shanghai was not only spacious but elastic, and in good working order.

was, as Mr. Franson explained, to do itinerant work;
" that is to be of the Thousand Mr. Taylor has prayed to the
Lord about—to do just that work."

They are prepared to go from place to place preaching the
Gospel, distributing tracts and Bibles, as the Lord may lead
for at least three years . . . and not to marry during this time,
or even get engaged to marriage. . . . I suppose it best that
they procure Chinese clothes as soon as they arrive.

Their desire was to be associated with the C.I.M., just
as the Swedish and German Alliance Missions were, and to
be under the direction of Mr. Taylor and his representatives
no less than that of their own leaders. It was a large contribution, as it proved, to the ranks of the Mission.

Never can one of the writers forget coming down the long
verandah of the Mission-house with Mr. Stevenson that
February morning, in glorious sunshine, just as two young
men of pleasing appearance presented themselves at the
main entrance.

" They must be the Scandinavians," said the Deputy
Director, going to meet them ; for he had just been speaking
of Mr. Franson's party.

" How many are you ? " was a necessary question in
view of providing accommodation.

" We are thirty-five," came the astonishing reply, " and
there are ten more, or perhaps fifteen, who will be here next
week."

Thirty-five in one party, and more to follow ! hardly
could we take it in. But the dear fellows looked so happy,
and were so anxious to bring up all the others to share their
welcome, that there was no room for hesitation. The only
thing to do was to receive them, full though the house
seemed already, thankfully realising that they were given of
God in answer to prayer, part of the coming Thousand.

And who that was then in the Mission-house was not
cheered and blessed through the coming of the Scandinavian
Fifty ? Faith set to music was the atmosphere they carried
with them. To the accompaniment of their guitars and
hearts overflowing with praise, they taught us many a sweet
refrain from their Swedish hymns. Few of them could

speak much English, but they prayed with perfect freedom in our meetings, and though we could not understand—save where the oft-repeated " Chere Herre Jesu " or " Kina, Kina " came in—the sense of fellowship in Christ was very real.

It's best to go singing, to go singing all the way,

was one chorus they translated for us ; and no less characteristic was the postscript to a letter of united thanks they wrote on leaving Shanghai for their up-country destinations :

" March along—we are going to conquer ! We have victory through the Blood."

CHAPTER XXXV

DEEPENING THE CHANNELS

1891–1892. AET. 59–60.

YET with all this growth and encouragement, seldom had there been a time of more serious and widespread danger for foreigners in China, or of greater strain for Mr. Taylor as leader of the Mission. The Scandinavian Fifty had hardly gone singing on their way when riots began to break out all along the Yangtze valley. In place after place Mission premises were destroyed, and though the fury of the people was specially directed against the Romanists, all foreigners were more or less imperilled. Even in Shanghai it seemed uncertain whether the authorities would be able to restrain looting and violence, and little sleep was to be had on more than one hot summer night because a riot was expected before morning.

Mr. Stevenson, meanwhile, had been obliged to take needed furlough, after five years of heavy directorial responsibilities. This left Mr. Taylor in sole charge in Shanghai and unable to leave headquarters, gladly as he would have gone to the help of those in more difficult situations. It was the women workers of the Mission who were specially on his heart, the little groups alone in the interior, with no human protection or companionship save that of the native Christians ; and great was the comfort of letters such as the following :

" There has been a good deal of *iao-ien* (wild talk) since the riots," wrote Miss Mackintosh from the Kwang-sin river, " but we go quietly on as usual. ' Under His shadow ' there is perfect safety anywhere. The six Swedish sisters are here, and are getting along with the language. The sisters from Kwang-feng are here also during the heat, so we are a party of thirteen, and all well and happy. . . . ' Jesus Himself drew near.' "

" Jesus Himself drew near " : yes, that was the secret of peace at many a post of danger. One missionary, not of the C.I.M., was murdered while waiting for a steamer on the Yangtze,[1] and with him the Customs official (European) who had gone to his relief ; and everywhere rumours were most menacing.

" The great enemy of souls has been simply raging against missions in China," Mr. Taylor wrote to Mrs. Fagg in Hobart some months later. " I look on the recent riots as Satan's reply to the Conference appeal for a thousand additional workers. God will have His response, however ; and while the enemy is mighty, God alone is almighty."

His chief concern was that the Mission should stand for real faith at such a time, setting an example of quietness and confidence in God to the Chinese Christians.

" We are continually encouraging our converts to brave persecution and to suffer loss for Christ's sake," he wrote in a circular letter upon how to act in times of danger,[2] " and they are apt to think that it is easy for us to speak in this way, seeing that, as far as they can tell, we are well-off and exposed to no danger or loss. When, therefore, we are in danger they will mark our conduct very closely, and judge for themselves how far we really believe that ' Sufficient is His arm alone, and our defence is sure.'

" What a loss it would be if any of them should think that we relied more upon a gunboat or a band of soldiers than upon the living God ! Years of teaching would not impress them as our conduct at such times may do. Moreover their sympathy will be drawn out toward us when they see us willing to suffer for the Gospel, as they so often have to do. A time of danger is a grand opportunity for being an object-lesson to the native Christians."

For five long months, from May to October, the excitement continued, notwithstanding an Imperial proclamation

---

[1] Much sympathy was felt for the Wesleyans in the loss of this promising young worker, Mr. Argent of the Joyful News Mission, killed at Wu-süeh in May 1891.   [2] Dated June 17, 1891.

which had a good effect. With few exceptions, C.I.M. workers were enabled to remain at their stations, none of which were actually rioted, though many were seriously threatened. Prayer for rain in June was wonderfully answered, and again in October, when the Council Meetings were adjourned in order that all in the Mission-house at Shanghai might unite in waiting upon God for deliverance. The summer had been intensely hot, and nothing was so likely to quiet the people as steady, continuous rain, which was much needed. Prayer was earnest and definite therefore, in this connection, and three weeks later a letter from Mrs. Taylor recorded the definite answer : " Rain has been coming down almost all this month." The effect was just what was hoped for : crowds were scattered, and gradually the anti-foreign feeling died down for the time being, and normal conditions were restored.

Meanwhile burdens of a different nature were pressing more and more heavily. With a mission embracing so many workers, widely scattered over a vast territory, all to be counselled, guided, sustained by prayer, supplied with means and many of the necessaries of life, it was inevitable that much of care, if not anxiety, should come upon its responsible head in Shanghai. To his beloved friend the Home Director in London, Mr. Taylor wrote in June :

Even you, dear Mr. Howard, can scarcely realise what it is to be out here, to know and love our dear workers, to hear of their sorrows and difficulties, their disappointments and their strifes ; learning of sickness, needing arrangements for succour if possible ; receiving telegrams asking for direction in peril, or telling it may be of death ; accounts coming in of massacre and arson, and all the untold incidents of our ever-varying experience—not to speak of the *ordinary* responsibilities and the pecuniary claim of a mission now approaching five hundred in number. There is just one way to avoid being overwhelmed —to bring everything as it arises to our Master ; and He does help, and He does not misunderstand.

Often had the question of funds to be brought to the Lord at this time, for it was one that was causing Mr. Taylor no little exercise of mind. With a rapidly growing and encouraging work on the field, the income received in

England had been falling for two or three years. Believing as he did that every gift to the Mission was the outcome of a divinely given impulse, Mr. Taylor could not but search his own life again and again, and prayerfully consider every aspect of the work to see whether there might be anything hindering the blessing of the Lord in this respect. His heart was kept in peace about it and about all the pressure that was upon him, but apart from the daily miracle of sustaining grace it would have been far otherwise.[1]

And there were other trials that led to even deeper exercise of heart and mind. For the relation of the work in China to the Council at home had not yet passed beyond the experimental stage, in which questions were apt to come up that were difficult of settlement. The whole idea of the Mission in this connection—government on the field rather than from a distance—was so new and contrary to received traditions that it was no wonder it had to win its way gradually, and in face, at times, of criticism and questioning. To Mr. Taylor with his thorough grasp of the problems to be dealt with, nothing could be clearer than that the control of affairs in China must be vested in men of expert knowledge, leaders in whom their fellow-missionaries would have confidence, able to deal with matters effectively on the spot. It was easy to see that in the home centres the Directors and Councils must be free to apply the principles of the Mission to their own problems and decide their own line of action in accordance with them ; but it needed time and experience to make it equally plain that the China administration must be upon the same footing. In principle this had been conceded from the first ; but it was one thing to have confidence in Mr. Taylor's

[1] " I should feel anxious if the work were my work," he had written to a friend in England (Jan. 1891), " but it is the Lord's work ; and though I do not see my way, the Lord sees His way, and I am thinking of Miss Warner's hymn : ' My heart is resting, O my God, I will give thanks and sing,' etc. I never saw my way less, or felt more at rest."

And in February, to another correspondent : " I need your prayers for strength and guidance. I should feel very concerned at the present aspect of matters had I not a deep consciousness that God is with us, and that He will care and provide for His own work. Thank God, I never had more deep rest and manifest help than in this hour of need. ' The LORD reigneth,' how can we but rejoice ! "

management as long as matters were in his own hands, and quite another to transfer that confidence to the China Council. Yet this was a cardinal point in the organisation he was building up, sometimes amid much of trial and perplexity.

" Mr. Berger is quite right," he wrote to Mr. Stevenson in this connection (May '91), " that the supreme question is that of final headship, and it is equally clear to me that it can only be vested in China ; but great gentleness and patience will be needed to make the reasonableness of this clear to all. It is the Lord's work, and He Who is most deeply interested *will* help us."

To one of Mr. Taylor's tender, affectionate nature divergence of judgement from those he esteemed highly, and to whom the Mission was indebted for much self-sacrificing service, was peculiarly painful, especially when, as in the present case, it was long continued. But there could be no question of compromise upon so vital an issue.

" We may make mistakes in China," he wrote again to Mr. Theodore Howard (Aug. 28), " and no doubt mistakes have been made in the past ; but evils far more serious would result from abandoning what I am convinced are God-given lines for the C.I.M."

Much as it would have meant to him therefore, amid all the pressure of this period, to have had the full and sympathetic concurrence ultimately secured in these matters, there was nothing for it but to wait upon God and to wait His time. And meanwhile the whole situation was being thought out and prayed over, both in England and China, in a way that could not but strengthen the work in days to come.

" The Lord doubtless has His purpose in permitting it," Mr. Taylor wrote to Mr. Stevenson at the close of the year (Dec. '91), " and to learn any lesson He may have to teach us is more important than getting rid of the trouble."

What could have been more encouraging under the circumstances than just the outpourings of spiritual blessing, both in the spring of the year and at its close, with which

the Lord was pleased to cheer His servants in Shanghai ?
No one could relieve Mr. Taylor of burdens that pressed
the heaviest, but others might be channels of divine grace
through which the entire Mission should be refreshed.

Such a channel was Mr. Frost, now paying his first visit
to China.   Arriving with a party from Toronto in February,
he stayed till well on in the summer, making a considerable
journey round the nearer stations.   A conference of American
workers gathered in Shanghai to meet him proved a time
of real spiritual help.[1]   " We would see Jesus," the hymn
with which it opened, had to be modified ere the close to a
version more in keeping with radiant lives and faces :

> We *have* seen Jesus—the great rock foundation
> Whereon our feet were set with sovereign grace ;
> Nor life, nor death, with all their agitation
> Can thence remove us, as we see His face.

Early in the autumn Mr. Cassels arrived from his far
western province to attend the Council Meetings, and the
Misses Newcombe of the C.M.S.—soon to lay down their
lives for Christ's sake—came up from Foo-chow on a visit.
All these brought blessing to the resident staff and the
many coming and going in the Mission-house.   They spoke
much of the life that is " No longer I but Christ" in practical
reality, but best of all *they lived it*.   And is there anything
else so sure to awaken hunger in other hearts ?

" There is a real spirit of prayer and quickening in the Home
here, praise God ! " Mrs. Taylor wrote on November 7.

A week later Mr. and Mrs. Orr-Ewing arrived from
England, and with them Mr. Walter B. Sloan, whose way
had opened, after years of prayer, to join the Mission.
Before going on to An-king to commence the study of the
language, he gave in a series of Bible Readings some of the
deeper things learned in that waiting time.   The Word
was with power, and many of his hearers could have said
with Mr. Macartney of Melbourne :

The peace you enjoy has made me envious : I want to have

---

[1] Mr. Southey, who had just arrived from Queensland, and Mr. Taylor
also took part in this conference.

more of it, and from the same Source. This, I think, I can truly say—the absence of it, or the interruptions of it, make me more uncomfortable and unhappy than ever before. This, too, is a work of the Holy Spirit for which I am thankful ; but I long to pass completely from the reign of ever-recurring conviction to the reign of ever-increasing rest.[1]

Then a great uplift was given, as the year drew to a close, by the coming of a C.M.S. party with Mr. and Mrs. Heywood Horsburgh from England. These beloved friends had the sorrow of losing a precious child in Shanghai, but from stricken hearts only love and blessing flowed to others. The tide of spiritual life was deepening, and before they left for their new sphere, fifteen hundred miles up the Yangtze, several conversions had taken place in the C.I.M. Hall and on a British man-of-war lying in the river.

After that came a wonderful time, in which one and another were brought face to face with a question which revealed the heart's deepest need and opened up a whole world of blessed possibility. One young worker from the interior, for example, unavoidably detained in Shanghai, was present at these meetings, and stirred with a sense of need and longing as never before. Four years in China had taught her something of the joy and blessing to be found in deeper fellowship with the Master, but something also of the deadening influences of heathenism, the power of evil within as well as around her, and the blank despair of seeking to help others when her own soul was out of living touch with Christ. How she longed for " the exchanged life," the life she saw in others, but knew not how to attain. Praying in anguish no one suspected for light and help, it was the last Sunday before Christmas when a word was spoken that, under God, brought deliverance and made all things new. After the evangelistic service in the C.I.M. Hall, an entire stranger—a Christian seaman—came up to her and said earnestly :

" Are you filled with the Holy Ghost ? "

Filled with the Holy Ghost ? She remembered no

[1] From a letter to Mr. Taylor of a few weeks later, dated December 15, 1891.

more of the conversation, but that question burned deeper and deeper into her heart. This, then, was the explanation of all the inward failure, the sorrow that seemed unavailing, the purposes that came to nothing. God had made a provision, given a Gift that she had never definitely accepted. She knew that the Holy Spirit must be her life in a certain sense, for " if any man have not the Spirit of Christ, he is none of His." And yet, just as certainly, she knew that she was *not* " filled with the Spirit," and was experiencing little of His power.

But how afraid she was of being misled, of running into error and mistaking emotion for reality ! The Word of God was full, now she came to study the subject, of the personality and power of the Holy Spirit. The Acts of the Apostles—what was it but the acts of the Holy Ghost, transforming and quickening lives just as she knew she needed to be quickened and transformed ? Oh, yes, why had she never seen it ! It was indeed the Holy Spirit she needed ; the fulness of the Holy Spirit, to make unseen things real to her and impossible things possible. And there stood out in Gal. iii. 13, 14 the words :

" Christ hath redeemed us from the curse of the law, having been made a curse for us . . . that we might *receive* the promise of the Spirit *through faith*."

What was she doing with the infinite Gift purchased at such a cost ? She saw that just as Christ is ours by the gift of God, and yet we have each one personally to receive Him, so with the Holy Spirit. She saw that He too was a Person, just as real as the Lord Jesus, and to be just as truly welcomed by faith into the heart that cannot do without Him as a living link with the risen, glorious Lord. All the rest that can be told is that she took the step, though with fear and trembling—scarce knowing what it meant— and trusted the Holy Spirit to come in and possess her fully, just as she had trusted the Lord Jesus to be her Saviour. Feeling nothing, realising nothing, she just took God at His word, and then and there asked that the promise might be fulfilled, " When He is come (to you) He will reprove (or convict) the world of sin, of righteousness and of judgement." Her chief sorrow for many months had been that she seemed to have little power for soul-winning, and hardly knew of any who had been brought to Christ through her instrumentality. It was Christmas week, and believing that a real, a definite transaction had taken place alone in that quiet room, she asked in faith that God would give her to see the proof of it in actual conversions *every day that week*, in connection with meetings that were being held.

And every day that week the prayer was answered. More than twenty people, young and old, sailors, visitors, and residents in Shanghai, it was given her to help to a definite decision for Christ, while the joy and liberty of her own heart were so manifest that others could not but long for and seek the same blessing. All this meant much to Mr. Taylor. No encouragement could ever be, to him, so great as just to see the hand of God working in such ways. Going into the room where a young missionary lay dying— one he had been seeking to help—he found the extremity of human weakness overflooded with the glow of a wonderful triumph. Fear and distress were gone.

" She told me about the Holy Spirit," whispered the one who had so dreaded the dark valley, " and it was just what I needed."

For weeks and even months the blessing continued. Mr. Sloan returned to Shanghai for a second series of meetings ; and in various centres, foreign residents and members of other missions entered into fulness of life in Christ.

" God is working in our midst," Mrs. Taylor wrote in April (1892), " emptying and humbling one and another, and filling with the Holy Spirit. We are having frequent meetings full of liberty and power."

On the 16th of that month the Council, which was in session, was suspended, a minute being passed to record that,

Instead of meeting for conference, the China Council united with the members of the Mission in Shanghai in seeking for themselves, the whole Mission in China and the Home Councils, the filling of the Holy Spirit.

In answer to prayer the blessing spread. From distant

stations letters that took weeks in coming told of individual
missionaries, and whole groups in some cases, transformed
by the same renewing power, while from the young men's
training home came the tidings that not one of the students
remained unblessed.

" Here in Shanghai there have been some very hungry hearts,"
Mr. Taylor wrote in a circular letter to the members of the
Mission,[1] " and praise God He has been fulfilling to them the
promise ' He satisfieth the longing soul, and filleth the hungry
soul with goodness ' ; with the result that there have been more
conversions in connection with our work here, in a few months,
than for several years previously—some fifty persons, sailors
and residents as well as native servants, having accepted Christ.
From other places too we are hearing of quickening and ingathering, which we trust may be as droppings before the showers we
need.

" The supreme want of all missions in the present day is the
manifested presence of the Holy Ghost. Hundreds of thousands
of tracts and portions of Scripture have been put into circulation ; thousands of Gospel addresses have been given ; tens of
thousands of miles have been traversed in missionary journeys
but how small has been the issue in the way of definite conversions!
We as a mission have much need to humble ourselves before
God. There has been a measure of blessing among us and souls
have been saved, but where are the ones that chase a thousand,
or the two that put ten thousand to flight ? Where are the
once-thirsty ones, now filled, from whom flow rivers of living
water ? . . .

" Few of us, perhaps, are satisfied with the results of our
work, and some may think that if we had more, or more costly
machinery we should do better. But oh, I feel that it is *divine
power* we want and not machinery ! If the tens or hundreds we
now reach daily are not being won to Christ, where would be the
gain in machinery that would enable us to reach double the
number ? Should we not do well, rather, to suspend our present
operations and give ourselves to humiliation and prayer for
nothing less than to be filled with the Spirit, and made channels
through which He shall work with resistless power ? . . .

" Souls are perishing *now* for lack of this power. . . . God is
blessing *now* some who are seeking this blessing from Him in
faith. All things are ready, if we are ready. Let us ask Him to
search us and remove all that hinders His working by us in larger

---

[1] Dated March 29, 1892.

measure. If any of us have been tempted to murmur, to think or speak unkindly of fellow-workers ; if light conversation or jesting ' which are not convenient ' have been indulged in ; if we have allowed less important things to take time and attention that God's direct work should have had ; if our Bibles or secret prayer have been neglected, let us confess the evil before God and claim His promised forgiveness, carefully avoiding such occasions of weakness for the future. And having sought the removal of all hindrances and yielded ourselves up in fresh consecration, let us accept *by faith* the filling, and definitely receive the Holy Ghost, to occupy and govern the cleansed temple."

It was cause for great thankfulness to all concerned when, before the close of the year, deliverance was given in the matters of difficulty that had so long been under consideration. These had necessitated Mr. Taylor's return to England, and when it seemed that unanimity could not be reached by discussion of the problems, the whole time was given at more than one Council Meeting to united waiting upon God. After that the change was very marked. With certain wise concessions on Mr. Taylor's part, liberty for the China administration was fully and finally secured, and early in the new year (1893) it was evident that this prolonged period of trial was passing away.

Nobly had the home staff borne the strain of continually increasing demands upon them through the enlargement of the work. Arrangements that had been adequate when Mr. Broomhall became General Secretary, and the total membership of the Mission was only about a hundred, had necessarily ceased to be so. With five times that number on the field, the home department needed strengthening, and there seemed a possibility at last of securing one in every way fitted to relieve the situation. At the sacrifice of a life of direct missionary service, Mr. Walter B. Sloan consented to take up the responsibilities of Secretary in London as junior colleague to Mr. Broomhall. Mr. Marcus Wood also gave up returning to his much-loved work in China, that he might undertake meetings throughout the country, especially with a view to enlisting young men in the cause of foreign missions. Mr. Stevenson having returned to China, Mr. Taylor was able to remain for a time in England, to the encouragement of the Council and staff ; and best of all, the blessing of God was manifest in unmistakable ways.

As to the financial trial of the period, Mr. Taylor had written before leaving Shanghai :

It has been wonderful and beautiful to see how the Lord has helped us. Timely gifts from members of our own Mission, some of them representing much self-denial, and contributions from foreign residents and visitors have not infrequently in the day answered the prayers for the day, so that every need has been met. On one occasion a party preparing to go to a distant station had their packing completed, and the hour for departure was drawing near before the funds came in to take them forward. Repeatedly we have been without any funds for the general requirements of the whole Mission, though for particular objects there have been balances which, of course, could not be touched. Our hearts have been kept in peace, knowing that God's promises cannot fail ; and to the question, " Lacked ye anything ? " we can only reply as did the disciples of old, " Nothing, Lord."

Needless to say, there had been times of straitness in China when special prayer was called forth, times when the members of the Mission had been drawn to one another in quickened love and sympathy, and had learned fresh lessons of the overruling care of God. Such, for example, was the December day in 1891 when two thousand pounds was urgently needed for general purposes, and the cable announcing the month's remittance was due to arrive from England. Mr. and Mrs. Taylor were at work in the study as usual, a junior member of the Mission being with them when the telegram was brought in. With a brief pause for silent prayer he opened and read it, read it aloud, forgetful perhaps of the young worker to whom the moment was one of almost breathless suspense.

" A hundred and seventy pounds."

" One thousand seven hundred, perhaps ? " questioned Mrs. Taylor.

" No : a hundred and seventy."

In the silence that followed it seemed to the one who listened as if the heavens had fallen, or a chasm of measureless blackness had opened at her feet. A hundred and

seventy pounds, and a pressing need of two thousand!
Nearly five hundred missionaries, and no further cable for
a month!

How did he know just what that young heart was
experiencing? How could he be so at leisure from himself,
so sure of God and at rest in Him that his first thought was
for the faith of another? Turning in his chair, Mr. Taylor
held out his hand with fatherly kindness:

" Now you will watch," he said, and there was even a
touch of joyous confidence about the words, " You will
watch and see *what God will do*."

A special opportunity for God to work and for faith
to triumph—this was the immediate attitude, fully justified
by the events that followed. The deficiency was not made
up by any outstanding gift on this occasion, but in many
directions the hand of God was seen. Larger remittances
than usual were received from Australia and other centres,
while unexpected help was forthcoming in China, so that
by the end of the month an average remittance had been
sent to all the stations with more than an average sense
of the love and care of Him Who " abideth faithful," Who
even when our faith wavers " cannot deny Himself."

Shortly before the settlement of home difficulties, a
remarkable instance of the kind occurred in England which
brought great joy to all at Pyrland Road. It was the 3rd of
October (1892), and Mr. Taylor, returning from an absence in
Scotland, found that the remittance for September had not
yet been cabled to Shanghai, the Financial Secretary having
waited to consult him as to how best to dispose of the small
sum in hand. The Council was to meet that evening, and
the balance being wholly inadequate, Mr. Taylor suggested
delaying another day before sending the telegram, and
setting aside the ordinary business of the Council, that the
time might be given to waiting upon God for funds. The
September receipts, however, Mr. Fishe reminded him,
could not be added to in any case; so the telegram was
sent, and the matter was specially remembered at mid-day
when the household gathered for prayer. Late that afternoon a letter was received at Pyrland Road which turned

the Council Meeting into one of praise. Not only did it contain a cheque for five hundred pounds ; the cheque was accompanied by an unusual request. It was from a lady and gentleman who felt constrained, they said, to send that sum for *immediate transmission to China*. It was too late to despatch an additional cable that day, but early the following morning the good news was telegraphed on, reaching Shanghai, as it proved, at a critical moment.

The autumn meetings of the China Council were in progress, and very encouraging it was to find, when the minutes came to hand by mail, how faith had been strengthened and rewarded. On receiving the first small remittance, special thanksgiving had been made for past deliverances, and the matter very definitely committed to the Lord and left in His hands—it being noted that only about one-fifth of the requirements of the month had been met. Twenty-four hours later, as the Council reassembled, the second wire was received, and Mr. Stevenson was able to tell of a like sum of five hundred pounds which had reached him from another quarter. With glad and grateful hearts it was recorded that " the members of the Council rose and reverently sang the Doxology."

CHAPTER XXXVI

THE FORWARD MOVEMENT

1893–1894. Aet. 61–62.

NEVER since that October day in 1889, when the thoughts had come to Mr. Taylor that found expression in his pamphlet *To Every Creature*, had the subject been absent from his heart. Despite the many grave difficulties that had attended missionary work in China since then, as though the appeal of the Shanghai Conference for a thousand missionaries had aroused all the opposition of the powers of evil, he was assured that the purpose was of God, and had lost none of his first sense of responsibility to do all that in him lay to carry it into effect. Travelling, thinking, speaking, planning new premises to replace the long inadequate quarters at Pyrland Road, encouraging his fellow-workers by visits to the Continent and to Scotland, where the Glasgow Council was growing in helpfulness, he quietly kept in view the large reinforcements that would be needed if " every creature " in China were to hear the Gospel.

With a diminishing income in England and responsibilities already heavy in China, it might have seemed anything but a time for fresh advance. But the heart of the Mission was glowing with fresh blessing, so that there could not but be fresh and fuller response to all the known will of God. Just before the annual meetings of this year (1893) four days were given to a gathering of C.I.M. workers at Pyrland Road for Bible study and prayer. For spiritual power both these meetings and the anniversary services were very marked, and Mr. Taylor's attitude toward the financial problem was more than ever one of confident faith.

"I have often felt glad," he said in the evening meeting, "that I was a poor man ; that I had no money and could never promise anything to anybody ; but that I had a rich heavenly Father, and could promise them all that He would not forget them. And since I have been a father myself I have often thought of something more—that He *could not* forget them.

"There are now labouring with us, largely in the interior of China, five hundred and fifty-two Christian workers who have gone out, a large proportion of them, with no means of their own and with no guarantee of support from man, but every one of them with the guaranteed supply of every need : ' My God shall supply all your need, according to His riches in glory by Christ Jesus.' They have put it to the test ; and that our God does at all times fulfil this gracious promise is no small cause of encouragement.

"The living God still lives, and the living Word *is* a living Word, and we may depend upon it ; we may hang upon any Word God ever spoke or ever caused by His Holy Spirit to be written. Forty years ago I believed in the verbal inspiration of the Scriptures. I have proved them for forty years, and my belief is stronger now than it was then. I have put the promises to the test ; I have been compelled to do so, and have found them true and trustworthy."

In this spirit Mr. Taylor did not wait for the rise in income, which came with the latter half of the year, before taking steps in the direction of advance.

"Pray much for guidance for us," he wrote to Mr. Stevenson in November. "I do not think we are ready to appeal for a hundred men just yet, but we may be six months hence."

And a few weeks later :

"We are encouraged as to our Forward Movement. Yesterday either a promise or a sum of one thousand six hundred pounds was sent us towards it. God always prospers us when we go forward, does He not ? "

It was little wonder that Mr. Taylor felt the time had come for advance. With the enlarged staff at Pyrland Road, much in the way of development seemed possible. A visit to Germany in April and another in August had convinced him that many valuable workers for China might be added to those who had already gone out from Barmen as associates of the Mission.[1] He saw his way to organise, as he wrote to Mr. Stevenson, a thorough campaign throughout England, Scotland, and Ireland, specially with a view to calling forth young men for missionary service. The newly published *Story of the C.I.M.* was being widely read ; funds were encouraging, no less than ten thousand pounds having been received in little over a month for new undertakings ; and with the exception of a brief visit to America for the second Student Volunteer Conference, Mr. Taylor was looking forward to a steady spell of work at home such as he had not had since the days of the Hundred.

And just then, strange to say, a little cloud no bigger than a man's hand warned him that he was needed in China. It concerned the welfare and usefulness of one or more valued members of the Mission ; and Mr. Taylor's warm love for them personally, as well as his sense of responsibility for the work, decided him to go on from America to Shanghai to deal with the matter. While regretting the break in his programme at home, it seemed that only a brief absence would be necessary, and he allowed his name to stand as one of the speakers at Keswick for the following summer.[2]

The Student Conference at Detroit was memorable, when John R. Mott, Robert E. Speer, and other leaders fresh from college gave evidence of the gifts which have since been so remarkably developed in world-wide work for God.

" Our chief and only burden," Mr. Mott had written to Mr.

---

[1] At Barmen Mr. Taylor had the pleasure of seeing Messrs. Paas and Polnick in the midst of the encouraging work of which he had heard on their visit to Pyrland Road in February. At Frankfort-on-Main he was impressed with the Student Conference in which he took part, and with the earnest, aggressive efforts of Pastor Bernus, whose guest he was ; and at Heidelberg he was much attracted to a young minister in whose church he held two meetings—the Rev. H. Coerper, whose interest in China and love for himself personally were to bear rich fruit in days to come.

[2] Mr. and Mrs. Hudson Taylor sailed for New York on February 14, 1894, accompanied by Miss Geraldine Guinness, whose marriage to Dr. Howard Taylor took place on their arrival in Shanghai.

Taylor, in urging him to come over, " is that it may be a markedly spiritual convention. God has been with you in other gatherings, as well as in your regular work, and we have faith to believe that you would be a channel of great spiritual blessing in this continent and through it to the world, if you are at Detroit. . . . Have we not a right to expect that God will do mighty things during these days, if we comply with His conditions ? "

And He did do mighty things, through various instrumentalities. Never to be forgotten was one early morning hour when the great hall was filled with students only, who had come together because they were hungry for definite, abiding blessing. The message was the same that had brought help to many in Shanghai two years previously ; and as then, heart after heart discovered God's provision to meet all depths of failure and need. Years of devoted service on many a mission-field were to bear witness to the spiritual transactions of that hour.

A few weeks later, the matter having been prospered that had brought Mr. Taylor to Shanghai, he was about to leave again for home, eager to help in calling out men for the Forward Movement, when all unexpectedly he found himself claimed in quite another direction. Far away in the north of China complications had arisen which threatened the recall of all Scandinavian missionaries to the coast. A little band, unconnected with the C.I.M., had recently commenced work in a devoted spirit, but on lines so foreign to native ideas of propriety that grave and growing danger was the result. The workers themselves were too inexperienced to realise the state of affairs, but passing travellers had carried the tidings to Peking and the Swedish Foreign Office was on the point of taking action. Of this, warning was received by Mr. Taylor, and though he had nothing to do with the missionaries in question he could not but see how seriously the Scandinavian associates of the C.I.M. might be affected. To those who knew of the situation it seemed providential that the Director of the Mission was in China, as no one could have greater influence in the matter, or be more likely to command the confidence of the authorities in Peking.

But how, even if he gave up his return to England, could he reach those far-off stations in time to be of use save by travelling through the entire summer? It was already the end of April. In a few weeks the hot season would begin, and the journey was one that involved three or four months of overland travel. Little wonder Dr. Howard Taylor felt concerned, medically, when on returning to Shanghai from his wedding trip he found his parents gone and already on their way to the interior. Permission was obtained from Mr. Stevenson to follow them, and at Hankow the bride and bridegroom overtook the beloved travellers, who were preparing to set out by wheelbarrow to cross the mountains into Ho-nan. Railways there were none at that time in the inland provinces, and after the barrow stage must come even rougher travelling on spring-less northern carts. Exposure to the burning sun and tropical rains of midsummer were serious indeed, not to speak of the difficulty of obtaining food when villages are deserted during the harvest season.

" It may cost your life, dear father," pleaded his children, hoping that some other way might be devised of meeting the situation.

" Yes," was the reply, so gently made that it seemed no reproof, " and let us not forget—' We *ought* to lay down our lives for the brethren.' "

After this there was nothing more to be said, but they obtained permission to accompany him. An experienced escort had been provided in Mr. J. J. Coulthard, Mr. Taylor's son-in-law, whose wife and children had just sailed for England, and with Mrs. Hudson Taylor, who was not to be left behind, the family party numbered five.

It was May when they left Hankow, and September when they emerged again from the interior at the northern port of Tien-tsin. Five provinces had been traversed in whole or part, and all the mission-stations visited along their route. Warm, indeed, was the welcome received at these few and far-separated centres : for the rest, excepting Sundays, it was fourteen hours daily on the road—from dawn to dusk, all through the blazing heat—everywhere meeting crowds of accessible, friendly people, amongst whom no witness for Christ was to be found. Over and over again the travellers' hearts were saddened at having to leave groups of interested hearers who begged them to stay longer or promise to return and teach them more. The family relationships proved a source of endless interest. It was all so natural from the Chinese point of view, especially the daughter-in-law ! and everywhere people met them with a smile.

" Perhaps that is because we smile at them," said the bridegroom, who also had noticed the fact.

And certainly there was sunshine in the hearts and on the faces of the little party, despite the heat and dust, the weariness by day and broken rest at night, in inns compared with which a clean cow-shed at home would be luxury.

And what shall be said of the wheelbarrows—those characteristic Ho-nan conveyances, whose chief recommendation from the point of view of a wedding journey is that they are designed to carry two victims rather than one. Primitive springless constructions, they consist of a strong wooden frame with one large wheel in the middle, and handles both back and front. On either side of the wheel the passengers sit, facing backwards, and the whole is covered by a hood of bamboo matting. Food baskets and light baggage may be piled up in front, while inside the travellers' bedding is spread out, to save those poor unfortunates from being shaken and battered beyond possibility of endurance.

" As soon as we were in," wrote the youngest of the party, " one powerful young barrowman slipped the broad canvas strap across his shoulders, lifted and balanced the barrow—throwing us backward at a sharp incline—and called to the other man in front to start away. With a creak, a jolt, and a long, strong pull, the cumbrous machine moved slowly forward. The dust began to rise around us from the feet of the men and the wheel track in the sandy road. With a gasp we clung, as for dear life, to the framework of the barrow, jumbling heavily over ruts and stones. Dry and oil-less, the slowly revolving wheel set up a discordant wail ; large beads of perspiration stood out upon the forehead of the man scarcely a yard away from us, bending so determinedly to his task ; the friendly crowds disappeared in the distance, and our journey was begun."

Ten days of such travelling brought the party to Mr. Coulthard's station, the great, busy mart of Chow-kia-kow. Here the church members, seventy in number, were on the tiptoe of expectation. Mr. and Mrs. Shearer and their fellow-workers received the dusty pilgrims with loving hospitality, and late though it was, cards and letters of welcome poured in. The next day was Sunday, and at an early hour guest-halls began to fill with visitors. Among them came dear old Mr. Ch'en—dignified, keen, and irreproachably dressed in his pale silk gown, but moved to the heart at the prospect of meeting Mr. Taylor. As the latter left his room to go to breakfast, Mr. Ch'en stood in the courtyard to greet him, and very touching it was to see the bowings and interchange of courtesies, and the unaffected love and reverence with which the ex-Mandarin said, again and again :

" But for you, Venerable Sir, we should never have known the love of Jesus."

A letter beautifully penned on a large sheet of red paper further expressed his feelings :

I bathe my hands and reverently greet—

The Venerable Mr. Taylor, who from the beginning raised up the C.I.M. with its worthy leaders, elders, and pastors.

You, Sir, constantly travelling between China and the foreign lands, have suffered much weariness and many labours. . . . And in our midst you have shown forth the seals of your apostleship—2 Cor. xii. 11 (last clause) and 12 (first and second clauses). It is the glorious, redeeming grace of the Saviour that has blessed us, but it has been, Sir, through your coming amongst us and leading us in the true way ; otherwise we had not been able to find the gate whereby to enter the right path. . . .

God grant you, our aged Teacher, to be spared to await the coming of our Lord, when Jesus Christ shall become King of kings and Lord of lords (Rev. xviii. 14). We are assured, Sir, that you will certainly hold high office in the Millennial Kingdom, and reign with Jesus Christ a thousand years ; also that at the close of the Millennium you will closely follow Jesus when He ascends up to heaven.

Among our own household, and indeed throughout the little church in and around Chow-kia-kow, there is no one who does not esteem you highly.

Respectfully wishing peace,

The very unworthy member,

CH'EN named PEARLY WAVE.

I bow my head, and respectfully salute.

A feast for the whole household in handsome native style was sent round the following day, Mr. Ch'en feeling "unworthy" to invite the Venerable Chief Pastor to his "mean abode." The cooking he had himself superintended —" six basins of the largest size, containing prepared meats such as are used in ancestral worship." On hearing that Mr. Taylor had to avoid pepper, he prepared with his own hands special provisions for the road, which arrived with the following characteristic note :

Honourable and Most Reverend Mr. Taylor :

Ch'en of the Pearly Wave bows his head.

I write this respectfully to present to you some travellers' provisions—minced meat boiled in oil, spiced apricot kernels, and pickled water-melon. Be pleased graciously to receive these at my hands. Of the spiced meats, one kind without cayenne pepper is for the special use of the aged Teacher, the other with capsicum is for the consumption of Mr. Coulthard and your second princely son. I write this note on purpose to wish you peace.

1st day of the Midsummer moon.

The poorer Christians also could not do enough to express love and gratitude. A little collection made among themselves was expended on cakes and sweetmeats with much ornamental red paper ; and a few days later one dear old coolie came to the missionary-in-charge with a matter that was causing him exercise of mind. The travellers had passed on their way by that time, but he was following them daily in prayer.

" I have been thinking about the Venerable Chief Pastor," he said. " His life is so precious ! but he is far from strong. I am not old yet ; I might live another ten or twenty years

But Mr. Taylor —— Teacher, I want you to know : if I should die suddenly, it is because I have offered the remaining years of my life that they may be added to his life. It is not to be spoken about. It is just my heart's desire before the Lord." [1]

Doubtless the prayers of these dear Christians had much to do with the safety of the travellers, and the way in which Mr. and Mrs. Taylor were enabled to endure exposure and weariness, especially through the long weeks of the cart journey. For neither of them were accustomed to this strenuous form of exercise, and Mr. Taylor, having a sensitive back from concussion of the spine, found it decidedly trying. And then the heat ! So terrific was it that the rainy season, though it turned the roads into quagmires, was almost a relief. But that again brought its dangers, for rivers fed by mountain streams rose rapidly, and the fords were soon merged in swirling torrents. Yet it was urgent to press on, and the inns in which other travellers were likewise detained were of the most wretched description. After three days, therefore, in one place in which, despite the rain, Mr. Taylor preferred his cart to the evil-smelling rooms that offered the only alternative, it seemed desirable to set out as soon as the river began to fall.

The carters reached the ford and were about to cross, when, to their surprise and indignation, another driver came down the bank and plunged in before them. This was an unheard-of insult, for every carter knows that he must jog along for hours behind respectable fellow-travellers rather than pass them, unless invited to do so. Their rage, however, was appeased by the suggestion that after all it was just as well, as now they would see what sort of crossing the others would make. All went prosperously awhile. The mules waded out deeper and deeper, but managed to keep their footing, until in the middle of the stream they paused on a sandbank to rest. Then came intense excitement as they were seen to go down into the main body of

---

[1] This faithful friend, Dr. Howard Taylor's special coolie, was subsequently a great help in opening two new cities in Ho-nan to the Gospel —Chen-chow-fu and Tai-kang. His years were not shortened in the way he anticipated, for he outlived Mr. Hudson Taylor.

the stream. Higher and higher rose the water, until it crept into the cart. Jumping and yelling wildly, the men on the bank cried out :

" *Puh-chong, puh-chong!* It's all up! It's all up!"

And sure enough, the current had caught the vehicle. Over and over it turned, the mules disappearing from sight—first wheels uppermost, then again the battered covering—until there seemed no hope for those within. Had it been Mr. Taylor's party, little doubt lives would have been sacrificed, but the far tougher Chinese somehow survived and were dragged out at a bend in the river where the cart stranded on the opposite bank. Needless to say, our travellers did not attempt that ford. Taking a circuitous route they reached a ferry, by means of which carts and mules were carried safely across.

Much more might be told of the experiences of that journey ; of its answers to prayer in deliverances from danger, in blessing at the stations, in the sparing of Mr. Taylor's life when stricken down with overpowering heat ; of Mrs. Taylor's brave endurance and beautiful example ; of the attainment of the object in view, and the final visit to Peking to communicate results to the British Minister. But of even more interest to Mr. Taylor were the signs of progress on the vast and populous Si-an plain, as well as in other regions, in the work nearest of all to his heart. When he had crossed the plain with Mr. Beauchamp, eight years previously, travelling from Pastor Hsi's district to Han-chung, no light-centres had broken the darkness all around them for hundreds of miles. Now, station after station had been opened, and in the capital—long one of the most anti-foreign cities in China—the Scandinavian workers were gathered whom he had come so far to meet.

It was a wonderful change, all due under God to the devoted lives of a little group of pioneers, long homeless, scorned, and persecuted, for Christ's sake and the Gospel's. When Thomas Botham first went over from Han-chung, things were so hard that even he was discouraged. Yet he could not give up the task to which he felt himself called.

" I am willing to walk in the dark with God," he said
to his Superintendent, himself one of the first pioneers in
the province.

" In the dark with God," replied Mr. Easton ; " why,
dear Brother, in Him, with Him is ' no darkness at
all.' "

It was a good word with which to begin work on the Si-an
plain, and much he and his companions had need of it !
Joined by Mr. Redfern and a few months later by Mr. Bland,
the young men naturally took it for granted that they must
obtain a settled dwelling. Not so, however, the people of
the plain. No one would rent them a house, and every
effort in that direction aroused intense opposition. At
last it came to them—" the command is ' Preach the
Gospel.' Let us go everywhere and do that, and leave the
rest with God. If He wants us to have a house He will
give it, and give it in such a way as not to hinder His
work."

Twenty-two governing cities, sixty market towns and
innumerable villages formed their parish—a district extending over twelve thousand square miles, in which they were
the only missionaries—and from end to end of it they were
met with little but opposition. All they could do was to
move from place to place, staying as long as possible in any
inn willing to receive them, preaching on the streets, and
seeking by Christlike humility and love to recommend the
Gospel. It was work that told, and they were willing for
the cost.

When Mr. Botham married, his bride had already been
two years in China and was herself a missionary. Rejoicing
to " suffer hardship with the Gospel," she determined to
make the most of their splendid opportunity, and so much
sunshine did she bring into that toilsome life that her
husband was able to write :

I never feel so happy as when with all my worldly goods on
one donkey, and my wife on another, I set out to carry the
Gospel to some new place on the Si-an plain.

So liable were they to riots and disturbances that the
little company had to divide, and scarcely ever dared to

be more than two in a city at the same time. Even in the place where they were most at home, they might have been " foreign devils " indeed, to judge by the treatment accorded them in the streets, and the city gates were placarded with posters accusing them of atrocious crimes. For months they were troubled that they felt these things so keenly, until the passage came home to them, " Reproach hath broken my heart " (Ps. lxix. 20). Then it was all fellow-ship, deeper fellowship with the suffering Saviour—how it lighted their most humbling and painful experiences with joy !

Meeting Mr. Bland returning from a city in which they knew he must have had a hard time, they inquired what he had been able to do on this visit.

" I was able to praise the Lord," was the brave answer. And together they rejoiced in this victory of faith.

But their wanderings were not aimless. They were literally carrying out the Master's word, " When they per-secute you in this city, flee ye into another " ; but they took good care, as Mr. Botham put it, to " flee in a circle," so that coming back from time to time to the same places, the people became used to seeing them.

" Home still means an inn," he wrote months after their marriage, " I might almost say *any* inn, we are so accustomed to travelling."

And the great advantage was that the love and purity, the sweetness and grace of the Lord Jesus Christ in those lives " could not be hid," just because they were lived so openly among the people.

" And I, if I be lifted up, will draw all men unto Me," how true it was in their experience ! Two or three years sufficed to bring the change. Wonderful things were happening that we must not dwell on now, and returning from a journey on which they had met with attention and sympathy—crowds of listeners following them in nearly every place, and people actually bringing out chairs and tea into the streets—the new note of their thanksgiving was, " The darkness is passing away."

To this district the leaders of the Scandinavian Fifty had been sent, and arriving just as these devoted lives were beginning to bear fruit, they were ready to take advantage of the changed conditions. Station after station was opened with little difficulty, and the new workers, being men of faith and prayer, were enabled to hold their own even in the capital itself. Many a missionary had sought to obtain a footing in that important city, but it was reserved for Holman and his guitar to win the day. Surrounded by a crowd bent on mischief that had invaded his premises, he pleasantly asked the people if they would like to hear him sing. Taken by surprise they listened, as with musical voice and instrument he poured forth Swedish melodies. He was so quiet and friendly that they began to feel ashamed ; and finally, as he went on singing —crying to God in his heart for deliverance—the crowd gradually melted away.

It was to the city thus opened Mr. Taylor's party was drawing near. Ten miles away it was plainly visible, the turreted wall, gates, and towers standing out against the sunset sky. At the cross-roads two men in Chinese dress with big straw hats were waiting, who turned out to be Mr. Easton and Mr. Hendrikson. Charged with letters and the warmest of welcomes, they had come to escort the visitors, some into the city and some to the ladies' house in the west suburb. Riding before the carts in the gathering dusk, they led the way through little-frequented streets, and oh, the joy of that arrival without observation ! Seventeen days of heat and weariness since leaving the last mission-station had prepared the travellers to appreciate the comfort of those Christian homes far in the heart of China ; and, luxury of luxuries, they found in each house a well—plenty of clean, cool water at their very doors !

The helpful meetings of the conference can only be mentioned in passing, and the notable answer to prayer when Mrs. Botham's life was despaired of, four days' journey away, and after seventy-two hours of restlessness and fever she passed into a healing sleep the very evening special prayer was being made for her at Si-an. Although on account of this illness Mr. Botham could not be present, the Superintendent of the province was there with Mr. Bland, and definite arrangements were entered into with regard to the Swedish associates. A district, including the capital and extending north-west into the province of Kan-su, was set apart for them under the general supervision of Mr. Botham, one of their own leaders being appointed missionary-in-charge. It was a great joy to Mr. Taylor to see how those in Si-an-fu had grown and developed during the short time, little more than three years, that they had been in China, and to find that though he had to suggest restrictions that might have seemed irksome, the ties were but drawn the closer that united the Scandinavian Alliance workers with the C.I.M.

Very real was the consciousness of that love and unity as he spoke to them around the Table of the Lord in the last meeting of the conference. Dwelling on the secret of a fully satisfied life—the heart that knows what it is to drink of the Living Water—Mr. Taylor referred to the delight of a well in those days of midsummer heat.

" After our long thirsty journey," he said, sitting in the midst of those young workers, " what refreshment we have found in the cool, delicious water springing up in your own dwellings, always within reach ! We have never thirsted since coming to Si-an. And the Lord Jesus gives me a well, a spring of living water deep down in my own heart—His presence there at all times. What do we do with our wells ? We go to them and draw. Drinking, we do not thirst. So, having Jesus, drinking of the spring He gives, we need never thirst again.

" Oh, it is so blessed to learn that His promise is strictly true ! that ' shall ' means *shall*, ' never ' means *never*, and ' thirst ' means *thirst* : ' shall never thirst '—no, not at any time ! And it is to be a well springing up, overflowing in a constant stream of blessing. Yes, it is for me, weak and old and good-for-nothing as I am ; and it is for you, young, strong, and able. ' From him shall flow rivers of living water.' God grant you to find, as you travel over this wide plain, the truth of that word, ' Everything shall live whither the river cometh.' "

> Name of Jesus—living tide !
> Days of drought for me are past.
> How much more than satisfied
> Are the thirsty lips at last.

Reluctantly we must pass over the rest of the journey, scarcely touching upon Mr. Taylor's visits in the neighbouring province of Shan-si to districts he already knew to some extent. Mr. Folke and his fellow-workers of the Swedish Mission in China had occupied one important region previously without any witness for Christ, and very delightful it was to meet in the important city of Yün-cheng a circle whose home-friends and churches had received Mr. Taylor with so much cordiality in Sweden. Beyond this point the travelling was by moonlight, to escape the intense heat (120° in the carts) which had almost cost Mr. Taylor's life in coming from Si-an. Setting out toward evening, it was a comfort to feel that before the sun rose again a good stage would have been accomplished, though dangerous characters other than wolves were to be met with in the mountains or in the shelter afforded by tall-growing crops. Stopped one night in the shadow of an arch or shrine, they found that two men had accosted the foremost cart.

" Do you carry foreign travellers ? " was the question which startled them.

A moment later, however, the situation was explained by the inquiry in a cultured English voice, " Is this Mr. Taylor's party ? "

Pastor Hsi and Mr. Hoste ! Miles had they walked out together to meet the expected visitors, and warm indeed was the welcome with which they received Mr. Taylor once again, just where Mr. Hoste had parted from him eight years previously.

It was a week later when, the Ping-yang-fu Conference being over, Mr. Taylor was free to accept Pastor Hsi's hospitality and spend a day or two in his home. Having been there before, what was his surprise on arrival to be driven in through courtyard after courtyard, past house and farm buildings, till an open space was reached that looked like a threshing-floor. There stood an ample table covered with a clean white cloth and other preparations for a " foreign " meal. Overhead a brown awning, supported on a dozen or more wooden masts, formed a sheltering roof,

and in the background a building (could it be a barn?)
stood with open doors. To this Mr. and Mrs. Taylor were
led—and lo, a royal pavilion, a whole suite of apartments,
beautifully arranged, clean, cool, and ready for use !

With growing astonishment they explored its resources,
touched by evidences of loving thoughtfulness on every
hand. The central dining-room gave access to a large
sleeping apartment on one side, and to a couple of smaller
chambers on the other. All were comfortably furnished and
most inviting. Lamps were ready on the tables, fresh straw
mats completely covered the floors, new bamboo curtains as
well as coloured hangings protected doors and windows, new
white felt rugs were laid over fine white matting on each of
the beds. The tables were spread with red covers, and neatly
laid in the centre of each was a square of green oil-silk, beautifully rich in colour. Brass basins, shining like mirrors, were
placed upon little stands ready for use, with clean white
towels and new cakes of the best Pears' soap ! The whole
place, in a word, was so clean and attractive, so polished
and radiant, that they could hardly believe their eyes.

And there stood dear Pastor and Mrs. Hsi eager to see if
they were pleased, but disclaiming gratitude or remonstrance.

" It is nothing. It is altogether unworthy. Gladly
would we have arranged far better for our Venerable Chief
Pastor and his family."

Nothing could exceed the love and joy of that welcome,
in which the whole household took part. Pastor Hsi
himself brought hot water for washing, and kept the cups
filled with tea. He hastened the mid-day meal, covering
the table with good things, and insisted on waiting in
person, lest his helpers should not be quick enough to
anticipate every wish. Very touching it was to see his
eyes fill with tears, as Mr. Taylor tried to thank him again
and again, and to hear him say :

" What, sir, have you suffered and endured that we
might have the Gospel ! This is my joy and privilege.
How could I do less ? " [1]

---

[1] The beautiful suite of rooms was as new to Mr. Hoste as it was to
the travellers, and later on he let out the secret of the transformation

Gladly would we linger over changes that told of progress in the work, and all the development in spiritual things that Mr. Taylor rejoiced to witness. For harvest days had come in Southern Shan-si, of which he had seen the promise, and in spite of many problems the outlook was full of encouragement. Far away from the Western Chang village events were transpiring, however, that were to have an important bearing on Mr. Taylor's movements. Hastening to complete the matter he had in hand, the leader of the Mission was anticipating a speedy return to England to take up the Forward Movement he had reluctantly left in February. But there is an unseen Leader Whose great ends are served by all happenings and in ways we should least devise. The very day Mr. Taylor spent in the delightful hospitality of Pastor Hsi's home (July 25) witnessed the outbreak of war between China and Japan, and by the time he reached Shanghai it was evident that he could not absent himself from the scene of danger. Things were going badly for the Chinese, and there was no knowing when or how baffled rage against the enemy might react upon other "foreigners." All thought of leaving for England had to be abandoned, and the visit to China that had already lengthened out from weeks to months was prolonged indefinitely.

---

scene. The building really was a barn, consisting of nothing but a roof and three bare walls. The new front and windows, partitions, plastering, white-washing, and hangings had been put in expressly for their use, and the furniture carried from Pastor Hsi's own rooms across several courtyards. And all this for a visit of a day or two !

PART VIII

WORN OUT WITH LOVING

1895–1905. Aet. 63–73.

" We see JESUS who was made a little lower than the angels for the suffering of death, crowned with glory and honour ; that He by the grace of God should taste death for every man."

" He, the Lord of angels, became lower than the angels, and He Who was eternal and necessarily deathless took on Him a mortal frame in order to die. Yet we are told of Him that, being made a little lower than the angels, He was ' crowned.' This crowning was peculiar : it was that of tasting death for every man ; it was the glory and honour of suffering, of conquering him who had the power of death . . . by submission, not by resistance."—J. HUDSON TAYLOR.

" For it became Him, for whom are all things, in bringing many sons unto glory, to make the Captain of their salvation perfect through sufferings. For both He that sanctifieth and they who are sanctified are all of one : for which cause He is not ashamed to call them brethren."—Heb. II. 9, 10.

" Well, it is but a little while and HE will appear to answer all enigmas and to wipe away all tears. I would not wish, then, to be of those who had none to wipe away, would you ? "—J. HUDSON TAYLOR.

CHAPTER XXXVII

CAN YE DRINK OF THE CUP ?

1895. AET. 63.

WITH the close of the Japanese War in April (1895) came the close also of the period in which the thousand missionaries were looked for in response to the appeal sent out by the Shanghai Conference of 1890. As Chairman of the Committee to report results, Mr. Taylor was thankful to be able to state that not a thousand only, but one thousand one hundred and fifty-three new workers had been added to the missionary staff in China during that time—a wonderful answer to prayer that could not but call forth widespread thanksgiving. And yet, as he pointed out, it was far from final, in the sense of having attained the end in view. A great step forward had been taken, but it left the primary duty—that of making known the Gospel "to every creature" in China, in obedience to the Master's great command—still unfulfilled. For out of the eleven to twelve hundred new missionaries only four hundred and eighty were men ; and this number, divided among the forty-five societies which had sent them, would only give an average of ten to each. Clearly, as many of these societies were working in provinces on or near the coast, the addition of even this large number hardly affected the situation in the great waiting world of inland China. It was for these unreached millions Mr. Taylor pleaded still and with renewed urgency.

"An important crisis in China's history has been reached," he wrote on behalf of the Committee. "The war just terminated

537

does not leave her where she was. It will inevitably lead to a
still wider opening of the empire and to many new developments.
If the Church of Christ does not enter the opening doors, others
will, and they may become closed against her. . . . Time is
passing. If a thousand men were needed five years ago, they
are much more needed now. . . . In view of the new facilities
and enlarged claims of China, the next five years should see
larger reinforcements than those called for in 1890. Will not
the Church arise and take immediate and adequate action to
meet the pressing needs of this vast land ? "

In the same spirit he addressed himself to the home
circle of the C.I.M.—the friends long tried and proved,
whose fellowship in the work of the Gospel had made so
many an advance possible.

" A new call is given us to hasten the evangelisation of
China," he wrote on his sixty-third birthday, with reference to
the war and its outcome. " Let us remember the power we
possess in united prayer. . . ."

Touching upon many causes for thankfulness in the
development of the Mission, he continued :

" Now we have peace, we must look for large and immediate
reinforcements. We in the C.I.M. have been conscious that God
has been preparing us for this. Needed facilities have been
supplied, without which large reinforcements would have embarrassed us. . . . Never before were we so well prepared for
definite advance, and our hope and prayer is that now the war
is over we may have given to us many ' willing, skilful ' helpers,
men and women, for every department of missionary service.

" Continue to pray for us, dear friends, and to help us as
God may lead you. Thank God for the hundreds of souls being
reaped year by year, and ask that soon the annual increase may
be very much larger. Pray that only Spirit-filled missionaries
may be sent out, and that all of us here may overflow with the
Living Water." [1]

But the effect upon missionary work of the tragic events
which had transpired was to be serious and far-reaching.
Five years yet remained of Mr. Taylor's active service,
years which, though they brought no lessening of the sense
of responsibility that had come to him, raised unparalleled
difficulties in the way of carrying out the project so much

---

[1] From a circular letter dated Shanghai, May 21, 1895.

upon his heart. China had entered at last upon the troubled period of transition from her exclusive policy of centuries to the reluctant but inevitable acceptance of her place in the great family of nations. The change was not one that could take place easily; and the weakening, through loss of prestige, of the Imperial Government at Peking let loose forces of disorder in many parts of the country. Thus barely a week after the above letter was written Mr. Taylor began to hear of riots, persecutions, and rebellion, from the coast right out to the borders of Tibet. Sitting quietly at breakfast on Sunday the 1st of June a telegram was put into his hands which brought the startling tidings :

Riot in Cheng-tu.[1] All missions destroyed: friends in *ya-men*.

This was followed by another and another, until within ten days he learned of destruction in all the central stations of the Mission in that province, except Chung-king on the Yangtze, from which many of the refugees were being helped. At the same time bitter persecution broke out against the Christians in the Wen-chow district, one of the oldest and most fruitful in the Mission. Tidings kept coming of homes attacked and pillaged, families fleeing for refuge to the Mission compound, and a work that had taken long years to build up threatened with complete devastation.

Nor were these the most serious issues. They were symptomatic of general excitement and unrest. Gradually the facts were becoming known as to the defeat suffered at the hands of Japan, and loss of confidence in the ruling powers was the inevitable result. Secret societies were everywhere active, and a great Mohammedan uprising was reported from the north-west, where C.I.M. missionaries were the only foreigners. The disbanded soldiery—still armed and with arrears of pay due in many cases—were a serious menace, and with hundreds of fellow-workers in inland stations, Mr. Taylor had no little cause for concern.[2]

---

[1] The capital of the great western province of Sze-chwan.
[2] At the end of March 1895 the Mission numbered 621 members, settled in 122 central stations, 90 of which were in the eleven formerly unoccupied provinces.

Over a thousand miles from Sze-chwan and kept in
suspense for weeks until letters could reach him, he was
specially exercised about the Church of England district in
which the work had been full of promise. In that group of
stations alone the number of baptized believers had risen
from fifty to a hundred during the previous year ; and for
the time being they were deprived of their leader, Mr.
Cassels being at home on furlough. Would they be scattered
now, and the work—outcome of so much prayer—be brought
to a standstill ? Mr. Taylor believed not ; and in the midst
of his distress, on behalf of the native Christians as well as
his fellow-missionaries, he was enabled to rejoice as never
before in Ps. lxxvi. 10, " Surely the wrath of man shall
praise Thee : the remainder of wrath shalt Thou restrain."

Then as news began to be received from one district and
another, it was cheering to see this expectation fulfilled,
even in the most painful situations. Protected by Government officials, no lives were actually lost in Sze-chwan, and
not a few of the missionaries who had taken refuge with the
local Mandarins were allowed to return before long to their
dismantled dwellings. To their great joy they found in
some places that the converts had been witnessing so faithfully that new inquirers had enrolled their names and were
coming regularly for instruction. This was the case in the
capital (Cheng-tu) and in Mr. Cassels' station (Pao-ning),
where the Christians had braved all danger, and coming to
the wall of the *ya-men*, had sought to reassure their missionary
friends by calling out fearlessly : " We are all here ! Not
one of us has gone back."

In a lonely station among the hills, from which the ladies
had not been driven out, their house was guarded night after
night by Christian men who, unknown to them, volunteered
for the task ; and a woman of position in the district was
so concerned for their safety that she came twenty miles on
her crippled feet to make inquiries, finding far more than she
sought, for her heart was drawn to living faith in the Saviour
of whom she thus heard for the first time.[1]

---

[1] So great was the love of this woman for the things of God that she
frequently walked the long distance from her home to the Mission-station

Even when the worst came—the tragedy that was to make this summer memorable in the long conflict between light and darkness—it was immediately and wonderfully overruled for good. Hardly could any missionary then in China forget the thrill with which the news was received of the cold-blooded murder of the Rev. Robert Stewart with his wife and child and eight fellow-workers of the Church Missionary Society. Mr. Taylor was at Chefoo when it happened, engaged upon buildings for the growing schools, and was not slow to realise the full significance of the event. Never before had the protecting hand of God been so far withdrawn as to permit of such a sacrifice. Instances had occurred in which Protestant missionaries had laid down their lives one or two at a time, but they had been few and far between, and no women had hitherto been among the number. Now mother and children had alike been attacked, and most of the sufferers were young, unmarried women. Gathered at a hill-station for rest during the great heat, they had fallen a prey to the plottings of a secret society which apparently hoped to involve the Government in trouble. Whatever the cause or ultimate results, the realisation came home to many a heart that a new era had dawned that day (August 1), and that a great price might yet have to be paid for the triumph of the Gospel in China. But there was no faltering.

Not to demand reparation nor to mourn the loss sustained was the great meeting held that filled Exeter Hall to its utmost capacity, but simply to *pray for China* and seek divine guidance as to the future of missionary work in that land. Far from looking upon what had happened as a check, the Secretary of the Church Missionary Society expressed the conviction of all present when he said that it simply demonstrated China's unutterable need of the Gospel, and was thus a call and challenge to *advance*. No

---

to attend the Sunday services, starting on Saturday morning to be in time. Unable on one occasion to leave before evening, she set out to walk the whole of Saturday night, assuring her neighbours who remonstrated—urging the danger of wolves and brigands—that she would not be alone, the best of Protectors was with her. So she " sang hymns by the way, and was not afraid."

reference was made to the harrowing details of the massacre, though the names of the martyr-band were read with some touching allusions to family matters. Personal considerations were lost sight of in the presence of Him Who loved not His life unto death, that He might open the gates of Life to all mankind. Facing as never before what it must mean to follow Him in His redeeming work, the whole assembly bowed in prayer as the consecration vow of many a heart was sung :

> Were the whole realm of nature mine,
> That were an offering far too small ;
> Love so amazing, so divine,
> Demands my life, my soul, my all.

. . . . . .

At that very time, unknown to those who were praying for China, but not to Him Who was watching over all, another little band was in utmost peril, far in the heart of that great land. After a preparatory stage of several months the Mohammedan Rebellion had swept down upon the city of Si-ning on the borders of Tibet, where Mr. and Mrs. Ridley, their infant child, and Mr. Hall were the only foreigners. Ten thousand Mohammedans lived in the suburbs round the city, and it was a terrible night (July 24) when, contrary to vows and protestations, they turned upon their Chinese neighbours, and amid scenes of fearful carnage threw in their lot with the rebels. Already the city was filled with refugees, and the missionaries were working night and day to care for the wounded. Led by a beggar who knew the healing virtue of their medicines, they had found in the Confucian Temple hundreds of women and children who had made their escape from burning villages and the horrors perpetrated by their enemies. Groans and wailing were heard on every hand, and in the twilight of that summer evening they saw a mass of human suffering that was appalling. Burned from head to foot and gashed with fearful sword-cuts, scores of these poor creatures lay dying with not a hand to help them, for no one would go near even with food and water.

Then the missionaries understood why they had felt so

definitely that they ought to stay on in the city, when they might have made good their escape. This was the work for which they were needed, the work that was to open hearts to the Gospel as years of preaching had not done. With heroic courage they gave themselves to the task, and throughout all that followed never ceased their ministrations. Amid scenes passing conception they cared for the wounded of both sides—first in the seven months of Mohammedan frenzy, when the Chinese were falling before them in thousands, then in still more awful months of Chinese retaliation. With no surgical instrument but a pen-knife and hardly any appliances but such as could be obtained on the spot, they performed hundreds of operations, and treated over a thousand cases of diphtheria, not to speak of the dressing of wounds that occupied them from early morning till late at night.[1]

But for the help of a four-footed friend Mrs. Ridley could never have got through at all. For their servants left them at the beginning of the siege, and with the baby she was nursing and all the household work on her hands, she alone could attend to a large proportion of their patients, the women and girls. Full gallop her brave little donkey would go through the busy streets, the people gladly making way for the mother whose baby was waiting at home. Well they knew there was nothing she would not do to comfort the suffering and bind up broken hearts, while her own must be torn with anxiety. Ah, *that* was what they could not understand—the secret of her peace !

She herself could hardly understand it, as those fearful days wore on. Once, only once, her heart failed her—in the midst of an attack upon the city, when it seemed as though all hell were let loose, and that at any moment the defences

---

[1] It was wonderful how they were helped, for neither Mr. Ridley nor Mr. Hall had had medical training, and though Mrs. Ridley was experienced in sickness she was not a qualified nurse. Operations without chloroform that would have daunted many a strong man she bravely took her part in, and they never once lost a life by cutting an artery in the extraction of bullets, etc. Cotton wool and oil for burns, and common needles and silk for sewing up wounds they were able to buy in the city, as also the sulphur with which they treated diphtheritic patients. A foreign razor helped out the pocket-knife in surgical cases.

might fall. She was fully alive by that time to what it meant to be at the mercy of Mohammedan hordes. Had not infants been brought to her, scores of them, mutilated by their savagery? Alone in the house that night, her husband and Mr. Hall being out amid the panic-stricken people, a wave of terror swept over her. It was Dora, little Dora she thought of. For themselves it did not matter—but oh, her baby! Her happy, smiling, always-contented treasure! how could she bear to see—— ? But as she knelt beside the sleeping infant and cried to God, the Presence which is salvation so wrapped her round that all else receded and was forgotten.

" He gave me the assurance then," she said, " that no harm should come to us." And though it was many a long month before fighting and massacre were over, that agonising dread never returned.

To Mr. Taylor, far off in Shanghai, such knowledge as he had of the situation was peculiarly distressing. Neither letters nor money could be sent to these fellow-workers, and for months together no tidings of them were received. A remittance forwarded in the spring had got through before the siege commenced, but it was spring again when the next came to hand. Relief expeditions sent by the Government failed to reach the city, more than a thousand soldiers losing their lives in the attempt. Mr. Taylor did not know that Mr. Ridley had almost succumbed to an attack of diphtheria, that smallpox was raging in the city, and that neither bread nor coal was to be purchased at any price. A winter of seven months had to be faced, with the temperature below zero much of the time,[1] and so small was their supply of fuel that they had to eke it out with manure, and even so could only afford a fire at meal-times. Had he seen and known it all, Mr. Taylor's solicitude could hardly have been greater, however ; and so much was that little group upon his heart that not infrequently he rose two and three times at night to pray for them.

And it was wonderful how prayer was answered in their desperate situation. The ninety-first Psalm could hardly

---

[1] Si-ning lies in a valley 8000 feet above sea-level.

have a more striking commentary. God raised up friends for them, supplied their need when money was useless and kept them strong in faith, so busy helping others that they had little time to think of themselves. Without anxiety they saw their stock of flour coming to an end, sure that before the sack was empty more would be provided. They were thankful then to have no servants, for to have fed a household would have exhausted their resources much more quickly. They recognised a Father's loving care, also, in an unexpected gift that had reached them, carriage paid, to their door, shortly before the siege commenced—two packing-cases containing soups and jam, biscuits and tinned meat, cocoa, and above all an abundant supply of oatmeal. Many months they had been on the way from England, but One Who knew when they would be needed brought them safely and just in time.[1]

Another comfort was the serene health of little Dora. Nothing troubled her. She would say " ta " in her pretty smiling way when she heard the guns close by, and was happy in her mother's absence and unaffected by the strain through which the latter had to pass. Then the kindness of neighbours was no little help. An official (the Governor's Secretary) living in the same street gave nineteen taels toward the medical work, which purchased oil, wadding, and material for bandages ; and his wife, knowing that Mrs. Ridley had no time for cooking, invited her to run in when-ever she could for meals. Another lady used to send batches of bread from time to time, and when in the straitness of the siege she could no longer do so, she begged that her cook might make bread for the Ridleys from their own flour.

No one guessed how hard up they really were, because Chinese families in their position would always have reserve stores of grain. When the flour was running low therefore, they had to take very literally the promise, " Trust in the Lord and do good ; so shalt thou dwell in the land, and verily thou shalt be fed." Hardly welcome under the

---

[1] A like generous gift was sent to every station in the Mission, from Mr. J. T. Morton, a London wholesale provision merchant, who was becoming deeply interested in the Mission.

circumstances was a visit from one of the city magnates, for, being alone in the house, Mr. Ridley had to light the fire and prepare tea, excusing as best he could his poor hospitality.

Too polite to make any comment, the visitor was taken aback by his discovery, and going straight to the head Mandarin informed him that the foreigners who were doing so much to help others were without a servant of any kind. Four soldiers were immediately pressed upon Mr. Ridley to attend him and look after his " animals," with the result that he was obliged to explain his circumstances and that he really could not provide them with food.

Busy among his patients next morning, what was his surprise to see two men enter the courtyard each carrying a large sack of grain. These were set down amid the delighted onlookers, the bearers explaining that the Prefect had sent two hundred pounds of wheat as a small recognition of the virtuous labours of the missionaries. Presently two more soldiers came and carried the sacks to the mill, bringing back the flour. Long before that supply could be exhausted, a procession of six men in uniform appeared, each with his sack of wheat, which was also ground and returned in the shape of six hundred pounds of flour ! So that without asking help of any save of God alone, those children of His, so isolated and resourceless, were not only provided for but were enabled to feed many of the starving around them until the siege was over.

Meanwhile Mr. Taylor was making every effort to reach them with supplies. He knew they must be still alive because of the burden of prayer on his heart for them day and night, but for months there was no other encouragement to hope.[1] Not until the new year dawned (1896) did the longed-for message come that Si-ning was relieved and communication re-established, and even then the reign of terror was prolonged by the Chinese retaliation. Almost

[1] Writing to Mr. Easton, the Superintendent of the district, on October 30 (1895), Mr. Taylor said : " We are praying, I may literally say, night and day for our dear friends in Si-ning and in all the other Kansu stations. . . . I am almost hourly praying that God will give more souls this winter than have ever been given before in the north-west."

two years in all the fearful business lasted, eighty thousand people being actually massacred, not to speak of soldiers killed in battle or frozen upon the mountains.   But through it all the missionaries stayed at their post, proving themselves the friends of Chinese and Mohammedans alike, and winning love and confidence that brought wonderful opportunities for the Gospel.   All the country was open to them.   Wherever they went they found known and unknown friends, and the work they could not overtake emphasised afresh the need for large and immediate reinforcements.   But that belongs to a later period.

Anxiety about Si-ning was at its height when, in the middle of October, tidings reached Mr. Taylor in Shanghai that added a poignant element to the already full cup of 1895.   Troubles and dangers had followed one another in quick succession, but so far without loss to the Mission. Now it was cholera that had visited one of the nearer stations, carrying off a whole group of native Christians and foreign missionaries.   Nine deaths in all had taken place in ten days, leaving the bereaved community sorely stricken.

And there were circumstances that made the news peculiarly distressing.   Well did Mr. Taylor remember the young husband and wife he had welcomed to China only a few months previously, whose record in the Soldiers' Home at Litchfield proved them to be soul-winners of exceptional value, and the brave Scotch workers they had joined in the Wen-chow district, who had stood the brunt of the persecution already referred to in this chapter, sheltering in their home scores of the suffering Christians.   Could it be that of the four only one was left, and that to her had come the double bereavement of losing husband and child ?

Not so long before, it seemed, she had arrived in China, having put off her marriage with the full consent of her fiancé, that they might each give themselves to learning the language and becoming useful as missionaries before beginning life together.   The rule of the Mission in this respect had meant, for them, real sacrifice, for they had long been engaged and were everything to each other.   But amid the loneliness of those first days in China, she looked as well as lived the message engraved on the simple brooch she wore : " Jesus does satisfy."

Married after two years to Alexander Menzies, home had been to them a little bit of heaven, and their joy in one another had deepened with the coming of their baby boy. And now the letter lay before Mr. Taylor in which the mother tried to comfort *him* in her overwhelming grief.

" It is just possible," she wrote from Wen-chow, " that you may have heard of the honour that my God and Father has put upon me. Yes, He has trusted me to live without my beloved husband and darling child. They are not, for God has taken them. . . ."

Briefly she told the circumstances, sparing Mr. Taylor most of the touching details : the father reaching home from a journey to find himself just in time for the funeral of his little son ; the bleeding heart, so chastened in its sorrow that he could say to an intimate friend two days later : " Ah, man ! It has been a blessed time for me : the Lord has made it a sweet sacrament to my soul " ; the short, sharp fight for life after life on the Mission compound ; three schoolgirls taken, a man, a woman, and the missionaries caring for them to the last, regardless of their own danger ; then Mr. Menzies first to go, followed by Mr. and Mrs. Woodman within a few hours of each other.

" It would have been so easy for me to have joined my Treasures," she continued, " but our Father has willed it otherwise. My Treasures are gone and I am left alone—yet not alone : ' Nevertheless, I am *continually* with thee.'

" Dear Mr. Taylor, God has taken His workmen, but He will carry on His work. I do not know what He has in store for me, but I do know He will guide the future as He has the past. . . . I long more than ever to do His blessed will. He has taken my *all* : now I can only give Him what remains of life. He has indeed emptied me ! May it be only to fill with His love, compassion and power."

So the sweet fragrance went up to God, and the life more than ever given to the Chinese witnessed, as words never could, to the blessed reality—" Jesus does satisfy." Thus it was all over the field : sorrow worked blessing ; trials of faith resulted in deeper confidence ; the bond of love and unity in the Mission was strengthened, and a spirit of prayer was called forth that prepared the way for more of God's own working.

The encouragements of the year were also great and many. After a visit to the training homes in the spring, Mr. Taylor wrote with thankfulness :

My heart was much rejoiced at each place. Never have parties of brighter, more capable, more consecrated workers gone out from these homes than this year.

At Chefoo there was much to be thankful for in the growth of the schools, and the way in which Dr. Douthwaite's medical work had been prospered. Beginning with three thousand cases in the first twelve months, the dispensary was now attracting over twenty thousand out-patients annually, while in the hospital hundreds of operations were performed and in-patients cared for. A great opportunity had been afforded by the recent war with Japan, of which Dr. Douthwaite and his helpers had not been slow to avail themselves. At the commencement of hostilities, strange to say, the Chinese had no provision whatever for Red Cross work.

" When the attack was made on the port of Wei-hai-wei," said the Doctor, " the Chinese fled towards Chefoo, many of them very severely wounded and many dying on the way. Snow was deep on the ground, the winter being almost arctic in severity. The poor fellows, bleeding as they were, had no strength to reach a place of refuge. Many sought safety in their own native villages, but not one was allowed to remain. They were seized by their countrymen, carried off and thrown into the sea and actually drowned, lest they should become a burden.

" About two hundred poor creatures managed to reach Chefoo in an awful condition, their clothing saturated with blood. One man, I remember, had seven bullets through him ; another, with his knee-caps shattered, had walked all the way, forty miles ; a third, with a bullet right through his lung, had walked through that bitterly cold weather ; while some crawled most of the way on their hands and knees, their feet being frostbitten. Of those that reached Chefoo, we were able to take in a hundred and sixty-three, and care for them with all the kindness possible in our hospital."

The result was amazing gratitude and openness of heart. Prejudice was broken down that had long hindered the work of the missionary, and for Dr. Douthwaite and his helpers the admiration of soldiers and civilians knew no bounds. When the war was over, a General, with all his staff, on horseback came to the hospital, attended by a brass band and a company of soldiers, and with great ceremony put up a complimentary inscription, beautifully embossed in gold on a large lacquered tablet. And when the same military official learned that stone was needed for the foundation of the new Boys' School, he sent to Dr. Douthwaite saying that he would gladly supply it from his own quarry, and that his soldiers would be delighted to carry it to the Mission compound, where they had received so much kindness.

No less encouraging had been the answer to prayer with regard to the new building for the Boys' School. Conducted on the same principles as the rest of the Mission, prayer was the only resource when the young life at Chefoo overflowed all bounds, and with a hundred boys and girls in the three departments of the school as many more were waiting to be taken in. Five thousand pounds at least were needed to put up a new building for the senior boys; and while daily prayer was being made for this sum, and many were wondering where the money could possibly come from, a letter was received by Dr. Douthwaite, the Superintendent of the station, in which a fellow-missionary said :

The Lord has laid it on my heart to bear the entire cost of building the new school.

Well might the doctor write when the beautiful premises were completed, upon which Mr. Taylor was working this summer :

Truly, the history of this school proves that God answers prayers, and that miracles are not doubtful events of a by-gone age of superstition.

Another gift that brought great joy was one the generosity

of which far exceeded its financial value. In the old home at Hang-chow, Pastor Wang and his family had united in making an offering to the Lord which deeply touched Mr. Taylor's heart. Declining a settled salary that he might be on the same faith basis as the members of the Mission, Wang Lae-djün had yet been enabled to lay by for his only child a sum which to people in their position was considerable. His daughter's husband had long been his co-Pastor in the Hang-chow church, but while his gifts would have brought them affluence in a business career, it was all they could do to educate their large family on the income he received in connection with the C.I.M. But neither Pastor Ren nor his wife would consent to accept the savings of their father's lifetime.

A thousand dollars—how large a sum it seemed ! No : it must not be given to them or their children. The Lord had always provided for their needs, and would still provide. It was far too precious for any but Himself ; and to Him they would unitedly give it.

So, while the war with Japan was still going on, the dear old Pastor came up to Shanghai to see Mr. Taylor. Very moving it was to the latter to learn the object of his visit, and that the money which meant so much to him and his was to be used, through the Mission, for sending out evangelists to carry the glad tidings to those who had never heard.

To the dear old Pastor it was wonderful to see the extensive premises of the Mission in Shanghai, and hear of the progress of the work throughout the far inland provinces, remembering the early beginnings in the little house by the Ningpo canal to which his beloved missionary friend had brought home his bride. Deeply their hearts were still united in the supreme longing that the Lord Jesus should see of the travail of His soul and be satisfied through the gathering in to Him of the fulness of His redeemed from among the millions of China.

Even this year of trial stood out as one of thankfulness, because it proved by the blessing of God to be the most fruitful in soul-winning that the Mission had ever known.

" In the midst of our sorrows God has been working," Mr. Taylor wrote, looking back upon its experiences, " and it is no small joy to record that, notwithstanding all hindrances, and in some cases through the very trials reported, many souls have been brought to Christ, so that a larger number of converts have been baptized in 1895 than in any previous year."

Detained in Shanghai amid all the coming and going ; welcoming new workers from many lands, and hearing the simple, often touching stories of how God had led them ; feeling the throb of faith and love that pulsed throughout the far-reaching fellowship of the Mission, Mr. Taylor might indeed have said, with one of his helpers of this summer : " It seems to me that the Holy Spirit is working all over the world on behalf of China."

CHAPTER XXXVIII

AGAIN THE FORWARD MOVEMENT

1896–1899.   AET. 64–67.

IT was hardly to be wondered at that Mr. Taylor's physical powers, so long taxed to the utmost in the interests of the Mission, should begin to fail under the strain of periods such as this of his ninth visit to China. It was the heart burdens that told, even more than the responsibilities of his position in a time of political upheaval and general unrest. " Worn out with loving " was as true of him as of the ardent spirit of whom the words were written,[1] and his service was checkered now with times of weakness from which recovery was less complete and rapid than formerly. Little by little the scaffolding of his life was being taken down from about the work he had prayed into being. Not that those nearest to him recognised it, or if they did in moments of anxiety could reconcile themselves to the thought. But he himself had it steadily in view, and rejoiced in the growing usefulness of others, and the way in which provision was being made for leadership in days to come.

The internal organisation slowly developed, and at much cost was working well throughout the Mission. The appointment of Mr. William Cooper as Assistant Deputy Director in China was proving exceedingly helpful, his wise judgement and loving spirit making him invaluable at head-

---

[1] The Rev. Denholm Brash, the devoted pastor and evangelist, of whom his son presents so beautiful a picture in the Memoir entitled, *Love and Life*, published by Kelly & Co.

quarters.[1] Mr. Broumton also had joined the Shanghai staff, the financial department having been moved from Wu-chang in order to consolidate the work. Thus the completed buildings round the Mission compound were utilised to the utmost. More and more the C.I.M. was saving expense and caring for its workers through the business department, and in nothing was the practical value of its principles more evident than in the provision made in this and other ways for coming needs. Refusing none who seemed truly called of God, whatever their nationality, denomination, or previous training, the Mission had been given men and women with every sort of qualification for usefulness. If all had been theologians or members of learned professions, how could the practical working of so large and varied an organisation have been provided for ? As it was, when need arose for the formation of a diocese in Western China, there was a bishop to be found in the ranks of the Mission. There were superintendents for great districts, including Mr. D. E. Hoste, recently appointed to South Shan-si. There were financial experts for the management of complicated money matters ; stenographers to help with the burden of correspondence ; competent heads for postal, shipping, and business offices ; an architect and land surveyor for building operations ; doctors and nurses to care for their fellow-missionaries as well as for medical work among the people ; and last, but not least, qualified teachers for the increasingly responsible posts at Chefoo. And all these workers, each indispensable in their own department, were equally members of the Mission and called to spiritual service in China.

" We are a very large family, and rather mixed," said Mr. Cooper when the Mission numbered seven hundred, " but all

---

[1] With much gentleness of spirit, Mr. Cooper possessed strong individuality and was fearless as to his convictions. Mr. Taylor's relationship with the leaders in the Mission, and with this beloved friend in particular, may be judged from an incident that took place in the early days of the China Council.

" I do not like so often to oppose you," said Mr. Cooper on one occasion ; " I think I had better resign."

" No, indeed ! " was the reply, " I *value* such opposition : it saves me from many a mistake."

labouring in blessed harmony in this work of works. With a bond of union like this and a field like China, we can afford to sink our differences."

Of the interesting appointment of Mr. Cassels to the diocese of West China, Dr. Eugene Stock wrote as follows in his *History of the Church Missionary Society* :

The China Inland leaders heartily entered into the plan, and Archbishop Benson, who took a warm interest in it, appointed, at the suggestion of the C.M.S. Committee, and with all his usual graciousness, the head of the C.I.M. in Sze-chwan to be the new bishop. This was the Rev. W. W. Cassels, one of the Cambridge Seven of 1885, in whose goodness and wisdom all parties had learned to repose confidence. The first public announcement was made at the great Saturday missionary meeting at the Keswick Convention of 1895, and drew forth much prayerful interest and sympathy. The C.M.S. guaranteed the Episcopal stipend, and Mr. Cassels came on to the Society's roll of missionaries, while fully retaining his position in the C.I.M. He was consecrated on St. Luke's Day, October 18, 1895, together with Dr. Talbot, the present Bishop of Rochester ; and he sailed on that day week for China. From Shanghai he wrote a striking letter to the missionary workers in his new diocese, headed with these words : " I am but a little child " ; " Jesus called a little child unto Him, and set him in the midst " ; " A little child shall lead them." The arrangement has proved by God's blessing a singularly happy one.[1]

When Bishop Cassels reached China to take up his new responsibilities, Mr. Taylor missed the expected pleasure of meeting him in Shanghai. Broken down after a visit to Wen-chow, to which he had gone immediately upon hearing of the deaths through cholera, he had been obliged to take a few weeks' rest. This gave opportunity for a boat journey to several of the Che-kiang stations, and for refreshing intercourse with Mr. Frost, who was again in China. Accompanied by Mrs. Taylor, they went to the

---

[1] Mr. Stevenson being at home in England, Mr. Taylor was glad to leave the matter, as concerned the C.I.M., largely in his hands. While regretting the partial loss of Mr. Cassels to the Mission, inevitable through the enlargement of his sphere, " I cannot but think," he wrote to a member of the London Council, " that it will be for the advantage of China. Mr. Cassel's department is surpassed by nothing in the Mission for spirituality or success."

beautiful district of Chu-chow, occupied by the Barmen Associates of the Mission, and completed the arrangements for handing it over to these fellow-workers—an important step in the direction of division of the field. But Mr. Taylor was still so unfit for any pressure of work on his return to Shanghai that it was with thankfulness they looked forward to the visit to India he was to pay before long.

A former member of the Mission, Miss Annie Taylor, who had made a remarkable journey through Tibet, was urgently needing help with a band of inexperienced workers she had been the means of calling out. They were in Northern India, hoping to gain an entrance from the Darjeeling district to that long-closed land, and Mr. Taylor was to speak at the first Christian Student Conference in Calcutta on his way to join them. An unexpected gift received for their own use made it possible for Mrs. Taylor to accompany him, which in his poor state of health was no little comfort. It would have enabled them also to travel second class by French mail, had they chosen to spend it all upon themselves. But there were fellow-workers to think of ; and though third class meant separation in the cabins for men and women respectively, they were thankful for berths near the doors which were not far apart. Then at Hongkong, Mr. Taylor was able to write the following letters, among others, to Shanghai.

After completing our arrangements here and making up our accounts, I find we have a margin that will allow of our providing the ten pounds we spoke of as desirable for your expenses beyond Melbourne. As the Mission funds were low when we left, we are very thankful to be able to send this. I had rather no one knew of the little gift.

I find the kind gift received in Wen-chow more than covers my wife's travelling expenses ; and having come to Hongkong cheaply, we have the joy of being able to enclose a cheque for a hundred taels toward your journey. . . . Please do not let any one know of this, but cash the cheque yourself at the bank.

Few things are more precious in the records that remain than the frequency of such acts of loving ministry, at a cost that no one knew of save the Lord Himself, to whom first and most of all their gifts were offered.

But though prospered in their visit to India, and much refreshed by intercourse with workers in that great field, the needs of which profoundly impressed him, Mr. Taylor was in no condition to face a summer in China, and an absence of more than two years from England made it desirable for him to be again in touch with the home work. He returned therefore after the spring meeting of the China Council, thankfully leaving matters to the wise and helpful direction of Mr. William Cooper.

Great were the changes that had taken place, as the travellers were prepared to find ; the new headquarters of the Mission being now completed and occupied at Newington Green. Knowing they would arrive from Paris during the Saturday prayer meeting, they avoided mentioning the train by which they were coming, so that no thought of giving them a welcome might disturb the meeting. Friends were on the tip-toe of expectation, however, and a larger company than usual had gathered, the Mildmay Conference and the Jubilee of the World's Evangelical Alliance having brought many visitors to London. Leaving their cab at the entrance, it was with great interest Mr. and Mrs. Taylor walked up the private road from the busy London thoroughfare to the open door of the hall for meetings, over which, carved in stone, stood out the words which meant so much in the history of the Mission—" HAVE FAITH IN GOD." Entering quietly, they remained at the back of the room while prayer was going on, so that not until the meeting closed was it generally known that Mr. and Mrs. Taylor were present. The warm welcome they then received greatly delighted some of the Continental delegates of the Evangelical Alliance who were staying at the Mission-house.

For the new premises were spacious enough to contribute to the realisation of one of Mr. Taylor's cherished ambitions : that of being able, in measure, to discharge the debt of the Mission for hospitality in many lands, by receiving—whether in London, Shanghai, or elsewhere—those of the one great family to whom a home away from home might be a con-venience. Simple as it was in all its appointments, the London headquarters could accommodate quite a number

of guests, and in Miss Williamson a hostess had been found
as large of heart as she was full of sympathy with the ideals
of the Mission.[1]

Here, then, in the summer of 1896, Mr. and Mrs. Taylor
settled down for the last period, little as any one realised it,
of their active service in connection with the work in
England. Their children being scattered they no longer
needed a home of their own, and though with advancing age
they might have been glad of more of privacy at times,
they were thankful for the closeness of touch with their
fellow-workers afforded by the daily life of the Mission-house.

The retirement of Mr. Broomhall had made a change
they could not but feel in the London work. But Number
2 Pyrland Road was still his home, and the relations of love
and sympathy were unbroken. The step had been taken
during Mr. Taylor's absence, after twenty years of service,
on Mrs. Broomhall's part as well as his own, the value of
which was beyond estimation.

" Few probably are aware," Mr. Howard recorded in the
minutes of the Council, " of the immense amount of work accomplished by Mr. Broomhall in past days, when he was assisting
Mr. Taylor in the early and rapid development of the Mission,
and almost single-handed was doing the work now divided
amongst several—and the Council feels that no words of theirs
can adequately express all that the Mission owes to his untiring
energy and unbounded labours. And they cannot but recall
how, for years, it was the privilege of candidates for China to be
welcomed into the happy home circle of Pyrland Road, where
in Mr. and Mrs. Broomhall a great many of our members now
labouring in China found a second father and mother."

The responsible post of Secretary was now filled by Mr.
Sloan, and both he and Mr. Wood in the deputation work
were leaders to be relied on. Mr. Taylor thus found himself
free for the larger issues claiming thought and prayer, for
conference with Mr. Stevenson and the Council, and for
visits to Norway, Sweden, and Germany for personal intercourse with the representatives of affiliated missions. And

[1] Toward the erection of these premises Mr. and Mrs. Taylor had
themselves given £900, though only one or two members of the Council
were aware of the fact.

then, with returning strength, he was claimed for conventions
and meetings of all sorts just in the old way, from the
Highlands to Salisbury Plain, and from Gloucester and
Liverpool to the eastern counties.

To Mr. J. T. Morton, who was increasingly interested in
the work, he wrote somewhat later :

You kindly ask whether workers are offering freely and
whether our funds enable us to accept those so offering. I am
thankful to say that we have been enabled to send out all suitable
candidates, whom we felt to be sufficiently prepared for the
work. We have a number still in training, principally in
Edinburgh and Glasgow. . . . Sometimes during the past year
(1896) we have been straitened for funds for the support of
missionaries and of the general work, while freely supplied for
special objects. At these times God has helped us through, in
answer to much prayer. . . .

Thank you for your kind thought about myself. My aim is
to get every part of the work into such a condition that it can
be carried on without me, and with this in view I visit different
branches of it in turn. We are specially asking God to give us
an increased number of efficient leaders, and to preserve the
lives and health of those we already have.

Needless to say the Forward Movement, which had been
for a time in abeyance, was the chief burden on his heart.
Wherever he went he kept it to the front, pleading for full
consecration to Christ in view of His unconditional command,
" Preach the Gospel *to every creature.*" Busy indeed was
the winter (1896–1897) after his return from the Continent,
when he was strong enough to travel constantly and address
meetings in all parts of the country. Never had invitations
been more cordial or the hearts of the Lord's people more
open to him. Many who remembered his missionary appeals
in the days of their childhood had grown to maturity, and
those who remained of his first friends and supporters were,
like himself, far on in life's pilgrimage. No voice had quite
the ring for them of his voice ; no one was more welcome
in conferences or among the churches of all denominations
that had known him so long.

How they loved him in that warm, throbbing centre
of Christian activity St. George's Cross Tabernacle,

Glasgow ! Of his many visits, the Rev. D. J. Findlay wrote :

His ministry in public and in our home was made a rich blessing, and the atmosphere of the presence of God which always surrounded him was a precious benediction. The way in which he was ever ready to give place to other speakers and to plead and pray for other missions was specially helpful. One year he gave half the time set apart for his own address to Mr. Fanstone from South America, who launched the " Help for Brazil " effort on that occasion and obtained his first missionary on the spot.

More than once Mr. Taylor spoke to us at the Table of the Lord, and these were memorable occasions. Many remember with what overflowing joy, on his last visit (Sept. 1896), he led us in singing the chorus of which he was very full at the time :

> I am feasting on the Living Bread,
>   I am drinking at the Fountain Head ;
> For he that drinketh, Jesus said,
>   Shall never, never thirst again.

It was as always the need of others that occupied him most—the desire not to get but to give, to bring all whom he could influence into the rest and joy of abiding fellowship with Christ.

·" There are many hearts, everywhere, wanting to know more of the fulness of Christ," he wrote to Mr. C. G. Moore before a longer visit to Germany in the spring of 1897. " Ask with us a fresh anointing for this service of love."

Tired with the winter's work, he was glad to accept Mr. Berger's invitation to the south of France for a quiet week or two before beginning his Continental meetings. It was good to be with his loved friend once more, for whom the sands of life were running low,[1] and to put into practice the injunction of which he had himself written a few months previously :

---

[1] During Mr. Taylor's next visit to China, Mr. Berger passed swiftly and painlessly into the presence of the Lord he loved, on the 9th of January 1899. Few expressions of his thoughtful sympathy in the work had been more precious to Mr. Taylor than his gift a few years previously of £4000 to commence a Superannuation Fund for the members of the Mission. To this Fund, any profits from the sale of the present volume, as from *Hudson Taylor in Early Years*, are devoted.

On my birthday I received your cheering note and card, for both of which my heart thanks you. May I send back the same message—" *Rest, in the Lord* " ?

> Bear not a single care thyself,
> One is too much for thee ;
> The work is mine, and mine alone,
> Thy work is—rest in me.

You will notice, perhaps, that I have put in a comma after the word " Rest," for I think that sometimes we run on in thought to the end and forget the first part of the sentence. Rest, as if nothing more were said. When you need it, rest in body ; rest always in spirit. Rest as one " in Him " alone can, and as all such can afford to ; for one with Him, all things are ours. Rest in His love, power, strength, riches. Ah, what arms to enfold, what a heart to lean upon !

Limits of space forbid more than a brief mention of that important visit to Germany, in which Mr. Taylor was joined by Mr. Sloan for the months of March and April. In addition to the Barmen Mission, whose workers Mr. Taylor had recently visited in China, there was a newer movement at Kiel which he was glad to strengthen. Started as a branch of the C.I.M. and subsequently developed as the Liebenzell Mission, this work was destined to great usefulness, and both its leaders and those of the older Barmen Mission gave Mr. Taylor a cordial welcome and many opportunities for speaking about China.[1]

---

[1] Of the origin of the Liebenzell work and Mr. Taylor's visit of the previous summer, Pastor Coerper wrote :

" When in 1896 the dear Hudson Taylor came to see me at Essen, his clear simple testimonies were a great joy and inspiration for me and others. He was just then helping to form a German branch of the C.I.M., as there was much interest for the Mission in China in districts not attainable for the Barmen Alliance Mission. He mentioned the matter to me several times, asking me to join him in prayer about it. How I longed to offer myself for this work ! But I did not feel free to do so, fearing that I might be following merely the desires of my own heart. When in 1899, however, the call came to me quite clearly . . . to take charge of the work, the Lord had opened the way and had made me willing to devote my life to Him for this service."

The Liebenzell Mission, still (1918) under the care of Pastor Coerper, has twelve central stations and sixty missionaries in the province of Hunan (Associates of the C.I.M.) with almost a thousand church members. It has also nineteen representatives in the South Sea Islands. All that such figures mean of prayer, labour, and self-sacrificing gifts at home, as well as devoted service abroad, the Lord only knows. It is a privilege to record

In Berlin their meetings were chiefly under the auspices of the Y.M.C.A., which had invited them for a Student Conference.   Generously entertained by Count Pückler, they were kept busy for ten days in the capital, some of the meetings doing much to deepen friendly relations.   For the C.I.M., as they discovered, was none too favourably regarded in certain quarters.   Its interdenominational basis did not commend it to leaders of Societies connected with the State Church, and the accounts that had reached them of its growth and faith principles were hardly credited.   It was, thus, in a somewhat uncertain frame of mind that prominent ministers and secretaries gathered in the drawing-room of Mrs. Palner Davies (*née* Baroness von Dungern) to meet the visitors, interested specially in seeing what sort of person " the renowned Hudson Taylor " might be.

" The stranger who stood in our midst," wrote the Baroness, " was not of an imposing appearance, and his fair curly hair made him look younger than he really was."

The time was largely given, we learn from her charming letter, to questions through interpretation, and her anxiety as hostess is frankly confessed.   For she was conscious, as Mr. Taylor could not be, of the critical attitude of not a few present, who regarded him as rather a free-lance in the sphere of missions.

" But how beautifully," she exclaimed, " this heavenly-minded man was able, in the humility of his heart, to conquer all the hidden prejudice against him and his work ! "

That as leader of the C.I.M. he received workers from various denominations was the first point on which explanation was desired.

Only recently the Mission had accepted a number of highly-educated and well-gifted young men who were members of the State Church.   How, then, were they able to work together with Methodists and Baptists, etc. ?   It was also in the mind of the questioners that Mr. Taylor himself had been connected with

___

here that nowhere in connection with the C.I.M. has the spirit of Christ been more manifest in these ways, or more steadfastly maintained, than in the Barmen and the Liebenzell Missions.

Baptists, and that he was the son of a Methodist preacher, which, with regard to his orthodoxy, made the strongly Lutheran clergy look upon him with suspicion.

To all this Mr. Taylor replied that, in our chief aims, we are all one in Christ ; also that China is large enough, and the workers can be distributed over the various provinces so that each denomination is able to retain its particular order of Church government. " Only recently," he stated, " we have been glad to welcome an English Bishop (one of our own number) for Western China, so that our missionaries from the State Church are not lacking the care of a spiritual guide and head. The great work of the mission-field, which is a call to us all, overrides theological differences, and our motto remains, ' All one in Christ. . . .' "

Just when the Director of the Gossner Mission had shaken his silver-white head and remarked to his neighbour in an undertone, " Such a mixture of Church and Sectarians would be impossible with us," Mr. Taylor continued :

" It is remarkable how the Lord Himself has chosen His instruments, so that even the most insignificant, in His hand, are able to be ' to the praise of His glory.' Surely it goes as in creation : there are strong and beautiful oak-trees, but there are also little flowers of the meadow ; and both the oak and the flower have been placed there by His hand. I myself, for instance, am not specially gifted, and am shy by nature, but my gracious and merciful God and Father inclined Himself to me, and I who was weak in faith He strengthened while I was still young. He taught me in my helplessness to rest on Him, and to pray even about little things in which another might have felt able to help himself "

Instances were mentioned from his early experiences— such as the giving away of his last half-crown, the only coin he possessed in the world, when he was living alone in lodgings and scarcely knew where the next meal was to come from.[1] To know God for himself as the Hearer and Answerer of prayer had been the preparation, in view of his life-work, that he felt all-important.

He knew the desire of my heart, and simply trusting like a child, I brought all to Him in prayer. Thus I experienced, quite early, how He is willing to help and strengthen and to fulfil the desire of those who fear Him. And so in later years, when I prayed the money came.

---

[1] See *Hudson Taylor in Early Years*, pp. 132-138.

He then told how the passage, " Owe no man anything save to love one another," had raised the question in his mind, " Are we entitled to make exceptions in work for the Kingdom of God, and continuously to sigh under the oppression of debt ? " His own conclusion had been that the words meant just what they said : that God is rich enough to supply " all our need " as it arises, and that He likes to do so before we run into debt much better than afterwards ; and he gave instances to show how, trusting Him to fulfil His own Word, and neither spending money before it was received nor making appeals for help, the seven hundred missionaries of the C.I.M. were actually sustained.[1]

" Will you please tell us," was then asked, " whether it is true that after you had moved a large audience by putting the need of missionary work to their hearts, and some one arose to make a collection, you went so far as to hinder it ? "

" I have done so more than once," replied Mr. Taylor. " It is not our way to take collections, because we desire to turn aside no gifts from other Societies. We receive free-will offerings, but without putting any pressure upon people. After such a meeting they can easily find opportunity, if they wish, to send their gifts --which so far has been done freely."

" We have heard," remarked a clergyman, " that in that way some quite large sums are sent in ; but *we* aim at training our congregations to systematic giving. . . ."

" That is a very important matter," answered Mr. Taylor. " However, one is led so, while another is led otherwise. Each must act according to his light. As I said before, for my weakness' sake the Lord has acknowledged my way of working and praying, but I am far from advising any one to copy me. You do well to train individuals, to train the whole Church to systematic giving. . . ."

---

[1] In times of financial straitness Mr. Taylor more than once took occasion to remind his fellow-workers of this principle. " The position of faith is incompatible with borrowing or going into debt, or forcing our way forward when the Lord closes the door before us," he wrote in November 1898. " If we propose a certain extension for which the Lord sees the time has not come, or which is not in accordance with His will, how can He more clearly guide us than by withholding the means ? It would be a serious mistake, therefore, to refuse to listen to the Lord's ' No,' and by borrowing or going into debt do the thing to which He had objected by withholding the needed funds or facilities. All the work we are engaged in is His rather than ours ; and if the Master can afford to wait, surely the servant can also."

Other questions were still raised, until I at length interposed, saying that Mr. Taylor had promised to be present at another meeting that same evening, and it might be well to spare his strength. He had been standing, by his own request, while for over an hour we had been sitting comfortably round him. Just then a sunbeam touched his face, so full of joy and peace, bringing a brightness as from above—and I could only think of Stephen, who saw heaven opened and Jesus at the right hand of God. One present bowed his head, covering his eyes with his hand, and I heard him whisper : " We must all take shame before this man."

" Yes," the white-headed Professor replied to my suggestion, " you are quite right ; we will not trouble our friend any further." And rising he crossed the room, put his arm round Mr. Taylor's neck and kissed him.

Summer days in England, after Mr. Taylor's return from the Continent, found him more than ever occupied with meetings. Not that he was equal to the strain, but funds were low for the general purposes of the Mission, and he was never one who could pray without working to the limit of his powers. That limit was reached before the Keswick Convention, however. Suffering severely from neuralgia and headache, he was obliged to cancel his engagements and accept the doctor's verdict—complete rest, and absence from the Mission for several months to come.

The wonderful air of Davos, in Switzerland, proved just the tonic he was needing, and there in the early autumn Mr. Taylor heard of an answer to prayer that helped to confirm his recovery. He had been much exercised about a financial difficulty that had arisen, due in part to the arrangements for special support in the new branches of the Mission. To deal with it, he would have to visit America as well as China and perhaps Australia, and he was planning such a journey, when a gift of no less than ten thousand pounds for the general fund relieved the situation and sent him rejoicing on his homeward way.

And there was more to follow. The generous donor, Mr. J. T. Morton, had been in failing health for some time, but it was a shock to hear of his death within a few days of the above-mentioned gift, and almost more so to learn that he had bequeathed to the C.I.M. a fourth part of his residuary estate—a share which could not be less and might be a good deal more than *a hundred thousand pounds*. This noble legacy for evangelistic and education work was to be treated as income and not as an endowment.

Overwhelmed with thankfulness and a deep sense of responsibility, Mr. Taylor could not but connect the great trust thus committed to the Mission with the great task yet to be accomplished in China, in obedience to the divine command. Ten thousand pounds a year for ten years or longer —for the money was to be paid in instalments—what might it not accomplish toward this end ? And so it came to pass that articles under the title of " The Forward Movement " began to appear in *China's Millions*, and before the year was out (1897) he was on his way to Shanghai, full of longing to see the inauguration of an evangelistic effort that might spread throughout all the provinces.

From certain points of view the outlook was definite before him, though just as indefinite from others. He saw with perfect clearness the dangers to which so large an accession of means exposed the Mission, and deeply felt the need for an increase of spiritual power. Not with silver and gold could precious souls be won, or men and women fitted to be messengers of the cross of Christ. A fresh baptism of the Holy Spirit, the Spirit of Calvary and Pentecost, was the supreme need, and for this he prayed as never before. And he did more than pray. Knowing how much blessing had been given through " Winter Missions " in India, he approached the leaders of the Keswick Convention about similar work among the native Christians in China, if the thought approved itself to the missionary body in that great field. For it was not the C.I.M. only that was upon his heart, it was all China. He longed to see the eighty thousand communicants of all Protestant churches quickened with new life and fired with zeal for the salvation of their fellow-countrymen.

" We missionaries could not take part in such a movement," he wrote, " without being greatly refreshed and strengthened ; and the fresh anointing would prepare us to arrange among ourselves for the division of the field, and for assisting and guiding the native evangelists whom the Holy Spirit might thrust forward, and the missionary evangelists whom we expect the same Holy Spirit would call from the homelands."

A Forward Movement in spiritual power and blessing was the object most of all upon his heart.

" We are not immediately appealing for new workers," he continued with regard to the Inland Mission—" our first need being to prepare for them in China, and the most important preparation of all a spiritual one."

CHAPTER XXXIX

EVEN SO, FATHER

1898–1900   AET. 66–68.

And except life itself be cast in the scale,
No life can be won, no cause prevail.

MORE and more it was to China's Christians, filled with
the Spirit of Christ, that Mr. Taylor looked for the evangelisation of China.   In his second article on the Forward Movement, written from Shanghai (March 1898), he asked much
prayer that the Keswick deputation, to whom a cordial
welcome had been sent by Dr. Muirhead in the name of
the missionary body, might be enabled to come out without
delay, and that

. . . in the meantime the Spirit of God may work mightily,
preparing the heathen for the Gospel and the converts for fuller
blessing, likewise raising up from among them evangelists,
called, qualified, and constrained to preach the Gospel, as well as
live out the Christ-life.

"There are eighty thousand Protestant communicants in
China," he had written in his earlier paper, "and possibly as
many more candidates and probationers.   Besides these there
are a still larger number who are convinced of the truth of
Christianity, though they have not yet grace and courage to
confess Christ.   If there were a widespread outpouring of the
Holy Spirit, all these might speedily be swept into the fold, and
the effect in China of a quarter of a million earnest, active, holy-
living Christians would be very great." [1]

---

[1] Mr. Taylor's thought, as set forth in these papers, was that centres
should be arranged for, in charge of experienced missionaries, to which
the new workers (foreign) should go on arrival for study of the language
and training in evangelistic method, and to which they could return from

But though the work was theirs, and without them could never be carried to completion, Mr. Taylor equally felt the need for Spirit-filled missionaries and many more of them, especially evangelists. Never before had he seen his way so clearly as far as money was concerned, but that very fact only made a revival of spiritual blessing the more urgent. Ten or twelve thousand pounds annually, in addition to current income, to be spent as it was received and to be spent in China, was a serious responsibility. It meant not only great possible development, but great possible difficulty at the end of the period when, the last instalment having been paid, the new undertakings would have to be carried on. Mr. Taylor had no doubt whatever but that the whole thing—the form of the bequest as well as the gift itself—was of God, and had no hesitation in accepting it ; but he saw that to go forward and enlarge the work without an increase of faith, prayer, and spiritual power, which alone could make it fruitful and sustain it, would be to court disaster.

" There probably never was a time when we needed divine guidance more than at present," he had written to Mr. Stevenson before leaving England. " We sorely need fresh life infusing into every part of our work, without which this large legacy

time to time for rest and refreshment after their itinerations. Chinese evangelists should also have training and Bible study in such centres.

" A special Itinerant Missionary Evangelistic Band would then be required," he wrote, " willing to consecrate five years of their lives to itinerant work, without thought of marriage or of settling down till their special work is accomplished. The work would be arduous, involving much self-denial, but it would bring with it much blessing and great spiritual joy, as the command, ' Preach the Gospel to every creature,' was being obeyed : in keeping of His commandments there is great reward (see Psalm xix. 11).

" The workers, when ready, would go out two and two, *i.e.* two missionaries and two native helpers, to previously arranged districts, to sell Scriptures and Gospel tracts, and to preach the Glad Tidings. Living together in the same inns, for companionship and fellowship, they would often separate during the day, one missionary and native brother going in one direction, and the other two in another, and meeting again at night, to commend to God the work of the day, as before setting out they had unitedly sought His blessing. Two-thirds to three-quarters of their time being thus occupied, the remainder would afford opportunity for bodily and spiritual rest and refreshment, for continuing the Chinese studies of the missionaries, and the systematic Bible studies of the native helpers. As the work progresses the number of these centres would need increasing."

which has been left us may prove the greatest misfortune we have had for a long time."

It was with this double thought in view therefore—a Forward Movement, based upon real accessions of spiritual blessing—that Mr. Taylor came out for his tenth visit to China, accompanied by Mrs. Taylor, Miss Soltau of the Women's Department in London, and Miss Bessie Hanbury —a little company who knew the way to the Throne. How serious was the call to prayer they could not but realise from another consideration very present to their minds.

" If the Spirit of God work mightily," Mr. Taylor wrote on the journey, " we may be quite sure that the spirit of evil will also be active. When the appeal for a thousand new workers went forth from the Missionary Conference of 1890, the enemy at once began a counter-movement, and riots and massacres have from time to time followed as never before."

Not that this was any argument for holding back. It simply meant that whatever was undertaken must be begun, as it could alone be continued, *in God.*

One year and nine months now lay before Mr. Taylor of this last period of his active service in China (Jan. 1898 to Sept. 1899). He as little as those about him realised it to be the last, and yet in tracing its experiences one cannot but be conscious of the finishing touches God was putting to the life labours of His servant. He was present at all the Council Meetings of this period, for example, with one exception. Seven times the leaders of the Mission gathered to meet him, and he was enabled to come into touch, through them, with a large part of the work. Many questions of difficulty were settled, and some problems of long standing happily solved. Then the important question of the Forward Movement was dealt with in ways that told of God's own working.

" Before leaving home," Mr. Taylor wrote in this connection, " we were greatly cheered by the promise of Ps. xxxii. 8, ' I will instruct thee and teach thee in the way which thou shalt go.' We felt we were going forward in this matter not knowing when, how, or where God would have the new work begun, but assured that, *in the way*, needed light and leading would be given ; and we have not been disappointed."

Quite apart from previous planning, experienced workers had met in Shanghai from England, America, the Continent of Europe, and the interior of China, and after the January and April Council Meetings all was arranged for a beginning to be made in the accessible province of Kiang-si, with its ninety-nine governing cities, capitals of counties, in very few of which the Gospel was as yet being preached.

The tide of spiritual blessing, too, was rising, even before the arrival of the Keswick deputation. He who delights to use " the weak things " had found a cleansed and empty vessel which He was pleased to fill to overflowing with His own Spirit.

" I go forth in conscious weakness," Miss Soltau had written of her visit to China, " feeling my need of His abundant life for the untried way."

Drawing on the promised fulness, she had begun the journeys which were to occupy thirteen consecutive months, taking her over six thousand miles in all, to forty-four mission-stations, in every one of which she was made a blessing. Some years before, from her responsible post in London, she had written to a near relative :

The work is always increasing ; and were it not for the consciousness of Christ as my life, hour by hour, I could not go on. But He is teaching me glorious lessons of His sufficiency, and each day I am carried onward with no feeling of strain or fear of collapse.

And so it was in China. Fatiguing journeys, lack of quiet and home-comforts, extremes of winter cold and summer heat, and at each station the demands of heart-to-heart interviews with beloved workers, many of whom were like her own children, as well as of frequent meetings with the missionaries or Chinese Christians who flocked around her—all were met in the same spirit of dependence upon the resources of the Lord Himself. Thus there was no breakdown, no hindrance to carrying out a full programme ; and from station after station Mr. Taylor had

the joy of receiving just the tidings he longed for.   From
the young men's training home at An-king he heard through
Mr. Stevenson of Miss Soltau's visit as " a truly remarkable
season."

"The Holy Spirit was poured out upon all present," Mr.
Taylor wrote, " and every one of the missionaries and students
received extraordinary spiritual help.   Such a Pentecostal
season had never been experienced there before.   This, surely,
is what we need, for ourselves and for our native brethren."

With regard to his own usefulness, it was doubtless a
trial to Mr. Taylor that he was prevented through ill-health
from joining in these meetings.   For several months after
his arrival he was confined more or less to his room, but
amid outward limitations he was learning much of the
divine alchemy that for brass can bring gold and for iron
silver, teaching in so many ways the lesson that His strength
is "*made perfect* in weakness."   To Dr. A. T. Pierson, whom
he had visited in America, and who had since been laid
aside by serious illness, Mr. Taylor wrote in April :

Ah, how much pains the Lord takes to empty us and to show
us He can do without us !   My experience has not been yours,
of suffering pain for any long periods, but of great prostration
and weakness, so that I have had to decline all public work since
reaching China.   In a quiet way I have been able to think and
pray over many matters, and to confer with many of our workers.
Some important arrangements have been made, which will, I
believe, bear fruit in the future, and I trust some lessons have
been learned.   May we both be better fitted for any service the
Lord may call us to, or for His own blessed appearing, which
surely is very near !

On our way out my wife came across a little verse in *Hymns
of Tersteegen and Others* which we have often thought of since :

> He told me of a river bright
> Which flows from Him to me,
> That I might be, for His delight,
> A fair and fruitful tree.

It is very simple : but has He not planted us by the river of
living water that we may be *for His delight,* fair and fruitful to
His people ? . . .

Sometimes God can carry on His work better without us
than with us. .   . Then, again, the best work is not always done

with large numbers. Our Lord fed the five thousand on the mountain-side, and eternity may show results we shall not know of till that day, but the record does not tell of much immediate outcome. On the other hand, He fed one woman at the well of Samaria, and immediately, through her, brought multitudes to His feet. So, do you not think, the Lord may see fit to call us away from the thousands, and do perhaps His best work through us to tens or even units, whom we may meet by the way?

May He lead you, dear Brother, and continue to bless you more and more. I am increasingly thankful that " My Father is the Husbandman." There are " under-shepherds " ; but no prentice hand trains the branches of the True Vine, nor cleanses nor prunes them.

Dr. Pierson had not been able to join the Keswick deputation to China, but the Rev. Charles Inwood came, fresh from a wonderful time of blessing on the Continent. Accustomed to speaking through interpretation and to leading his hearers step by step from the elements of truth into fuller and deeper experiences, he was just the teacher needed, and from autumn to early summer he and Mrs. Inwood laboured without intermission as Miss Soltau was doing, their united service covering almost the entire period of Mr. Taylor's visit. One year and five months altogether these special meetings continued, Mr. Inwood in particular finding a wide sphere outside the Inland Mission. Travelling over ten thousand miles—north and south and far up the Yangtze to Chung-king—he had " precious fellowship with every missionary society in China," and found that year stand out, in spite of toil and danger, as the brightest he had ever spent in the Master's service.

Mr. Taylor meanwhile had wonderfully gained in strength, and even before Mr. Inwood's arrival had been able to take several journeys, and by meetings and correspondence to forward the same important end. While detained in Shanghai he had met over two hundred members of the Mission, and subsequently in visits to Chefoo and the new hill-station at Ku-ling had had opportunity for ministry to a large circle. But his letters went further still, carrying much of the blessing that sustained him and which he thankfully realised to be accessible to all.

" Go forward in the strength of the Lord, and in the sufficiency that comes from Him alone," he wrote to one who needed encouragement, " and thank Him for your conscious insufficiency, for when you are weak, then He can be strong in you.

" Do not be afraid to let His light shine through you ; do not be afraid to let even a trickling overflow, overflow. Do not let any self-consciousness prevent your being at God's disposal for any message He may want you to give at any time, to any one. Never mind what people think about you ; perhaps they will only think about Him, not about you at all, and thank Him for His ministry, though it may come through you. If at any time you are conscious of failure or sin, or even if you stand in doubt about anything, confess it at once to Him, and accept His promise of immediate cleansing and restoration. The moment you switch on electricity, the light shines or the power is manifested, just as before it was switched off,—though in spiritual things the power of God may be manifested differently at one time from another. I do pray for you. My very heart goes out in prayer on your behalf, and I never was more thankful to God for you than I am now." [1]

No pains seemed too great if he could lead a soul into fuller blessing, and not least, his own children.

" With regard to many truths, there are two aspects to be borne in mind," he wrote to his daughter a few weeks later, " the divine and the human. This is so of the question of being filled with the Spirit. The command ' be filled ' etc., points us to the human side. What do we mean when we say that a loving mother is ' full of her baby ' ? Some leave their babies to the nurse and do little or nothing for them themselves, going occasionally to amuse themselves with their children, but finding their principal enjoyments apart from them altogether. But the mother full of her baby is very different. Her heart, her time, her life are given to the child. Very much in the same way, the ' mind of the Spirit ' spoken of in Romans viii. 6 (R.V.) means letting the Holy Spirit fill us and have us.

" Now the heart can no more be filled with two things at the same time than a tumbler can be filled with both air and water at the same time. If you want a tumbler full of water to be filled with air, it has first to be emptied of the water. This shows us why prayer to be filled with the Spirit is often gradually answered. We have to be shown our sins, our faults, our prepossessions, and to be delivered from them. Faith is the channel

---

[1] Written from Ku-ling, Sept. 2, 1898.

by which all grace and blessing are received ; and that which is accepted by faith, God bestows in fact. Being filled does not always lead to exalted feeling or uniform manifestation, but God always keeps His word. We have to look to His promises or rest in them, expecting their literal fulfilment. Some put asking in the place of accepting ; some wish it were so, instead of believing that it is so. We have never to wait for God's giving, for God has already ' blessed us with all spiritual blessings in heavenly things in Christ.' We may reverently say, He has nothing more to give ; for He has given His *all*. Yet, just as the room is full of air, but none can get into the tumbler save as far as the water is emptied out, so we may be unable to receive all He has given, if the self-life is filling to some extent our hearts and lives."

Gradually, as 1898 wore on, the outlook with regard to social and political conditions became increasingly disquieting. While souls were being saved in larger numbers than ever before and spiritual blessing given, the political unrest which had been growing since the Japanese war, and the bitterness of feeling due to the aggressions of foreign powers were hastening a crisis the nature of which was but too evident. The countermove Mr. Taylor had anticipated as likely to hinder widespread evangelistic effort was taking serious form. Too hasty attempts on the part of the young Emperor to introduce reforms had thrown the country into a ferment ; open discussion in the European press of the " partition of China " was goading the authorities to desperation ; and the Imperial Government had so lost influence with the people that, as Mr. Taylor wrote in July, there seemed " little hope of averting a complete collapse." A powerful rebellion had broken out in Western China in the spring of the year, which was still unsubdued ; local uprisings and riots were of frequent occurrence ; and finally the Dowager Empress, at the head of the reactionary party, had resumed the reins of government, visiting with dire retribution the over-zealous reformers, and consigning the hapless Emperor to virtual imprisonment in " the inner apartments." This had taken place in September, and now in quick succession drastic measures were being taken to reverse the policy of recent years and to curtail the pretensions of foreigners. Needless to say, this sudden change of front on the part of the Government encouraged anti-foreign feeling throughout the country; and as almost the only Europeans in the interior were missionaries, it was against them particularly that hostilities were directed. The situation was fraught with peril, and could not but give rise to serious apprehensions.

"Leave God out of count," Mr. Frost had written for the November *China's Millions*, "and fear might well possess and overwhelm us. Bring God into account and there is perfect peace for us at home and for our beloved missionaries in China. . . . Satan is mighty, but God is almighty. Not one thing can man do that God does not allow to be done, and one outstretching of His glorious arm can subdue every enemy. . . . For thirty-two years of the Mission's history He has preserved life in the face of threatened dangers, so that up to the present time, in spite of robbers, bandits, and rioters, not one person has been called on such accounts to pass through death. And further, suppose He should allow this long record of divine interposition to be broken, would He be less strong to keep in the hour of death than He has been in the days of life? We do not speak lightly; but thinking of God and of His mighty acts, and with the past in view, though faced in thought with martyr fires and rack and sword, we know that God can keep His own, and we believe that He would do so, now, as in the days of old."

That for thirty-two years God had so watched over the Mission that no life had ever been lost through violence or accident or in travelling was a very real comfort to Mr. Taylor. Frequently in his letters of this troubled year he calls attention to the fact, which was indeed a remarkable one, considering the pioneering work accomplished in all the inland provinces, and that there was scarcely a moment of the day or night in which journeys were not being taken, either by land or water. Shipwrecks had occurred once and again at sea, and more often on the rapids of the Yangtze; but though loss of property had been permitted, as also in many a riot, life and limb had been protected in every case, often in most wonderful ways. Indeed, there had grown up in Mr. Taylor's mind a restful confidence in God that He *would* thus protect His servants in the

Mission, especially defenceless women, working alone in their stations, at a distance often from the nearest missionaries. He rejoiced in their faith and devotion no less than in the blessing that rested on their labours. At this very time (1898–1899) despite persecution and threatened danger, two hundred and fifty converts were received into church membership in the ladies' stations on the Kwang-sin River, while a thousand inquirers were under instruction as candidates for baptism. Such a result from the labours of a few young women in a few brief years, with quite a small, though growing, band of native leaders, was indeed cause for thankfulness.[1]

To a woman also had been given success in the difficult and dangerous task of effecting a settled residence in Hu-nan, so long the most anti-foreign province in China. With a single native helper and a Chinese woman-companion she had walked quietly over the border from Kiang-si, under the very eyes of the soldiery sent to guard the frontier, but who never dreamed of connecting those dusty wayfarers with the dreaded foreigner they were to intercept ! During his recent visit to England Mr. Taylor had been rejoiced by a letter (1896) from this brave Norwegian worker saying that the Lord Jesus had taken up His abode in the hearts of some of the people over the border, and that if *she* should be put out, *He* could not—for hearts that have once received Him are not likely to give Him up. But a new day had dawned for Hu-nan. Miss Jacobsen was not put out. On the contrary, the Rev. George Hunter, Dr. Keller and others were so prospered in similar efforts that this very period of uneasiness and trouble witnessed the opening of centre after centre, until the C.I.M. alone had *four* settled stations in the province. From Cha-ling-chow, Dr. Keller wrote at the close of 1898 :

We have from twenty to forty quiet, attentive hearers at our morning services. Yesterday, Sunday, we held a longer meeting,

---

[1] " They are weak enough for God to use," Mr. Taylor had written of similar workers in Shan-si, " and they believe in being filled with the Holy Ghost. They seek a blessing with fasting and prayer, and they do not seek in vain. The people feel that there is power in connection with their work."

about sixty being present.   We have quite a few callers, and they
all drink tea with us without hesitation.   Is not this rather
unusual ?   Everything seems peaceful and quiet.   Oh, let us
praise Him !   Reports are brought to us of some harsh talk in a
large students' hall near here—threats to kill our landlord and
loot his premises, and afterwards make an assault on us.   We are
in God's hands, and He is almighty. . . . Pray for us.

By this time Mr. Taylor was on his way up the Yangtze
to the far west of China.   Despite the rebellion in Szechwan,
which was still in progress, and the unquiet state of the
country everywhere, Mr. and Mrs. Inwood were to attend
the conference of West China missionaries to be held at
Chung-king in January (1899) and Mr. and Mrs. Taylor
had decided to accompany them.   The journey, first by
steamer and then by native boat hundreds of miles up the
Yangtze, was no little undertaking in mid-winter, especially
to those unaccustomed to the rapids ; but much help was
found on the way at the various homes and business centres
of the Mission, at which every possible arrangement was
made for the comfort of the travellers.   Very different
had been Mr. Taylor's earlier experiences before the Mission
had any business organisation, when in the midst of pressing
work and responsibilities he had to look after such affairs
himself, or risk their miscarrying.   Of one journey, happily
not a long one, he retained a feeling recollection—when the
willing but unbusinesslike fellow-worker to whom he had
entrusted his belongings (being so busy himself that he
hardly knew how to get off) arrived with his coolie at the
landing-stage just as the vessel was steaming away.   Mr.
Taylor, after waving farewell to his baggage, had to sleep
on bare boards that night—making the best, as he said, of
a shoe and an umbrella for a pillow and the cold wintry
air for a coverlet.   Now, things were on a very different
footing, and no one appreciated the change, or the sacrifice
at which able and devoted missionaries were facilitating
the work of others, more than the leader of the Mission who
had himself known so much of " serving tables."

But not all the loving care of fellow-workers by the
way could keep from him the heavy tidings received at

Hankow of the first martyrdom in the ranks of the C.I.M. Away in the distant province of Kwei-chow the tragedy had occurred, when William S. Fleming, from Australia, had been murdered with his friend and helper, P'an, a convert from the Black Miao tribe they were seeking to evangelise. In trying to protect the latter, Mr. Fleming's own life had been sacrificed; and while thanking God for the spirit in which he had met his brief but terrible end, Mr. Taylor realised with a straitened heart something of what it meant that such an event should have happened.

" How sad the tidings ! " he wrote to Mr. Stevenson on the 22nd of November : " blessed for the martyrs but sad for us, for China, for their friends. And not only sad, but ominous ! It seems to show that God is about to test us with a new *kind* of trial : surely we need to gird on afresh ' the whole armour of God.' Doubtless it means fuller blessing, but through deeper suffering. May we all lean hard on the Strong for strength . . . and in some way or other the work be deepened and extended, not hindered, by these trials."

" Deepened and extended, not hindered "—how often in the months that followed the thought must have been turned into prayer as his own way was increasingly hedged about with difficulty. The conference at Chung-king proved a time of blessing. Attended by seventy to eighty missionaries of various societies it gave opportunity for Mr. Inwood's helpful ministry, and brought Mr. Taylor into touch with Bishop Cassels, Dr. Parry, and other leaders in the C.I.M. work. But the visits he and Mrs. Taylor hoped to pay to many of the western stations had to be abandoned. In the first place, a fresh outbreak of the Yü Man-tze rebellion made travelling extremely dangerous ; and further, a serious illness brought Mr. Taylor so low that his life was almost despaired of. Nursing him night and day, Mrs. Taylor at last saw that all that could be done was unavailing. It seemed as if, at any moment, his heart might fail. Realising what it would mean to the Mission if he were taken suddenly, with no one in view to fill his place, she had been holding on to God in prayer and faith for his recovery.   Now, in the silent room, she could only kneel and cry :

"Lord, we can do nothing ! Do what Thou wilt. Undertake for us."

When he next spoke, knowing nothing of her prayer, it was to whisper, "I feel better, dear " : and from that time he recovered.

On the return journey to Shanghai he regained a measure of strength, but the summer (1899) had to be spent either on the hills or at Chefoo.   It was a matter of concern to Mr. Taylor that the men for the Forward Movement seemed to be volunteering so slowly.   Some had been sent out and some had offered from the ranks of the Mission in China, including his own youngest son, but quite a few were yet needed to make up the first twenty, though the money to sustain them was waiting in abundance.   Contrasted with former experiences, such as the answers to prayer in connection with the Seventy and the Hundred, this seemed the more remarkable, and could not but confirm Mr. Taylor's life-long conviction that in God's work the silver and the gold, though very necessary, are of secondary importance.   Still, the disturbed state of the country reconciled him to patience.   Things seemed to be going from bad to worse politically.   The anti-foreign movement fostered by the Dowager Empress was growing in power, and it might be long before normal conditions were restored. Meanwhile a promised visit had to be paid to Australia and New Zealand, and then to New York for the Œcumenical Missionary Conference.   This journey, Mr. Taylor hoped, would greatly help the Forward Movement, as well as call forth much prayer for China.

A tender and special interest necessarily attaches to those spring and summer days that witnessed his last ministries in scenes and to fellow-workers long held dear. So unconscious was he that his work in China was drawing to a close that he entered heartily into plans for building a cottage to which he and Mrs. Taylor could retire for rest from the busy Mission-house at Shanghai.   This little summer home, the only dwelling they ever planned for themselves, consisted of a sitting-room and two small bedrooms, over kitchen and servants' quarters, with an upstairs verandah on three sides. The latter was the great attraction, for from it the well-wooded hills stretched away in beautiful vistas to the plain two thousand feet below. Cool even on summer nights, the spot seemed ideal for a sanatorium, and Mr. Taylor had purchased a strip of the hill while property up there was still of little value. It was soon, however, to become a favourite resort for foreign residents, and a service of steam-launches brought it within two days of Shanghai.

Thus it was that Mr. and Mrs. Taylor found themselves in the old home at Hang-chow once more, for having missed the north-bound launch they had just time to go down while waiting for the next train of boats to start. The visit was only for a few hours, but how many recollections it brought ! More than thirty years had elapsed since the *Lammermuir* party had found shelter in the house next door, beginning there the work that had now spread to the most distant provinces. Fuh Ku-niang, the bright-faced girl who had been the first to visit the women in their homes, and had led many to the Saviour, was still remembered and loved. Long had she borne with her husband the burden and heat of the day. Its working hours were numbered now. How gladly would they have spent them to the last with the dear old Pastor in the care of the church, and in soul-saving work which had always had a first place in their hearts. But the Mission needed them, needed them in some ways more than ever, and in service to their fellow-workers all those last weeks and months were filled. No one could sympathise, counsel, or comfort as they could ; no one had so sure an access, by way of the Throne, to other hearts.

In much perturbation of spirit, for example, one devoted worker had come down to Shanghai in May, determined to leave the Mission unless the principle of not appealing to Consuls for redress could be so far set aside in his case as to admit of his wrongs being righted in connection with a recent riot. Mr. Taylor greatly valued both the brother in question and his work. He knew him to be a man of intense convictions and strong feelings, and being warned of his attitude by Mr. Stevenson, who had travelled with him, gave himself specially to prayer, and delayed the interview for a day or two. It was a case for putting into practice his own words :

What is spiritual ministry ? It is that if you see me to be wrong you are able by prayer, by spiritual power, by tact, by love, forbearance and patience to enlighten my conscience, and thus cause me gladly to turn from my mistaken course to the right one.[1]

Meanwhile the young missionary, eager and impatient as he was, began to see things, somehow, in a different light. Though no word was said against his position, he could not but feel as he reconsidered the matter that it was, perhaps, rather out of keeping with the spirit of Christ. He little knew that Mr. Taylor, who seemed too busy to spare him a few minutes, was spending not minutes but hours in earnest pleading on his behalf. But that hidden influence did what no reasoning, far less exercise of authority, could have accomplished.

" Before the interview took place, or Mr. Taylor said a word to me on the subject," he recalled with thankfulness, " my whole position was changed. I saw I had been utterly wrong, and that the C.I.M. principle was right, even in such a peculiar case as mine. During our first conversation, Mr. Taylor did not refer to the matter. He talked about other things, asking my opinion as to the use of certain drugs, and when the dinner-bell rang said that he would like to have further talk with me that afternoon at three o'clock.

" I felt guilty over taking up so much of his time, and so, though I had resolved not to open the subject, I decided to tell

---

[1] " Though we cannot scold people right we may often *love* them right," he had written to Mr. Stevenson before leaving England. " It will not do for us to lose expectant faith and Holy Ghost power, and let those whom God gives us drift away, if prayer and fasting, pains and patience will hold them together. . . . We must claim from God by faith the love and spiritual power that will make men *wish* to obey. . . . I do long for myself and for all of us to be more filled with the Spirit, and thus fitted for God's work. Then we shall always overflow with love, joy, peace, gentleness, and all the fruit of the Spirit, and every one will be attracted and helped as far as possible."

him frankly of my change of position. At the appointed hour I went to him and said :

" ' Mr. Taylor, I feel I ought to let you know at once that I see things differently, and am prepared to submit the whole matter to you and act as you may direct.' "

It was a manly decision, worthy of a strong character, and Mr. Taylor's relief was so great that he could only exclaim, " Thank God ! "

" This experience was a crisis and turning-point in my life," continued Dr. Keller. " It taught me in a most practical way how even strongly formed purposes can be changed and men's hearts influenced by prayer alone. I have always felt that surrenders made and principles accepted at that time, together with real changes in character that then took place, were God's direct and gracious answer to Mr. Taylor's prayers." [1]

Then at Chefoo that summer Mr. and Mrs. Taylor had many opportunities of coming into touch with the staff and pupils of the three flourishing schools. The month spent in their midst was full of interest.

" Over a hundred and fifty children," Mrs. Taylor wrote, " all in good health and doing well in their work, is something to be thankful for."

---

[1] When Dr. Keller was willing to accept Mr. Taylor's advice and help, the latter arranged for a more experienced missionary, the Rev. Ed. Pearse, to go to the capital of the province and call on the Governor to make a friendly representation. This, by the blessing of God, proved entirely successful. The Governor sent a deputy to Cha-ling-chow, who arranged with the local authorities to repair the house and re-establish the missionaries according to Chinese law. In order that the landlord might be fully compensated, Dr. Keller waived all claim to indemnity.

" Every one was delighted with this arrangement," the Doctor wrote after his return, " and all the secretaries and petty officials in the *ya-men* rushed in to thank us for our gracious treatment of the Chow (the local Mandarin). From this time the Chow and his family were our warm friends. I became their family physician . . . and the Chow himself came to Chang-sha (the capital) years after to be treated by me in his last illness. They proved the sincerity of their friendship at the time of the Boxer uprising. After the Italian priests had been killed at Heng-chow, a band of soldiers came over to Cha-ling and wanted to kill me. The Chow protected me for a week in his *ya-men*, and at last, when things got beyond control and his own life was in danger, he got me away by night, and sent me with a strong escort safely to Kiang-si. A year later we went to Chang-sha, and our kindly reception there, together with the confidence and friendship of the officials which were such a help to us, were largely due to the settlement at Cha-ling made in answer to Mr. Taylor's prayers. '

Delighting in the happiness of the boys and girls, Mr. and Mrs. Taylor never tired of watching their games and seeing all they could of them personally.   Foundation Day was a great occasion.   A boat race in the early morning, followed by cricket and tennis matches, prepared the young folk to enjoy the quiet noonday hour with plenty of singing and an address from Mr. Taylor.   After tea, under the willows, several photographs were taken, and the cool of evening brought a delightful " social " in the quadrangle.

" It was a warm, moonlit night," wrote Mrs. Taylor, " and the lights in the room near the pianos were all that was necessary. One of the teachers, Miss Norris, is a beautiful musician, and with songs and recitations the pleasant day ended."

In the serious work of the schools with all that it involved for the teachers of strenuous, self-denying labour they were still more interested.   Few could realise better what it meant to have the constant care of so many young lives in a climate and amid surroundings that were often trying. The strain upon patience and endurance was great indeed, and to no members of the Mission did Mr. and Mrs. Taylor's hearts go out in deeper sympathy.   Writing to the ladies in the Girls' School especially, Mrs. Taylor said, as they were leaving the beautiful harbour for the last time (June 26, '99) :

I do love and value you, and am so glad to know you better ! Though we have left, our hearts are still with you, and we would fain have had longer together.   I do thank you for giving me your confidence, and I want to send to all of you a good-bye message : it is this : *Determine to prove what faith and love will do.* " Grip God," as Mr. Inwood says, for one another.   Believe that God will make you helpers, each one to all the rest.   Covet earnestly to put joy into one another's lives, and by love conquer all that otherwise would be trying.   Our calling in Christ Jesus is to live supernatural lives, to be " more than conquerors " day by day.   Yield yourselves to God to be more fully indwelt, and to serve only in His strength, and then expect Him to do all that you need, for " nothing shall be impossible to you. . . ."

Only take firm hold of God, for yourselves and for one another, and look out to see what God will do.   You have His Almightiness amongst you always, for everything. . . . More and ever more of Christ in our lives, more of dependence upon Him, is the remedy for every lack, the solution of every difficulty.

To the last this loving ministry was maintained, by letters and in other ways, so that it was difficult to get off to the steamer even when their luggage was on board and they were starting for America via Australia and New Zealand. Mr. Taylor was still writing letters when Mrs. Taylor left for the dock—letters of sympathy and comfort to one and another whose needs were upon his heart. It was midnight before he could tear himself away, a fine night in September. Only Mr. Stevenson accompanied him, the Mission-house being all asleep and farewell said some hours before. Together they went by rickshaw through the quiet streets, and alone Mr. Stevenson returned to the heavy responsibilities that awaited him.

For events were moving with startling rapidity, now, to the *dénouement* of 1900. Mr. Taylor was still in the midst of his campaign in Australia, joined by the writers, when the Dowager Empress put forth the inflammatory edict with which that fateful year opened. Posted up in every city of importance, those burning words lost nothing through the free translation given by scholars to the great mass of the illiterate. It was seen to be war to the death, and the secret society of patriotic " Boxers," pledged to the extermination of all foreigners, flourished under Imperial protection till the movement spread like wildfire throughout the land.

By this time Mr. Taylor and his party, having found warm friends and addressed many meetings in New Zealand, had crossed the Pacific to California, and were on their way to New York, where they were among the speakers expected at the Œcumenical Conference. From all parts of the world representative missionaries and others gathered for this great occasion, and much prayer was made for China, where the situation was becoming desperate. After the Conference, sending his son and daughter-in-law before him, that they might take part in the annual meetings of the Mission in London, Mr. Taylor remained on for further work. Concern

about the state of things in China and an over-full programme when he was single-handed proved just too much,
and brought about a rather serious breakdown.

England was reached in June, and under a feeling of
urgency that she hardly understood, Mrs. Taylor arranged
for the continuation of their journey to the quiet spot
among the mountains where Mr. Taylor's health had been
so wonderfully restored some years previously. He was
quite unable for meetings or correspondence, and consented
to the course that offered best prospect of recovery, thankful to leave the work in London, as in Shanghai, so well
provided for. At Davos they had found warm friends in
an English lady and her husband, Mr. and Mrs. Hofmann,
who received visitors in a homelike Pension at moderate
charges. Simply writing to say they were coming, the
travellers set out—a few days only before the prayer meeting at Newington Green, at which Mrs. Hofmann herself
was present, when the first announcement was made of
the terrible events even then transpiring in China. Had
Mr. and Mrs. Taylor delayed for that meeting or for a reply
from the Villa Concordia, they probably would never have
reached the shelter of that quiet home. For when the
telegrams began to come they could not have left London.
The Boxers had already entered Peking, and the work
of destruction was begun. Hundreds of Christians were
massacred, and war openly entered upon by the Chinese
authorities. The Foreign Legations were in a state of siege,
and Imperial decrees had gone out commanding viceroys
and governors everywhere to support the rising.

Hearing that Mr. Taylor would already be at Davos,
Mrs. Hofmann hastened back to do all in her power to help
and comfort in that time of sore distress. And there it
was the blow fell, and telegram after telegram was received
telling of riots, massacres, and the hunting down of refugees
in station after station of the Mission—until the heart that
so long, in joy and sorrow, had upheld these beloved fellow-
workers before the Lord could endure no more, and almost
ceased to beat. But for the protection of that remote
valley where news could, in measure, be kept from him,

Hudson Taylor would himself have been among those whose lives were laid down for Christ's sake and for China in the oversweeping horror of that summer. As it was he lived through it, holding on to God.

" I cannot read," he said when things were at their worst; " I cannot think; I cannot even pray; but I can trust."

CHAPTER XL

WATERS OF REST

1900–1904. AET. 68–72.

*The Lord hath His way in the whirlwind and in the storm . . .
and He knoweth them that put their trust in Him.*

In the Mission-house at Ping-yang-fu (South Shan-si) the
little party of foreigners were preparing for flight—facing
the desperate journey of a thousand miles overland, through
a country teeming with " Boxers," to the nearest place of
safety. The white-haired native pastor, so infirm with age
that he could hardly walk, had come to bid them farewell,
and was talking with one of the ladies, when an urgent
message called him out. A friend, in real concern, begged
him to return home immediately. It was at the risk of
his life he was showing sympathy with foreigners. An
Imperial Edict had just arrived saying that they and all
connected with them were to be utterly destroyed, and his
only safety lay in keeping out of sight. Calmly the old
man returned to his missionary friends, and finished what
he had been saying with the words :

" *Kueh neng mieh ; Kiao mieh-puh-liao* " : " Kingdoms
may perish ; but the Church can never be destroyed."

And in this confidence he and hundreds of other Chinese
Christians sealed their testimony with their blood.[1]

Among those who escaped in Pastor Hsi's district was
one dear old man who held a very simple creed. He had

---

[1] Pastor Hsi would doubtless have been among the number had he not
passed away four years previously. Seng, ordained with him in 1886,
was the Pastor of the Ping-yang church above referred to.

long been a leader in the opium-refuge work and had seen much of the power of God. All over the countryside people knew the value of his prayers and would send for him in sickness or trouble. Yet Li Pu-cheo was no scholar : he could not even read. But one thing he did know beyond a doubt—that the Lord Jesus was risen from the dead, and that therefore *everything was possible*.

Before the terrible summer of 1900, this had been his ground for expecting deliverance in and through every trial. Was some village cause in danger, the chapel looted, and the Christians scattered ?

" But I knew that Jesus rose from the dead," he would say with quiet confidence.

Because of that glorious fact the little church no less would rise. And neither before nor after those long months of anguish was he disappointed.

For Mr. Taylor too, as we have seen, nothing remained but sheer and simple faith. " Lord, *Thou* hast been our dwelling-place in all generations." Long had he found strength and sufficiency, his one unchanging rest, in GOD, and that Refuge did not fail him now. Everything was falling about him, everything that is that could be shaken ; but there are " things that cannot be shaken," and they held fast amid the storm. The confidence of a lifetime— trust in the infinite faithfulness of our Father in heaven —had not been in vain. *All* His ways are love and light, light and love, for " In Him there is no darkness at all."

" Before I had children of my own," Mr. Taylor had often said, " I used to think, God will not forget me ; but when I became a father I learned something more—God *cannot* forget me."

In the last analysis is it not just that love, that Father-heart, we must fall back upon ? Amid the darkness and confusion and all the havoc wrought by sin I may see nothing, understand nothing, be able to do nothing, not even to pray at times ; but GOD I know. All is intelligible from His standpoint, all necessary, working out the highest good.

"I trusted in Thee, O Lord: I said, Thou art my God. My times are in Thy hand."

Leaving China for the last time a few months previously, Mr. Taylor had written to one in trial—written at midnight just as he was going to the steamer:

The Lord Himself will undertake for you and help you. . . .

> Leave God to order all thy ways,
>   And hope in Him whate'er betide;
> Thou'lt find Him in the evil days
>   Thy all-sufficient strength and guide:
> Who trusts in God's unchanging love
> Builds on the rock that naught can move.

And this he and those he bore upon his heart were to prove as never before.

But how he suffered as the days and weeks went by in the sufferings he was unable to lessen or even directly share! For more than thirty years he had always been the first to hasten to scenes of calamity and danger, never sparing himself if he could succour the fellow-workers he so truly loved. And now in the hour of their supreme trial he had to stand aside, and be willing to be nothing and do nothing, save as he could cry to God on their behalf.

"Day and night our thoughts are with you all," Mrs. Taylor wrote in July. "My dear Husband says: 'I would do all I could to help them; and our Heavenly Father, Who has the power, *will* do for each one according to His wisdom and love.'"

He could not write himself. Indeed, when the worst news was coming, in the middle of August, life seemed to ebb away so fast that he could scarcely cross the room alone, and his pulse fell from seventy or eighty to only forty per minute. Anguish of heart was killing him, and it was only by keeping the tidings back in measure that the slender thread of life held on. With the relief of the Legations and the flight of the Court from Peking (August 14) the Boxer madness began to pass away, and Li Hung-chang was called again to the helm, to pilot his distracted country through the complications with foreign Powers. But before that time the Inland Mission had a martyr-roll of over fifty of its members, while not a few who survived had suffered even more than those whose lives had been laid down. Fifty-eight in the C.I.M. alone perished in that terrible crisis, besides twenty-one children of the Mission, martyred with their parents or dying under sufferings the latter were enabled to survive. But in all the correspondence of the period not one bitter feeling can be traced against their persecutors, not one desire for vengeance or even for indemnification. The spirit of that tender mother who—dying after weeks of brave endurance on the journey to Hankow, having lost one little one by the way and witnessed the prolonged sufferings of others— whispered to her husband, " I wish I could have lived, I wish I could have gone back there, to tell the dear people more about Jesus," seemed rather to animate all hearts.[1]

As to the difficult question of compensation, Mr. Taylor had from the first advised that no claim should be made by the Mission, and that even if offered none should be accepted for injury to life or person. Later on when, besides a heavy indemnity and other punitive measures, retribution of a fearful character was inflicted by certain of the Powers, he went further, fully agreeing with the Councils that indemnification for Mission property also should be declined, though individuals were left free to accept compensation for personal losses if they so desired. This action, though criticised in certain quarters, was warmly approved at the British Foreign Office and by its Minister in Peking, who sent a private donation of a hundred pounds to the Mission in expression of his " admiration " and sympathy.

When with returning strength Mr. Taylor was able to bear more detailed knowledge of what had taken place, not one page of journals or letters did he spare himself as these came to hand. Snow had fallen on the mountains when he sought his daughter-in-law one bright October morning where she was working on the manuscript of

---

[1] A precious heritage to the people of God is found in the full story of the Boxer crisis as it affected the Inland Mission, told by Mr. Marshall Broomhall in his *Martyred Missionaries of the C.I.M.*, by the Rev. A. Glover in *A Thousand Miles of Miracle in China*, and by Mr. C. H. Green in his equally touching record of personal experiences, *In Deaths Oft*.

Pastor Hsi. A mail had just been received with tidings from Pastor Hsi's own district, which had moved him deeply. Tears overflowed as he paced the little room, telling of what he had been reading—last letters from his dear friend Miss Whitchurch and her companion, Miss Searell, written only the day before they met death alone in their distant station.

" Oh, think what it must have been," he broke in on the sad recital, " to exchange that murderous mob for the rapture of *His* presence, *His* bosom, *His* smile ! "

" They do not regret it now," he continued, when able to command his voice, " ' A crown that fadeth not away.' They shall walk with Me in white, for they are worthy.' "

A little later, speaking of his longing to go to Shanghai to be with the refugees gathered there.

" I might not be able to do much," he said, " but I feel they *love* me. If they could come to me in their sorrows and I could only weep with them, it might be a comfort to some."

Tenderly his daughter-in-law tried to tell him how much such sympathy would mean, and that there was no one in the world who could give it as he could, but even that was almost more than he could bear.

Prevented thus from being himself in China, it was a great comfort to Mr. Taylor that Mr. Stevenson was not without the help of one manifestly prepared of God for this emergency. Mr. Cooper, whose return from the north he had been eagerly anticipating, had fallen by the headsman's axe, and it seemed as if nothing could make up to the Mission for the loss of so wise and prayerful a leader, whose experience and powers of sympathy fitted him to be a help to the Chinese Christians no less than to his fellow-missionaries. But by Mr. Taylor's wish and arrangement, Mr. D. E. Hoste had come down from Ho-nan, of which he was then Superintendent, and was spending the summer at Shanghai. He was thus at hand when the pressure upon Mr. Stevenson became overwhelming, and was able to give invaluable assistance. Feeling that his own life might be cut short at any time, Mr. Taylor cabled out in

August, appointing Mr. Hoste as Acting General Director of
the Mission.   This was no hasty step taken in an emergency.
For years he had been looking to the Lord for guidance as
to his successor, and had seen with thankfulness Mr. Hoste's
growing fitness for the position.   There had been no uncertainty in Mr. Taylor's mind, even before he left China,
as to the answer to his prayers ; and though the appointment of Mr. Hoste was not made public until some months
later, when Mr. Stevenson's approval and that of the London
and China Councils had been cordially expressed, Mr.
Taylor had the comfort of feeling that an important step
had been taken to safeguard the interests of the whole work.

Another cause for thankfulness was the spirit that
breathed through many a letter that found its way to
Mr. and Mrs. Taylor at Davos.

" I have been writing," he said toward the close of the year,
" to some of the relatives of those we have lost, to comfort them
in their sorrow, and to my surprise they forget their own bereavement in sympathising with me."

How much it meant to him that fathers and mothers
should not only write in a spirit of resignation, but should
send gifts for the work, and even wish that others of their
children might be called to missionary service, will readily
be understood.   In reply to a letter of loving sympathy
from Shanghai, signed by three hundred members of the
Mission, he wrote in December (1900) :

As we have read over your signatures one by one we have
thanked God for sparing you to us and to China.   The sad
circumstances through which we have all suffered have been
permitted by God for His glory and our good, and when He has
tried us and our native brethren He will doubtless reopen the
work at present closed, under more favourable circumstances
than before.

We thank God for the grace given to those who have suffered.
It is a wonderful honour He has put upon us as a mission to be
trusted with so great a trial, and to have among us so many
counted worthy of a martyr's crown.   Some who have been
spared have perhaps suffered more than some of those taken, and
our Lord will not forget.   How much it has meant to us to be
so far from you in the hour of trial we cannot express, but the

throne of grace has been as near to us here as it would have been in China. . . .

When the resumption of our work in the interior becomes possible we may find circumstances changed, but the principles we have proved, being founded on His own unchanging Word, will be applicable as ever. May we all individually learn the lessons God would teach, and be prepared by His Spirit for any further service to which He may call us while waiting for the coming of the Lord.

It was not until the following summer (1901) that Mr. Taylor was obliged to abandon his cherished hope of returning before long to China. A little accident in the Chamounix Valley, where he was regaining a measure of strength, brought on his old spinal trouble, and for many months he was more or less crippled. It seemed impossible, at first, that such a small thing would develop serious consequences—only a slip on the pine-needles on a wooded slope. But it proved God's answer to His servant's prayer for guidance, by gently closing the way.

A visit to England some months later brought happy intercourse with friends at the Mission-house and in other circles, but was too much of a strain because of its very interests. It was all Mr. Taylor could do—just before his seventieth birthday—to return to the quieter surroundings of Switzerland, thankful for the relief of the simple, retired life which enabled him and Mrs. Taylor to serve the Mission still by prayer and correspondence.

Glad to be near their beloved friend, Mrs. Berger, it was by the Lake of Geneva they made their home at length, in the hamlet of Chevalleyres above Vevey. No railway climbed the hillside then, nearer than the village and castle of Blonay, whose grey old tower looked out on a scene of ever-changing beauty. Further up toward the wooded heights of the Pleiades an attractive though simple Pension was found among meadows and orchards. Entering at the back, from the level of the road, the south rooms on the ground floor were raised a storey above the garden. This was just what Mrs. Taylor was seeking. A little sitting-room and bedroom, with a front balcony and a closed-in verandah toward the sun-rising, offered just the accommodation needed; while the moderate charge of four and a half francs a day included meals served in their own apartment. But best of all was the kindness of Monsieur and Madame Bonjour and their parents in the old home next door, who from the first seemed specially drawn to these visitors.

Here, then, they came to stay in the summer of 1902; and here they found loving care and sympathy that almost made them feel as if they were among their own people. From the dear old Count and Countess at the château to the peasants who met them in their daily walks there came to be hardly a face that did not brighten or a heart that did not warm toward the white-headed missionary and his devoted companion. Love radiated from their lives, despite the restrictions of an unfamiliar language, and it is safe to say that that love was never more warmly responded to than in this last resting-place on their earthly pilgrimage.

" My beloved husband is very frail," Mrs. Taylor wrote a few weeks after settling in. " I am thankful he can be so quiet here and comfortable. We are looking forward to seeing Mr. Hoste."

Little by little, as their stay was prolonged, the Pension became quite a resort for English guests, many friends coming for longer or shorter visits because Mr. and Mrs. Taylor were there. This afforded delightful society and opportunities for united prayer about China. That little corner sitting-room became, indeed, a C.I.M. centre up among the mountains, the precious influence of which was felt in many distant places.

" It was not so much what your father *said* but what he *was* that proved a blessing to me," wrote Mr. Robert Wilder of that winter. " You may remember the words of Emerson, ' Common souls pay with what they do, nobler souls with what they are.' Your father bore about with him the fragrance of Jesus Christ. His strong faith, quietness, and constant industry, even in his weakness, touched me deeply. It was a privilege to spend six months with him in the same house at Chevalleyres. To see a man who had been so active compelled to live a retired life, unable to pray more than fifteen minutes at a time, and yet remaining bright and even joyous, greatly impressed me. I remember his saying, ' If God can afford to lay me aside from active service, surely I should not object.' Not one single complaint or murmur did we ever hear from his lips. He was always cheerful—rejoicing in the flowers by day and studying the stars at night."

One reason for the quiet happiness of those days was that changes and partings were over, and the two who had known so much of separation could be together at last and have time to enjoy one another's society. For they were lovers still, and fitted in perfectly with each other's needs. At first they were able to be out a good deal together, delighting in little excursions by rail and steamer and in the long, patient climbs that ended in a glorious outlook from some favourite height. By degrees it came to be others who accompanied Mr. Taylor in his longer walks, however, Mrs. Taylor finding sufficient excuse for staying oftener at home. Her strength was not what it had been, but she did not wish him to be anxious. In Miss Williamson, who managed to leave the Mission-house for months at a time that she might cheer their solitude, he had a companion whose love for the mountains was as unfailing as his own. And always—writing at the table or knitting by the window —Mrs. Taylor was ready for their return with the welcome cup of tea and cheery news of visitors or letters. Then there were long hours in developing the photographs taken and studying the flowers gathered. The keenness of Mr. Taylor's pleasure in these simple enjoyments as well as his delight in nature and the everyday intercourse of friendship were remarkable. His capacity for happiness was like that of an unspoilt child. Time never hung heavy on his hands ; and while unable for any but easy reading, his love for the Word of God remained the same. In this seventy-first year of his life he read the Bible through from beginning to end, for the fortieth time in forty years, and rejoiced in the various renderings Mrs. Taylor loved to gather from the French and other versions.[1] His corre-

[1] From his own experience Mr. Taylor said : " The hardest part of a missionary career is to maintain regular, prayerful Bible study. Satan will always find you something to do when you ought to be occupied about that—if it is only arranging a window-blind ! "

spondence was carried on almost entirely through her pen, the letter-books that remain showing how closely they were in touch with friends in many parts of China and all over the world.

Until the autumn of this year (1902) Mr. Taylor retained his position as General Director of the Mission, receiving regular reports from Mr. Hoste, Mr. Stevenson, and others. Once and again Mr. Frost and Mr. Sloan came over to Switzerland to see him, and on their second visit the latter was appointed Assistant Director of the Mission in England. Then, when Mr. Hoste arrived from China (November 1902), Mr. Taylor felt that the time had come for laying down responsibilities for which he was no longer equal. Many problems were pressing in connection with the reconstruction and rapid development of the work. Opportunities were wonderful, and the seed sown in tears and watered with blood was giving promise of an abundant harvest. The blessing of God had signally rested on the appointment made two years previously, and knowing he had the full concurrence of all the Directors and Councils, Mr. Taylor felt only thankfulness in resigning to Mr. Hoste the full direction of the Mission. The change had come about so gradually that to many it was hardly felt, Mr. and Mrs. Taylor remaining in all but name as closely connected with the work as ever, but to Mr. Hoste it meant a heavy increase of responsibility. Waking next morning in his little room at Chevalleyres, in the grey November twilight, it all came over him :

" Now I have *no one*—no one but God."

But the love and confidence of all his fellow-workers went out to him afresh when the appointment became known, many writing in the spirit of Mr. Orr Ewing's previous letter : " I am thankful that you have been led to select, perhaps, the most prayerful man among us."

That Mr. Taylor deeply and painfully felt his inability to labour as he had formerly was evident to those who saw below the surface. While preparations were being made one morning for an excursion to the Matterhorn, he learned that one of the family felt she must remain at home to press on with important writing. Coming to the little study, he spoke so tenderly about the disappointment, and about its being for Jesus' sake. That was the true joy of life—to do all for Jesus' sake. Sacrifice and labour were alike sweet when it was for Him.

" Yes," he added after a pause in which she could not but think how much he had known of that joy, " yes, but it's hardest of all to do *nothing* for His sake."

Yet he rejoiced in and shared the experience of his beloved friend the Rev. Charles Fox, whose own long fruitful day was drawing to a close :

> Two glad services are ours,
>   Both the Master loves to bless ;
> First we serve with all our powers,
>   Then with all our feebleness.
> Nothing else the soul uplifts
>   Save to serve Him night and day ;
> Serve Him when He gives His gifts,
>   Serve Him when He takes away.

In this spirit Mr. Taylor met with fortitude the last great sacrifice of his life, when a little cloud came up unexpectedly that threatened to darken the whole horizon. It was a telegram in July (1903) that first informed the writers of serious trouble, and brought them from their deputation work to the stricken hearts of those they loved so well. An internal tumour had discovered itself, and Mrs. Taylor, whose mother had died of cancer, was facing a terrible fear. In that remote Swiss hamlet they felt the need of their doctor-son, and he was thankful to call in a specialist of world-wide fame who was just then visiting Europe and " happened " to be in Switzerland. A Christian man of no ordinary devotion, Dr. Howard Kelly was a member also of the American Council of the C.I.M., so that the providence of his being just then accessible was very comforting, one of many evidences of the tender care of God at this time.

For it *was* cancer ; though in the merciful ordering of circumstances about them Mr. and Mrs. Taylor never knew it, and even the fear passed away. Not that they were in any way deceived as to the diagnosis. When the case was investigated under chloroform it was found that an operation would be useless, the disease being too far advanced. Having committed themselves unreservedly to the guidance of God through the specialists, including the skilful Dr. Roux of Lausanne, they never questioned further, thankfully concluding that an operation was *not necessary*. The growth must therefore be a simple tumour, and their relief was so great that nothing but thankfulness remained. It was very wonderful, but so in keeping with the " quietness and confidence " of their whole lives that it did not seem strange.

" Loving kindness and tender mercy " was indeed the crowning of the years that remained (1903–1904) that might have been so full of pain and apprehension. To those who knew what lay before them it was a daily miracle to see, instead of a troubled sunset, the path growing brighter and brighter to the perfect day. Nothing was changed or marred of their happy life together. Dying of cancer, she was still taken up with those around her, not with herself, still continued her loving ministries and correspondence, still lived for her husband and for China, and in her days of weakness and suffering did but count the more on God.

> Be glad of thy helplessness, Belovèd ;
> And if thou needs must long,
> Let it be only for the rest of weakness
> In the Arms for ever strong.

．　　．　　．　　．　　．　　．

The winter was spent in Lausanne to be near Dr. Roux, and fully did Mrs. Taylor appreciate the comforts of a home in the city with an electric tramway to the very door. The English church and the frequent visits of friends were a help while she was able to go about more or less freely ; and then, as greater weakness came on, how good it was to return to the spring flowers and all the peace and beauty of Chevalleyres ! Back in their old quarters and surrounded as before with loving care, their cup seemed to run over. Never had the news from China been more cheering.

" God is greatly helping Mr. Hoste in directing and developing the work of the Mission," Mr. Frost had written after his visit to Shanghai in February. " There is an unusual spirit of unity and devotion among the workers, both native and foreign. Openings and opportunities abound as never in the past, and souls are being won to Christ and gathered into the churches of the Mission in ever-increasing numbers."

Mr. and Mrs. Taylor were rejoicing also in an accession of means which enabled them to make a number of unexpected gifts at this time. It seemed as if the Lord must have hastened the winding up of legal proceedings in Australia, so that the residuary estate of her uncle yielded this fifteen hundred pounds while she was still able to use it for the advancement of His kingdom. Giving had been, to her, the luxury of life, and she was to have the joy of giving to the last. Several cheques for a hundred pounds found their way to the treasuries of the Mission, with words of loving cheer, while the letters that went with other gifts were just as much from the heart. To the Secretary of the Church Missionary Society she wrote, for example :

My beloved husband and I have much pleasure in sending a little contribution toward your funds. We sympathise with you much in the trial and crisis you are in, and pray that God may raise up many more friends for the dear C.M.S., and may enable those who do give to do so more adequately.

And her last gift to the Rev. John Wilkinson expressed the deepest interest in his work among the Jews.[1]

Thus, then, came the beauty of their last spring and summer days together.

" You ask about my health," she wrote before leaving

---

[1] Work among God's ancient people occupied a special place in the prayerful sympathy of both Mr. and Mrs. Taylor ; and Mr. John Wilkinson, founder of the Mildmay Mission to the Jews, recalled an interesting phase of their long friendship. Taking advantage of a New Year's Day spent at home (1897), Mr. Taylor went round to Mr. Wilkinson's house with a brotherly note enclosing a gift for the Mission. " *To the Jew first,*" were the words with which the cheque was accompanied. Mr. Wilkinson's warm heart was touched, and he immediately wrote a brotherly reply, enclosing his own cheque for the same amount, with the words : " *And also to the Gentile.*" This helpful interchange of sympathy was kept up ever after, the only change being that each doubled the amount of their contribution.

Lausanne (March 1904). " Well, I have got thin and weak, and have more or less of discomfort at times. I vary a good deal, but am so thankful to be able to keep about. The Lord's loving kindness and tender mercies are new every morning. The clever and kind Dr. Roux has given me a remedy which is helping me, and I am able to rest as I need and have every comfort.

" All the way ' He shall choose,' Who knows what is really best, and Who loves evermore. My beloved husband keeps very frail. . . . We match one another very well—both so thankful for a quiet life without strain. We have many pleasures and such kind friends ! "

And after their return to Chevalleyres :

May 2 : I had been thinking yesterday morning whether we were not too comfortable here, and free from the rubs of ordinary life, and the Lord gave me His answering message through *Daily Light*, so sweetly : " My people shall abide in a peaceable habitation, and in sure dwellings, and in quiet resting-places " (Is. xxxii. 18). He had told me when we were here before that this was one of His " resting-places." Anything more peaceful it would be impossible to find down here, and nature is so lovely now. I am sitting on the verandah, and all around are cherry-trees in blossom and little songsters flitting about, while the grass is just one vast nosegay of flowers : narcissus and forget-me-nots are just now our favourites.

The long chair on the verandah was a great comfort, and in it more and more time came to be spent.

" I have weary days often," Mrs. Taylor wrote to Mrs. Broomhall at the end of May, " but am not suffering as I did. It is so good to know that all is chosen for one in infinite love. We received such a good report on Saturday of the work in China. I read it aloud at tea-time, and we rejoiced and thanked God."

May 31 : It is so good to have the summer before us. . . . The news from China was never more encouraging.

June 7 : Dear Howard reached us last Saturday, and we hope to have him mostly with us now, for a while. It relieves the strain on my dear husband about me as nothing else could. I do very fairly, night and day, except for the weakness which makes it difficult to get across the floor now. The LORD has " our times " in His hand, and it is well.

June 8 : I have just to rest in Him now. My busy days are all past ; and I can only talk to Him about you busy toilers in His vineyard.

June 8 : Our dear Amy is here, caring for us very lovingly.

Howard spent a few days with us, on his return from China. He and Geraldine have been doing and will do deputation work in England, coming to us for a little while in the summer, *D.V.*, and Howard being available should we need him. No, my dear husband had no bronchitis in the winter, not even a cold. We do not know what lies before us ; but we know Him, and that all will be well.

June 24 : My strength seems ebbing fast away. I trust I may not linger on in a quite helpless condition ; but however it is, it will be all right.

By the end of June the dear invalid was obliged to give up the effort of dressing, which she had kept on with as long as possible, not to break the family circle. A visit from his younger son, Charles, was a great comfort to Mr. Taylor at this time, and the bright companionship of his daughter Amy, who was helping with the nursing. If anything troubled Mrs. Taylor it was the fear of being a burden to these loved ones, and under the circumstances it seemed difficult to arrange for a trained nurse. But for this too, although it never became a need, the Lord provided. To Mr. Frost, who was of the inner circle of her corre-spondents, Mrs. Taylor wrote on the 30th :

The Bonjours are eager to do anything for us at any time, and the servants are like-minded. The chambermaid speaks English, and is a very nice, trained nurse. If I come to need night atten-tion, I am to have her altogether, and the Bonjours will get some one else. Could anything be kinder, seeing she is most acceptable and capable in this busy house. The Lord is good and does make His children kind !

" Since I have not attempted to get up, I have been better in some ways," she wrote in the middle of July ; " and with the French windows open on to the verandah I get view and air, while the open door into the sitting-room keeps me in touch with the others. I could not be better cared for or happier. It is just a peaceful, quiet time, though in weakness and sometimes pain."

I have been praying, often, " Let GOD arise " ; it seems to be all that is needed anywhere.

I am nearly Home—what will it be to be there !

It is all goodness and mercy, and will be to the end.

The Lord is taking me slowly and gently, which is such a mercy for dear father's sake.

One precious letter from that borderland reached her daughter-in-law at Keswick, where she was fulfilling a last engagement before hastening to the dear mother's side.

July 16 : Here in my quiet room I hope to bear you up next week amid the thronging multitudes. I am learning lessons of the sweet power of helplessness and dependence ; and perhaps you too are learning them spiritually, in another way. Oh, that one had always been quite dependent in one's service !

" Leaning upon her Beloved " it is always " coming up," and the restfulness and the guidance and the full supply and the deep satisfaction in Him are all secured. May He enable us to ask big things for His glory.

It will be lovely to see you here afterwards, if the Lord will ; but I only live by the day now, not knowing what the next may bring. " My times are in Thy hand," so blessed that it is so ! You will know the comfort that dear Howard is, and Amy and dear father—all so loving and ready to spoil me in everything. So tenderly the Lord is dealing with us ! there seems nothing to wish for, only to praise.

CHAPTER XLI

HIS WAY IS PERFECT

1904–1905. AET. 72–73.

AFTER that the end came quietly. A few more helpful messages and letters, showing how her heart went out to loved ones near and far ; a last gift to the Mission of a hundred pounds as " a thank-offering for mercies received and expected " ; a few days so peaceful and tender that those about her caught the reflection in those deeply-shining eyes of a Presence to them unseen, and then the silent crossing of the swift, dark river.

" No pain, no pain," she said repeatedly, though for some hours the difficulty in breathing was distressing. Toward morning, seeing Mr. Taylor's anguish :

" Ask Him to take me quickly," she whispered.

Never had he had a harder prayer to pray ; but for her sake he cried to God to free the waiting spirit. Five minutes later the breathing became quiet—and in a little while all was peace.

> Before the world, O soul, I longed for thee,
> And still I long, and thou dost long for Me ;
> And when two longings meet, for ever stilled,
> The cup of love is filled.

But for him the desolation was unutterable. On the wall of the little sitting-room hung a text, the last purchase they had made together, and many a time during the days that followed did he look up through his tears to the words in blue, shining out from their white background :

" Celui qui a fait les promesses est fidèle." [1]

" MY grace is sufficient," had been almost her last words
to him, and then—" He will not fail." Upon this certainty
he rested now in the desolation he had so little strength to
endure, remembering her constant joy in the will of God,
and that, as he recalled again and again, "she never thought
anything *could* be better."

Cheered by the companionship of his niece, Miss Mary
Broomhall, Mr. Taylor remained on in the Pension that
had become a second home. Week by week he gathered
strength for the walk down to Blonay Castle and the village
and church of La Chiesaz, where his loved one lay sleeping.
It was a lovely spot—the grey old tower of the church,
draped in crimson creepers, seen through the branches of
a spreading cedar, with all the background of lake and
mountains. There Mr. Taylor spent many an hour, plant-
ing seeds and flowers, or quietly resting before he turned
to climb the hill again.

He was not without congenial society at Chevalleyres
that winter, some old friends from Toronto making a stay
of several months and entering into all his interests with
kindness that could not be exceeded. A decided improvement in health encouraged him to hope that with the spring
he might even think of returning to China ; and the desire
gaining ground, the writers were set free to accompany
their father by way of America.

On Mr. Taylor's seventh visit to the United States we
must not dwell, save to say how great was his interest in
the new centre of the Mission in Philadelphia. In the
pleasant suburb of Germantown almost a fortnight was
spent as the guests of Miss C. L. Huston, close to the Mission-
house which her generosity and that of Mr. H. C. Coleman,
a member of the American Council, had provided. Very
refreshing was the intercourse with these beloved friends,

---

[1] To a friend called to pass through similar sorrow Mr. Taylor wrote
on August 6, one week after his own bereavement : " You may have
noticed the French version of Heb. x. 23, ' *Celui qui a fait les promesses
est fidèle* ' (' Faithful is He who made the promises '). All we have to do
is to look out with patience to see how He will prove it true."

as well as with the larger circle who welcomed the coming of Mr. and Mrs. Frost into their midst, and found the Mission-house to be a centre of blessing. There in the Saturday prayer-meeting, and in the church of the Rev. D. M. Stearns near by, Mr. Taylor was able to give brief addresses.

" Every remembrance of your dear father stirs my heart," wrote Dr. Stearns a few months later, " and awakens new gratitude to God for that Sunday morning when you and he sat in the little church at Germantown, knelt together at the chancel-rail to commemorate our Lord's death, and afterwards stood by me (your dear father standing between us) while he gave my people an after-Communion message—reminding us that, in love, the Lord Jesus Christ had died for us, and that His love can never die.   In all my twenty-five years' ministry I never saw any one so moved at the thought of the love of God, and in receiving the emblems of our Lord's body and blood, as your dear father was that morning. . . . I have wondered whether he commemorated our Lord's death again, after that, in the little while that remained before his Home-going ? "

How short the interval was to be, and how full of precious experiences, no one anticipated.   Only six weeks lay before him in China, but frail though he was for the long journeys undertaken, there was no sign that the end was near, and least of all did he himself expect it.

Landing at Shanghai on the 17th of April (1905), he was welcomed by a representative company at the Mission-house, for the Spring Council Meetings were in session. Mr. Hoste and Mr. Stevenson were there, together with some who had come through the worst of the Boxer outbreak, and from the Che-kiang stations Mr. Meadows had come up, whose association with Mr. Taylor went back to the old days of the Ningpo Mission.   The love and veneration for their leader of these long-tried friends was beautiful to see, as were also the tokens of welcome from far and near—the flowers that filled his rooms, the comforts forethought had provided, and the letters of love and sympathy that flowed in.

Easter was spent with Miss Murray at Yang-chow, home of so many memories !   There and at Chin-kiang, the old headquarters of the Mission, early prayers and longings could not but come to mind—now abundantly fulfilled. How weak the human instrumentality had been all through! "A work of God," that alone explained it; and a remark Mr. Taylor made before leaving the training home was long remembered. "We cannot do much, but we can do a little, and God can do a great deal."

From the new Mission-house near the hills at Chin-kiang it was an easy walk to the cemetery overlooking the river, where in the long-ago years that seemed somehow not far away he had laid his heart's best treasures. There the names of four of his children were engraved beside their mother's; and the memories were sweet rather than sorrowful, for the partings were long since past and reunion must be at hand. To a group of young workers just setting out for inland stations he spoke a few words of loving counsel:

It is a great privilege to meet many of you here. I have met many here in days gone by. My dear wife died by me here. . . . In spirit our loved ones may be nearer to us than we think; and He is near, nearer than we think. The Lord Jesus will never leave nor forsake us. Count on Him: enjoy Him: abide in Him. Do, dear friends, be true to Him and to His Word. He will never disappoint you.

"You may be tired often and lonely often," he said to one in parting, "but the Lord knows just how much each cup costs. Look to Him; He will never disappoint you."

Steamer to Hankow was an easy stage that brought him once again to that busy centre of the Mission at which there was so much coming and going for the far interior. Here the welcome was just as warm as at Shanghai, Mr. and Mrs. Lewis Jones lavishing love and care on the dear traveller, and old friends of other Societies gathering round him with every token of affection. It was touching to see the meeting of the veteran Dr. Griffith John, still in the ripeness of his strength, with one whose course had run parallel with his own for nearly fifty years in China. He seemed to remember Mr. Taylor's love of music, and sang hymn after hymn with him in his own home, with all the old Welsh fire. Dr. W. A. P. Martin, too, came over from

Wu-chang to join the circle, a friend of very early Ningpo days, the missionary life of the three together amounting to no less than a hundred and fifty-six years.[1]

The journey to Hankow having been accomplished in safety, Mr. Taylor felt encouraged to go a little farther and make trial of the new railway running northward to Peking. If he could only reach one or two of the stations in Ho-nan, it would be so good to be right in the interior again! Thus with no definite plan, but looking to be guided day by day, he set out, every arrangement being made with the utmost helpfulness by those in charge of the Business Department.[2]

" It was so interesting at all the wayside stations to notice the pleasure the sight of dear Father called forth," wrote one of his companions. " Whenever he appeared at the window or on the platform, young and old seemed drawn to him, and looks of kindliness and interest made even the dullest faces attractive. Every one seemed anxious to show him attention. The Belgian officials kindly arranged for us to sleep on the train at night, to save him the trouble of going to an inn, and all along the way he was the centre of smiling interest.

" Once before on just such a May morning we had left Hankow on the same journey, but then it was by barrow, and many a weary day lay between us and our destination. Now, two weeks of strenuous travelling was replaced by a run of twenty-four hours. It was a wonderful change, and as we glided swiftly over the iron

---

[1] Dr. Martin, who reached China in 1850, was seventy-eight years of age; Mr. Hudson Taylor, who arrived in 1854, was seventy-three; and Dr. Griffith John, who arrived in 1855, was a year older. They were photographed together at Hankow on the 29th of April 1905.

[2] With reference to the Business Department, Mr. W. E. Geil, author of *A Yankee on the Yangtze*, wrote to Mr. Stevenson after his journey across China : " I am emphatically endorsing (in my book) the management of the missionary merchandise by the C.I.M. Never have I seen the people's money made to go so far as under your wise administration. As to my own accounts, without exception they were promptly, politely, properly attended to. In an age of commerce and high-pressure commercial enterprises worked by vast combinations, it is good to find equally wise methods applied to the gifts of the Church in this economical and wise distribution. . . . I have been impressed too when among the C.I.M. workers by a spiritual atmosphere saturated with two good things, kindness and common sense. . . . Your missionaries receive very small pay, but never once have I heard complaint, and never has salary been mentioned but the ready reply has come, ' It is sufficient.' God bless the self-sacrificing missionaries in Inland China."

THREE CHINA VETERANS.

W. A. P. Martin, D.D.   Griffith John, D.D.   J. Hudson Taylor, M.R.C.S.

To face page 608.

road we felt as if there must be a rude awakening. But no, it went on and on, fresh surprises meeting us at every point, until only six hours after leaving Hankow we steamed through the long tunnel under the mountains between Hu-peh and Ho-nan, and found ourselves once again in that familiar province."

A delightful visit at Yen-cheng, a station to which the railway brought them, gave Mr. Taylor the opportunity of seeing something of the work of Australian members of the Mission. In Mr. and Mrs. Lack he found missionaries after his own heart, and so also in Mr. and Mrs. Joyce in the neighbouring station to which he ventured on, though it involved an overland journey. A night, indeed, had to be spent in an inn, which was an outstanding experience for its strangeness and yet familiarity—just an ordinary wayside inn like so many hundreds Mr. Taylor had known in earlier days.

" We made dear Father as comfortable as we could," continued the story written at the time, " and though he was very weary he seemed to enjoy the Chinese supper and arrangements, and was full of interest in the people who thronged about us listening to the Gospel. After he had gone to rest a touching little incident happened, which we did not hear of until morning.

" It was between ten and eleven at night, and we were all soundly sleeping, when Mr. Joyce, who had come to meet us, was awakened by some one calling him outside the window. It proved to be one of his own church members, who had heard in his village not far away of our being in the inn that night, and had come over after his long day's work to pay his respects to the Venerable Chief Pastor. Mr. Joyce explained that Mr. Taylor was now sleeping ; that the journey had tired him very much, and that it would hardly do to awaken him.

" ' Never mind, never mind,' said the visitor, though much disappointed. And then, fumbling with something he was carrying, he pushed a little bundle through the paper window.

" ' Why, what is this ? ' asked Mr. Joyce.

" ' Oh, nothing ! It is only my poor little intention. It is my duty to provide for the Venerable Pastor while he is near our village.'

" It was two hundred cash, money the dear man had brought for our expenses at the inn. And when he had given it he slipped away, leaving us all to rest. We were so sorry in the morning not to have seen him ; but on Sunday he came in to the services and Father was able to thank him in person."

The Sunday at Hiang-cheng was full of interest ; and as heavy rains came on, an easier method of returning to the railway was suggested. Hour by hour the river rose behind the Mission-house, until with a good current boats were going down stream cheerily. On one of these, in company with Mr. and Mrs. Joyce and their children who needed change, the journey was made, and instead of parting when the railway was reached Mr. Taylor decided to go right on to a station where his daughter (Mrs. Coulthard) had been the first lady missionary. Sunday the 14th of May was spent at this important place, and there Mr. Taylor preached a sermon two miles long, which would never be forgotten. The home of Mr. and Mrs. Brock, in which Mr. Taylor's party were entertained, was at a considerable distance from Mr. Shearer's compound, where the principal services were held, and the question arose as to how Mr. Taylor was to cross the city that hot summer morning. A beautiful sedan-chair with eight bearers had been sent over from a neighbouring station, in the hope that he might be persuaded to go over on Monday to visit the ladies working there. It would have been easy to let four of the men carry him through the crowded streets to the meeting. But no, Mr. Taylor would not hear of it ! Not to set such an example had he come up to Ho-nan. If he went to church at all, he would walk ; and walk he did, the whole way there and back. One of his companions carried a folding chair, and when Mr. Taylor was too tired to go further he just sat down and rested.

" ' *Tsa puh k'iah ko kiao lai ?* ' ' Why don't you bring a sedan-chair ? ' exclaimed the people who gathered in crowds about him ; which gave an opportunity for explaining that Sunday was God's day of rest, and that it was His will that men should keep it holy. Great was the astonishment with which onlookers heard that there was, even then, a sedan-chair with bearers waiting at the Mission-house, but that the white-haired missionary would not use it, on this account. It was a theme for several little discourses by the way, and went further to impress the meaning and duty of Sabbath-keeping on the Christians than many a sermon could have done."

And so, just a step at a time, the way opened and Mr. Taylor was led on until he had visited five of the centres in Ho-nan, meeting with the missionaries from as many others. To his companions the latter part of the journey was of special interest, as the two stations to which he travelled by sedan they had had a part in opening. Oh, that familiar road—how often they had traversed it in all weathers! Every tree and house looked just as they had seen them scores of times, until they neared the first of the two cities (Chen-chow-fu) and there something unusual arrested their attention.

Right in front of us on the main highway a crowd of men and boys were gathered near a table, and as they stood there in the sunlight, several bright gleaming objects held up in their hands puzzled us not a little. They looked like the instruments of a brass band : but surely that could hardly be ? Then in a moment it flashed upon us—they were the Christians from Chen-chow-fu who had come out to meet us. The table we now saw was spread with refreshments for dear Father on his journey. The glittering objects shining in the sun were four large golden characters held up to greet him—the motto to be fixed on a banner they were probably preparing to present when he arrived.

And so it proved. For in a few minutes they were all about us, the love and enthusiasm of their welcome defying description. The beautiful characters, *Nui-ti en-ren*, were their chosen greeting to dear Father—literally " Inland China's Grace-man," or " Benefactor of Inland China."

A little farther on a group of women Christians met us, and when we reached the house inside the city we found the whole courtyard covered in, with a broad platform arranged at one end, draped in red, and welcome written large on everything. When the red satin banner was hung up over the platform, and the crowd of smiling, happy, hearty friends trooped in for the afternoon meeting, filling every corner to overflowing, it was a beautiful sight, not soon to be forgotten.

Oh, the happy days spent there, how they live in our memory ! Dear Father was much among the Christians, and spoke to them once or twice by interpretation. At a Christian Endeavour meeting we were all presented with silver badges, and enrolled as members of the Chen-chow branch. Father was very pleased

with the way in which it was done, and wore the sign of membership on his coat right on to the end.

At Tai-kang, the last station visited, the same love and lavish
kindness were displayed. Some of the Christians hired a cart
and came to Chen-chow, a whole day's journey, to meet us. On
the way they passed a letter-carrier, who said that Father was
not well and that he would have to turn back without visiting
their city. Upon this the Tai-kang friends were greatly distressed, and stopped in the middle of the road to pray that the
Lord would strengthen him and help him to undertake the
journey.

" Oh, Lord, what have we done," they said, " that the Venerable Pastor should come thousands of miles from the other side
of the world, and after months of travelling stop short just one
day's journey from our city ? Oh, Lord, we too are his little
children ! Help him to come on and visit us."

Great was their joy a few hours later, when they reached
Chen-chow, to find a baptismal service in progress, and Father
taking part and addressing the newly received believers, and to
hear that he had already made up his mind to go on to Tai-kang
next day. What a journey that was, in their escort ! Kuo
Lao-siang, a very Greatheart, bore us along in triumph ; insisted
on paying himself all expenses by the way, and delighted us hour
after hour by the story of all the Lord had done for the Tai-kang
Church since we left it seven years ago, and especially during the
troubles of 1900.

Outside the city gate the Christians met us, with Mr. Ford
and Mr. Bird, their missionaries. Mr. and Mrs. Joyce had
arrived already, so we were a large party—old friends and fellow-
workers, reunited after long years. With hearts full of thankfulness we recalled early experiences, hopes, and prayers ; how the
Lord brought us through the terrible riot of 1896, and how He
had blessed and increased the work ever since.

Time fails to tell further of those happy days at Tai-kang ;
of the long talks and meetings with the Christians, the beautiful
banner they too presented to dear Father ; the return journey all
the way to Yen-cheng and much besides. One meeting at Chow-
kia-kow, however, must be mentioned. We found ourselves
there for a Sunday, and as it happened for Sunday the 21st of May.
The Christians came to know it was Father's birthday, and to our
surprise prepared a beautiful scarlet satin banner to present to
him, bearing the inscription, " *O man greatly beloved.*" He was
not well enough to walk to church that day, so they all gathered
at Mr. Brock's for an afternoon meeting. Numbers had come in
from the country and from distant out-stations, a dozen or more

of the leading men being present from all over the district. One after another they rose and made little addresses to dear Father, some of them very heart-moving. He spoke to them too for a few minutes.

It was Friday the 26th of May when the party reached Hankow once more, the thirty-ninth anniversary of the sailing of the *Lammermuir*. In the train on the way down they had had precious times of prayer, joined by Miss af Sandeberg, whose relatives had been the first to show Mr. Taylor hospitality in Sweden. At Hankow Dr. Whitfield Guinness, among others, was waiting to meet them, and with thankfulness for the three and a half weeks in Ho-nan they sought renewed strength from the Lord and guidance as to the next stage of their journey.

And oh, how tender was His watchful care over every step of the way that remained! Only eight days were left of dear Father's earthly pilgrimage, five in May and three in June—and then the " far more exceeding and eternal weight of glory." If only we had known! But He knew who was planning all.

After a quiet Sunday in Hankow, Mr. Taylor decided to go on by steamer to Chang-sha, capital of the province of Hu-nan, which he had never visited. First of the far inland provinces the Mission had attempted to enter, it had been the last in which settled residence had been obtained, and for more than thirty years Mr. Taylor had borne it specially upon his heart in prayer. Only since the troubles of 1900 had it been fully opened, and he greatly desired to see the work of Dr. Keller and others in the capital, described with graphic interest by Dr. Harlan Beach in a recent number of *China's Millions*. Strangely enough, when all arrangements had been made and the berths taken, unlooked - for circumstances prevented their travelling among the native passengers as Mr. Taylor wished.

It was the last, last journey dear Father was to take in China ; the days were very hot and the nights trying, and it was to be made as cool and comfortable for him as possible. Nothing would have persuaded him to travel foreign passage had the less expensive accommodation been available, but the matter was taken out of our hands. The Japanese steamer for which we were waiting ran aground in the Tong-ting lake, and a wire was received in Hankow saying it was quite uncertain as to when she would arrive.　We were expected at Ch'ang-sha for Sunday, and the only thing to do was to take the China Navigation Company's steamer sailing that same evening, and even then waiting off shore.　But it had to be by saloon cabin, as they do not issue tickets to foreigners travelling Chinese passage.　Thus when we went on board it was to find a beautiful new boat, the best on the upper river, the kindest of captains and officers, and the entire saloon accommodation at our disposal.　We were the only foreigners on board, and under the circumstances nothing could have been more delightful.

Those two days with Captain Hunter on the s.s. *Shasi* could hardly have been more perfect.　Dear Father was just himself, and though the weather was intensely hot he enjoyed the cool saloon, the comfortable chairs on deck, and the fresh breezes.　It meant much to him to have us all with him and to see the friendship between the younger members of our party deepening,[1] and his joy in the answer to the prayers of a life-time in the opening of China's last unreached province to the Gospel was very great.

As they crossed the far-reaching lake and steamed up the river, passing well-built cities, beautiful pagodas and temples, rich plains covered with ripening crops, and noble mountain ranges near and distant, they could not but think of all the toil and prayer of years gone by, of buried lives and dauntless faith, richly rewarded at last in the change that was coming over the attitude of the people.　Until eight or nine years previously there had not been one Protestant missionary settled in the province.　None had been able to gain a footing.　No fewer than a hundred and eleven missionaries were to be found there now, connected with thirteen societies, working in seventeen central stations and aided by a strong band of Chinese helpers.

It was Thursday afternoon the first of June when we reached the capital (Chang-sha) and were welcomed by our dear friends Dr. and Mrs. Keller and Dr. Barrie.　Twenty minutes in chairs brought us to the Mission-house, in which we felt quite at home already, having carefully studied Dr. Harlan Beach's ground-plan and article.　Of the two days that followed, how can I write?　They were so calm and peaceful, so full of interest and encourage-

---

[1] Miss J. af Sandeberg and Dr. Whitfield Guinness were engaged a few days later.

ment, so rich in love and sympathy and the tender care that surrounded our beloved one, that our hearts overflow on every remembrance of the Lord's goodness up to the very end.

Friday was a quiet, restful day. It rained all the morning and we could not go out. After lunch, chairs were called and we visited the T'ien Sin Koh, a lofty building on the highest point of the city wall. Father was delighted with the wonderful view of mountains, plain, and river, surrounding the city outspread at our feet. He climbed to the second story without being overtired, and afterwards went to see the site for the new hospital—several acres of land in a good situation that the Governor hopes to give for the work of our medical mission.

On Saturday, Father did not come down to breakfast, but was dressed and reading when we carried up his tray. He was to speak to the Chinese friends that morning, so as soon as the daily service was concluded he went to the Chapel and said a little through interpretation. They were deeply interested in seeing him, many of them having just read the *Retrospect* translated by Mr. Baller into Chinese. Mr. Li the evangelist responded, expressing the love and joy with which they welcomed him to Chang-sha.

That afternoon a reception had been arranged to give all the missionaries in the city an opportunity of meeting Mr. Taylor, and before the time appointed he came down seasonably dressed in a suit of Shantung silk.

It was cool and pleasant in the little garden on to which the sitting-room opened, and tea was served on the lawn, surrounded by trees and flowers. Father went out and sat in the midst of the guests for an hour or more, evidently enjoying the quiet, happy time, and interested in the photographs that were being taken.

After all had left, Howard persuaded him to go upstairs, and as we were busy sending our things to the steamer (we were to walk down ourselves on Sunday evening after the service) Dr. Barrie remained with him for half an hour. It was a still evening, and while they were talking Father rose and crossed the room to fetch two fans. One of these he handed to Dr. Barrie, who exclaimed :

" Oh, why did you not let me bring them ? "

" I wanted to get *you* one," was the reply, in a tone which deeply touched his companion.

Speaking of the privilege of bringing *everything* to God in prayer, Dr. Barrie said that he was sometimes hindered by the feeling that many things were too small, really, to pray about.

Father's answer was that he did not know anything about it—about such a distinction, probably.   Then he added :

"There is nothing small, and there is nothing great : only God is great, and we should trust Him fully."

When the evening meal was ready Mr. Taylor did not feel inclined to come down, and a little later he was preparing to go to rest when his son brought him his supper. While waiting for him to be comfortably settled, his daughter-in-law spent a few minutes alone on the little roof-platform which is such a pleasant addition to many Chang-sha houses.

Twilight had fallen then, and darkness veiled the distant mountains and river.   Here and there a few glimmering lights dotted the vast expanse of grey-roofed city.   All was silent under the starlit sky.   Enjoying the cool and quietness I stood alone awhile, thinking of Father.   But oh, how little one realised what was happening even then, or dreamed that in less than one half-hour our loved one would be with the Lord !   Was the golden gate already swinging back on its hinges ?   Were the hosts of welcoming angels gathering to receive his spirit ?   Had the Master Himself arisen to greet His faithful friend and servant ? What was happening, oh, what was happening, even then, over the sleeping city ?

Knowing nothing, realising nothing, I went down.   Dear Father was in bed, the lamp burning on the chair beside him, and he was leaning over it with his pocket-book lying open and the home letters it contained spread out as he loved to have them. I drew the pillow up more comfortably under his head, and sat down on a low chair close beside him.   As he said nothing, I began talking a little about the pictures in the *Missionary Review* lying open on the bed.   Howard left the room to fetch something that had been forgotten for supper, and I was just in the middle of a sentence when dear Father turned his head quickly and gave a little gasp.   I looked up, thinking he was going to sneeze. But another came, then another !   He gave no cry and said no word.   He was not choking or distressed for breath.   He did not look at me or seem conscious of anything.

I ran to the door and called Howard, but before he could reach the bedside it was evident that the end had come.   I ran back to call Dr. Keller, who was just at the foot of the stairs. In less time than it takes to write it he was with us, but only to see dear Father draw his last breath.   It was not death—but the glad, swift entry upon life immortal.

" My father, my father, the chariots of Israel and the horse-men thereof ! "

And oh, the look of rest and calm that came over the dear face was wonderful ! The weight of years seemed to pass away in a few moments. The weary lines vanished. He looked like a child quietly sleeping, and the very room seemed full of unutter-able peace.

.   .   .   .

Tenderly we laid him down, too surprised and thankful to realise for the moment our great loss. There was nothing more to be done. The precious service of months was ended. Mr. Li and other Chinese friends went out to make arrangements, but we could hardly bring ourselves to leave that quiet room. All the house was still, hallowed by a serenity and sweetness that hardly seemed of earth. Though he was gone, a wonderful love and tenderness seemed still to draw us to his side. Oh, the comfort of seeing him so utterly rested. Dear, dear Father, all the weariness over, all the journeyings ended—safe home, safe home at last !

One by one or in little groups the friends who were in the house and the dear native Christians gathered round his bed. All were so impressed with the calm, peaceful look that lingered on his face, and many touching things were said, showing that even in these short days the sweetness and simplicity of his life had won their hearts.

" Oh Si-mu," whispered one dear woman as she left the room, " ts'ien ts'ien wan-wan-tih t'ien-shi tsieh t'a liao ! " (thousands and myriads of angels have welcomed him)—and in a flash one almost seemed to see it.

Last of all a dear young evangelist and his wife, a bride of eighteen, came up. They had journeyed in from an out-station on purpose to meet us all, and especially Father, whose Retrospect they had been reading. Arriving in the afternoon while tea was going on, they did not like to ask to see him, and when the guests had left he was tired. So they put it off till morning, as we were to spend Sunday with them all. And then, suddenly, they heard of his departure to be with the Lord.

Full of sorrow, they sent in to ask if they might come and look upon his face. Of course we welcomed them, telling them all that had happened and how grieved we were that they had not seen him earlier in the day. Together they stood beside the bed in silence, until the young man said :

" Do you think that I might touch his hand ? "

Then he bent over him, took one of Father's hands in his and stroked it tenderly, while to our surprise he began to talk to him just as if he could hear.   He seemed to forget us and everything else in a great longing just to reach the one who still seemed near, and make him feel his love and gratitude.

" *Lao Muh-sï, Lao Muh-sï,*" he said so tenderly (Dear and Venerable Pastor), " we truly love you.   We have come to-day to see you.   We longed to look into your face.   We too are your little children—*Lao Muh-sï, Lao Muh-sï.*   You opened for us the road, the road to heaven.   You loved us and prayed for us long years.   We came to-day to look upon your face.

" You look so happy, so peaceful !   You are smiling.   Your face is quiet and pleased.   You cannot speak to us to-night. We do not want to bring you back : but we will follow you. We shall come to you, *Lao Muh-sï.*   You will welcome us by and by."

And all the time he held his hand, bending over him and stroking it gently, his young wife standing by.

Downstairs, meanwhile, another touching scene was taking place.   Mr. Li and others who had been out to make arrangements returned, bringing a coffin and bearers and everything necessary for the last journey.   They had hoped when first they learned of dear Father's Home-call that he would be buried in Hu-nan, and had rejoiced to think that in this way they might keep him among them still.   But when it was explained that we must leave at once for Chin-kiang, as his family grave was there, and he had always wished to be laid beside his loved ones should he die in China, they set aside their own desire and did all they could to forward our departure.

When everything had been brought to the house they sent word to my husband asking if they might speak with him.   He went at once, and was touched by the many evidences of their thought and care.   Then, gathering round him, they said that they had wished to obtain a more beautiful coffin, but had been obliged to be satisfied with the best they could find ready-made ; that he need not ask the price, for it was their gift, the gift of the church ; for if they could not be allowed to keep the Venerable Chief Pastor in Hu-nan, they must at any rate do everything for him at their own expense.

It was a great surprise, but they would take no denial.   Had not the Lord brought their beloved father in the faith to Chang-sha, and permitted them to look upon his face ?   From their midst had he not been translated ?   Hu-nan Christians had been the last to hear his voice, to receive his blessing.   Theirs must be the privilege of providing for his last needs.

Yes, it was beautiful and right.   It meant a large sum to them, and they would feel it.   But the joy of sacrifice was in their hearts, and we could not but stand aside and let them do as they would. So Hu-nan hands prepared his last resting-place, Hu-nan hearts planned all with loving care—one little company of the great multitude his life had blessed. Not in vain, ah, not in vain the faith and toil and suffering, the ceaseless prayer and soul-travail of fifty years. Inland China open everywhere to the Gospel proclaims the faithfulness of God, and these strong Hu-nan men with hearts as tender as children's, these women with tear-dimmed eyes helping in the last ministries of love, attest the gratitude of a redeemed and blood-washed company no man can number.

By the mighty river at Chin-kiang they laid him, where it rolls its waters two miles wide toward the sea. Much might be said of the love and veneration shown to his memory; of Memorial Services in Shanghai, London, and elsewhere ; of eulogies in the public press ; of sympathetic resolutions passed by missionary and other societies, and of personal letters from high and low in many lands. From the striking tribute of a High Church Bishop in *The Guardian* to the tender reminiscences of fellow-workers, many were the written and spoken words that showed him to have been not only " the heart-beat felt throughout the Mission," but a vital force of life and love in every part, one might almost say, of the body of Christ. But the voices that linger longest are those he would have loved the best—the voices of Chinese children singing sweet hymns of praise as they laid their little offerings of flowers upon his resting-place.

" Thus one by one the stars that are to shine for ever in God's firmament appear in their celestial places, and the children of the Kingdom enter upon the blessedness of their Father's house not made with hands."

CHAPTER XLII

PRAYERS YET TO BE ANSWERED

ADONIRAM JUDSON, the Apostle of Burma, less than two weeks before his death, heard of a definite answer to prayers he had offered with great earnestness long years before, and which had seemed to be unheard. His heart had been deeply burdened about the Jewish people—so much so that he had even sought to found a mission in Palestine for their benefit—but nothing came of it. And then, only a few days before he passed away, he learned from a daily paper of the conversion of a number of Jews in Trebizond through a tract concerning his own life-work, and that they had sent to Constantinople asking for a Christian teacher. With tears in his eyes the veteran missionary exclaimed :

I never was deeply interested in any object, I never prayed sincerely and earnestly for anything, but it came. At some time, no matter how distant a day, somehow, in some shape, probably the last I should have devised, it came. And yet I have always had so little faith. May God forgive me . . . and cleanse the sin of unbelief from my heart.

Prayers yet to be answered—how rich the inheritance Hudson Taylor left to the land he loved, to the Church of God in China for which his life was given ! In one sense the prayers of that life-time had indeed been answered.

> He sowed with tears :
> He laboured, suffered, strove for one great field,
> And saw it yield,
> His every hope of half a hundred years.[1]

---

[1] From an In Memoriam poem by his niece, Miss Marian Fishe, now Mrs. J. L. Rowe.

But in another sense do not those prayers lie beyond us yet, marking out wide possessions upon which the foot of faith has trodden, possessions still to be possessed ?

Nothing could have been more definite than Mr. Taylor's own conviction as to the thoughts that had come to him in 1889. Once he had seen it he could never doubt again the Master's will and purpose that " every creature " in China should hear the glad tidings of salvation. Through all the years that followed, though hindered again and again, and postponed for a time by the Boxer crisis, his purpose never wavered.

" This work will not be done without crucifixion," he said in the C.I.M. Conference of May 1890, " without consecration that is prepared *at any cost* to carry out the Master's command. But, *given that*, I believe in my inmost soul that *it will be done*. If ever in my life I was conscious of being led of God, it was in the writing and publication of those papers, the first of which came out in November of last year."

The time had not come for it then, as events were to prove, but who shall say that the time has not come for it *now* ? Many are the indications that these are the lines on which the Spirit of God is working. A recent survey of missionary operations in China during the last ten years reveals nothing more clearly than the new spirit of evangelism which is taking hold of the Chinese Church. In the province of Ho-nan, for example, with its twenty-five millions—the province in which Mr. Taylor spent more than half his last brief visit to China—all the Societies and churches are at the present moment united in an effort to carry the Gospel to every home and " every creature " within a period of five years. At the beginning of 1917 this forward movement was entered upon, its definite aim being " to enlist the co-operation of every Christian in Ho-nan and bring the Gospel to the ears of every non-Christian in the province " within the time agreed upon. And this effort, which will command the prayerful sympathy of all who long for the coming and kingdom of our Lord Jesus Christ, is but part of the larger movement which in varying degrees is making itself felt throughout China.[1]

Equally encouraging are the tidings that come from Hu-nan, where the Floating Bible School is proving an effective method cf developing soul-winners. Started by Dr. Keller, from whose home in Chang-sha Mr. Hudson Taylor had passed to his reward, this remarkable movement has for its aim " the speedy and thorough evangelisation of the twenty-two millions " of that province by means of itinerant bands labouring in connection with all the Societies. Taking advantage of the waterways which abound, the students of the Bible School—who must be men of a living faith in Christ and a serious call to His service—spend most of the year with a trained Chinese leader, visited by their missionary superintendents, on a boat large enough to accommodate twelve or more.[2] On the invitation of the missionary in charge they go to a given

[1] On this subject the *China Mission Year-Book* (1917) gives definite and most encouraging testimony. Following the great evangelistic meetings among students held by Dr. John R. Mott and Mr. Sherwood Eddy (1913 and 1915), which evoked a response undreamed of before among the educated classes to the character and claims of Christ, has come a " new vitality in evangelistic work," fostered by the " Special Committee on a Forward Evangelistic Movement," of which Bishop Price of the C.M.S. (Fukien) is Chairman and Dr. Warnshuis the National Evangelistic Secretary.   Such a movement, uniting all Societies labouring in China, is new indeed, and so is the Week of Evangelism it has promoted —" the first attempt ever made to mobilise the spiritual forces of the Chinese Church in a united evangelistic movement " (p. 343).

In their report for 1917 the Forward Evangelistic Committee states : " Wherever this national Week of Evangelism was thoroughly prepared for and carried through with energy, the churches have been awakened and found themselves able to move forward on a wide front.   As stated in last year's report, the purpose was to create a persistent, organised, and enthusiastic missionary endeavour in the whole Church, among both pastors and lay-people, of which this Week of Evangelism would be but the beginning.   This ideal still remains to be achieved, and the programme which the Committee recommends for the ensuing year contains proposals for a continuation of this effort."

[2] The course of study, which is thoroughly supervised and systematic, " covers two years and includes Biblical introduction, book, chapter, and topical Bible study, Bible doctrine, outlines of church history, music, the preparation of Gospel addresses, and individual training in chapel and street preaching, and in personal work.   Much care is taken to foster a deep prayer life in each worker, real, living fellowship with God, and a consciousness of absolute dependence on the indwelling Holy Spirit for a holy life and fruitful service."

district and take whatever time is necessary to reach its entire population, whether in town or country, with the Message of Salvation.

" We now have three parties at work," Dr. Keller wrote in 1917, " and we hope to add three more parties this year. In hundreds of homes the people have given up idolatry, and have accepted Christ as their Saviour and Lord. Bible-study classes have been formed ; new churches have been organised, always by the missionary of the district, never by our men ; and many thousands who never heard the Gospel before have had their misconceptions cleared away, their prejudices broken down, and their hearts opened to the Gospel message."

Then once a year the bands gather together for two months of special study in their Autumn Bible School among the mountains, where a famous shrine (Nan-yoh) attracts hundreds of thousands of pilgrims annually. There the students are joined by pastors and evangelists from all over the province who come up for rest and spiritual refreshment, and take part in the " intense, fruitful, heart-to-heart work " carried on among the pilgrims, a large proportion of whom are earnest, religiously-inclined young men. Forty thousand personal conversations were recorded in 1916, and many cases of conversion of the deepest interest. These methods of training and work, Dr. Keller believes, could be adapted to the special needs of other provinces, and would go far to solve the problem of the evangelisation of China in this generation.

In the Bible Mr. Taylor used up to the time of his Home-going a little map was found, traced on thin paper, of the province of Kwei-chow, showing the stations especially in which the work among the tribes-people was beginning. Often prayed over, that fragment of paper bears its silent testimony to the longing of his heart after those wild, neglected children of the mountains—living at enmity with their Chinese neighbours, worshipping demons and charms, and bound by the grossest superstition and sin. Coming home on his first furlough from Kwei-chow, Mr. James R. Adam, who had been doing what he could among the Miao people round An-shun, met Mr. Taylor in Dundee in the home of Mr. William Scott. The work was difficult though full of promise, and how to follow it up Mr. Adam hardly knew, with the charge of the station on his hands. Yet there seemed no prospect of fellow-workers. What was Mr. Adam to do ? Should he give up the effort to reach the tribes-folk, and confine himself to work among the Chinese ?

" Never shall I forget your dear father's kindness," he wrote, " that last time I met him. With affectionate sympathy he wished me Godspeed in this work among the Chinese and Miao, telling me to go on as I had been doing and to do the best I could for both."

Little did either of them think as they parted in Dundee of the answer that was to be given to their prayers ; of the wonderful movement that, beginning in the An-shun district, was to extend to the adjacent province (Yun-nan), gathering many thousands of these simple mountain people into the kingdom of God, and raising up from among them ardent missionaries to carry the Gospel on from tribe to tribe in ever-widening circles of blessing.

" The sun has never risen upon China without finding me at prayer," Mr. Taylor could say of long years of his labours in that land ; and perhaps no part of those labours had more to do with the results we see to-day. But he not only prayed. The foregoing pages have revealed a little of what lay behind those prayers. " I do want to give up myself and you too, darling, for the life of the Chinese and of our fellow-workers," he wrote to Mrs. Taylor in one of their many separations : and, " Notice, in 1 Cor. i. 18, the connection of the Cross with power. Do not many lives lack power because they do not love the Cross ? May your life be full of the power of God, and mine."

The needs that moved him, the command that revealed the yearning of the heart of Christ—Whom we, too, call Master and Lord—remain the same to-day. Great changes have come and are coming in China. New methods are needed in missionary work to meet the new conditions, and are being prayerfully developed and applied. But the great underlying facts remain the same. Idolatry has not lost its hold. Writing from the far north-west (June 1918), a member of the Mission tells of Guilds in one city numbering thousands of men and women sworn to regular worship at stated times. In one of these some fifteen hundred women are pledged to go to a certain temple on the second and sixth of every month, "where they kneel upright on the verandahs and in the courtyard, each holding a stick of incense between the two hands raised to the level of the forehead. This position has to be maintained and prayers recited until the stick of incense has burned away—quite a long process." And offerings of money must be made on every one of the stated worship days, which go to the building and beautifying of temples and making fresh idols. And this is only one city out of hundreds that have as yet no resident missionary. Do the people need light in their darkness? Do they not care about the unknown future and what becomes of the soul? Is it for them too that the precious blood was shed which alone can cleanse from sin and bring us nigh to God? And what shall be said of the responsibility that rests upon us if, knowing these things, we are not doing our utmost—whether by prayer or gifts or personal service—to bring to them too the knowledge which is life eternal?

Much is being done ; but much more is needed if the present opportunity—perhaps the most glorious that has ever come to Christian men and women—is to be dealt with faithfully. "When China is moved," Napoleon used to say, "it will change the face of the globe." China *is* moved, is moving : shall it not be home to the heart of God?

"We must advance upon our knees," said Bishop Cassels in view of the needs, the possibilities of that vast country. "There must be a fresh taking hold of God in prayer. . . . I thank God that this Mission lives upon prayer. But I say, God will do 'a new thing' for us when there is a new spirit of prayer among us. God will do 'a new thing' for us when there is a new spirit of consecration among us."

If the one whose steps we have followed through a life of toil and sacrifice, yet of radiant joy in fellowship with Christ, could speak to us to-day from " the exceeding and eternal weight of glory," would he not say again as he said in the midst of the fight :

There is a needs-be for *us* to give *ourselves* for the life of the world—as He gave His flesh for the feeding of the lifeless and of living souls whose life can only be nourished by the same life-giving Bread. An easy-going non-self-denying life will never be one of power.

Fruit-bearing involves cross-bearing. " Except a corn of wheat fall into the ground and die, it abideth alone." We know how the Lord Jesus became fruitful—not by bearing His Cross merely, but by dying on it. Do we know much of fellowship with Him in this ? There are not two Christs—an easy-going one for easy-going Christians, and a suffering, toiling one for exceptional believers. There is only one Christ. Are you willing to abide in Him, and thus to bear much fruit ?

Would that God would make hell so real to us that we cannot rest ; heaven so real that we must have men there ; Christ so real that our supreme motive and aim shall be to make the Man of Sorrows the Man of Joy by the conversion to Him of *many* concerning whom He prayed, " Father, I long that those whom Thou hast given Me be with Me where I am, that they may behold My glory."

INDEX

Aborigines, movement among the, 346, 624

Accomplishing the Impossible, 216

Adam, James R., 623

Administration questioned, 107

Alcock (Sir Rutherford), Ambassador, 154, 158, 160

America, numerous applicants, 452

America's contribution of missionaries, 471

America's financial contribution, 471

American branch, concern in England, 460

American branch idea, 450

American workers first, 441

A Missionary Band, 378

An-hwei—
    Meadows enters the province, 158
    C.I.M. Superintendent appointed, 394

An-King—
    riotous uprising, 179
    centre of men's training home, 180
    Conference, 366
    training home principal appointed, 394
    first meeting of superintendents, 420

Anniversary meetings, first, 279

Anniversary meetings, the twenty-first, 428

" Appeal for Prayer," the, 265

Appeal for the " Seventy," 360

Appeal for the " Thousand," 487

Appealing for funds discouraged, 257

" A *present* Saviour," 148

Argent, Mr., murder of, 504

A Thousand Miles of Miracle in China, 591

Audiences, some eccentricities, 100

Australasia, C.I.M. beginnings, 488

Australia, Mr. Taylor's visit, 490

Australian Council formed, 490

Australian party, first, 496

Auxiliary Council formed, 466

Aveline, Mr., 104

A Yankee on the Yangtze, 608

Ballard, Mr., 322, 324

Baller, F. W.—
    call to China, 220
    arrival in Shanghai, 245
    describes his early experiences, 246-8
    trained at Harley House, 262
    escorts ladies to Shan-si, 313
    escorts lady workers into West China, 331
    reference to women of Hu-nan, 340
    appointed principal of training home, 394
    in Shan-si, 403

Baptisms, early, 111

Barmen Alliance Mission, 556, 561

Barnardo, Dr., 56

Barrie, Dr., 615

Basket, entering Hang-chow by a, 130

Baptisms and progress, 255

Baptisms, first record year, 552

Baptisms in Temple, 307

Beach, Dr. Harlan, 613

Bead mat, message of a, 151

Beauchamp, Lady, 315

Beauchamp, Montagu—
    joins the Mission, 381
    goes to Sze-chwan, 413
    travelling with Mr. Taylor, 414
    visits Australia, 490

Bedside Council meetings, 267

Bell, Mr. Henry, 12

Berger, W. T.—
    his conversion, 25
    first meeting with Mr. Taylor, 25
    consecration to missionary service, 26
    undertakes to represent the work at home, 37
    weekly and noonday prayer meetings at Saint Hill, 71
    home ministry, 103
    his letters, 104
    difficulties in administration, 107
    correspondence *re* Yang-chow riot, 161
    letter to Mr. Taylor on his bereavement, 207
    unprecedented difficulties, 209

THE END